# Revisiting *Crimes of the Powerful*

Frank Pearce was the first scholar to use the term "crimes of the powerful." His ground-breaking book of the same name provided insightful critiques of liberal orthodox criminology, particularly in relation to labelling theory and symbolic interactionism, while making important contributions to Marxist understandings of the complex relations between crime, law and the state in the reproduction of the capitalist social order. Historically, crimes of the powerful were largely neglected in crime and deviance studies, but there is now an important and growing body of work addressing this gap. This book brings together leading international scholars to discuss the legacy of Frank Pearce's book and his work in this area, demonstrating the invaluable contributions a critical Marxist framework brings to studies of corporate and state crimes, nationally, internationally and on a global scale.

This book is neither a hagiography nor a review of random areas of social scientific interest. Instead, it draws together a collection of scholarly and original articles which draw upon and critically interrogate the continued significance of the approach pioneered in *Crimes of the Powerful*. The book traces the evolution of crimes of the powerful empirically and theoretically since 1976; shows how critical scholars have integrated new theoretical insights derived from post-structuralism, feminism and critical race studies; and offers perspectives on how the crimes of the powerful – and the enormous, ongoing destruction they cause – can be addressed and resisted.

**Steven Bittle** is an Associate Professor of Criminology at the University of Ottawa, Canada.

**Laureen Snider** is an Emeritus Professor of Sociology at Queen's University, Kingston, Ontario, Canada.

**Steve Tombs** is Professor of Criminology at The Open University, UK.

**David Whyte** is Professor of Socio-legal Studies at the School of Law and Social Justice, University of Liverpool, UK.

## Crimes of the Powerful
Gregg Barak
*Eastern Michigan University, USA*
Penny Green
*Queen Mary University of London, UK*
Tony Ward
*Northumbria University, UK*

*Crimes of the Powerful* encompasses the harmful, injurious and victimizing behaviours perpetrated by privately or publicly operated businesses, corporations and organizations as well as the state mediated administrative, legalistic, and political responses to these crimes.

The series draws attention to the commonalities of the theories, practices, and controls of the crimes of the powerful. It focuses on the overlapping spheres and inter-related worlds of a wide array of existing and recently developing areas of social, historical and behavioural inquiry into the wrongdoings of multinational organizations, nation-states, stateless regimes, illegal networks, financialization, globalization and securitization.

These examinations of the crimes of the powerful straddle a variety of related disciplines and areas of academic interest, including studies in criminology and criminal justice; law and human rights; conflict, peace and security; economic change, environmental decay and global sustainability.

### Uncovering the Crimes of Urbanisation
Researching Corruption, Violence and Urban Conflict
*Kristian Lasslett*

### State-Corporate Crime and the Commodification of Victimhood
The Toxic Legacy of Trafigura's Ship of Death
*Thomas MacManus*

### Market Criminology
State-Corporate Crime in the Petroleum Extraction Industry
*Ifeanyi Ezeonu*

### Revisiting *Crimes of the Powerful*
Marxism, Crime and Deviance
*Edited by Steven Bittle, Laureen Snider, Steve Tombs and David Whyte*

For more information about this series, please visit: www.routledge.com/Crimes-of-the-Powerful/book-series/COTP

# Revisiting *Crimes of the Powerful*

## Marxism, Crime and Deviance

Edited by Steven Bittle,
Laureen Snider, Steve Tombs
and David Whyte

LONDON AND NEW YORK

First published 2018 by Routledge

2 Park Square, Milton Park, Abingdon, Oxon OX14 4RN
52 Vanderbilt Avenue, New York, NY 10017

*Routledge is an imprint of the Taylor & Francis Group, an informa business*

First issued in paperback 2021

Copyright © 2018 selection and editorial matter, Steven Bittle, Laureen Snider, Steve Tombs and David Whyte; individual chapters, the contributors

The right of Steven Bittle, Laureen Snider, Steve Tombs and David Whyte to be identified as the authors of the editorial material, and of the authors for their individual chapters, has been asserted in accordance with sections 77 and 78 of the Copyright, Designs and Patents Act 1988.

All rights reserved. No part of this book may be reprinted or reproduced or utilised in any form or by any electronic, mechanical, or other means, now known or hereafter invented, including photocopying and recording, or in any information storage or retrieval system, without permission in writing from the publishers.

Notice:
Product or corporate names may be trademarks or registered trademarks, and are used only for identification and explanation without intent to infringe.

Publisher's Note

The publisher has gone to great lengths to ensure the quality of this reprint but points out that some imperfections in the original copies may be apparent.

*British Library Cataloguing-in-Publication Data*
A catalogue record for this book is available from the British Library

*Library of Congress Cataloging-in-Publication Data*
Names: Bittle, Steven, 1968– editor. | Snider, Laureen, 1944– editor. | Tombs, Steve, editor.
Title: Revisiting crimes of the powerful : Marxism, crime and deviance / edited by Steven Bittle, Laureen Snider, Steve Tombs and David Whyte.
Description: 1 Edition. | New York : Routledge, 2018. | Series: Crimes of the powerful | Includes bibliographical references and index.
Identifiers: LCCN 2018006415 | ISBN 9780415791427 (hardback) | ISBN 9781315212333 (ebook)
Subjects: LCSH: Commercial crimes. | Corporations—Corrupt practices. | Organized crime. | State crimes. | Political corruption.
Classification: LCC HV6768 .R485 2018 | DDC 364.16/8—dc23
LC record available at https://lccn.loc.gov/2018006415

ISBN: 978-0-415-79142-7 (hbk)
ISBN: 978-0-367-48295-4 (pbk)

Typeset in Bembo
by Apex CoVantage, LLC

This book is dedicated to Frank Pearce: friend, teacher, colleague and inspiration.

# Contents

| | |
|---|---|
| *List of figures* | x |
| *List of contributors* | xi |
| *Foreword by Frank Pearce* | xviii |
| *Acknowledgements* | xxxii |
| *Revisiting Crimes of the Powerful: an introduction* | xxxiii |
| STEVEN BITTLE, LAUREEN SNIDER, STEVE TOMBS AND DAVID WHYTE | |

## SECTION I
## Theoretical and conceptual excursions

1

**1 Conceptualization, theoretical practice and *Crimes of the Powerful***

3

JON FRAULEY

**2 Law: ideological whitewashing and positive enabling of coercion**

20

HARRY GLASBEEK

**3 Underworld as servant and smokescreen: *Crimes of the Powerful* and the evolution of organized crime control**

32

MICHAEL WOODIWISS

**4 Shadow boxing against the crimes of the powerful**

45

MARGARET BEARE

**5 Between force and consensus**

60

VINCENZO RUGGIERO

viii Contents

6 Developing Pearce's new materialism 73
NICK HARDY

7 Theorizing fiscal sacrifices in zombie capitalism:
a radical Durkheimian approach 87
RONJON PAUL DATTA

8 Power, crime and enclosure: capital accumulation in
the twilight of the neoliberal SSA 102
RAYMOND MICHALOWSKI

## SECTION II
## Crimes of the powerful research: empirical dimensions 117

9 Marx reloaded for the 21st century: capitalism, agency
and the crimes of the powerful 119
KRISTIAN LASSLETT

10 The imaginary social order of corporate criminal liability 131
LIISA LÄHTEENMÄKI AND ANNE ALVESALO-KUUSI

11 Global capital, the rigging of interbank interest rates
and the capitalist state 143
GREGG BARAK

12 Pipelines, presidents and people power: resisting
state–corporate environmental crime 157
ELIZABETH A. BRADSHAW

13 Pesticideland: Brazil's poison market 174
STÉFANIE KHOURY

14 No criminology of wage theft: revisiting "workplace
theft" to expose capitalist exploitation 188
PAUL LEIGHTON

15 Prying into the pockets of public figures 202
SCOTT POYNTING

16 The crimes of the powerful and the Spanish crisis 217
IGNASI BERNAT

Contents  ix

17 Crimes of globalization and Asian dam projects: powerful institutions and slow violence 231

DAVID O. FRIEDRICHS

## SECTION III
## New developments in crimes of the powerful research 243

18 An extension of Frank Pearce's work on crimes of the powerful: "demystification" and the role of our consent 245

DAWN L. ROTHE AND VICTORIA E. COLLINS

19 Debtfarism, predatory lending and imaginary social orders: the case of the U.S. payday lending industry 257

SUSANNE SOEDERBERG

20 Failure to protect: state obligations to victims and state crime 270

LAURA FINLEY

21 "Punitive reformation": state-sanctioned labour through criminal justice and welfare 283

JON BURNETT

22 Imperialism: the general theory of crimes of the powerful 297

BIKO AGOZINO

23 Frank Pearce and colonial state crimes: contributions to a research agenda 309

JOSE ATILES

24 Organized irresponsibility, corporations and the contradictions of collective agency and individual culpability 322

DEAN CURRAN

*Index* 335

# Figures

|  |  |  |
|---|---|---|
| 8.1 | New enclosure movements power dimension | 111 |
| 16.2 | Spanish mortgages 2003–2016 | 223 |

# Contributors

**Biko Agozino** is a Professor of Sociology and Africana Studies at Virginia Tech, USA. He was educated at Edinburgh University (PhD), Cambridge University (MPhil) and University of Calabar (BSc). He is the author of *Counter-Colonial Criminology: A Critique of Imperialist Reason* (London, Pluto Press, 2003) and of *Black Women and the Criminal Justice System: Towards the Decolonisation of Victimisation* (Aldershot, Ashgate, 1997), among other works. He directed and produced *Shouters and the Control Freak Empire*, winner of the Best International Short Documentary, Columbia Gorge Film Festival, USA, 2011. He blogs at www.massliteracy.blogspot.com.

**Anne Alvesalo-Kuusi** is Professor of Sociology of Law at the University of Turku, Finland. She has studied extensively in the area of corporate crime control and criminal policy. Her areas of interest also include the misuse of migrant labour and border criminology. At the moment she is the principal investigator of the research project Securitization in Finnish Legislation funded by the Finnish Academy.

**Jose Atiles** is a Postdoctoral Researcher at the Centre for Social Studies of the University of Coimbra, Portugal, and an Adjunct Professor of Philosophy at the University of Puerto Rico, Mayagüez Campus. Dr Atiles' research focuses on the socio-legal and philosophic-political analysis of the role of law and exceptionality in the context of U.S.–Puerto Rican political, economic and colonial relationships. Currently Dr Atiles is working on a book manuscript entitled *Colonial State of Exception as Economic Policy: The Puerto Rican Case*, which analyses the role of exceptionality and law on the Puerto Rican fiscal and economic crisis.

**Gregg Barak** is Professor of Criminology and Criminal Justice at Eastern Michigan University, USA. He received his PhD in criminology from UC Berkeley in 1974. In 2003, he became the 27th Fellow of the Academy of Criminal Justice Sciences, and in 2007 he received the Lifetime Achievement Award from the Critical Division of the American Society of Criminology

(ASC). Barak is the author and/or editor of numerous books on crime, justice, media, violence, financial crime, homelessness, human rights and related topics. His *Theft of a Nation: Wall Street Looting and Federal Regulatory Colluding* received the 2012 Outstanding Publication Award given by the White Collar Crime Research Consortium of the National White Collar Crime Center, and his *Unchecked Corporate Power: Why the Crimes of Multinational Corporations are Routinized Away and What We Can Do About It* received the 2017 Outstanding Book Award from the Division of White Collar and Corporate Crime of the ASC.

**Margaret Beare** is Professor of Law and Sociology at York University, Toronto, Canada. She is the author of six single or co-edited books on organized crime, corruption and policing and, in addition to the article in this volume, has a forthcoming 2018 corruption-related article: "Internal Enemies, Legitimate and Illegitimate Enterprises," *Handbook of Organized Crime and Politics*, Edward Elgar Publishing.

**Ignasi Bernat** has lectured in the areas of criminology and sociology at the University of Girona (Spain) and at the University of Surrey (UK). His work focuses on economic crimes and how power relations shape the role of the state on those crimes primarily through Marxist and decolonial theory. He has published in *Critical Criminology,* the *Oñati Journal of Emergent Socio-Legal Studies* and *Crítica Penal y Poder*.

**Steven Bittle** is an Associate Professor of Criminology at the University of Ottawa, Canada. His research and teaching interests include crimes of the powerful, corporate crime, corporate criminal liability, safety crimes and the sociology of law. He has published in *Law and Policy, Crime, Law and Social Change, Critical Criminology, Critical Sociology* and *Capital and Class,* among others. He is the author of *Still Dying for a Living: Corporate Criminal Liability after the Westray Mine Disaster* (2012, UBC Press), which received the 2014 Publication of the Year Award by the National White Collar Crime Research Consortium.

**Elizabeth A. Bradshaw** is an Associate Professor of Sociology at Central Michigan University, USA, where she teaches in the Social and Criminal Justice concentration. Much of her research focuses on state–corporate environmental crime within the fossil fuel industry, as well as social movements as a form of resistance against crimes of the powerful. Her research has been published in multiple edited books and journals, including *Theoretical Criminology*, *State Crime Journal*, and *Critical Criminology*.

**Jon Burnett** is a Lecturer in Criminology at the University of Swansea, UK. He has published widely on issues relating to forced labour, penal power, racism and neoliberalism. He is a member of the Council of the Institute of Race Relations.

## Contributors xiii

**Victoria E. Collins** is an Associate Professor in the School of Justice Studies at Eastern Kentucky University, USA. Victoria's research and teaching interests include state crime, white-collar crime, transnational crime and violence against women. Victoria has published a book with Routledge (Taylor & Francis) titled *State Crime, Women and Gender*. Some of Victoria's recent publications have appeared in journals such as *Social Justice*, the *International Journal of Law, Crime and Justice*, *International Criminal Law Review*, *Critical Criminology*, *Contemporary Justice Review*, and *The Australian and New Zealand Journal of Criminology*.

**Dean Curran** is an Assistant Professor of Sociology at the University of Calgary, Canada. He has previous degrees in economics and the philosophy of the social sciences and a PhD in sociology. His research areas include social theory, risk and inequality, and he has publications in the *British Journal of Sociology*, *Economy and Society*, *Antipode*, *Journal of Risk Research*, *Journal of Classical Sociology*, *European Journal of Social Theory* and a 2016 book with Palgrave Macmillan, *Risk, Power and Inequality in the 21st Century*.

**Ronjon Paul Datta** studied sociology at Trent University, Queen's University and Carleton University, earning a Governor General of Canada Academic Gold Medal for his doctoral work on Foucault and politics at Carleton. Presently, he is an Assistant Professor and member of the Graduate Faculty, specializing in social theory, in the Department of Sociology, Anthropology and Criminology at the University of Windsor, Ontario, Canada. He also worked at The University of Alberta (meriting a Bill Meloff Memorial Teaching Award), Mount Allison University, Queen's University, The University of Ottawa and Carleton University. He has published on a variety of topics, including metatheory, zombie capitalism, Durkheim and religion, Foucault, cosmopolitanism, anti-security, Deleuze and justice, among others. Additionally, Paul is co-founder of the Canadian Network of Durkheimian Studies and serves on several advisory boards. His current research explores nominalism and axiology, as well as radical Durkheimian analyses of suicidality.

**Laura Finley** is Associate Professor of Sociology & Criminology at Barry University in Miami, Florida, USA. She is the author, co-author or editor of twenty books, as well as numerous journal articles and book chapters. Dr Finley is also a syndicated columnist with PeaceVoice. In addition to her scholarly work, Dr Finley is actively involved with a number of organizations focused on peace, justice, human rights and gender equality.

**Jon Frauley** is Associate Professor of Criminology at the University of Ottawa, Canada, where he teaches courses on social and criminological theory, epistemology and methodology and creative analytics. He is fortunate, and grateful, to have completed his doctoral studies under the direction of Frank Pearce. Jon's work can be found in the *British Journal of Criminology*, *Social & Legal Studies*, and *Critical Criminology*, among others. He is editor of and contributor to *C. Wright Mills and the Criminological Imagination: Prospects for Creative Enquiry* (Routledge, 2015) and (with Frank Pearce) *Critical Realism and the Social Sciences: Heterodox Elaborations* (University of Toronto Press, 2007). He is the author of *Criminology, Deviance, and the Silver Screen: Fictional Realities and the Criminological Imagination* (Palgrave 2011).

**David O. Friedrichs** is Distinguished Professor of Sociology, Criminal Justice and Criminology at the University of Scranton (Pennsylvania, USA). He is the author of *Trusted Criminals: White Collar Crime in Contemporary Society* (4th ed.) (Cengage 2010), *Law in Our Lives: An Introduction* (3rd ed.) (Oxford University Press 2012), co-author (with Dawn L. Rothe) of *Crimes of Globalization* (Routledge 2015) and (with Isabel Schoultz and Aleksandra Jordanoska) of *Edwin H. Sutherland* (Routledge 2018), and editor of *State Crime* (Ashgate 1998). He served as President of the White Collar Crime Research Consortium (2002–2004) and received its Outstanding Publication Award in 2011. In 2005 he received the Lifetime Achievement Award of the Division on Critical Criminology of the American Society of Criminology. He has been a Visiting Professor at a number of universities, including the University of South Africa, Flinders University (Australia), the University of Western Australia and Stockholm University.

**Harry Glasbeek**, BA, LLB (Hons.) University of Melbourne, JD (Chicago), Professor Emeritus and Senior Scholar, Osgoode Hall Law School, York University, has taught at the universities of Melbourne and Monash in Australia and the University of Western Ontario in Canada. From 1974 to 1996 he was a Professor at Osgoode Hall Law School. After retirement, until 2013, he spent six months of the year as a visitor and Adjunct Professor at Victoria University. He has written books on Australian labour law and Australian evidence law, on Canadian labour law and Canadian evidence law, as well as more than 130 articles on tort law, labour law, bills of rights, legal education, corporate law, corporate criminality, corporate social responsibility and occupational health and safety. His last two books, the 11th and 12th, are *Class Privilege: How Law Shelters Shareholders and Coddles Capitalism* (Toronto: Between the Lines, 2017) and *Capitalism: A Crime Story* (Toronto: Between the Lines, 2018).

**Nick Hardy** is an Assistant Professor in the Department of Sociology at the University of New Brunswick, Canada. His work focuses primarily on social ontology, critical realism and post-structuralism (mainly through the work of Michel Foucault). He has published in *Rethinking Marxism, Foucault Studies* and *The Journal for the Theory of Social Behaviour*, among others, and is currently working on a book manuscript discussing the presence and place of materialism in Foucault's archaeological and genealogical theory.

**Stéfanie Khoury** is Research Associate at the University of Liverpool (UK). Her research focuses on violations of human rights by corporations and the lack of corporate accountability in international human rights law. Her academic interests include researching the powerful, critical socio-legal studies and qualitative research methods. She is co-author of *Corporate Human Rights Violations: Global Prospects for Legal Action* (Routledge, RIPE Series, 2017).

**Liisa Lähteenmäki** works as a post-doctoral research fellow at the University of Turku, Finland, Faculty of Law. She is also a fellow in the Turku Institute for Advanced Studies (TIAS) during 2018–2020. Her research interests are regulation and deregulation of employment, occupational safety crimes and empirical research of law. Her most recent publications include "Corporate Criminal Liability and Abolitionism – An Unholy Alliance of Corporate Power and Critical Criminology?" in *Justice, Power and Resistance* 1(1), 2017, together with Anne Alvesalo-Kuusi and Steven Bittle.

**Kristian Lasslett** is Professor of Criminology at Ulster University, Northern Ireland. His research employs a range of investigative methods to interrogate the systems, actors and transactions which facilitate grand corruption, large-scale land theft and human rights abuses in the extractives sector. He has pioneered a range of data analysis tools, including investigative social network analysis and transaction mapping. His first book, *State Crime on the Margins of Empire,* was published in 2014 by Pluto Books, and his second book, *Uncovering the Crimes of Urbanisation*, was published in 2018 by Routledge.

**Paul Leighton** is a Professor in the Department of Sociology, Anthropology and Criminology at Eastern Michigan University, USA. He is a co-author with Jeffrey Reiman of *The Rich Get Richer and the Poor Get Prison* (11th ed., 2016). He is also a co-author, with Gregg Barak and Allison Cotton, of *Class, Race, Gender & Crime* (5th ed., 2018). Leighton co-authored, with Donna Selman, *Punishment for Sale: Private Prisons, Big Business and the Incarceration Binge* (Rowman & Littlefield, 2010). He is a past President of the Board of SafeHouse and is currently on the advisory board of the food pantry serving the university.

**Raymond Michalowski** is a sociologist, Arizona Regents Professor and faculty member in the Department of Criminology and Criminal Justice at Northern Arizona University, USA. He is the author of books and articles on an eclectic variety of topics, including state–corporate crime, immigration rights, criminological theory and motorcycle pilgrimage. He lives on several acres of Arizona desert scrubland with his wife, Jill, and a varying assemblage of dogs, cats, motorcycles and boats.

**Frank Pearce** is a Professor Emeritus at Queen's University, Canada, where, for many years, he taught sociology. He has researched, taught and published in two distinct but overlapping areas: Sociological Theory and the Sociology of Law, Crime and the State. His appreciative but critical engagements and elaborations of the theoretical concepts of Karl Marx, Emile Durkheim and Michel Foucault have helped him develop a complex understanding of capitalist social formations; see, for example, *The Radical Durkheim* (1990/2010) and *Critical Realism and the Social Sciences: Heterodox* elaborations (with Jon Frauley, 2009). His more empirical work has focused on the roles that states play in reproducing a range of different capitalist societies, this requiring an engagement with current analyses of specific societies, a detailed knowledge of their history and a creative deployment of sociological theory. This strategy was particularly evident in *Crimes of the Powerful: Marxism, Crime and Deviance* (Pluto Press 1976) and in *Toxic Capitalism: Corporate Crime and the Chemical Industry* (with Steve Tombs) (1998). He has collaborated and is still collaborating with other scholars in the struggle against corporate crime.

**Scott Poynting** is Adjunct Professor in the School of Social Sciences and Psychology at Western Sydney University, Australia, and in the School of Justice at Queensland University of Technology. He co-edited (with David Whyte) the December 2017 special issue on "Corruption Downunder" of the *International Journal for Crime, Justice and Social Democracy*, and is co-editor (with Monish Bhatia and Waqas Tufail) of *Media, Crime and Racism* (Palgrave, 2018).

**Dawn L. Rothe** is a Professor and Chair of the School of Justice Studies at Eastern Kentucky University, USA. She is the author or co-author of 10 books and over seven dozen peer-reviewed articles and book chapters that address crimes of the powerful, neoliberalism, power and inequality.

**Vincenzo Ruggiero** is Professor of Sociology at Middlesex University in London, UK, where he is also Director of the Centre for Social and Criminological Research. Since 2010 he has published the following books: *Penal Abolitionism* (2010), *Corruption and Organised Crime in Europe* (co-edited) (2012), *The Crimes of the Economy* (2013), *Punishment in Europe* (co-edited) (2013), *Power and Crime* (2015) and *Dirty Money: On Financial Delinquency* (2017).

**Laureen Snider** is an Emeritus Professor of Sociology at Queen's University, Kingston, Ontario, Canada. Recent publications include *About Canada: Corporate Crime* (Fernwood, 2015); "Interrogating the Algorithm: Debt, Derivatives and the Social Reconstruction of Stock Market Trading," *Critical Sociology*, 24 February 2014, at http://crs.sagepub.com/content/early/2014/02/21/0896920513504603; "Law, Regulation and Safety Crime: Exploring the Boundaries of Criminalizing Powerful Actors" (with Steven Bittle), *Canadian Journal of Law & Society*, June 2015; and "Examining the Ruggie Report: Can Voluntary Guidelines Tame Global Capitalism?", *Critical Criminology*, 21: 177–92.

**Susanne Soederberg** is a Professor of Global Political Economy in the Department of Global Development Studies at Queen's University in Canada. She is the author of several books, including *Corporate Power and Ownership in Contemporary Capitalism* (2010) and *Debtfare States and the Poverty Industry* (2014).

Her current book project maps the socio-spatial, institutional and material processes of survival in contemporary capitalism through an exploration of rental housing insecurity (including evictions, debt and homelessness) in Berlin, Dublin and Vienna.

**Steve Tombs** is Professor of Criminology at The Open University, UK. He has a long-standing interest in the incidence, nature and regulation of corporate and state crime and harm and has published widely. He has long worked with the Hazards movement in the UK, and is a Trustee and board member of Inquest.

**David Whyte** is Professor of Socio-legal Studies at the School of Law and Social Justice, University of Liverpool, UK. His research and teaching interests are focused on the connections between law and corporate power. His most recent books are *The Violence of Austerity* (Pluto, 2017, ed. with Vickie Cooper) and *Corporate Human Rights Violations: Global Prospects for Legal Action* (Routledge, 2017, with Stéfanie Khoury).

**Michael Woodiwiss** is a Senior Lecturer at the University of the West of England, UK. He has written, edited and co-authored many books and articles covering topics such as bootlegging, drug trafficking, criminal money management, official corruption and many types of corporate and financial crime. He co-edited *Global Crime Connections* with Frank Pearce in 1993 and is the author of *Organized Crime and American Power* (2001) and *Gangster Capitalism* (2005). His most recent publication is *Double Crossed: The Failure of Organized Crime Control* (2017). Currently he is working with a legal scholar, Mary Young, on a project that will identify and analyse the links between U.S. and UK efforts to control organized crime and the effects of these efforts, particularly anti-drug trafficking efforts, nationally, regionally and globally.

# Foreword

## Autobiographical context for *Crimes of the Powerful*

I think I can take it for granted that readers of this book will have read *Crimes of the Powerful: Marxism, Crime and Deviance* – abbreviated henceforth to (*CotP*) – or some of my other writings on corporate, organized and state crime. It is worth noting that when I wrote this book, many Marxists considered "crime and deviance" to be a relatively uninteresting topic and that most criminologists were either relatively uncritical supporters of law and order, or were concerned with diagnosing and providing treatment for the pathologies with which criminals allegedly were afflicted. Criminologists were relatively dismissive of Marxism, charging it with being merely ideological. In this chapter I would like to provide some context for understanding how it came about that I felt impelled to write sociologically about crimes of the powerful in the mid-1970s and why I think it is of continuing interest today.

The chapter is a rewritten version of the keynote speech I gave to participants at the conference on "Revisiting *Crimes of the Powerful*" which took place in Toronto on 25 and 26 May 2017. In what follows, I will be referring to some of my life experiences as they relate to the creation of the *CotP* text. I will try to show, by weaving them together, how these experiences and my responses to them helped and continue to help me understand the connections between what C. Wright Mills famously called personal troubles and public issues. Indeed, writing this autobiographical essay has helped me explain better to myself why these experiences had such strong effects on my personal, political and intellectual development.

## My family life

*To begin at my beginning:* I was born into a typical British working-class family. Both of my parents were brought up in rural hardship; they knew the meaning of poverty. My paternal grandfather was a farmer who married three times, was widowed twice and fathered eight children. His first wife died while at a relatively young age, having already given birth to a daughter. His second wife also died at a relatively young age, a victim of the influenza epidemic of 1919, but not before she had given birth to two boys, including my father, and a daughter. His father remarried again; this time there were three children, another girl and two more boys; the third wife outlived him. He developed a small dairy business which sadly he lost during the economic Depression. This was, in part, because he gave many of his poorer customers credit with the knowledge that many would not be able to pay their bills. He was aware that their pressing need to feed their families did not disappear because they lacked the income to buy for them the necessities of life.

The Pearce family grew up in a village near Bristol. Initially, my father worked in an orchid house on a large estate, similar to that portrayed in the TV series *Downton Abbey*. In the mid-1930s, realizing there was little future for him in this occupation, he joined the army as a regular soldier. He was assigned to work in a unit dedicated to developing tank warfare, was rapidly promoted to sergeant and remained a sergeant until he left the army. He was also an extremely good footballer who played for the army national team and won numerous trophies.

My mother was Irish, born in Garnish, County Cork, into a large family that did not exactly embrace English rule; one of her female relatives was a captain in the IRA. My mother's father was a fisherman and farmer who married a local girl. They emigrated to America, where he worked in the Montana copper mines, and they started a family. Soon they were a family of five. But their eldest child died tragically in a house fire there. They returned to Ireland, and my grandmother gave birth to another six children. My grandfather had contracted chronic emphysema, very possibly from workplace exposures, and from which he eventually died. Two more of my mother's siblings died in tragic circumstances: one was killed in a mining accident in Wales and the other was murdered in Central Park, New York, in what may have been what we now identify as a homophobic hate crime. The ability and willingness to work hard did not guarantee basic life security or a minimally adequate income.

My parents met in the early 1940s when my mother was working "in service" as a cook. They married, and within a few years my sister and I were born. My father was still in the army, so we had what passed as reasonable housing accommodation. Having survived the Second World War, my father was posted to Egypt, to the Suez Canal, where he caught tuberculosis. He was in a sanatorium for two years. My mother kept working part-time as a cleaner. Eventually my father was able to leave the sanatorium, and shortly thereafter he was medically discharged from the army, with instructions to undertake only light work. Because of his ill health and limited formal education, he was now an unskilled man, with extremely limited employment options. The family could no longer live in army accommodations, so my parents had to find another house to rent. This was no easy task, but my father and mother persevered and managed to rent from the council a modest but well-built, pre-war red brick house in a small council estate of 50 or so houses in Farnborough, Hampshire.

Money was always tight for my family. Fortunately for us all, they were both very good at managing money, were personally quite abstemious and in their different spheres of responsibility were more than competent. We were always well fed, well housed and well clothed. They also looked after my mother's brother's wife as she succumbed to cancer, and they took on the responsibility of bringing up her two children: a 6-year old girl and a 15-year-old boy. They also helped my mother's brother find a house to rent less than a mile away from us. Unfortunately, he never contributed to his children's keep, which placed an additional burden on my parents although they never complained about it.

Both of my parents were thoughtful, well-informed and caring people. Of the two, my mother had a deeper understanding of the injuries, evident and often hidden, of class and of racial prejudice; after all, she was an Irish Catholic. She was also a fighter. My father was more easy-going and less confrontational. In our household the newspaper was *The Daily Mirror* which at that time generally supported the Labour Party; the radio and TV programs we listened to and watched were predominantly broadcast by the BBC. All of us in our own ways paid attention to, and sought to understand, current events and the world in which we lived.

## Education and evaluation

In my early years as a schoolboy, I spent an agreeable amount of time both in and out of my parents' gaze. There was a large park about five minutes away from my home. One day, aged six, I met a boy named Brian there. We got on well. We were playing by his house on the other side of the park from mine. At about 5:00 p.m. his mother came out; seeing us playing she said to my new friend, "teatime, it's 5 o'clock." Spontaneously, he asked if his new friend, Frank, could come to tea, too. She responded by saying, "No, you have to have a bath after tea tonight." Brian responded, "But that is not until 6:30." She turned to me and said, "I would think your mother will be making tea for you too. Where do you live?" I pointed to the other side of the park, "In the council houses," I said proudly. She said, "I think you should play with the children where you live rather than coming all the way over here." I thought this was puzzling but I knew grown-ups were strange. I told my mother. She was livid. "Bloody snob," she said. "She thinks because we are working class you aren't good enough to play with her son." I felt sad because I had upset my mother; later when I understood what had occurred, I felt hurt and angry. This was the day I learnt that I was working class.

Meanwhile, my sister and I had begun attending St. Patrick's School, an underfunded small local Catholic school, run by nuns with some non-religious male and female teachers. One problem with the school was its overemphasis on religion. We were continually exposed to renderings of the doctrines and ritual performance of the Catholic Church. Pupils, however, received only rudimentary instruction in science, mathematics and the English language. This was particularly significant because at that time all school children were required to write what was known as the 11-plus examination.

The results of this exam "snapshot" at the age of 11 were taken to be an accurate index of the relative abilities of different children and to be accurate predictors of their possible academic prowess. These were assumed to provide reliable assessments of the kind of careers they could rationally envisage for themselves. These results were hugely consequential, at least for working-class children. It was assumed that their destiny was to join the workforce and become unskilled or semi-skilled workers where they would be subject to an authoritarian work regime. On average, middle-class children were recorded as performing much better than working-class children. These outcomes were not surprising if one pays attention to the actual ways in which resources were distributed between and within schools. The size of classes and the mode of instruction were appropriate to rote learning but hardly to independent thinking. The kinds of conduct and forms of relationships to self and to others which were endorsed were typical of professional middle-class culture but not intrinsic to the capacity to learn. As Michel Foucault argued, the function of much education was to "discipline and/or punish."

In contrast to the situation of the mostly working-class parents who had little choice about where their children went to school, middle-class parents were able to buy houses in areas where the relative quality of the schools – defined by the percentage of students who passed the 11-plus examination – was significantly better than schools in other areas.

Those who passed the 11-plus obtained access to a relatively well-funded local education grammar school, where they could acquire a rigorous, albeit uncritical, education. Those from working-class families who continued to do reasonably well at their grammar school generally had imbued many of the values found in their middle-class milieu almost by "osmosis" and had learnt how to play some of the games that came "naturally" to the middle-class majority. However, a tendency among adolescents to see the world somewhat ironically meant there were always cognitive escape routes away from conformism.

There were reparative actions available to middle-class parents whose children were unable to do well at the time of the 11-plus. They could pay to go to private schools. Some of these, the "public schools," were extraordinarily expensive and had quite high academic standards. The rest, the smaller private schools, could provide an approximation to a grammar school education. My school, the Farnborough Salesian College, was one of the latter schools, at least for non-Catholics. The students were a hybrid mixture of Catholic boarders and both Catholic and non-Catholic day school students. Most of the formal teaching was done by priests. Catholic boys who passed the 11-plus examination could either go to the local non-denominational grammar school or the local private Catholic school as dayboys and have the bulk of their fees paid by the state. This was not an option for non-Catholics who had failed the 11-plus examination; there were no grants for them. My parents believed this school – which was much smaller than the local grammar school – to be the better option for me, so I became a pupil there.

However the process of changing schools was not without its own difficulties. I felt at home in St. Patrick's school. I was reasonably well adjusted, I could take care of myself and I was accepted by the other kids. My neighbourhood had seemed equally safe, but unfortunately I began to be bullied by a cousin of some of the local boys who were a couple of years older. He was a frequent visitor, the same age as them, and, like them, much bigger than me. He rather sneakily intimidated me while telling his cousins that I was a "wimpy" liar when I complained to them. This went on for some time, but when he suddenly stopped coming around, the bullying stopped as well. I never knew why he stopped visiting his cousins, but it was a great relief. I had survived. But the incident made me feel helpless and hopelessly vulnerable. It called into question my loyalties and my self-identification.

The route to my new school was past my old school and whereas I had joined with my schoolmates in teasing the "sallies" as we called the Salesian boys, now I was being treated as one myself. I was not sure who or what I was, although I was certainly uncomfortable being a working-class boy in such a middle-class school. I experienced many of the other students as cliquey and as often overbearing in their self-confidence. The violence of some of the teachers, particularly those who wore a white clerical collar but who were not yet ordained as priests (and might never be), was terrifying. That is not to say that all of the teaching staff were violent. But the headmaster had the legally endorsed right to inflict corporal punishment on the student population.

In retrospect, I believe that in response to these difficulties, I attempted to find different ways to change my relation to my situation. First, at age 13, it seemed to me that I wanted to be a priest and, with my parents' approval and their financial support, I successfully applied to go to a junior Salesian seminary in Cheshire, for what turned out to be a painful experience. An implicit motivator may have been if I can't beat the middle classes and I don't want to join them, is there an institution which will allow me to "leap-frog" over them by becoming one of the "holy men"? Incidentally, I remember discussing with my fellow seminarian classmates the relative violence of the different Catholic teaching orders. It is notable that nobody condoned any of the violence but there was general agreement that the Christian brothers were the worst. In light of subsequent courtroom revelations about the physical abuse, including sexual abuse, that the Christian brothers inflicted on the children over whom they exercised authority, this was a particularly astute assessment.

After two years, the priests decided they didn't want me! The Father Superior warned me that I had an excess of pride. Thank goodness that was partly true. I escaped what would have been for me a dreadful mistake. True, I learnt how to concentrate intensely, not least to be able to read Charles Dickens' *Bleak House* and to find pleasure in mastering ideas and solving intellectual puzzles. But I was already non-conformist. I was outraged that the seminary censored the news and only posted excerpts from two right-wing newspapers: *The Daily Telegraph* and *The Times*. When in the reading room of the local public library, looking for alternative news sources, I discovered and read *The Daily Worker*, the communist party newspaper that I knew about but had never actually seen. I was now a rebel, and this seemed a more natural identity for me to embrace when I returned to my local Salesian College.

My rebelliousness deepened. This was particularly true after I did very well in my ordinary-level public examinations, my GCEs, at age 16. Although I performed well in both arts and sciences, because neither my parents nor I wanted me to be parachuted into the much larger grammar school, I needed to continue my education at the same school. However, I was forced to study only the natural sciences in my advanced-level examinations, when I wanted to focus on arts subjects. My own interests were sacrificed "for the good of the school." My resentment found its strongest expression in my critical reaction to the "Apologetics" class taught by a senior priest. I was sent to the headmaster's office where he asked me what I believed was the problem with that particular course. I responded by saying: "In one of his proofs for the existence of God, Saint Thomas Aquinas states that 'because an infinite series of causes is impossible, there must be an uncaused cause, and that is God.'" "But," I said, "in our scientific work we use the concept of infinite series all the time. Who has the right to simply declare it impossible?" Given that the headmaster had a chemistry degree, I expected some rational answer. Instead, he said: "Go and pray to your guardian angel as you did when you were a child." The only word that could possibly describe my reaction was "flabbergasted." For me, it was another nail in the coffin of religion.

Like many adolescent boys, I was fascinated by sex and I was aware that I was very lucky to have missed out on priesthood-based celibacy. Meanwhile in the wider world, Penguin, the major publisher of paperback books, was prosecuted for publishing D. H. Lawrence's, *Lady Chatterley's Lover*. During the well-publicized trial, the prosecuting counsel asked the jurors whether they would be happy for their wives and servants to read such a book. In response, the media was derisive. The prosecution failed, but Penguin's victory did not necessarily mean the end of prosecution of sexually explicit books because few authors had the artistic credentials of D. H. Lawrence. But many people were certainly offended by the patronizing tone of the trial. I took a somewhat obsessive interest in news involving sexual topics and particularly scandals like the Vassal case and the Profumo affair.

## Scandals and scapegoating

The British press in the early 1960s had something of a passion for spy stories. The British government had successfully identified and nullified a Soviet-controlled group of spies known as "The Portland Spy Ring"; captured and imprisoned the spy George Blake; and identified the relatively junior civil

xxiv Foreword

servant, John Vassal, as a mole for the Russians. Vassal had been sexually active in clandestine homosexual milieus while working for the British government in Russia and had been identified as a homosexual and potential mole by the Russian Secret Service. They used a combination of "the carrot and stick" to force him to spy for them when he returned to Britain. The "stick" was the threat of revealing to his superiors his clandestine sexual activities. Homosexual acts were illegal in both Britain and Russia, and generally there was active hostility to homosexuals in both countries. (I analysed this homophobia in my 1973 article "How to Be Immoral and Ill, Pathetic and Dangerous All at the Same Time: Homosexuality and the British Press"). Anybody in politically sensitive government employ who did not confine their sexual life to the marriage bed was seen as potentially unreliable.

In 1963 John Profumo, the Secretary of State for War in Harold Macmillan's straight-laced Conservative government, was accused of having had a sexual relationship two years earlier with a "would-be model," Christine Keeler, who at that time was 17 years of age. When questioned in the House of Commons, Profumo denied "any impropriety," but this denial simply could not fly; there was too much evidence to the contrary, including a love letter from Profumo to Keeler.

This liaison was represented by the Labour Party opposition as a potential security breach because at the same time she had been involved with Profumo, Christine Keeler was also in a sexual relationship with a member of the Russian Embassy, Yevgeni Ivanov, believed to be a spy. The Profumo affair was like a comic opera written by Gilbert and Sullivan and adapted by Berthold Brecht – with a stock set of characters based on widely circulated stereotypes. Christine Keeler was friendly with Mandy Rice-Davies, another "would-be model." Both were also "friendly" with Dr Stephen Ward, something of an outsider, a hanger-on, to Lord Astor's hedonistic aristocratic circle. Ward was an osteopath, hence a practitioner of fringe medicine (he had graduated from a minor American university and his qualifications were not recognized in Britain.) Stephen Ward was successfully prosecuted for "procuring," that is, introducing people to each other who subsequently engaged in extra-marital sex. He was found guilty and allegedly hanged himself, although there has long been speculation that he was murdered by MI5, one of the British Secret security services. More recently many similar questions have been asked about the death of Dr David Kelly, a nuclear weapons inspector, who was found dead in the aftermath of the invasion of Iraq.

Another of Keeler's lovers was Peter Rachman, a property speculator and slum landlord and a major contributor to the Conservative Party's war chest. Also, in a separate scandal, it was reported in the press that at an orgy, a cabinet minister, allegedly Reginald Maudling, had served guests food while naked except for a mask. It was also intimated that there were possible royal connections to the Profumo affair, hinted at in *The Daily Mirror*'s two-page banner headline "Prince Philip and the Profumo Scandal – Rumour Utterly Unfounded."

In the witch-hunts of the 1960s, no rumour was too wild to be given currency. But the level of secrecy over the activities of the royal family, politicians, judges and the police was extraordinary and legally sanctioned. On the other hand, it was always possible that someone "in the know," if encouraged by money from the tabloids, would leak snippets of information to them. The hopeless task of controlling the flow of this information created a situation rife with speculation. Often, it seemed that the only way to make sense of scandalous events was to project on them one's own prejudices. I was not exempt from this, but what I rightly took away from my following of the Profumo affair closely was a recognition that there was little relation between what governments and their official spokespersons said, what press barons claimed to be the case and what actually happened. There was clearly an "imaginary social order," a phrase that I coined in *CotP*.

## Learning to be critical and teaching critically

I survived the ordeal of school; I secured entrance to an undergraduate degree course in chemistry at University College London (UCL). In those days fees were usually paid by the state and a living allowance was virtually automatic for successful applicants. I loved living in London, it was (and is) such a great city, but I now wanted to study politics and economics. Having passed my key chemistry exams, it was possible to get an extra year's grant, which I was awarded. But I was informed that it was for studying the social sciences at the University of Leeds. I was devastated, as it meant leaving London.

This was one of those many occasions when a fate against which I initially fought made a brilliant choice for me. Yorkshire, I soon loved; the Yorkshire people had more aphorisms and wittier folk sayings than anywhere I have been – but it was the flourishing student culture and low cost of living that knocked me out.

I felt that, unbeknownst to "the boring old Edwardians," their long political reign was ending. It would not taint those of us who knew that we were a radically different generation. I felt that I was living in Monty Python's Flying Circus. I had begun to realize that Eric Idle, John Cleese and the rest of the crew were incapable of being deferential. It was no wonder then that deference for my generation was virtually inconceivable. So was gravity.

To understand the significance of the 11-plus examination in the narrowing of the future possibilities for working-class people, it is useful to look at the relationship between class and university education for my cohort of university entrants. In the early 1960s, only 6% of young people went to university; for young people as a whole, for every student who went to university, 15 would not go there. Furthermore, 75% of those who became university students came from the 25% of the population who were middle or upper class; 25% were from the 75% who were working class; the middle- or upper-class 20-year-old was ten times more likely to be at a university than a working-class 20-year-old.

At the age of 20 I had discovered in Leeds a brilliant, creative community. Here it was possible to watch in a leisurely way the films of Ingmar Bergman and Jean Luc Godard; to enjoy concrete poetry; to listen to jazz, blues and "sweet soul music"; to organize against right-wing complacency; to live communally; and to build organizations premised on minimal hierarchy and participatory democracy. It was a "socialist cornucopia." My organizational involvement was mainly with the syndicalist groupuscule, *Solidarity*, a small British outpost of the much more fashionable French *Socialisme ou Barbarie*, which featured Jean Francois Lyotard and Paul Cardan (aka Cornelius Castoriadis).

Having graduated, I moved back to London and started teaching at Polytechnic of North London. Life went on as before, but more intensely. My Polytechnic was notable for the extent to which we demanded a thoroughgoing democratization so that all affected by any set of decisions had a right to have a vote in the decision-making process. It was deeply anti-authoritarian politics. There were also demands that Marxist and other radical thinkers be read and discussed. In Sociology, many of us read approvingly Marx's "Theses on Feuerbach" citing in particular the 11th thesis: "The philosophers have only interpreted the world, in various ways; the point is to change it." This was read in a way that expanded its possibilities – we believed that the material relations obscuring and, in turn, hidden by the routine workings of commodifying processes could be revealed. However, we also believed that identifying the impact of these processes required a self-reflective orientation to the ways that we were using concepts, particularly because these were developed through imaginative theorizing, including the development of new concepts. Such theorizing needed to be rendered coherent, non-eclectic and empirically supported.

At that time, in and beyond the university there was a *passionate seriousness* about developing an accurate understanding of how society actually worked. This meant that left-wing scholars of all ages took seriously the discourses of a wide range of academic disciplines. To use our current language, ontological, epistemological and ethical issues were seen as important, and there were attempts to be rigorous in specifying and developing the nature and the content of conceptual systems. There was a commitment to determining the nature of phenomena, to discover and render rigorous the most appropriate methods to understand and analyse them. Many were exploring the different forms that social life had taken and could take whilst identifying and challenging the forces that blocked these possibilities. There was an especial concern with the significance of different levels of substantive equality and inequality and the possibilities of participatory democracy in institutional and interpersonal relations.

Importantly, there was an awareness that both theory and empirical analysis play essential roles in understanding the world and developing strategies to transform it, ideally, into societies where all members could easily secure the material necessities of life, leaving them freer to choose which of their talents to develop, for their own good and in friendly support of like-minded others. Marxism was the main reference point for both my interlocutors and myself. I learned a great deal from reading Marx himself, sometimes independently, but often while guided by humanistic, Hegelian, revolutionary and/or structuralist Marxist discourses – all contributed to a time of great intellectual creative effervescences.

At this time, it certainly seemed to me that Marx quite often changed the meaning and significance of his concepts (e.g. his definition of capitalism, and the lists he made of the number and nature of modes of production). I was already sufficiently influenced by Saussure to recognize that the advocates of a humanist Marx often worked with an essentialist conception of discourse, treating changes in the meaning of a word/concept as a development of or a correction of an enduring word/concept, thereby assuming that these changes only modified the accidental attributes of the word/concept while leaving its kernel/essence intact. Rather, I had begun to understand that the very meaning of a word/concept was defined by the sets of words/concepts of which it was a part, gathered together and organized and deployed within distinctive discursive formations. In other words, the degree of continuity in the meaning of a word/concept in different texts had to be established, not assumed. But this could be a difficult process. After all, there was no consistency in the way that Marx's statement that "men make history, but not under conditions of their own choosing" was used in his concrete analyses of different societies. To claim to know the "central discourse in Marx" or that there was a "true Marx" while other Marxisms were heretical, seemed to me foolhardy. Such judgements denied the significance of the task of analysing different empirical worlds and of investigating how different forms of revolutionary practice could subvert relations, which concealed many of the modes of exploitation and oppression continuously at work.

I will return briefly to the struggles within the academic milieu. While making no claims that it was more important than any other academic institution, the Polytechnic of North London was a particular target of repression. Although this was partly internal, due to some divisions among faculty, it was also orchestrated by forces external to the polytechnic. The recently appointed principal of the institution, Terence Miller, was no friend of participatory democracy. It was rumoured that he was connected to the Special Branch and that he may have been rewarded for his role in safeguarding what were termed "British interests" in Rhodesia. And, of some relevance, for a long period, the first question that the extremely right-wing Minister of Education, Keith Joseph, asked of his staff when he arrived at his office was "What has been done about Polytechnic of North London?"

A late recruit to the Sociology Department was Caroline Cox, a militant Christian and co-author of a grossly inaccurate book, *The Rape of Reason*. Ignoring all the usual guidelines for the process, she was appointed by the administration to be head of the department. She subsequently became an important public spokesperson for Thatcherism. Indeed, Margaret Thatcher elevated her to the House of Lords as Baroness Cox, where she continued campaigning for right-wing causes. There was no reason for any hidden conspiracy, the Right was free to do what it wanted to do, the mass media were certainly not concerned about democracy and established procedures and "the rule of law" mattered not a whit.

However, in the annals of oppression and resistance, what happened in British higher education is of relatively little significance. For revolutionary politics, including university politics, and for the struggle against organized repression, Latin American Marxism surely has the most to teach us. In 1973, I had been teaching summer school in a still very radical California when the CIA-sponsored murderous coup placed Pinochet in power in Chile. In contrast to the conventional reporting by the major networks, radical networks provided heart-breaking testimony on what actually took place. This provided irrefutable evidence of how the United States dominated Latin America. However autonomous and seemingly "democratic" its component countries appeared, the limits of their freedom were made evident by the destruction of Allende's democratic socialist project. For me personally, this was a major event that inspired *CotP*.

Without going into further detail, this and variations of it remained my world until about 1976, the year *CotP* was published.

## *Crimes of the Powerful*: continuities, challenges and aftermaths

*CotP* is a book of applied Marxist theory. It is an historical materialist analysis of the nexus of institutions and social relations required if a capitalist mode of production is to be produced and reproduced.

As a Marxist, I argue that what are often described as free-market societies are better described as capitalist societies and more precisely as capitalist modes of production and their enabling social formations comprising capitalistic economic relations and the social, legal and political institutions that can secure their conditions of existence. In capitalism a minority of the population owns most of the wealth, including the means of production, and the mass of the population do not own enough resources to survive without engaging in wage labour, working for others. Capitalists exist as individual owners of means of production, where they employ particular wage labourers, and as members of a class of capitalists, with whom they share an interest in maintaining capitalistic economic relations, a legal system that prioritizes absolute property rights over labour rights, a socio-political system that at best is a paternalist and pseudo-democratic system, and at worst a potential Chile. But all capitalistic social formations require subjection to the hegemony of a capitalist ruling class.

In capitalist economies surplus value is extracted from the working class by a system of unequal exchange. When workers and capitalists confront each other at the bargaining table, the vastly greater resources of the capitalists compared to the extremely limited resources of workers mean that the capitalists are in a position to impose a settlement in which the workers receive only a fraction of the value added by their labour power. Exploitation takes place in the production process. More value is added by the socially necessary labour that workers contribute to the production processes than the value of the commodities required to reproduce themselves and their families – the value of what Marx calls labour power. This surplus value is appropriated by the capitalist class. Such a mode of production can take various forms, and in all instances the owners benefit at the workers' expense.

These processes are concealed in part by an ideology that occludes the exploration of fundamental conditions of existence of this mode of production – for example, that workers on the whole will have scant opportunity to become self-employed because the capitalist class monopolizes the means of production. In 21st-century capitalism, the relationships are particularly unequal because production is organized oligopolistically. The American economy has long been a classic example of oligopolistic capitalism. The implications of this are a major concern of *CotP*.

If anything, the global economy has become even more oligopolistic since *CotP*'s publication 40 years ago. Similar ideologies are still at work, aided by a now 24-hour global news cycle. Repression has always played an important role in maintaining the capitalist status quo. Current incarceration rates of Afro-Americans constitute a stunning manifestation of this. Hence, ideological mystification and state repression must be seen as conditions of existence for a capitalist mode of production to sustain itself. Thus, a combination of inequalities in resources, ideological obfuscations and state-organized repression must be seen as intrinsic to capitalism. Capitalism necessarily projects an imaginary social order.

In the years and now decades following the publication of *CotP*, reading Althusser and Foucault's writings on discourse and discursive formations profoundly changed my way of reading and judging texts, including Marxist theory. But this has involved no simple endorsement of Althusser or Foucault. I have never felt a need to simply be swallowed-up by any one theoretical position, although Marxism, in one or another of its variants, has always played a major role in my thinking. As those who have read my work and conversed with me over the years will know, I have always and continue to engage with the challenge of new ideas, and my thinking has never been static. After writing *CotP* there was an additional change: I developed a way of working which allowed me to welcome dialogue with certain complex non-Marxists, including, most notably, Emile Durkheim. As I read it, Durkheim's work is in many ways complementary to Marx; for example, Durkheim's discussion of fatalism and the forced division of labour provides a way to understand the anomic condition which led people to vote for Trump in the 2016 U.S. election.

Although my analytic reference point is deeply sociological, I believe that Marxist theory remains the most powerful analytic for examining the workings of capitalist economies. However, like the rest of contemporary social thought, it has developed new concepts and categories to make sense of the changing global order and its consequences for the societies in which we live and the kinds of lives that are made possible (or impossible). If I were to rewrite *CotP* today, I would explore inequalities of gender, disability, and racialization, as well as class, and my framework would be more global and more environmental. However, the basic critical vision which informed *CotP* when I wrote it remains essentially unchanged. The animating ideal was perhaps best articulated in 1848 in the *Communist Manifesto* when Marx and Engels envisioned a society on whose banner are written the words "the free development of each [is] the condition for the free development of all."

## Acknowledgments

This article is a rewritten version of the talk I delivered to open the first session of the conference on "Revisiting *Crimes of the Powerful*" which took place on 25 and 26 May 2017, at Osgoode Hall, York University. This conference came about as a consequence of a series of discussions between Steve Bittle, Laureen Snider, Steve Tombs and Dave Whyte about how to memorialize the 40th anniversary of Pluto Press's publication of *CotP*. It was decided that a suitable marker would be the publication of a book of essays written by authors for whom the encounter with *CotP* has been noteworthy and of some lasting significance.

When Margaret Beare became aware of these plans, she suggested that the Social Sciences and Humanities Research Council (SSHRC) of Canada might be willing and able to support this initiative by funding a conference dedicated to further developing the growing corpus of work of radical and scholarly work, of which *CotP* is an example. This corpus is notable for its fusion of sophisticated social theorizing, rigorous empirical research and practical proposals for legal and other kinds of reform. She made a successful application to SSHRC to fund a conference on "Revisiting *Crimes of the Powerful*" which she then organized. This turned out to be a very exciting, cooperative and constructive conference. For this I am grateful to Margaret, who is herself a significant figure in the study of organized crime, particularly in Canada and more globally. I also want to give thanks to Mike Woodiwiss, who has spent many years studying organized crime in the United States and who has used this conference as a place to positively evaluate my critique in *CotP* of the view that Al Capone ran Chicago. Capitalists organize themselves as a class and control and influence political institutions as a class; they generally learn that if they become the dominant class, that ruling a complex society requires the development of a complex division of labour with different institutional forms achieving somewhat different tasks. Although they always seek to impose their interests as requiring most attention, they also realize that there are advantages in allowing a certain freedom to other institutions, for example, governments and churches. In 2004 Mike presciently coined the phrase "gangster capitalism" as a way of characterizing the economic system currently dominating our lives.

In addition to those I have already thanked I want to mention a number of faculty now working in Canadian universities who as graduate students worked with me to develop fresh ways of thinking about social theory and about crime's place within such theory. I am thinking in particular of Ronjon Paul Datta at the University of Windsor, Danica Dupont at Queen's University, Jon Frauley at the University of Ottawa, Nick Hardy at the University of New Brunswick, Fredericton and Dean Curran at the University of Calgary. Intellectual work, after all, is inescapably a collective endeavour – something that, as Durkheim would have said, is qualitatively different from, and often greater than, the sum of its parts. This is particularly true when the intellectual production emerges out of long-term relationships between comrades, colleagues, faculty and graduate students. But bear in mind that in a sense there is rarely a single author of any particular text; rather, there are collective authors. In this case there are four other contributors to my thought and to my capacity to write the words I have written: my personal assistant and good friend, Kat Flanagan; my sister, Patricia Reddy; my dear friend, Lorna Weir; and my demanding but ever-kind interlocutor, Tara Milbrandt.

Frank Pearce

# Acknowledgements

As editors, we would like to thank all the contributors, with whom it's been a pleasure to work – a far from standard experience in putting together an edited collection. Special thanks also go to Gregg Barak, Tom Sutton and Hannah Catterall for their support in getting this collection into print, as well as to Margaret Beare and all of the staff and volunteers (especially Saana Ahmed, Lielle Gonsalves, Jasmine Hebert, Hannah Malik and Sarah Pedigo) who put so much work into organising the conference "Revisiting *Crimes of the Powerful* – A Global Conversation on Capitalism, Corporations and Crime" at Osgoode Hall Law School in May 2017. It was integral to the success of this book – and a total pleasure to attend. Thank you also to the Social Sciences and Humanities Research Council of Canada (Connection Grant # 611-2016-0409), the Jack and Mae Nathanson Centre on Transnational Human Rights, Crime and Security, Osgoode Hall Law School, York University and the Department of Sociology, Queen's University for providing financial and in-kind support for the conference.

In addition, we would like to acknowledge the friendship and support of our colleagues in the Department of Social Policy & Criminology at the Open University, in Sociology, Social Policy & Criminology at the University of Liverpool, the Department of Criminology at the University of Ottawa and the members of the European Group for Deviance and Social Control. We also thank our family and friends who over the years have been important to us both personally and intellectually. Steve Tombs and Dave Whyte would particularly like to thank Joe Sim (sorry you could not join us in this venture Joe, until the next time), Dani Jimenez, Alejandro Forero, Pablo Ciocchini and Roy Coleman; Steven Bittle would like to thank his family, Ruth and Finley, as well as Katherine Lippel and Jennifer Quaid; and Laureen Snider would like to thank her family, especially grand-daughter Soleil who kindly waited until after the conference to be born.

# Revisiting *Crimes of the Powerful*

## An introduction

*Steven Bittle, Laureen Snider, Steve Tombs and David Whyte*

More than 40 years have passed since the publication of Frank Pearce's seminal book, *Crimes of the Powerful: Marxism, Crime and Deviance* (*CotP*). In it, Pearce incisively interrogates crimes of the powerful in the United States, while also critiquing liberal orthodox criminology, particularly in relation to labelling theory and symbolic interactionism, and offering key Marxist insights into the complex relations between crime, law and the state in the reproduction of the capitalist social order. *CotP* was ground-breaking work: to our knowledge Pearce was the first to use the term "crimes of the powerful." In our opinion, the book never garnered the attention it deserved, a fact owing to the ongoing neglect of crimes of the powerful in criminological thinking and general academic antipathy towards Marxism that became prevalent in the years following its publication. At the same time, however, Pearce's work has been a tremendously productive influence for many critical scholars working in the field. In this respect, even though much has changed socially, politically and economically since *CotP* was first published, an ongoing and seemingly endless list of crimes of the powerful globally, along with neoliberal capitalism's continued dominance, generating massive inequalities for all but the economically powerful – the 1% – provides fertile ground for reflecting on Pearce's work and its continued relevance in the contemporary context.

The chapters in this collection bring together scholars working in a variety of disciplines, including criminology, sociology, law, socio-legal studies, political science and history who have been influenced by *CotP*. This book is not intended as a hagiography, nor does it seek to represent all the areas of social scientific interest which have appeared since *CotP*'s publication. Instead, the book collects together original contributions with academic merit which develop or supplement some of Pearce's key insights and concerns. The goal is thus to extend and explore Pearce's work in ways that help us understand and challenge contemporary forms of crimes of the powerful in all of their (dis)guises. In this introduction we explore some of the main themes of *CotP*, situating those themes within the current capitalist conjuncture.

## The real and the imaginary social order

Throughout *CotP* Pearce reminds us of the imaginary social order that is reproduced through the complex and varied relations within and between states and corporations. A key point for Pearce (2015) is that the maintenance and reproduction of the capitalist social formation requires continuous effort to ensure "the transformation of consciousness and the conditions of existence of those who live in such societies." Nowhere does this argument presuppose a process that is "planned or automatic in outcome." It is instead a story of how capitalism "comes through societies and relations to produce economic reductionism" (Pearce 2015). In so doing an illusionary portrayal of society is constructed in that the material realities of life under capitalism are, indeed, significantly different from what is officially claimed through liberal democratic speak. Within this imaginary social order one finds a number of inter-locking elements: an economy based on private property with many competing businesses, each with many shareholders, an economy where ownership and control are separated; an economy where only the most efficient and innovative corporations become dominant. If they were not the most efficient, the argument goes, the market would eliminate them (1976: 94). As Pearce (1976: 96) argued,

> the common sense picture of the . . . American economy and of the relationship between large corporations and the government. . . [is] illusionary and misleading. The degree of concentration and the extent of the control of the market means that the large corporations continually violate antitrust-laws.

Several essential points flow from Pearce's notion of the "imaginary social order" that remain relevant today and which are highlighted both later and throughout the chapters in this collection. Of particular note is that, as Pearce suggested, the nature and extent of these illusions are reinforced through a series of social relations that not only include states and corporations in their efforts to reproduce capitalist ideals, but also a general indifference within academe to scrutinizing crimes of the powerful. Academics have generally sustained the deep-seated ideological belief that what is "good" for the economy is automatically a positive sum gain for all of society. As Pearce observed in *CotP*, it is difficult to understand the reproduction of the capitalist social order without reflecting on the refusal of much of academe to conduct research on crimes of the powerful. In this respect, it is necessary to revisit Pearce's critique of orthodox criminology and its relevance for interrogating the neoliberal dominance that has taken root over the past three decades.

## The limits of orthodox criminology

As Pearce argued: "within sociology, and particularly within criminology, the serious study of the state and its agents and of the activities of the ruling class is virtually non-existent" (1976: 158). Pearce expressed particular concern with the limitations of labelling theory and symbolic interactionism (SI), two "critical" modes of thinking that emerged in the early 1970s which represented a turn from an individualist criminology fixated on blue-collar crime towards one that addressed societal and state reactions in (literally) creating criminals. The problem, according to Pearce, was that labelling and SI remained transfixed by criminology's tendency to operate as a "policy science" which effectively reinforced the "assumptions made by government bureaucracies" that a clear distinction could be made between "normal and deviant" behaviour (Pearce 1976: 25). Although labelling and SI questioned the unequal application of criminal and deviant labels, they ignored the underlying consensus-based idealism that made it possible to look down the social hierarchy at the so-called "nuts, sluts and perverts" (Liazos 1972) and ignore crimes of the powerful. Labelling and SI thus remained circumscribed by state-dominated definitions of crime and deviance.

Of course much has changed in criminological thinking since labelling and SI; detailed discussions relating to gender, race and intersectionality are absent from *CotP*.[1] At the same time, we also note the general absence of analyses of patriarchy, racism and other forms of intersectional oppression in the literature of "crimes of the powerful" *since* the publication of *CotP*. There is no good reason for this, especially when we recognize that patterns of victimization in workplaces and in communities are always gendered and always shaped in relation to racialized structures of vulnerability. There are some scattered exceptions that show how women's vulnerability as consumers and as workers is central to understanding the unequal distribution of corporate crime victimization along lines of class *and* gender (Croall 1995; Szockyj and Fox 1996; Wonders and Danner 2002; Wonders and Danner 2015). There are also contributions that place colonialism at the centre of their analysis (Agozino 2003; Lasslett 2014). But such contributions remain relatively rare since our work remains siloed in a category that deals with the "economy" or the state's administration of the economy as a sphere of study that is separated from the literature on other forms of oppression. This is undoubtedly a major failure in the scholarship since the publication of *CotP*.

A different, but related, failure is that as a discipline criminology still fails to interrogate categories of crime as social constructions (Snider 2000). This failure is particularly germane in light of what Box (1983) characterized more than 30 years ago as the "collective ignorance" of criminology towards corporate crimes and crimes of the powerful. And although moments of crisis such as the 2007–2008 global financial meltdown typically generate "new" criminological interest, the bulk of such studies approach problems of global capital as aberrations – that is, the immoral decisions of a few corrupt individuals in an otherwise effective, essential system of production (Tombs 2016). Or they make passing reference to these "deviant" acts before retreating back to the world of "real" crimes (Tombs and Whyte 2015). In this sense the discipline of criminology continues to dance to its own tune, fetishizing the crimes that have preoccupied it since its inception.

Pearce also critiqued labelling and SI theories for producing a pluralized account of power. Although more radical forms of labelling (for example, Becker 1967) recognized that not all groups in society benefited equally from the existing social order, they failed to ask what made certain groups the targets of labelling and not others. Even if radical pluralism demanded "fairness" in the process of labelling acts as criminal or deviant, it lacked the analytical tools to unpack this claim. Labelling theories generally viewed power as the (unequal) interaction between competing interests rather than a structurally flawed "struggle of ideas and class forces" integral to the reproduction of the capitalist social formation. For Pearce (ibid. 31), Lemert's argument that radical ideas failed to materialize in American society because they were not seen as practical or realistic for/by the majority of the population, and therefore state responses to radicalism were sometimes understandable, was particularly instructive: it revealed the failure of labelling theory to interrogate the relations of power that *supported* official "overreactions" to all radical ideals seen as threats to the social order. The powerful anti-socialist interests behind McCarthyism in 1950s United States are a case in point, as are the corporate forces behind heavy-handed state responses to anti-globalization protests associated with various G-8 and G-20 summits. As Pearce (1976: 35 – emphasis original) noted in underscoring the role of the state in quelling social unrest, "there are circumstances where, if left unrepressed, *socialist ideas will spread because of their relevance*," a fact that can and does necessitate state intervention by hegemonic interests to (re)secure the status quo.

The aforementioned tendencies of labelling and SI to incorporate official definitions of crime and deviance within the context of pluralist thinking resulted in little analytical space to contemplate the role of the state in resecuring the capitalist social order. As we shall see, Pearce could not have known that, as he launched this critique, the state would slip even further from academic scrutiny due to the post-modern turn taken by many social sciences in the next decade. Indeed, Pearce's critique of pluralism is even more relevant today given the dominance of post-modern and post-structuralist schools that position power within a multitude of relations that exist throughout the social body. As Coleman et al. (2009) argue, over the last 30 years the state has been "gradually airbrushed out of critical analysis," giving way to new forms of "liberal speak" that focus on forms of power that emanate though different governmental and non-governmental institutions, therein obscuring the role of the state in reproducing the social formation. However, as Pearce foregrounded, and as many of the contributions in this collection demonstrate, the state is a *process*, not a thing, that "provides the arena for the organization of social forces" that are constantly in flux and necessarily drawing from both "'public' and 'private' interests" (Coleman et al. 2009: 9).

## Neoliberalism

To comprehend the reasons why the state further disappeared from academic scrutiny requires some consideration of the "tectonic shift in public policy"

(Fudge and Cossman 2002: 3) that was underway as Pearce was writing *CotP* and which he and others have since analysed and described as "neoliberalism." In November 1979, the election of Ronald Reagan in the United States and of Margaret Thatcher in the United Kingdom officially launched the religion of neoliberalism, which "swept across the world like a vast tidal wave of institutional reform and discursive adjustment" (Harvey 2007: 23). Subsequently across much of the capitalist world, a form of highly idealized free market economics was adopted within which the state was said to be of diminishing relevance, as markets and private capital were "freed" from state interference.

Now, some four decades later, with neoliberal ideology still intact, the state is at once *less* visible but also *more* visible than was the case when Pearce made this observation. Through privatization, deregulation and downsizing, states have handed responsibility for formerly public goods and services to private capital, creating new markets and new terrain upon which profit can be generated. Though moments of exposure for the capitalist state – such as frauds and industrial disasters – have forced re-regulation in some of these sectors, state, neoliberal and academic "experts" have talked states into irrelevance. As we discuss in more detail later, such "experts" insist that states no longer directly intervene in any form of economic activity. Yet at the same time, the essential role of the state in responding to crises engendered by private capital has highlighted the inherent contradictions within neoliberalism, intellectually, economically and politically. State intervention in saving the powerful from their frauds and disasters has become a key point of vulnerability for neoliberal ideology and practice. As "post"-crisis states have repackaged private debt into national debt and reframed private corporate recklessness into public profligacy and lassitude, they have ironically recast the corporation from a potential problem to the only hope of economic recovery. Thus governments, not least the UK government, now claim the 2007–2008 meltdown of the economy (created by the misdeeds of the private sector) forces them to create greater "freedom" for markets, opening up ever greater terrain for private capital to colonize. In fact, however, these so-called private–public partnerships are overseen by national and local states, albeit through a complex myriad of contractual and interorganizational relationships – so that if scratched, the surface appearance of private delivery reveals only too clearly the essential imbrication of corporate and state structures.

The advent of neoliberalism also ushered in a period of official state antipathy to government regulation of business (deemed "interference"). The disciples of neoliberalism, dedicated to setting business "free," pursued policy agendas that lowered corporate taxes, increased globalized trade, abolished tariffs, privatized many formerly public services (for example, water, energy and transportation) and drastically increased financialization – the practice of applying a monetary (exchange) value to everything that can be touched (tangible goods, services, natural resources) or imagined (futures, derivatives, intangible concepts and processes). The process of financialization has been enforced across the globe by the Washington consensus and the institutional architecture of IFIs (international financial institutions) and international trade agreements that enforced it. This set of institutional arrangements that Stephen Gill describes as a "new constitutionalism" (Gill 1995: 412) imposes disciplinary neoliberalism through a system of policy appropriation and surveillance mechanisms. Over the subsequent decades those processes have produced a mammoth increase in inequality within and between states, and not coincidentally in political, economic and cultural corporate power. And in one contribution to analysing the overall structure that produced corporate crime in the neoliberal period, Laureen Snider (2000) noted that strategies of accumulation realigned the balance of social forces in capitalist economies in a contradictory form. On one hand, neoliberalism created fertile conditions for producing corporate crimes. On the other hand, it diminished our capacity to describe and respond to them. Corporate crime, for Snider, was effectively being defined out of existence by neoliberal ideals and the policies that followed those ideals. In Pearce's terms the international nature of regulation itself was creating an illusion of corporate crime's disappearance.

It is with these neoliberal forms of regulation in mind that we return to Pearce's work in *CotP* and, in particular, his position that we must dissect bourgeois law in order to comprehend how corporations and powerful corporate actors regularly avoid legal scrutiny, for it is "only by understanding why certain actions are *not* prohibited by law . . . that we can make sense of the social relationships inside the capitalist world system" (Pearce 1976: 80). For Pearce this included an understanding of laws that are introduced to address the abuses of corporate power, but also those which ultimately, although not automatically or necessarily, reproduce dominant class interests. There is a section of *CotP*, for instance, where Pearce empirically documented how labour laws were used to "pre-empt" the "radical potential of an increasingly powerful trade union movement" and were safely ignored once trade unions were co-opted. Likewise, Pearce outlined the passage, revision and enforcement of anti-trust legislation in the United States, laws putatively designed to force companies to compete openly and fairly in the "free" market. He argued that these and similar laws are only passed when levels of social unrest threaten the capitalist status quo. When such a threat is recognized, business then becomes actively involved in shaping the legislation it can no longer prevent, in ways that guarantee the continued "stability, predictability and security" of a viable (read "profitable") capitalist system. Thus the approach of corporate CEOs to regulation is always "calculative" (Pearce 1976: 84) – corporations obey as much law(s) as they deem necessary for their continued existence and prosperity and no more. Pearce then showed the tiny number of prosecutions launched against major corporations since the three key American anti-trust statutes, the Sherman Act (1890), the Clayton Act (1914) and the Federal Trade Commission Act (FTC) (1914), were passed and argued that government action had done little to impede the formation and growth of monopolies and much to preserve and dramatize "an imaginary social order" (Pearce 1976: 90) where rich and powerful lawbreakers are subject to the same punishments as the poor and powerless. A similar pattern has emerged since the early 2000s with the introduction of corporate criminal liability and corporate manslaughter laws in countries such as Canada, the United Kingdom and Australia: these measures have also, thus far, been largely unenforced, symbolic measures which have failed to hold corporations and corporate executives to account for negligently killing workers and/or members of the public (Bittle 2012; Tombs and Whyte 2007 and 2015; Tombs 2013 and 2016).

However, as Pearce argued, law's failure to hold powerful individuals to account does not mean that law is a tool of capital, but that it is a site of struggle where powerful class interests and subjects are reproduced. In this sense he urged us to understand why certain laws were formed or not formed, the ways in which they were conceptualized (including the conditions that made it possible, even necessary, to contemplate criminal laws in the first place) and the ways in which these laws are (or more aptly are not) enforced, therein helping to reveal both the factors that downplay the seriousness of corporate crime and the social relationships in contemporary capitalism that help (re)produce or (re) secure this outcome. This struggle over the meaning of law and its outcomes has particular relevance within the context of neoliberalism.

In American anti-trust law, for instance, the neoliberal shift led to intense, endless battles among academics (primarily economists, lawyers and business gurus) over how, when and whether governments should intervene to prevent business monopolies. When the Democratic Party was in power, enforcing anti-trust laws was generally favoured (and to some degree practiced); under Republican governments it was not. This does not mean anti-trust laws have remained unchanged since 1976 – penalties for law breakers have been regularly increased. (There is no downside to appearing "tough on corporate lawbreakers" if the laws are not enforced; indeed such actions reinforce Pearce's imaginary social order.) Thus the maximum fines and jail terms under the Sherman, Clayton and FTC acts now stand at $100 million and/or six years imprisonment and/or fines of twice the amount gained by the conspirators or lost by their victims if either amount is over $100 million (Kobayashi 2001). And after more than four decades of both Democratic and Republican regimes, the American economy today is more dominated by oligopolies and monopolies than ever. For example, three leading companies, Kraft, Pepsi and Nestle, dominate worldwide food production; Airbus and Boeing control the aircraft market; Microsoft, Sony and Nintendo control the video console market. In the United States, six movie studios reap 87% of all motion pictures revenue; four wireless providers control 89% of the cellular market; four airlines – Delta, United, Southwest and American/USAir – control the American airline industry.

The effects of neoliberal capital are also evident in the nature and scope of corporate regulation globally. Corporate infrastructures – and the power bases upon which they depend – have their origins in the material practices of nation-states. Thus, it is national governments that establish the juridical and administrative framework for corporations, transport and communication infrastructures and that organize diplomatic relationships with states to enhance opportunities for import, export and investment and so on. States help to constitute capital, commodity, commercial and residential property markets; help to produce different kinds of "human capital"; constitute labour markets; regulate the employment contract; constitute economic enterprises through the rules of incorporation; specify the rules of liability; and so on (Tombs and Whyte 2015). But a close reading of the historical origins of all of those apparently *national* infrastructural sources of corporate power must also be understood in the context of *international* political economy. Though the principle of limited liability arguably originated in 15th-century England, it was a tightly restricted privilege, granted to a select few. It was not until the early 19th century that the modern form of the corporation began in the United States, the UK and France, and states began conferring unlimited liability freely. The result was an exponential increase in the infrastructural powers of corporations. By the dawn of the 20th century all European states had legislated to create their corporations in the same image. This process occurred because of the structural advantages in production and trading that the limited liability corporate structure provided to owners and the competitive advantages accruing to states that employed this model of property investment. Thus, a model that had its origins in national debates and national legislatures followed a logic that was given force at the level of international political economy.

The emergence of the limited liability corporation – which afforded owners exceptional privileges of immunity from the risk of investment – provides a clear example of how regulation plays a creative and enabling role for regimes of capital accumulation at the level of the global economy. Here we find similar processes and practices that enable the formation of particular capitals to be reproduced. Thus, *lex mercatoria* (the laws and norms that have evolved to cover commercial law and arbitration), global trade agreements (such as those established in the World Trade Organization [WTO]) and bilateral agreements on market access (such as the Transatlantic Trade and Investment Partnership) provide key examples of how the coercive and infrastructural power of states combines to shape the conditions for capital accumulation. The architecture of international sources of regulation shows that the lines of separation across state power and corporate power are not easily drawn. Corporate power in this sense is wholly reliant upon a series of regimes of permission (Whyte 2014; Bernat and Whyte 2015), including the permission to trade as a separate entity; the permission to structure ownership in particular ways; investment regimes which permit particular privileges; the permission for corporations to act as holders of "rights"; and so on.

Those privileges and rights in turn are guaranteed by policy and practice, and central to the policy effort are IFIs such as the World Bank, the International Monetary Fund and the European Central Bank. Those institutions impose conditions on an increasing number of nation-states that rely upon access to credit that, in turn, enhances the structural domination of the world's largest corporations. The power to employ workers, to buy and sell goods and services, to deal in financial markets, to transform future surplus value into capital on stock markets are also only possible as a result of a broader complex of *international* regimes of permission that are guaranteed and underwritten by nation-states, but which are guided by norms of conduct that are part of a complex international recognition of a very particular legal form of the corporation as the principal economic actor.

## Academic knowledge claims

Once again, academic knowledge claims have played an integral role in reinforcing the global rights and privileges of the powerful by giving them legitimacy. Regulatory orthodoxy today, in sociology, business, law and criminology, asserts that the state has been decentred, replaced by fragmented, networked power where the state shares power with a range of actors and institutions, creating governance systems where power is fleeting and fluid. As Parker and Nielsen (2009: 46) put it: "the distribution of power at both national and global levels is shaped by interactions between state-based regulation, business activity and civil society" And: "state power [today] is often not about imposing sovereign will, but about building networks" (Braithwaite and Drahos 2000: 31–2). The "plural, de-centered and networked nature of regulation" (Parker and Nielsen 2009: 47) ("network governance") means that "trust and empowered reflexivity" have replaced state coercion (Davis 2011: 8; Beck 1992; Giddens 1984; 1990). In this new social order, universal, more democratic risks pervade modern social systems: rich and poor suffer equally from climate change, nuclear war, financial meltdowns and polluted air. Structurally based inequality, for these theorists, is not a central, nor even for some even a present, concern.

At the policy level scholars studying business regulation have interpreted governance theories to mean that even the most powerful states cannot adequately police corporations or markets. Thus, in well-intentioned attempts to find some way of controlling corporate criminality without abolishing capitalism (seen as an unrealistic, impossible goal), regulatory scholarship has adopted a version of the liberal "middle way" described earlier. Regulators can be most effective in a neoliberal, globalized world, it is argued, if they concentrate their resources on the sectors and sub-sectors where risks of non-compliance are greatest and the consequences of the most dire forms of law breaking or the businesses most "at risk" of offending. This "regulation school" (Tombs 2012) assumes that corporations in general accept dominant moral values and legal commitments and are inherently risk averse; therefore, regulators should help them comply through advice and education, rather than resorting to punitive law enforcement. Full, vigorous enforcement of regulatory laws should be reserved for businesses that repeatedly fail to comply and the hypothesized small number of "bad apples" (firms which should, in any case, have been identified by the risk assessment exercise). Regulation must become a process of negotiation and compromise, not a unitary – and particularly not a punitive – response (Parker and Nielsen

2009: 48). This strategy, known as "risk-based responsive regulation," has been adopted in most of the capitalist world.

The problems with such an approach have been highlighted in the legions of corporate crimes that have emerged where mainstream, blue-ribbon corporations – those that standard risk assessments would have deemed low risk and therefore not worthy of regulatory scrutiny – have blatantly and intentionally disobeyed laws. Because their offences typically escape the regulatory gaze, they have generally been discovered by accident, by investigative reporters, crusading politicians or activist groups. For example, in September 2015, Volkswagen admitted that for decades it had been installing "defeat devices" designed to give fraudulent emission ratings. These devices, put in some 11 million diesel cars (the Audi, Golf, Jetta, Passat, Beetle), consisted of inserting software that allowed polluting vehicles to pass U.S. restrictions under the Clean Air Act. The cars were actually emitting 40 times more nitrogen oxide than allowed. This crime was uncovered not by the regulatory agency, but by researchers at Western Virginia University allied with an independent not-for-profit agency, the International Council on Clean Transportation. After they reported the results of their research in May 2014, the Environmental Protection Agency took another 14 months to take definitive actions against VW (Dingman 2015).

One might also consider the financial crisis of 2008, where high-risk, fraudulent acts by the world's leading financial institutions sent global markets crashing. Virtually overnight world gross domestic product (GDP) declined 6%, $25 trillion was obliterated from capital markets and millions of people lost their jobs and retirement prospects and experienced profound attacks on their life chances. In the decade leading up to the crash, investment bankers, in a never-ending quest for ever higher profits (and bonuses), invented numerous speculative, unregulated financial instruments. Foremost among these (and not coincidentally key factors in the credit collapse of 2008) were mathematically based ways of hiding risk by conceptualizing, bundling assets of varying worth and selling them through financial products such as credit default swaps (CDS), collateralized debt obligations (CDOs) and mortgage-backed securities (MBSs). Despite receiving numerous tips and evidence of wrong-doing from variously situated whistle blowers (Taibbi 2013), the U.S. Securities and Exchange Commission repeatedly failed to restrain, restrict or punish the responsible parties – who were, of course, the blue-ribbon mainstream banks. And to this day although sizeable fines have been levied against some corporations and investment banks, not a single corporate executive has served a day in prison for these activities. The enormous ideological, symbolic and life-threatening power of the sovereign state to criminalize and sanction, so overused against traditional law breakers, has been kind to those whose greed and fraud cause globalized social harm.

The field of regulation, then, is no longer ignored by criminology or sociology. However, the neoliberal turn it has taken fails to recognize the criminogenic nature of the for-profit corporation. Power thus remains pluralized, as

Pearce pointed out more than 40 years ago; something to be controlled and adjusted through continuous technical fixes to regimes of regulation.

## *Crimes of the Powerful* and beyond

In perhaps one of the most commonly quoted passages of *CotP*, Pearce (1976: 105) noted that "[o]nce criminal activity is viewed as one amongst other strategies used by corporations, then one is forced to analyse the overall structure in which they act." In this respect Pearce challenged us to unearth the vulnerabilities and contradictions of capitalism's imaginary social order, both as a means of challenging the many and extensive harms caused by society's most powerful individuals and the institutions that they own and control and to, ultimately, contemplate a different, more equitable society. As Pearce (2015) himself recently noted, *CotP* was meant as a "tentative analysis" that would lead to more "comprehensive accounts of State(s), economy (ies) and ideology (ies)." It is within this spirit that this collection reflects on the continued relevance of *CotP* more than 40 years after its publication and the ways in which it helped spawn new generations of scholars and activists who study and challenge the crimes of the powerful.

Key to these efforts, in the short term, is fostering an understanding that the capitalist status quo, particularly in terms of the interdependence between state and private capital, is dynamic, always in flux, far from secure and constructed on the bases of shifting historical, legal and political foundations. The bank bailouts – and the increasingly obvious imbrication of states and corporations in the still-unfolding post-crisis settlements – certainly remain a moment of exposure for states and corporations, threatening the tales of their independence, indeed, tales skilfully and feverishly spun over decades as part of the wider construction of neoliberal ideology (Peck 2010). As noted earlier, the reassembling of the international capitalist economy has seen widespread state rhetoric regarding the essential role of private capital in "recovery," calls for a reduced state, calls demanding that more "public" functions be handed to "private actors" because of a claimed fiscal crisis. But this game is far from over. It has created risks for state and capital. It generates new forms of disjuncture between the real and imaginary social orders. And it is this space between the real and the imaginary that Peck has identified as the fundamental "curse" of neoliberalism: namely, it can live neither with, nor without, the state. As Peck puts it, "For all its creativity, neoliberal discourse has never provided an elemental answer to this question" (2010: 65). And nor can it.

There are, thus, a series of vulnerabilities integral to the still-unfolding post-2007–2008 settlements between the interdependent state and capital, not least around regulation and enforcement, which allow strategic exploitation as part of a counter-hegemonic challenge. For instance, one feature of the neoliberal period is that some of the key *illusions* of the liberal democratic order have become much more difficult to sustain. Perhaps most obvious is the formal separation – the reification – of the public and private spheres. It is assumed that in liberal democratic systems, public policy making is insulated from the corrupting influence of private interest; the political order is based upon the formal constitutional segregation between public and private spheres. It is this barrier that ostensibly ensures that governments protect the public interest. Liberal democracy is therefore a system of political organization that does not recognize any conflict between the realization of political and economic freedoms, or between the realization of public and private interests. Yet those narratives of formal organization are historically fragile and vulnerable to exposure for the illusionary myths that they are. The neoliberal period has intensified the challenge to the credibility of this illusion.

Perhaps the formally separate relationship between public and private spheres has never been entirely successful at masking the embeddedness of states in markets (Polanyi 1944/1957). But the point is that these contradictions have become more visible under contemporary capitalism. Because neoliberal capitalism conceptualizes the main role of government as facilitating the profitability of business, it encourages closer collaboration between government and capital at an institutional and individual level. An increasingly visible manifestation of this process is the "revolving door" that facilitates the movement of personnel between public and private sectors and provides the social networks that are ultimately used to concentrate power in social elites. In some industrial sectors, revolving-door appointments make it difficult to draw a formal distinction between "public" and "private"' interest (Whyte 2015).

The early 2000s also witnessed the development of a body of work that importantly challenged this reification and foregrounded the state–corporate relation as a means of understanding the production of corporate crime. This literature focuses on the close, and often symbiotic, relationship between state/public actors and private actors (normally large corporations). In doing so, it consistently points to the structure of political economy that creates particular conditions that produce corporate crime (Kramer et al. 2002; Kramer and Michalowski 2006; Lasslett 2014). In this sense, the literature has responded to Pearce's call to analyse the overall structures in which corporations act. As *CotP* made very clear, corporate crimes are not the result of a breakdown in the regulatory function of states; they occur as part and parcel of a process of corporate power mongering and, in the main are tolerated and encouraged by states (see also Bittle 2012; Snider 2015; and Bittle and Snider 2006). In other words, corporate crime occurs not because the state is disobeyed, but generally because the state is *obeyed*. After all, processes of regulation are only ever partially concerned with the "control" of crime or illegalities. In most contexts, regulatory systems are ultimately unable to resolve conflicts and crises, but can merely repackage them in ways that allow governments to, temporarily at least, retain some control over the amelioration of corporate harms (Tombs 2012; Tombs and Whyte 2015; Whyte 2004). In this sense, the term "regulation" should be understood as a matter of how capitalist social orders are governed and normalized (Aglietta 2000).

Other vulnerabilities that have emerged post-2007–2008 present important strategic opportunities for launching a counter-hegemonic challenge. First, the mystification of private efficiency risks being increasingly exposed as corporations are seen to fail to deliver goods and services in new markets. It may become more apparent that new markets created through re-regulation necessarily result in no more, and often ostensibly less, efficient delivery of goods and services (Goodman and Loveman 1991; Simms and Reid 2013).

Second, if corporations are generally inefficient entities benefitting from economies of scale coupled with market power – rather than any competitive superiority per se – the extending reach of private corporations increases the opportunity structures for and likely incidence of harm and crime, and so renders them, again, vulnerable. Indeed, consistent and mounting evidence of corporate harm and crime (see Mokhiber 2003; Violation Tracker n.d.) may increasingly call into question not simply the probity, but may combine to signify the recidivism, of key private players within specific market sectors.

Third, even if the "willingness" on the part of state institutions to "control" corporations exists, the ability to respond effectively to these crimes and harms is limited. More specifically, the very existence and visibility of such corporate oligopolies undermines central claims of neoliberalism and indicates clearly and consistently the limitations of state claims to be able to regulate such markets, corporations or even contracts.

Fourth, it is not just that states are increasingly dependent upon oligopolistic sectors in which a handful of companies dominate for the delivery of basic services; they have become increasingly reliant upon local and national-state contracts for a significant proportion of their income. This is such a level of state dependency that it might best be summed up by the term "corporate welfare" – and it is, of course, antithetical to claims of efficiency, competitiveness and so on. To expose corporate welfare is to expose these central claims, while at the same time opening up a potentially much wider, and socially and politically volatile, contestation over who or what is a benefit scrounger, parasitic on the state, kept alive only by handouts from general taxation.

Taken together, the new forms of and increasing interdependence of states and corporations undermine a central plank of "laissez-faire" discourse – that is, the separations between market and state, economy and politics, private and public. All of these dichotomies are highly ideological, and none bear much relationship to the reality each claims to signify, nor in fact ever could. But they have been highly significant, crucial in fact, to sustaining claims for the superiority of private capital.

As Crouch has argued, one effect of the elevated status of corporations under neoliberalism has been the placing of a greater onus on corporations to provide moral and political leadership. Thus, increasingly, the

> argument that the job of business is just business, and nothing to do with morality or politics, falls to the ground; leading firms are of their own accord, and sometimes virtually officially, taking on moral and political roles. The very ideology that proclaimed the autonomy and superiority of economic motivations has produced complications for those same motivations.
>
> (Couch 2011: 369)

This expectation will most certainly lead to demands being made upon corporations and states which neither is capable of meeting. The rhetorical embrace by many corporations of "corporate social responsibility" exemplifies this development. As the lines which separate the phenomena denoted within each of these couplets become increasingly blurred, what then remains of the claims of neoliberalism? They can still be advanced, of course, but here the disjuncture between the "imaginary" and the "real" social order becomes ever greater. This risks not simply exposure, but also poses very specific challenges.

In short, we may be witnessing a period of increasing corporate vulnerability, which is simultaneously an increasing exposure for the state, the institutions of which paved the way for, maintain and pronounce the superiority of the "private sector." After all, corporate power is far from absolute; corporations must constantly reposition themselves, particularly following major corporate disasters and crises, to (re)secure their hegemonic role as an essential component of the "free" market system. As Tombs and Whyte (2015: 2–3) note, this process entails significant and ongoing work on the part of corporations, with the support of states, to ensure what they call the "synoptic effect of corporate power" that disciplines all of us into seeing the corporation as a "natural and permanent social institution." It is here that *CotP*'s messages, which are revisited in the chapters that follow, remain an important corrective to dominant ways of thinking (academically, politically, socially) that are still fixated on working within the confines of capitalism and which dismiss discussions of social change as "idealistic" (Bittle 2015). To embrace the non-deterministic Marxian thinking that underpinned Pearce's work then and now means that we can never predict when counter-hegemonic struggles will erupt into more fundamental change (Althusser 1971 [2001]). As Pearce (2015) recently argued in reflecting back on the transformative thinking that underpinned his work in *CotP*

> a consolation from [a Marxian] analysis is the conclusion that the current mode of producing goods is neither the only way, nor the best way, of providing for human needs or the necessities of life. They are not required for humanity to live comfortably and safely. Producing plentiful and nutritious

food and other necessities of life could be achieved by organizing societies and institutions that are egalitarian and democratic with open systems of communication and high general levels of education, in other words, in socialist societies.

## Conclusion

This overview has highlighted the changes and the continuities in capitalist economies since the publication of *CotP* – a period of neoliberal globalized capitalism during which the power of corporations has exponentially increased, the democratic welfare state (inadequate as it was) has been systematically and thoroughly dismantled and inequalities within and across societies have widened enormously. We have also explored some of the legitimators and enablers of this social order, including mainstream academic criminology and its continuous refusal to study crimes of the powerful or the capitalist state. But as this book demonstrates, critical scholarship nevertheless thrives. The chapters which follow variously explore, update and extend the theoretical implications of *CotP*; empirically document the various forms of destruction which corporate/state alliances have inflicted on vulnerable populations and environments; and highlight new directions, both theoretical and empirical, that *CotP* scholars are studying today.

## Note

1 Pearce has, however, wrestled with these issues in later publications. See, for example, Dupont and Pearce (2001); Pearce and Frauley (2007).

## References

Aglietta, M. (2000) *A Theory of Capitalist Regulation: The US Experience*. London: Verso.

Agozino, B. (2003) *Counter-Colonial Criminology: A Critique of Imperialist Reason*. London: Pluto.

Althusser, L. (1971 [2001]) *Lenin and Philosophy and Other Essays*. New York, NY: Monthly Review Press.

Beck, U. (1992) *Risk Society: Towards a New Modernity*. London, UK: Sage.

Becker, H. (1967) "Whose Side Are We On?" *Social Problems*, 14(3): 239–247.

Bernat, I. and Whyte, D. (2015) "Entendiendo Los OríGenes Del Crimen Estatal-Corporativo: un análisis de los desastres del Prestige y Morecambe Bay." *Revista Crítica Penal y Poder*, no. 9, September: 255–278.

Bittle, S. (2012) *Still Dying for a Living: Corporate Criminal Liability after the Westray Mining Disasters*. Vancouver, BC: UBC Press.

—— (2015) "Beyond Corporate Fundamentalism: A Marxian Class Analysis of Corporate Crime Law Reform." *Critical Sociology*, 41(1): 133–151.

Bittle, S. and Snider, L. (2006) "From Manslaughter to Preventable Accident: Shaping Corporate Criminal Liability." *Law and Policy*, 28(4): 470–496.

Box, S. (1983) *Power, Crime and Mystification*. London, UK: Tavistock.

Braithwaite, J. and Drahos, P. (2000) *Global Business Regulation*. Cambridge: Cambridge University Press.

Coleman, R., Sim, J., Tombs, S., and Whyte, D. (eds.) (2009) *State, Power, Crime*. London, UK: Sage Publications.

Couch, C. (2011) *The Strange Non-death of Neoliberalism*. Cambridge, UK: Polity Press.

Croall, H. (1995) "Target Women: Women's Victimisation From White Collar Crime," in R. Dobash and L. Noaks (eds.) *Gender and Crime*. Cardiff, UK: Cardiff University.

Davis, J. (2011) *Challenging Governance Theory: From Networks to Hegemony*. Bristol: The Policy Press.

Dingman, S. (2015) "Volkswagen's Deception, and How It Was Discovered." *Globe and Mail*, 22 September 2015. Online. Available HTTP: https://www.theglobeandmail.com/news/national/volkswagens-deception-and-how-it-was-discovered/article26489354/ (accessed 26 March 2018).

Dupont, D. and Pearce, F. (2001) "Foucault Contra Foucault: Rereading the Governmentality Papers." *Theoretical Criminology*, 5(2): 123–158.

Fudge, J. and Cossman, B. (eds.) (2002) *Privatization, Law and the Challenge to Feminism*. Toronto, ON: University of Toronto Press.

Giddens, A. (1984) *Constitution of Society: Outline of the Theory of Structuration*. Berkeley: University of California Press.

Giddens, A. (1990) *Consequences of Modernity*. Stanford, CA: Stanford University Press

Gill, S. (1995) "Globalisation, Market Civilisation and Disciplinary Neo-liberalism." *Millennium: Journal of International Studies*, 24(3): 399–423.

Goodman, J. and Loveman, G. (1991) "Does Privatization Serve the Public Interest?" *Harvard Business Review*, November–December. Online. Available HTTP: https://hbr.org/1991/11/does-privatization-serve-the-public-interest (accessed 20 August 2017).

Harvey, D. (2007) "Neoliberalism as Creative Destruction." *Annals of the American Academy of Political and Social Science*, 610(1): 21–44.

Kramer, R. and Michalowski, R. (2006) "The Original Formulation," in R. Michalowski and R. Kramer (eds.) *State-corporate Crime: Wrongdoing at the Intersection of Business and Government*. New Brunswick, N.J.: Rutgers University Press

Kramer, R., Michalowski, R. and Kauzlarich, D. (2002) "The Origins and Development of the Concept and Theory of State-Corporate Crime." *Crime & Delinquency*, 48(2): 263–282.

Lasslett, K. (2014) *State Crime on the Margins of Empire: Rio Tinto, the War on Bougainville and Resistance to Mining*. London, UK: Pluto Press.

Lemert, E. (1951) *Social Pathology*. New York: McGraw-Hill.

Liazos, A. (1972) "The Poverty of the Sociology of Deviance: Nuts, Sluts, and Perverts." *Social Problems*, 20(1): 103–120.

Mokhiber, R. (2003) "The Top 100 Corporate Criminals of the Decade." Online. Available HTTP: www.informationclearinghouse.info/article3676.htm (accessed 4 October 2017).

Parker, C. and Nielsen, V. (2009) "The Challenge of Empirical Research on Business Compliance in Regulatory Capitalism." *Annual Review of Law and Social Science*, 5: 45–70

Pearce, F. (1976) *The Crimes of the Powerful: Marxism, Crime and Deviance*. London: Pluto Press.

——— (2001) *The Radical Durkheim, Second Edition*. Toronto, Canadian Scholars' Press International.

——— (2015) "Marxism and Corporate Crime in the 21st Century." Red Quill Books Interview Series #3. Interviewed by Steven Bittle. Posted 2 February 2015. Online. Available HTTP: http://redquillbooks.com/wp-content/uploads/2015/02/Interview-with-Frank-Pearce-2.pdf. (accessed 10 August 2017).

Pearce, F. and Frauley, J. (eds.) (2007) *Critical Realism and the Social Sciences: Heterodox Elaborations.* Toronto, ON: University of Toronto Press.

Peck, J. (2010) *Constructions of Neoliberal Reason.* Oxford: Oxford University Press.

Polanyi, K. (1944/1957) *The Great Transformation: The Political and Economic Origins of Our Time.* Boston: Beacon.

Simms, A. and Reid, S. (2013) "'The Private Sector is Superior': Time to Move on From this Old Dogma." *The Guardian,* 25 April. Online. Available HTTP: www.theguardian.com/commentisfree/2013/apr/25/private-sector-superiority-mythbuster (accessed 1 October 2017).

Snider, L. (2000) "The Sociology of Corporate Crime: An Obituary (or: Whose Knowledge Claims Have Legs?)." *Theoretical Criminology,* 4(2); 196–206.

Snider, L. (2015) *About Canada: Corporate Crime.* Winnipeg, MB: Fernwood.

Szockyj, E. and Fox, J. (1996) *The Corporate Victimisation of Women.* Boston: Northeastern University Press.

Tombs, S. (2012) "State-Corporate Symbiosis in the Production of Crime and Harm." *State Crime,* 1(2): 170–195.

——— (2013) "Still Killing With Impunity: Corporate Criminal Law Reform in the UK." *Policy and Practice in Health and Safety,* 11(2): 63–80.

——— (2016) *Social Protection after the Crisis: Regulation Without Enforcement.* Bristol, UK: Policy Press.

Tombs, S. and Whyte D. (2007) *Safety Crimes.* Cullompton, Devon, UK: Willan Publishing.

——— (2015) *The Corporate Criminal: Why Corporations Must Be Abolished.* London, UK: Routledge.

Taibbi, M. (2013) "Why Didn't the SEC Catch Madoff? It Might have been Policy Not to." *Rolling Stone,* 31 May 2013. Online. Available HTTP: www.rollingstone.com/politics/news/why-didnt-the-sec-catch-madoff-it-might-have-been-policy-not-to-20130531 (accessed 4 October 2017).

Violation Tracker (n.d.) Online. Available HTTP: www.goodjobsfirst.org/violation-tracker (accessed 4 October 2017).

Whyte, D. (2004) "Corporate Crime and Regulation," in Muncie, J. and Wilson, D. (eds.) *The Student Handbook of Criminology and Criminal Justice.* London, UK: Cavendish.

——— (2014) "Regimes of Permission and State-Corporate Crime." *State Crime Journal,* (3)2: 237–246.

——— (2015) "Introduction," in Whyte, D. (ed.) *How Corrupt is Britain?* London: Pluto

Wonders, N. and Danner, M. (2002) "Globalisation, State-Corporate Crime and Women: The Strategic Role of Womens' NGOs in the New World Order'," in Potter, G. (ed.) *Controversies in White Collar Crime.* Cincinnati, OH: Anderson.

——— (2015) "Gendering Climate Change: A Feminist Criminological Perspective." *Critical Criminology,* 23(4): 401–416.

# Section I

# Theoretical and conceptual excursions

The articles in Section I explore, update and extend the theoretical implications of *Crimes of the Powerful (CotP)*. Jon Frauley begins with a close and critical reading of *CotP*, demonstrating how Pearce's work provides an "empirically grounded and exemplary work of sociological theorizing," followed by Harry Glasbeek's powerful argument that activists and scholars focus too much on the corporation, a vehicle of capitalism, and too little on the capitalists themselves, the human beings who benefit from and control corporations. Michael Woodiwiss and Margaret Beare present case studies that trace the links between organized crime, corporations and the capitalist state: Woodiwiss shows how the myth of Al Capone and the mammoth super-criminal organization was used to facilitate anti-democratic, anti-radical, anti-union policies in the United States; Beare's study of corruption scandals in Canada shows that professionals and corporations are embedded in and enablers of (if not actual partners in) criminal corruption schemes, not duped or "infiltrated" victims of racketeers. Then Vincenzo Ruggiero reveals how a combination of coercion, legitimacy, violence, secrecy, consensus and hegemony are used by powerful groups to achieve their aims and overcome obstacles – that is, to exercise power. Nick Hardy applies the social theory Pearce developed in *CotP* and (with Steve Tombs) in *Toxic Capitalism* to examine the interplay between social structures (including organizational structures) and discourses in Canada's nuclear industry. Next, Ronjon Paul Datta synthesizes *CotP* with Pearce's *Radical Durkheim* (2001) to understand "how they got away with it," how financial sacrifice and state cutbacks in public goods, services and benefits following the 2007–2008 fiscal crisis and the bailout of the very financial institutions that caused the crisis were justified morally and politically. The final article in this section, by Raymond Michalowski, incorporates three macro-level theories – globalization, social structures of accumulation and social sources of power – into one framework to explain capitalist expansion under neoliberalism into spatial, political and biospheric spheres. Michalowski exhorts critical scholars to situate our analyses of crimes of power in this broader setting and examine the intersections of economic, political and ideological power.

# Chapter 1

# Conceptualization, theoretical practice and *Crimes of the Powerful*

*Jon Frauley*

Situated alongside classics such as *The New Criminology* (Taylor et al. 1973) and *Policing the Crisis* (Hall et al. 1978), Frank Pearce's (1976) *Crimes of the Powerful* (*CotP*) offers a path-breaking analysis of capitalist democracy and an advance over dominant past and present empiricist forms of enquiry within the sociology of law and crime. It offers theoretical and empirical analysis of the criminogenic processes and connections found within capitalist democracies obfuscated by official, mass media and scholarly accounts of the nature of these societies. A seminal and prescient book, *CotP*'s themes – collusion between states and corporations and their anti-democratic practices; the political and economic utility of crime, selective law enforcement and prosecution; the provisional nature of both the state's and the limited liability corporation's adherence to the rule of law; and the anaemia of empiricist analysis – remain important and timely. Especially apt is the extensive analysis of "radicalism" in the United States, the political and economic role of law and its enforcement, as well as the complicity of positivists and symbolic interactionists in reproducing a conventional and conservative portrayal of these and other activities. This conventional veneer, stemming from "the moralising empiricism of journalists and the political naivety of corporate liberals" (Pearce 1976: 158), covers and shelters the darker, illiberal underside of capitalist democracies.

*CotP* is concerned with crime "in a different way" from conventional empiricist enquiry, emphasising the internal (i.e. necessary) relations that bind the capitalist state, ruling class and organized crime. This "different way," driven by a more adequate "theoretical framework for analysing the problem" of organized crime in corporate America (Pearce 1976: 158), offers a more robust description and incisive conceptualization of capitalist democracy and the nature of the relationship binding the state to the for-profit limited liability corporation. Composed of three essays, Chapter 1 offers immanent critique of empiricist sociology to explain *why* Marxist concepts are analytically more adequate. The second and third chapters are a demonstration of *how* Marxist method can be used to produce a more robust and more adequate analysis of capitalist democracies and deepen our knowledge of the nature of elite deviance, especially in how the organizational structure of capitalist states operates to stabilize the political and economic basis of criminogenic conditions and class domination. Overall, *CotP* illustrates the significance of the procedure of conceptualization for producing theoretically rigorous and sophisticated, yet empirically guided sociological accounts of social phenomena.

To my mind the book was wrongly and misleadingly classified in such a way as to marginalize its theoretical and methodological contribution to the sociology of law and crime.[1] The cataloguing indicates that the book's subject matter is "crime," yet the entire book is a protracted argument against the legitimacy of "crime" as an object of sociological investigation (and, by implication, that criminology is not a legitimate discipline).[2] Additionally, its tripartite organization was thought to undermine the book's cohesiveness (Jones 1979; McMullan 1978; Michalowski 1979; Quinney 1978; Roy 1977; Weitzer 1979). Chapter 1 was thought to be overly theoretical, whereas the second and third chapters were thought to be empirical, leading to confusion about the overall relationship between them. Some interpreted the book as a substantive study of corporate and organized crime, whereas others viewed it as a contribution to Marxist criminology. I think the theoretical practice that subtends the text and the relationship between "theory" and "empirics" proffered by Pearce was misunderstood. It ought to be revisited, however, in light of the current intellectual malaise and regression that characterises much of (critical) criminology today.[3]

This chapter demonstrates *CotP* is far more complex than has been recognized. Three things are emphasized: *First*, *CotP* has not been given its due as it has been mainly read as a substantive work primarily concerned with "crime," even though Pearce is adamant crime is not a sufficient object of or concept for sociological enquiry and criminology is not a viable discipline. *Second*, the book is a theoretical work that takes the activities of the capitalist state and limited liability corporation as empirical referents to be more adequately conceptualized. In so doing the poverty of the empiricism that underwrites both correctionalist and interactionist sociology is illustrated and the analytic value of Marxist epistemology and concepts demonstrated. *Third*, Pearce makes a methodological argument in an exemplary way, showing the value of escaping from empiricist practices of "theory" and "methodology." Relational analysis is advocated to produce the theoretically robust and empirically adequate accounts of social phenomena that can inform transformative social practice.

## Conceptualizing law, regulation and the powerful in a capitalist democracy

Discussing legislation aimed at regulating commercial enterprise and organized crime and the selective enforcement of such laws, Pearce convincingly illustrates law, crime and crime control are used strategically by both the state and corporation to secure profit and growth (Pearce 1976: 105). Crucially, with

## Conceptualization and theoretical practice 5

respect to the operation of the state and corporations, he shows democracy and the rule of law enjoy only a "provisional status" (Pearce 1976: 51, 60).

> By 1914 the major foundations for the new social order were well established: big business was consolidating its control over the major political parties, much of the wind had been taken out of radical movements because "something" had been done, and the legal structure was one that would help rather than hinder the actions of these powerful men. However, their commitment to this legal system was and is pragmatic, their attitude being determined by whether it helps them to realize their goals [of profit and growth] and the consequences of ignoring it.
>
> (Pearce 1973: 25)

This tentative commitment to democracy is particularly glaring with respect to American anti-trust laws and prosecutions of corporations for violation of these laws, as well as the state response to "radicalism" in the post-war period. This activity and much more helped to reproduce the dominant and powerful mythologies that sustain U.S. capitalism.

The outcry about the dangers of anarchy often links together actions like crimes of personal violence, property offences strikes and political demonstrations, and the last two are often condemned for violating the "rule of law." The laws which regulate social life, then, are seen as the product of the democratic process; their interpretation is undertaken by an independent judiciary and their enforcement by an impartial police force (Pearce 1976: 50–51).

In the second and third chapters Pearce scrutinizes law making, enforcement and prosecution in the United States, illustrating in detail the mythological role played by the doctrine of the rule of law and how this serves to obfuscate the provisional commitment to democracy.

> Corruption and partiality within the police, the class bias of the judiciary, and the use of harassment, terror and violence of both a legal and illegal kind against socialists better describes the workings of the law within these societies. The "rule of law" only has meaning when there is a period of social quiescence when democratic debate takes place within a set of assumptions that includes the sanctity of capitalist private property.
>
> (Pearce 1976: 51)

Pearce shows empirically the major commitment of capitalist enterprise to profit and growth and the "willingness to sacrifice democracy when it interfered with corporate action [and that this] underlines the tenuous and provisional nature of their commitment to democratic institutions" (Pearce 1973: 20, 36; 1976: 103).[4] In other words "the capitalist's loyalty to democracy is only provisional" (Pearce 1973: 20; 1976: 60). Consequently, and crucially, as the U.S. state and limited liability corporations are intertwined, *the state can evince only a provisional adherence to the rule of law* and ends up being a handmaiden to commerce.

> The American state may be formally democratic but it is so constrained and beholden to corporate capital that it is very narrow in the interests it pursues and often cruelly indifferent to the well-being of most citizens at home and abroad. Sometimes this involves illegal activities, often it means creating a legal framework which allows and, indeed, encourages the destructive activities of corporate capital.
>
> (Pearce and Tombs 2002: 185–186)

Illustrated is how the conventional account of the rule of law, democracy and, importantly, the development of American capitalism "cannot explain significant features of American society either now or at the beginning of this century" (Pearce 1973: 19). In analysing the relatively low number of prosecutions of corporations under existing anti-trust and labour laws "compared to the degree of violation" (Pearce 1976: 90) and with respect to the growth of commercial enterprise, such legislation is argued to "have a function other than that of regulating business activity" (Pearce 1976: 90). For example, Pearce examines the Export Trade Act of 1918 that allowed for monopolies with respect to some foreign markets yet the Sherman Act of 1890 expressly forbade monopolies. Additionally, in some cases big business *supported* anti–big business acts, such as with the Chicago slaughterhouse owners supporting the Meat Inspection Act of 1906. Moreover, as large corporate enterprise has not been confined to the United States, since WWI, according to Pearce, corporations "have been involved in the administration and direction of American foreign policy" (1973: 34; 1976: 94). In this regard corporations have strategically helped to present the United States' foreign relations "in terms of her commitment to the 'free world' – a world of democracy and free enterprise" (1976: 101). Given the inability of the conventional account to explain these discrepancies, a more plausible explanation is: "Government regulation provided means by which monopoly could be achieved against dangerous competitors and without the dangers of popular reactions" (Pearce 1973: 23; 1976: 87–88). As "state neutrality" and "rule of law" are marshalled to represent and even legitimate criminality, they mask that powerful and anti-democratic corporate actors are actively involved in consolidating economic and political power and, in shaping U.S. foreign policy, meeting their own interests of profit and growth (1976: 94, 102; 1973: 34).

These and other inconsistencies (see his discussion of labour law, 1973: 30–33) and the strategic use of state governance and the rule of law to reproduce corporate power have not been adequately explained by positivists or interactionists. "On closer analysis," Pearce argues, "the common-sensical picture of the nature of the American economy and of the relationship between large corporations and the government, proves to be illusory and misleading" (Pearce 1973: 30), especially as the "continuing success of these large corporations cannot be explained by them having a competitive superiority through the relative cheapness of their products" (Pearce 1973: 29). Law making, enforcement and prosecution do not

Conceptualization and theoretical practice **7**

adhere to the rule of law, but merely serve to "dramatise an 'imaginary social order' and hence to legitimate the economic structure by a misleading portrayal of its nature" (Pearce 1976: 90, 93). At the same time this dramatization "vindicate[s] the claim that the state is neutral, in that it seems that every group, no matter how powerful, is subject to the will of the majority" (Pearce 1973: 26). Such an "ideological picture of the nature of capitalist society" is central to reproducing forms of domination that are freely and willingly accepted.

The "imaginary social order" is conceptualized by Pearce (1976: 104) as "[the] 'ideological' portrayal of American society as being a democratic free-enterprise system, wherein the majority rationally control the legislature and the government." This ongoing display perpetuates a mythology that contains these, among other, key articles of faith:

- the economy is based on private property with many shareholders;
- the economy's central feature is the pursuit of profit in a competitive market;
- large corporations are self-governing and achieve their growth naturally as an outcome of being efficient;
- large corporations invest most money in research and development;
- corporations are beneficent;
- the market is self-regulating and competition is central to this efficient form of regulation;
- managers can remain "community-conscious" as ownership and control are separate.

(Pearce 1976: 94)

This "ideological picture of the nature of capitalist society" (Pearce 1976: 100) insulates the "real social order" – "a monopoly capitalist system, with a certain degree of state control of the industrial infrastructure, but where the state itself is ultimately dominated by the ruling class" (Pearce 1976: 66) – from critique. What is obfuscated by this *doxic* account of capitalist democracies is that great economic power is concentrated in anti-democratic entities, that capitalist societies are oligopolies, that the massive economic power of large multinational corporations dwarfs most Western states and, in turn, this shapes how states utilize law making, enforcement and prosecution (which more often than not directly or indirectly props up these powerful entities).

Normalization and naturalization are important components of societal reproduction and operate through the creation and (selective) enforcement of laws, especially those targeting street crimes, which in turn help to reinforce the hegemony of lifestyles consistent with capitalism (Pearce 1976: 66; 1973: 15). However, as important as law and enforcement are to this process, we must also enquire into what is *not* prohibited and why.

> But it is not enough to ask why laws have been passed (and whether they are implemented). We must also query why they have not been

> passed (1973: 34, 37) . . . . For it is only by understanding why certain actions are *not* prohibited by law . . . that sense can be made of the social relationships inside the capitalist world system (Pearce 1973: 15) . . . . This means that one must no longer focus primarily on the strategies by which prosecution is avoided, but rather on the effects of different kinds of crime, and thereby explain why the state wishes to prosecute certain offences and not others (Pearce 1973: 18) . . . the major determinant of police action is the relationship between the criminal activity and the "real social order." Actions that pose a real threat to this must be controlled, e.g., embezzlement or lower-class attacks on private property . . . police action by the state stabilizes the system by mystifying the people.
>
> (Pearce 1973: 37–38)

An exclusive focus on law making, enforcement and criminal activities – and especially the very restricted liberal legal-political understanding that criminologists tend to use, which perpetuates the myth of the rule of law, state neutrality, democracy and social atomism – makes a great many sociological and criminological enquiries parochial and thus inadequate, especially given capitalism is an international system (Pearce 1976: 26, 101). One can only understand crimes of the powerful, Pearce argues, by situating these activities within "society as a whole" and by specifying the place of the state within this structure (Pearce 1976: 50, emphasis added), thereby "redefining these as actions which, at a particular time, *were the most effective way to help realise the dominant goals of profit and growth*" (Pearce 1976: 102). Highlighting this "discrepancy between the world (legitimate as well as criminal) portrayed by official agencies and the mass media" (Pearce 1973: 15) and the "real social order" enables Pearce to produce a more truthful but much darker understanding than that of conventional liberal accounts of capitalist democracy.

The "naïve and misleading" imaginary social order is not only to be found in accounts circulated by mass media and in the official rhetoric of the state (including in law) (Pearce 1973: 29; 1976: 94). Importantly, as Pearce shows, empiricist and parochial scholarly accounts of law, crime and social control also perpetuate a distorted and misleading view. To offer a radical account, it is necessary to move beyond a focus on appearances and therefore beyond empiricist epistemology and analyses that are guided by liberal legal-political categories. Pearce aims to

> integrate the study of crime into the study of social life, and to drop the common-sensical categories that have inhibited the full development of an adequate criminology. . . . Once criminal activity is viewed as merely one amongst other strategies used by corporations, then the overall social structure within which they act must be analysed.
>
> (Pearce 1973: 34, 38)

Contrasting "the 'imaginary' social order in America, where it is portrayed as being a pluralist, democratic, free-enterprise society, [wherein the majority rationally control the legislature and the government] with a more adequate (i.e., better theorized) description of its nature" (Pearce 1973: 16; 1976: 80–81), Pearce illustrates that Marxist epistemology, concepts and method are much more adequate to conceptualizing "the nature of American society" and hence can be used to provide a "more sophisticated analysis" (Pearce 1976: 82; 1973: 15).

## Epistemology, methodology and critique

To illustrate the advances in employing Marxist epistemology and methodology, Pearce subjects symbolic interactionism, a dominant explanatory system, to immanent critique to reveal its weaknesses. In so doing he also demonstrates the method to be employed in Chapters 2 and 3, where it is utilized to analyse the state–corporation nexus. As Edwin Lemert was a major criminological interpreter of the work of G.H. Mead (the founder of symbolic interactionism) and important to the emergence of labelling theory, Pearce subjects his work to extensive evaluation to illuminate the limitations of interactionism and a pluralist conception of society. Critiquing Lemert's conventional understanding of "society" and "radicalism",[5] Pearce states:

> One of the functions of the cold war myths generated by the Western Allies after the Second World War was to achieve stability and to maintain the international empires, if necessary by force of arms. . . . McCarthyism and Truman's cold war policies helped make the American public accept intervention in world affairs. . . . Soon after, McCarthy fell from power. Even if the internal communist threat seemed real to J. Edgar Hoover, the head of the FBI, his hysterical propaganda mystified the nature of radicalism and [led] people to believe that the problem was one of a foreign origin rather than something which related to an indigenous American tradition.
>
> (Pearce 1976: 36–37)

This contrary view to Lemert's conventional account highlights not only the inadequacy of Lemert's conceptualization but also how the latter serves to simply mystify the nature of radicalism and capitalist democracy. In general, interactionist accounts of capitalist democracy (e.g. Kituse, Erikson and Goffman), including those radical variants (i.e. the "radical pluralism" represented by Becker and Matza), aid in reproducing the criminogenic relations that bind the state and corporation and are not useful for promoting meaningful social transformation.

> Thus whilst Lemert identifies with ruling class interests, Becker can at best be a somewhat righteous and reactive critic. Marxism, on the other hand, can help in the transformation of these repressive societies.
>
> (Pearce 1976: 48)

Empiricist sociology is analytically impotent for revealing deep-seated connections that tether states and corporations in the process of naturalizing and reproducing forms of domination and exclusion. Impotent scholarship simply obscures the illiberal underside of capitalist regimes of wealth extraction and hoarding and their concomitant harmful externalities.

> Whether social scientists attempt to explain crime and deviance in general or some specific example of it such as the use of illegal drugs, they are importing into their explanations the kinds of assumptions made by governmental bureaucracies. . . . Whether they accept the judgements of the powerful or give a sympathetic ear to the complaints of the oppressed, deviancy theories allow their field of study to be circumscribed by the givenness of social definitions.
>
> (Pearce 1976: 26, 45)

Additionally, this scholarship is shown to be apolitical, ahistorical and overly humanist, displaying a tradition of class-blindness. Class struggle and the convergence of the interests of the liberal state with those of capital are overlooked (Pearce 1976: 35).

Class blindness and accepting the liberal legal-political view of law and crime, radicalism and society evince for Pearce an aversion to taking seriously "the struggle of ideas and class forces that ultimately determined the drift of American history" (Pearce 1976: 30). Lemert, Pearce holds, avoids the arguments – the ideas – of radicals themselves in his analysis of radicalism. That this history is made up of such struggles is lost on Lemert as he "fails to put their beliefs in context by relating them to socio-economic conditions under which radicals lived" (Pearce 1976: 34). Pearce (1976: 35) insists we ought not disregard "the understanding developed by the people who are actually in the situation being analysed." The struggle over ideas is an important component of the making of history and the installing of hegemony; thus, the production of consciousness is an important element in understanding capitalist social relations and the reproduction of the forms of domination that are endemic to capitalist societies.

Pearce shows criminalization of radicalism in the United States (i.e. McCarthyism, anti-union sentiment) could not have been because radicals posed a threat requiring the sort of punitiveness witnessed, as the conventional view holds, since "being alien and marginal, they must, almost by definition, be impotent" (Pearce 1976: 34).

> When the ruling class's control of the state is linked with its recognition that there is no necessary unanimity of interest within society and of the spread of a commitment to socialism, then the societal "over response" can be seen to have exhibited a hidden rationality.
>
> (Pearce 1976: 35)

Here law is one mechanism for creating "unanimity of interest" and a collective consciousness. As with his discussions of anti-trust and labour laws, he persuasively argues the basis for law, criminalization and policing is not the imagined "will of the people" but rather the "hidden" or embedded logic of capital, social life reduced to commercial enterprise.

Importantly, it is not only empiricist interactionist accounts of capitalist democracy Pearce takes issue with, indicating some Marxist accounts are also inadequate as they are overly deterministic, leaving little room for human agency. As Pearce makes clear, these accounts, such as those of Paul Hirst, are also seriously hampered because they avoid the struggle over ideas, leaving little to no room for consciousness in their accounts. However, as Pearce argues, the production of hegemonic forms of consciousness is indicative of a struggle over ideas and must be accounted for. Thus, we have some structuralist Marxist accounts that eschew any role for consciousness, whereas interactionist sociologists are methodological individualists and cannot grasp the broader relations and processes that sustain hegemonic forms of consciousness.

Pearce is not only interested in illustrating that Marxist social theory is better able to help us reveal and analyse hidden and deep-seated facets of contemporary capitalist democracies. He is committed to the interactionist concern with consciousness and the transformative power of human agency and is critical of those strands of Marxist theory that downplay this. The interactionist emphasis on consciousness, he suggests, should be retained to strengthen structural analysis of the relationship between the capitalist state, corporations and organized crime.

> Those who treat the subjective views held by people in situations as if they are irrelevant epiphenomena are distorting Marxism. The construction of a scientific model that lays bare the unrecognised consequences of actions, and which specifies the limiting factors that structure these actions even when not consciously recognised, does not involve a denial that such a system is dependent on the actions of men.
>
> (Pearce 1976: 55)

He (1976: 55) adds in a footnote, "This is to say that a great deal can be gained for Marxism by a critical use of the subjectivist sociologists, of interactionism and ethnomethodology." Subjective understandings contain important expressions of the "social conditions under which men live [and which] determine the limits of their possible actions" (Pearce 1976: 55; see Pearce 1985). Thus, the actor's point of view is an important reproductive element as action is animated by the imagined social reality, shaped as it is under particular historical, economic and political conditions. As one is shaped by the particularity of these conditions, we would expect one's understanding of the world to provide some access to the social relations of production and the limits to the range of action which accords with the structure of institutions (see Pearce 1976: 53–55).

Pearce is very clear that we need to identify and connect subjective and objective features of social life, as both combine to form capitalist democracy. *CotP* does this in revealing how "capitalist economic relations tended to subordinate the complexity of social life to its one dimensional logic with a crippling effect on the potential creativity and diversity of human life" (Pearce 2001: xv). This concern with subjectivity in part derives from the influence of György Lukács' (1971) understanding of Marxist method, the conception of "totality" and history, and Marx's distinction between "appearance" and "essence" (see Geras (1965) on the latter). Pearce discusses the influence of Lukács in the preface to the second edition of his subsequent book, *The Radical Durkheim* (2001: xv), and in an interview with Steve Bittle for Red Quill Books (2015). During the time he wrote *Crimes of the Powerful*, he was "sensitised" to the issue of social action – in part through left Weberian sociology and in part through engagement with student politics at the University of Leeds – as a "puzzle and that we cannot simply assume that we know what it means" (2001: xiv). Growing disenchantment with Weberian and post-Marxist theory, especially for limitations to developing a strategic theory of transformative practice, led him to a "phenomenological Marxism" which included, among others, the work of Lukács (Pearce 2001: xv).[6] Unlike some structural Marxist accounts, the Lukáscian Marxism that informs *CotP* requires that we retain an emphasis on human consciousness. Pearce (1976: 54) argues what may be a "naïve apprehension of reality cannot be ignored." All social institutions (i.e., ideological apparatuses)

> are important for the maintenance of the attitudes and forms of life compatible with capitalism and require the control, and if possible the elimination, of rival 'life styles'. . . .The strategy of stressing the normality of certain ways of life and the abnormality of others is an important function of the ideological apparatus.
>
> (Pearce 1976: 66)

Dialectical materialism, Lukács (1971: 5–6) argues, is crucial "to puncture the social illusion" encouraged by the capitalist social structure. This practice "will help us to glimpse the reality underlying it" (Lukács 1971: 6). Importantly, "dialectics insists on the concrete unity of the whole" (Lukács 1971: 6). For the dialectical method, states Lukács (1971: 3), "the central problem is to change reality" and this is "the central function of theory," or more rightly the practice of conceptualization. For we must first "provide real knowledge of what goes on in society" (Lukács 1971: 15) apart from what is presented to us before we can formulate viable strategies for change (Lukács 1971: 225). This is the chief function of the dialectical method, to help the working class better "understand a situation so that, armed with this knowledge, it could act accordingly" (Lukács 1971: 225). Lukács' contributions are less toward a particular theory of Marxism as he was "more concerned with the nature of theory as such" (Craib 1984: 172). According to Craib (1984: 171; see also Craib 1976), Lukács was "concerned to make Marxism a more subtle method of analysis." The emphasis is on the procedure of conceptualization as method. Theory for Lukács is intimately bound up with practice – analytical as well as social – and thus "theory is the articulation and working out of this experience" (Craib 1984: 174). One must recognize "that consciousness – agency – has an independent role to play" in the formulation of explanations and for transformative practice (Craib 1984: 171). The critical working out (i.e. conceptualization) of our experience within history and the totality of capitalist society is liberatory because it can lead to new and transformational practices.

Further, the distinction made by Pearce between the "imaginary" social order and the "real" social order draws to some degree on Lukács' notion of reification (1971; see also Albritton 2003; Arato 1972; Craib 1976; Pitkin 1987; Postone 2003).

> Though Marx scarcely used the term [reification], Lukács claims that the idea of reification is central to his thought. And Marx certainly did use a number of terms in the same general conceptual region, such as "objectification," "estrangement," "alienation," "ideology," "mystification," and "fetishism."
>
> (Pitkin 1987: 264; see also Arato 1972)

Thus the formulation by Pearce that the "secret" and "hidden rationality" of capital is contained in the "real social order" that is reproduced through the dramatization of law making, enforcement and prosecution argues that we have been led to misrecognize the nature of capitalist democracies (and, by implication, have misrecognized "crime" as an obvious or natural object for scientific study). This misrecognition is perpetuated by the conventional accounts of mass media, state officials and the empiricist and uncritical formulations offered by a great many sociologists and criminologists. These latter tend to employ liberal political-legal categories to frame their analysis of the social world which allows "their field of study to be circumscribed by the givenness of social definitions" (Pearce 1976: 26, 45).

> Reification, then, is a misapprehension of the world, an "ideological phenomenon," in which reality is "falsified" or hidden under a deceptive "covering" (or "husk") that must be uncovered. Lukács says that "the basic methodological thought" underlying *Capital* is the undoing of this reification, "the reconversion of economic objects from things back into concrete human relationships" that are capable of being transformed by human choice and action.
>
> (Pitkin 1987: 266; see Geras 1965)

For Lukács and other Marxists, "[the] hidden reality of the social world is that all these different parts make up a whole in a constant process of development.

Reification prevents us from grasping this," as we often and wrongly hold various parts of our society are separate from one another and can be studied as such (Craib 1984: 177).

> Consequently the producers experience themselves as, subject to such impersonal forces, powerless. But in advanced capitalism, Lukács argues, such fetishism extends beyond factory workers and bourgeois political economists into all aspects of everyone's life: people lose awareness of their capacity for agency.
>
> (Pitkin 1987: 265)

Thus there is a need for a non-empiricist epistemology and relational analysis to reveal, identify and connect what are perceived as fragments to reconstruct the broader dynamic whole.

The imaginary social order as a reified order is one level or strata of material reality manifested in part through people's understanding and everyday practices. An ideological order is a symbolic order, but is also the product of what Marx called "objectification." It is a product of human labour, but has come to be understood as separate from us, experienced as alienated; in this it is "thingified." This means that this representational order is naturalized as an independent order and comes to be thought of as something that is beyond human control and which is coercive. What is exemplified here is the idea that conscious acting subjects are simultaneously objects organized into processes of production and consumption. Reification has an objective and subjective side, so people's consciousness is shaped as part of the process of thingification. These different domains must be studied together. This is why Pearce argues to "integrate the study of crime into the study of social life" (1973: 34) and "society as a whole" (1973: 38; 1976: 50) and in so doing account for both structural-institutional domains as well as consciousness and its formation.

The criminal justice system, law and myths about fairness, equality and justice are all products of this process of reification. These products of human labour have come to be understood as separate from us and as having power over us; therefore, they are naturalized as timeless and universal (as without a history). These do have coercive qualities, but they are not natural or timeless and therefore can be changed. Any viable *social* practice of transformation, though, needs to be based on an adequate *sociological* practice that can produce a well-conceptualized ontology of capitalist democracy. The radical analysis proffered by Pearce is explicitly designed to show us this. In uncovering the "secret" – the obfuscated logic of capital that degrades human beings and which authorizes and animates collusion between capitalist states and corporations, including their provisional commitment to democratic practice – Pearce is able to connect these different domains of social reality that escape empiricist enquiry and conventional accounts of capitalist democracy.

## CotP and the "new" criminology

It is worth noting that although Pearce's text is superior in many ways to Taylor, Walton and Young's (TWY) (1973) now-classic *The New Criminology*, it has not achieved the same status. *CotP* is far more theoretically rigorous, has an empirical referent and illustrates the advances to be had through employing Marxist concepts and methods.[7] Of all the initial reviews of *CotP*, Quinney (1978: 83, emphasis added) offers the fullest appreciation: "Pearce is most interested theoretically and substantively in the control mechanisms within the capitalist system" and the substantive chapters "demonstrate, through the presentation of further material . . . and detailed criticism, the superiority of Marxist analysis. With this *method* we are able to discover the kinds of questions *not* raised by positivist (or correctional) criminology." I think Quinney is correct to emphasize the methodological aspect of the text, as this is what makes it distinctive and superior to *The New Criminology* but also posed a challenge to and confused empiricists (including many self-identified critical and radical scholars).

Bankowski et al. (1977) suggest TWY attempt to rescue criminology and its object "crime" as part of their radical "fully social theory of deviance." However, there is nothing radical about maintaining a liberal legal-political category as central for organizing sociological enquiry. Pearce's argument against this and his argument for why criminology is not adequate as a stand-alone discipline is much more radical and is in keeping with Marxist dialectics. As Bankowski et al. (1977) and Currie (1974) have noted, TWY do not *demonstrate* the superiority of Marxism over other approaches because they do not employ dialectics or utilize Marxist social theory to conceptualize the nature of any empirical referent.

> [I]t still remains for Taylor, Walton and Young to systematically argue for, and demonstrate the superiority of, Marxism over other social philosophies, theories and practices. It is simply not enough to use Marxism as a resource because Marxism is supposed to be radical. Assertions should never replace argued cases.
>
> (Bankowski et al. 1977: 43)

Bankowski et al. (1977: 38, 40) further suggest TWY tend to adopt the epistemological, empirical and moral relativism embedded in interactionism. Likewise, Currie notes the failure by TWY to move beyond assertions is the result of what he deems a hostility on their part toward Marxism, landing them closer to the radical interactionist deviance theory that Pearce has shown to be empiricist, ahistorical, apolitical, atomizing and conventionalist. Further, Currie criticizes TWY for paying too little attention to the social consequences or implications for social change of their position.

> The book has the overall tone of an academic debate, rather than a moral and political confrontation. But criminology hasn't simply been

an academic matter. Criminological theory has sometimes (though not always) been closely connected to repressive penal or quasi-penal programs that have oppressed and humiliated real people . . . the absence of analysis of the practical consequences of theories of crime distorts the authors' view of their theories themselves. It's hard to adequately assess the political implications of a theory without looking at the way in which the theory has been put into practice . . . abstracting criminological theory from its social and political context, the authors obscure the sense in which conventional criminology has functioned as part (a small part, perhaps, but significant one) of a larger strategy of liberal State intervention into the crisis of advanced capitalist society.

(Currie 1974: 110)

What is at issue here is praxis. Pearce *does* illustrate the "social consequences" of both empiricist and Marxist sociology: the former cannot yield sociological knowledge that can underwrite a transformative social practice. Marxist epistemology and methodology, however, are capable of this. Our consciousness, shaped as it is by the dominance of an imperative to overproduce and overconsume, drives us to accept as natural inequalities and exploitation and to engage in practices that reproduce this condition. However, social transformation is not unobtainable. Collectively, as the exploited and marginalized gain knowledge of their conditions of existence, they can make conscious decisions as to how to deploy this knowledge to formulate practical strategies for positive transformation of those conditions. Currie (1974: 112–113) argues TWY downplay the role of the consciousness of actors beyond reacting to social control, whereas in Pearce the formation of (class) consciousness is fundamental for understanding and explaining societal reproduction and transformation. It is crucial to understand the conditions under which hegemonic forms of consciousness emerge but also the content of that consciousness. The history of capitalism in many ways can be read as a history of "strategies used by the capitalist class in their struggle against the development of a socialist consciousness amongst the working class" (Pearce 1973: 43). As TWY's text does not offer a radical sociology, it cannot provide a foundation for transformative praxis. When we compare this now-classic text to *CotP* it is clear the latter is far more conceptually and methodologically radical. It is puzzling, then, why *The New Criminology* is routinely taken to be a work of radical scholarship. This might have something to do with the pervasiveness of empiricism (and/or meta-theoretical ignorance) within sociology and criminology where it is routinely manifested in the work of even self-identified critical scholars. As with labelling theory (i.e. "radical" interactionism), TWY look radical in comparison to positivist enquiry but share with it an empiricist epistemology. In comparison to a Marxist epistemology, labelling theory and *The New Criminology* look less than radical. We must break from the straightjacket of empiricist conceptions of theory and methodology, as these foreclose the possibility of imaginative, creative and transformative practice.

## Conclusion

Although criminology routinely deals with very complex social and political objects such as criminalization and crime control, is itself situated within a complex of political apparatuses (e.g. education, work, law), and criminologists contend to be able to say something of value about abuses of power and authority as well as crime and criminality, within criminology there is a dearth of equally complex, non-empiricist analytic procedure. Pearce is explicit about the importance of conceptualization for the sociology of law and crime, as it is this procedure that distinguishes explanatory social science from descriptive empiricist varieties of enquiry driven by operationalization (see Frauley 2017). It is an important yet neglected methodological procedure for producing rigorous theoretical and empirically robust descriptions and explanations and for exercising a maximum amount of control over the process of collecting, interpreting and explaining the significance of both qualitative and quantitative data, important especially given that social scientists have the heavy burden of studying phenomena within open systems (Blaikie 2000; Sayer 1992). We can read *CotP* as a contribution to the epistemological and methodological development of criminology, and there is much about *CotP* that can and should be built upon. It is critical that sociologists and criminologists do just this to produce incisive and adequately conceptualized accounts of capitalist democracy in order to challenge "faith in this unreal world" (Pearce 1976: 93).

## Notes

1  The Library of Congress classification is as follows: "Crime – US; Commercial Crimes – US; White Collar Crime – US; Organized Crime – US."
2  Pearce is adamant that the "validity" of separating "crime" from other social phenomena is questionable on the basis of the interdependence of social institutions (Pearce 1976: 62). My use of "criminology" denotes a subfield of sociology, not a stand-alone discipline.
3  Today post-modernism, left realism, peace making, and cultural criminology, among others, are included in many accounts of "critical" criminology, yet these are empiricist, rely on a conventional account of phenomena and eschew political economy and relational analysis. See Coleman, Sim, Tombs and Whyte (2009) and Russell (1997, 2002)
4  Most recently, drawing on the work done in *CotP*, with Tombs in *Toxic Capitalism* (1998) – specifically drawing on the idea that corporations and states *sacrifice* democracy at the altar of capital – and on his work on Durkheim (2001), the *Collège de Sociologie* and the concept of "the sacred" (2003a,b, 2006), Pearce has produced a "sociology of sacrifice" in which he draws parallels between the ritualized practices of Aztec human sacrifice and U.S. imperialist forms of sacrifice "to show that on a deeper level there are significant similarities between them" (Pearce 2010: 52; see also Pearce 1996).
5  The discussion of radicalism is timely given current events in the United States where the idea that radicalized Muslims from the Middle East threaten U.S. freedom and democracy is gaining traction and is a major plank in the current president's political platform. Here, as Pearce notes, media and political rhetoric have "mystified the nature of radicalism and lead people to believe that the problem was one of a foreign origin rather than something which related to an indigenous American tradition" (Pearce 1976: 37). See Friedman (2016), Ybarra (2015), Wilner and Dubouloz (2010), Bazelon (2017).

6 Some indication as to Pearce's thinking on the contours and limitations of Weberian sociology and his sympathetic reading of the relationship between Hegel and Marx is given in Pearce (n.d.-a, n.d.-b).
7 It is vital to eschew an empiricist understanding of "method" here (i.e. techniques of data collection and interpretation) and understand "conceptualization" as central.

## References

Albritton, R. (2003) "Superseding Lukács: A Contribution to the Theory of Subjectivity," in R. Albritton and J. Simoulidis (eds.) *New Dialectics and Political Economy*, 60–77. New York: Palgrave Macmillan.

Arato, A. (1972) "Lukács' Theory of Reification." *TELOS*, 11: 25–66.

Bankowski, Z., Mungham, G. and Young, P. (1977) "Radical Criminology of Radical Criminologist?" *Contemporary Crises*, 1: 37–52.

Bazelon, E. (2017) "Department of Justification." *New York Times Magazine*, 28 February. Online. Available HTTP: www.nytimes.com/2017/02/28/magazine/jeff-sessions-stephen-bannon-justice-department.html (accessed 10 December 2017).

Blaikie, N. (2000) *Designing Social Research*. Malden, MA: Polity Press.

Coleman, R., Sim, J., Tombs, S. and Whyte, D. (2009) "Introduction: State, Power, Crime," in R. Coleman, J. Sim, S. Tombs and D. Whyte (eds.) *State Power Crime*, 1–19. Thousand Oaks, CA: Sage.

Craib, I. (1976) "Lukács and the Marxist Criticism of Sociology." *Radical Sociology*, 17: 26–37
——— (1984) *Modern Social Theory*. New York: Harvester Wheatsheaf.

Currie, E. (1974) "Beyond Criminology: A Review of the New Criminology." *Crime and Social Justice*, 2: 109–113.

Frauley, J. (2017) "Synoptic Vision: Metatheory, Conceptualisation, and Critical Realism." *Canadian Journal of Sociology*, 42(3): 293–324.

Friedman, U. (2016) "What If the Terrorists Are Already Here?" *The Atlantic*, 2 July. Online. Available HTTP: www.theatlantic.com/international/archive/2016/07/america-terrorism-national-security/489872/ (accessed 10 December 2017).

Geras, N. (1965) "Essence and Appearance: Aspects of Fetishism in Marx's Capital." *New Left Review*, 1: 69–85.

Hall, S., Critcher, C., Jefferson, T., Clarke, J. and Roberts, B. (1978) *Policing the Crisis: Mugging, Law and Order and the State*. New York: Macmillan.

Jones, K. (1979) "Crimes of the Powerful and Beyond: An Essay Review." *Contemporary Crises*, 3: 317–331.

Lukács, G. (1971) *History and Class Consciousness*. Cambridge, MA: MIT Press.

McMullan, J. (1978) "Review of *Crimes of the Powerful*." *Canadian Journal of Sociology*, 3(3): 376–377.

Michalowski, R. (1979) "Crime and a Theory of the State: The Adolescence of Radical Analysis." *Criminology*, 16(4): 561–580.

Pearce, F. (n.d.-a) "Notes on Hegel, Feuerbach and Marx." Unpublished manuscript.
——— (n.d.-b) "Weberian Sociology: An Exegesis and Critique." Unpublished manuscript.
——— (1973) "Crime, Corporations and the American Social Order," in I. Taylor and L. Taylor (eds.) *Politics and Deviance*, 13–41. Middlesex, England: Penguin Books.
——— (1976) *Crimes of the Powerful: Marxism, Crime and Deviance*. London: Pluto Press.
——— (1985) "Neo-Structuralist Marxism on Crime and Law in Britain: A Review." *The Insurgent Sociologist*, XIII(1/2): 123–131.

—— (1996) "'Gifts of Blood' or Contingent Necessity: An Aleatory Materialist Exploration of the Defeat of the Aztec/Mexica by the Conquistadores." Paper presented at *The Gift: Theory and Practice – International Conference*. Trent University. Peterborough, Canada.

—— (2001) *The Radical Durkheim* (2nd ed.). Toronto: Canadian Scholar's Press.

—— (2003a) "Introduction: the Collège de Sociologie and French Social Thought." *Economy and Society*, 32(1): 1–6.

—— (2003b) "Off With their Heads: Caillois, Klossowski and Foucault on Public Executions." *Economy and Society*, 32(1): 48–73.

—— (2006) "Foucault and the 'Hydra-Headed Monster': The Collège de Sociologie and the two Acéphales," in A. Beaulieu and D. Gabbard (eds.) *Michel Foucault and Power Today: International Multidisciplinary Studies in the History of Our Present*, 115–137. Oxford, UK: Lexington Books.

—— (2010) "Obligatory Sacrifice and Imperial Projects," in R. Kramer, R. Michalowksi and W. Chambliss (eds.) *State Crime in the Global Age*, 45–66. Portland OR: Willan Publishing.

—— (2015) "Marxism and Corporate Crime in the 21st Century." Red Quill Books Interview Series #3. Interviewed by Steve Bittle. Online. Available HTTP: http://red quillbooks.com/wp-content/uploads/2015/02/Interview-with-Frank-Pearce-2.pdf (accessed 15 December 2017).

Pearce, F. and Tombs, S. (1998) *Toxic Capitalism: Corporate Crime and the Chemical Industry*. Burlington, VT: Ashgate.

—— (2002) "States, Corporations, and the 'New' World Order," in G. Potter (ed.) *Controversies in White Collar Crime*, 185–216. New York: Routledge.

Pitkin, H.F. (1987) "Rethinking Reification." *Theory and Society*, 16(2): 263–293.

Postone, M. (2003) "Lukács and the Dialectical Critique of Capitalism," in R. Albritton and J. Simoulidis (eds.) *New Dialectics and Political Economy*, 78–100. New York: Palgrave Macmillan.

Quinney, R. (1978) "Review of *Crimes of the Powerful: Marxism, Crime and Deviance*." *Insurgent Sociologist*, 8(1): 83–84

Roy, D. (1977) "Review of *Crimes of the Powerful: Marxism, Crime, and Deviance*." *Sociology*, 11(2): 395–396.

Russell, S. (1997) "The Failure of Postmodern Criminology." *Critical Criminology*, 8(2): 61–90.

Russell, S. (2002) "The Continuing Relevance of Marxism to Critical Criminology." *Critical Criminology*, 11: 113–135.

Sayer, A. (1992) *Method in Social Science: A Realist Approach* (2nd ed.). New York: Routledge.

Taylor, I., Walton, P. and Young, J. (1973) *The New Criminology: For a Social Theory of Deviance*. New York: Routledge and Kegan Paul.

Weitzer, R. (1979) "Review of *Crimes of the Powerful*." *Contemporary Sociology*, 8(2): 251.

Wilner, A.S. and Dubouloz, C.J. (2010) "Homegrown Terrorism and Transformative Learning: An Interdisciplinary Approach to Understanding Radicalization." *Global Change, Peace & Security*, 22(1): 33–51.

Ybarra, M. (2015) "Majority of Fatal Attacks on U.S. Soil Carried Out by White Supremacists, not Terrorists." *The Washington Times*, 24 June. Online. Available HTTP: www. washingtontimes.com/news/2015/jun/24/majority-of-fatal-attacks-on-us-soil-carried-out-b/ (accessed 12 December 2017).

# Chapter 2

# Law

## Ideological whitewashing and positive enabling of coercion

### *Harry Glasbeek*

I had to teach workplace health and safety regulation in my labour law course. It was obvious that many of the incidents that gave rise to workers' injuries, diseases and deaths might easily have been designated as criminal offences. They rarely were. Even though I had read Frank Pearce's *Crimes of the Powerful* (*CotP*), the combination of the importance of corporations as employers and my lawyer's instincts led me to surmise that it was the legal nature and attributes of the corporation that inhibited the normal deployment of otherwise universally applicable law.

I engaged in the debates around the difficulties created by the doctrines of legal personality and limited liability for the attribution of legal responsibilities to corporations; I participated in the complicated discussions about how to make corporations, as corporations, more easily criminally responsible; I joined in exchanges about whether it made sense to impose more positive legal duties on corporations and their senior functionaries to prevent harms to stakeholders other than shareholders, and in discussions about whether it was logical to make legal demands that corporations be operated in the best interests of the larger public.

Eventually, I began to see the obvious. The investigators and policy makers engaged in these debates have had considerable successes. There have been many *legal* reforms, and there continue to be calls for even more effective reforms to improve corporate governance and to raise awareness about the need for corporate actors to be more socially responsible. Yet the number of harms inflicted by corporations and those acting through them, many of which exact a terrible toll, never seems to diminish. Facts on the ground have delivered their verdict to me. I have been looking in the wrong place for amelioration. Pearce had suggested as much. The title of the book made it clear that he was pointing to structured-in power, rather than to a legal tool, as the source of the uneven application of law.

This piece pivots around three of the points Pearce made in *CotP* (1976) and which now inform my work:

(i) Pearce observed that the gap between law's portrayal as the defender of a system of shared values and the actual conditions that law allows to prevail is vast and needed to be documented (63);

(ii) He rejected the conventional proposition that, because we appear to have mature democratic practices, we must be taken to have consciously chosen a free enterprise system. Pearce asserted that there was no consensus and that one set of actors, capitalists, constitute a ruling class that has a special relationship to the state. That relationship needs to be interrogated (66);

(iii) He urged us to look beyond the shared understandings of legal institutions and to ask why it is that some laws are passed and some laws are not passed (101).

This chapter is a sketch of my current lines of inquiry based on these insights. I am pursuing the idea that a combination of law's ideological starting points and ideologically counterintuitive specific pro-private profit-maximization laws works to serve capitalists. This points to a systemic privileging of one class' interests. I posit that it is not the corporation per se that leads to the difficulties confronted by anti-capitalists. The corporation, the legal tool, is one cog (albeit an important one) in a much larger machine that pushes the state and its laws to serve and privilege the capitalist class.

## Taking Pearce seriously

### *Law and voluntarism – assuming away the coercion of workers*

There is a huge wealth gap between the owners of the means of production, the capitalists, and the owners of labour power, the workers (Piketty 2014; Mcdonald 2014). It suits capitalists to have this divide maintained and, if possible, deepened. Law extends a large helping hand to capitalism. One of law's ideological starting points is that exchanges of goods and services between sovereign individuals, if not coerced by physical force, duress or fraud, constitute an expression of the to-be-respected autonomous choices of individuals acting in their own interest. On this basis, Anglo-American law holds that the ensuing voluntarily agreed-upon terms and conditions are to be enforced without any further questioning of the contract.

To apply this starting point to the exchanges that create employment relationships should be counterintuitive. Yet that is what law does. Willfully blinding itself, law assumes that those without any means other than their own bodies and minds are just as sovereign and free as those who own the means of production with whom they must deal. Yet the latter can choose not to invest their property, whereas the former have no freedom not to sell their assets, their minds and bodies. It is true, of course, that it is not the law per se that forces workers to sell their capacities to some wealth owner; their concrete conditions do that (Higgins 1911; Farwell 1906).

The lack of challenge to law's ideological starting position is a triumph of form over substance. But this does not satisfy law: it gives oomph to the capitalist-favouring ideology with positive laws. Should workers choose not to sell any of their capacities to profit seekers, the rules of legally created welfare regimes usually will make them ineligible to receive life-sustaining benefit payments. In the actual world, in the capitalist world, workers must find employment (or exploit themselves, a choice that more often than not leads to a precarious living). To enforce employment agreements as if they are just a species of discretionary commercial transactions, as if they are just like, say, a contract between a retailer and the purchaser of a pickled herring, is perverse. Yet this is the default position for all Anglo-American employment contracts, no matter what kind of specialized legal regime regulates them.

If left to bargain as individuals, the gross imbalance in bargaining power leads to miserable terms and conditions of employment for workers. They must turn to the only strength they have, their numbers, and engage in political struggles to get some legitimacy for collective bargaining regimes, to win some legislation setting minima below which their terms and conditions should not sink. They have had to appeal to legislators who have had to be more responsive to public sentiments and demands than the defenders of free contract doctrines, the judges, have been (Ruegg 1905). The gains they made have been very important, but they are seen as interferences with the natural state of things rather than inviolable rights. The primacy of the ideology of individual contract making has remained intact. Its retention makes it legitimate for the owners of the means of production to seek to have those anti-individualist, state interventionist, protections removed on the basis that, not only do they make for inefficiencies, but also, because they offend our deepest value, the sacrosanct nature of individual decision making. Capitalists' fight-backs do not have to struggle for political legitimacy, and they are ceaseless. Today they are called austerity policies. Under neoliberalism there are many employer successes as union strength and legislated protections are wound back (Smith 2015; Tucker 2014).

The legal assumption that work-for-wages contracts are voluntary ones is a fateful one. With a sweep of its invisible hand, law hides the reality of capitalist relations of production. The assumption that a bargain between economically very unequal individuals is voluntary and should be enforced by law signifies that private economic superiority is not seen as a source of coercion that affects legal equality. The potential for private, as opposed to state, coercion is marginalized by legal ideology. Only political rebellious struggles will lead to some interventions, which I argue are Band-Aids rather than cures. This starting point, namely that the decisions by the wealth-less to work on certain terms and conditions are to be taken to be voluntary and acceptable to them, has enormously important consequences for the regulation of capital–labour relations in particular and for the regulation of capital in general.

### Schizophrenia – when it is necessary to pass laws to beef up the fantasy of hands-off voluntarism?

The comparison between discretionary commercial contracts and contracts of employment is not only ill based because of the way the latter, unlike the former, are forced to accept deals they would not choose if they were truly sovereign human beings, it also is illogical because what workers sell and employers buy are not commercial objects like, say, pickled herrings. Workers sell their capacities, their intelligence, physical attributes and dexterities, their skills and talents, their willingness to use these characteristics – that is, they sell parts of their very being. Their interest in the subject matter of the contract is very different to that which a seller of a pickled herring has in the dead fish. Naturally, as sellers, workers want to sell as little of their personal attributes for as much as they can. Employers, having bought an unquantifiable amount of human capacity, need to get as much out of the human traits bought as possible for as little as possible. There is a built-in conflict about who is to control how much of the essence of human beings.

Employers are advantaged by any increase in the competition for scarce jobs by, say, immigration or the ability to employ workers in far-away countries or by any reduction in the needed talents and skills required by the use of technologies. The greater the pool of would-be desperate non-wealth owners, the greater will be the employers' ability to discipline (please mark the word!) their work forces into doing more for less. This is why employers oppose trade unions which minimize competition among workers and resist legislative strictures such as minimum wage or maximum working hours laws, all of which undermine employers' efforts to get more for less. Here law's starting assumption that voluntary decision making by sovereign individuals should rule employment contracts helps employers. Law also intervenes actively to ensure that employers get additional leverage over workers.

In Anglo-American jurisdictions, the judiciary has been the prime promoter of the mythology that employment contracts are to be respected as voluntary ones. It is the same judiciary that reads feudal, worker-subjugating terms into these supposed voluntary agreements between equal sovereigns. Every contract of employment, unless it contains something specifically to the contrary, places an enforceable legal duty on the employees to exercise a reasonable amount of skill and effort, to act in good faith and with fidelity for the employers' business interests and to obey all reasonable commands issued by employers. This applies to all employment arrangements, whether they are the result of individual bargaining or of collective bargaining by unionized employees. It applies to all other regimes that regulate employment relations, such as employment standards, human rights or health and safety provisions (Glasbeek and Drache 1992, Glasbeek 1987). The ubiquity of these read-in duties reflects the point made earlier to the effect that the private individual contract doctrines and ideology constitute the default position of law's regulation of capital/labour relations.

All of these imposed duties have contestable meanings, but, in essence, they are legal tools that enable employers to make better use of the personal qualities that workers have sold to them. A right to exercise legally sanctioned demands over the minds and bodies of workers made sense in a political economy in which workers had the status of serfs whose fate depended on the whims of their lord. It is not justifiable in a liberal political economic system that prides itself on the *de jure* equality of every human being. One way to justify it is to argue that the reading in of terms and conditions of subordination is that workers would have agreed to them if they had been asked to do so. This, of course, would amount to an acknowledgment that workers are so desperate that they must surrender their individuality to the employing class. But this would endanger the central fantasy that contracts of employment are truly voluntary arrangements. It is easier, therefore, to pretend that contractual duties that subjugate employees are natural and normal and do not require justification.

This should not be an easy stance to maintain. After all, the imposition of these duties directly gives employers legal permission to be authoritarian. Employers can punish workers for failing to meet these duties. When employment has been created by means of a basic common law contract between an individual employer and individual employee, it still is, as it always was, proper for an employer to rely on the breach of one of these duties as a just cause to terminate the relationship. This starting position has been modified by legislation in some (but not all) jurisdictions in recent years. Where legislative gains have been made by workers, employers may not automatically dismiss duty-breaching workers because they can claim to have just cause to do so; they may have to abide by some of the protective rules unionized workers had won (England and Christie 2005; Sack 1999). These union-won protections do not mean that employers cannot discipline workers for violations of their duties.

Where special protections have been won, a sophisticated jurisprudence has been crafted to regulate those gains. As noted, employers can no longer automatically dismiss workers for breaches of duties, but they are not left without remedies. Workers can be reprimanded, suspended with pay or without pay for varying periods, forced to apologize, put into re-education programmes or be dismissed for breaches of their duty to exercise care, be of good faith and fidelity and be obedient to all reasonable orders (Mitchnick and Etherington 2006; Brown and Beatty 1984). The goals of this specialized area of jurisprudence are said to be specific deterrence, general deterrence and corrective justice (Adams 1979). There emerges an intriguing parallel between state power and the coercive power given to employers by a private ordering regime allowed room to breathe by the state's legal system. This endorses Pearce's suggestions about the need to study the special relationship between capital and the state and the extent to which the wealth-owning class is a ruling class.

In the event, a finely calibrated punitive system has evolved, supposedly on the basis that it stops employers from acting tyrannically. Under this refined system of education, reform and punishment of their workers, employers are prevented from acting directly on their built-in economic advantage. On the other hand, it helps employers create a work culture that suits them very well (Glasbeek 1987, 1984). The law deems employers entitled to control the behaviour of the inherently rebellious employed classes who want to retain their personal autonomy. It is hard to miss the parallel between the state's and capitalists' power to control and punish subjects. Employers have been given the legal tools to establish a quasi-criminal justice regime. Unsurprisingly to lawyers, the salient factor in determining whether an employment relationship exists is whether one party exercises control over the other. A superior-inferior nexus between parties who are assumed to be legal equals is, paradoxically, the legal hallmark of employment (Kahn-Freund 1972; Woods Task Force 1968).

The story thus far is that:

(1) The employing classes' ability to coerce is normalized by assuming that the voluntary nature of employment in a capitalist political economy is not to be questioned;

(2) This averts a legitimacy problem, as coercion in a supposed liberal polity is unacceptable. Even the state's power to coerce is to be constrained by clearly defining what kind of conduct is worthy of criminalization and stigmatization and by a multitude of procedural safeguards for those to be subjected to state power (LRCC 1976). Most often the state's right to use force against its citizens is said to be justified only when those citizens have breached a shared moral value and/or inflicted an intolerable harm. These criteria are rather vague, as one person's notion of morality may differ sharply from another's, and as the gravity of harm is relative to the value of the objectives achieved when inflicting it (Devlin 1965; Hart 1963). But one thing appears plain – agreed-upon moral wrongs inflicting serious harm, such as murder, assault and fraud are, in part at least, perceived to be immoral because they involve coercion. In this context, to acknowledge the coercive nature of employment contracts would/should present a grave problem. This is why so much is done to pretend that employment contracts are voluntary, freely consented to agreements made between equally sovereign individuals;

(3) After pretending that there is no worrisome coercion arising out of employment contract making, law then ensures that employers have direct coercive powers to help them advance their profit-chasing agenda. In the employment context, this extraordinary legal intervention is portrayed as natural, as normal, as being for everyone's good. Capitalists are given dispensations by the state and law.

### Enter the corporation – doubling (tripling or more) up on coercion by legal intervention

Having built-in economic coercion as a neutral aspect of the modes of production, law gives that coercion more bite by promoting the incorporation of profit-chasing firms. First, corporations are aggregations of a number of inorganic assets derived from various sources and capitalists. The size of the assets they control and the number of people they employ exacerbate the power capitalists as individuals would likely get from an imbalance in economic wherewithal. Second, the legal treatment of the incorporated firm as if it is just another person in Anglo-American jurisdictions, despite the collectivization of assets and people that give it life, entitles it to have its employment contracts (and other contracts) treated as voluntary ones. This makes life even more perilous for the working class than it would otherwise be. One aspect of this is worth noting here.

The corporate firm is the legal equivalent of any one worker. Just as a worker may withdraw her capital – that is, her mind and body – at any time, so may the corporation. But the worker's right to act collectively is strictly limited by law. A union may not ask its members to withdraw services collectively – that is, to strike – unless very strict conditions are met. It is true that the corporation, as an employer, cannot lock out its workers without meeting similar (but less stringent) requirements. This equivalence in legal treatment is deceiving. The corporate employer as an individual can always withdraw its capital. It is, law says, merely an individual doing as it likes with its property. This gives corporate employers a tremendous additional advantage in the economic bargaining game. Note as an aside, it is the same capacity to withdraw its assets at any time from anywhere, as any individual might her mind and body, which gives capitalists an enormous advantage in the electoral, lobbying and regulation designing spheres. In popular terms, the withdrawal of property by the corporate sectors is known as a capital strike, but not a strike that attracts legal regulation or restrictions.

Third, the law allows shareholders to limit their liability for corporate losses to the amounts they have invested in the corporation. If the corporation cannot meet its obligations, there is no way for a creditor to look to the shareholders for redress. This makes shareholders, as a group, indifferent to the creation of risks to others by the corporation. This indifference is deepened by the fact that shareholders have been deemed by law not to have any operational functions. This means that not only will their fiscal responsibilities for bad outcomes be limited, but also that they are immunized from being saddled with any personal civil or criminal responsibility for wrongful corporate conduct undertaken on their behalf. This is extremely dangerous to the rest of us. Corporate directors are legally bound to act in the best interests of the corporation, and in today's circumstance, this is taken to mean the best interests of the shareholders (Ireland 2005), the very same shareholders who do not have to care how profits are pursued. This is a driver of harmful behaviour towards customers, to the environment, to workers and their communities. Profits, and thereby share values, may be increased by not taking steps to prevent injury to those stakeholders.

Shareholders are, it is assumed, happy when the value of their shares improve. They do not have to care how that desire is met. They do not mind whether it comes at the expense of the long-term viability of the corporation and, therefore, of its workers; they do not mind whether it comes because the corporation is engaged in the production and sales of harm-inflicting and socially undesirable goods and services, such as arms, tobacco, alcohol, the running of private prisons, laying pipelines through indigenous peoples' lands, displacing people from their environment as extraction industries ravage a countryside, gouging the public so that only the rich can have access to needed medical supplies or attention, knowingly manufacturing shoddy goods that harm and pollute, exploiting their economic power to set up supply chains which they know will lead to vulnerable people being treated abominably – it turns out to be dead easy to attract investors to corporations that engage in these all-too-common anti-social ways. Moreover, shareholders are likely to discipline directors and executives who do not do their utmost to maximize profits, even as this is likely to lead to ugly, often illegal, behaviour. As well as the stick, they use the carrot: they reward directors and executives if they push, aggressively, unethically, to improve share values by giving them a piece of the thus enriched share pie.[1] Unsurprisingly, there is a mass of literature that establishes that unethical and wrongful behaviour is the norm rather than aberrational (Tombs and Whyte 2015; Pearce and Tombs 1998; Snider 1993; Mokhiber 1988; Ferguson 2012; Taibbi 2014; Glasbeek 2002).

Corporations are a site where profit-hungry capitalists have been given a licence to be irresponsible and to encourage irresponsibility. Their preferred tool, the legal corporation, is ideally suited to help them pursue the capitalist agenda at the rest of society's material, political and cultural expense (Glasbeek 2007). It is tempting, therefore, to think of the corporation as a misused tool that ought to be fixed so that it cannot be so abused. But as the next section demonstrates, those kinds of reforms do not confront the more fundamental issue: the state and its law will continue to aid flesh-and-blood capitalists to attain their goal of the private accumulation of socially produced wealth. The legal regulation of capitalist relations of production is aimed at keeping the regime alive and well, even as some political pressures are felt to reform its current favourite instrument.

### Regulatory law: inhibited by the legitimation of economic power and the persistent fantasy of voluntarism

Governments rely on individual wealth-chasing capitalists to generate the overall welfare that governments need to produce. Capitalists are to be encouraged. But as anarchic, self-seeking individuals, some/many may well act inefficiently and/or bring the regime into disrepute. An old and dramatic example is provided by Danuta Mendelson (2015), who records that, in mid-19th-century England, more than 50% of children employed in some industries had lost fingers and had hands crushed and that, by 1854, in some large factories, up to one-fourth of children were seriously crippled or deformed. Reforms were needed.

Governments have to step in to curb profit seekers' inefficient externalization of costs and the loss of legitimacy for the capitalist enterprise that may accompany such foolish behaviour. The laws set standards. They are to be enforced by punishing violators. The intent, however, is not to inhibit the investment of wealth by its owners. To the contrary: the purpose of regulatory laws is to promote and facilitate entrepreneurial activities while limiting the political danger of too many ugly outcomes. A delicate balancing act is to be performed that, in the end, relies on a number of highly contestable assumptions.

We are to be happy that owners of wealth are willing to deploy their property. Regulatory standards are set on the basis that workers, consumers, communities and their environments freely, willingly, indeed contentedly, accept some, but not all, of the risks the chase for private profits creates for them. There is no acknowledgment that inequality in the ownership of the means of production means that most of us have no choice but to accept those risks. Once again, voluntarism is assumed, built-in coercion ignored. A corollary to this spurious assumption is that because virtuous profiteers do not set out to do harm, they are not to be perceived as unethical, stigmatizable, criminal, actors when things go wrong. They should be treated with kid gloves. The more reckless among them, those who violate known standards, should be re-educated; direct enforcement and punishment is to be a last resort. Engagement in risk regulation, as opposed to direct enforcement of existing laws, has taken a firm hold on policy makers' imaginations. This legislative quasi-criminal scheme is less stringently enforced than is the private ordering disciplinary regime operated by the employing class.

The line of thinking that deems potential investors of their capital as benefactors to whom all should be grateful and be prepared to give incentives means that state regulators should seek their cooperation when planning to fetter their operations. Entrepreneurs are consulted about the standards they are to meet. An unholy combination emerges. The would-be regulatees, bent on profit maximization, have a natural desire to hide the risks of their operations and to stress the benefits they will yield. As they possess most of the information about risks and benefits, and because governments need to please them, the ensuing regulations set the bar much lower than it would be if saving workers' lives were the main consideration. Two points need to be stressed.

The premise is that, below this low protective bar, workers, consumers, communities and their environments have agreed to any harms profit-seeking undertakings inflict. The most they may be entitled to is some compensation, usually coming out of an insurance fund to which they contribute. The huge bulk of those harms are born by non-capitalists, those who do not have a true choice as to what work they do, where they live or what products or services they can afford to buy. The harms are seen as outcomes of unfortunate accidents, unintended consequences, although, in fact, they are the results of a plan to satisfy greed in a profit-maximizing manner. And should the injuries be the result of a breach of any regulated standard, it is most unlikely that the punishment imposed will meet any notion of justice that the majority of people share. One contemporary "for instance" is the lamentations about the "too big to fail, too big to jail" refrain sung in the wake of violations of financial regulations. So obvious is this lack of direct enforcement that occasionally governments are forced to pretend to give criminal law proper more bite (*The Flinders Journal of Law Reform* 2005; *Policy & Practice in Health and Safety* 2013). These efforts are not intended to have much impact, as is shown by the very low rate of prosecutions under the novel schemes devised (Glasbeek 2013, Bittle 2013).

This sketch demonstrates that there are structural barriers safeguarding capitalism from the normal rules said to lie at the heart of the liberal state. Although the size and anonymity bestowed by the corporate firm help maintain these structural barriers, the barriers are there to help capitalists, whether their enterprise is incorporated or not. This points to the special relationship between the dominant class, on the one hand, and the state and its law, on the other.

## Conclusion

It is clear from this account why the corporation is seen as the enemy by anti-capitalist intellectuals and activists. It is understandable that efforts are expended on minimizing the adverse impacts of the special legal attributes of the corporate firm and that reformers seek to exert pressures on the corporations that so influence our economic, political, social and cultural spheres, to persuade them to go easy on us, to be more socially responsible. Serious activists try to tame the corporation. Well and good. But this does not address the fundamental problems Frank Pearce rightly asked us to resolve. The relations between capital and the state and the unbalanced application of law they entail will still be in place if the corporation is less useful to capitalists. The starting points will be unchanged and capitalists will remain free to find other means to maintain themselves as the ruling class, to be treated as an exceptional class. Once again, Pearce pointed us in a useful direction. He stressed that capitalism is essentially based on the calculative nature of capitalists, on the nature of flesh-and-blood capitalists, not corporations. He referred to *the* capitalist's characteristics, to the fact that *he* wants control over *his* environment (1976: 84).[2] It is time to take this idea that the problems of capitalism arise from the drive and scheming of human capitalists be taken seriously. A single-minded focus on the corporation, rather than the human beings, who benefit from and control their actions may be leading scholars and activists astray. I am trying to think about the implications.[3] I owe Frank Pearce a deep intellectual debt.

## Notes

1 Space forbids an argument to be elaborated, but note that here I am excluding the thousands of shareholders who hold equities as a means of saving to ensure themselves against the vicissitudes of life in a polity that does not provide adequate social welfare. They are not capitalists as that word is used in the text. Mostly they hold shares indirectly and exert no influence; the institutions that hold on their behalf do, but they behave more like direct and controlling shareholders than their beneficiaries might desire.

2 At that time, academics were less sensitive to the need for gender-neutral language, but this may not have been the case in Frank Pearce's writing as then, and as still largely is the case, more often than not, males ruled the roost.

3 See *Privileging Class: How Law Shelters Shareholders and Coddles Capitalism* (2017, Between the Lines).

## References

Adams, G.W. (1979) *Grievance Arbitration of Discharge Cases, A Study of the Concept of Industrial Discipline*. Kingston: Industrial Relations Centre, Queen' University.

Bittle, S. (2013) "Cracking-down on Corporate Crime? The Disappearance of Corporate Criminal Liability Legislation." *Policy and Practice in Health and Safety*, 11(2): 45–62.

Brown D. and Beatty, D. (1984) *Canadian Labour Arbitration*. Canada Law Book Co.

England, G. and Christie, I. (2005) *Employment Law in Canada*. Carswell.

Farwell, L.J., *Devonald v. Rosser*, [1906] 2 K.B. 728, 743.

Ferguson, C.H. (2012) *Predator Nation: Corproate Criminals, Political Corruption, and the Hijacking of America*. New York: Crown Business.

*The Flinders Journal of Law Reform* (2005) Special Edition, Industrial Manslughter, 8 (1).

Glasbeek, G. (1984) "The Utility of Model Building: Collins' Capitalist Discipline and Corporatist Law." *Industrial Law Journal*, 12: 133.

———— (1987) "Labour Relations' Policy and Law as a Mechanism of Adjustment." *Osgoode Hall Law Journal*, 25: 179.

———— (2002) *Wealth by Stealth: Corporate Crime, Corporate Law, and the Perversion of Democracy*. Toronto: Between the Lines.

———— (2007) "The Corporation as a Legally Created Site of Irresponsibility," in H. Pontell and G. Geis, (eds.) *International Handbook of White-Collar and Corporate Crime*. New York: Springer.

———— (2013) "Missing the Targets – Bill C-45: Reforming the Status Quo to Maintain the Status Quo." *Policy and Practice in Health and Safety*, 11 (2): 9–23.

Glasbeek H. and Drache, D. (1992) *The Changing Work Place: Reshaping Canada's Industrial Relations System*. Toronto: James Lorimer.

Hart, H.L.A. (1963) *Law, Liberty and Morality*. New York: Vintage Books.

Higgins, J. (1911) *Federated Engine-Drivers and Firemen's Association of Australia v. The Broken Hill Propriety Company Ltd*, 5 C.A.R. 12.

Ireland, P. (2005) "Shareholder Primacy and the Distribution of Wealth." *Modern Law Review*, 68(1): 49–81.

Kahn-Freund, O. (1972) *Labour and the Law* (2nd ed.). London: Stevens & Sons.

Law Reform Commission of Canada. (1976) *Our Criminal Law*. Ottawa: Information Canada.

Lord Devlin. (1965) *The Enforcement of Morals*. Oxford: Oxford University Press.

Mandelson, D. (2015) *The New Law of Torts* (3rd ed.). Oxford: Oxford University Press.

McDonald, D. (2014) *Outrageous Fortune: Documenting Canada's Wealth Gap*. Ottawa: Canadian Centre for Policy Alternatives.

Mitchell Sack, S. (1999) *Getting Fired*. New York: Time Warner Pub.

Mitchnick, M. and Etherington, B. (2006) *Labour Arbitration in Canada*. Toronto: Lancaster House.

Mokhiber, R. (1988) *Corporate Crime and Violence: Big Business Power and the Abuse of Public Trust*. San Francisco: Sierra Club Books.

Pearce, F. (1976) *Crimes of the Powerful: Marxism, Crime and Deviance*. London: Pluto Press.

Pearce, F. and Tombs, S. (1998) *Toxic Capitalism: Corporate Crime in the Chemical Industry*. Aldershot: Ashgate.

Piketty, T. (2014) *Capital in the Twenty-First Century*. Cambridge, MA/London: The Belknap Press.

*Policy & Practice in Health and Safety* (2013) Special Issue on Corporate Criminal Liability, 11(2).

Report of the Task Force on Labour Relations (Woods) (1968) *Canadian Industrial Relations*. Ottawa: Privy Council.

Ruegg, A.H. (1905) *The Law Regulating the Relations of Employers and Workmen in England*. London: W.W. Clowes.

Smith, P. (2015) "Labour Under the Law: A New Law of Combination, and Master and Servant, in 21st Century Britain?" *Industrial Relations Journal*, 46(5–6): 345–364.

Snider, L. (1993) *Bad Business: Corporate Crime in Canada*. Toronto: Nelson.

Taibbi, M. (2014) *The Divide: American Injustice in the Age of the Wealth Gap*. Melbourne/London: Scribe.

Tombs, S. and Whyte, D. (2015) *The Corporate Criminal: Why Corporations must be Abolished*. London/New York: Routledge.

Tucker, E. (2014) "Shall Wagnerianism Have No Dominium?" *Osgoode Legal Studies Research Paper 49*.

## Chapter 3

# Underworld as servant and smokescreen

## Crimes of the Powerful and the evolution of organized crime control

*Michael Woodiwiss*

*Crimes of the Powerful (CotP)*, published in 1976, was the first book to make the case in any depth that the phenomena known as "corporate crime" and "organized crime" were not mutually exclusive. In the section on "Organized Crime in Historical Context," Frank Pearce debunked the idea that the Mafia was a centralized, super-criminal organization that lay behind virtually all organized criminal activity in the United States and was therefore a threat to national security. He then argued that gangsters, far from being dictators in their various cities and fields of activity, were better described as servants to local, corporate and governmental elites. There was no doubt, Pearce argued, that Al Capone, for example, was a powerful man in 1920s Chicago, but "there is equally no doubt that when he started to interfere with the interests of corporate capital, the limitations of his power became clear" (Pearce 1976: 130).

Pearce's insight into the limitations of Capone's power has since been confirmed by historical and criminological research. Capone never bossed Chicago or even his many gangster partners. On the contrary, as the legal scholar Mark Haller has demonstrated, "The group known to history as the Capone gang is best understood not as a hierarchy directed by Al Capone but as a complex set of partnerships." Capone, his brother Ralph, Frank Nitti and Jack Guzik formed partnerships with others to launch numerous bootlegging, gambling and vice activities in the Chicago Loop, South Side and several suburbs, including their base of operations, Cicero. These various enterprises, Haller continues, were not controlled bureaucratically. Each, instead, was a separate enterprise of small or relatively small scale. Most had managers who were also partners. Coordination was possible because the senior partners, with an interest in each of the enterprises, exerted influence across a range of activities (Haller 1995: 237).

Like other criminal entrepreneurs, Capone did not have the skills or the personality for the detailed bureaucratic oversight of a large organization. Criminal entrepreneurs like Capone are "instead, hustlers and dealers, for whom partnership arrangements are ideally suited. They enjoy the give and take of personal negotiations, risk-taking, and moving from deal to deal" (Haller 1995: 225–253).

The historian James D. Calder has also demonstrated that the story of Al Capone's rise and fall as a Chicago gangster has always depended upon the selective dissemination of federal agency records, particularly records of the Internal Revenue Service (IRS). IRS records of the Capone case remained sealed from public access, and only selective releases have been made to journalists, film producers and historians over the years. "There is no definitive history of Al Capone's involvement in organized crime." What we are left with remains, as Calder put it, "government-crafted history." The released documents have done little or nothing to justify descriptions of Capone as a supercriminal.

This contribution builds on Pearce's analysis to make the case that the idea of supercriminal organizations, outside the mainstream of American society, controlling organized crime, such as the one that Capone allegedly headed, acted as a smokescreen to conceal anti-democratic, anti-radical tendencies within the American state. The Capone story is used to track the evolution of organized crime control to the Organized Crime Control Act of 1970. This was a series of measures that were justified by the claim that organized crime was a threat to national security and, once applied, diminished the legal protections of Americans such as the right to a fair trial. Under the criteria of the act, as noted presciently by Pearce in 1976,

> most black militants and many white radicals would be liable for classification as Dangerous Special Offenders. The high risk of arrest experienced by all poor black people, the degree of state harassment of members of organisations such as the Black Panthers on the one hand, and on the other, the possibility of conviction for narcotic offences of white militants recruited from a counter-culture . . . would see to that. The conspiracy provision is so flexible and extensible as to include almost any criminal offense.
> (Pearce 1976: 158)

Calder was only half-right when he called the Capone story governmentcrafted history. The representatives of big business, mainly in the guise of the privately funded Chicago Crime Commission (CCC), led the way in creating a caricature of Al Capone that would be a key part of the process that would, much later, justify the draconian Organized Crime Control Act of 1970.

The serious effort to investigate Capone had begun on 18 October 1928, when President Calvin Coolidge authorized the special intelligence unit of the U.S. Bureau of Internal Revenue to begin an investigation into the gangster's income tax affairs (Hoffman 1993: 32–33). The effort intensified after St. Valentine's Day 1929 when the killing of seven men associated with the bootlegger "Bugs" Moran was thought by many to be Capone's work. Soon afterwards, a deputation of Chicago business interests, led by Frank Loesch of the CCC, went to Washington to ask President Herbert Hoover to intervene. Hoover from then on kept constant pressure on Andrew Mellon, Secretary of the Treasury, to go after Capone, somewhat ironically given that Mellon later testified before Congress that he used thugs like Capone to break workers' unions in building up his family's empire in aluminium and was also found to have been evading taxes on a scale that made Capone's tax infractions seem minimal (Russo 2001: 495).

Loesch and the CCC are usually described in the organized crime literature in fulsome terms as brave, upright "crusaders" against crime. Loesch, the CCC's most prominent publicist during the 1920s, was a corporate lawyer who, like many of his White Anglo Saxon colleagues, believed strongly that only his class, race and faction possessed honesty and integrity (Cohen 2004: 269). Loesch was also one of the first to articulate the crudely xenophobic interpretation of organized crime that came to dominate popular and professional perceptions of the problem. In a speech to students at Princeton University in 1930, Loesch proclaimed, "It's the foreigners and the first generation of Americans who are loaded on us. . . . The real Americans are not gangsters . . . the Jews [are] furnishing the brains and the Italians the brawn" (Russo 2001: 45).

Shortly after his speech, Loesch had a colleague from the CCC bring him a list of "the outstanding hoodlums, known murderers, murderers which you and I know but can't prove." He selected 28 mainly Irish, Italian and Jewish men from the original list, and as he related, "I put Al Capone at the head and his brother [Ralph] next. . . . I called them Public Enemies, and so designated them in my letter to the Chief of Police, the Sheriff, every law enforcing officer" (Bergreen 1994: 365–366). Calling certain criminals "Public Enemies" was an early step in the process of framing organized crime as a national security issue that could have no other solution than repression.

After Loesch and his allies' trip to Washington, a coordinated attack was launched. The federal government wanted to "get Capone" to show that ultimately the state was the only "big shot." His arrest and imprisonment for tax evasion in October 1931 was orchestrated by the Intelligence Unit of Elmer Irey, chief of the United States Treasury Enforcement Branch, aided in significant ways by a group of businessmen who became known as the "Secret Six" owing to a desire to operate anonymously. "Secret Six" money, for example, enabled one of Irey's chief investigators, Pat O'Rourke, to buy gaudy clothes in "gangster styles": a white hat with a snap brim, several purple shirts and checked suits. He also used "Secret Six" money to rent a room at the Lexington Hotel, a Capone hang-out, reading newspapers or playing dice games with bodyguards (Bergreen 1994: 154). The money also helped Treasury agents produce informants and collect documentary evidence.

Crime writer Gus Russo's verdict on Loesch and the "Secret Six" is accurate and damning:

> [T]he Chicagoans "crusade" was in large part a self-serving exercise in hypocrisy. . . . (It) was another xenophobic lynch mob that had no qualms about establishing its fortunes on the backs of musclemen. . . . Their civic activism was a barely concealed attempt to improve their own business

fortunes by getting the gangs off the streets in time for the upcoming World's Fair.

(Russo 2001: 45)

At the trial, the only defence his lawyers could offer was that Capone had not known that money from illegal businesses was taxable. He was sentenced to 11 years in a federal penitentiary (Kobler 1971: 312–330).

For a few years during the 1920s, Capone and his partners had made a great deal of money in scores of businesses that illegally provided Chicagoans opportunities to drink alcohol, gamble and visit prostitutes. After Capone was convicted of tax evasion in 1931, his career was over. He served most of his sentence at Alcatraz, located on a small island in San Francisco Bay. In 1936 Capone was reported as "dodging death" as fellow prisoners were threatening to kill him, allegedly for not buying a boat for them to escape on (*Pittsburgh Sun Telegraph* 1936).

On 16 November 1939 Capone was released after having served seven years and having paid all fines and back taxes. By then he was suffering from paresis derived from untreated syphilis. He spent some time in hospital before retiring to his Florida home, where his doctor described him as having the mentality of a 12-year-old. He died due to a stroke and pneumonia on 25 January 1947. He was said to have died penniless – certainly his children did not lead affluent lives (Kobler 1971: 362). His departure from Chicago's criminal world made no impact on the organization of bootlegging, gambling and prostitution – Chicagoans continued to pay for these goods and services, and corrupt networks continued to supply them.

The representatives of big business, mainly in the guise of the CCC, the "Secret Six" and the press, led the way in creating a Capone of demonic proportions. Loesch of the CCC, in his efforts to exaggerate Capone's importance, often revealed another agenda – an anti-union agenda. Testifying before a judiciary committee in 1932, for example, he made the often-repeated and rarely challenged claim that "fully two thirds of the unions in Chicago are controlled by, or pay tribute to, Al Capone's terroristic organization." No substance was offered to support the claim beyond Loesch's allusion to "those who know the situation" believed it (Omaha World-Herald 1932). Many authors in the years that followed chose to repeat the claim without taking the trouble to substantiate it. However, most unions were as honestly or dishonestly run as the business organizations that backed the CCC. By the 1920s some did begin to ape the tactics of businesses during strikes and enrolled gangsters to break the heads of strikebreakers. Both sides in these cases used violence and deceit and in every way possible fought to win (Hutchinson 1972: 19–22).

Capone had been virtually unknown to reporters until 1926 when he first featured in many newspapers as a possible suspect in the killing of a Chicago prosecutor William McSwiggin. In May the *San Diego Union* referred to Capone as "leader of a beer running gang" (*Union* 1926). In October, the

*Atlanta Chronicle* referred to him as "reputed king of the Cicero underworld" (*Chronicle*, 1926). Cicero at that time was a suburb of Chicago with a population of around 50,000. In November 1927, the Cleveland *Plain Dealer* had him as "one of the five gang leaders to escape death in the gang war of extermination two years ago" (*Plain Dealer* 1927). The following month, however, *The Daily Independent* of Murthysboro, Illinois, along with hundreds of other newspapers across the land, promoted him to "King" of Chicago (*Daily Independent* 1927). After that time newspapers more often regarded him as "king," "czar" or "emperor" of Chicago rather than as a simple "gang leader." Capone, according to the *Tampa Tribune* in June 1928, was "the sinister figure of an underworld czar more powerful than constituted authority, an emperor of racketeers whose subjects traffic in every vice shunned by decent society" (*Tribune* 1928).

In the years that followed thousands more books, magazine articles, documentaries and films similarly reflected Capone's imaginary supremacy over Chicago, a city of nearly 3 million during Capone's brief period of successful criminal activity. The version of the Capone story that most writers prefer to present to Americans and the rest of the world is that he was "King" of Chicago. The only substance for these claims about Capone's supremacy is, as in the case of his New York contemporaries Charles "Lucky" Luciano and Meyer Lansky, repetition and unsourced speculation.

Nevertheless, Capone would have probably remained a figure of mythic nostalgia associated only with the television and movie films of *The Untouchables* and, more recently, *Boardwalk Empire*, if not for the intervention of one of Loesch's CCC successors, Virgil Peterson. During the 1940s, as Capone's mental health deteriorated and the press began to pay him minimal attention, Peterson represented the gangster as the founder of the criminal dynasty in Chicago that had come to control gambling. This claim could not be substantiated, but it made the Capone story useful to an emerging narrative. This presented the history of organized crime in America in a version that edited out the "crimes of the powerful." By the 1950s, for example, industrialists such as John D. Rockefeller, once considered to be "robber barons" who employed gangsters and thugs to keep their laborers under control, were more likely to be called "captains of industry or "business pioneers."

Peterson took over the running of the CCC in 1942 and revived its influence through crime control recommendations aired in the *Journal of Criminal Law and Criminology* and more popular journals and news releases. "The more diligently Peterson studied organized crime and gambling," according to the historian William Moore, "the more closely they seemed to merge in his mind, and he shortly became convinced that there was not only a historical but a necessary relationship between the two." Peterson's thesis, articulated in the press and in two influential books published between 1945 and 1951, was that gambling was immoral and unproductive, whether legal or illegal, and that it should be defined as a security threat because two criminal syndicates, one based in Chicago, the other in New York, controlled it. Peterson called the Chicago-based syndicate the "Capone syndicate" even though Capone by then had been criminally inactive for two decades and he had never, as Haller demonstrated, headed a singular syndicate. People who Capone knew, including his cousins Rocco and Charles Fischetti, were involved in illegal gambling activity after Capone's incarceration, but that does not prove that the scores of criminal entrepreneurs involved in off-track bookmaking, for example, constituted one supercriminal organization founded by Al Capone (Moore 1974: 88–90).

Peterson's thesis, however, was accepted by the press and, more significantly, by a Senate committee appointed to investigate organized crime in 1950 and 1951. The chair of this committee, Estes Kefauver, at the conclusion of the hearings, wrote a book entitled *Crime in America* which acknowledged Peterson's contribution and elaborated on his anti-gambling argument, most closely in a chapter entitled "Chicago: The Heritage of Al Capone," which told what had now become the standard story of Capone's "rule" over Chicago being ended by the Internal Revenue Service but continued without Capone by, in Kefauver's words, "the Capone syndicate . . . run pretty much by a 'corporation'" (Kefauver 1952: 52–53).

Kefauver's investigative committee held televised hearings in several cities and gave undeserved substance and respectability to the claims of Peterson and a number of sensationalist journalists. Together they supported narratives about organized crime that have no supporting evidence. These narratives tended to consist of claims that organized crime became centralized during and just after Prohibition by Capone in Chicago and Charles "Lucky" Luciano in New York before jumping from these claims to the idea that the Mafia came to dominate organized crime in America from the end of the Second World War onwards. As America became a national security state, it was in the interests of some in positions of influence that people believe that organized crime in America was run by a foreign super-criminal organization.

The committee's *Third Interim Report* traced the history of the Sicilian Mafia and its "implantation" into America and then made the following frequently quoted but usually unexamined assertions:

> There is a nationwide crime syndicate known as the Mafia, whose tentacles are found in many large cities. It has international ramifications.
>
> Its leaders are usually found in control of the most lucrative rackets of their cities.
>
> There are indications of a centralized direction and control of these rackets, but leadership appears to be in a group rather than in a single individual.
>
> The Mafia is the cement that helps bind the Costello-Adonis-Lanksy syndicate of New York and the Accardo-Guzik-Fischetti syndicate of Chicago as well as smaller criminal gangs and individual criminals throughout the country.

> The Mafia is a secret conspiracy against law and order which will ruthlessly eliminate anyone who betrays its secrets. It will use any means available – political influence, bribery, intimidation, etc. – to defeat any attempts on the part of law enforcement to touch its top figures or to interfere with its operations.
>
> (US Congress 1951: 147–150)

The Kefauver report did not attempt to substantiate the crude analysis contained in these excerpts. Once the report had been issued, however, it, rather than the cheap sensationalism of journalists who paraphrased it, added the illusion of weight and coherence to the idea that organized crime was a centralized entity and alien implant.

The only evidence the report offered for its Mafia conclusions were stories about Capone and his cousin Charlie Fischetti and a number of drug trafficking stories supplied by the Federal Bureau of Narcotics involving Italian American gangsters. Neither these stories nor any testimony at the hearings were at all convincing about the idea of a centralized organization dominating or controlling organized crime. In fact, virtually all of the hard evidence produced by the committee contradicted its Mafia conclusions. The committee found men with different ethnic origins at the head of criminal syndicates around the nation and that there was frequent contact and cooperation between gangsters of different ethnicities. The ethnic origins of the suspected syndicate figures called before the committee were fairly equally divided between Jewish, Irish and Italian. Even in the committee's own choice of the two most powerful syndicates in the country – the Costello-Adonis-Lansky syndicate of New York and the Accardo-Guzik-Fischetti syndicate of Chicago – only Tony Accardo represented the Sicilian "cement." Meyer Lansky and Jacob Guzik were Jewish, and Frank Costello, Joe Adonis and Charles Fischetti, like Capone, had parents that originated in mainland Italy. All significant gangsters had been born or at least nurtured in America. The networks of illegal activities that the committee described cut across ethnic designations and always depended on the compliance of local officials. The evidence the committee uncovered showed that gambling operators in different parts of the country had sometimes combined in joint ventures, in the same way as businessmen everywhere, and had made a lot of money for themselves and for public officials (Moore 1974: 113).

Based on the conclusions about the structure of organized crime in America, the committee made 22 recommendations to combat crime in inter-state commerce. These included a number of acts tightening up existing anti-gambling legislation, the establishment of a Federal Crime Commission and proposals related to regulation of immigration and deportation. Most of the proposals for new legislation generated little enthusiasm in Congress and were dropped. The Kefauver Committee was essentially a show put on to maintain support for existing anti-gambling and anti-drug policies, and it produced only one recommendation that had long term significance. The Committee's Recommendation XII reads:

> Penalties against the illegal sale, distribution, and smuggling of narcotic drugs should be increased substantially. There is an alarming rise in the use of narcotics, particularly among teen-agers, who begin with marijuana and gradually become hopeless addicts to heroin and cocaine. The average prison sentence meted out to narcotics traffickers is eighteen months, and, as Narcotics Commissioner Anslinger told us, "short sentences do not deter." The committee endorsed the commissioner's recommendation that the law be amended to fix a **mandatory** (emphasis added) penalty of at least five years' imprisonment for dope peddlers and others engaged in commercial aspects of the narcotics of the narcotics traffic, on conviction for a second offence. Passage of such a bill has been recommended by the House of Representatives' Ways and Means Committee.
>
> (Kefauver 1952: 249)

This recommendation was in support of Congressman Hale Boggs, a White supremacist from Louisiana. Boggs had introduced a bill to increase all drug-offense penalties, with mandatory minimums of two years for a first offense, five years for a second offense, and ten (to twenty) for third and subsequent repetitions. Making the length of prison sentences for drug offenses mandatory diminished the role of judges, hit Black and minority defendants hardest because enforcement was directed mainly at them and eventually led to prisons that were overcrowded and incubators of the prison gang phenomenon of the 1980s through to the present.

The construction of the U.S. federal government's perspective on organized crime has recently become clearer with documents made available on the Internet that had previously only been made available to FBI agents. The so-called "Mafia Monograph" was a secret document prepared by the FBI's Central Research Section after the Appalachian meeting of Mafiosi in 1957 and meant only for limited distribution amongst federal law enforcement officials. It was a hastily put together and poorly sourced study of the origins, nature, and activities of the Mafia in Sicily and the United States and became a kind of "bible" for the top echelon of federal law enforcement, including, of course, J. Edgar Hoover (FBI Records 1958). The monograph featured a description of Al Capone as "crime king" of Chicago and the Capone gang, after his incarceration, as "a criminal organization with a menacing power surpassing that of the Mafia in Sicily," citing Peterson's *Barbarians in Our Midst* to substantiate these nonsensical assertions. From 1957 on the federal government, mostly represented by the FBI and informed by its Mafia bible, continued to make illogical and unchallenged efforts to "prove" its thesis of the centralization of organized crime. These efforts included the televised testimony of a lowly Mafia "soldier" Joe Valachi in 1963 and the often-debunked claims of prominent criminologist,

Donald Cressey, that "Mafia" and "organized crime" were virtually synonymous. Thus, far-fetched claims about Capone's omnipotence and long-lasting influence somehow acted as context for ideas about the Mafia controlling organized crime and thus threatening national security. These ideas, through a process described elsewhere (Woodiwiss 2001: 227–311), were key to the passage of the Organized Crime Control Act of 1970 and the subsequent development of organized crime control policy.

The laws contained within the 1970 act gave federal policemen more scope to spy on and suppress political dissent, as well as facilitating the control of despised minority groups. To begin with, Nixon's administration used its new powers more actively against anti–Vietnam War protestors and other radicals than Italian American or any other gangsters. Between 1970 and 1974, in particular, grand juries, along with increased wiretapping and eavesdropping powers, became part of the government's armoury against dissent. A list of abuses during these years includes harassing political activists, discrediting "non-mainstream" groups, assisting management during strikes, punishing witnesses for exercising their Fifth Amendment rights, covering up official crimes, enticing perjury and gathering domestic intelligence. These abuses were documented by a group of lawyers and concerned citizens known as the Coalition to End Grand Jury Abuse and submitted to the House of Representatives Judiciary Subcommittee, which was considering grand jury reform in the summer of 1976. Titles I and II of the act, for example, had changed the immunity provisions for grand jury witnesses. Previously once a witness had been immunized, the witness could never be tried on the subject of his or her testimony. The new laws, based on fears about a nebulous Italian American criminal conspiracy, changed this to a form under which witnesses in grand jury proceedings could be forced to testify on a grant of immunity and still be liable for prosecution for the events they described. This change, among others, allowed prosecutors from the Internal Security Division of the Department of Justice to call large numbers of dissenting Americans before special grand juries. These prosecutors, according to Senator Ted Kennedy, were "armed with dragnets of subpoenas and immunity grants and contempt citations and prison terms." "These tactics," Kennedy continued, "are sufficient to terrify even the bravest and most recalcitrant witnesses, whose only crime may be a deep reluctance to become a government informer on his closest friends and relatives" (Block and Chambliss 1981: 204–208).

In the years immediately following Watergate, checks were put on this type of repressive government behaviour, but the mood changed again after the inauguration of Ronald Reagan as president in 1980.

In 1982 Reagan announced a plan intended to "end the drug menace and cripple organized crime." The plan did not achieve either aim, but the high-level corruption and suppression of dissent using organized crime control powers continued.

Among the mountains of evidence of corruption uncovered during the Iran-Contra scandals, a Senate subcommittee in 1989 stated that the U.S.-supported

Contra-rebels used drug money in their efforts to overturn the Nicaraguan government (US Senate 1989: 36). This was confirmed by CIA Inspector General Frederick P. Hitz in 1998 (Hitz 1998). Extensive drug trafficking by America's chosen allies, in other words, was known to U.S. government agencies ostensibly engaged in a war to suppress drug trafficking.

At the same time as the country was officially engaged in its ambivalent war against drugs and organized crime, Reagan administration officials were using organized crime control powers to infiltrate church meetings and wiretap church phones in Arizona and Texas. The intention was to monitor the efforts of some religious groups to provide "sanctuary" to Central American refugees. These refugees were primarily from El Salvador and Guatemala, countries whose regimes had the active support of the U.S. government despite much documented evidence of the violent suppression of dissent. For a single set of indictments, 40,000 pages of secretly taped conversations involving priests and nuns were compiled. No prison sentences resulted, but the harassment had successfully intimidated the "sanctuary" movement (Shapiro 1984).

More recently, in 2012, FBI documents obtained by the Partnership for Civil Justice Fund (PCJF) using Freedom of Information Act requests revealed that from its inception, the FBI treated the Occupy Wall Street (OWS) movement as a potential criminal and terrorist threat even though the agency acknowledges in documents that organizers explicitly called for peaceful protest and did "not condone the use of violence" at Occupy protests. FBI offices and agents around the country were conducting surveillance against the movement even as early as August 2011, a month prior to the establishment of the OWS encampment in Zuccotti Park, New York. According to Mara Verheyden-Hilliard, executive director of the PCJF, "These documents show that the FBI and the Department of Homeland Security are treating protests against the corporate and banking structure of America as potential criminal and terrorist activity." On 19 August 2011, for example, the reports showed that the FBI in New York was meeting with the New York Stock Exchange to discuss the OWS protests a month before they began. By September, prior to the start of the OWS, the FBI was notifying businesses that they might be the focus of an OWS protest. Two other revelations were:

- Documents show the spying abuses of the FBI's "Campus Liaison Program" in which the FBI in Albany and the Syracuse Joint Terrorism Task Force disseminated information to "sixteen (16) different campus police officials" and then "six (6) additional campus police officials." Campus officials were in contact with the FBI for information on OWS. A representative of the State University of New York at Oswego contacted the FBI for information on the OWS protests and reported to the FBI on the SUNY-Oswego Occupy encampment made up of students and professors;
- Documents released show coordination between the FBI, Department of Homeland Security and corporate America. They include a report by the

Domestic Security Alliance Council (DSAC), described by the federal government as "a strategic partnership between the FBI, the Department of Homeland Security and the private sector," discussing the OWS protests at the West Coast ports to "raise awareness concerning this type of criminal activity."

The DSAC report on this secret collaboration between American intelligence agencies and their corporate allies illustrated additional ways in which organized crime control powers could be adapted to suppress challenges to the American power structure,.

Since *CotP* was published in the 1970s, repression of the poor in America was put on an assembly line scale as courts filled the prisons, mainly with African Americans and other minorities. The numbers of convictions for crime in the United States, much of it drug related, drastically increased. State and federal legislatures hugely increased the penalties for criminal violations. In New York, for example, Governor Nelson Rockefeller pushed through the so-called "Rockefeller Laws," enacted in 1973. These dictated a mandatory minimum sentence of 15 years' imprisonment for selling just two ounces (or possessing four ounces) of heroin, cocaine or marijuana. In addition, the new, enhanced sentences were frequently made mandatory. The concept of mandatory minimum sentences with the consequent diminution of the judge's role in cases was, as noted earlier, introduced to the American system by White supremacist Hale Boggs with the support of anti-organized crime crusader Estes Kefauver.

Former judge, Jed S. Rakoff, writing in *The New York Review of Books*, made the case that there is an imbalance of power in today's American criminal justice system. He showed that the prosecutor had all of it during plea bargaining processes, whereas the defender and the judge had none. A plea bargain, he writes is much like a "contract of adhesion" in which one party can effectively force its will on the other party. "The result," he concludes, "is that, of the 2.2 million Americans now in prison – an appalling number in its own right – well over two million are there as a result of plea bargains dictated by the government's prosecutors, who effectively dictate the sentences as well." The unintended consequence of mass imprisonment has been, as noted earlier, the proliferation of prison gangs, and whichever way this form of organized crime evolves, it is likely to be destructive.

Just as one of Capone's homes, Alcatraz, symbolized the war on crime during the 1930s, perhaps the warehouse in Chicago known as Homan Square best symbolizes the repressive policies associated with America's recent wars on drugs and organized crime. Spencer Ackerman, writing in *The Guardian*, has revealed that for more than a decade, Chicago's police brought thousands of people under arrest to their detentions and interrogations warehouse at Homan Square. This was a complex accommodating narcotics, vice and intelligence units for the Chicago police that has also served as a secretive facility for detaining and interrogating thousands of people without providing access to attorneys. Chicago police, particularly from the Bureau of Organized Crime, could use their headquarters for incommunicado detentions and interrogations without attracting significant public notice. Ackerman reported that

> Police used punches, knee strikes, elbow strikes, slaps, wrist twists, baton blows and Tasers. . . . The injured men are among at least 7,351 people – more than 6,000 of them black – who . . . have been detained and inter-rogated at Homan Square without a public notice of their whereabouts or access to an attorney.
>
> (Ackerman 2015)

Tales about Capone and other gangsters were woven together to portray organized crime as a national security threat rather than as a part of America's social, political and economic systems. This organized crime mythology helps explain why America now has incommunicado detentions, millions of convictions without juries, wholesale use of eavesdropping, wiretapping, entrapment techniques, urine tests, hair tests and much more in a country with a written Bill of Rights guaranteeing the rights to privacy and due process of law. These rights have been diminished by campaigns that manipulated public fears about organized crime and drugs, while the crimes of the powerful continue to harm more people, as many chapters in this collection demonstrate.

This contribution therefore, following Pearce, has used the Capone story, and the manipulation of the Capone story, to illuminate ways in which gangster activity served the interests of the American elite.

## References

Ackerman, S. (2015) "Homan Square Revealed: How Chicago Police 'Disappeared' 7,000 People." *Guardian*, 19 October.

Bergreen, L. (1994) *Capone: The Man and the Era*. New York: Simon & Schuster.

Block, A.A. and Chambliss, W. (1981) *Organizing Crime*. New York: Elsevier.

Calder, J.D. (1992) "Al Capone and the Internal Revenue Service: State-sanctioned Criminology of Organized Crime." *Crime, Law and Social Change*, 17.

*Chronicle* (Atlanta) (1926) "Al 'Scarface' Capone Wants to See End of Chicago Gang Murders." 14 October.

Cohen, A.W. (2004) *The Racketeers' Progress: Chicago and the Struggle for the Modern American Economy, 1900–1940*. New York: Cambridge University Press.

*Daily Independent*, Murthysboro, Illinois. (1927) "A King With a Gun For a Sceptre." 13 December.

FBI Records: The Vault. (1958) *Mafia Monograph*. Online. Available HTTP: https://vault.fbi.gov/Mafia%20Monograph (accessed 10 January 2018).

Haller, M.H. (1995) "Illegal Enterprise: A Theoretical and Historical Interpretation," in Nikos Passas (ed.) *Organized Crime*. Aldershot: Dartmouth.

Hitz, F.P. (1998) Inspector General, Central Intelligence Agency Before the House Committee on Intelligence Subject – Investigation of Allegations of Connections between the CIA and the Contras in Drug Trafficking to the United States. Online. Available HTTP: https://en.wikisource.org/wiki/Statement_of_CIA_Inspector_General_to_The_House_Committee_On_Intelligence_-_March_16 (accessed 10 January 2018).

Hoffman, D.E. (1993) *Scarface Al and the Crime Crusaders: Chicago's Private War Against Capone*. Carbondale and Edwardsville: Southern Illinois University Press.

Hutchinson, J. (1972) *The Imperfect Union: A History of Corruption in American Trade Unions*. New York: E.P. Dutton.

Kefauver, E., (1952) *Crime in America*. London: Victor Gollancz.

Kobler, J. (1971) *Capone: The Life and World of Al Capone*. London: Coronet, 1971.

Moore, W. (1974) *The Kefauver Committee and the Politics of Crime*. Columbia: University of Missouri Press.

Pearce, F. (1976) *Crimes of the Powerful: Marxism, Crime and Deviance*. London: Pluto.

*Pittsburgh Sun Telegraph* (1936) 12 February.

*Plain Dealer* (Cleveland) (1927) "Gang Chiefs Free in Chicago War," 23 November.

Rakoff, J.S. (2014) "Why Innocent People Plead Guilty." *New York Review of Books*, 20 November.

Russo, G. (2001) *The Outfit: The Role of Chicago's Underworld in the Shaping of Modern America*. London: Bloomsbury.

*San Diego Union* (1926) "Gang Chief Escapes by Narrow Margin." 9 May.

Shapiro, S. (1984) "Nailing Sanctuary Givers." *Los Angeles Daily Journal*, 12 March.

*Tribune* (Tampa) (1928) "Capone and the Miami *News*." 28 June.

US Congress. (1951) Senate Special Committee to Investigate Crime in Interstate Commerce (hereinafter called the Kefauver Committee), 82nd Congress, *Third Interim Report*, Government Printing Office, Washington DC.

US Senate. (1989) Subcommittee on Terrorism, Narcotics and International Operations of the Committee on Foreign Relations, *Drugs, Law Enforcement and Foreign Policy*. Washington, DC: Government Printing Office.

Woodiwiss, M. (2001) *Organized Crime and American Power: A History*. Toronto: University of Toronto Press.

*World-Herald* (Omaha) (1932) "Says Capone Seeks Liberty by Politics." 25 March.

# Chapter 4

# Shadow boxing against the crimes of the powerful

*Margaret Beare*

This chapter examines crimes that are economically profitable but also have a significant bearing on and/or nexus with state interests. Historically, most analyses of crime, as well as enforcement efforts, were – and remain – largely focused on the money-grubbing pursuits of the drug traffickers, small-time "accidental" money launderers, the in-your-face outlaw biker outfits, and the ethnic-based "alien" conspiracies of organized criminals. With his classic *Crimes of the Powerful* (*CotP*), Frank Pearce joined a few others (Bell 1960; Albini 1971; Schelling 1971; Chambliss 1978) to uncover the role of capital amid the political corruption of bureaucrats and government officials, the exploitation and monopolization of corporations, and the endurance and seemingly impervious status of mob-controlled unions.

We are talking about those perpetrators of criminal businesses, financial manipulators and corrupt politicians who became segregated from the stereotypical organized crime mobsters by Edwin Sutherland's introduction of so-called "white-collar crime" during his 1939 speech to the American Sociological Society.[1] We forget that concepts like organized crime are social constructs. To quote Robert K. Merton: "Our conceptual language tends to fix our perceptions. . . . The concept defines the situation, and the research worker responds accordingly" (1967: 145). This new "white-collar" concept had a direct and immediate impact on how researchers as well as the public and sanctioning authorities dealt with data related to crime in general. More specifically, changes occurred in terms of our understanding as to who committed "real" crimes (as distinguished from those of a lesser category, now referred to as white-collar crimes), under what conditions, and what sanctions (if any) were appropriate to these now-distinct categories of crimes. With this shift in focus *from* the criminal activity *to* the people, a false binary was created between what was understood as real crime and this lesser form of illegal activity.

This is the *first* of three shifts in focus that I argue undermine our ability and our willingness to seriously combat economically motivated financial crimes – that is, white-collar/corporate crimes and corruption. The *second* shift in focus was from the criminal *act* to the criminal *intent*. I argue that highlighting the economic imperatives of "economic" crimes dilutes perceptions regarding its seriousness – that is, not "really" criminal in nature but merely driven by profits. In fact, the economics involved are often used to justify the crimes. As Vincenzo Ruggiero points out, the powerful attributes of offenders allow their otherwise unethical or criminal conduct to be redefined. These successful violators may "present themselves as philanthropists" – that is, creating jobs for the underclasses, bettering the wider society. The conduct is sanctioned based on what Ruggiero calls an appeal to a higher principle – an appeal based on economics rather than legal or moral principles (2015: 102).

The financial schemes that eroded pension funds, took away peoples' homes and brought banks to the point of collapse or, alternatively, the death of 1,130 people in the Rana Plaza collapse were presumably mitigated by the fact that corporate managers were only chasing profits and did not intend to cause the deaths and financial havoc.[2] However, punitive fines as a criminological tool ignore the fact that in 2014, the "big six" U.S. banks made a record-breaking $152 billion in profits despite paying spectacular multibillion-dollar fines (Bank of America $77.09B; JPMorgan Chase $40.12B; Citigroup $18.39B). Three of the four largest financial institutions are 80% bigger today than they were before they were bailed out.[3] This focus on economics generates the lazy and flawed assumption that deterrence can be ensured by removing economic motivations rather than pursuing punitive and possibly criminal measures.

Finally, in reference to a third shift, I have argued that the enablers of corporate and political crimes, including service industry professionals, lawyers, brokers and accountants, are as much a part of the criminal operations as are the more traditional "Mafia" participants. These schemes often involve the interweaving of legitimate and illegitimate participants and/or enterprises (Beare in press: 2). However, this focus on individual actors has the unintended result of shifting attention further away from the pervasive nature of such crime – that is, the crimes of capital and the capitalist system. Together, these three shifts move attention away from the "social embeddedness" of capital that facilitates and rewards, *and will continue to facilitate and reward*, these forms of high-stakes financial and corporate crimes.

Our focus must now shift to this social embeddedness of capital. This chapter looks beyond individuals to see the role of capital in massive corruption schemes. Canadian corruption inquiries plus large-scale infrastructure swindles will be used to illustrate the truth of Pearce's argument that the interests of big business, consolidated corporations and the political influence that they wield are what determine a society's ability to police organized crime (in every form, including tax evasion, money laundering and financial frauds), corporate crime and political corruption, and not the often-claimed lack of legislative powers or adequate resources.

Given their diverse profiles, what term best describes the criminals involved in ongoing corporate, financial and political corruption schemes involving ill-gotten gain? The Charbonneau Commission into corruption in construction in Quebec (Quebec 2015, henceforth called the Commission report) referred to the participants in the corruption schemes as "organized crime" but then divided organized crime into two categories: Mafia-type traditional criminal groups, and non–Mafia-type groups which included participants who traditionally might have been labelled white-collar offenders (Commission report: 168). A footnote in the report acknowledges that Michael Levi's testimony to the Commission supported the idea that "organized crime can also apply to legitimate companies who engage in criminal activities" (Commission report: 50–51, 58–59). The distinction between these two categories purportedly lay in the use of violence: the Mafia-type groups were violent, whereas members of the non-Mafia category were claimed not to be "characterized by use of violence, threats of violence and control of territory" and were not necessarily career criminals but were instead "contractors, officials, politicians, and professionals" (Commission report: 170). However, evidence of violence and intimidation practiced by both groups refuted this differentiation (Beare in press).

Further to this definition, the Commission report argued that "infiltration" by organized crime into the construction industry/political corruption schemes takes two forms. First, it may come from the outside, that is, Mafia-type groups "creeping" into the legitimate economy. Second, infiltration can refer to the criminal groups that develop inside an industry, that is, the non–Mafia-type criminals: the construction bosses, union officials and politicians who participate in the schemes (Commission report: 171).[4] Therefore, all of the participants were "organized criminals," but, once again, the corporate and political participants were deemed less serious.

Despite the pressing need to develop a better term that includes *all* of the partners in the schemes, the term "organized crime" as a concept is too sullied by overuse and misuse with ambiguity as to who is or is not an organized criminal. "Corporate crime" may be too narrow to capture the facilitators and non–white-collar or corporate participants. Robert Blakey, who drafted the U.S. Racketeer Influenced and Corrupt Organization Statute (RICO), used the term "racketeer" both in the title of his statute[5] and to explain the wide array of diverse criminals charged under the statute. He argued that in a network of criminals involved in an ongoing criminal conspiracy where everyone was profiting, everyone deserved the same "criminal" label: "If officials operate like racketeers then they *are* racketeers regardless of the colour of their collars" (Blakey 1983, quoted in Beare 1996).

While discussing "crimes of the powerful," the term racketeer is perhaps the most suitable. The simplest definition of "racketeer" is someone who makes money from a dishonest or illegal activity – or from a legal activity but dishonestly. My focus will be on racketeering within the financial and construction industries. Daniel Bell argues that "racketeering is shaped by the market" (1965: 222), and he makes specific mention of the construction trades or any trade where "waiting time" can be expensive. Racketeers, like legitimate businesses, attempt to gain the maximum control possible by managing the "choke points" of an industry. In the construction industry, gaining control of the concrete supply and delivery process, a time-sensitive activity, places the rest of the construction process at the racketeer's mercy.[6] However, cement is not the only choke point: contacts or conspirators within government who help get contracts and ensure the continued winning of lucrative contracts are of equal value and have the same effect of allowing the work to begin or to continue. Likewise, having sophisticated legal or financial advisors who effectively serve as a "choke point" for any enforcement investigation into the racketeer's off-shore dealings will also serve to allow profits to flow.

As Bell notes (1965: 177), complex social relations give rise to and explain how racketeering can flourish in an industry. In this sense, construction might be the "perfect storm": there are large, often multimillion-dollar contracts at stake; multiple unions; oversight by conceivably competing private and public oversight bodies; competing teams of lawyers; numerous and competing financial institutions; political constituency interests; political campaign funding interests;[7] and key contracting bureaucratic positions. Finally, the nature of construction tasks requires specialized knowledge of not only the costs involved in construction, but also makes it equally easy to manipulate calculations of the risks that must be covered by the contracts.

Across Canada, large-scale hospital redevelopment projects have been particularly vulnerable to corruption and criminal frauds of various sorts. In 2016, the federal government announced a $125 billion infrastructure spending plan (Curry 2016). The details of a Phase 1, $300 million development plan is one example of the network of players involved in each project. By my count, the said project had the Etobicoke Healthcare Partnership and Infrastructure Ontario working with six separate law firms, with teams headed by at least 13 different lawyers, in addition to a team of financiers, which included a trust company, an international bank, a Canadian bank and a Canadian Life Assurance Company. Of course, all of these professionals sit above or off to the side of the contractors, friends of contractors, bureaucrats and politicians who all have an interest in the project. Similar mega-projects are currently taking off across the country. The federal government has stated that they are taking somewhat of a hands-off approach to infrastructure funding, with an emphasis on local decision making and local (municipal and/or provincial) procuring and monitoring. However, there is a fairly wide variation in terms of the structures and expertise that are in place to handle these responsibilities. As Charbonneau illustrates, jurisdictions that one might imagine would have the most experience have proven to be vulnerable to corruption and large-scale financial crime. This is the world of the PPP (public–private partnerships), where the private partnerships are global in nature and law firms advertise their specialized teams of "infrastructure lawyers" and boast the range of their global reach.[8]

## The rules/the players/the game

### The rules

By introducing the "participation/facilitation" offense the 2001 Canadian criminal association legislation (*Canadian Criminal Code* s.467.11(1)) allows "white-collar" racketeer participants, enablers/facilitators, corrupt politicians and bureaucrats to be seen as partners in various criminal conspiracies and therefore liable for criminal prosecution. This legislation thereby extends the category of who is or is not an organized criminal beyond the "usual suspects." However, the key is the discretion given to the state to charge or exclude these participants.

Crimes committed by corporations are hard to "police," and various chapters in this volume look at these barriers to prosecution. There is little to show as "achievement" in the fight against economically motivated crime. Take the example of corruption. The first stumbling block is the issue of definitions and evidence. In Canada, as in the United States, a *quid pro quo* exchange must be proven for a successful criminal prosecution. Meeting the standard of proof beyond a reasonable doubt of the element of the offense pertaining to bribery of officers and judicial officers, fraud against the government, municipal corruption, selling or purchasing office, influencing or negotiation appointments and/ or secret commissions all require some type of proven *quid pro quo* exchange (*Canadian Criminal Code*: Sections 119–125). For example, in overturning the guilty verdict against a former Virginia governor who had been convicted on multiple counts of public corruption, the U.S. Supreme Court judge in 2016 opined that, although the case was distasteful, without evidence of a clear *quid pro quo* exchange, there was a greater danger in a broad interpretation of the U.S. federal bribery statute used in the case than in the deeds committed by the governor.[9]

Basically, the legislation is ill designed to prosecute corporate or political corruption and criminal conduct, and enforcement tools are too blunt, if not actually captured or compromised by the industry. In 2015, for example, when facing fraud charges from the RCMP, SNC-Lavalin president and chief executive Robert Card was reported to have said that the criminal charges could result in "dismemberment" of the company or possibly a sale to a foreign owner, with the additional threat that "the company could move its headquarters if it falls out of favour in Canada" (Blackwell et al. 2015)[10].

To understand corruption and how it works, one must look beyond the strictly legal definitions – beyond evidence that documents a strict qud pro quo exchange. The Charbonneau Commission defined corruption as a clandestine exchange between private and public actors where one can gain an unfair advantage and the other can provide the benefit. The testimony from Charbonneau shows a pattern of ongoing "normalized" exchanges that achieve invisibility due to their gradual normalization as the way things are done. One must look for these ongoing patterns of exchange that reveal a corrupted industry within a corrupted political system rather than a one-off corrupted individual. The Commission exposed the "political-construction-union-Rizzuto (Mafia)" exchange environment that had continued for over a decade.

Although we might worry about the instances when accountability is lacking and no one seems to care, it is equally serious when there are attempts at accountability and the efforts are futile. Regulatory schizophrenia is reflected in the inability of states to hold corporations and/or their directors and top management criminally liable for the harms they inflict. As Tombs and Whyte argue, the protection of individuals in corporate crime cases shows "a form of criminal law that can barely mask its inherently structural class bias." This bias is written into the legal fabric of laws and courts and is underlined by the clear preferences for corporate prosecution as opposed to individual prosecutions in regulatory cases. Few courts, for example, have demonstrated the willingness to pierce the "corporate veil" and go after the human agents behind the offending decision making of the corporation (Tombs and Whyte 2015: 85). As such, criminal prosecution can only occur when harm and crime are seen as central to corporate activity, not as a marginal occurrence (Tombs and Whyte 2015: 158, 170). In those situations the state might be forced to respond.

### The players: collars of many colours

Most large-scale financial schemes, scams and thefts involve a "nest" of lawyers, accountants, political elite, business and agency executives and, in one case discussed later, a high-profile forensic firm and the Canadian Revenue Agency. Perhaps more telling of the embeddedness of the power elite with the state are situations where the state's agencies directly facilitate the crimes of the powerful.

At least four recent reports have drawn attention to Canada's failure to make the beneficial ownership structure of corporations transparent. First, the 2016 Financial Action Task Force (FATF) "peer" review of Canada noted that the identification of beneficial ownerships procedures remained a problem. Businesses and professionals who are otherwise obligated to comply with anti-money laundering and counter-terrorism financing (AML/CFT) obligations are not required to identify beneficial ownership or to take special measures with respect to foreign politically exposed persons (FATF 2016). Second, a report by the International Bank for Reconstruction and Development and the World Bank (2011) looked at the use of front companies and the abuse of corporate opacity to conceal corruption. It concluded that despite commitments to the UN Convention against Corruption and international AML/CTF standards to improving the transparency of legal entities and other arrangements, a "legal fog" covers the definition of "beneficial ownership" (including distinctions between a legal person and a natural person). This report ranked Canada 70th in terms of ability to access information on companies – below Sri Lanka, El Salvador and Bahrain. Third, Transparency International (Transparency International 2015, 2016) classified the Canadian framework as "weak" along with Australia, Brazil, China, South Korea and the United States.[11] The report notes that Canada does not mention ultimate control and limits the exercise of direct or indirect control to the equivalent of a percentage of share ownership. This makes the country "one of the most opaque jurisdictions, globally, in terms of identifying corporate ownership."[12] Finally, OpenCorporates (n.d.) ranked Canada as one of the worst countries in terms of openness and the detail available to the public on corporations, their licenses, ownership, shareholders and directors.[13]

This criticism of Canada reached a high public peak with the media coverage titled *Snow Washing* with headlines such as "Signatures for sale: Paid to sign corporate documents, nominee directors serve to hide companies' real owners" (Oved and Cribb 2017). Once again, revelations from the Panama papers revealed the role played by Canada in money laundering and/or tax avoidance/evasion. The authors noted: "Canada's corporate registration systems – federally and provincially – are shrouded in the same kind of secrecy that exists in tax havens such as the British Virgin Islands, Panama and the Bahamas" (Cribb and Oved 2017). Canada's "good reputation" as a responsible international citizen serves as an attraction to those wishing to exploit the various loopholes. Names were found on public registries that had nothing to do with the companies' "real" owners and yet served to legitimize the international taxation agreements that lead to no taxes being paid in any country (Anderson 2017).

### Enablers with benefits. . .

Although corporations are certainly benefiting from the tax abuse and other invisibility advantages, who are the enablers driving these schemes? According to John Christensen, founder and executive director of the Tax Justice Network of financial researchers, the aggressive marketing of this tax abuse industry is driven by specialist law firms, financial advisors, accounting firms and banks (Cribb and Oved 2016). This recognition of the power of the powerful to define situations was best described by Doreen McBarnet:

> Manipulating the law to escape control yet remain legitimate is an option more readily available to large corporations and "high net worth" individuals than to the mass of the population.
>
> (1992: 71)

According to McBarnet: "Creative compliance will be found in any area of the law in which those subject to it have the motivation and the resources – in terms of money and/or know-how – to resist legal control *legally*" (2001). She contends that even if there are "big stick" enforcement tools that can be directed at non-compliance, they only can be used once the issue of compliance vs. non-compliance is determined. This is where the big guns of the corporations and their legal teams can intervene. She argues that issues related to compliance have largely to do with corporate attitudes "far from seeing the law as an authoritative and legitimate policy to be implemented, see it as a material to be worked on, to be tailored, regardless of the policy behind it, to one's own or one's client's interests. And it requires active legal work" (2001: 6).[14]

"Active legal work" proves to be a major advantage to high-net-worth clients. In Canada, the exclusion of lawyers from mandatory suspicious reporting has been confirmed. In February 2015, a seven-member bench of the Supreme Court agreed that lawyers should be excluded from mandatory reporting requirements prescribed by Canadian legislation following the FATF recommendations. Five judges also found that a lawyer's duty of commitment to their clients' interests was a principle of fundamental justice, and requiring lawyers to report on their clients' activities or to permit state agents to access confidential information without proper legal authority would violate that principle (*Canada (Attorney General) v. Federation of Law Societies of Canada*, [2015] 1 SCR 401, 2015 SCC 7 (CanLII)). Lawyers for the government and the law societies fought over this decision for several years. At stake was the claim to the "exceptional" status of law and lawyers and their power as a lobbying group; that the interests of the law societies prevailed was therefore not too surprising. However, the lawyers' incentives also include "profit": in Canada, defence lawyers may take their professional fees from the forfeitable criminal proceeds of their clients. These two provisions throw into question the sincerity of those in government who purport to push the anti–money laundering and anti-corruption initiatives.

The services of lawyers in financial and corporate dealings are essential and can prove particularly useful in concealing the true source of funds through the use of legal trust accounts, use of nominees and facilitating the transfer of funds to tax havens. Likewise, solicitor–client privilege is powerful and restricts the ability of law enforcement to gather information from law offices (Beare and Schneider 2007). The 2015 evaluation of Canada by the FATF concluded that all high-risk areas in Canada were covered except legal persons and arrangements, especially nominee shareholding arrangements.[15]

Lawyers are not the only "enablers with benefits" that the state vests with powers to undermine enforcement against crimes of the powerful. Accountants – especially forensic accountants – serve their powerful corporate clients with the blessings of the state, even when the activities appear to be contrary to the law, the spirit of the law and, in the case that follows, even against the interests of the accommodating state agency. One high-profile case involving the Canada Revenue Agency (CRA) and KPMG forensic firm and a "sham" offshore tax scheme on the Isle of Man should have enraged the public. A "leaked" memo outlined the conditions under which the CRA was offering a secret amnesty deal to the multimillionaire clients of KPMG. The Canadian Broadcast Commission (CBC) received a copy of the confidential agreements that CRA had sent to KPMG, which passed them on to their wealthy clients who were offered a "deal" to voluntarily self-identify and pay their taxes with no additional fines, penalties or criminal charges.[16]

The CRA stated that the agreements would be terminated if the KPMG clients spoke to others about the secret offer. This deal – as documented by the investigative reporters and disclosed during Finance Committee hearings – did not apply to lower-income/middle-class investors who had, like the wealthy clients, followed the same faulty advice of their accountants. In their cases, they were faced with back taxes, heavy fines and, in some cases, criminal charges. Why was the deal secret? The CRA acknowledged that it would not be advantageous for the tax-paying public to learn that there were different systems of accountability at work! Why would the CRA do this? The explanation is easy. The self-identification of the wealthy clients would result in some tax revenue that otherwise would remain hidden in off-shore accounts. The amnesty process would free up the CRA to go after the smaller clients who would not have the resources to engage in long court battles with high-priced lawyers.[17] The advantage that the wealthy investors held was therefore twofold: large resources that the tax collectors wanted brought back to Canada *and* large financial resources that would have made it expensive, difficult and perhaps futile for CRA to fight in court.

Among the documents subpoenaed during the Finance Committee inquiry was a simple half-page template titled *Declaration of Gift*. "Clients with more than $5 million vow to give away their money 'absolutely and irrevocably' to a company on the Isle of Man." CRA concluded that this lacked credibility and was itself a scam intended to justify the Isle of Man tax evasion scam. The inquiry material indicated that the KPMG lawyers and accountants were, even in advance of CRA becoming alert to the scam, preparing their "creative compliance" arguments. Emails between KPMG officials referred to some of their defences: that is, CRA would not be able to prove that the "gifted" money was the same money that was being returned to Canada, and also that it was likely too many tax years would have elapsed before any conviction would be possible (Cashore et al., 6 June 2016).

KPMG ran the scam for over 10 years and charged $100,000 per client to set up their accounts under the Isle of Man plan – earning KPMG between $1.5 million and $1.6 million. As far as the Finance Committee could determine, KPMG was charging approximately 15% commission on the invested money. The Finance Committee found it near impossible to get any clear information due to the diverse legal protections: KPMG representatives claimed attorney–client privileges and the CRA claimed privacy concerns (Caron 2016).

### The game: advantage goes to the racketeers. . .

What are the main criminal "markets" for the powerful? Financial crimes of the powerful involve "big money" – amounts that make most of the proceeds from traditional organized crime operations look amateurish. Internationally, countries have bought into the need to target foreign corrupt practices, and significant fines have resulted. The Panama papers warned us all that we were also vulnerable locally. When these complicated, symbiotic and multilayered reflexive relationships between high-profile individuals and corporations with states, regulatory agencies, politicians and bureaucrats are left unexamined, they result in seemingly inexplicable phenomena such as the corporate and political corruption conspiracies that are allowed to continue undeterred for decades.

There are few ways to look inside the continuing criminal conspiracies of the powerful. One way is via commissions of inquiries with subpoena powers. However, an examination of the factors that determine when or if an inquiry is called reveals its own power dynamic – periodically, for usually political reasons, the near-normative corrupt behaviour is transformed into a "scandal." When opportunity arises, the party out of power will perform the *outrage dance* and demand that action be taken to curb the abuse, but nothing will fundamentally change – the dancers will merely change partners.

Two Canadian commissions – Charbonneau and Gomery[18] – provide us with examples of the political "use" of corruption inquiries. In both of these inquiries, the revelations – mostly known before the inquiries – resulted in changes of government political parties, with the deemed corrupt "old" party being ousted and replaced with one that promised to be clean, transparent and concerned with taxpayer resources. The impact on actual corruption is less certain. As Chambliss argued, corruption is exposed when those with power will benefit from the exposure: "Each political party exposes some but not all the dirty linen of the other" (1988: 205).

The criminal activities that led up to the 2015 Quebec Charbonneau inquiry into corruption in the construction industry were widely acknowledged to have been near business as usual for over 20 years. Although there is a legal culture that imposes barriers to exposing corruption among the powerful, there is also a social culture that develops between and among those who have unrestricted opportunities and, in most cases, the resources to work on the edges, if not on the clear criminal side, of operations. The investigative reporting of the KPMG and the CRA "deal" illustrated the close social as well as lobbying links between the political masters and KPMG officials.

The Charbonneau inquiry into corruption in the construction industry in Quebec reached the conclusion that "*a culture of impunity*" took over a vast section of Quebec's public tendering in construction in which organized crime, political figures and bureaucrats, political parties, unions and entrepreneurs worked together to skim public funds for illicit ends: modern-day "political machines." A decade prior, the federal Gomery sponsorship inquiry concluded that the party in power (Liberals) engaged in bribery and collusion without remorse and perpetuated a partisan, corrupt contracting system that made friends rich and paid party bills. The report referred to the development of a "*culture of entitlement*" (Travers 2005). The numerous books and articles that have tried to understand what happened inside Enron before its collapse repeatedly refer to a cult-like *culture of greed and invincibility*.[19]

The main lesson learned from these inquiries was to stay away from corruption inquiries! Critics during the Charbonneau inquiry referred to the "Gomery Effect" (Gyulai 2015) as serving to warn the Charbonneau Commission of the consequences of digging too deep. Therefore, in addition to individual costs for whistle blowers or organizations that "step up" to point at the corruption, there are potential political consequences. When "something is done about it," it tends to be done with an eye fixed on power relations. Although perhaps it is true that "no one likes corruption," no one truly wants to do very much about it. Too many people benefit from it or are intimidated by those who do. This is true at the international, domestic and municipal levels.

Non-governmental organizations (NGOs) and small private companies must go through extensive paperwork and security/reference checks to apply for miniscule amounts for small contracts. Yet once one moves into this other zone, the oversight too often falls to connections – not just one's own connections but also the connections of one's legal and financial advisors. Infrastructure will be the big market in the coming years in Canada and, seemingly, other Western countries; P3s (private–public partnerships) will be the main way these contracts will be processed. If holding tax-evading/avoiding individuals accountable is too hard or too expensive, how much harder is accountability in the large multimillion- or even billion-dollar projects involving international corporations? The state will have a vested interest in getting the projects completed, but at the same time, each project will have tentacles that reach out to additional political interests, and the greatest good will be seen to merge corporate, state and elite interests.

Even firms that violate the foreign anti-corruption rules are not necessarily sanctioned at home – York University in Toronto received a $20 million donation for the creation of the Dahdaleh Institute for Global Health. The Panama Papers confirmed that Dahdaleh served as "the mystery middleman" known as "Consultant A" in a series of U.S. court documents that lay out a decades-long kickback scheme involving global aluminium giant Alcoa and government officials in Bahrain. The U.S. officials allege that Dahdaleh "enriched himself" with $400 million in markups via the paying of bribes. These revelations did not, however, stop him from receiving an honorary doctorate from York in 2016. At that commencement ceremony, he advised the graduates to "[a]ppreciate the power of trust, staying true to one's values and giving back to the community."[20]

## Advantage to the racketeers. . .

Western societies, with no great impact, continue to announce their various wars on drugs, poverty or perhaps even on crimes in a generic sense. Seldom, if ever, is there a war on corruption; no one really wants to go after high-stakes financial crimes. Given a key regulatory aim of a state is to maintain the status quo, the preservation of the interests of the capitalist system will be a priority. As such, even a "crackdown" protecting the interests of workers and consumers will not significantly harm the long-term interests of the capitalist class. I shall leave the final words to Frank Pearce, who forces us to examine the "legitimating functions of the imaginary social order" versus the "real social order" and appreciate with historical examples the gap between rhetoric and actions when it comes to appreciating the purpose of various forms of regulation and the actual targets that are envisioned when they are framed and implemented (1976: 66, 159).

## Notes

1  There is a body of literature that examines the process by which "mobsters" became seen as a separate category from corporate/business criminals. See Smith (1991) for an analysis of this evolution. See also Sutherland (1983) for a full discussion of white-collar crimes.

2  In addition to those killed, 2,000 others were injured in the Rana Plaza collapse. A Toronto-based class action firm is currently pursuing a proposed class action on behalf of the survivors, the families and estates of the victims against Loblaws and the workplace inspection company, Bureau Veritas.

3  Issues – Reforming Wall Street. https://berniesanders.com/issues/reforming-wall-street/

4  On the one hand, the Commission is to be credited for recognizing the serious nature of non-Mafia criminal conduct by designating it as "organized crime." However, by retaining the distinction between the two categories of organized criminals, the Commission fell into the trap of treating some crimes as "more serious" than others.

5  One assumes the title was not *strictly* selected to incorporate Blakey's attraction to gangster movies and the Enrico Caesar 1931 character in the Edward G. Robinson movie *Little Caesar* – with the final lines "Mother of mercy, is this the end of Rico?"

6  Suspicions were raised regarding Donald Trump's relationships with NYC Mafia when it was noted that there was something a little peculiar about the construction of Trump Tower and subsequent Trump projects in New York. Instead of steel girder construction or pre-cast concrete, Trump chose ready-mix concrete. The advantages are that it can speed up construction, but it must be poured without interruption. One needs assurances that there would be no union actions that would cause even a brief labour slowdown. It is alleged that those assurances would have had to have come from a concrete company controlled by Mafia chieftains Anthony "Fat Tony" Salerno and Paul Castellano (Johnston 2016).

7  See Teachout, Zephyr (2014) *Corruption in America*. Cambridge: Harvard University Press, for a description of the increasing role of lawyers and lobbyists in the move toward the "legalization" of massive campaign donations and their impact on government policies. See also the U.S. Supreme Court of the United States, *Citizens United v. Federal Election Commission*, appeal from the United States district court for the District of Columbia, No. 08–205 for the details of the landmark US case that determined that laws that prevented corporations and unions from using their general treasury funds for independent "electioneering communications" (political advertising) violated the US Constitutional, First Amendment's guarantees.

8  See Denton's home page. "Infrastructure and PPP in Canada": www.dentons.com/en/find-your-dentons-team/industry-sectors/infrastructure-and-ppp/regional-sectors/infrastructure-and-ppp-in-canada.aspx.

9  In September 2014, the jury found Robert McDonnell guilty on 11 corruption counts and his wife Maureen guilty on 8 corruption counts. One year later, that decision was reversed (Supreme *Court of United States McDonnell v. US*) (the judgement of the Court of Appeals was vacated).

10  There have been an array of separate fraud and corruption cases brought against SNC-Lavalin. The case that involved the McGill University Health Centre's new $1.3-billion super-hospital had not yet gone to trial as of April 2017. A separate case resulted in charges being dismissed due to the methods by which the RCMP had obtained their wiretaps – see Gallant (2017).

11  Transparency International 2015 and 2016. The various country frameworks were measured against the G20 Beneficial Ownership Transparency Principles adopted by the G20 in November 2014.

12  The quote is attributed to Transparency International Canada's Peter Dent (Seglins, Houlihan and Dubinsky 2017).

13 Together these negative evaluations of Canada focussed on the lack of transparency regarding "beneficial ownerships" and also the exclusion of lawyers from mandatory reporting of suspicious transactions.

14 See also McBarnet (1984, 1992).

15 Lawyers have responded that they now have developed their own anti–money laundering rules and that they will try to verify the identification of their clients.

16 The CBC and the *Fifth Estate* ran two separate programmes documenting this arrangement between KPMG and Revenue Canada: KPMG and Tax Havens for the Rich: The Untouchables. 3 March 2017; June 2016. See also Rosen and Rosen 2017.

17 KPMG is fighting CRA in federal court over the agency's attempt to obtain all client names and documents related to the investment scheme, and the debate continues as to whether KPMG will be charged.

18 Quebec 2015; Canada 2005, Gomery Commission Report, (Phase 1) 2006 (Phase 2) Parliament of Canada.www.parl.gc.ca/Content/LOP/researchpublications/prb0560-e.htm

19 At Enron following the collapse, one comment referred to the Enron "culture of cleverness" which allowed, encouraged and pressured the employees to see themselves as unconstrained by rules.

20 The York website listed the numerous national and international accomplishments of this Canadian business magnate based in the United Kingdom.

# References

Albini, J. (1971) *The American Mafia: Genesis of a Legend*. New York: Appleton-Century-Crofts.

Anderson, M. (2017) "The Shell Game: Canada's Lax Disclosure Laws Open Door to Tax Fraud, Money Laundering: Transparency International Warns against Country Becoming a 'haven for corrupt capital.'" Online. Available HTTP: The Tyee.cahttps://thetyee.ca/Opinion/2017/01/02/Canada-Disclosure-Laws/

Beare, M. (in press) "Internal Enemies, Legitimate and Illegitimate Enterprises," in Allum, Felia and Gilmour, Stan (eds.) *Handbook of Organized Crime and Politics*. Cheltenham, UK: Edward Elgar Publishing.

Beare, M. (1996) *Criminal Conspiracies, Organized Crime in Canada*. Nelson Toronto, Canada.

Beare, M. and Schneider, S. (2007) *Money Laundering in Canada: Chasing Dirty and Dangerous Dollars*. Toronto: University of Toronto Press.

Bell, D. (1965) *The End of Ideology* (originally published in 1960). New York: Free Press.

Blackwell, R., McFarland, J. and Van Praet, N. (2015) "'Very damaging' Fraud Charges: What's Next For SNC-Lavalin?" *The Globe and Mail*. 19 February. Online. Available HTTP: www.theglobeandmail.com/report-on-business/snc-lavalin-fraud-charges-threaten-companys-reputation/article23103760/

Blakey, G.R. (1983) Comments to the Reparative Sanctions International Consultative Workshop. Hosted by the Department of the Solicitor General. Unpublished proceedings (January) and 1982. Presentation to the Symposium on Enterprise Crime Proceedings. Hosted by the Department of the Solicitor General. Quoted in M.E. Beare 1996. *Criminal Conspiracies, Organized Crime in Canada*. Nelson Canada.

Canada. (Attorney General) v. Federation of Law Societies of Canada, [2015] 1 SCR 401, 2015 SCC 7 (CanLII) Online. Available HTTP: www.canlii.org/en/ca/scc/doc/2015/2015scc7/2015scc7.html Canada (A.G.) v. Charbonneau; [2012] Q.J. No. 3457

Canada. (2005) Gomery Commission Report, (Phase 1) 2006 (Phase 2) Parliament of Canada. Online. Available HTTP: www.parl.gc.ca/Content/LOP/researchpublications/prb0560-e.htm

Caron, G. (2016) "Tax Evasion Will Persist Until Parliament Hill Steps Up." *Huff Post Politics*, 25 August 2016. Online. Available HTTP: www.huffingtonpost.ca/guy-caron/tax-evasion-kpmg_b_11665574.html

Cashore, H., Ivany, K. and Hwang, P. (2016) "CBC Investigates Isle of Man Tax Dodge Could Violate Income Tax Act, KPMG Insiders Cautioned." *CBC News*. Posted: 6 June 2016.

Chambliss, W. (1988) *On the Take* (2nd ed.). Bloomington, IN: Indiana University Press (originally published 1978).

Cribb, R. and Oved, M.C. (2016) "The Secrecy Specialists behind Panama Papers' Canadian Offshore Dealings." *Toronto Star*, 9 May 2016. Online. Available HTTP: www.thestar.com/news/world/2016/05/09/the-secrecy-specialists-behind-panama-papers-canadian-offshore-dealings.html

Cribb, R. and Oved, M.C. (2017) "Snow Washing: Canada Is the World's Newest Tax Haven." *Toronto Star*, 25 January 2017.

Curry, B. (2016) "The $125 Billion Question." *The Globe and Mail*, Monday, 21 March. Online. Available HTTP: www.theglobeandmail.com/news/where-will-125-billion-in-infrastructure-spendinggo/article28228477/

FATF: Anti-Money Laundering and Counter-Terrorist Financing Measures in Canada. 2016. Online. Available HTTP: www.fatf-gafi.org/media/fatf/documents/reports/mer4/MER-Canada-2016.pdf

Gallant, J. (2017) "Judge Acquits SNC-Lavalin Execs, Says RCMP Relied On 'Gossip'." *The Toronto Star*. 10 February 2017. Online. Available HTTP: www.thestar.com/news/gta/2017/02/10/judge-acquits-snc-lavalin-execs-says-rcmp-relied-on-gossip.html

Gyulai, L. (2015) "'Cautious' Charbonneau Commission Report Lets Public Draw the Conclusions." *Montreal Gazette*. 27 November 2015. Online. Available HTTP: http://montrealgazette.com/news/local-news/john-gomery-cautious-charbonneau-commission-report-lets-public-draw-the-conclusions.

Johnston, D.C. (2016) "Just What Were Donald Trump's Ties to the Mob?" *Politico Magazine*. 22 May 2016. Online. Available HTTP: www.politico.com/magazine/story/2016/05/donald-trump-2016-mob-organized-crime-213910

McBarnet, D. (1984) "Law and Capital: The Role of Legal Form and Legal Actors." *International Journal of the Sociology of Law*, 12 (3): 231–238.

——— (1992) "It's Not What You Do But the Way that You Do It," in D. Downes (ed.) *Unravelling Criminal Justice*. London: Macmillan.

——— (2001) "When Compliance Is Not the Solution but the Problem: From Changes in Law to Changes in Attitude." Working Paper no 18, August 2001, Centre for Tax System Integrity Research School of Social Sciences Australian National University Canberra, ACT. Online. Available HTTP: https://openresearch-repository.anu.edu.au/bitstream/1885/41635/2/WP18.pdf.

Merton, R.K. (1967) *On Theoretical Sociology: Five Essays, Old and New*. New York: Free Press Paperback.

OpenCorporates (n.d.) "The Closed World of Company Data: An Examination of How Open Company Data Is in Open Government Partnership Countries." Online. Available HTTP: http://opencorporates.com/downloads/ogp_company_data_report.pdf

Oved, M.C. and Cribb, R. (2017) "Signatures for Sale." *Toronto Star*, 26 January 2017. Online. Available HTTP: http://projects.thestar.com/panama-papers/canada-signatures-for-sale/

Pearce, F. (1976) *Crimes of the Powerful: Marxism, Crime and Deviance*. London: Pluto Press.

Quebec. (2015) Rapport final de la Commission d'enquête sur l'octroi et la gestion des contrats publics dans l'industrie de la construction. Novembre 2015. Commissioners, France

Charbonneau with Renaud Lachance. Bibliothèque Nationale du Canada. Online. Available HTTP: www.ceic.gouv.qc.ca/fileadmin/Fichiers_client/fichiers/Rapport_final/Rapport_final_CEIC_Integral_c.pdf ["Commission report"]

Rosen A. and Rosen, M. (2017) *Easy Prey – Investors*. Kingston, ON: McGill-Queen's University Press.

Ruggiero, V. (2015) *Power and Crime*. London: Routledge.

Schelling, T. (1971) "What Is the Business of Organized Crime." *Journal of Public Law*, 20: 71–84.

Seglins, D., Houlihan, R. and Dubinsky, Z. (2017) "'Tax haven' Canada Being Used by Offshore Cheats, Panama Papers Show." *CBC News*, 24 January 2017. Online. Available HTTP: www.cbc.ca/news/investigates/panama-papers-canada-tax-haven-1.3950552

Smith, D.C. (1991) "Wickersham to Sutherland to Katzenbach: Evolving an 'Official' Definition for Organized Crime." *Crime, Law & Social Change*, 16(2): 135–154.

Sutherland, E.H. (1983) *White Collar Crime: The Uncut Version*. New Haven: Yale University Press.

Teachout, Zephyr (2014) *Corruption in America*. Cambridge: Harvard University Press.

Tombs, S. and Whyte, D. (2015) *The Corporate Criminal: Why Corporations Must be Abolished*. London: Routledge Press.

Transparency International. (2015) Just for Show: Reviewing G20 Promises on Beneficial Ownership. Online. Available HTTP: www.transparency.org/whatwedo/publication/just_for_show_g20_promises

Transparency International: Canada. (2016) No Reason to Hide: Unmasking Owners of Canadian Companies and Trusts. Online. Available HTTP: www.transparencycanada.ca/wp-content/uploads/2016/08/TIC-BeneficialOwnershipReport-Interactive.pdf

Travers, J. (2005) *Toronto Star*, 2 November 2005. Online. Available HTTP: https://media.curio.ca/filer_public/ae/62/ae62a992-8dd6-41cc-9426-d0d1fb0f5433/gomery.pdf

U.S. Supreme Court of the United States, Citizens United v. Federal Election Commission, appeal from the United States district court for the District of Columbia, No. 08–205.

U.S. Supreme Court of United States McDonnell v. US (no.15–474, decided 27 June 2016) www.supremecourt.gov/opinions/15pdf/15-474_ljgm.pdf

World Bank. (2011) *The Puppet Masters: How the Corrupt Use Legal Structures to Hide Stolen Assets and What to Do About It*. Prepared by: E. van der Does de Willebois; E.M. Halter; R.A. Harrison; J. Won Park; J.C. Sharman. Online. Available HTTP: https://star.worldbank.org/star/sites/star/files/puppetmastersv1.pdf

Chapter 5

# Between force and consensus

*Vincenzo Ruggiero*

In the formulation of Bertrand Russell (1975), power is the production of intended effects. The element of intention, or "will," is also stressed by Max Weber (1978: 943), who defines power as "the probability that an actor in a social relationship will be in a position to carry out his own will despite resistance." We have here two key components of power: the capacity to perform purposive action, on the one hand, and the ability to overcome obstacles, on the other. In social theory we find numerous descriptions of the functioning and the process of actualization of these two components. This contribution intends to provide an outline of this process.

The capacity to produce intended effects is what distinguishes powerful from powerless individuals and groups, with the former being granted a wide range of choices and potential actions to be carried out (Bauman 1990). Power, in this sense, derives from the number and diversity of choices available and the ability to predict their outcomes. In making choices and acting, however, the powerful may turn the actions performed by others into means for their own goals, and this can be realized through coercion or legitimacy. The crimes of the powerful, in the analysis proposed later, are enacted through varied combinations of coercion, legitimacy, violence, secrecy, consensus and hegemony. After an attempt to examine some such combinations, this contribution will discuss the viability of social and institutional responses to the crimes of the powerful.

## Coercion

Classical sociology distinguishes between military societies and industrial societies, respectively characterized by the spirit of conquest and the spirit of cooperation. In the evolutionary perspective of Spencer (1885) and Comte (1953), the predominance of the latter type of societies will determine the decline of warfare. Cooperation, therefore, seems to exclude coercion. Even in a Marxist vision, the main sources of social control can be attributed to the "free" exchange between labour and industrial capital, whereas violence, structurally implicit in that exchange, may also characterize collective class struggle, ultimately culminating in revolutionary force.

The pioneering contribution of Frank Pearce (1976) can be located in this tradition of thought. Pearce explains why there is a discrepancy between "official portrayals of reality and what is actually taking place" (1976: 80), and in discussing the international activities of corporations makes a radical break from traditional criminology. He describes the hidden processes that preside over the "distribution of criminal activity and the nature of the social response to this," contrasting the "imaginary social order" associated with presumably pluralist and democratic societies with the description of their real nature. His is an effort to unveil how coercive social relationships are embedded in a specific power rationality.

Paradoxically, it is from other traditions of thought that power as pure coercion is theorized. Conservative right-wing thinking, inspired by Manichean juxtapositions, distinguishes between good and evil in the moral realm, beautiful and ugly in aesthetics, profitable and unprofitable in economics and friend and enemy in politics (Schmitt 1976, 1985). This categorical distinction separates the political from the ethical, isolating power as a distinct entity to be studied in its own terms. Power presupposes the existence and creation of strangers, others, enemies, and is necessarily exercised through conflict. A form of warfare, it generates violations, excesses and crimes in routine acts aimed at keeping the evil, the ugly and the other at a distance (Hausgaard 2009).

Although this polarization may describe the antagonistic relationships within party politics in democracy, the violence on which such polarization is based is the legacy of the birth and expansion of state power. Large-scale violence proved to be the most efficient tool for the extraction of resources, the accumulation of capital, the drawing of national borders and the forging of identities (Tilly 1985). Notions such as humanity, justice, progress and civilization provided powerful ideological devices in this process, legitimizing invasion and conquest and allowing the subjugation of reluctant aliens and their coercive assimilation into "humanity": "when you have to deal with beasts you have to treat them as beasts" (Hausgaard 2009: 286).

There was no end to war and conquest, as external violence turned into disciplinary devices addressed at internal others so that their effects were inscribed in institutions, in social inequality and in the bodies themselves of each and every one of us (Foucault 1980). In brief, the control of the means of production proceeded simultaneously with the control of the means of destruction. However, although naked power exemplified by a military apparatus deters and terrorizes, forcing individuals to do things that they would not otherwise do, it also aspires to designate a supreme moral authority. Violence, in other words, is an expression of, and simultaneously aims to generate, hegemony. Violent crimes committed by powerful individuals and groups are inspired by a similar aim.

That the two components of power, coercion and hegemony, are intimately connected is clear in Max Weber's (1978) argument that domination may be established by virtue of "a constellation of interests" and by virtue of "authority."

The former falls in the economic domain and derives from the possession of resources and marketable goods: this type of domination determines the conduct of those devoid of possessions, who nevertheless remain formally free and motivated simply by the pursuit of their reproduction. Monopolies, it is implied, are the extreme forms of this type of domination. The latter type is exemplified by patriarchal, magisterial or princely power; therefore, it "rests upon the alleged absolute duty to obey, regardless of personal merit or interests" (Lukes 1986: 30). Domination by virtue of constellation of interests, as Weber postulates, often turns into domination by authority, as material possessions are transformed into duty to obey on the part of the dispossessed.

Frank Pearce identifies, among the components of this process, the differentiated attention attracted by crimes committed by the dispossessed and crimes committed by the powerful, suggesting that concentrating on the former is functional in maintaining class systems. "Firstly, it strengthens the dominant individualist ideology," by depicting crime as the result of personal, rather than structural, inadequacy. Secondly, by criminalizing the disadvantaged, it neutralizes "their potential for developing an ideologically sophisticated understanding of their situation" (Pearce 1976: 81).

The crimes of the powerful within the framework delineated so far are routine expressions of power itself, chains of events and actions that reinforce authority in social and institutional spheres. There are, however, other modalities through which power can commit crime – for example, by reducing the cognitive area of those subjected to it. Rulers are bound to limit and select social demands, and they do so by choosing the issues and the areas to which their responses are addressed (Luhmann 1975, 1985). For power, decisions are important, but just as important are the decisions that are not made, the proposals that are never considered, the innovative ideas that are somehow always out of the question. "Ruling a country means controlling the political agenda, defining what is thinkable and unthinkable, and this work is always done behind the façade of democratic politics" (Walzer 2004: 24). Selective and reductive activities turn into impunity when crimes of the powerful are committed; this is because citizens interact with the sources of power only sporadically and in extremely limited spheres of social life. They, therefore, are the recipients of injunctions, of binding decisions transmitted to them, but the complexity of their condition does not allow them to orient themselves politically and ethically. By providing such orientation to citizens, in brief, power reduces the autonomy of their judgment, thus making its crimes invisible (Ruggiero 2015). Coercion and selection, in this case, also entail a degree of concealment and/or secrecy.

The selective process through which coercion is concealed, therefore, entails the control of agendas so that the field of the dominated is structured and narrowed by the dominators. Whereas in Marx this process is accompanied by the development of a "false consciousness" on the part of the dominated, in Weber it leads to an authoritative power of command that exacts obedience through the acceptance of the norms it imposes.

In brief, it is extremely hard to draw a neat difference between coercive power strategies and consensual exercise of authority, as the analysis of the concept of hegemony may confirm.

## Hegemony and secrecy

Structures of dominancy are constituted through norms that acquire hegemony thanks to customary social practice. A dynamic of this process is clearly described by John Dewey (1997: 4) in his analysis of "how we think." Thoughts, he argues, grow up unconsciously and "without reference to the attainment or correct belief."

> From obscure sources and by unnoticed channels they insinuate themselves into acceptance and become unconsciously a part of our mental furniture. Tradition, instruction, and imitation are responsible for them.
>
> (Dewey 1997: 4)

But such thoughts, Dewey specifies, are prejudices, that is, prejudgments, not judgments proper that rest upon a survey of evidence. In a Weberian sense, it is not only thoughts, but every sphere of social order which is profoundly influenced by structures of dominancy. These structures are taken for granted, although, at times unobtrusively, they privilege certain specific ideas and interests. We can also term these thoughts and structures as "meaning systems," historical *a priori* that help people make sense of their world.

Pearce's work on the crimes of the powerful endorses this Weberian view, when he stresses that "the capitalist loyalty to democracy is only provisional." In his view, "meaning systems" that privilege specific ideas and interests revolve around the acquisition of profit.

> This explains how capitalism has successfully developed in pre-democratic countries such as nineteenth-century Britain; how it has coexisted with militaristic and fascist regimes in Japan and Germany; and how at present many of the countries with investments by, or trade with, US business have dictatorial regimes.
>
> (Pearce 1976: 85)

In Gramsci's surprisingly enduring analysis, consensus and hegemony are closely related to the point of almost overlapping. Supremacy of a social group, he argues, manifests itself in two ways: as domination and as intellectual and moral leadership (Gramsci 1971). Domination aims at subjugating, or even liquidating, rival groups. However, it is leadership that allows the exercise of power, as moral and intellectual values are widely spread, shared and ultimately internalized even before power itself can be exercised. Conflicts between social groups result in the victory of the party which "captures" the mind and the political sensibility of the enemies, thus absorbing them in a hegemonic culture. Some groups, according to Gramsci, "for reasons of submission and intellectual subordination, adopt a conception of the world which is not their own but is borrowed from another group" (Gramsci 1971: 327).

Focusing on current developed democracies, there are two major, intertwined, domains in which hegemony needs to be achieved, namely the domain of economic life and that of international relations. Although not distinctively separable, in the former, at issue is the dominant philosophy of neoliberalism, whose perpetuation must rely on support or, at least, on silent consensus. In the latter, hegemony has to manifest itself by making violence, particularly in the form of war, an acceptable version of Gramsci's domination. Let us briefly examine the two domains separately.

"Freedom" in labour markets consists of the encounter between those who use others as means to their ends and those who allow themselves to be used in that manner. "The superb meeting point of these two freedoms is called employment" (Lordon, 2014: ix). This coerced freedom implies a form of capture, which consists of getting individuals to act on behalf of the capturer while closing down other avenues of their reproduction. In a formula indebted to Marxist analysis:

> If the primary meaning of domination consists in one agent's having to pass through another to access the object of desire, then evidently the employment relation is a relation of domination.
>
> (Lordon 2014: 12)

Hegemony, in this realm, may be achieved through the dissociation of the figure of the consumer from that of the employee, with the former becoming predominant at the cost of life indebtedness. Domination through employment, moreover, tends to increase with the relocation of business, whereby the employees are forced to compete with colleagues scattered across the world who accept lower salaries and therefore a lower level of consumerism. Such competition generates uncertainty and fear, transforming the labour force into a fluid mass to be forged and governed as a component of a portfolio, as a mere asset at the disposal of investors. Consensus and hegemony thrive on threat, which incorporates a degree of violence and, at the same time, on forms of social control that seem to render violence unnecessary.

It could be argued that hegemony, in this case, is achieved thanks to a degree of secrecy, which characterizes many operations in contemporary global markets. Companies are constituted by multiple layers of concealment: they may be based in a tax haven, be controlled by a sister company in a Western European country, possess large interests in another company in Asia and be managed by one located in the United States. Secrecy describes not only the financial aspects of operations, identifiable as the concealment of profits and the evasion of taxes, but also the very productive processes in which companies engage.

Resources, practices, peoples, monies, entire productive operations are "moved from one national territory to another, and they are wholly or partly hidden from the view of the public and/or public authorities" (Urry 2014: 9).

Considering the domain of international relations, consensus and hegemony may be mobilized through the depiction of invasions as democratic missions. The crimes of the powerful perpetrated at the international level, in this way, become celebrations of democratic values, although wars against undemocratic enemies require that the very democratic principles allegedly inspiring them be jettisoned. The several terrorism legislations drawn up in recent years, for instance, appear to imply that the defence of freedom requests the sacrifice of giving up freedom. Simultaneously, in the name of universalistic values, some humans are placed outside the universe of moral obligation, while it is ultimately the aggressors who draw the line between legitimate and illegitimate coercion.

Concealment and secrecy as components of hegemony are also determined by the considerable distance (geographical, relational, functional or simply cultural) between the parties. The victims of international aggressions and other crimes become invisible, their suffering and even their death fail to produce reactions but spawn insensitivity and result "in eyes turned away from a silent ethical gaze" (Bauman and Donskis 2013: 9). Our gaze is spared cruel spectacles, and we are reassured that such spectacles will never enter our private domain. As Dal Lago (2012) remarks, since 1991 Western countries led by the United States have fought in Iraq, Bosnia, Somalia, Serbia, Afghanistan, Iraq again, Libya, Pakistan, Syria and so on. Yet we may feel that we have never been at war, a feeling of indifference unprecedented in history. The word "war" is prohibited; in its place we have "peacekeeping operations" or "protecting civilian populations." Soldiers are advised to present themselves as social workers.

## Ostentation

Hegemony and violence, as I have argued earlier, may be intertwined and at times hidden behind threat and the exercise of fear. Secrecy is a variable in this equation, although the crimes of the powerful are at times characterized by its reverse, ostentation, that strengthens the position of those who commit them. The variable ostentation, however, appears to be applicable to certain types of crimes of the powerful more than to others, as it becomes clear when considering that not all crimes of the powerful are immune to prosecution. If some such crimes were left unprosecuted, it is maintained, "capitalism might well collapse" (Pearce 1976: 81). Long-term interest may prevail over immediate easy profit; therefore, "one crucial question that must be asked is what effects do these crimes, and the public awareness of them, have on the social order": "actions that pose a real threat to this must be controlled" (Pearce 1976: 104).

On the other hand, the suggestion that these crimes are motivated by the mere pursuit of profit depicts only a partial picture. The crimes of the powerful, in reality, are foundational events, in the sense that they transform rules, experiment with new procedures and, ultimately, act as legislative tools. They establish a new type of morality and legitimacy by creating precedents and decriminalizing conduct. Invasion of "evil" countries, torture, the use of prohibited weapons, extraordinary rendition and the like are examples of non-monetary crimes that transform the international law by violating it. At the domestic level, discriminatory and violent policing may possess the same characteristics, as it does not incorporate a direct monetary element, but aims to augment the power of the perpetrators. The crimes of the powerful, in this sense, are signals that indicate the "conatus" of power to grow indefinitely and unchallenged. As such, they are bound to showcase their exploits and dynamics and to advertise their pursuit of non-legal mechanisms of cooperation. Secrecy would not allow for the emission of signals.

People engage in signalling games in order to show that they are desirable partners in cooperative endeavours. Such games establish behavioural regularities and guarantee the predictability of the effects of interactions. Good or bad reputations, depending on the signaller, are built as people attempt to publicize their skills and potential to benefit others in joint ventures. When criminals send signals, they find the way of displaying their credentials, identifying each other, advertising the goods they trade and their reputation (Gambetta 2009). Law-abiding people, similarly, identify possible partners by signalling their own reputation as cooperative individuals. Powerful criminals, however, may value the immediate benefit of their behaviour more than its reputational consequences, thus discounting the future heavily. Violators, at times, may also be motivated by the fact that others cannot afford to ostracize them and that even their bad reputation will not reduce the desire of others to interact with them: at times cutting off relationships with violators can result in loss (for example, cutting links with investment banks). This perception is caused by the idea that those who violate social norms are wealthy and powerful enough to be able to afford violations and that they deserve cooperation or imitation.

The pursuit of profit is, therefore, accompanied by the desire to be imitated and expand the range of potential or actual accomplices.

> A common modern form of hubris is for increasingly successful people to violate norms until they go too far and are finally shunned by anyone whose cooperation they would find desirable. They violate norms as a challenge: it is their way of saying: you need me more than I need you.
>
> (Posner 2000: 28)

More than secretive or conspiratorial, the crimes of the powerful, in this case, must be visible, they must signal values and goals, solicit imitation or even admiration.

Ostentatious violators of social norms include conventional as well as powerful criminals, both implicitly declaring their loyalty to their own system of values as alternative systems to the dominant ones. What is important to note, therefore, is that such violators may trigger "herd behaviour," namely imitative conduct based on the observation that the behaviour of violators is undeniably successful. In such circumstances, shaming violators by communicating their undesirable character proves ineffective, as it is unlikely to provoke genuine ostracism. Even the peers of violators will hesitate to act as whistle blowers, fearing the loss of future opportunities that interactions with them will certainly bring. In brief, the act of shaming is often too costly. In extreme cases, even formal punishment may fail to build a bad reputation for those punished, who can instead use it as a "badge of status," a sign of distinction which augments rather than dents their popularity.

Under the circumstances just alluded to, discarding the future is indeed justified, as popularity and admiration augur well for further crimes to follow. In other cases, however, the future is a key concern of powerful criminals, who may identify "uncertainty" as a crucial aspect of their life. They may be led to crime by their occupational culture, but also by what they perceive as their contingent condition, by the assessment of their uncertain status and the forecast of future developments. The crimes of the powerful, therefore, could be partly deemed the outcome of fear for the future. Fear, however, is also an element of power itself. As Poggi (2001: 11) has perceptively argued:

> Power has to do with the future, with expectations, with hopes and fears. In this sense, it has anthropological significance. . . . Hobbes was right in saying that humans alone, among animals, can feel tomorrow's hunger today. We can think of power as a way of confronting and controlling the inexorable sense of contingency and insecurity generated by our awareness of the future.

The crimes of the powerful, then, are the result of an obsessive relationship of powerful individuals and groups with their future; they are forms of accumulation and accretion of the power they already possess inspired by fear that in the future events may lead to them losing it. This fear makes the distinction between immediate easy profit and long-term interest extremely difficult to draw, at least from the point of view of the perpetrators.

### Homo juridicus

Responses to the crimes of the powerful may combine legal and social action. Let us see the difficulties both types of action may encounter.

According to one tradition of thought, the criteria according to which crime is distinguished from other forms of conduct reflect the interests of the powerful social strata rather than social consensus on what distinguishes right from wrong acts. Legal categories, from this perspective, are politically charged and the elites are only concerned with norms that protect and expand their privileges (Chambliss and Mankoff 1976). By contrast, the liberal idea of the law reflects a form of atomistic individualism whereby persons stand before the law as abstract holders of rights, as legal persons, irrespective of status and social background. Critical legal thinkers, however, would also argue that the disadvantaged may at times benefit from the law as a set of guarantees to be used for the improvement of their condition (Fine 2013). As genuine repositories of democratic values, the laws are completely disregarded by power when it engages in the sole task of appropriating wealth, pursuing the "ugly dream" and the "empty desire" to have money beget money (Arendt 1973: 143–144). Positive law, in this context, may create obstacles to the endless expansion of power and support the enjoyment of the fundamental rights characterizing the human condition that no tyrant can take away. Arendt refers to the relevance of speech and of human relationships expressed through political activity, which are denied by certain power arrangements. This denial, in her view, destroys the polity and expels humans from humanity itself (Arendt 1973: 297).

Fighting the illegality of the powerful by resorting to their own laws may sound paradoxical, unless one considers that the powerful routinely violate their own principles and the values they officially profess. Positive law, therefore, may be used to restore collective wellbeing and forge rules for non-exploitative interactions. Positive law is said to erect boundaries and establish channels of communication within communities which are continually endangered by the new people being born into them. "With each new birth, a new beginning is born into the world, a new world has potentially come into being" (Arendt 1973: 465). The stability of the laws is necessary vis-à-vis the constant motion of all human affairs, a motion which can never end as long as humans are born and die. The laws protect us from new and unpredictable conducts and events; they constitute for our political existence what memory is for our identity:

> [T]hey guarantee the pre-existence of a common world, the reality of some continuity which transcends the individual life span of each generation, absorbs all new origins and is nourished by them.
>
> (Arendt 1973: 466)

Crimes committed by authorities demolish the boundaries and channels of communication constituted by laws; they abolish the fences of laws between humans, taking away their freedom and destroying their political possibilities. From Arendt's perspective, the crimes of the powerful could be regarded as the result of a deficit of control or vigilance over positive law. The limited guarantees powerless groups are granted are not sufficiently safeguarded and defended by their bearers. Overlooking such guarantees is a mistake, Arendt warns, and fighting the crimes of the powerful does not mean changing the laws so that they favour the powerless, but defending those limiting and restraining the powerful. The fight, in a nutshell, is for the conservation of humanity, as the powerful tend to create a system in which humans are superfluous (Adler 2005).

Positive and rational law, according to this analysis, constitutes a crucial patrimony to be protected. The law, it has been argued, connects our mental universe with our physical existence, thus fulfilling the anthropological function of instituting us as rational beings. It is by transforming each of us into a *Homo juridicus* that "the biological and symbolic dimensions that make up our being have been linked together" (Supiot 2007: ix). On the other hand, we know that it is often through the law that juridical persons are annihilated. This is why establishing certainty in law may help identify and thwart abuses and crimes of power. The crimes of the powerful, by contrast, thrive when certainty of meaning is discarded as unrealistic, when law is deemed a mere technique of domination and when, as a consequence, every "value choice" is associated with individual morality and excluded from the legal sphere. In these cases "law's essential quality is neglected, namely that it can temper the most varied forms of political power or technological prowess with a measure of reason" (Supiot 2007: xxv).

## Acting in concert

It could be objected that reliance on law risks reinforcing a false notion of equality and that no meaningful social change can be achieved through tribunals. Nonetheless, the appeal to use legislation as a tool to temper power and its crimes, read from another angle, hides or implicitly encourages political action, agency and participation. In this sense, it is a call to mobilization or, at least, to critical thinking. This call may transmit a modicum of confidence (a Gramscian optimism of the will?) in contexts characterized by "flight from the world," populated by "absent persons" who turn away from collective concerns (Sloterdijk 2016). Perhaps this is what Arendt had in mind when, while worrying for societies that appear to engage in a sort of psychological strike against reality, proposed a radically alternative view of power. The notion of law as a potential tool for social change, therefore, must be linked with what she describes as the capacity to act in concert.

This formulation entails that power and coercion are not just different, they are opposites, with the former being "power to" and the latter "power over" (Lukes 1986: 71). "Power to" is primarily derived from the fostering of autonomy in collaborative endeavour through virtuous politics (Arendt 1970). It is a manifestation of genuine, undistorted communication among citizens, which allows for a kind of co-dependent autonomy (Klusmeyer 2015). Of course, we are back to Aristotle's notion of humans as political animals who realize their essence as members of the polis by facilitating autonomy through collaboration with others. But we are also very close to contemporary elaborations and collective practices.

The necessity of niche experiments that tackle inequality has been advocated within the mounting debate around transition thinking and post-capitalism (Bailey et al 2009; De Angelis 2007; Linebaugh 2008; Hardt and Negri 2009). The two concepts are associated with the ability to think how social change can occur and how "niches," where innovation takes place, may turn into "regimes," where rules and relationships shape daily practices and announce what is possible (Chatterton 2016). Post-capitalist transition experiments are said to be the result of widespread indignation for the conduct of the elite and contain an emphasis on the "commons," which in their simple historical form referred to the resources governed by those who depended on them. The commons today also refer to socially produced goods such as knowledge and information. "The shared attribute is that these entities are collectively owned and managed [. . .] The commons, then, is made real through the practice of communing" (ibid: 5). This daily building of post-capitalist transitions, carried out through experimentation, transformation and direct democracy, is perhaps a process that makes the notion of law as a tool of social change plausible.

Acting in concert implies the waging of a "war of manoeuvre" rather than a "war of position," a military metaphor used by Gramsci (1971) to contrast ultimate violent confrontation with the creation of a new hegemonic block. Law and action in concert may stem the process turning all social groups, as Sloterdijk (2016: 27) warns, into "sects as substitute forms of extended families [. . .] functioning like church congregations." The creation of a new hegemonic block is an alternative to a situation so described:

> Our society is trying, at least at points where liberal thinking occurs, to move from totalitarian inclusiveness to a pluralism of exclusive groups. That is, society is dissolving into a patchwork of exclusive minorities that are not easy to enter.

> (ibid: 28)

## Conclusion

The crimes of the powerful are the result of the different features displayed in the exercise of power itself: coercion, legitimacy, violence, secrecy, consensus and hegemony. In this contribution these components have been examined as blends, variable mixtures that, irrespective of the different contexts, aim at increasing social polarization. Even naked power exercised through military force, it has been argued, attempts to mobilize consensus and legitimacy leading to its expansion. Secrecy does play a role in this process, but so does ostentation, as the crimes of the powerful consist of signals, marks of omnipotence that lend themselves to imitation and, at times, admiration. Hegemony, therefore, can be achieved through crime. Domination, in its turn, is expressed through the pursuit of crude interest and the simultaneous shaping of moral authority. It is for this reason that, when confronted with the law, powerful offenders react with indignation, feeling that they cannot submit to the ordinary normativity imposed on others. In response, a notion of power as the capacity to act in concert has been advanced, one that turns the indignation of the powerless into social action.

# References

Adler, L. (2005) *Dans les pas de Hannah Arendt*. Paris: Gallimard.

Arendt, H. (1970) *On Violence*. London: Allen lane.

——— (1973) *The Origins of Totalitarianism*. San Diego: Harcourt Brace.

Bailley, I., Hopkins, R. and Wilson, G. (2009) "Some Things Old, Some Things New." *Geoforum*, 41: 595–605.

Bauman, Z. (1990) *Thinking Sociologically*. Oxford: Blackwell.

Bauman, Z. and Donskis, L. (2013) *Moral Blindness: The Loss of Sensitivity in Liquid Modernity*. Cambridge: Polity.

Chambliss, W. and Mankoff, M. (1976) "Preface," in Chambliss, W. and Mankoff, M. (eds.) *Whose Law? What Order? A Conflict Approach to Criminology*. New York: John Wiley.

Chatterton, P. (2016) "Building Transitions to Post-Capitalist Urban Commons." *Transactions*, 41 (4): 403–415. doi: 10.1111/tran.12139.

Comte, A. (1953) *Cours de philosophie positive (vol. VI)*. Paris: Gallimard.

Dal Lago, A. (2012) *Carnefici e spettatori. La nostra indifferenza verso la crudeltà*. Milan: Raffaello Cortina.

De Angelis, M. (2007) *The Beginning of History*. London: Pluto.

Dewey, J. (1997) *How We Think*. New York: Dover Publications.

Fine, R. (2013) "Marxism and the Social Theory of Law," in Banakar, R. and Travers, M. (eds.) *Law and Social Theory*. Oxford: Hart.

Foucault, M. (1980) *Power/Knowledge*. Brighton: Harvester Press.

Gambetta, D. (2009) *Codes of the Underworld: How Criminals Communicate*. Princeton and Oxford: Princeton University Press.

Gramsci, A. (1971) *Selections from the Prison Notebooks*. Chicago: International Publishing Corporation.

Hardt, M. and Negri, A. (2009) *Commonwealth*. Cambridge: Harvard University Press.

Hausgaard, M. (2009) "Power and Hegemony," in Clegg, S.R. and Hausgaard, M. (eds.) *The Sage Handbook of Power*. London: Sage.

Klusmeyer, D.B. (2015) "Violence, Law, and Politics: Hannah Arendt and Robert M. Cover in Comparative Perspective." *Criminal Justice Ethics*, 34 (3): 312–337.

Linebaugh, P. (2008) *The Magna Carta Manifesto: Liberties and Commons for All*. London and New York: Verso.

Lordon, F. (2014) *Willing Slaves of Capital. Spinoza and Marx on Desire*. London and New York: Verso.

Luhmann, N. (1975) *Macht*. Stuttgart: Ferdinand Enke Verlag.

——— (1985) *A Sociological Theory of Law*. London: Routledge.

Lukes, S. (ed.) (1986) *Power*. Oxford: Basil Blackwell.

Pearce, F. (1976) *Crimes of the Powerful: Marxism, Crime and Deviance*. London: Pluto Press.

Poggi, G. (2001) *Forms of Power*. Cambridge: Polity Press.

Posner, E.A. (2000) *Law and Social Norms*. Cambridge: Harvard University Press.

Ruggiero, V. (2015) *Power and Crime*. London and New York: Routledge.

Russell, B. (1975) *Power: A New Social Analysis*. London: Allen and Unwin.

Schmitt, C. (1976) *The Concept of the Political*. Rutgers: Rutgers University Press.

Schmitt, C. (1985) *Political Theology: Four Chapters on the Concept of Sovereignty*. Cambridge: MIT Press.

Sloterdijk, P. (2016) *Selected Exaggerations*. Cambridge: Polity.

Spencer, H. (1885) *Principles of Sociology*. London: Williams and Norgate.

Supiot, A. (2007) *Homo Juridicus: On the Anthropological Function of the Law*. London/New York: Verso.

Tilly, C. (1985) "War Making and State Making as Organized Crime," in P.B. Evans, D. Rueschemeer and T. Skocpol (eds.) *Bringing the State Back In*. Cambridge: Cambridge University Press.

Urry, J. (2014) *Offshoring*. Cambridge: Polity.

Walzer, M. (2004) *Politics and Passion*. New Haven: Yale University Press.

Weber, M. (1978) *Economy and Society*. Berkeley: University of California Press.

# Chapter 6

# Developing Pearce's new materialism

## Nick Hardy

This chapter takes a developmental look at some of the social theory employed in Frank Pearce's *CotP* (1976) and his later book (co-authored with Steve Tombs) *Toxic Capitalism* (1998). As such, it does not take an explicitly criminological approach but instead examines and develops elements of Pearce's complex and nuanced social theory which he utilizes when analysing social phenomena. Specifically, *CotP*'s "imaginary social relations" (1976: 80, 94), and *Toxic Capitalism*'s first- and second-order relations (1998: 133) will be examined with regard to the nuclear industry.

## Pearce's critical realism

In their excellent co-edited collection, Frauley and Pearce (2007) outline the principles of critical realism (CR). In a nutshell CR offers three major things. First, an *ontology* arguing that reality is *stratified*. This is CR's innovative way of delineating the world: a huge background of entities with a range of capacities interact at certain points and produce a range of possible effects and outcomes, from which humans experience only a small subset.[1] The second is an *epistemology* arguing that although knowledge is necessarily imperfect, scientific inquiry offers the best means so far for humans to gain usable knowledge about the world.

Third is an understanding that human agents engage in social interaction from largely non-voluntary, pre-existing socio-structural positions that provide (or suppress) certain abilities and powers. This is why CR (Bhaskar 1986, 2005, 2008) developed the transformational model of social action (TMSA). For critical realists the TMSA outlines how a social actor begins from a particular social position (with all the impediments and empowerments associated with it), undertakes an action – including contact with structures and other social agents – and then finishes, most likely, at largely the same position from which they started (although there is the possibility that they finish in a worsened or possibly bettered position). It is through the TMSA that CR argues human agents reproduce/reform the social structures they use in social interaction.

However, in a number of developmental critiques – such as Benton (1998), Frauley and Pearce (2007), Pearce (2007), and Elder-Vass (2012b) – the argument is formulated that CR does not pay enough attention to what we may call here "dormant" social structures and the effect that they can have on social relations. This is especially true in the TMSA: there is no recognition, these critics argue, of relevant dormant capabilities contained in some social structures that may, even when left unactivated by a particular agent, have an effect upon that agent's social interaction. An example of a dormant capacity might be one country's (suitably sized and equipped) army to invade another country's territory: the army *has* this capacity, even if it is not presently exercising it. Utilizing Benton's criticism of Bhaskar, Pearce argues "there can be power-relations where powers – for example, the full coercive powers of the state – can be available to certain agents and, even when not exercised. . ., remain very much in reserve" (Pearce 2007: 47). What Pearce and others achieve from this critique is to make explicit that the capabilities of social agents *are more than just the abilities contained in individual social agents themselves*. Instead, a social researcher must look more broadly for explanation, necessarily including an analysis of social structures.

A distinction should be made at this point between social structures and social relations. A *social structure* should be understood as being generated through the form and shape of the dispersal of entities and resources repeated over time.[2] Examples of this might be the formal structure of an organization (e.g. which positions hold what abilities) or even the distribution of economic wealth. *Social relations*, meanwhile, are more expansive and include the interactions that take place in the context(s)/environment(s) created by social structures *as well as by* other entities, objects and human agents. To give an analogous example that illustrates both, an architect designs and then a builder constructs a house (a structure), but the occupants of the house can choose to use each room in a variety of different ways (interactive relations). Although some rooms have proposed uses designed into them (e.g. a sink and oven in one, a bath and shower in another), the design only *shapes*, not predetermines, the use of each room. Social structures shape social relations to varying degrees, but structures do not absolutely determine relations.

To summarize the points made earlier, Pearce's CR offers a focus upon the powers and capacities generated by the particular form of social structures themselves. By focusing attention upon dormant/unactivated powers in social structures, a line of questioning is opened up that views the *combination* of structures and human agents as being important. However, what CR needs in its analysis is a more nuanced understanding of how structures and their associated discourses interact to achieve these effects. It is to this point that this discussion now turns.

## Disambiguating social structures and social relations: humans, discourses and the extra-discursive

An important corollary question to the discussion earlier is what, exactly, can be understood to be the relationship between social structures and social relations, to then understand how they (dis)empower human agents? It is here that we may turn to another of Pearce's ongoing theoretical engagements: the work of Michel Foucault. This may seem a roundabout way of answering the structure/relations question, but Foucault's answers form an important part of Pearce's theoretical insights. In Foucault's work there is a continuous (if not heavily emphasized) distinction between discourse and the world external to it (Foucault 1972, 1980b, 1994a, 1994b, 2003; Hardy 2011). Discourses exist within structured "environments" (called discursive formations) where only certain people, concepts and things can, respectively, speak, be utilized and be spoken about. In this way, discourse is neither day-to-day speech (*parole*), nor is it formal language itself (*langage*) (Hardy 2013). Instead, Foucault understands discourse to be a number of linked statements that together end in one or more conclusions; these conclusions then become axioms and rest within a wider grouping of axiomatic conclusions until (possibly) later successfully challenged. "The discursive," therefore, exists as a social product (for there are no discourses in nature), albeit a social product that has an internal coherence and structure external to individual human will and intent.

The extra-discursive is, unsurprisingly, all that exists external to discourse. This includes the material world, which is affected by discourse, as well as that which is not (e.g. the sickness of a patient in a hospital is as much the extra-discursive as is wood crafted into a table as is the Andromeda galaxy). The importance of the extra-discursive is not only that it exists *independently* from discourse (even if it is affected by discourse), but also that it exists as a counterbalance to the discursive: without the extra-discursive, Foucault's ontology is nothing more than social constructionism. And it is precisely because of the effects of the extra-discursive that Foucault is able to account for a large number of instances of change in discourses; and with changes to discourses and the extra-discursive, there follows a change to social relations.

Yet a problem with Foucault's position is that the discursive/extra-discursive split largely excludes human agents. For much of Foucault's work, humans exist as the terminus of two distinct types of power relations. The first is control over the human body and its abilities; this is why Foucault argues that there is an "investment. . . [in] the body by power" (1980a: 58). The second is the continued construction of subjectivity – that is, what it means to "be" human in a particular society – an ongoing process corresponding to the discourses associated with the dominant group(s) in a society at a particular time. For instance, Foucault identifies a "bourgeois" subjectivity that is becoming increasingly normalized in (Global North) societies (1991); however, it still comes into conflict with the remnants of the preceding religious discourses on subjectivity. Similarly, a bourgeois form of bodily power, disciplinary power, comes into conflict with previous (and some later) forms of power relations. So where do human agents fit in a Foucaultian account? In Foucault's thinking, humans do not exist as truly autonomous and free-willed agents, but, rather, undertake social actions from within constrained and corralled social positions.

So how does the discussion of discourse, the extra-discursive and human agents aid our wider discussion of developing Pearce's conception of power relations and social interaction? If the Foucaultian position is combined with the earlier discussion of social structure and social relations, a more nuanced picture can be drawn. The Foucaultian approach understands the discursive, extra-discursive and human agents existing in a combination; a combination that creates an environment of competing forces that appears stable only because of the tension exerted by the current dominant group (Foucault 2003). However, this still does not give sufficient account of social action, so it is here that CR's TMSA model of humans situated within a particular social position is useful. With theoretical labour, the CR and Foucaultian positions can be integrated (Hardy 2011; Pearce and Woodiwiss 2001; Elder-Vass 2011) and, when done so, open up a much more ontologically vibrant possibility for social analysis.

## Recombinant nature, technologies and social structure to social relations

If the combination of CR and Foucaultian theory is understood as being "vibrant" in this way – because it offers an understanding of the conduct of human agents *along with* the wider "social" elements of the discursive and the extra-discursive (while, importantly, not giving human agents an assumed primacy in altering either structure or relations at will) – then the question now falls to examining how it is that social structures are formed and how they affect social relations.

An excellent example of an answer to this question can be found in the environmental critical realism of Raymond Murphy (2002, 2004, 2007, 2009, 2016) and his arguments conceptualizing what he terms *recombinant social relations*. Murphy distinguishes between three forms of non-human relations: *pristine nature* (entities and environments unincorporated into human social relations), *primal nature* (entities and environments incorporated into human social relations but in an almost totally unaltered state) and finally *recombinant nature*. "Recombinant nature" is where humans rearrange "nature's dynamics and materials" in order to promote certain social ends (Murphy 2007: 149). Murphy argues that recombinant relations are the "technologies" that humans develop and utilize.

The realist approach of Murphy's analysis is threefold. The first is that "beliefs about nature – including scientific knowledge – are analysed as fallible social constructions that result in practices with different consequences, depending on their interaction with nature's autonomous dynamics, and these consequences then affect discourse about nature" (Murphy 2007: 146). The second is that natural objects contain powers in their own right (i.e. their powers are not socially constructed, even if they are understood through socially produced knowledge). The third is that natural powers and forces can "slip their leash" (Turner 1978: 158, cited in Murphy 2004: 253), escaping their "primal" or "recombinant" enmeshment as part of social and institutional structures. As Murphy argues, critical realist environmental sociology seeks to move "beyond the culture/nature divide" by investigating the interaction between social constructions and natural constructions (Murphy 2007: 148).

It is worth noting that the argument for recombinant social relations recognizes the independence of natural entities (even when recombinant), including their inherent powers and capabilities. But this is not to claim some level of "choice agency," "consciousness" or "essence" on their behalf. Rather, it recognizes that they have powers and capabilities inherent to the particular entities that they are – for example, plutonium-187 emits neutron radiation and does so whether present in pristine nature or as part of recombinant nature as the product of the fission decay of uranium-256 in a nuclear reactor core. This position rejects both of what Murphy terms the "hard" and the "nominalist" social constructionist accounts – that is, that human knowledge either makes the world or that knowledge is a system separate from the real world and has no influence upon it (Murphy 2004).

The concept of recombinant nature highlights the distinction between humans, discourses, (reconfigured) natural entities and the social structures within which they become recombined. It is from the interrelations (what we may call the "enmeshment") between the four that created social relations. This distinction is theoretically important as it moves beyond just a discursive/extra-discursive divide and begins to conceptualize what the "bridge" may be between the discursive and the extra-discursive.[3] Recombinant nature is precisely those naturally occurring processes and powers that are altered in some way(s) and then integrated by humans into social structures. The "bridge" element in the concept of recombinant nature is found in the articulation of *where* the powers and capabilities of non-human entities are generated *whilst still conceptualizing them as part of social structures or social relations.* The processes and powers of extra-discursive entities are not "just" acting *externally* onto/into social structures/relations; they are important and necessary components *of* social structures/relations – albeit ones that may "slip the leash" of human control.

An example of this could be the 2011 earthquake and resulting tsunami that struck Japan and leading ultimately to the failure of containment mechanisms in the reactors at the Fukushima nuclear plant (e.g. Thomas 2012). The sea defences outside the nuclear plant failed due to the tsunami being higher than expected (waves on previous occasions had been successfully repelled). The resultant meltdown of the cores at three of the Fukushima reactors and the fire at the spent fuel storage pond at the fourth reactor occurred because the "normal" recombinant technological structures failed, as did the various back-up safety mechanisms. For a critical realist, the tsunami breaching the sea defences, the consequent meltdown of the reactor cores and the combustion of the on-site stored nuclear waste involved natural processes breaking their "recombinant" state – that is, their containment within social structures acting as management

## 78 Nick Hardy

systems – and operating their inherent (and highly destructive) powers almost freely. Recombining Fukushima's nuclear entities back into human social structures/technologies is extremely difficult, for they have changed their form and many are now too virulent to be recombined and so can only – hopefully – be contained.

## Looping effects and "enmeshment"

With the concept of recombinant nature, theorists can begin to identify the component parts of particular social structures (from institutions to Murphy's "technologies") and how they lead to the establishment of particular social relations, that is, the (inter)actions of human agents based upon the powers and capabilities gained by (or removed from) them by social structures. Yet, and despite the utility of the concept of recombinant relations, it does not fully account for the "stability" found in social relations: how is it that many social structures are so enduring? Accounting for this stability is important because it lays bare the reliance many discursive relations have upon the extra-discursive in order for them to form and operate. Attention should be paid to what may be termed the *continuous reaffirmation* that discourses have with the extra-discursive (it is worth noting that it is the need for this continual re-association between discourses and the extra-discursive that makes social structures/relations so fragile). In the following discussion Ian Hacking's concept of "*looping effects*" between discourses and human subjects will be examined before being reworked and extended to an argument that there is a level of *enmeshment* between discourses and the extra-discursive. It is this enmeshment that enables the stability of inter-effects between the discursive and the extra-discursive.

Hacking (1995, 2002, 2006) has outlined a process he terms a *looping effect*. When a group becomes defined in some way – which Hacking terms the creation of a "kind" of people (e.g. juvenile delinquents, autistic children, obese people, etc.) the group becomes an object for knowledge. But when knowledge is generated about a kind, it precipitates a change in that kind (although not necessarily in conformity with the knowledge held about them). This is ongoing, Hacking argues, as change necessitates the generation of new knowledge, which then precipitates further change in the kind, which then prompts new knowledge, etc.

> To create new ways of classifying people is to change how we can think of ourselves, to change our sense of self-worth, even how we remember our own past. This in turn generates a looping effect, because people of a kind behave differently and are different. That is to say the kind changes, and so there is new causal knowledge to be gained and, perhaps, old knowledge to be jettisoned.
>
> (1995: 369)[4]

An effect of this is that each kind of people ("category" in Hacking 2002) has its own unique history in terms of its constitution and development.

> Each category has its own history. If we wish to. . . [partially] describe such events, we might think of two vectors. One is the vector of labelling from above, from a community of experts who create a "reality" that some people make their own. Different from this is the vector of the autonomous behaviour of the person so labelled, which presses from below, creating a reality every expert must face.
>
> (2002: 111)

There is a high level of correspondence with Foucaultian theory in Hacking's argument (which Hacking himself highlights).[5] What Hacking's looping effect allows us to do is generate the importance of the *iterative* processes that occur in social interactions, including the *generative* outcomes of these interactions – that is, that relations can change *because of* the inherent instability of those relations.

If Hacking's argument is extended beyond the discursive-to-human and taken to the discursive-to-object, we can begin to articulate the *creative* processes of discourses to extra-discursive objects, as well as the *instability* inherent in the resultant social structures/relations. Developing Hacking's argument in this way gives us two points: (1) that discourse is an important component of shaping and maintaining the social world; and (2) that we can identify both "type" and "particular" versions of objects and entities.

(1) Discourse is undisputedly a large component of social relations. Discourse can include the motivation(s) for undertaking acts (Bhaskar 2005; Elder-Vass 2012a), the creation of "frames" which create "types" of things (Hacking 1995), even to altering practices (Bourdieu 1977). The importance of discourse to material objects is, therefore, that discourse affects the form, complexity and even the skill of human interaction with material objects. The place and form of material objects as components in social relations are, in part, the product of the discourses that engage with them;

(2) However, for CR – and, in a way, for Foucault too – objects and entities have certain attributes that are the result of the constitution *of* those entities (e.g. the attribute of a dog to bark: the dog did not "acquire" the ability to bark, all things being equal; the dog *has* the ability to bark because it is a dog). Thanks to Hacking's use of Foucault's bio-political arguments (Hacking 2002), we can delineate "types" of things ("dogs") from particular individual things ("that dog"). This allows for an argument to expand that although there are characteristics of type (e.g. "dogs have the capability to bark"), there are individual circumstances where the type characteristics do not hold true ("that dog does not bark because its vocal cords were removed due to illness"). Therefore, we can say that particular social relations may accentuate, suppress or modify type capacities and attributes in

certain ways, thus making them into a multitude of particular things. This is a (brutally reduced) version of Foucault's bio-politics: a general set of types containing specific individual examples.

The outcome of altering Hacking's argument in this way is to highlight the repeated processes involved in reaffirming the position of humans, non-humans and material objects in social structures. Importantly, this reaffirmation does not produce a multitude of the same "type" of object – instead, different types of things can be identified in their "particular" structural positions. The combination of the altered TMSA model, the discursive/extra-discursive divide coupled with the idea of recombinant nature and finally looping effects generates a theoretical position where a background of social structures can be identified as being present and upon which social relations form. We may term this the *enmeshment* of the different components.

## Accounting for social change

One of Pearce's enduring theoretical commitments has been his continuous argument that social theory should not rely on humanism as its core explanatory component. "Humanism," using Kate Soper's (1986) account, explains social change as the product of some combination of human will, rationality, intent, action or endeavour. Pearce (2001: 21, 40) rejects humanism precisely because it downgrades the non-human components of the social world outlined in the larger argument earlier – thus undeservedly reifying humans as exceptional – but also because, as Margaret Archer (1995) argues, it "elides" social structures and their powers into the conceptual category of human agents. By emphasizing, as Pearce does, the "situatedness" of human agents within social structures, he is able to account for *both* human actions (which, to note, are important to any explanatory account – they are just not inherently the primary factor) and the larger social structures and social forces which give shape and position to those actions. To give a simple example: when a person goes from home to work during an average Canadian winter, they do so in temperatures somewhere between −10°C and −30°C. To make this journey possible without their resulting death en route, they must employ a range of other components to make it possible: from warm clothing, to transportation, to the very transportation infrastructure itself (i.e. snow-clear roads). This is not to even mention the economic, legal and political systems, as well as the corporate institutional form, that expect and require some people to be at work, at a certain time, on particular days.

Yet with this in mind, how can the argument so far account for social change if it is not initiated and driven by intentional human actions? For if most important elements are argued to be external to social actors, do social actors have any role at all? There is not enough space here to give this answer the depth that it deserves, but it would not be too glib to use Marx's pithy observation that "[humans] make their own history, but not spontaneously [or] under conditions they have chosen" (1983: 287). Social agents find themselves (dis)empowered to varying degrees based upon their social position; for example, societies with capitalist economies give human agents with monetary wealth a multitude of advantages vis-à-vis an agent without. In order for the agent without wealth to obtain even some of the advantages held by the wealthy agent, they must utilize different strategies and, even then, they have no assurances of success. But even this example is of avenues of change *within* particular social structures. To account for larger social change, it is helpful to examine the later work of Louis Althusser.

In an engaging and thought-provoking series of discussions, (2006), Althusser outlines his understanding of social structural change. Terming it *aleatory materialism* (i.e. "chance" materialism), he argued that social structures change because of the aleatory interactions they have with other social structures, nature and human agents (see Hardy 2012). Change can consist of small variations (which are usually subsumed back into the wider structural form with little effect) but also large variations, producing much larger effects. What his argument entails is that social structures, that is, the (semi-)stable interlinkages of discursive, material and human components, make it difficult for single or multiple human actors to alter them. Instead, most social change occurs at moments when there is flux and instability within social structures because of $n$-components "failing" to reproduce their necessary effects as part of the social structure. It is at these moments of instability that human agents are most effective at provoking "change."

## Enmeshment and hazardous nuclear waste

The argument made so far for identifying, theorizing and then developing Pearce's understanding of the fabric of social relations (and so the world in which the crimes of the powerful exist) has been as follows. First, Pearce's distinction between imaginary and real social orders was highlighted, as was his distinction of first- and second-order causes. This was adapted with his critical realism to give an account of humans-situated-in-structures and the (dis)empowerment that occurs because of it. Pearce's adaption of Foucaultian theory was outlined to distinguish between discourse, the extra-discursive and human subjects. To adapt Pearce's account, Murphy's concept of "recombinant nature" was utilized to show the inherent powers and effects of non-human entities. Following this, Hacking's argument for "looping effects" was utilized but also extended to include non-human entities. Finally, a non-humanist argument was briefly outlined that accounted for social change even if human agents are not reified as primary actants. At this point it may be helpful to give an illustrative example that draws together this development of Pearce's theory.

Hazardous nuclear waste is an unavoidable by-product from operating nuclear reactors using uranium or plutonium for fuel. The answer of what to do with nuclear waste has ranged, country by country, from reprocessing (to extract useful elements from the waste) to developing long-term storage facilities. Reprocessing is beset with multiple problems – mostly to do with the sheer toxicity of the waste being handled – and long-term storage capacity has only been developed in a very small number of countries. Finland, at the Onkalo geological repository deep in its southwest coast, is the first country to begin construction of such a storage facility; at the end of construction the series of underground storage chambers will sink over 500 metres into the ground to store waste for at least 100,000 years. It is expected the site will become operational around 2025 and continue operating until finally sealed shut in 2120 (Gibney 2015).

Canada began seriously considering long-term storage in 2002, with the establishment of the Nuclear Waste Management Organization (NWMO), itself established by the Nuclear Fuel Waste Act (2002). The NWMO is a not-for-profit group consisting of the three provincial power providers with nuclear power stations (Ontario Hydro, Hydro-Québec and New Brunswick Power) and Atomic Energy Canada Ltd. (AECL). In 2017 eight potential sites were being studied as potential areas for an underground long-term storage facility.[6] So how come, with large reactors coming online in Canada since the 1950s, has it taken this long to begin developing a plan for long-term hazardous waste storage in Canada?

Using the theoretical framework outlined earlier, we might begin to lay out a brief, and tentative, answer. The particular structure of the "nuclear fuel cycle" – mining, fuel fabrication, energy-producing reactors, waste handling and waste storage – will produce a number of second-order structures (i.e. certain priorities, tendencies and commonalities). But it is worth noting that only some of this form will be in response to the extra-discursive virulence of the recombinant radioactive elements used. Other parts of the structure take their shape from the wider economic, political and social structures surrounding the nuclear industry. For instance, as Pearce and Tombs (1998: 133–135) argue, a "for profit" second-order structure (i.e. the profit motive in capitalism) in an industry will create particular pressures upon how a corporation considers externalities (i.e. events, entities and circumstances beyond which it need not concern itself) and safety (i.e. of employees, civilians and the environment).[7] They note several factors that are relevant to how a corporation operates, for instance, one of which is the length of *time* over which a corporation is expected to make profit: the longer the time, the greater the likelihood of a higher safety orientation. Another area is union representation for employees: if a workforce is unionized, then operational safety is higher.

So how did Canada – with a state-controlled nuclear energy commissioning and oversight body (AECL), with unionized nuclear workforces, and with long-term goals in sight – end up with no plan for storing nuclear waste? First, the discourses generated about and around nuclear energy are never totally resonant with the extra-discursive materials with which they engage. Using

Murphy's and Hacking's adapted arguments, entities (be they human or non-human) do not fully cohere with the discourses associated with them.[8] This explains the discrepancy between what was said about nuclear energy (e.g. scientific triumphalism, energy "too cheap to metre," future economic and commercial success, etc.) and the unforgiving reality of radioactive entities.

Second, beyond discourses per se, the structure of the industry itself arguably promotes certain tendencies in the "actions" of the institutions and human subjects within it. By enabling the compartmentalization of the industry (i.e. into discrete industrial sectors), the effects of one area are able to be offset through the assumption that another area will be able to solve the problem (in this case, waste) at a later time. This spatial and temporal (i.e. space/place and time) displacement of adverse effects allows decisions to be made that might otherwise have been taken or made differently.

Third, and building slightly upon the first point, the problem with radioactive entities (even at the "low-intensity" end of the spectrum) is that they require constant and careful replication of their enmeshment into social relations. The "ease" of dealing with nuclear energy never came to pass; reality always comes to "bite back" (or "slip the leash") against human attempts to contain it. The complexity of the recombinant structures required to successfully contain nuclear waste is such that it requires much more dedicated effort not to only maintain recombinant enmeshment, but also even to design and to explore the *possible* forms of that enmeshment (e.g. viable long-term storage sites).

## Conclusion

In the space available, this discussion sought to outline and then develop Frank Pearce's argument for the structure and the complexity of the social world, before sympathetically developing it with homologous arguments from similar areas of social theory. The end result is an understanding of Pearce's theory that shows the huge contribution that both *CotP* and *Toxic Capitalism* made to the sociology of powerful actors – namely, that power originates from the social positioning of a human subject or a corporate institution, manifesting itself as the ability to partially produce, maintain or even to reduce the social position of both oneself and of others. This is achieved through (re)forming social structures and thus affecting the social relations that form around them.

## Notes

1  The largest of the three stratified levels is what CR calls the *real*; it is here that entities exist with many (if not all) possessing any number of attributes and capabilities, which CR terms *mechanisms*. If and when these entities interact, they do so in *events* that take place at the mid-level of stratification, which CR calls the *actual*. Finally, at the lowest level, there is the *empirical* where humans have their *experience* of the world.
2  This is a mixture of arguments from Marx and Foucault. Marx's argument was that the driving forces of any epoch could be understood through its *mode of production*. The term "mode

of production" was itself, however, only ever a shorthand for two distinct concepts: the *tools/means* of production and the *relations* of production (Marx 1983, 158–161). Industrial capitalism, for instance, has the tools/means of industrial factories but the social relations of a capitalist economy. There was nothing to stop society using those same tools/means but organizing them as industrial socialism or, even, industrial communism. Foucault's argument was from his technique for articulating discursive formations: they cannot be fully understood from just their content, nor the agents articulating them, nor their concepts, but, instead, the "shape" of the dispersal of their various elements (Foucault 1972: 10).

3 This "bridge" was only implicit in Foucault's work and, as such, leads to many problems in establishing a clear ontology for his arguments.

4 And precisely because the looping effect is *ongoing* and contains the very real possibility that the kind moves *away* from knowledge held about them makes it different from symbolic interactionism's "labelling theory" (Hacking 1995: 369).

5 Especially, for example, Foucault's polyvalence of discourses (1990: 100–102).

6 They are (1) Blind River, Elliot Lake, and surrounding area; (2) Central Huron; (3) Hornepayne and surrounding area; (4) Huron-Kinloss; (5) Ignace and surrounding area; (6) Manitouwadge and surrounding area; (7) South Bruce; and (8) White River and surrounding area (NWMO 2017, "Study Areas").

7 Pearce and Tombs (1998: 133–135) go to great lengths to emphasize that there is not a direct inverse relationship between profit and safety (i.e. the greater the profit, the lower the safety).

8 This is most definitely at the "second-order" level of social structures. The assumptions made about nuclear energy were/are a backdrop that partially determines the range of actions available to subjects within this particular discursive setting. N.B. This is also similar to Foucault's distinction between *connaissance* and *savoir:* the former is broadly approximate to "actively applied knowledge," the latter as "axiomatic knowledge."

## References

Althusser, L. (2006) "The Underground Current of the Materialism of the Encounter," in F. Matheron and O. Corpet (eds.) *Philosophy of the Encounter: Later Writings, 1978–87*, 163–207. London; New York: Verso.

Archer, M.S. (1995) *Realist Social Theory: The Morphogenetic Approach*. Cambridge; New York: Cambridge University Press.

Benton, T. (1998) "Realism and Social Science: Some comments on Roy Bhaskar's 'The Possibility of Naturalism'," in M. Archer et al. (eds.) *Critical Realism: Essential Readings*, 297–312. London: Routledge.

Bhaskar, R. (1986) *Scientific Realism and Human Emancipation*. London: Verso.

——— (2005) *The Possibility of Naturalism: A Philosophical Critique of the Contemporary Human Sciences* (3rd ed.). London; New York: Routledge.

——— (2008) *A Realist Theory of Science* (2nd ed.). New York: Verso.

Bourdieu, P. (1977) *Outline of a Theory of Practice*. Cambridge: Cambridge University Press.

Elder-Vass, D. (2011) "The Causal Power of Discourse." *Journal for the Theory of Social Behaviour*, 41(2): 143–160.

——— (2012a) *The Reality of Social Construction*. Cambridge: Cambridge University Press.

——— (2012b) *The Reality of Social Construction*. Cambridge, UK: Cambridge University Press.

Foucault, M. (1972) *The Archaeology of Knowledge*. New York: Pantheon Books.

——— (1980a) "Body/Power," in C. Gordon (ed.) *Power/Knowledge: Selected Interviews and Other Writings, 1972–1977*, 55–62. 1st American ed. New York: Pantheon Books.

—— (1980b) "The Confession of the Flesh," in C. Gordon (ed.) *Power/Knowledge: Selected Interviews and Other Writings, 1972–1977*, 194–228. 1st American ed. New York: Pantheon Books.

—— (1991) *Discipine and Punish: The Birth of the Prison*. London: Penguin.

—— (1994a) *The Birth of the Clinic: An Archaeology of Medical Perception*. New York: Vintage Books.

—— (1994b) *The Order of Things: An Archaeology of the Human Sciences*. New York: Vintage Books.

—— (2003) "Nietzsche, Genealogy, History," in P. Rabinow and N.S. Rose (eds.) *The Essential Foucault*, 351–369. New York: New Press.

Frauley, J. and Pearce, F. (2007) *Critical Realism and the Social Sciences: Heterodox Elaborations*. Toronto: University of Toronto Press.

Gibney, E. (2015) *Why Finland Now Leads the World in Nuclear Waste Storage*. Online. Available HTTP: www.nature.com/news/why-finland-now-leads-the-world-in-nuclear-waste-storage-1.18903 (accessed 26 February 2017).

Hacking, I. (1995) "The Looping Effects of Human Kinds," in D. Sperber, D. Premack and A.J. Premack (eds.) *Causal Cognition: A Multidisciplinary Debate*, 351–383. Oxford: Oxford University Press.

—— (2002) *Historical Ontology*. Cambridge, MA: Harvard University Press.

—— (2006) "Making Up People." *London Review of Books*. London, UK.

Hardy, N. (2011) "Foucault, Genealogy, Emergence: Re-examining the Extra-discursive." *Journal for the Theory of Social Behaviour*, 41(1): 68–91.

Hardy, N. (2012) "Theory From the Conjuncture: Althusser's Aleatory Materialism and Machiavelli's Dispositif." *Décalages: An Althusser Studies Journal*, 1(3): 1–33.

—— (2013) "A History of the Method: Examining Foucault's Research Methodology," in B. Dillet, I. Mackenzie and R. Porter (eds.) *The Edinburgh Companion to Poststructuralism*, 95–121. Edinburgh, UK: Edinburgh University Press.

Marx, K. (1983) "The Eighteenth Brumaire of Louis Bonaparte," in E. Kamenka (ed.) *The Portable Karl Marx*, 287–323. New York: Viking: Penguin Books.

Murphy, R. (2002) "The Internalization of Autonomous Nature into Society." *The Sociological Review*, 50(3): 313–333.

—— (2004) "Disaster or Sustainability: The Dance of Human Agents with Nature's Actants." *Canadian Review of Sociology/Revue canadienne de sociologie*, 41(3) : 249–266.

—— (2007) "Thinking Across the Nature/culture Divide: An Empirical Study of Issues For Critical Realism and Social Constrcutionism," in J. Frauley and F. Pearce (eds.) *Critical Realism and the Social Sciences: Heterodox Elaborations*, 142–161. Toronto: University of Toronto Press.

—— (2009) *Leadership in Disaster: Learning For a Future with Global Climate Change*. Montreal, QC; Kingston, ON: McGill-Queen's University Press.

—— (2016) "Conceptual Lenses to Bring into Focus the Blurred and Unpack the Entangled." *Environmental Sociology*, 2(4): 333–345.

Nuclear Fuel Waste Act (2002) S.C. 2002, c.23. Online. Available HTTP: http://laws-lois.justice.gc.ca/eng/acts/N-27.7/page-1.html (accessed 28 March 2018).

NWMO (2017) *Study Areas*. Online. Available HTTP: https://www.nwmo.ca/en/Site-selection/Study-Areas (accessed 8 June 2017).

Pearce, F. (1976) *Crimes of the Powerful: Marxism, Crime, and Deviance*. London: Pluto Press.

—— (2001) *The Radical Durkheim* (2nd ed.). Toronto: Canadian Scholar's Press.

——— (2007) "Bhaskar's Critical Realism: An Appreciative Introduction and a Friendly Critique," in J. Frauley and F. Pearce (eds.) *Critical Realism and the Social Sciences: Heterodox Elaborations*, 30–63. Toronto: University of Toronto Press.

Pearce, F. and Tombs, S. (1998) *Toxic Capitalism: Corporate Crime and the Chemical Industry*. Aldershot, Hants, England; Brookfield, VT: Ashgate/Dartmouth.

Pearce, F. and Woodiwiss, T. (2001) "Reading Foucault as a Realist," in J. Lopez and G. Potter (eds.) *After Postmodernism: An Introduction to Critical Realism*. New York: Athlone Press, 51–62.

Soper, K. (1986) *Humanism and Anti-humanism*. London: Hutchinson.

Thomas, S. (2012) What Will the Fukushima Disaster Change? *Energy Policy*, 45(0): 12–17.

Turner, B.A. (1978) *Man-made Disasters*. London: Wykeham.

# Chapter 7

# Theorizing fiscal sacrifices in zombie capitalism

## A radical Durkheimian approach

*Ronjon Paul Datta*

> While all social life requires some sacrifice, not all sacrifices are necessary and just.
>
> (Pearce 2010: 48)

In "Obligatory Sacrifice and Imperial Projects," where he analyses the political economy of killing in the Aztec and American empires, Pearce begins by discussing Durkheim's earliest conception of sacrifice; it concerns the moral subjection of children: "children are 'forced to take into consideration interest other than their own, to make sacrifices and dedicate themselves to the good of the family'" (Durkheim in Pearce 2010: 46). Substituting "working-class and their dependents" for "children," and "finance capital" for "family" is the basis for the formulations developed here. I theoretically synthesize Pearce's sociology of crime in capitalist societies with his radical Durkheimian theory of sacrifice, one that is quite some way from his caricature of Durkheim in *Crimes of the Powerful* (Pearce 1976: 47, hereafter *CotP*). I hope to contribute to a broadened conception of the moral dynamics of contemporary capitalism in which the rhetoric of fiscal sacrifices is imbricated.

Fiscal sacrifices and the renewed valorization of "austerity" have followed in the wake of the extraordinary measures used to bail out financial firms that were key agents in precipitating the 2007–2008 global financial crisis (hereafter, GFC). Such economic sacrifices subject people to cuts to public goods, services and hard-won benefits (Streeck 2017: li, 23). Doing so secures accumulation conditions for capitalist enterprises grown frail or even collapsing, reflecting the formation of a "zombie capitalism" with its legions of "living-dead" firms and households so indebted they are unlikely to ever become solvent (Botting 2013; Datta and MacDonald 2011). However, that such sacrifices are imposed by fiscal policy while juxtaposed with "bailouts" for financial firms is symptomatic of discrepancies in capitalist moral reasoning. Pearce's *theorem* that the reproduction of capital requires "continuous effort" (*CotP*: 56) is helpful here. This effort is needed because of the real concrete contradictions that capitalist production creates, ones that it can also frequently exploit (cf. *CotP*: 54). My central contention is that fiscal sacrifices are a moral-political patch on the contradictions in zombie capitalism producing a primitive accumulation of the future by capital. I draw on the sociology of capitalism in *CotP*, one that also partially informs Pearce's work on sacrifice (2010: 52; see also Pearce 2001). I follow Pearce's (2001) neo-Althusserian theoretical methodology designed to investigate the discursive production of questions and ways of "picturing" the social world in coherent and comprehensive, if heterodox, ways (see Woodiwiss 2005; cf. Datta, Frauley, and Pearce 2010). This sociological sensibility at the core of Pearce's approach requires sustained, careful and reflexive scholarly engagement; constant attention to empirical referents; and the crafting of rational accounts of contingent social formations. The aim is to conceptualize societies as complexly articulated totalities (in Althusserian terms, the "Real-Concrete") that cannot be known empirically but rather must be produced conceptually (in Althusserian terms, the "Concrete-in-Thought") to adequately explain social phenomena and events.

## *Crimes of the Powerful* in a new conjuncture

The GFC compelled renewed normative consideration of capitalism (see Lazzarato 2015; Streeck 2017; Panitch and Gindin 2012; Brown 2015). It also drew popular attention again to the moral deficiencies in capitalism in which firms that received billions in government bailouts continued to pay handsome bonuses to their employees (Barofsky 2012). Successful films like *The Big Short* are now enduring collective symbols that "*dramatise an imaginary* [capitalist] *social order*" (*CotP*: 93), providing evidence that the "collective conscience" (Pearce 2001: 20–22) has been pricked, leading to a commonplace reprobation of the "banksters" (Pontell et al. 2014: 13). And, although *CotP* was written at a time in which modern finance capital was in its relative infancy (see Phillips 2008: 29ff; Harman 2009: 277ff) – Pearce makes but one reference to finance (*CotP*: 61) – the basic structure and dynamics of the capitalist mode of production (hereafter, CMP) conceptualized by Pearce have not changed. The drive in the CMP remains ongoing accumulation even in the face of the concrete contradictions of uneven development, social and political struggles and more and less organized and successful resistance. Bailouts are a striking example of the "protection of the means of production" by the state (*CotP*: 57). The framework in *CotP*, however, needs further development, especially in an Althusserian direction to better theorize the linkage between contradiction and reproduction (Althusser 2014). In contemporary rescue packages, the protection of the means of production occurs by securing the means of *financial production* in order to reproduce the means of *consumption* to stimulate demand and complete exchanges. The state ensures that banks are "liquid" enough so they have money to lend to consumers and firms who then finance purchases without thereby imperilling the lender's own balance sheet. Through the genius of finance, capital in the aggregate gets its cut twice: first in the exchange moment

Theorizing fiscal sacrifices 89

(paying for the commodity), and second in the cost of borrowing that can be securitized as an income stream for investors. They may even get a third cut with lobbied reductions in business taxes. State institutions thus demonstrate that they play a key role in the "reproduction of social life" (*CotP*: 49–50) and "are not separate from society, over and above it, but are an integral part of the mode of production" (*CotP*: 58). Alas, the Marxist sociology of *CotP* has not inspired criminological considerations of the wrong-doing or harms surrounding the GFC (Tombs 2015: 62).

## Situating zombie capitalism

I define zombie capitalism as a condition in which heavily indebted socio-economic entities that would normally be left to "die" (declared insolvent and/or liquidated) are given a "second [undead] life" (cf. Botting 2013; Datta 2017) via inventive schemes like rolling over debt, government loan guarantees and central banks offering extraordinarily low interest rates to borrowers. The widespread inability to pay was linked to flat, or frequently declining, household incomes relative to the cost of living. The gap was covered by increased borrowing made possible by liberalized and massively expanded credit markets, a trend that took hold in the mid-1970s (Streeck 2017; Phillips 2008; Harman 2009; Panitch and Gindin 2012). However, this eventually created a structural weakness in the demand capacity, undermining the value of physical assets like mortgaged houses for want of those who can actually afford them, causing housing markets and investment vehicles derived from them to crash, the effects of which hit global financial markets hard. By the moral logic of capital, large banks that securitized such debts should have been "left to die" because of poor business practices instead of being rescued (cf. Peek and Rosengren 2003; Onaran 2011).

Zombification is done for many reasons, including the need for goods and services and sustaining employment (e.g. a firm's failure would spike unemployment and generate political backlash). Some argue that zombifying schemes deprive "healthy" entities (e.g. firms, individuals and societies) of the creativity and assets being consumed by such zombies, thus entrenching the misallocation of social resources (i.e. "inefficiency") (Bryan 2016; see also Quiggin 2010). Some zombie firms are able to service debt but then lack a surplus required for investment and innovation (Pym 2012), at which point, strictly speaking, they are no longer capitalist firms. This current situation has complex origins rooted in significant shifts in the global political economy involving the de- and re-regulation of finance and banking since the late 1970s (Panitch and Gindin 2012; Harman 2009). The problems of a global system hampered by extensive debt and the proliferation of indebted entities remain. "Zombies in this guise do not mark a breaking point, but the condition of living on after being broken" (Botting 2013; cf. Roubini in Durden 2013). This capitalism cannot function healthily according to its own criteria, but neither does it seem capable of

## Problematizing bailouts

"Bailouts" were a significant indicator of the severity of the GFC even though they have accompanied the rise of private debt in the United States since the early 1980s (Phillips 2008: 40–41, 55). Indeed, "[d]uring the last 20 years, all of the nearly 100 banking crises that have occurred internationally were resolved through bailouts at the taxpayer's expense" (Woll 2013: 613).

The bailouts were about states using their power to restore the workings of financial institutions by repairing their balance sheets after the housing bubbles burst (Besley and Hennessy 2009). Negative market and public reactions to bank failures were decisive as evinced by the shock caused by the run on the British bank Northern Rock, a major mortgage lender, in September 2007 (*The Economist* 2007). More instructive was the serious fallout from the failure of the U.S. investment bank Lehman Brothers on 15 September 2008, that sent markets reeling. "[I]nvestors immediately questioned both the government's commitment and organizational capacity to support the private institutional pillars of the financial system" (Panitch and Gindin 2012: 314–315). This reaction showed governments that bailouts were necessary to avoid major social crisis (see also Pontell et al. 2014: 8, 11). The most (in)famous bailout programme is the American $700 billion "Troubled Asset Relief Program" (TARP) for purchasing "large quantities of the 'troubled' mortgages and mortgage related bonds" (Barofsky 2012: 24). The total U.S. government commitment to TARP is an astounding $16.8 trillion (Collins 2015).

The GFC and massive bailouts showed again that economic life was suffused with morality and imbricated in complex social totalities (Fourcade et al. 2013; Lazzarato 2011; Brown 2015). Under normal conditions, according to capitalist morality, "if [firms] were not efficient, the market would ruthlessly remove them; the market breeds efficiency; competition is central to the system" (*CotP*: 94). Neoliberalism, as a broadly normative project informed by economics as a *moral* discourse, adopted such logic and aimed to extend it to society as a whole (Brown 2015), seeing *markets as the most economical and efficient means for morally regulating society*. Neoliberals sought to revitalize morality by challenging the deresponsibilizing tendencies of the welfare state "in which individuals refuse to accept responsibility for tackling risks resulting from their own choices and instead transfer responsibility and blame to others" (Hunt 2003: 184). Anglo-American neoliberalism in particular views open competitive markets as a technology to constitute "responsible" citizens who think through the consequences of their actions, typically by monetizing outcomes and their evaluation (do the right thing and you make money; do the wrong things and you lose money). Such consequences are deemed to follow naturally from markets properly constituted by the state (cf. Tombs 2015: 68). Yet as the GFC showed, contracts for debt obligations were a *deresponsibilization* technique: buyers of securitized debt were to do their due diligence to protect their investment, whereas mortgagers themselves didn't when intending to sell the debt (i.e., sell the income stream from the mortgage to some other investor).

The bailouts thus raised issues about "moral hazard" because they erase the adverse consequences (e.g. bankruptcy) that are supposed to follow from poor business decisions. Offloading debt obligations as a deresponsibilization technique was coupled with *deconsequentialization* since bailed out firms were not allowed to fail – "mercy" and "forgiveness" don't capture the moral logic here given the lack of an admission of moral responsibility on the part of the immediate causal agents. The issue is not only that sales incentives, immediate income generation, conflict of interest (in the case of bond ratings agencies) and fraud were involved in the GFC (cf. Pontell et al. 2014; Phillips 2008). Rather, moral hazard "encapsulates the idea that misplaced incentives lead self-interested individuals to rely on others for their own benefit, to 'free-ride' on public insurance" (Woll 2013: 611; cf. Streeck 2017: 89).

The bailouts showed that there were constitutive class exceptions to the rule of the marketization of morals. These firms are treated as legal persons having moral agency possessing wide degrees of freedom for activity by right (Pearce and Tombs 1998: 40–41). But they are not just like any other firm or juridical subject because, as the crisis that emerged in the wake of the Lehman Brothers failure showed, they are necessary to the system while also dependent on that system. Regulation presupposes an entity *cum* moral agent with degrees of freedom to act and contemplate the consequences of actions. *Necessity*, as in "too big to fail," means that we are dealing in a more fundamental kind of entity. It is then not an issue of "responsibilization" or "deresponsibilization" but of what can be called "pre-responsibilization," "beyond good and evil." "Necessity" implies that entities of this kind should not be allowed degrees of freedom such that they would undermine their own existence or *conditions of existence* as was the case with the self-interested, highly levered investments of banks that resulted in the generation of massive systemic risk.

Bailouts reveal the discrepancy in the morality–state–market relationship and dominant neoliberal discourse about it (Fourcade 2013: 623). Although some contend that the discrepancy is between morality at the level of the individual financial firm and the "collective moral responsibilities of the financial industry" as a whole (Woll 2013: 611; cf. *The Economist* 2013), it is really a matter of the *displacement of morality by security*. Apparatuses of security are about establishing the very conditions of possibility of governing, law and regulation to constitute permissible paths of development while managing sources of uncertainty (Foucault 2007: 33). Large financial services firms were shown to be part of the apparatuses of security because they are necessary to capitalist social stability. Zombification in the form of bailouts thus is a result of capitalist security in that "the capitalist requires an environment which is predictable, and as much as possible under his [sic] control"' (*CotP*: 84). Although security may have displaced market morality, "morality" in the general political economy returns in the guise of "fiscal sacrifice."

## Rethinking Durkheim's theory of sacrifice

Political theorist Wendy Brown (2015) suggests that sacrifice is a necessary supplement to neoliberal rationality, "something outside of its terms, yet essential to its operation" (210). Radical Durkheimianism provides a way to develop Brown's insight to analyse the moral logic involved in economic sacrifices. The first Durkheimians sought a general theory of sacrifice, one able to account for commonalities among its different types (e.g. personal, expiatory, atoning, etc.) (Hubert and Mauss 1981; Durkheim 1995). Durkheim understood sacrifice as a foundational institution, one combining collective representations and obligatory practices (ways of acting prescribed by the group) that are expressed through myths about exemplary conduct. In sacrifice, members affirm their commitment to the group and the system of reciprocal obligations shared by members. They do so by giving up something valued by the donor and the group; egoistic interests of the individual person are thus first sacrificed because one cannot simply do what one will with what one has. This means more than laying aside one's appetites and preferences because the group to whom the individual belongs values what is given up. In religion, this system of values is communicated and rationalized in an organized way by a priest sub-group or individual that is itself "sacred," set apart from the rest of the community (Durkheim 1995: 35). Sacrifice thus inherently involves an obligatory *exchange* in the medium of communal values regulated by an exclusive minority group. Conversely, what is thus proscribed is a one-way relationship of being a "taker" from group life. But although one is obliged to give something, demonstrating the transcendence of egoistic individualism on the part of the donor, *one in the end receives more than one gives* (Durkheim 1995: 345). One becomes more than a slave to one's appetites and can instead become a moral being (Pearce 2010: 48), a communally recognized person capable of thinking in generalities and thus capable of participating in organized life with others. Sacrifice is thus a cyclical, microcosmic mechanism for the reproduction of society (Durkheim 1995: 342).

Pearce's retheorized Durkheimianism attends in particular to "the role played by sacrificial discourses and sacrificial practices" in the Aztec empire and the more recent American imperium (Pearce 2010: 45), quite some way from Durkheim's concern to theorize the conditions of emergence of a just, democratically socialist republic! Pearce thus unwittingly provides a different leverage point for engaging with Durkheim. The conventional French model of sacrifice (see Hubert and Mauss 1981) involves a sacrificial triangle of a sacrifier, a sacrificer and a victim. The "sacrifier" is the originator, and generally believed to be the benefactor, of the sacrifice; it is the desire of the sacrifier that gets the process going. The "sacrificer" "is a person or a collectivity who arranges and possibly presides at a sacrifice" (Pearce 2010: 49). The sacrificer is the agent of the sacrificial ritual (Pearce 2010: 50) and conducts it by killing, destroying or otherwise consuming the offering on behalf of the sacrifier. Last is the victim offered up by the sacrifier to the sacrificer for removal from the mundane world. Pearce broadens this model of the sacrificial triangle to include the recipient of the sacred that he calls a "*superior sacred other*" such as a god or value. He thus defines sacrifice as

> an act or acts by which a sacrifier gives up something it values to a *superior sacred other*, sometimes through a ritual officiated by a sacrificer, in the hope of creating for itself and sometimes for designated others a right relation with the superior [sacred] other and possibly to receive benefits that the latter can bestow.
>
> (Pearce 2010: 49)

Somewhat modifying Pearce's model (2010) by recourse to other Durkheimian work (Pearce 2001; Datta and Milbrandt 2014), one gets the following schema for analysing sacrifice:

**Sacred/profane**: a constitutive division between what pertains to the power of the group (the sacred) vs. that which pertains to individual interests and desires and is without a concern for the group per se (the profane); reflects the group's imposition of the moral primacy of the sacred over the profane;

**Cosmic order**: beliefs about powers affecting human fates, including more and less rational beliefs about how the world could end (crisis); it is emergent from conventional social practices that attach collective representations to their empirical and practical referents;

**The sacrificial triangle**: sacrifiers, sacrificers, and victims;

**Societally superior sacrifier**: "[e]lite individual or institution that can in part appropriate the sacrifice" (Pearce 2010: 50), for example, a priestly caste (e.g. Hubert and Mauss 1981: 43);

**Community/group**: the symbolically constituted totality, regulated by mechanisms of inclusion and exclusion, that serves as the referent of a sacrificial act;

**Recipient(s)**: "the superior [sacred] other that can be a sacred or common/mundane individual, collective, being, or ideal";

**Rituals**: articulated combinations of beliefs, practices and their subjects in a combination imposed in an obligatory way on participants;

**Beneficiaries**: "[d]esignated individual(s) or collectivity(es)" (e.g. priests and their households that use sacrifices to sustain themselves);

**Hierarchy**: distinctions within the community relative to their access to sacred things; the hierarchy is made sacrosanct by ongoing sacrifices thus reproducing an existing regime of values and institutions;

**Effects**: generating a form of solidarity (shared fate) among the various but unequally positioned groups in the community, plus the articulated "complex effects that may differ for different groups".

(Pearce 2010: 50)

Pearce's model thus serves as a stimulus for investigating a broader political economy of sacrifice, here applied to rhetoric about economic life itself.

## Analysing "expropriative" sacrificial logics in contemporary fiscal discourse

Defending calls for deficit reduction in the United States in 2011, Democratic House Leader Nancy Pelosi stated that "it is clear we must enter an era of austerity; to reduce the deficit through shared sacrifice" (Brown 2015: 275, n. 21). There are significant examples of similar rhetoric used by U.S. President Obama and Italian critics of former Italian Prime Minister Mario Monti, to its journalistic use by social commentators in widely read periodicals (Brown 2015: 276–276; Streeck 2017). In Canada, moral arguments about austerity, cuts and the greater good have been part and parcel of political culture since the early 1990s (McQuaig 1996; McBride 2005). These sacrifices have significant impacts on the lives of workers especially and "may entail sudden job losses, furloughs, or cuts in pay, benefits, and pensions, or it may involve suffering the more sustained effects of stagflation, currency deflation, credit crunches, liquidity crises, foreclosure crises, and more" (Brown 2015: 210–211). In the United States, such sacrifices include "cutbacks to the US court system" (Brown 2015: 277, n. 26) and for Southern Europe, "accepting persistent high rates of joblessness combined with life-threatening cuts in social protections and services" (Brown 2015: 212). Ongoing austerity and fiscal sacrifices typically generate other kinds of deficits around public infrastructure and failures in costing for the depreciation of public goods (Streeck 2017). Similar rhetoric is found in a variety of cases, including Japan (Harding 2015) and Britain (Sparrow 2015), among others. For instance, as governor of Puerto Rico, Rosselló, stated,

We cannot allow them to make us choose between paying police, teachers and nurses or to pay the debt . . . We must all share the responsibility and the sacrifice so then we can share in the benefits of a growing Puerto Rican economy.

(in Gamboa 2015; cf. Robles 2017)

Such sacrificial discourse predominantly refers to either fiscal measures, concerning governments' budget priorities and balance sheets, or is oriented to the household, addressing people as tax-payer-citizen-worker-consumers required to engage in some form of "noble self-sacrifice" (cf. Pearce 2010: 50), ostensibly done in the interest of the greater good and for the sake of their children, lest they be saddled with payments on government debts extending well into the future (McQuaig 1996; McBride 2005; Lazzarato 2015). Sacrificial discourse comes to have hegemonizing effects through "interpellation" (cf. Hubert and Mauss 1981: 31). The process of interpellation refers to the hailing of people as subjects who thus come to recognize themselves as imbricated in an existing set of social relations to which they are already practically subordinated, enabling and constraining their capacities to act (Althusser 2014: 189–190). Consent to this political economy of economic sacrifice starts with people's recognition that the "hail" about making "sacrifices" is actually addressed to them, thus instanciating an existing normative frame of reference concerning the valorization of capital accumulation.

Sacrificial interpellators, calling for fiscal and other economic sacrifices, use authoritative economics discourse to change the normal basis of the political economy, ostensibly for the good of the group, to differently appropriate and deploy resources to address a "crisis" that threatens the social order. An interpellative hail is made to the public, and its acceptance then constitutes the addressee as the sacrifier who "freely" accepts their role in being the agents and sustainers of this sacrificial desire. One key effect here is the reproduction of people's subjugation to dominant economics discourses about what shapes a shared political economic fate. In the case of zombie capitalism, this hailing was done by politicians, economists, pundits, columnists and journalists.

I call such fiscal and economic sacrifices "expropriative" because this process reflects state powers of "expropriating property"; what is taken can be accomplished through taxation or the diminution of government goods and services by right, but without, as in the Durkheimian account, people *getting more in return*; *people get less, and they know it*. What is got in return is "security," meaning securing reproduction conditions for some form of capitalist development. In accepting the hail, the public as workers, consumers, citizens, taxpayers and benefactors of public goods, quickly becomes the "sacrifier." Once the address is acknowledged, economic and fiscal sacrifices can thus be subsequently recoded as expressing the people's desire even while being constituted by the successful production and circulation of the hail. *Societally superior sacrifiers* in the form of capitalist enterprise, the ostensible creative dynamism of market virtue, and the capitalist state emerge. A range of *sacrificers* is also interpellated, including politicians and public-sector administrators as budget makers developing austerity measures and implementing cuts. Individuals and households, charitable groups and non-governmental organizations (NGOs), either left picking up the slack or dealing with cuts to grants, end up in a similar, if coerced, role.

Sacrificial interpellation first hails the public as the *sacrifier* and then calls on them to play the next role as *sacrificer* in belt-tightening: *responsibility for cutting trickles down and out* through the population, perversely democratizing agential participation in the political economy. Hailing people as those who care about the next generation shows how people's *present actualities* are subordinated to an abstract better future, *governing them through that future.* Thus, there is some appeal to "self-interest" concerning opportunity costs extending into the future. People are also hailed in neoliberal terms as utility-maximizing consumers (ones who may have to cut back on some purchases) and thus predominantly as *Homo economicus*, rather than as active political subjects and citizens (Brown 2015). In classic ideological form, such calls for sacrifice are purportedly "shared" (are "universal") when as bailouts have shown, they are not; indeed, the "universality" of the address to "the people/public" devolves to the practicalities of a multitude of particular households, *depoliticizing* the economy of sacrifice and austerity which deals in what is to be done with a "surplus" of value *already* extracted by the state in the form of obligatory taxation and revenue streams. The result appears as the "sociological imagination" in reverse: in sacrificial interpellations, people are shown to be *less important* than a bigger political economic system (cf. Brown 2015: 217).

The process is completed as it *devolves, disperses and dilutes* the concentrated and accumulated concrete contradictions of finance capitalism to the individual level in which the work of the reproduction of labour power in the broader population becomes more precarious: insecurity for people is a security technology for capital accumulation as people, largely left to their own devices absent adequate state assistance, are "incentivized" to innovate, or create, or do whatever to survive (cf. Datta 2011). Such accumulation techniques are analogous to "racketeering" (*CotP*). A protection racket is one in which "a local strong man forces merchants to pay tribute in order to avoid damage – damage the strong man himself threatens to deliver" (Tilly 1985: 37; Pearce 2010: 59; cf. Tombs 2016: 10). In zombie capitalism such fiscal sacrifices involve an exchange by which a surplus is expropriated in the interests of the "greater good," meaning security for capital accumulation: one gets protection from the worst vicissitudes of finance capitalism (bank runs, civil collapse, barbarism) via the state, but people must give something up while getting nothing in return, *except the non-event of a socio-economic catastrophe.* This further reveals that we are dealing in the realm of "security" (Datta 2011), the political economy of the "virtual," thus becoming a new front in the class struggles of the twenty-first century.

Victimization and blame (carrying with it issues of responsibility) is complex in zombie capitalist expropriative sacrifices. Cuts to public services mean that people also hold the third position in the sacrificial triangle itself, being the victim of cuts. Women workers, significantly represented in public-sector employment, are disproportionately affected by government cutbacks, layoffs, unemployment and precarity (Oksala 2013), whereas mid-career men facing financial hardship in particular see their suicide rate increase (Phillips and Nugent 2014; Coope 2014). People at times blame themselves (Claydon 2014), but this cannot account for inflationary pressures from housing (inflated by finance capital–driven credit market expansion) and education.

Theorizing fiscal sacrifices 97

However, as households aim to manage daily life and cost pressures, blame has been frequently directed at politicians, and politics itself is sacrificed. Water privatization in Britain is a telling case in point: "Conservative and Labour governments have discovered that when they give powers to private companies, and those private companies screw up, voters blame the government for giving the power away, rather than the companies for misusing them" (Fisher 2009: 62). In turn this has given traction to populist rejections of the expert agents of discursive authority (anti-intellectualism as a dialetical opposite to the post-political dominance of expert administration [cf. Datta 2011]) and their institutions become victimized too, as zombie capitalism eats some "brains."

Moral distortions follow from the deresponsibilization of two groups: (1) sacrificial interpellators and (2) sacrificers. Once the public recognizes themselves in the call to make sacrifices, the *public* becomes the *sacrifier* and hence responsible for sustaining the desire for economic sacrifices. This shifts responsibility from the experts recommending sacrifices and makes it possible for experts to absolve themselves because the public has accepted the hail and is the purported benefactor and sustainer of the sacrificial desire in this form of perverted form of trickle-down "agency." A similar process is at work when it comes to executing cuts: *the public does it to themselves* when clamouring for tax breaks to help repair household balance sheets. The devolution of responsibility from those in positions of dominance and authority to the public generates an effect with an unexpected "use": *the cunning of neoliberal reason*. A rejection of politics and expertise means that people increasingly take matters into their own hands to get by. But this is precisely what the dreams and schemes of expert neoliberal programming aim for (cf. Datta 2011). In turn, as people accept their overdetermined positioning as sacrifiers, sacrificers and victims, they continue to depoliticize, given the practical immediacy of their struggles (cf. Brown 2015; Althusser 2014: 220). This has a further use for dominant political classes given how this devolution of sacrificial agency involves the displacement of politics by *ethics* now tied to the valorization of personal finance (Mulcahy 2016), returning to the financial services industry to borrow or for investment vehicles to compensate for weakened public provisions (cf. Streeck 2017: 38–46).

What fiscal sacrifices do, while providing a zombified "resurrection" for the finance side of the security apparatus, is transform the locus of accumulation and the divorce of "the producer from the means of production" (cf. Marx 1967: 714), patching over the accumulated contradictions of this most recent phase of capitalism. It is no longer simply a matter of "M–C–M'" (money, commodity, more money), but rather a modified circuit in which labour power becomes commodified differently through securitization and virtualization (e.g., calculations about likely performance). Today, workers in wage labour produce themselves not only as labour power, but also as a performance distribution profile ("P") concerning probabilities of income generation and payment to generate this new circuit: "M–P–C–M'" (cf. Datta and MacDonald 2011). Certainly, an appropriation of surplus labour occurs in the present, but with indebtedness (household and public) and securitization, workers will owe into the future and thus the "divorcing" of workers from the means of production *in the future* is already a done deal. This is a structural claim on potential value to be produced *whatever that is*: what is produced substantively, how, etc., is inconsequential from the point of view of capital. What is appropriated is not simply *value* in the future (we cannot know what or how something will be valued in the future), but rather the real potential of subjects to think, create and produce concretely and shape their circumstances and fates, including politically, to constitute different futures. Thus is yielded a "metaphysics of morals" peculiar to contemporary zombie capitalism, resulting in the discursive *primitive accumulation of futures* that *govern the potentials in the present* as they continually pass into actuality.

## Conclusion

In stressing the complex and contradictory nature of capitalist social formations, *CotP* reminds us that concrete contradictions continuously trip up the purportedly rational capitalist accounts of social dynamics and morality. I have aimed to extend Pearce's sensibilities about the moral inconsistencies in capitalism to theorize how the state assists in the reproduction of a zombie capitalism unable to survive on its own. The rhetoric of sacrifice in the economic domain reveals itself to be a ruse for gaining control of a surplus and providing a moral gloss on those so deprived and victimized by cuts. The consequence is a structure of the ongoing primitive accumulation of people's futures while securing paths of capital accumulation couched in a contradictory discourse about the moral necessity of sacrificing for the greater good.

## Acknowledgements

The radical Durkheimianism articulated here has developed in the context of countless conversations about Durkheim, Althusser, Foucault, capitalism and law with Frank Pearce. I learned my theoretical method from Frank while he supervised my MA thesis on Durkheim, Foucault and the sacred in the Department of Sociology at Queen's University; he remains a most trusted interlocutor and dear friend. I thank Frank, Jonathan Frauley, Steve Tombs, Ariane Hanemaayer, Dean Curran, David Whyte, Steve Bittle and participants at the *Revisiting the Crimes of the Powerful Conference*, York University, 2017, for helpful discussions and critiques.

## References

Althusser, L. (2014) *On the Reproduction of Capitalism*. New York: Verso.

Barofsky, N. (2012) *Bailout: How Washington Abandoned Main Street While Rescuing Wall Street*. New York: Free Press.

Besley, T. and Hennessy, P. (2009) "The Global Financial Crisis: Why Didn't Anybody Notice." *British Academy Review*, 14 (November): 8–10.

Botting, F. (2013) "Undead-Ends: Zombie Debt/Zombie Theory." *Postmodern Culture*, 23(3).

Brown, W. (2015) *Undoing the Demos*. New York: Zone Books.

Bryan, B. (2016) "'Zombie Companies' Are Killing the Economy, So We Should Just Let them Collapse." Online. Available HTTP: www.businessinsider.com/zombie-companies-killing-us-economy-2016-3

Claydon, J.E. (2014) *What's the Charge? Perceptions of Blame and Responsibility for Credit Card Debt*. D.Phil Thesis. The University of Sussex.

Collins, M. (2015) "The Big Bank Bailout." Online. Available HTTP: www.forbes.com/sites/mikecollins/2015/07/14/the-big-bank-bailout/#1963a3d42d83

Coope, C. et al. (2014) "Suicide and the 2008 Economic Recession: Who Is Most At Risk? Trends in Suicide Rates in England and Wales 2001–2011." *Social Science & Medicine*, 117: 76–85.

D'Altroy, T.N. (2002) *The Incas*. Oxford: Blackwell.

Datta, R.P. (2011) "Security and the Void: Aleatory Materialism contra Governmentality," in George Rigakos and Mark Neocleous (eds.) *Anti-Security*, 217–241. Ottawa: Red Quill Books.

Datta, R.P. (2017) "Zombie Capitalism and the Collective Conscience: Between Bataille and Agamben." *Interdisciplinary Approaches to Surviving the Zombie Apocalypse*, 1: 59–73. Online. Available HTTP: https://ojs.uwindsor.ca/ojs/leddy/index.php/iasza/article/view/4916/4229

Datta, R.P., Frauley, J. and Pearce, F. (2010) "Situation Critical: For a Critical, Reflexive, Realist, Emancipatory Social Science." *Journal of Critical Realism*, 9(2): 227–247.

Datta, R.P. and MacDonald, L. (2011) "Time for Zombies: Sacrifice and the Structural Phenomenology of Capitalist Futures," in C.M. Moreman and C.J. Rushton (eds.) *Race, Oppression and the Zombie*, 77–92. Jefferson: McFarland.

Datta, R.P. and Milbrandt, T.H. (2014) "The Elementary Forms of Religious Life: Discursive Monument, Symbolic Feast." *Canadian Journal of Sociology*, 39(4): 473–522.

Durden, T. (2013) "The Case Against QE: Zombie Banks, Companies, Households, and Governments." Online. Available HTTP: www.zerohedge.com/news/2013-01-25/case-against-qe-zombie-banks-companies-households-and-governments

Durkheim, E. (1995) *The Elementary Forms of Religious Life*. New York: The Free Press.

*The Economist* (2007) "The Bank that Failed." Online. Available HTTP: www.economist.com/node/9832838

———— (2013) "The Euro Zone: Europe's Other Debt Crisis." Online. Available HTTP: www.economist.com/news/leaders/21588366-its-not-just-sovereign-borrowing-there-are-too-many-zombie-firms-and-overindebted

Fisher, M. (2009) *Capitalist Realism: Is There No Alternative?* Zero Books.

Foucault, M. (2007) *Security, Territory, Population*. New York: Palgrave Macmillan.

Fourcade, M., Steiner, P., Streeck, W. and Woll, C. (2013) "Moral Categories in the Financial Crisis." *Socio-economic Review*, 11(3): 601–627.

Gamboa, S. (2015) "Puerto Rico Governor: We Can't Let Our Debt Bring Us to Our Knees." Online. Available HTTP: www.nbcnews.com/news/latino/puerto-rico-governor-we-cant-let-our-debt-bring-us-n384121

Harding, R. (2015) "Shinzo Abe Sacrifices Economic Leverage for Political Advantage." *The Financial Times*, Online. Available HTTP: www.ft.com/content/5e09a966-a2fe-11e5-bc70-7ff6d4fd203a

Harman, C. (2009) *Zombie Capitalism*. London: Bookmarks Publications.

Hubert, H. and Mauss, M. (1981) *Sacrifice: Its Nature and Functions*. Chicago: University of Chicago Press.

Hunt, A. (2003) "Risk and Moralization in Everyday Life," in R. Erickson and A. Doyle (eds.) *Risk and Morality*, 165–192. Toronto: University of Toronto Press.

Lazzarato, M. (2011) *The Making of Indebted Man*. New York: Semiotex(e).

——— (2015) *Governing by Debt*. New York: Semiotext(e).

Marx, K. (1967) *Capital: Volume 1*. New York: International Publishers.

McBride, S. (2005) *Paradigm Shift: Globalization and the Canadian State (Second Edition)*. Winnipeg: Fernwood Books.

McQuaig, L. (1996) *Shooting the Hippo: Death by Deficit and Other Canadian Myths*. Toronto: Penguin Books.

Mulcahy, N. (2016) "Entrepreneurial Subjectivity and the Political Economy of Daily Life in the Time of Finance." *European Journal of Social Theory*, 20(2): 1–20.

Oksala, J. (2013) "Feminism and Neoliberal Governmentality." *Foucault Studies*, (16): 32–53.

Onaran, Y. (2011) *Zombie Banks: How Broken Banks and Debtor Nations Are Crippling the Global Economy*. New York: Bloomberg Press, Kindle Edition.

Panitch, L. and Gindin, S. (2012) *The Making of Global Capitalism*. New York: Verso.

Pearce, F. (1976) *Crimes of the Powerful*. London: Pluto Books.

——— (2001) *The Radical Durkheim, Second Edition*. Toronto: Canadian Scholars' Press International.

——— (2010) "Obligatory Sacrifice and Imperial Projects," in W. Chambliss, R. Michalowski, and R.C. Kramer (eds.) *State Crime in the Global Age*. New York: Routledge.

Pearce, Frank and Tombs, Steve. (1998) *Toxic Capitalism: Corporate Crime and the Chemical Industry*. Aldershot: Ashgate.

Peek, J. and Rosengren, E.S. (2003) "Unnatural Selection: Perverse Incentives and the Misallocation of Credit in Japan." Working Paper 9643, National Bureau of Economic Research, Cambridge, MA.

Phillips, J.A. and Nugent, C.N. (2014) "Suicide and the Great Recession of 2007–2009: The Role of Economic Factors in the 50 US States." *Social Science & Medicine*, 116: 22–31.

Phillips, K. (2008) *Bad Money: Reckless Finance, Failed Politics, and the Global Crisis of American Capitalism*. New York: Viking

Pontell, H.N., Black, W.K. and Geis, G. (2014) "Too Big to Fail, Too Powerful to Jail? On the Absence of Criminal Prosecutions After the 2008 Financial Meltdown." *Crime, Law and Social Change*, 61(1): 1–13.

Pym, H. (2012) "'Zombie' Companies Eating Away at Economic Growth." Online. Available HTTP: www.bbc.com/news/business-20262282

Quiggin, J. (2010) *Zombie Economics*. Princeton: Princeton University Press.

Robles, F. (2017) "Fiscal Fears Grip Puerto Ricans Facing 'Sacrifice Everywhere'." *The New York Times*, Online. Available HTTP: https://nyti.ms/2phuIW0

Sparrow, A. (2015) "David Cameron Sees Tax Cuts Worth £7bn as a 'reward for sacrifice'." *The Guardian*. Online. Available HTTP: www.theguardian.com/politics/2015/jan/26/david-cameron-tax-cuts-reward-for-sacrifice

Streeck, W. (2017) *Buying Time: The Delayed Crisis of Democratic Capitalism, Second Edition*. New York: Verso.

Tilly, C. (1985) "War Making and State Making as Organized Crime," in Peter Evans, Dietrich Rueschemeyer and Theda Skocpol (eds.) *Bringing the State Back In*, 169–187. Cambridge: Cambridge University Press.

Tombs, S. (2015) "Crisis, What Crisis? Regulation and the Academic Orthodoxy." *The Howard Journal of Criminal Justice*, 54(1): 57–72.

———— (2016) *Social Protection after the Crisis: Regulation without Enforcement.* Cambridge: Polity Press.

Woll, C. (2013) "The Morality of Rescuing Banks." *Socio-economic Review*, 11(3): 610–614.

Woodiwiss, A. (2005) *Scoping the Social*, New York: Open University Press.

# Chapter 8

# Power, crime and enclosure

## Capital accumulation in the twilight of the neoliberal SSA[1]

*Raymond Michalowski*

Some writers are stenographers. Before they write, they know what it is they want to say. For me, writing is exploratory. It is a process of discovering what I know. In the mid-1970s, I wanted to know how an emerging Marxist criminology might apply to the full range of typical criminological topics, from street crime to corporate crime, from law making to policing, from prisons to the creation of subjectivities. So I began writing. The eventual outcome was a critical criminology textbook (Michalowski 1985), although that had not been my original plan.

A number of Marxist criminologists, including Bill Chambliss, Tony Platt, Paul Takagi and Richard Quinney, left important signposts to follow on my journey of discovery. However, because I was most interested in the relationship between corporate power, law and social harm, it was Frank Pearce's (1976) *Crimes of the Powerful* that best showed me a path toward the clearing I was looking for. It was from Frank that I learned to appreciate the ironic ways corporate regulations often increase rather than diminish corporate power. His analyses also challenged my residual belief in the efficacy of state regulation that, like a palimpsest, lurked beneath my critique of capitalist corporations. *Crimes of the Powerful* deepened my recognition that capital accumulation, however regulated, inevitably generates crime and social injury and that strategies for regulatory control, at best, can only reduce corporate harms at the margins. Frank's attention to the politics of corporate control planted the seeds of what would eventually grow into the state–corporate crime model that Ron Kramer and I developed as a framework for studying crimes of the powerful (Michalowski and Kramer 2006).

What makes Frank Pearce's influence on both my early and later work unique is that, unlike the more established scholars who influenced me back in the day, Frank is an age-peer, but one who was always a step ahead of my thinking. A peer who always taught me something new. The analysis of enclosures and expulsions generated by neoliberal capitalism that follows owes an intellectual debt that reaches all the way back to *Crimes of the Powerful*.

As I continue a wandering path toward understanding how intersections of corporate and state power generate both familiar and new forms of social harm,

Power, crime and enclosure 103

I am grateful to Frank Pearce for pointing me toward this path. It is curious to think that Frank and I, as well as our other critical criminology age-peers are now the "senior" scholars. My hope is that scholars much younger than us continue to discover the depth and the value in Frank Pearce's work, just as I did, and do.

## Theorizing enclosure and expulsion

What follows is an abbreviated version of efforts to bring together three theoretical themes for *seeing* and analysing how new forms of enclosure and expulsion have become routine components of capital accumulation in the market-above-all political economy known as neoliberalism. These themes are neoliberal globalization, social structures of accumulation (SSA) and social sources of power.

When I speak of enclosures and expulsions I am referring to two dimensions of the same process or, metaphorically, two sides of the same coin. *Enclosure* is the process of denying one or more social group(s) previously established ownership and/or use of some tangible or intangible element of social life and the transference of that access to some other group(s). The established character of the access being denied may reside in custom, culture, law or some combination of these.

The concept of "enclosure" is most often linked to analyses of English practices between the 16th and 18th centuries that denied serfs access to historically common lands and then transformed those lands into pasturage for sheep to facilitate expansion of emergent capitalist markets for wool (Marx 1887/1977; Neeson 1996; Yelling 1977). Contemporary transfers of land from traditional owners/users to transnational corporations or state control through neoliberal development schemes bears similarities to these earlier enclosure movements (Evans 2005; Linebaugh 2014). However, by the late 20th century, enclosures involved much more than *terra firma*. Thus, the definition of enclosure is applicable beyond land rights to arenas such as political participation, public services, cultural patrimony and ecosystem survival (Ilcan 2009; Willy 2011).

Whereas enclosure is the denial of access to present or future users of something of value, *expulsion* is the objective removal of those who currently have access by denying them structural positions that would enable them to continue their traditional usage of social spaces that are now enclosed. This may seem to be a distinction without a difference. However, I suggest it has theoretical utility. In contemporary nation-states, the first step in denial of access to some and its transference to others is typically accomplished through the creation of new laws or reinterpretations of established ones. In many instances, however, this denial must also be enforced if legal enclosure is to have practical import. That is, those who have been denied legal access must be materially or metaphorically "thrown out" of whatever physical or social space they enjoyed that allowed them to access to the now-enclosed space. Thus, it is useful to keep in mind that most enclosures signal the onset of expulsion of someone or something, just as most expulsions signal some type of enclosure in pursuit of "primitive accumulation" (Marx 1977: 915).

## Neoliberal globalization

Neoliberal globalization is the project of creating a hemisphere-wide, broadly integrated system of capitalist production and distribution based on the proposition that capitalist accumulation projects, unfettered by regulations, should be free to penetrate the material, labour, commodity and knowledge markets of all countries (Dardot and Laval 2014). According to this framework, the capitalist market system must be free to commodify large portions of the remaining commons, whether in the form of material resources, cultural patrimony, political power or creative productions.[2] There have been many different interpretations and analyses of this process.[3] My specific concern here, however, is the ways that neoliberal enclosures and expulsions have generated avoidable, harmful social conditions. These include:

(1)  The human suffering caused by increased inequality, austerity, new forms of dispossession, primitive accumulation and "primitive disaccumulation" (Burowoy 2009; Klitgaard 2011; Magdoff 2013; Livingston 2010).
(2)  Erosion of the political capacity of citizens of putatively democratic states to shape state behaviour as a result of:

i.   Increased control of finance capital over governmental decisions (Judis 2001; Hassen 2016; Mayer 2016; Potter and Penniman 2016);
ii.  Growing power of the "executive" function in political states (Sassen 2009);
iii. Increased privatization of formerly public functions such as education, law enforcement, utilities and even fighting wars, turning them into corporate revenue streams that allow little to no citizen oversight or control (Bakker 2010; Kahn and Minnich 2005; Obinger et al. 2016; Ravitch 2013).

(3)  Accelerated environmental harm, up to and including, the threat of ecocide posed by global climate change resulting from the unregulated growth project of the global state–corporate nexus (Higgins 2012; Kramer 2012; Lynch and Stretesky 2012).

## SSA theory

The political economy of neoliberal globalization and its harms has been theorized from a number of different perspectives.[4] For reasons too complex to unpackage here, I suggest that social structure of accumulation (SSA) theory is particularly useful in understanding enclosures and expulsions. SSA theory frames neoliberalism as another stage in the evolution of institutional frameworks designed to facilitate capitalist accumulation, while simultaneously managing the class conflicts and structural crises endemic to capitalist social systems. As a theory of capitalist transformations, SSA theory provides tools for thinking *prospectively* about how the relationships among capital, states, labour and civil society change in the search of relations of production and governance conducive to the accumulation of capital and levels of social stability necessary for that accumulation to take place.

Beginning in the early 20th century, economists observed extended business cycle patterns lasting from 40 to 60 years from peak to peak (Kondratieff 1935). While these "long waves" were apparent, they were undertheorized to the point that the historian Eric Hobswam (1999: 87) opined that the idea of long waves "convinced many historians and even some economists that there is something . . . we don't know what."

Well before Hobswam's observation, David Gordon, Richard Edwards and Michael Reich (1982) sought to more fully theorize the "what" behind Kondrotiev's long waves. They proposed that each wave contains within it a particular configuration of social institutions that, for a time, is able to facilitate robust accumulation of capital, but that eventually loses its vitality to do so. This results in a period of economic *decay*, followed by a period of *exploration* characterized by attempts to find a new institutional structure that will stimulate a return to strong economic growth. This leads to a period of *consolidation*, in which a new configuration of institutions emerges to facilitate robust accumulation. Although refined over time, particularly by Kotz, McDonough and Reich (1994), SSA theory retained this basic formulation for some time.

SSA theory is a *sociological* theory, not a purely economic one. It directs us to identify the constellation of institutions that serve to facilitate accumulation and/or stabilized class relations during periods of consolidation, and do so less effectively during periods of decay and exploration. As David Gordon (1980: 17) proposed:

> The interdependencies among the individual institutions [that constitute an SSA] create a combined social structure with a *unified* internal structure of its own – a composite whole, in effect, *whose intrinsic structure amounts to more than the sum of the individual institutional relationships.*
>
> [Emphasis added]

Since the end of the Federal Period, the United States has been characterized by four distinct SSAs: an era of laissez faire capitalism from the 1830s to the 1890s, an era of monopoly capitalism from then until the 1930s, an era of regulated capitalism from the 1930s until the 1980s and the present era of neoliberal capitalism whose full-blown emergence is often associated with the conservative turn signalled by the rise to power of Ronald Reagan in the United States and Margaret Thatcher in Britain.[5] Each of these periods is characterized by a distinct set of relations among private sector capital, the state, labour and civil society.

By the early 2000s, it was becoming apparent that the rate of economic growth generated by the neoliberal SSA was not much stronger than the decay phase of the SSA it replaced. Martin Wolfson and David Kotz (2010: 211) addressed this apparent anomaly by theorizing that SSAs "are best understood as institutional structures that (temporarily) stabilize class contradictions" and that although the increased power of capital over labour in the neoliberal SSA "should translate into a higher share of profit in total income, it does not follow that growth will be faster." From this perspective, although reductions in the return to labour, primitive accumulation and debt-fuelled extraction of wealth from the working class may boost returns on investments in stocks and other "financial instruments" while inflating salaries of CEO "superstars," they are more about facilitating unequal distribution than growing the "real economy" (Boyer 2010; Picketty 2014; Soederberg 2014).

## The neoliberal SSA

Key characteristics of the neoliberal SSA are reductions in government oversight of economic practices (deregulation), a shift of the economic centre of gravity from goods production to banking facilitated by restructuring of rules governing investment services (financialization), increased conversion of public services into for-profit companies (privatization) and increased disaggregation of material and media consumption (individualization) (Kotz and McDonough 2010). Globalization, in turn, is the effort to implement these strategies on a worldwide basis through reduction or elimination of tariffs and other trade barriers by subjecting national development strategies to international financial discipline; supporting governments willing to collaborate in the project of weakening laws and practices designed to protect workers, local markets and environments; and marketizing and monetizing much of what had once been the commons. The desire for global capitalist integration is not new (Braudel 1992; Gunder-Frank 1978). However, in the latter decades of the 20th century, technological advances in transportation and communications brought the goal of deep global integration closer than any time before.

The project of neoliberal globalization forged a new world order in which the accommodations between corporate capital accumulation, labour and the 20th-century welfare state characteristic of regulated capitalism were scuttled in favour of a Shumpetarian global order based on weakening regulatory controls at all levels, and reducing Keynesian-era commitments to social welfare in order to facilitate capital accumulation through intensified exploitation of people, land and the biosphere (Jessop 1993; Kotz 2015). Increased commodification of the commons was essential to this process insofar as it was a repository of potential profit in a world of shrinking resources. By globalizing neoliberal ideology and practices, the neoliberal SSA created a *liebenswelt* that in many countries increasingly framed economic and social life primarily in free-market terms (Castree 2010; Green, Ward and McConnachie 2007; Nathan et al. 2004; Shipley 2016).

## Power and the neoliberal SSA

The neoliberal SSA is characterized by a state–corporate "symbiosis" (Tombs 2012) in which economic power is linked to and dependent upon both the executive power of the political state and the ideological power of the "extended state" in which civil society produces and disseminates conceptual frameworks supportive of existing structural arrangements (Gramsci 1971). I propose that a useful way of analysing the dynamics of power in the neoliberal SSA is through a tripartite model that recognizes the intersections of economic, political and cultural power (Mann 2012a).

Analyses of power in both political sociology and international relations typically begin with Weber's (1948: 180) ideal-typical definition of power as "the ability of an individual or group to achieve their own goals or aims when others are trying to prevent them from realizing them." Weber went on to identify three primary sources of "authority," that is, the *legitimated* exercise of power: traditional authority, charismatic authority and rational/legal authority.

More recently, Nye (2004) proposed a distinction between hard and soft power. In the context of international relations, which is Nye's primary focus, hard power is the application of military/police might to compel obedience, or the use of superior economic resources to coerce or bribe compliance with interests of power holders' interests. Soft power, by comparison, is the ability to attract people to do what those exercising power wish. Legitimation, in the Weberian sense, is central to soft power. As one analyst of soft power notes, "If a people or a nation believes our objectives to be legitimate, we are more likely to persuade them to follow our lead without using threats and bribes" (Armitage and Nye 2007: 6).[6]

Sociological and criminological inquiries into the harms committed by corporations and states typically emphasize the role of *hard power* in facilitating these transgressions. These analyses tend to focus on the ability of states to compel compliance through the use or threat of overt force, or the capacity of corporations to use coercion and bribery to achieve their goals (Lasslett 2014). Critical analysts also typically view these uses of power as wrongful, even though this wrongfulness is frequently not recognized, either in law or by wide swaths of ordinary publics (Agnew 2011; Michalowski and Kramer 2006; Green and Ward 2004). This suggests that analyses of the relationship between power and harm would benefit from deeper consideration of the role of soft power in the production of consciousness regarding state–corporate harms. That is, how do economic and political actors legitimate the harms that result from their actions, thus making *avoidable* harm appear as *necessary* harm?

Some years ago, I analysed the role of soft power in establishing a "business-friendly" regulatory climate in North Carolina, a climate that was the first step in a chain of events that eventually led to the death of 22 people in a fire at a chicken processing plant (Aulette and Michalowski 1993). This analysis suggested the importance of understanding how the construction of ideological frames that come to be accepted as the "rules of the game" serve to legitimate harm-producing exercises of power.

Analysts often conceptualize architectures of power in which different forms of power inhabit different social spaces; different floors of a building, if the imagined social design is hierarchical, or adjacent and connected buildings, if the vision is a more horizontal social edifice. Or, if one takes a Foucaldian approach, like the electrical or communications networks that keeps a building or a city linked into a common grid (Castells 2009). Whatever the preferred architecture, both hard and soft power are typically viewed as operating in one of three registers: economic power, political power or cultural power. In everyday life, however, the practice and experience of power *always occurs at the intersection of these different forms of power*. That is, "[t]he economic is always political. The political power is always economic [and] both economics and politics are always cultural" (Michalowski 2009: 305.) Thus, theories of power are most useful when they avoid assigning causal primacy to any one of these forces. Their relative impact will vary by time and locus. Sociological analyses of power should seek to identify the ways in which the registers of power intersect and magnify one another, as well as the ways in which, periodically, they also conflict with one another.

Addressing the debate over the causal importance of economic versus political organization, Michal Mann (2012b: 17) similarly agues "Advanced capitalist states are not political *rather than* economic phenomena: they are both, simultaneously." I would also add the inverse: Economic institutions are not economic *rather* than political, they are simultaneously both. Corporations and other economic institutions and practices are themselves political creations, licensed by the state, dependent on it for protection, and are frequently key political actors that shape the state and its production of cultural products (e.g. education curricula).

Mann (2012a) articulates what he terms an "IEMP model" of social power in which power takes four forms: ideological power, economic power, military power and political power. Collectively, according to Mann, these constitute the net of power in any society, although the specific role and particular location of each in this network vary in different configurations of human social order. My approach here is similar to and owes much to Mann's model. However, I approach social power as a three-part configuration consisting of economic power, political power and cultural power. I treat military power as a subset of political power insofar as military power is usually the expression of antecedent arrangements of political power, whether that power is manifest in a formal political state or some nonstate entity such as a revolutionary force.

Economic power is the ability to organize production, extract value and determine distribution of the resulting social product, thereby shaping the concentration or dispersal of that production.

Political power is the organization of rule making such that rules can be promulgated and enforced over some geographically dispersed population. Political power may be derived from relations of affinity, relations of authority or relations of force and includes the rule-making power of corporations as well as governments.

Cultural power is the organization of consciousness, including the creation of subjectivity, causal narratives of the past and predictive narratives of the future. Cultural power resides in its ability to create a consciousness that will act in accordance with that ideology.

In each of these cases power resides in the ability to *organize* the relevant resources. The more effective the organization, the more powerful the outcome (Mann 2012a).

Whenever we talk about corporations and corporate harm in the neoliberal SSA (or any SSA), we are talking about the organization of power within specific structures organized around the mandate to facilitate capital accumulation. For this reason, it is easy to imagine that the problem of corporate harm is primarily a problem arising from economic organization. However, if we consider the dynamics of new projects of enclosure and expulsions to accumulate capital in the neoliberal SSA, we can more readily see how these projects engage all three forms of power: economic, political and ideological.

## Enclosure, expulsions and the neoliberal SSA

The concept of a new enclosure movement and its conceptual twin, new patterns of expulsion, refers to the neoliberal project of transforming "the commons" into private property, with broad, socially transformative consequences

The new enclosure movement, however, is not a reconstruction of medieval history. The commons currently being enclosed are not the garden and grazing plots of medieval serfs (Ince 2014). Although one element of the "new enclosure movement" does, indeed, involve the expropriation of land and resources from their traditional beneficiaries, the contemporary enclosure movement is about much more than real estate. It involves the privatization of public goods once managed through welfare states, transforming them into new corporate revenue streams, the increased corporate penetration into spheres of once-private life, efforts to surround the digital commons with private property fences in order to monetize inter-space and a narrowing of the life-space for many living things as ecosystem assaults radically alter the biosphere as we know it.

Here, I want to consider three of these enclosures:

(1) *Spatial enclosure* is characterized by the large-scale resource acquisition by corporations seeking new inputs for capital accumulation. These enclosures most closely model earlier enclosure movements that displaced peoples from traditional access to property and other resources in order to create new and more concentrated sources of capital accumulation. New spatial

enclosures most often occur in less developed nations of the Global South or on Indigenous lands in the Global North, dispossessing traditional residents from their established ways of life. Typical mechanisms for new spatial enclosures are land grabs, water grabs and green grabs, that is, sequestering land for ostensible "conservation" purposes (Borras et al. 2011).

(2) *Political enclosure* is characterized by walling off of public spheres through the increased privatization of formerly state functions such as education, security and services. Citizens are essentially expelled from political spaces that previously enabled them to exert greater control over these formerly public spheres. Political enclosure includes and is fuelled by growing dominance of finance capital in political processes (Boyle 2003).

(3) *Biospheric enclosure* involves a reduction in the total space for biotic life. As the planet becomes increasingly shrouded by greenhouse gasses and poisoned in its air, land and water, the biospheric space that can support life shrinks. The consequence is an expulsion of ever-larger numbers of species and individuals from the biosphere, that is, as Sassen (2014) notes, they are expelled "from life itself."

These are not the only arenas of enclosure. Snider (forthcoming 2018), for example, examines how neoliberal practices have increased the institutional control of time.

## Power, networks and new enclosures

Figure 8.1 blends the four lines of inquiry– globalization, SSA, social power and new enclosure movements – by linking specific enclosures generated by the neoliberal SSA to specific forms of power essential to their operation. This array is meant to be illustrative rather than exhaustive of contemporary enclosures and expulsion. I offer it as a sensitizing, conceptual snapshot of the power dynamics inherent in neoliberal SSA's use of enclosures and expulsions as accumulative strategies and as a map toward future inquiry.

Space does not allow for a detailed discussion of the specifics of the individual cells in Figure 8.1. What I hope to convey with this array, however, is how new enclosures are embedded in multidirectional *networks of power*. For instance, land grabs have typically been analysed *primarily* as economic phenomena because they involve the corporate acquisition of access to large tracts of land to facilitate capital accumulation through agricultural production of food and/ or biofuels (Borras et. al. 2011). These acquisitions, however, depend on multiple intersecting forms of power. For sure, the corporations involved wield both persuasive and coercive economic power, often to gain *political* cooperation from host governments (Michalowski and Kramer 1987). However, as Cotula et al. (2009: 4) observe, although the private sector may be the dominant player, land grabs frequently require "support from government, and significant levels of government-owned investments." Land grabs both manipulate and sometimes struggle against the social and legal power embedded in traditional land

| | Enclosures/<br>Expulsions | | |
| --- | --- | --- | --- |
| | *Economic* | *Political* | *Ideological* |
| *Spatial*<br>Land grabs<br>Water grabs<br>Green grabs | FDI<br>Corruption<br>Financialization<br>Structural<br>   adjustment | Legal titles<br>Patents<br>Trade agreements<br>Tax incentives | Excess land<br>Capital shortfalls<br>Food/oil<br>   shortage<br>Title security<br>Green needs |
| *Public Sector*<br>Education<br>Welfare cuts<br>Deregulation | Campaign<br>   funding<br>Research<br>   funding<br>Think-tank<br>   funding<br>Corruption<br>Media influence | Privatization<br>Tax policies<br>Regulatory capture | Fiscal crisis<br>Deservedness<br>Efficiency<br>Free choice |
| *Biospheric*<br>GMO<br>Climate change<br>Species loss | Scientific<br>   agenda<br>   setting<br>Research/think<br>   tank/campaign<br>   funding<br>Corruption | Patent law<br>Funding/tax<br>   policies:<br>Roads vs. public<br>   transportation<br>Fossil fuel vs.<br>   alternatives<br>Pro-consumption | Food shortage<br>Fundamentalism:<br>   Dominion<br>Science<br>Denialism |

*Figure 8.1* New enclosure movements power dimension

tenure systems of target countries (Kabia 2014). The explosion in land grabbing that began in the early 2000s was facilitated by international political power manifest in neoliberal free trade agreements (Magdoff 2013). Land grabs also typically deploy the ideological power embedded in research claiming to show better, more "scientific" ways to increase yields and/or narratives that identify lands of traditional land users as "underutilized" (Schneider 2011).

My central point here is that enclosures and expulsions occur at specific intersections in complex grids of power. Given this, I suggest that analyses of crimes of power should always consider the network of power relations in which these harms are embedded, rather than focusing on any single dimension of it.

## Conclusion

As I noted at the beginning, the neoliberal SSA seems to be nearing its sell-by date. If we take the 1970s as an approximate starting point, we are now nearly 50 years into a cycle that lasts typically from 40 to 60 years. The present SSA peaked in 2008, just before the onset of the Great Recession, and has since been characterized by decay of efficacy, as indicated by the tepid recovery and the rising class conflict. This means, as David Kotz (2015) notes, "The crisis of neoliberal capitalism has made it vulnerable to replacement by something else."

The recent rise of nationalist and/or populist political trends in many of the nations of the Global North that initiated a worldwide neoliberal SSA may signal the beginning of what SSA theorists term a "period of exploration." Global capitalism integrated large portions of the world economy. In doing so, it intensified inequality and consequently alienated the disadvantaged in the Global North, while simultaneously immiserating some population sectors in the Global South while boosting others. We stand at a moment of multiple possible future trajectories. We may be returning to an era ruled by capitalist oligarchs similar to the Gilded Age, as Picketty (2014) contends. The rise of racist nationalism and anti-globalization populism in some developed nations may signal a return to a world constructed around competing national spheres of influence – the arrangement that sparked World War II. Or neonationalism may prove to be a temporary and unsuccessful attempt to find the "something else" that Kotz refers to. Perhaps, we will see a return to regulated capitalism. Or an increase in vicious, predatory capitalist practices that intensify the enclosures and expulsions. Or a long, slow slide into capitalist entropy as Streek (2014) predicts. Whatever pathways eventually emerge, however, the key changes will occur at the intersections of power that characterize the existing, increasingly troubled, neoliberal SSA.

## Notes

1  I would like to thank Dr. Susan Carlson and Dr. Nancy Wonders for helpful commentary on an earlier draft of this chapter.
2  Commodification of the commons frequently involves transforming formerly free indigenous knowledge into fungible property under patent authority (Mgbeoji 2006).
3  For detailed analyses of globalization from divergent perspectives see *inter alia*: Aguirre, Volker and Reese (2006), Dierks (2001), Friedman (2007), Harvey (2015), Kagarlitsky (1999), Robinson (2014), Sassen (1998), Stiglitz (2003).
4  See *inter alia:* Friedman (2012), Hartnett and Stengrim (2006), Iadicola (2008), Jha (2006), Kargalitzky (2003), Petras and Veltmeyer (2001), Picketty (2014), Rodrik (2012), Sassen (2006), and Stiglitz (2003).
5  There is some debate among SSA theorists whether neoliberal globalization constitutes a new SSA or is a new institutional structure that falls short of facilitating the level of accumulation associated with SSAs (McDonough 2010). In either case, however, it is clear that the configuration of power among capital, labor and states changed in fundamental ways beginning in the 1980s (Wolfson and Kotz 2010).
6  I exclude Nye's (2004) concept of "smart power," which some treat as a third "ideal type" of power, because as even Nye (2009) notes, it is essentially a combination of soft and hard power in which typical tools of hard power (e.g. the military) are sometimes used for "soft" purposes such as nation building, and soft tools, such as propaganda, are often used to support hard-power efforts to destroy opposition.

## References

Agnew, R. (2011) *Toward a Unified Criminology: Integrating Assumptions about Crime, People and Society*. New York: NYU Press.

Aguirre, A. Jr., Volker, E. and Reese, E. (2006) "Neoliberal Globalization, Urban Privatization, and Resistance." *Social Justice*, 33(3): 1–3.

Armitage, R. and Nye, D. (2007) *Commission on Smart Power: A Smarter, More Secure America*. Washington, DC: Center for Strategic and International Studies.

Aulette, J. and Michalowski, R. (1993) "Fire in Hamlet: A Case Study of a State-Corporate Crime," in K.D. Tunnell (ed.) *Political Crime in Contemporary America,* pp. 171–206. New York: Garland.

Bakker, K. (2010) *Privatizing Water: Governance Failure and the World's Urban Water Crisis*. Ithaca, NY: Cornell University Press.

Borras Jr., S., Hall, R., Scoones, I., White, B. and Wolford, W. (2011) "Towards a Better Understanding of Global Land Grabbing: An Editorial Introduction." *Journal of Peasant Studies*, 38(2): 209–216.

Boyer, R. (2010) "The Rise of CEO Pay and the Contemporary Social Structure of Accumulation," in McDonough, Reich and Kotz (eds.) *Contemporary Capitalism and its Crises*, 215–238. New York: Cambridge University Press.

Boyle, J. (2003) "The Second Enclosure Movement and the Construction of the Public Domain." *Law and Contemporary Problems*, 66: 33–74.

Braudel, F. (1992) *Civilization and Capitalism, 15th–18th Century, Vol. I* (Siân Reynold, Trans.) Berkeley, CA: University of California Press.

Burawoy, M. (2009) *The Extended Case Method: Four Countries, Four Decades, Four Great Transformations, and One Theoretical Tradition*. Berkeley: University of California Press.

Castells, M. (2009) *The Rise of the Network Society: The Information Age: Economy, Society, and Culture Volume I*. New York: Wiley-Blackwell.

Castree, N. (2010) "Neoliberalism and the Biophysical Environment: Theorising the Neoliberalisation of Nature." *Geography Compass*, 4(12): 1734–1746.

Cotula, L., Vermeulen, S., Leoarnar, R. and Keely, J. (2009) *Land Grab or Development Opportunity?* London: IIED/FAO/IFAD.

Dardot, P. and Laval, C. (2014) *The New Way of the World: On Neoliberal Society*. London: Verso.

Dierks, R.G. (2001) *Introduction to Globalization: Political and Economic Perspectives for the New Century*. Chicago: Burnham.

Evans, P. (June 2005) "The New Commons vs. The Second Enclosure Movement: Comments on an Emerging Agenda for Development Research." *Studies in Comparative International Development*, 40(2): 85–94.

Friedman, T. (2007) *The World Is Flat 3.0: A Brief History of the Twenty-first Century*. New York: Picador.

Friedman, T. (2012) *The Lexus and the Olive Tree: Understanding Globalization*. New York: Picador.

Gramsci, A. (1971) *Selections from the Prison Notebooks of Antonio Gramsci*. (Hoare and Smith, Trans.) London: Lawrence and Wishart.

Green, P. and Ward, T. (2004) *State Crime: Governments, Violence and Corruption*. London: Pluto Press. Green, P., Ward, T. and McConnachie, K. (2007) "Logging and Legality: Environmental Crime, Civil Society, and the State." *Social Justice*, 34 (2): 94–110.

Gordon, D. (1980) "Stages of Accumulation and Long Economic Cycles," in Terence K. Hopkins and Immanuel Wallerstein, eds., *Processes of the World System*. Beverly Hills: Sage, 9–45.

Gordon, D., Edwards, R. and Reich, M. (1982) *Segmented Work, Divided Workers: The Historical Transformation of Labor in the United States.* Cambridge: Cambridge University Press.

Gunder-Frank, A. (1978) *World Accumulation, 1492–1789.* New York: Monthly Review Press.

Hartnett, S. and Stengrim, L. (2006) *Globalization & Empire: The U.S. Invasion of Iraq, Free Markets, and the Twilight of Democracy.* Tuscaloosa, AB: University of Alabama Press.

Harvey, D. (2015) *Seventeen Contradictions and the End of Capitalism.* New York: Oxford.

Hassen, R.L. (2016) *Plutocrats United: Campaign Money, the Supreme Court, and the Distortion of American Elections.* New Haven: Yale University Press.

Hobswam, E. (1999) *Age of Extremes: The Short Twentieth Century 1914–1991.* London: Abacus.

Higgins, P. (2012) *Earth is Our Business: Changing the Rules of the Game.* London: Shepheard-Walwyn.

Iadicola, P. (2008) "Globalization and Empire." *International Journal of Social Inquiry*, 1(2): 3–36.

Ilcan, S. (2009) "Privatizing Responsibility: Public Sector Reform under Neoliberal Government." *Canadian Review of Sociology*, 46(3): 207–234.

Ince, U.O. (2014) "Primitive Accumulation, New Enclosures, and Global Land Grabs: A Theoretical Intervention." *Rural Sociology*, 79(1): 104–131.

Jessop, B. (1993) "Towards a Schumpeterian Workfare State? Preliminary Remarks on post-Fordist Political Economy." *Studies in Political Economy*, 40: 7–39.

Jha, P.S. (2006) *The Twilight of the Nation State: Globalization, Chaos and War.* London, England: Pluto Press.

Judis, J. (2001) *The Paradox of American Democracy: Elites, Special Interests, and the Betrayal of the Public Trust.* New York: Routledge.

Kabia, F. (2014) "Behind the Mirage in the Desert – Customary Land Rights and the Legal Framework of Land Grabs." *Cornell International Law Journal*, 47: 709–734.

Kagarlitsky, B. (1999) *New Realism, New Barbarism: Socialist Theory in the Era of Globalization.* London: Pluto Press.

Kahn, S. and Minnich, E. (2005) *The Fox in the Henhouse: How Privatization Threatens Democracy.* Oakland, CA: Berrett-Koehler Publishers.

Klitgaard, K. (2011) "Degrowth and the Social Structure of Accumulation." Proceedings of the New York State Economic Association, Vol. 4. Online: www.nyecon.net/nysea/publications/proceed/2011/Proceed_2011_p088.pdf May 2015.

Kondratieff, N. (1935) "The Long Waves in Economic Life." *Review of Economic Statistics*, 17(6): 105–115.

Kotz, D. (2015) "A Great Fall: The Origins and Crisis of Neoliberalism." *Dollars and Sense* (November/December). Online. Available HTTP: http://dollarsandsense.org/archives/2015/1115kotz.html.

――― (2015) *The Rise and Fall of Neoliberal Capitalism.* Boston: Harvard University Press.

Kotz, D. and McDonough, T. (2010) "Global Neoliberalism and the Contemporary Social Structure of Accumulation," in McDonough, Reigh and Kotz (eds.) *Contemporary Capitalism and its Crises*, pp. 93–120. New York: Cambridge.

Kotz, D., McDonough, T. and Reich, M. (1994) *Social Structures of Accumulation: The Political Economy of Growth and Crisis.* Cambridge: Cambridge University Press.

Kramer, R.C. (2012) "Carbon in the Atmosphere and Power in America: Climate Change as State-corporate Crime." *Journal of Crime and Justice*, 36(2): 1–18.

Lasslett, K. (2014) *State Crime on the Margins of Empire: Rio Tinto, the War on Bougainville and Resistance to Mining.* London: Pluto Press.

Linebaugh, P. (2014) *Stop, Thief!: The Commons, Enclosures, and Resistance.* Oakland, CA: PM Press

Livingston, J. (2010) "Primitive Disaccumulation?" Online. Available HTTP: https://politicsandletters.wordpress.com/2010/10/14/primitive-disaccumulation/.

Lynch, M. and Stretesky, P. (2012) *Exploring Green Criminology: Toward a Green Criminological Revolution.* New York: Routledge.

Magdoff, F. (2013) "Twenty-First-Century Land Grabs: Accumulation by Agricultural Dispossession." *Monthly Review,* 65(6). Online. Available HTTP: http://monthlyreview.org/2013/11/01/twenty-first-century-land-grabs/.

Mann, M. (2012a) *The Sources of Social Power Volume 1: A History of Power from the Beginning to AD 1760* (2nd ed.). New York: Cambridge University Press.

——— (2012b) *The Sources of Social Power Volume 4. Globalizations, 1945–2011.* New York: Cambridge University Press.

Marx, K. (1877/1977) *Capital: A Critique of Political Economy. Volume 1,* Chapter 27. Moscow: Progress Publishers.

——— (1977/1877) *Capital: A Critique of Political Economy. Volume 3,* Moscow: Progress Publishers.

Mayer, J. (2016) *Dark Money: The Hidden History of the Billionaires Behind the Rise of the Radical Right.* New York: Doubleday.

McDonough T., Reich, M. and Kotz, D.M. (2010) *Contemporary Capitalism and its Crises.* New York: Cambridge University Press.

Mgbeoji, I. (2006) *Global Biopiracy: Patents, Plants, and Indigenous Knowledge.* Ithaca, NY: Cornell University Press.

Michalowski, R. (1985) *Order, Law and Crime.* New York: Random House.

——— (2009) "Power, Crime and Criminology in the New Imperial Age." *Crime, Law and Social Change,* 54(3–4): 303–325. Michalowski, R. and Kramer, R. (Feb 1987) "The Space between Laws: The Problem of Corporate Crime in a Transnational Context." *Social Problems,* 34(1): 34–53.

——— (2006) *State-Corporate Crime: Wrongdoing at the Intersection of Business and Government.* New Brunswick: NJ: Rutgers University Press.

Nathan, D., Kelkar, G. and Walter, P. (eds.) (2004) *Globalization and Indigenous Peoples in Asia.* Thousand Oaks, CA: Sage.

Neeson, J.M. (1996) *Commoners: Common Right, Enclosure and Social Change in England, 1700–1820.* Cambridge, UK: Cambridge University Press.

Nye, Joseph. (2004) "Soft Power and American Foreign Policy." *Political Science Quarterly,* 119(2).

Nye, J. (2009) "Get Smart: Combining Hard and Soft Power." *Foreign Affairs* (July/August). Online. Available HTTP: www.foreignaffairs.com/articles/2009-07-01/get-smart.

Obinger, H., Schmitt, C. and Traub, S. (2016) *The Political Economy of Privatization in Rich Democracies.* New York: Oxford University Press.

Petras, J. and Veltmeyer, H. (2001) *Globalization Unmasked: Imperialism in the 21st Century.* London: Zed Books.

Picketty, T. (2014) *Capital in the 21st Century.* Cambridge, MA: Harvard University Press.

Potter, W. and Penniman, N. (2016) *Nation on the Take: How Big Money Corrupts Our Democracy and What We Can Do About It.* New York: Bloomsbury Press.

Ravitch, D. (2013) *Reign of Error: The Hoax of the Privatization Movement and the Danger to America's Public Schools.* New York: Knopf.

Robinson, W. (2014) *Global Capitalism and the Crisis of Humanity*. New York; London: Cambridge.

Rodrik, D. (2012) *The Globalization Paradox: Democracy and the Future of the World Economy*. New York: W.W. Norton.

Sassen, S. (1998) *Globalization and Its Discontents*. New York. The New Press.

——— (2006) *Territory, Authority, Rights: From Medieval to Global Assemblages*. Princeton, NJ: Princeton University Press.

——— (2009) "Beyond Party Politics: The New President and the Growth of Executive Power." *Dissent* (Winter). Online. Available HTTP: www.dissentmagazine.org/article/beyond-party-politics-the-new-president-and-the-growth-of-executive-power.

——— (2014) *Expulsions: Brutality and Complexity in the Global Economy*. Cambridge, MA: Harvard University Press.

Schneider, A.E. (2011) "What Shall We Do without Our Land? Land Grabs and Resistance in Rural Cambodia." Paper presented at the International Conference on Global Land Grabbing, 6–8 April 2011, Sussex, UK. Online. Available HTTP: www.iss.nl/fileadmin/ASSETS/iss/Documents/Conference_papers/LDPI/49_Alison_Schneider.pdf.

Shipley, T. (2016) "Enclosing the Commons in Honduras." *American Journal of Economics and Sociology*, 75(2): 456–487

Snider, L. (2018) "How Do I Discipline thee: Let Me Count the Ways . . . Or Tightening the Screws on the 99%," in Judy Fudge and Eric Tucker (eds.) *Law with Glass: Essays inspired by Harry Glasbeek*. Halifax: Fernwood, forthcoming.

Soederberg, S. (2014) *The Debtfare States and the Poverty Industry: Money, Discipline and the Surplus Population*. London: Routledge.

Stiglitz, J. (2003) *Globalization and Its Discontents*. New York: W.W. Norton & Company.

Tombs, S. (2012) "State-Corporate Symbiosis in the Production of Crime and Harm." *State Crime Journal*, 1(2): 170–195.

Weber, M. (1948) *From Max Weber: Essays in Sociology*, ed. H. Gerth and C.W. Mills, New York: Oxford University Press.

Willy, C. (2011) "The New Enclosure Movement: How Can We Verify Abuse?" Future Challenges. Online. Available HTTP: https://futurechallenges.org/local/ gesperspectives/the-new-enclosure-movement-how-can-we-verify-abuse/ (accessed 20 September 2015).

Wolfson, M. and Kotz, D. (2010) "A Reconceptualization of Social Structure of Accumulation Theory," in McDonough, Reich and Kotz (eds.) *Contemporary Capitalism and its Crises*, 72–92. New York: Cambridge University Press.

Yelling, J.A. (1977) *Common Field and Enclosure in England 1450–1850*. New York: Palgrave Macmillan.

# Section II

# Crimes of the powerful research

## Empirical dimensions

The nine chapters which constitute Section II collectively underscore the breadth, depth and extent of crimes of the powerful enabled by globalization. Kristian Lasslett uses *CotP* and Marx's *Capital* to theorize the link between structural conditions and agency, then applies these factors in a case study of the actions taken by executives of a mining company in Papua New Guinea, sponsoring war crimes when intractable local resistance clashed with capitalist profit-making imperatives. Liisa Lähteenmäki and Anne Alvesalo-Kuusi document that even in Finland, one of the few countries to pass and enforce corporate criminal liability laws, individuals rather than corporations are charged, fines are miniscule and blame is too often shifted to low-level employees. Thus power relations remain unchallenged while the illusion of equal justice is maintained. Gregg Barak analyses the apparent immunity from punishment enjoyed by global financial institutions and multinational corporations through a study of the worldwide rigging of interbank interest rates (the Libor scandal), showing how capitalist state apparatuses of social control increasingly privilege the interests of global capital over the welfare of global citizens. Elizabeth A. Bradshaw's study of resistance by environmental and indigenous activists to the construction of the Dakota Access (oil) Pipeline also focuses on complex and contradictory efforts by states – here the U.S. federal state – to uphold both capitalist accumulation/profit maximization imperatives *and* respect citizens' wishes (as well as its own rhetoric on climate change). In the end citizens won, but the victory was symbolic, short-term and quickly overturned by a new federal government. Meanwhile, Stéfanie Khoury looks at crimes of the powerful in Brazil, where the federal government has allied with agribusiness corporations (themselves allied with the dominant political class) to make Brazil a world leader in the production and use of agro-toxins – with dire effects on the health and wellbeing of the vast majority of Brazilians. Paul Leighton focuses on enablers of crimes of the powerful in the academic discipline of criminology, asking why scholars have ignored the massive, $550 billion annual theft perpetrated by employers on the employed. Scott Poynting uses Pearce's comments on the ways that deeper structures of systemic power are masked by the scandalization of corruption to illuminate how the case of former New South Wales government minister Eddie Obeid was subjected to a process of ideological mystification. In so doing, Poynting shows how the Obeid case was not an aberration, but an archetypal consequence of a neo-liberal political system that has routinized some forms of corruption. Ignasi Bernat's case study of mortgage lending concessions made by the Spanish state before and after the fiscal crisis of 2007–2008 locates crimes of the powerful within the financialization of the economy. The state then becomes an instrument to assist corporations to "squeeze yet more corporate profitability within the frame of the neoliberal turn." The final chapter in this section, by David O. Friedrichs, excoriates criminologists for ignoring the harms perpetrated by immensely powerful international financial institutions such as the World Bank and the International Monetary Fund, which privilege profits over safety, social and environmental standards and impose huge damage on the Global South through mandatory structural adjustment agreements.

Chapter 9

# Marx reloaded for the 21st century

## Capitalism, agency and the crimes of the powerful

*Kristian Lasslett*

Frank Pearce's *Crimes of the Powerful* enjoys pioneering status for a diverse range of compelling reasons (Pearce 1976), one of which is its serious engagement with Marxist theory both as a tool of critique in criminology and as a framework for understanding the drivers which lie behind the crimes of the powerful. Yet Pearce was writing this seminal contribution when Marx's ideas had reached a high point in their influence on the social sciences in Western academic institutions. In a few short years, post-modernism and post-structuralism would call into question "grand-narrative" theory, which has marginalized Marx's work.

Although for a period mainstream academic tendencies precipitated a turn away from Marx, Pearce's original intervention germinated a small but serious engagement with Marx's ideas within the crimes of the powerful scholarship. Indeed, in their 2002 paper, "Unmasking the Crimes of the Powerful," Tombs and Whyte observe:

> The labour theory of value and the theory of surplus value, the necessarily antagonistic relationship between classes, the inherent tendency of capitalism to expand, destructively, whilst at the same time reproducing the contradictions upon which it is founded, all seem to be crucial tools for understanding and engaging with the trajectories of the world.
>
> (2002: 222)

Two years later Green and Ward (2004) published the keystone text *State Crime*, which again points to the value of Marxist theory as a device for explaining elite deviance.

Since then Marx's works have enjoyed something of a revival. The 2008 global financial crisis saw his writings being quoted in the popular press, with approval, while sales of *Capital* are said to have soared. We have also witnessed adept popularizes of Marx's thought broaden this process of theoretical renewal – David Harvey, Slavoj Žižek and Yanis Varoufakis are notable examples. For those who believe in the enduring intellectual and emancipatory value of Marx, these vectors are to be welcomed, as fragile as they may be in practice.

Yet as Marx noted in the preface to *Capital*, "there is no royal road to science, and only those who do not dread the fatiguing climb of its steep paths have a chance of gaining its luminous summits" (1976: 104). The challenge that is now set for crimes of the powerful scholarship which aims to cultivate an expanded engagement with Marx is translating this broad appreciation of the latter's work into an active programme of research that appropriates in a critical and creative fashion the scientific canon Marx generated – in its entirety – applying it to fertilize understandings of state and corporate crime in its regionalized trajectories. This task, in part, demands a sensitive theoretical balancing act that uncovers the threads that connect objective conditions of existence with historical struggles and events powered by human agency.

In this respect Pearce notes:

> The social conditions under which men live determine the limits of their possible action. The nature of group identification and what are seen as the historical possibilities within these situations will affect the historical development of these societies. Those who treat the subjective views held by people in situations as if they are irrelevant epiphenomena are distorting Marxism.
>
> (1976: 55)

The following chapter aims to build on this important insight, looking in particular at how *Capital* can be interpreted not only as a critique of political economy, but an important contribution to theories of human agency and the latent criminogenic potentials which can be actualized by human beings acting under certain concrete conditions. To do this, a summary will be offered of the philosophical framework Marx developed to steer his critical engagement with political economy. This will establish a vantage point for framing *Capital* as a theoretical treatise that offers important insights into how identity, capacities, values and ideas emerge within human subjectivities, giving rise to the possibility of agency taking historical forms that drive the waste of life, ecosystems and wealth. To evidence *Capital*'s applicability to this micro level of analysis, examples will be drawn upon from the author's research into state and corporate crime in Papua New Guinea.

## The philosophical foundations of Marx's political economy

In the preface to *A Contribution to the Critique of Political Economy*, Marx remarked of his unpublished book – *The German Ideology* (Marx and Engels 1968) – which he co-authored with Engels, "we abandoned the manuscript to the gnawing criticism of the mice all the more willingly as we had achieved our main purpose – self-clarification" (1971: 22). *The German Ideology* was not the only intervention from this period that aided self-clarification. *The Poverty of Philosophy* (Marx 1978a), *The Economic and Philosophical Manuscripts of 1844* (Marx 1959) and *The Holy Family or Critique of Critical Critique* (Marx and Engels 1957) also stand out as texts where Marx laid the foundations for his future theoretical trajectory.

A close reading of these volumes reveals an emerging philosophical framework that reimagines ontology, epistemology and methodology in a way that is congruent with a materialist modality of dialectical thought. Critically, during this period of reflection and inquiry, Marx developed an understanding of human nature – a theory of being and self-actualization – that is critical to reading his later work, *Capital*. In the absence of this philosophical link, *Capital* remains a powerful treatise on the laws and tendencies of capitalism as an economic system, but once the link is made, it also becomes a vehicle for thinking about how humans value their world, connect and relate to each, develop capacities and identities and express different forms of social agency.

Owing to spatial limitations, only an elliptical presentation of Marx's philosophy is possible here. To that end, it ought first to be noted that one of the most fundamental features of existence pointed to in Marx's philosophical inquiry is captured by the category totality. That is, all matter, however complex or simple, cannot exist in an isolated, atomized form, even if this appears to be the case on the surface of things. From a dialectical position, atomization and isolation would negate the possibility of matter possessing any definition or characteristics, which is what distinguishes being from non-being. Accordingly, Marx argues that all matter exists within systems of relations, which give the constituting elements of a system their concrete features.

Applied to human society, it follows that one of the most elementary constituting parts of *social* systems, human beings, are in their infant form, potential in the state of becoming. It is only once this human potential is actualized within a particular system of social relationships that human beings develop concrete capacities, sensibilities and ideas, that is the substance of human agency. Mediating social relationships and self-actualization are practice and culture (Mikhailov 1980). Social systems generate productive, political and social practices, around which rich human cultures develop, which as whole allows technique and knowledge to be transferred to new generations. Out of this process of cultural transference and practical application, humans in a state of becoming develop concrete agency powers through which to make history.

But as is the case with Marx's thought, this ontological conception is laced with a contradiction. Although the human ability to actualize potential is *facilitated* through modalities of life activity that emerge out of historically evolving social relations, these relations can also place *limits* on how potential is actualized. To that end, Marx observes in *The Poverty of Philosophy*, "[i]n principle, a porter differs less from a philosopher than a mastiff from a greyhound. It is the division of labour which has set a gulf between them" (1978a: 120).

These social relationships can also amplify and supress different human capacities in uneven, historically distinct ways – creating contexts, for instance, where personal "greed" is so heightened, it appears a determining factor in precipitating economic crisis. Accordingly, from a philosophical and emancipatory perspective, making sense of these relationships and how they shape the historical actualization of human subjectivity becomes a core concern for Marx, which manifests in a twin track of political economy and political commentary that marked his intellectual career.

However, if we are to understand the social relationships which underwrite our agency powers, Marx argues, a process of methodological prioritization must take place. That is, although social reality exists as a totality, the human mind can only begin to appropriate this interconnected whole gradually and methodically. This process of gradual appropriation, Marx (1973) contends, must begin with the most elementary social relationships underpinning human communities before incrementally appropriating more complex relational sequences. To that end, he argues, it is the social relationships through which human beings produce the material substances essential to their sensuous existence, both essential (sustenance, shelter) and cultivated (enjoyment, culturally mediated consumption), that forms the elementary foundations of society. Theorization, therefore, must begin with these structures before contending with more complex political, cultural and legal relationships. The latter are not mere epiphenomena; they are also determinate forces that must be thought about. However, their concreteness cannot be fully unravelled without first appreciating the elementary processes they emerge out of.

In that light, *Capital* is a text which theorizes the elementary social relationships that underpin capitalist societies. However, it is also an attempt to think more richly about the historically developed social regimes that convert human potential into differentiated concrete subjectivities, that drive social contention, struggle and change. Reading *Capital* this way has important implications for how we apply Marx to crimes of the powerful scholarship. On that note, the broad contours of *Capital* will now be traced, before we then look at some concrete examples which demonstrate its capacity to inform analyses that link criminogenic events underpinned by contentious expressions of agency power to the broader structures of capitalist society.

## *Capital* and the crimes of the powerful

Marx's seminal theoretical work begins at the moment of production, which is primarily the focus of volume I. It then expands to consider economic circulation as a totality in volume II, before considering the mechanisms which condition how revenues are distributed, which is the subject of volume III. The latter two volumes were unfinished at the time of Marx's death, and further planned iterations, including one on the state system, had not been started.

If we turn first to volume I, Marx (1976) begins the work by theorizing the social relationships which give commodities – goods produced for market – of many different types a common substance that underpins their exchange value. To that end, he argues, the common substance is human labour time – that is, each commodity requires a certain exertion of human effort, which can be measured temporally. Marx observes "what exclusively determines the magnitude of the value of any article is therefore the amount of labour socially necessary, or the labour-time necessary for its production" (1976: 129). To this he adds "socially necessary labour-time is the labour-time required to produce any use-value under the conditions of production normal for a given society and with the average degree of skill and intensity of labour prevalent in that society" (Marx 1976: 129).

Having set out his labour theory of value, Marx then considers the hidden basis of the revenues enjoyed by different stratas of the bourgeoisie. To that end, he argues, the owners of labour power (i.e. workers) sell their capacity to generate value in exchange for wages. The difference between what the worker is paid in wages and the value they can produce in the contracted time constitutes the elementary basis of surplus value, which through a series of mechanisms eventually congeals in revenue forms accruing to the capitalist class. The rate of surplus value extraction can be increased in a variety of ways, Marx argues, such as extending the working day, decreasing wages or cheapening the price of labour through efficiency gains in the production of the means of consumption essential to labouring households.

If we now shift attention to volume II of *Capital*, here Marx (1978b) broadens his focus from the moment of production in order to think about how it forms part of a broader whole, which he labels the circuit of industrial capital. Any attempt to explain this circuit must be rooted in Marx's particular conception of capital. For Marx, the latter was a process, not a thing – although it, of course, assumes numerous phenomenal forms. From this vantage point, capital is congealed value, which is deployed in order to expand itself through the extraction of surplus value, which renders a result wherein the original value is retained and expanded upon through an augmentation provided by labour. To prosecute this valorizing journey capital must both assume, and then successfully transit from, a number of phenomenal forms.

A mass of value begins the circuit of industrial capital in the money form. It then must make the transition to productive capital. This demands that value successfully transforms, through market exchange, into labour power and means of production. Once labour power and the means of production have been unified in the production process, value can then make the next transition into commodity form. However, the latter should now be pregnant with a mass of surplus value provided gratis by labour. The total mass of value and surplus value congealed in the commodity form, if it is to complete the valorizing journey, must be brought to market and returned back into the money form. As a result, the circuit of industrial capital can then be renewed on growing scales.

Of course, important conclusions can be drawn from this valorizing journey. It points to the key role played by financial and merchant capital in organizing the conditions essential to industrial capital's valorization. Furthermore, innovations introduced by each sector can potentially expand the mass of surplus value extracted from labour through compressing circulation time and switching value rapidly into new profitable arenas of production. The circuit of industrial capital also draws attention to the ever-present potential within capitalism for crisis. Barriers which emerge that prevent value's effervescent transformation into different forms essential to its valorization can trigger periods of social paralysis, demanding radical interventions of a remedial or revolutionary nature.

Turning now to volume III, it ought first to be noted that Marx (1981) begins this iteration of *Capital* with an important theoretical observation that concretizes key insights developed in volume I. Critically, he points to social mechanisms which mediate the distribution of surplus value. Put simply, although surplus value is generated by living labour, it does not follow that sectors which employ large volumes of living labour accrue significant profits, whereas those industries where the ratio of labour to means of production is more modest realize less profit. To the contrary, Marx argues that surplus value is redistributed through mechanisms which create a tendency towards a general rate of profit, which is hooked to size of the total capital invested. As a result, Marx observes, the connection between labour and profit is obscured in the eyes of the capitalist, given that the means of production are seemingly as much a source of profit as is labour.

In volume III, Marx considers further mechanisms which inform how value/ surplus value become articulated at a granular level, in particular, revenue forms, including profit of enterprise, interest and ground rent. A key point to emphasize here is that the surplus value generated at the moment of production is sifted through a range of market-mediated mechanisms which can see it realized, for instance, in the form of interest, without the financier being aware of their revenue's debt to the exploitation of labour.

The presentation thus far is a broad sketch of what is an enormously complex and unfinished theoretical treatise. And it is one Marx developed, in part, to think more richly about the relationships that structure how human beings differentiate from abstract potential into heterogeneous concrete forms, with particular capacities, interests and sensibilities. This application of *Capital* is apparent from the text itself. In it Marx explicitly looks at the way in which concrete subjectivities emerging from this system of practice express their agency powers through activities that demonstrate an indifference towards human life and suffering (see Lasslett, Green and Stańczak 2015).

For example, in volume I Marx considers how an economic system which pivots on the extraction of surplus value, enforced through the disciplinary mechanism of competition, generates human beings who exhibit a greater loyalty to the extraction of labour time than to the guardianship of children. When examining the reaction of English manufacturers to proposals which would place a modest brake on the exploitation of child labour, Marx observes:

> Capital ... began a noisy and long-lasting agitation. This turned on the age-limit of the category of human beings who, under the name "children,"

were restricted to 8 hours of work and were subject to a certain amount of compulsory education. According to the anthropology of the capitalists, the age of childhood ended at 10, or, at the outside, 11. The nearer the deadline approached for the full implementation of the Factory Act, the fatal year 1836, the wilder became the rage of the mob of manufacturers.

(1976: 392)

To use another example, later in volume III, Marx reflects on the practical implications that flow from a general rate of profit. In short, individual capitalists can innovate and realize higher-than-average profits through "efficiency savings" obtained from the frugal handling of labour *or* means of production. This, Marx contends, has had a monstrous effect. Its reverberation within the personas of those managing capital has triggered calculations which count the squandering of human life and limb as an acceptable cost of heightened profit. The pathology engrained into industrial capitalists is emphasized by Marx when tracing the managerial resistance mounted to safety measures introduced by the Factory Act of 1844. He observes:

> The factory-owners of the time formed a 'trade union" to resist the factory legislation, the so-called "National Association for the Amendment of the Factory Laws," based in Manchester, which collected a sum of more than £50,000 in March 1855 from contributions on the basis of 2 shillings per horse-power, to meet the legal costs of members prosecuted by the factory inspectors and conduct their cases on behalf of the Association. The object was to prove "killing no murder" if done for the sake of profit.

(1981: 183)

Marx notes that in some cases the cost of introducing the requisite safety measures was cheaper than the association's fees, such was the demonstrated devotion of industrialists for protecting capital's freedom to expand at the cost of human life.

It is easy to frame these passages, of which there are many in *Capital*, as just empirical material for a theoretical thesis centring on productive relations. This is true in part. On the other hand, these passages are also theoretical, in as much that Marx is teasing out concretely the forms of brutalizing indifference that become expressed in the powers of human agency when subjectivities become articulated through practices emerging from capitalist social relations.

Of course, Marx's analysis in this respect was far from exhaustive. There remains ample scope to think in greater detail how the dynamic processes constitutive of capitalism foster historical forms of agency that promote arrangements and practices conducive to diverse social harms. In order to demonstrate this point, we will now turn to an exemplary case taken from the author's research in Papua New Guinea.

## The organic composition of capital and state–corporate crime

The exemplary case centres on a decade-long war (1988–1997) which took place on the island of Bougainville, an autonomous region which forms part of Papua New Guinea (see Lasslett 2014). At the heart of this conflict was contention over a copper and gold mine operated by the Rio Tinto subsidiary, Bougainville Copper Limited (BCL). When the war was sparked in 1988–1989 by rural resistance to the mining operation – articulated in a campaign of industrial sabotage – the mine was generating "36 per cent of export earnings, and 24 per cent of total government revenue" (Namaliu 1995: 61). The Papua New Guinea government responded to this campaign of industrial sabotage, perpetrated largely by customary landowners and disenfranchised local mine workers, by deploying paramilitary units, before calling out the defence force. Papua New Guinea's military attempted to quell local resistance through a sharp and focused campaign of state violence directed against rural communities in the mine area, which featured extra-judicial killings, village burnings, internment and torture (Amnesty International 1990). Local resistance, which had initially been prosecuted through protests and sabotage, rapidly transformed into an armed campaign prosecuted by the Bougainville Revolutionary Army. This laid the groundwork for a protracted struggle that is estimated to have taken as many as 20,000 lives.

The mine operator, BCL, has been lauded in the literature for its good corporate citizenship, which had been an explicit feature of the company's corporate culture since the 1960s (Dorney 2000; Oliver 1991). Indeed, during the life of the mine, BCL attempted to maintain good relationships with customary landowner communities through the provision of infrastructure, employment, investment in local entrepreneurship, public services and scholarships and by offering compensation rates above the legally mandated rate (Lasslett 2014). According, to BCL's Chairman (1971–1979) Frank Espie: "[c]ontrary to some impressions, the Chairman of a multinational company can be a responsible citizen . . . I am best able, in the long run, to ensure the return on my shareholders' investment by conducting our business in a way which satisfies local requirements" (King 1978: Appendix II).

Although this approach precipitated an inter-class bloc of workers, managers and business owners loyal to the mine, it failed to dilute a sizable mass of rural farmers and low-level mine workers, who resented the incision which the operation had made into their land, environment, culture and sovereignty (Iruinu 2015). When the latter's resistance escalated during 1988–1989 the company worked closely with the Papua New Guinea security forces. Indeed, BCL provided the military with a range of logistic assets, even though they were abreast of the human rights abuses being produced by the government's counter-insurgency campaign (Lasslett 2014). The collaboration was so close, BCL's (1989) the managing director pointed military command towards community leaders who should be targeted.

A critical question was triggered as these data emerged through investigative fieldwork. Specifically, why would a company which professed a long-standing commitment to good corporate citizenship abruptly shift tactics in this way? Theoretical guidance was drawn from an ontological reading of *Capital*. Critically, in volume I, Marx makes a distinction between variable capital and constant capital. The former constitutes the portion of industrial capital that has assumed the form of labour power, whereas the latter captures the portion absorbed within the means of production. By uniting with the means of production, living labour gradually transfers the value latent in the former into the commodity form, with an addition of surplus value provided by the worker.

In the mining sector, the ratio of variable to constant capital, which Marx calls the organic composition of capital, assumes a particularly lopsided form. A large-scale open cut mine in a remote location, such as the one operated by BCL, requires a significant expenditure of constant capital, which is gradually absorbed into the commodified mineral output through the application of labour power over a period measured in decades. Owing to this particular organic composition essential to the mining industry, a culture and professional repertoire can be found within corporate operators that places a strategic emphasis on securing a legal, tax and social governance regime that will endure in a predictable and calculable fashion for the mine's lifetime. BCL's chairman (1971–1979), Frank Espie, remarked during the mine's development, "there is no point in our starting an operation unless we are able to negotiate a reasonable and enduring agreement" (cited in King 1978: 100).

Critically, in this respect, mining capital requires states that are prepared to wield power in service of governing agreements. As one BCL executive noted, in a nod to the Indonesian government, a state whose record is a notably brutal one:

> It so happened on one trip I went to Indonesia, there was a couple of thousand illegal miners working up the creek, and they were going to start occupying our lease. So I went to the guys in Jakarta and said "we have a problem, we are going to build a mine for four or five hundred million bucks, and these guys are getting in the road." They said "it will take us three months but we will fix it." So they gave notice to these people that they had to be gone in three months, and they all were with a few exceptions, and the army moved the rest out.
>
> (BCL Official A 2006)

It is reasonable to conclude then that circulating industrial capital – of a particularly lopsided composition – grounded in a political system of nation-states generates within mining corporate practitioners an acute sensitivity towards any form of occurrence that may threaten the mine governance regime's durability, whether it be political turbulence or local resistance – a fact which was attested to by BCL's senior management in a consistent manner during interviews conducted by the author. One general manager remarked, "[W]ell if you have a shoe factory, and somebody wants you to go, you pack it up and move it. All you leave is the slab on the ground, you take the shed, you take the equipment, you take the market, you take the suppliers, everything else goes with you. But with a mine you can't do that" (BCL Official B 2006).

Accordingly, when protests, and then industrial sabotage, were employed by a mass social movement mobilizing against the mine, BCL management demonstrated a pathological commitment to the Bougainville Copper Agreement, the formal instrument which had governed the mining operation and buttressed by national legislation. Senior managers felt that any concession to a social movement which eschewed negotiating through invited forums stipulated in the agreement would set a precedent which would gradually erode its durability (BCL Official C 2006). In effect, to concede the possibility that communities might express sovereignty over the local political economy outside of the filter mechanisms "liberal" democratic regimes offer – which channel resistance into a prescribed range of outcomes – represented an existential danger in light of the particular way mining capital spatially agglomerates and economically accumulates. A decisive and swift response from the government's security forces was, in BCL's view, the only viable method for disciplining landowning communities in a way that ensured they internalized a respect for the socio-legal regime essential to mining capital's valorization. This would help fashion a context where contention outside a certain set of circumscribed avenues was not simply viewed as strategically undesirable by mine opponents, but rather such alternative paths for expressing landowner sovereignty would not be seen at all (i.e. a non-possibility).

Despite this political-strategic orientation, during interviews BCL managers professed and demonstrated profound personal connections with Bougainville, its culture and communities. Yet they suffered no visible cognitive dissonance when pressing home the sound rationale for the company's decision to adopt a hard-line approach when dealing with protesting communities. The primarily failure managers pointed to was on the Papua New Guinea government's part, who in their opinion did not act decisively, or with enough vigour, to abruptly curtail the resistance.

This points to the uneven ways in which positionality within a set of social relations can heighten some loyalties while diluting others. In this case, the loyalty corporate agents felt to alienated social processes – amplified by the disciplinary edifice of organizational frameworks that had emerged around the actors – exerted greater influence over their behaviour than personal values and sentiments at the centre of their expressed personhood. The theoretical challenge in this context is to treat subjectivity seriously as an active materially embedded process which affects the course of history, but at the same time, being careful to conceptualize the many concrete threads that link actualizing subjects to the relations they are immersed within.

In so doing, it is possible to better explain, for instance, the apparent paradox in BCL's shift from good corporate citizen to sponsor of war crimes.

Management's considerable investment in good corporate citizenship, and then subsequently, the military operations, were in fact different sides of the same coin. The former practice was designed to cement the mine regime's local durability by winning loyalty from influential local stakeholders. And it had enabled those actors who actualized their human potential through many years of service as company managers to build identities that were self-consciously connected to the host society and culture. Nevertheless, this happy marriage could only last for as long as latent class contradictions did not rupture into overt antagonism, for a crucial reason: BCL was administered by corporate managers whose careers had centred for decades on efficiently transiting value – impregnated with surplus value – from its productive form to its commodity form, in a context marked by a particular high ratio of constant to variable capital. Consequently, a professional culture and disposition had emerged – buttressed by organizational structures within the company – heavily focused on tenure and security.

Under the weight of this force, corporate managers expressed their agency power through means that demonstrated a preparedness to risk the safety of landowner communities in order to both preserve the existing sums of value embedded in the mine and to secure future operating conditions essential to profitability. Personal loyalties to communities and local cultures, which had been fed to an extent by the company's corporate social responsibility, proved impotent.

## Conclusion

Back in 1976, Pearce warned against deterministic applications of Marxism, which ignore the crucial role played by human agency. For contemporary crimes of the powerful scholarship, this warning remains of enduring importance. If we are to move beyond explanations that focus on the immediate set of acts and processes which underpin particular criminal events, we must build methods that help us to better understand the dialectical relationship between the immediate facts and a deeper social ontology that underpins human communities.

This chapter contends that Marx developed a philosophical standpoint that, with clarity, traces the mediated relationship between historically developed social relationships underpinning human societies and the specific way human potential actualizes into concrete forms of agency, exhibiting particular capacities, interests, values, sensibilities and ideas. Accordingly, in *Capital* Marx makes a conscious effort to link the sets of social practices emerging from capitalist productive relations to certain expressions of agency, which have exhibited a notable indifference to human suffering.

It follows then that a post-capitalist project which wishes to end these heightened forms of inhumanity must be driven by strategies that consciously confront the ontological reality of social being by taking seriously the connection between self-actualization, agency powers, social practice, productive relations and historical change. Such a project and movement, in short, must harness the history-making powers which humans enjoy to bring about social relationships and associated forms of life activity that can actualize historical forms of agency that endow human beings with an acute sense of loyalty and connection to other human beings on a global scale, and the natural world we are fundamentally tied to, from which a more ethical culture can flourish. The reform of capitalism is merely a palliative option. Capitalism's transcendence, if we are to take Marx's social ontology and political economy seriously, is the only sustainable method for countering the predatory and inhumane practices our current mode of production systemically generates.

## References

Amnesty International. (1990) *Papua New Guinea: Human Rights Violations on Bougainville 1989–1990*. London: Amnesty International Secretariat.

Bougainville Copper Limited. (1989) Meeting Minutes, 13 July.

Bougainville Copper Limited Official A. (2006) Personal Communication, 13 September.

Bougainville Copper Limited Official B. (2006) Personal Communication, 26 October.

Bougainville Copper Limited Official C. (2006) Personal Communication, June 7.

Dorney, S. (2000) *Papua New Guinea: People, Politics and History Since 1975*. Sydney: ABC Books.

Green, P. and Ward, T. (2004) *State Crime: Governments, Violence and Corruption*. London: Pluto Press.

Iruinu, B. (2015) Personal Communication, 5 August.

King, H.F. (1978) *The Discovery and Development of the Bougainville Copper Deposit*. Melbourne: Conzinc Riotinto of Australia.

Lasslett, K. (2014) *State Crime on the Margins of Empire*. London: Pluto Books.

Lassett, K. Green, P. and Stańczak, D. (2015) "The Barbarism of Indifference: Sabotage, Resistance and State–Corporate Crime." *Theoretical Criminology*, 19(4), 514–533.

Marx, K. (1959) *Economic and Philosophical Manuscripts of 1844*. Moscow: Progress Publishers.

———— (1971) *A Contribution to the Critique of Political Economy*. London: Lawrence & Wishart.

———— (1973) *Grundrisse: Foundations of the Critique of Political Economy*. Middlesex: Penguin Books Ltd.

———— (1976) *Capital*, Vol. 1. Middlesex: Penguin Books Ltd.

———— (1978a) *The Poverty of Philosophy*. Moscow: Progress Publishers.

———— (1978b) *Capital*, Vol. 2. Middlesex: Penguin Books Ltd.

———— (1981) *Capital*, Vol. 3, Middlesex: Penguin Books Ltd.

Marx, K, and Engels, F. (1957) *The Holy Family or Critique of Critical Critique*. London: Lawrence and Wishart.

———— (1968) *The German Ideology*. Moscow: Progress Publishers.

Mikhailov, F. (1980) *The Riddle of the Self*. Moscow: Progress Publishers.

Namaliu, R. (1995) "Politics, Business and the State in Papua New Guinea." *Pacific Economic Bulletin*, 10(2): 61–65.

Oliver, D. (1991) *Black Islanders: A Personal Perspective of Bougainville 1937–1991*. Melbourne: Hyland House Publishing.

Tombs, S. and Whyte, D. (2002) "Unmasking the Crimes of the Powerful." *Critical Criminology*, 11(3): 217–236.

# Chapter 10

# The imaginary social order of corporate criminal liability[1]

*Liisa Lähteenmäki and Anne Alvesalo-Kuusi*

In 1976, Frank Pearce argued that state involvement in crime control is not determined by considerations of legality or illegality. Instead, he claimed, the criterion for igniting the state's repressive apparatus is the extent to which the actions and persons defined as harmful undermine the prevailing social order. In capitalist societies, the social order – the way of life the ruling class considers appropriate for members of society, one that is compatible with the ideology of private wealth accumulation – is maintained via law and institutional communication (Pearce 1976: 66). Pearce's notions of a real and an imaginary social order are essential here. According to Pearce, an imaginary social order is an illusionary description of a society in which the actual material realities of life underlying capitalism – inequality, the indifference shown to the sufferings of the working class and the limited attention paid to their health and welfare compared to the protection afforded the ruling class and its possessions – are obscured (Pearce 1976: 67).

Despite the persistence of the simulated order, laws aimed at punishing corporations are sometimes nonetheless passed, and powerful corporations are indeed prosecuted, as Pearce and others (e.g. Alvesalo-Kuusi and Lähteenmäki 2016; Bittle 2012; Tombs 2013) have demonstrated. These sporadic acts of criminalization and prosecution are, however, nothing but a spectacle, which ultimately serves the needs of the state and powerful corporations to strengthen the imaginary social order by the "occasional punishment of the powerful" (Pearce 1976: 93). This chapter will contribute to the analysis of this reproduction of the imaginary social order by demonstrating, through empirical data, how this spectacle is used to obscure the real social order.

The goal of this chapter is to scrutinize the crimes of the powerful in today's Finland, focusing on occupational safety crimes, which we define as crimes committed by an employer or a representative thereof that violate Finnish safety at work legislation. For our purposes, Pearce's observations regarding the dominant individualistic ideology, that is, the prevailing beliefs and practices surrounding the understanding of the "criminal" whose criminality is believed to be caused by his or her inadequacies (Pearce 1976: 77–82), are particularly important. We argue that even though the Finnish state did react to the crimes of the powerful by enacting corporate criminal liability (CCL) legislation, and despite the law being enforced to some extent, the overall picture – that harmful corporate action is effectively disciplined via the criminal justice system – is flawed and has served to dramatize the imaginary social order which is based on the idea of crime being committed by individuals only.

Aiming to answer Frank Pearce's call to reveal the imaginary social order, throughout this chapter we revisit the empirical findings of our recent "Corporate Criminal Liability in Finland" research project. In our study, we first scrutinized the 22-year-long formulation of CCL legislation in Finland by examining legislative documents. In addition, we investigated the concrete enforcement of CCL and analysed, both qualitatively and quantitatively, 154 occupational safety crime cases, in which 161 corporations were sentenced to pay a corporate fine (see Alvesalo-Kuusi and Lähteenmäki 2016; Lähteenmäki et al. 2016). Our study revealed that the law, the legal decisions and their reasoning and the regulation and punishment of serious corporate malpractice are all a mere spectacle.

The chapter begins with the story of the legislative process and continues by addressing the court data. Finally, we discuss the relevance of our findings in revealing the reinforcement of the imaginary social order and contemplate their relevance for making change in the "real" social order.

## The long road to a vitiated CCL

In recent decades, many democratic nations have advanced their means to curb the crimes of the powerful through either administrative or criminal law (e.g. Almond 2013; Bittle 2012; Mongillo 2012). In the wake of European Union membership, and following other Western countries, Finland imposed CCL in 1995. For the first time, after 22 years of contemplation, the Finnish state signalled a structural readiness to target powerful corporations with criminal law (cf. Alvesalo and Whyte 2007).

When discussions on CCL legislation were first initiated in Finland during the 1970s, social matters such as environmental and occupational safety issues were considered to be especially in need of legal protection. In addition, throughout the years of Finland's contemplation of this issue, the country's political wind blew from the left, and the labour movement and other civic non-governmental organizations (NGOs) were active in initiating law-making processes. The left-wing social democratic party, SDP, and the Centre Party, of rural origin, took the majority in the Finnish Cabinet (see Alvesalo-Kuusi and Lähteenmäki 2016).

The legislative process to impose CCL in Finland was far from expeditious. As the law aimed to bring powerful corporate actors to justice, resistance against this was resilient and influential. The employers' lobby judged the legislative proposals as "anti-employer" and as *criminalization of entrepreneurship.*" In their comments on the proposals, the employers – backed by the legal profession – strongly promoted an understanding that the definition of crime "*cannot include economic activity.*" "*Criminal sanctions should be aimed at real criminals,*" demanded the lobby, emphasizing the divide between "real (individual) criminals" and business actions that were presented as, first and foremost, benevolent and advantageous. Furthermore, the lobby declared that it was "*unnecessary*" to punish corporations, as individuals were already liable for crimes committed through the operations of a corporation. The lobby also declared that the legislator's main argument for enacting CCL – to emphasize the liability of the corporation, not merely those in subordinate positions, by "*placing liability where it belongs*" – was essentially "*flawed legislative reasoning,*" as it bypassed the central and immutable criminal law principle of *mens rea* – the guilty mind. For the legal profession, CCL represented a step back in time for the same reason: discarding individual accountability for a model that emphasized collective responsibility would also, according to the jurists, result in moral corrosion.

Under heavy lobbying and a declining economy, the right-wing government elected in 1991 ended up proposing CCL legislation with only discretionary sentencing. This meant that it was up to the courts to decide, on a case-by-case basis, whether to sentence a prosecuted corporation. According to the government, the discretionary system made it possible "*to avoid unnecessary and costly processes.*" Besides, CCL was only intended to be used on a few "*serious crimes,*" further stressing the steadfastness of individual guilt.

This law, and discretionary sentencing in particular, was even criticized by the legal profession, as it formed a stark exception in the Finnish legislation. The enacted law nevertheless stipulated that "a legal entity *may be sentenced* to a corporate fine in a case in which a person or persons, acting on behalf of, or for the corporation, commits a crime or an omission" (Penal Code 1995, Section 9:2). The rule of *mens rea* was further emphasized by an explicit formulation: "*Corporations do not, in the same sense as natural persons, commit crimes*" (Bill 95/1993: 16).

Corporations thus avoided the label of criminal, as the law was based on the idea of corporate liability on the behaviour of individual perpetrators: corporations could be punished but were not established as guilty, as they were not regarded as having the intentional mind needed to commit crimes. Moreover, only a handful of offences were covered by the purview of CCL – mainly offences against the capitalist order, such as bribery, insider trading and industrial espionage. A major exception was environmental crimes. Safety crimes, in contrast, did not come under the scope of CCL, as their inclusion, according to the government, "*would have sent an incorrect message to business*" (see Alvesalo-Kuusi and Lähteenmäki 2016).

Although the process and the debate ultimately resulted in the possibility to punish corporations, the law was seldom enforced. During 1995–2000, the prosecuting authorities made only nine CCL claims and only five prosecutions were successful (mainly financial crimes). At the same time, sentencing individuals for safety crimes – mainly middle management – continued as usual. The formulation of the CCL law itself, its compulsive fixation with individual liability and guilt and the special discretionary sentencing system accorded to the corporations, acted as disincentives to its enforcement. The law thus created a spectacle that on the outside communicated the state's interest in the crimes of the powerful, but in reality silenced the fact that the corporations were unlikely to ever be punished.

Discretionary sentencing was finally removed from the law in 2003. At the same time, occupational safety crimes were added to its scope. This amendment took place under a left-wing cabinet. Today, the majority of the approximately 40 yearly corporate fine sentences are imposed for occupational safety crimes. However, only a few corporations are ever convicted, and even when they are, the punishments tend to be very lenient, as we demonstrate in the next section.

## An empirical enquiry into the CCL in (non)action

With regard to all criminal offences in Finland, punishment is aimed at individuals about 58,000 times a year, whereas corporations are punished approximately 40 times. In cases of occupational safety crimes, the majority of sentences are directed at individuals, whereas corporations are only sentenced in every fourth case (OSF 2017; Niemi 2016: 5). However, 90% of all corporate fine sentences are imposed for occupational safety crimes. In order to scrutinize the reality of punishing corporate offences, we analysed every judicial decision concerning a safety crime and involving a corporate fine, from each district court, court of appeal and the Supreme Court in Finland during 2010–2014. The number of cases was 154 and the number of corporations fined was 161.[2] In Finland, CCL is executed as a corporate fine, which is a lump-sum fine, varying between 850 and 850,000 euros.

During 2010–2014, the average corporate fine for a safety crime was 10,700 euros, the most frequently imposed fine being 5,000 euros and the single highest fine being 180,000 euros. Looking at the punished corporations, we found that 54% had a net yearly revenue of over 10 million euros at the time of sentencing, and only 13% were generating long-term losses. An analysis of the companies making a profit revealed that the fine usually constituted *less than 0.1% of their annual profit*, the most lenient case being 0.0015%. In addition to 161 corporations, 288 individuals were convicted in the cases under scrutiny: 26% of the convicted individuals were top managers, 38% middle managers and 33% supervisors. The average fine imposed on an individual was 27 day-fines[3] (approximately 1,170 euros), which equals 2.7% of an average Finn's annual salary.

In the cases under scrutiny, a total of 131 people were injured and 12 were killed. The most common injuries were fractures or amputations of limbs or digits. The omissions leading to injury most often included a lack of supervision over work methods and a lack of training at the worksite. In 20% of the convicted corporations, another industrial accident or near-miss situation had already occurred before the incident leading to the conviction in our data.

We will now take a closer look at the court decisions. In the course of our analysis, we observed three ways in which the reactions of the criminal justice system contributed to maintaining the imaginary social order: the silencing of repeat corporate offending, the simulated severity of corporate punishments and the blaming of the victim by stressing individual choice and liability.

## Silencing corporate recidivism

Our data include eight companies were convicted more than once during the five-year period under scrutiny. Four of these companies were fined as often as three to four times, and the remaining four were fined twice.

According to the Finnish Penal Code (6:5:5), repeat offending constitutes grounds for increasing the punishment if the criminal history of the offender, the relation between the previous and the new offence or the similarity between the offences shows that the offender is clearly heedless of the prohibitions and commands of the law.[4] Generally, when sentencing individuals for "traditional" crimes, recidivism is the most prevalent reason for increasing the punishment (Lappi-Seppälä and Niemi 2012: 365).

To obtain a detailed picture[5] of how the courts take corporate recidivism into account, we did a comparison of each company's two consecutive sentences. When analysing the amount of the fines in these pairs, we saw that in most cases, the latter sentence was no stricter than the former. In six of the cases, the fine was the same or even smaller than that in the former sentence. Only in two cases was the corporate fine higher in the latter sentence.

What is of importance here is that repeat offending was not taken into account by the courts when they decided on the amount of the fine, or in the description of the events. Rather, the courts more often reasoned that negligence was *"an isolated event that did not express general disregard for safety regulations."* Consequently, they did not consider the offence particularly blameworthy, but instead stressed other legally binding responsibilities as a testimony of corporate respectability and due solicitude for occupational safety.

For instance, in a case in 2014, in which an employee was severely injured with broken ribs resulting in a six-week medical leave, a consolidated corporation was sentenced in the Court of Appeal. In its decision, the court pointed out *"that the omission, in its entirety, is not a minor one."* Nevertheless, it also stressed that the corporation had invested in safety measures and had, *after the accident,* launched a special campaign to promote safety. Furthermore, the court emphasized that the case involved a subcontracting company that had also neglected its responsibilities. The court reduced the corporate fine from the original district court decision of 60,000 euros to 20,000 euros. A further reason for reducing the fine, explained the court, was the fact that the victim had previously worked on the same site in similar tasks, stressing the responsibility of the victim. The decision did not mention that the consolidated corporation had been convicted of a safety crime twice before in 2010 and once in 2014.

Another repeat offender, a consolidated corporation that had been sentenced earlier for both a safety crime and for violating anti-trust regulations, was given an 8,000-euro corporate fine in a case in which an employee was injured after falling, resulting in permanent brain damage. The court, in contemplating the amount of the fine, pointed out the safety training that the corporation had provided its employees, and that the *"employer had specifically obligated the employees"* to repost all the safety defects they encountered. The corporation had thus *"strived to minimize the safety hazards."* According to the court, the corporation had not been negligent. The fact that the corporation had partially taken into consideration what the law stipulated was acknowledged in the decision as a sign of due diligence (c.f. Bittle and Snider 2011: 381). Similar accounts of corporate compliance were given on several occasions to justify the reduction of the fines, whereas in the main, the courts kept quiet about the corporations' previous and similar offences.

The only cases in which the earlier sentences of a given corporation were even mentioned in the decisions made were those concerning two companies that were both sentenced to a corporate fine twice during the same year, and a company that was fined twice during a period of two years. Nevertheless, for the first two companies, the corporate fine was less than the mean of all corporate fines (10,700 euros). The district court simply stated in its decisions that *"an identical accident took place in the operations of the company only somewhat earlier and the district court has taken this into account in measuring the fine."* The first company was fined 6,000 euros on both occasions and the second 8,000 euros. The third company was first fined 5,000 euros in 2012, and then 15,000 euros in 2014. In this case, the court stated in its latter decision that *"both the length of the omission and the fact that the corporation had a previous sentence of having serious safety shortages, justifies a substantial corporate fine."* In this case, substantial meant 8.7% of the company's one-year profit. All in all, this was the only ruling in which the significance of repeat corporate offending was explicitly acknowledged, even though corporate fine sentences are registered at the Finnish Legal Register Centre, stay in the register for five years and are always available for the courts to check while deliberating over punishment.

### Punishing the shop floor (but not those in power)

The Finnish Penal Code (9:2) states that a corporation is sentenced to a corporate fine if a person who is part of its statutory organ or other management, or who exercises actual decision-making authority, has been an accomplice in an offence, allowed to commit the offence, or if the care and due diligence necessary to prevent the offence have not been observed in the operations of the corporation. The law thus bases the idea of punishing corporations on the wrongdoings of the management, stressing that culpability and liability lie where the actual decisions are made. This was the essential thrust behind corporate criminal legislation in the first place, as well as for criminalizing work safety omissions altogether. Despite this initial idea of "placing liability where it belongs," only 26% of the sentenced individuals represented top management; that is, management with actual decision-making authority. The individuals who bore the burden were mainly middle and low-level managers (71% of the sentenced individuals).

When analysing the court decisions, we found that a general rule seemed to prevail that the courts applied to direct liability onto the lower levels of the hierarchy (see Saloheimo 2003). According to the courts, top management was not responsible for day-to-day operations but rather "*for economic or tangible prerequisites and organizational preconditions*," which included, for example, the recruitment of qualified lower-level managers. Further, middle management was described as "*taking care of drawing up safety regulations and making suggestions regarding safety equipment*." Supervisory-level management was then "*in charge of supervising safety and safety instruction*." In most cases, the omissions were described as "*neglecting the supervision and instruction of the employees*". The rule thus placed liability at the middle or supervisory level.

One of the most telling examples of placing the blame on low-level managers was a case in which an employee was exposed to toxic chemicals over a long period and developed a toxic cerebral disease. The middle manager who was prosecuted testified in court that from the very beginning of his employment, he had tried in several ways to develop safety practices and search for appropriate protection against the chemicals used in the victim's work. The court stated clearly in its decision that even though the middle manager had tried to resolve the safety shortages, the corporation had underestimated and belittled the dangers of various toxic solvents. This attitude reflected, according to the court, "*a general disregard for safety*," which had continued for over a decade. However, despite this, the middle manager was sentenced, whereas top management was not even prosecuted. The corporation was also fined. So although the law depicts an imaginary social order in which those with power bear the responsibility and are disciplined, in reality, it is those in subordinate positions who are focused upon, found guilty and punished. Top management sits behind the corporate veil (c.f. Tombs and Whyte 2015) and is seldom punished directly.

Finally, we also found that the weight of the burden of fines was much heavier on the shop floor level than at the corporate level. Although the corporate fine is a lump-sum fine, to compare the individuals' sentences to those of the corporations, we recalculated the corporate fines in terms of day-fines. On average, the mean corporate fine was 10,700 euros, whereas the mean annual result of the corporations was 10.1 million euros. Using the day-fine formula, we calculated that with a 10.1 million "income," a one day-fine should be approximately 14,000 euros. This means that corporations paid only 0.76 day-fines compared to individuals' 27 day-fines. Hence, for the individuals, the fine was, on average, 35 times higher than that of the corporations. If the corporations had borne the same responsibility as the individuals, the mean corporate fine should have been as high as 379,000 euros.

## Blaming the victim (and obscuring dubious corporate culture)

Our final observation regarding the imaginary social order deals with blaming the victim. Finnish legal commentaries have confirmed the main principle that the contributory role of the victim should *not* be taken into account when deciding on culpability, on whether a safety crime has been committed by the employer's representative or on whether the corporation should be punished (e.g. Nuutila 2006: 151). The behaviour of the victim should be taken into consideration only if the actions of the victim/employee have been *unpredictable and unforeseen*. In addition, only if the victim's contribution to the events is *exceptional* can it be taken into account as a mitigating factor when punishment, such as a corporate fine, is decided on (Penal Code 6:6:2).

All in all, in 88 cases (57%), the defence representatives stressed the victim's responsibility in the occurrence of the incident. In 18 cases, the court also stated that the victim had played some form of contributory role in the incident. While contemplating the amount of the corporate fine, the court explicitly mentioned the victim's contribution as a mitigating factor in five cases.

Our analysis of all 18 cases in which the court at least mentioned the victim's contribution revealed that the mean corporate fine was 7,047 euros, thus below the mean of all the cases (10,700 euros). It thus seems that regardless of whether the court explicitly considered the victim's contribution a mitigating factor, it reduced the amount of the fine, contrary to the established interpretation of the law.

Blaming the victim is not surprising when this is done by an accused corporation. It is historically common for corporate representatives to refer to an accident-prone and reckless worker (c.f. Tombs 1991; Tombs and Whyte 2007). In our data, corporate agents often defended themselves by claiming to "*not know*" of the actual methods and actions that the employees performed in their daily operations, because workers may "improvise" in their practices. However, they also referred to the extensive experience and proficiency of the employees, claiming that it was the employees who did not want supervision or guidance. It is indicative of the real social order that the courts stress the role of the victim even when the description of the events, verified in the judicial decision, tell a story of collective arrangements – accepted by the employer – that are upheld primarily to save time; that is, money. Unlawful ways of speeding up production are often also encouraged by the fact that the employee's salary may depend on production.

In several cases, senior employees had taught unlawful and dangerous working methods and procedures to the newcomers, namely to be able to work more "efficiently." In some cases, the unlawful ways of working were selected and maintained because of strict timetables dictated by the management, which,

# The imaginary social order    139

if not achieved, would mean extra costs for the corporation. These facts were candidly told in the testimonies. Nevertheless, the court in these 18 cases turned a blind eye to this dubious corporate culture and stressed instead the actions of individuals.

The common denominator in the five cases in which the victim's actions explicitly affected the fine was the saving of time. For example, in a case in which three people – two mid-level managers and one foreman – and the company were fined, safety rules had been ignored for a very long time. The court stated that the unlawful work method had become *a common habit*, applied by several employees. This habit involved operating a lamination machine without protective devices and cleaning it without turning off the machine. This, according to the employees, was easier and quicker. One of the employees described the situation as a treadwheel, implying that there was no other option if you wanted to keep up with production. The management had formally forbidden the procedure, but was nevertheless aware that it was "normal practice." According to the documents, the injured worker "*knew it was forbidden,*" as he was previously instructed by a colleague "*not to do it as I do it.*" The court stated that the contribution of the victim had played a part in the incident, because "*he had knowingly acted*" against safety instructions. The company was fined 5,000 euros, but the court stated that in deciding on the fine it had considered the mitigating circumstances (the victim's actions) and the good economic standing of the company, a factor which usually would, according to the law, increase the fine.

The law governing occupational safety (OSH Act 2:8; 41:2) clearly states that employers shall design and choose the measures necessary for improving working conditions and put them into practice by adopting *safety measures that have general impact before individual measures.* Access to the danger zones of machinery or work equipment should be restricted *by means of their construction, placement, guards or safety devices, or by other suitable means.* Judicial decisions also stress that guidance, warnings or instructions alone cannot replace technical and general safety measures (see also Hahto 2004: 329) and that it is the employers' responsibility to *constantly monitor* that, for example, safety guards are actually used.

Nevertheless, in cases in which the contributory role of the employee is acknowledged, it is mainly the actions or "human error" of the employee that "causes" or "results in" the injury. It is the employee who "*takes risks,*" "*acts negligently*" or "*uses methods that are forbidden.*" In describing the actions of the employees, the courts use wording that conveys the impression that the employees *choose* to act against the regulations. Individual managers are pictured as failing to ensure safety, but the corporations, even when found not to have taken the care necessary for the prevention of the offence, are most often described as "*striving to attend to safety matters*" or "*generally law-abiding*" and that offences are found to be "*one-off exceptions.*" Corporations did not "*knowingly*" commit unlawful actions. Even when proven as neglecting the law, the omissions were minimized, as the judicial documents revealed that safety omissions were regularly of a long-term nature. The average duration of the crime (in cases in which duration was reported, N = 90) was as long as 525 days. In several judicial decisions, the court had nevertheless reported the duration of the crime as the date of the incident, even when the testimonies made it clear that the omission had continued "for decades." Moreover, lengthy omissions did not result in higher fines either (see Lähteenmäki et al. 2016).

## Conclusion

The developments described here present the ongoing reproduction of an imaginary social order witnessed in many contemporary societies. Repeatedly looking for the individual "real criminal" instead of structural violence and institutional law breaking has a double effect, as the law holds on to the principle of *mens rea* while the courts effectively obscure problematic corporate cultures. The law and its enforcement thus effectively work to ignore both the actual decision making in safety matters as well as the social reality of the employees who are not, ultimately, immune to social and economic pressures, and are seldom able to choose the circumstances under which they work.

We argue that the legislative process itself represented a spectacle, only cosmetically changing the social order of criminal liability: the Finnish state enacted a law that declared a readiness to punish corporations in the same way as individuals. However, when the law was being made, powerful employers and lawyer lobbies succeeded in blocking the opportunity to critically examine the very foundations of law making and criminal law. The fact that the law excluded the workings of corporations from the ontology of the crime and based corporate liability on the actions of individuals was discussed as a moral issue, not as an issue of (in)justice. Corporations' essential complexity and lawful capability to shift liabilities was thus left unchallenged, while the law was celebrated in the bill as "placing liability where it belongs."

On the level of enforcement, the Finnish CCL essentially maintains the imaginary social order in three ways. First, the discourses in court documents contribute to the "responsibilization" of individuals rather than of powerful corporations. Although it is reasonable to think that actions and omissions require some form of agency or some directing mind, the fact that this mind and agency is most often found in the ranks of individual middle- or low-level managers serves to uphold the imaginary social order in which everyone is rewarded according to their aptitudes. Some just seem to be "bad apples" in an overall legitimate, well-policed and functional system, where corporations "strive" to deliver beneficial results that serve the entire community. As quoted by the courts, the middle and low management willingly, with deliberation, take on responsibilities, even in cases when they do not possess the means to alter the corporation's problematic safety culture. Thus, top management is often not even investigated, as for the police, this "voluntary" responsibility and the apparent "closeness" to the victim in the line of command effectively reveals the guilty parties (see Alvesalo-Kuusi 2011; Alvesalo and Whyte 2007). Further, as the courts keep silent about corporate recidivism, and as in the majority of the cases the corporations are not even prosecuted, the primacy of individual liability and the idea that criminality is caused by personal inadequacies are reinforced.

Second, since 2003, the number of CCL convictions has indeed increased, and currently annual convictions total approximately 40. These figures give the impression that the law is delivering on its promises. The average corporate fine, 10,700 euros, further conveys the spectacle: individuals are punished with approximately an 1,170-euro fine, which means that powerful corporations are paying 10 times more! Information regarding the true effect of the fine on the financial standing of a corporation – constituting often less than 0.1% of the annual turnover – is not readily available to the public, so the illusion of corporations being equally subject to punitive measures as individuals is reinforced.

Third, blaming the victim works towards the same ends. Here, too, the neoliberal ideal of free choice overrides social and institutional restrictions. By blaming the victim and turning a blind eye to power relations, the courts end up creating only a simulated justice.

Despite the impression of nothing new since the initial publication of the *Crimes of the Powerful*, we are nevertheless seeing some light at the end of the tunnel. Our faint optimism stems from the Supreme Court decision in a case in 2014, which resulted in a considerable corporate fine (180,000 euros). This case, in which no one was actually injured but in which the court acknowledged the gross negligence of safety regulations by one of the leading construction companies of the country, might mark a crack in the dominant individual ideology. As the Supreme Court rulings establish general guidelines to be applied later, we have at least some hope that future punishments will truly acknowledge the harm that corporations inflict. On the other hand, one exception in a long line of disregard of the sufferings of the working people may only represent yet another spectacle, too. It nevertheless remains our duty as researchers to raise and make public the inconsistencies between the real and the imaginary social order.

## Notes

1 This work was supported by the Academy of Finland grant number 283553.
2 In some cases, two corporations were sentenced for the same offence/omission. This was in cases of, for example, subcontracting as both companies were held liable.
3 The Finnish day-fine system is used when sentencing individuals and is based on a formula that takes into account the annual income of an individual (which is first divided by 12, then by 60).
4 In order to be considered recidivism, the new crime should take place five years after the initial conviction at the most (e.g. Tapani and Tolvanen 2016: 86–87).
5 We left out the oldest sentences of the companies that were sentenced more than twice and focused on the most recent one and the preceding one. This way the time between the two convictions was at least 5 months and 33 months at the most.

# References

Almond, P. (2013) *Corporate Manslaughter and Regulatory Reform*. Basingstoke: Palgrave Macmillan.

Alvesalo, A. and Whyte, D. (2007) "Eyes Wide Shut: The Police Investigation of Safety Crimes." *Crime Law and Social Change*, 48(1): 57–72.

Alvesalo-Kuusi, A. (2011) "Investigating Safety Crimes in Finland," in J. Gobert and A.-M. Pascal (eds.) *European Developments in Corporate Criminal Liability*, 175–188. Abingdon: Routledge.

Alvesalo-Kuusi, A. and Lähteenmäki, L. (2016) "Legislating for Corporate Criminal Liability in Finland: 22-Year Long Debate Revisited." *Journal of Scandinavian Studies in Criminology and Crime Prevention*, 17(1): 53–69.

Bill 95/1993 (1993) Government Bill to the Parliament to Enact Legislation Concerning Corporate Criminal Liability.

Bittle, S. (2012) *Still Dying for Living*. Vancouver & Toronto: UBC Press.

Bittle, S. and Snider, L. (2011) "Moral Panics Deflected: The Failed Legislative Response to Canada's Safety Crimes and Market Fraud." *Crime, Law and Social Change*, 56(4): 373–387.

Hahto, V. (2004) *Uhrin myötävaikutus ja rikoksentekijän vastuu*. Helsinki: Edita.

Lähteenmäki, L., Koistinen, H., Alvesalo-Kuusi, A., Tapani, J. and Janhonen, M. (2016) "Yhteisösakot ja niiden mittaaminen työturvallisuusrikoksissa." *Lakimies*, 7–8: 1054–1079.

Lappi-Seppälä, T. and Niemi, H. (2012) "Kontrolliviranomaisten toiminta," in *Rikollisuustilanne 2011*, 297–402. Helsinki: Oikeuspoliittinen tutkimuslaitos.

Mongillo, V. (2012) "The Nature of Corporate Liability for Criminal Offences: Theoretical Models and EU Member State Llaws," in A. Fiorella (ed.) *Corporate Criminal Liability and Compliance Programs, Vol 2: Towards a Common Model in the European Union*. Jovene Editore. Online. Available HTTP: www.academia.edu/6224944/The Nature of Corporate Liability for Criminal Offences Theoretical Models and EU Member State Laws.

Niemi, H. (2016) *Seuraamusjärjestelmä 2015 – Tiivistelmä*. Kriminologian ja Oikeuspolitiikan Instituutti. Katsauksia 12/2016. Helsinki: Helsingin Yliopisto. [Referred 12.6.2017] Online. Available HTTP: https://helda.helsinki.fi/handle/10138/164423.

Nuutila, A-M. (2006) "Työrikossäännökset," in Teoksessa A. Alvesalo and A.-M. Nuutila (eds.) *Rangaistava työn turvattomuus*, 127–205. Espoo: Poliisiammattikorkeakoulu.

OSF. (2017) Official Statistics of Finland: Prosecutions, Sentences and Punishments [e-publication]. ISSN=2343–1679. Helsinki: Statistics Finland [referred: 1.3.2017]. Online. Available HTTP: www.stat.fi/til/syyttr/index_en.html.

Pearce, F. (1976) *Crimes of the Powerful: Marxism, Crime and Deviance*. London: Pluto.

Penal Code (1995) Finnish Penal Code 1889/39, Amendment 1995/743 Corporate Criminal Liability.

Saloheimo, J. (2003) *Työturvallisuus – perusteet, vastuu ja oikeussuoja*. Helsinki: Alma Talent.

Tapani, J. and Tolvanen, M. (2016) *Rikosoikeus: Rangaistuksen määrääminen ja täytäntöönpano*. 3. uudistettu painos. Helsinki: Talentum.

Tombs, S. (1991) "Injury and Ill-health in the Chemical Industry: De-centring the Accident-Prone Victim." *Industrial Crisis Quarterly*, (5): 59–75.

——— (2013) "Still Killing With Impunity: Corporate Criminal Law Reform in the UK." *Policy and Practice in Health and Safety*, 11(2): 63–80.

Tombs, S. and Whyte, D. (2007) *Safety Crimes*. Cullompton: Willan.

——— (2015) *The Corporate Criminal: Why Corporations Must Be Abolished*. Abingdon: Routledge.

# Chapter 11

# Global capital, the rigging of interbank interest rates and the capitalist state

*Gregg Barak*

The controlling crimes of capital, such as the ones perpetrated by global financial institutions and multinational corporations, are often the beneficiaries of criminal impunity and the processes of normalization. In part, these legal relations have to do with the nature of the modern corporation, a 19th-century capitalist invention that established the corporation as a person. More fundamentally, these legal relations have to do with the contradictions between the enforcement of the criminal law, on the one hand, and the enforcement of capital accumulation, on the other hand.

In the case of the latter, the historical enforcement of capital accumulation has usually, if not always, exceeded the criminal enforcement of powerful corporate wrongdoing. Over time and in relation to economic development or capital expansion, various forms of criminal accumulation, worker exploitation and consumer fraud have remained beyond incrimination. Not free of the rules of social control altogether, many of these violations have been subject to civil law and administrative regulation (Barak 2012, 2017).

In the case of the former, for example, the U.S. Supreme Court in 1886 (*County of Santa Clara v. Southern Pacific Railroad*), building on earlier rulings which had decided that corporations were citizens but only for the purposes of court jurisdiction, ruled that a corporation was entitled to the same benefits as a real person under the equal protection clause of the 14th Amendment. The Court has also declared that the owners or shareholders and the directors, executives and employees do not actually constitute the corporation as a person. By definition this legal fiction allows a corporation or the "corporate person" to borrow money, enter into contracts and sue for damages. It also permits corporations and their owners, shareholders and so forth to be sued without subjecting themselves to any personal liability.

Succinctly, the corporate person has the same rights as a real person. Unlike a real person, however, the corporation has only limited rather than full liability. In other words, in deference to the demands of capital accumulation, on the one hand, and to the risks involved in capitalist expansion, on the other hand, bourgeois legality has rigged the consequences of the "free" enterprise system and the treatment of incorporated entities. The effects have been that corporate persons are allowed to profit from both their licit and illicit activities without any serious negative outcomes in the case of the latter. Thus, these legal relations reinforce the "risk-taking" illegalities and help to prevent some corporate persons from becoming socially responsible and law-abiding citizens.

As framed in this chapter, some crimes are certainly an expression of power mongering, or actions that are either irresponsible and/or tyrannical by definition. However, not all crimes are inherently both, nor are they all central or complex features of power mongering in capitalist states. As for the aetiology of the crimes of the powerful, we have two types of power mongering occurring. The first involves the world of global finance and multinational corporations, and the second involves the crime control apparatus of the capitalist state. A further distinction needs to be made between irresponsible and tyrannical power mongering. In other words, although it is rather simple to equate these actions with the charges of irresponsibility, it is another thing altogether to equate these actions with charges of tyranny. To do so is to fundamentally deny agency to individual capitalist state actors and attitude to collective social and political bodies, actions or inactions. These processes of social control may not necessarily be democratic. However, they are not without political consensus, social denial and tolerance of the crime and crime control actions free from coercion, force or despotic corporatism (Ruggiero 2017).

In the case of the worldwide interbank rate rigging that has persisted over time, these crimes of the powerful or of global banking behemoths could very well have been charged, convicted and subjected to the corporate death penalty and its senior officers subjected to the career death penalty. In a few words, the capitalist state apparatuses of crime and crime control still have a choice: if they want to, they can provide the resources, hire the investigators and prosecutors and pursue those powerful perpetrators on behalf of a sizable class of victims from a myriad of financial and economic violations. So far, however, the majority of political enforcers or social controllers have chosen not to. At the same time, more than a few myths are floating around and serving to debunk the actual possibility of law enforcement-prosecutorial option. Perhaps providing the most cover to these non-enforcers of the criminal law is the mega myth of all that the financially global institutions and multinationals are simply too big to fail or too big to jail (Ramirez and Ramirez 2017).

These perpetrators of the crimes of the powerful – corporate and state – are sometimes separated from the other and sometimes they are tied together in their unlawful transactions, political cover-ups or whitewashing of their otherwise criminal illegalities and penal obligations. In making distinctions between the activities and commitments of global capitalists and capitalist states, there is the recognition that global capital and the capitalist state are not one and the same, though their interests are usually intertwined. Accordingly, the normalization and routinization of these crimes of the powerful are viewed less about how "crimes" are a central and complex feature of power mongering and more about how crimes of accumulation perpetrated by industries, technologies and financial institutions are of powerful enough value to regularly bend the means of capitalist state apparatuses to the wills of the political economies of global capital.

The forthcoming accounts of criminal impunity for the worldwide rigging of the interbank interest rates, or why the present-day neoliberal state apparatuses regularly decriminalize and fail to adequately regulate the illegal and harmful behaviours of powerful corporate actors generally, supports Frank Pearce's partial thesis that capitalist states do not typically pursue those crimes that do not threaten the profitability, wellbeing or systems of capitalist accumulation and reproduction. Concurrently, capitalist monopolies of the past or capitalist oligarchies of the present generally "manage to keep their anti-social acts hidden from public scrutiny, or, failing that, have them dealt with administratively" (Pearce 1976: 61).

## The capitalist state's relationship to criminalization and the economies of capital

Capitalist states possess the power not only to tax and redistribute assets and incomes, but also to monitor and influence other non-economic institutions, such as law enforcement, education, health care, intelligence, the military and communications. What is ultimately criminalized or not in capitalist economies, such as whether or not fraudulent interbank interest rates are crimes, is also one of the primary functions and purposes of the capitalist state apparatus of social control. As for the capitalist state's role in relation to the various forms of criminality and criminalization, whether these crimes are committed by the powerful or the powerless, most of these offenses are expressions of the ways in which capitalist societies are organized.

As capitalism creates conflicts and contradictions, as capitalism shapes social institutions, identities, and actions capitalism also influences the types of crimes and types of crime control we have (Barak 1998, 2009; Chambliss 1988; Lynch et al. 2000; Michalowski 1985; Pearce 1976; Spitzer 1975; Taylor et al. 1973). Similarly, those crimes of the powerful that promote the accumulation and reproduction of capital are typically not subject to and/or are ignored by criminal laws and legal processes that often serve to conceal, enable or facilitate what Richard Quinney (1977) labelled the "crimes of domination and repression." By contrast, those crimes of the powerless that are "dysfunctional" and threaten the accumulation and reproduction of capital are subjects of laws and legal processes that reveal, inhibit or obstruct what Quinney labelled the "crimes of accommodation and oppression." Or, within the classic logic of the "theory of law and social control" (Black 1976) and from the stance of "constitutive criminology," the crimes of the powerful and the crimes of the powerless in capitalist societies are reciprocally related to each other as both crime and crime control are reflections of the total production of the cultural and structural relations of power differentials and hierarchical relationships (Henry and Milovanovic

1996). Legalistically, multinational or transnational corporate crimes refer to those illegal actions or to those legal obligations ignored by international business organizations or by individuals working on behalf of these corporations and usually, but not always, by the capitalist state. Sociologically, these multinational corporate harms also refer to those organized behaviours that injure or victimize people, animals or environments, whether or not these are legally defined as crimes.

Contemporary capitalist economies are typically market-driven systems with varying degrees of state intervention and governmental regulation into the affairs of capital reproduction. There are also the less common mixed or planned economies where private, public and/or state ownership of capital coexist. Concerning the latter forms in the contemporary world order, Quebec has been for the past two decades moving toward a social economy with fair markets. Canada's second-largest province with 8.2 million people currently has more than 7,000 cooperative or non-profit organizations. These socially oriented enterprises in Canadian dollars are currently ringing up $17 billion in annual sales. They hold $40 billion in assets, employ nearly 225,000 people and make up approximately 10% of the province's gross domestic product (GDP) (Walljasper 2017).

In virtually all of the developed political economies today, whether "free enterprise" or "welfare state" capitalism, varied forms of democracy and socialism are at work there. Since the 1980s, most of the key areas of market activity, including oil, food, finance, pharmaceuticals, tobacco, aircraft, defence contracting, utilities, energy, insurance, hotels and mining, have become oligopolized. Regardless of its formation (i.e. mercantile, industrial, service, financial), the capitalist mode of reproduction "rests on the fact that material conditions of production are in the hands of non-workers in the form of property in capital and land, while the masses are only owners of the personal conditions of production, of labor power" (Marx 1875).

For more than the past century and a quarter, the "social relations of production" or the degrees of competition, roles of intervention and regulation and the scope of state versus private ownership of property have varied, depending on the arrangement of mixed working models of capitalism. Presently and for the foreseeable future the capitalist forces of production, including those means of globalization, financialization and oligopolization are propelling the spread of neocolonial extraction, consumer markets and the contouring of technological services.

In making sense out of imperialism in the context of the aftermath of the Industrial Revolution, Rosa Luxemburg in her posthumous work, *The Accumulation of Capital* (1913), argued that accumulation of wealth was impossible in an exclusively capitalist environment fraught with contradictions of development. For capital to grow, it has to expand into non-capitalist strata and nations: without the "constant expansion into new domains of production and new countries," the survival of capitalism is unlikely because "the global drive to expand leads to a collision between capital and pre-capitalist forms of society," resulting in violence, war and revolution (quoted in Walker 2015). Satyajit Das, in *The Age of Stagnation: Why Perpetual Growth Is Unattainable and the Global Economy Is in Peril* (2016), argues that in a post-industrial, technologically advanced world the "forever-expanding" global economy has become increasingly overridden with debt that contributes to slow- or no-growth economies.

Regarding the slowdown worldwide in the growth and accumulation of capital that was occurring before and which was exacerbated by the banking crisis of 2008, the global financial system now has a multitrillion-dollar problem that seems to be having a long-term effect on weakening both developed and emerging economies. A decade after the financial meltdown, the signs of threat posed by the overload of bad debt and unpaid toxic loans are getting worse. For example, by the winter of 2016, some financial analysts estimated that China's troubled credit had already exceeded $5 trillion, or the equivalent of about one half of the size of the nation's annual economic output. In Europe, the debt in bad loans was exceeding more than $1 trillion. And in South America's biggest banks, toxic debt was also on the rise (Eavis 2016).

Over time, whenever debt overtakes consumption due to the periodic crises in capitalism or following periods of economic growth and/or new rounds of technology, the demands for profits or for the intensification of surplus value in the reproduction of capital has depended on a combination of skill, effort and entrepreneurship, on the one hand, as well as on the application of force, fraud, violence, corruption and state power, on the other hand. In the latter instances, as during the European decline of late feudalism and the early rise of market capitalism, circa 1000 to 1500 AD, before there was the appropriation of land and compiling of stocks, the primitive accumulation of capital resulted from the Enclosure movement, or the "thefts of the commons" by the landed gentry. Their "booty," or what would become the initial stockpiles of wealth, were held by nobles and aristocrats who with the assistance of developing nation-states and armed with laws, militia, patents and corruption were able to use violence against peasants and workers in order to seize both personal property and land (Polanyi 1944).

Once again, where the rate of profit has fallen, colonization of non-capitalist sectors has always been one potential accumulation and reproduction of capital, such as the extensive oil extraction in the Global South today. Referring to what Marx had termed surplus wealth, Hannah Arendt also argued in *The Origins of Totalitarianism* (1951) that the Industrial Revolution had created enormous fortunes, or what she called "superfluous wealth," for capitalists with little or no domestic utility for reinvesting in profitable markets. As a consequence, this contradiction of expansion and crisis in European capital set the stage for decades of financial and real estate fraud in the business sector that victimized artisans, tradesmen and small merchants, and which was accompanied by economic depressions, massive unemployment and corrupt nation-states. Outside of Europe, the crisis in unrestrained markets and capital reproduction set the stage for the imperialism to come. By the 1870s, these capitalists had secured the services of their states to protect their international investments by force. This re-alliance of corporate–state power enabled "the productive use of superfluous capital" and "the employment of superfluous men as soldiers and sailors," as well as "supervisors or workers in the new colonies, or in the transportation of imports and exports" (Walker 2015).

More recently, one has to look no further than the economic crises of 1929 and 2008 to appreciate the many ways that capital accumulation and the avoidance and/or accommodation of financial crises have been aided not only through the relations of monopoly, oligopoly, fraud and corruption, but also by the continuous expansion into non-capitalist sectors vis-à-vis the privatization of the social commons both at home and abroad. Domestically, for example, capitalists and Tories alike in Great Britain are intent on privatizing the National Health Service (NHS). Although the NHS operates in a market society, it has not historically been a part of the process of capital accumulation. The free-marketers there are looking "at the way the US medical/drug system works for the benefit of the rich and they want that for themselves" (Walker 2015). Similarly, free-marketers and their political allies in the United States, for example, have been struggling for nearly two decades to transform the public educational system into a cash cow for private gain. Likewise, portions of the public prison system and all of the immigrants awaiting deportation in the United States have already become subjects to or objects of the privatization and accumulation of capital.

In the supranational legal relations beyond the turn of the 21st century, the crime control apparatuses, augmented by super-technologies and securitization, are reflective of bourgeois legal orders where capitalist states not only possess vast monopolies over the use of surveillance, force and intelligence, but they also enjoy joint sovereignties over the currency and the law, all striving to reproduce not-in-lockstep the hegemony of global capital. Additionally, capitalist states have the ultimate power of eminent domain over private and public property. This power is especially important as the shrinking commons both locally and globally have become increasingly deferential not only to the needs of capital accumulation and reproduction, but also to the contemporary neoliberal policies and practices of austerity, privatization and structural adjustment.

Finally, by way of collaboration between central banks and treasury departments, or what David Harvey (2014) labels the "state-finance" nexus, these capitalist states are fulfilling their key supportive roles as managers of both capital and monetary policies. Or, in the words of Alan Greenspan (2013), the longest-serving chair of the U.S. Federal Reserve Board, 1987–2006, the dominant economies of the world have become integrated networks of global megabanks all dependent on capitalist states for their very survival. At the same time, the rest of this chapter explores the crimes of financial accumulation, specifically those that revolve around the establishment of interbank rates first exposed by the Libor scandal and how the markets, interest rates and loans affected by these fraudulent interbank rates were neutralized by the capitalist state without any real harm or specifically criminal sanction coming to bear on those perpetrators involved and without any remedy or compensation whatsoever coming to pass for the mass of victims harmed by these fraudulent activities.

## The rigging of interbank interest rates: an epidemic of global fraud exposed by the Libor scandal

The London Interbank Offered Rate, or Libor, scandal that came to light in 2012 was a series of fraudulent rate submissions by those banks who submit interest rates for calculating an average interest rate used as a measure of the cost of borrowing between banks, as well as setting a benchmark for interest rates worldwide. The Libor rigging or manipulating of interbank interest rates was by no means isolated, as similar riggings and the non-criminal enforcements of these violations of the securities codes were occurring worldwide in relation to both the Libor and other interbank rating systems. These interest riggings have also been connected to widespread insider trading of securities.

The Libor calculating process and those of similar interbank rates measured elsewhere in the world, such as the Japanese Tokyo Interbank Offered Rate (Tibor) or the Belgium-based Euro Interbank Offered Rate (Euribor) work like this. A number of very large banks, typically not fewer than 7 and not more than 18, are asked what interest rate they would have to pay to borrow money for a certain period and in a certain currency. Their responses are collected with a percentage of the lowest and highest tossed out before the averages are calculated, creating the rates (O'Toole 2012).

Concerning the criminal and civil violations of the Libor that were committed before, during and after the Wall Street implosion, these fraudulently submitted rates and the monies derived from these exceeded by orders of magnitude any financial scam in the history of markets. As one of the civil complaints read: "[B]y surreptitiously bilking investors of their rightful rates of return. . . [d]efendants reaped hundreds of millions, if not billions, of dollars in ill-gotten gains" (Ibid.). In the United States alone, the early estimated costs to the states, counties and local governments came to at least $6 billion in fraudulent interest payments, not counting $4 billion that governments spent to unwind their positions exposed to rate manipulation (Preston 2012). In public responses, there were calls for resignations, criminal prosecutions and stricter regulations of the financial sector. In addition, numerous civil lawsuits were filed by a diversity of plaintiffs, ranging from mutual funds to the city of Baltimore that claimed they had "lost profits on Libor-based securities due to banks' artificial suppression of the rate" (O'Toole 2012). Defendants in these legal cases included the Bank of America, JPMorgan, Credit Suisse, HSBC and Citigroup.

It should be pointed out that before the short-lived outrage developed, the Libor in the global world of finance was considered the "gold standard" for benchmarking interest rates. That is to say, when the Libor went up, monthly interest payment rates were inclined to go up. When the Libor went down, some borrowers enjoyed lowered interest rates. However, pensioners in general as well as those who had invested in mutual funds would lose money by earning less in interest. Similar to "insider trading" in the stock market, having advance knowledge or information of Libor rates can not only affect the value of a security or a commodity, but its manipulation can also be used to make lucrative profits off of trades.

In terms of the routinization of these rigged rates, court documents have revealed that at the Royal Bank of Scotland (RBS), among senior traders it was common practice to make requests to the bank's rate setters as to the appropriate Libor rate. Testimony from documents filed in Singapore by one RBS trader, Tan Chi Min, claimed that the Libor fixing process amounted to an "interest rate cartel" where rates could be globally manipulated. In his court affidavit, Min maintained further that senior traders at RBS were not only aware of the rate manipulation, but that they also supported such actions. Messages from one Barclays Capital (BCS) trader also revealed that for each basis point or .01% the Libor was moved, those involved could net a couple of million dollars (Eagle 2012).

In 2012, there was roughly $10 trillion in loans – including credit cards, car loans, student loans and adjustable-rate mortgages – as well as some $350 trillion in derivatives that were all tied to the Libor. In July of that year, the United Kingdom–based investment bank BCS paid $453 million in a settlement with U.S. and UK regulators, admitting that their traders had submitted fraudulent bank rates for their costs of borrowing between 2005 and 2008. These traders had "repeatedly requested that their colleagues in charge of the Libor process tailor the bank's submissions to benefit the firm's trading positions. Barclays staffers also colluded with counterparts from other banks to manipulate rates" (O'Toole 2012). Additionally, during the height of the global financial crisis, between late 2007 and early 2009, BCS made artificially low Libor submissions because the bank was afraid that if its submissions were too high, then it would get punished in the markets as their investors would question the bank's health.

As former U.S. Assistant Attorney General Lanny Breuer was quoted as saying, regarding a settlement with UBS Financial Services, the real reason that Barclays had rigged the Libor rate was to "maximize profits" and to "hide its weakness" during the crisis. At the UBS press conference, he also had this to say,

> Make no mistake: for UBS traders, the manipulation of LIBOR was about getting rich. As one broker told a UBS derivatives trader, according to the statement of facts appended to our agreement with the bank, "mate yur getting bloody good at this libor game . . . think of me when yur on yur yacht in Monaco wont yu."

> (Breuer 2012)

Make no mistake: the manipulation of Libor was also about accumulating capital and expanding the net wealth of UBS.

On 11 December 2012, the U.S. Department of Justice (DOJ) announced that HSBC Holdings, a British multinational banking and financial services company based in London and ranking as the fourth-largest bank in the world with total assets of $2.67 trillion, had agreed to forfeit $1.25 billion and to pay $665 million in civil penalties for violating the Bank Secrecy Act, the International Emergency Economic Powers Act and the Trading With the Enemy Act. It is also worth noting that in the settlement, the DOJ had also agreed not to criminally prosecute HSBC for alleged terrorist financing. One week later, UBS, Switzerland's biggest bank, settled with U.S., UK and Swiss regulators for a sum of $1.5 billion for manipulating interest rates and for criminal charges against two former traders. The global investigation of these traders involved more than a dozen banks and brokers (Brush and Mattingly 2012).

In fact, regulators found that the Zurich-based bank made "more than 2,000 requests to its own rate submitters, traders at other banks and brokers to manipulate rate submissions through 2010" (Ibid.). According to the Financial Services Authority, there were at least 45 bank employees, including some managers, who knew of the persuasive practice and another 70 people who were included in open chats and messages where attempts to manipulate the Libor and Euribor were discussed. In 2011, Japanese regulators had also temporarily suspended some of UBS and Citigroup's transactions "after finding that both banks had attempted to influence Libor rates and the related Tokyo Interbank Offered Rate" (O'Toole 2012).

Besides these multinational banks, other global banks were involved in this kind of collusion and submission of fraudulent interbank interest rates. Back in March 2011 the *Wall Street Journal* reported that U.S. regulators were investigating Bank of America and Citigroup for manipulating the Libor. Eleven months later, in February 2012, the U.S. Department of Justice announced that it was launching a criminal investigation into widespread Libor abuse. In July 2012, the UK Serious Fraud Office announced that it too was opening a criminal investigation into Libor. Not only was the UK looking into BCS' fraudulent submission rates but also those of 20 other major banks.

During the same month and year, the Canadian Competition Bureau (CCB) announced that it was carrying out an investigation into the Canadian branches of the RBS as well as HSBC, Deutsche Bank, JPMorgan Bank and Citibank for "price fixing" around the yen-denominated Libor rate. A federal prosecutor for the CCB stated that interest rate derivative traders "at the participant banks communicated with each other their desire to see a higher or lower yen LIBOR to aid their trading positions" (Beltrame 2012).

By the end of 2015, more than a half-dozen banks had paid out more than $10 billion to settle charges with regulators for fraudulent rate submissions. However, in the face of all the accusations against dozens of multinational or global banking giants, and in the midst of a worldwide interest rate rigging epidemic in the financial services industry, there were very few traders who were actually indicted and subsequently criminally prosecuted for securities frauds (Smith 2015). There were no CEOs or chairmen of the boards who faced any type of criminal charges. Although a number of them, bowing to political pressure, found it necessary to resign their leadership positions.

Despite the lack of difficulty in convicting these multinational financial criminals for their habitual violations of the Libor, pretty much like the history of high finance crimes in general, these securities fraudsters have for all intents and purposes been routinized away and decriminalized. Like the capitalist state's responses to the epidemic of securities frauds in the financial services industry that led up to and caused the Wall Street meltdown, the social control of these criminals has primarily been subject to conciliatory settlements with the feds or to compensatory civil relief for select groups of investors. Rarely have the benefactors of these defrauding schemes been subject to any kind of penal sanction.

In terms of compensation for the victims of Libor, plaintiff investors and municipalities initially filed a series of class actions in New York. Eventually homeowners claiming that they, too, had been victimized by the Libor manipulations joined these lawsuits. They argued, in effect, that their mortgage repayments were made more expensive than they would have been. As a consequence, in many instances home were foreclosed and repossessed by the lenders (Salvatore 2015).

In one class action suit filed in New York, Annie Bell Adams and her four co-lead plaintiffs explained how their subprime mortgages were securitized in Libor-based collateralized debt obligations and sold by bankers to investors. The class action alleged that traders at 12 of the biggest banks in Europe and North America were "incentivized to manipulate the London interbank offered rate to a higher rate on certain dates when adjustable mortgage interest rates were reset" (Kavoussi 2012). According to the complaint, the result was that subprime homeowners between 2000 and 2009 ended up paying more. Alabama-based attorney, John Sharbrough, at the time of the filing stated that the number of plaintiffs could be as high as 100,000 and that each of them may have lost thousands of dollars. These plaintiffs held what had been called Libor Plus adjustable-rate mortgages. Moreover, accordingly to the Office of the Comptroller of the Currency there were at least 900,000 outstanding U.S. home loans that originated between 2005 and 2009 with an unpaid principal balance of $275 billion that were indexed to Libor (Wilson 2012).

Estimates of how much banks were going to end up paying in Libor lawsuits once ranged from a low of $7.8 billion to a high of $176 billion. However, in the spring of 2013, a federal judge dismissed most but not all of the Libor lawsuits against 16 banks, including JPMorgan Chase and Bank of America, in part, because the plaintiffs "couldn't jump through all of the necessary hoops to show how they had been harmed by violations of U.S. antitrust laws" (Gongloff 2013). Although the judge found that plaintiffs had lacked standing to sue under relevant anti-trust laws as well as the Racketeer Influenced and

Corrupt Organizations statues, he let some claims proceed under different laws. For example, he made it possible for big institutional bond investors, including pension funds and money managers like Charles Schwab, to proceed. Similarly, lawsuits by derivative traders were allowed to go forward, which simply resulted in many of the defendant banking institutions settling their cases financially for fractions of what they made from their ill-gotten gains.

## Conclusion

The rigging of the interbank interest rates globally, the impunity for these financial crimes and securities frauds and the significant role of the capitalist state apparatuses in not pursuing those harms and injuries that do not threaten the profitability of capital accumulation and reproduction certainly support Pearce's partial thesis of impunity for the crimes of the powerful even, if not, the more instrumental and less structural analyses of the aetiology of crime and crime control that would represent the power mongering of capitalist states as one and the same as the power mongering of global capitalists.

Traditional rationalizations for not rigorously going after these crimes of capitalist control include, especially with respect to securities fraud, the myth that these violations are complex legal matters that are too difficult to prosecute and win when pitted against those more legally powerful mega financial institutions. The myriad of excuses for not criminally pursuing or even examining these crimes of the powerful are consistent with those views of the former attorney general of the United States, Eric Holder. As the AG for seven years, he maintained that to pursue, let alone criminally convict, these behemoth financial fraudsters would do more harm than good and that such efforts would not be in the best interests of both global producers and global consumers (Froomkin 2015).

Facilitating this neutralization, toleration and routinization of these crimes of the powerful are the capitalist states' apparatuses of social control (Barak 2015, 2016, 2017). Since Michel Foucault first introduced the concept of *dispositif* in the 1970s, the term has been translated and mentioned by others as well as by Foucault as a device, machinery, construction and deployment of things otherwise not talked about. These references include administrative, institutional and physical mechanisms of control. They also include knowledge structures, social narratives and ideological beliefs that function together to enrich and uphold power within a given social body (Agamben 2009).

Lastly, both indirectly and in conjunction with private justice/control through the utility of semi-autonomous agencies, individual capitalist states also include political networks of vested and competing interests that make up loosely affiliated and often ethically challenged bureaucracies whose discretionary powers are frequently executed in clusters of legally bound decisions that are normally subordinate to but are not dictated by either these crimes of the powerful or by global capitalism. Moreover, these capitalist state apparatuses of social control are far too complex and numerous to be mere instruments of capital that efficiently absolves the crimes of the powerful without any resistance or pushback. At the same time, although the interests of capitalist states are certainly not one and the same as those of capital, and may at times be at odds with the interests of capital, these capitalist states nonetheless increasingly protect the interests of global capital over the social and political interests of the vast majority of people worldwide.

## References

Agamben, G. (2009) *What Is an Apparatus? And Other Essays* (trans. D. Kishik and S. Pedatella). Stanford, CA: Stanford University Press, p. 14.

Arendt, H. (1951) *The Origins of Totalitarianism*. New York: Harcourt, Brace & Co.

Barak, G. (1998) *Integrating Criminologies*. Boston: Allyn and Bacon.

———— (2009) *Criminology: An Integrated Approach*. New York: Rowman & Littlefield.

———— (2012) *Theft of a Nation: Wall Street Looting and Federal Regulatory Colluding*. New York: Rowman & Littlefield.

———— (2015) "Introduction: On the Invisibility and Neutralization of the Crimes of the Powerful and their Victims," in G. Barak (ed.) *The Routledge International Handbook of the Crimes of the Powerful*, 1–35. London and New York: Routledge.

———— (2016) "Alternatives to High-Risk Securities Fraud Control: Proposing Structural Transformation in an Age of Financial Expansionism and Unsustainable Global Capital." *Crime, Law and Social Change*, 65(3): DOI 10.1007/s10611-016-9615-9.

———— (2017) *Unchecked Corporate Power: Why the Crimes of Multinational Corporations are Routinized Away and What We Can Do About It*. London and New York: Routledge.

Beltrame, J. (2012) "Canadian Connections to LIBOR Scandal Probed by Competition Bureau." *National Post*, 15 July. Online. Available HTTP: http://news.nationalpost.com/news/canada/canadian-connection-to-libor-scandal-probed-by-competition-bureau.

Black, D. (1976) *The Behavior of the Law*. New York: Academic Press.

Breuer, L. (2012) "Assistant Attorney General Lanny A Breuer Speaks at the UBS Press Conference." *Justice News*, 19 December. Online. Available HTTP: www.justice.gov/opa/speech/assistant-attorney-general-lanny-breuer-speaks-ubs-press-conference.

Brush, S. and Mattingly, P. (2012) "UBS $1.5 Billion Libor Settlement Signals More to Come." *Bloomberg Business*, 19 December. Online. Available HTTP: www.bloomberg.com/news/articles/2012-12-19/ubs-1-5-billion-libor-settlement-signals-more-to-come.

Chambliss, W. (1988) *Exploring Criminology*. New York: MacMillan.

Eagle Fried. (2012) "Barclays Pays a Heavy Price For Falsifying the LIBOR Submissions." *The Economist*, 30 July. Online. Available HTTP: www.economist.com/node/21557772.

Eavis, P. (2016) "Toxic Loans Around the World Weigh on Global Growth." *The New York Times*, 3 February. Online. Available HTTP: www.nytimes.com/2016/02/04/business/dealbook/toxic-loans-in-china-weigh-on-global-growth.html?emc=edit_th_20160204&nl=todaysheadlines&nlid=34985918&_r=0.

Froomkin, D. (2015) "Holder Defends Record of Not Prosecuting Financial Fraud." 16 October. Online. Available HTTP: https://theintercept.com/2015/10/16/holder-defends-record-of-not-prosecuting-financial-fraud/.

Gongloff, M. (2013) "Banks Win Big with Dismissal of Libor Lawsuits, But War Is Far from Over." *The Huffington Post*, 2 April. Online. Available HTTP: www.huffingtonpost.in/entry/banks-libor-lawsuits-dismissed_n_2994198.

Greenspan, A. (2013) *The Map and the Territory: Risk, Human Nature, and the Future of Forecasting*. New York: The Penguin Press.

Harvey, D. (2014) *Seventeen Contradictions and the End of Capitalism*. New York: Oxford University Press.

Henry, S. and Milovanovic, D. (1996) *Constitutive Criminology: Beyond Postmodernism*. London: Sage.

Kavoussi, B. (2012) "Annie Bell Adams, Foreclosure Victims, Sues Big Banks Over Libor Manipulation." 15 October. Online. Available HTTP: www.huffpostbrasil.com/entry/annie-bell-adams-libor-foreclosure-manipulation_n_1966528.

Lynch, M.J., Michalowski, R.J. and Groves, W.B. (2000) *The New Primer in Radical Criminology: Critical Perspectives on Crime, Power, and Identity*. St. Louis: Willow Tree Press.

Luxemburg, R. (1913) *The Accumulation of Capital*. London: Routledge and Kegan Paul Ltd (1951). Online. Available HTTP: https://www.marxists.org/archive/luxemburg/1913/accumulation-capital/ (accessed 28 March 2018).

Marx, K. (1875) *Critique of the Gotha Program*. Accessed from the Marxist Internet Archive, 15 February 2015. Online. Available HTTP: www.marxissts.org/archive/marx/works/1875/gotcha/ch01.htm.

Michalowski, R. (1985) *Order, Law, and Crime*. New York: Random House.

O'Toole, J. (2012) "Explaining the Libor Interest Rate Mess." *CNN Money*, 10 July. Online. Available HTTP: http://money.cnn.com/2012/07/03/investing/libor-interest-rate-faq/.

Pearce, F. (1976) *Crimes of the Powerful: Marxism, Crime, and Deviance*. New York: Pluto Press.

Polanyi, K. (1944) *The Great Transformation*. New York: Farrar & Rinehart.

Preston, D. (2012) "Rigged LIBOR Costs State, Localities $6 Billion." *Bloomberg News*, 10 October. Online. Available HTTP: http://ourfinancialsecurity.org/2012/10/afr-in-the-news-rigged-libor-costs-states-localities-6-billion/.

Quinney, R. (1977) *Class, State, and Crime: On the Theory and Practice of Criminal Justice*. New York: David McKay.

Ramirez, M.K. and Ramirez, S. (2017) *The Case for the Corporate Death Penalty: Restoring Law and Order on Wall Street*. New York: New York University Press.

Ruggiero, V. (2017) *Dirty Money: On Financial Delinquency*. Oxford, UK: Oxford University Press.

Salvatore, C. (2015) "Judge Trims Libor Claims Against Banks in NY Lawsuits." *Law 360*, 4 August. Online. Available HTTP: www.law360.com/articles/687361/judge-trims-libor-claims-against-banks-in-ny-lawsuits.

Smith, R. (2015) "Two Former Traders Found Guilty in Libor Manipulation Case." *The New York Times*, 5 November. Online. Available HTTP: www.nytimes.com/2015/11/06/business/dealbook/two-former-traders-found-guilty-in-libor-manipulation-case.html?_r=0.

Spitzer, S. (1975) "Towards a Marxian Theory of Deviance." *Social Problems* 22: 638–651.

Taylor, I., Walton, P. and Young, J. (1973) *The New Criminology: For a Social Theory of Deviance*. London and New York: Routledge.

Walker, E. (2015) "Capitalism Versus The Social Commons." *Nakedcapitalism*. Online. Available HTTP: www.nakedcapitalism.com/2016/01/capitalism-versus-social-commons.html?utm_source=feedburner&utm_medium=email&utm_campaign=Feed%3A+NakedCapitalism+%28naked+capitalism%29.

Walljasper, J. (2017) "A More Equitable Economy Exists Right Next Door." *Alternet*. Online. Available HTTP: www.alternet.org/local-peace-economy/canadas-equitable-economy-next-door.

Wilson, D. (2012) "BofA, Others Face Suit Over Libor-Tied Mortgage Plot." *Law 360*, 15 October. Online. Available HTTP: www.law360.com/articles/386531/bofa-others-face-suit-over-libor-tied-mortgage-plot.

# Chapter 12

# Pipelines, presidents and people power
## Resisting state–corporate environmental crime

*Elizabeth A. Bradshaw*

Within the fields of state crime, corporate crime, state–corporate crime and environmental crime (or green criminology), there has been a recent push to unify these concepts under the common banner of "crimes of the powerful" (see Barack 2015; Rothe and Kauzlarich 2016). However, little credit has been given to Frank Pearce's (1976) *Crimes of the Powerful: Marxism, Crime and Deviance* in laying a foundational framework for these concepts. Capturing the shifting relations between states and corporations under neoliberalism, Pearce's Marxist analysis of crime explains the exclusion of crimes of the powerful from the larger discipline of criminology while identifying key facets of the relationship between large corporations and the federal government under capitalism. Moreover, although research on green criminology has also adopted a similar Marxist framework for understanding crime, environmental harm perpetuated by state and corporate agents was left underexplored by Pearce (1976). Similarly, Pearce did not grant serious attention to the role of social movements in controlling the crimes of the powerful. This chapter will explore the relevance of Pearce's insights into the role of the state in mediating capitalist conflicts through a case study of resistance by environmental and Indigenous activists (known as "Water Protectors") to the construction of the Dakota Access Pipeline.

## Revisiting *Crimes of the Powerful*: insights on state-facilitation of corporate environmental harm

Pearce's (1976) analysis of the role of the state under capitalism can help explain the actions and reactions of federal agencies in response to widespread resistance against the Dakota Access Pipeline (DAPL). Exploring the complex meaning behind Marx's contention that "the executive of the modern state is but a committee for managing the common affairs of the whole bourgeoisie," Pearce stresses that the group holding the reins of governmental power may not in fact be ruling the country but instead may be representing the interests of a dominant segment of the ruling class (1976: 61). Although the primary objective of the state is reproduction of the capitalist economic system, government is just one institution comprising state power. Pearce (1976: 60) explains that

> These other institutions – the judiciary, the police, the army, etc. – often have quite a high degree of independence from the government. But, this does not mean that they are autonomous. The institutional and personal nexuses within which they are located guarantee that their personnel are committed to the interests of capitalism, and whatever political party is in power institutional inertia acts against social change.

Indeed, the response of the federal government to the demands of the Standing Rock Sioux Tribe (SRST) and Water Protectors varied greatly within and between agencies in the Obama administration. Under the Obama administration, the Army Corps of Engineers initially seemed to support granting Dakota Access, LLC, the easement to drill below Lake Oahe. However, the Environmental Protection Agency, the Department of Interior and the Advisory Council on Historic Preservation (ACHP) expressed concern about the lack of consultation with tribal nations and the failure to conduct a thorough environmental review. To be sure, these agencies were not opposed to further capitalist fossil fuel infrastructure development per se, but instead were concerned for the process by which the DAPL project was implemented. Initially reluctant to intervene, for months the Obama administration monitored the standoff between Water Protectors and Dakota Access, LLC – backed by law enforcement and private security – before making a public statement. It was not until the conflicts between police and demonstrators escalated and received significant national and international attention that the state interfered with capitalist interests.

As Pearce (1976: 66) argues, state intervention increases to the extent that resistance activities threaten to undermine the state-supported monopoly capitalist system. Deployment of police force is therefore most likely against actions that pose a real threat to the capitalist system, such as lower-class attacks against private property. During the standoff at Standing Rock, Water Protectors were met with militarized police and private security when they attempted to physically block construction of the DAPL through bulldozed sacred sites. As the pipeline pushed closer and closer to the encampments throughout fall 2016, the Morton County Sheriff's Department was tasked with protecting capitalist private property of Dakota Access, LLC, at the expense of water protection and human rights.

Giving the appearance that the state is influenced by the people, the state may occasionally pass laws that go against the interests of the rich. However, these appeasements function to neutralize popular political movements (Pearce 1976: 104–105). Using the power of the bully pulpit, President Obama pressured the U.S. Amy Corps of Engineers (USACE) to delay and deny granting the easement for Dakota Access, LLC. Because president-elect Donald Trump's intention to support the pipeline was obvious during his campaign, the actions taken by the Obama administration after the election appear to be little more than a symbolic gesture. Although this was viewed by some as a victory, the looming Trump presidency made many Water Protectors rightfully hesitant. Nevertheless, following the decision, many living in the resistance camps heeded the requests of the SRST to leave. Clearing resistance from the pipeline's path and neutralizing the threat to capitalist property, Obama's decision to deny the permit effectively dispersed the blockade erected by Water Protectors. Largely a politically timed symbolic gesture, the actions of the Obama administration did little to block the interests of fossil fuel capitalist elites and instead paved the way for its construction.

## Fossil fuels, climate change and state–corporate environmental crime

Governments and corporations are the most powerful organizations perpetuating environmental harm. However, Pearce's (1976) analysis did not grant significant attention to these types of harms. Uniting the fields of both green criminology and state–corporate crime, the concept of state–corporate environmental crime helps to unveil how and why government and business entities routinely engage in behaviour that harms both humans and non-humans alike.

Recognizing that governmental organizations play an important role in contributing to corporate harm, the concept and theory of state–corporate crimes relies on a political-economic framework to analyse the inter-relationships of powerful organizations. State–corporate crimes, according to Michalowski and Kramer (2006: 20), are defined as

> illegal or socially injurious actions that result from a mutually reinforcing interaction between (1) policies and/or practices in pursuit of the goals of one or more institutions of political governance and (2) policies and/or practices in pursuit of the goals of one or more institutions of economic production and distribution.

State–corporate crime can take on two different forms: state facilitated and state initiated. State-facilitated crime occurs when government agencies fail to regulate deviant business practices either due to direct collusion or in adherence to shared goals. State-initiated corporate crime, on the other hand, occurs when corporations employed by government agencies engage in organizational deviance at the direction of or with the tacit approval of government (2006: 20). Scrutinizing the nexus of government and corporate interactions, the concept and theory of state–corporate crime helps to advance Pearce's understanding of crimes of the powerful by further highlighting the inter-organizational mechanisms by which the state propagates harms implicit in capitalist production.

The field of green criminology explores the political-economic relationships between crime, harm and the environment. Within this perspective, the treadmill of production theory focuses on how human political economic systems, and specifically capitalism, produce environmental harm and ecological disorganization (Stretesky et al. 2014). More recently, a growing body of literature in both state–corporate crime and green criminology has begun to document the enormous social, physical, economic and environmental harm caused by anthropogenic climate change (Stretesky and Lynch 2009; White 2009, 2011, 2012; Lynch and Stretesky 2010; Agnew 2011, 2012, 2013; Spapens et al. 2014; White and Kramer 2015). As White (2012: 2) argues, present action or inactions on climate change and fossil fuels will be viewed by future generations as "the gravest of transnational crimes."

At the centre of the problem are unfettered fossil fuel development and the failure of governmental organizations to take effective actions to limit emissions of carbon dioxide. One particular theme within the literature on state–corporate environmental crime documents the extensive harm within different segments within the fossil fuel industry, including tar sands extraction (Smandych and Kueneman 2010), deepwater offshore oil drilling (Bradshaw 2014, 2015a, 2015b) and hydraulic fracturing (Doyon and Bradshaw 2015). Furthermore, increasing research on state–corporate environmental crime also highlights the role of nation-states and corporations in both failing to take action on global warming and actively stifling efforts to mitigate and adapt to climate change (Lynch et al. 2010; Kramer and Michalowski 2012; Kramer 2012, 2013, 2014; Brisman and South 2015; White and Kramer 2015). As these bodies of literature demonstrate, the state consistently strives to maintain the status quo of oil industry development even in the face of catastrophic climate change.

### Blockadia rising: environmental activism against climate crimes

Another important dimension left neglected by Pearce (1976) in *Crimes of the Powerful* is the role of resistance in challenging state and corporate domination. Environmental activism provides important social controls against state–corporate environmental harms by confronting acts and omissions that are already criminalized and prohibited, as well as events that have yet to be deemed formally harmful. White (2011: 150) asserts that the state plays an important role in shaping environmental activism and the tactics employed: "How different nation states act, react or do not act in relation to environmental issues helps to shape local, regional and transnational activist campaigns. It also provides impetus for the adoption of different kinds of strategies and tactics." Most environmental activism utilizes a combination of tactics and strategies involving confrontation, conciliatory or conventional actions (White 2013: 131). Examples of confrontational techniques include mass mobilizations and public demonstrations, protest actions, trespass and breaking in, sit-ins and office takeovers, symbolic use of media, blocking roads, eco-sabotage and riots. Strategies considered more conciliatory or conventional consist of behind-the-scenes negotiation or cooperation, petitions, leafleting, website, information table, lobbying of politicians, media advertising and press releases (White 2011, 2013). Four main areas of campaign activity that have been especially successful include campaigns and actions that directly disrupt company operations; corporate vilification campaigns that undermine their "green" image; campaigns against overseas customers of corporate products; and corporate campaigns targeting shareholders, investors and banks (White 2013: 133). Not exempt from participation in progressive social movements, Kramer (2013) stresses that criminologists also have an obligation to identify as criminal the harms perpetrated by states and corporations and must work to fight crimes against the environment.

As nation-states and conventional politics have failed to implement international treaties and climate summits, increasing numbers of young people concerned about climate are "flocking to the barricades of Blockadia" (Klein 2014: 295). According to Klein (2014: 294–295),

> Blockadia is not a specific location on a map but rather a roving transnational conflict zone that is cropping up with increasing frequency and intensity wherever extractive projects are attempting to dig and drill, whether for open-pit mines, or gas fracking, or tar sands oil pipelines.

While fighting for a deeper form of democracy that gives local communities greater control over natural resources, "these place-based stands are stopping real climate crimes in progress" (2014: 295).

Waging Blockadia, Indigenous peoples, landowners and environmental activists from across North America fought a four-year battle against TransCanada's proposed Keystone XL pipeline. The 1,179-mile pipeline would have carried 800,000 barrels a day of Canadian tar sands oil to the Gulf of Mexico, contributing an estimated 17% greater greenhouse gas emissions than the average U.S. crude oil. Serving as a rallying point for climate change activists, "rowdy greens" utilized more confrontational direct action techniques such as marches, mass arrests, lockdowns, blockades and tree sits to obstruct the Keystone XL pipeline (Bradshaw 2015b). The U.S. Department of State's (2014) environmental review and comments by the EPA acknowledged that further development of the Canadian tar sands caused by Keystone XL would represent a significant increase in greenhouse gas emissions. Promising to reject the pipeline if it would significantly contribute to climate change, President Barak Obama, advised by the State Department, ultimately decided that the infrastructure project would work against national interests and therefore declined TransCanada's permit on 6 November 2015 (White House 2015).

This temporary victory demonstrated that it was possible for social movements to prevent oil infrastructure projects using direct action techniques. Emboldened by the victory in blockading Keystone XL, Indigenous peoples and climate activists have come together to stop another pipeline project that threatens to poison the waters of millions of people and further fuel the problem of climate change.

## Resisting the black snake: Energy Transfer Partner's Dakota Access Pipeline Project

Spanning from the Bakken and Three Forks production region of North Dakota to Patoka, Illinois, the DAPL Project is a 1,172-mile pipeline system with the capacity to carry up to 570,000 barrels per day of fracked crude oil. The DAPL project is owned by Dakota Access, LLC, a joint venture of Phillips 66 and a joint venture of Energy Transfer Partners and Sunoco Logistics, which includes Enbridge and Marathon Oil (with a combined 37% stake). Providing Dakota Access, LLC, with $2.5 billion in loans to construct the pipeline, 17 banks have financed the DAPL project, including Citibank (which has been operating the books on the project), Wells Fargo, BNP Paribas, SunTrust, Royal Bank of Scotland, Bank of Tokyo-Mitsubishi, Mizuho Bank, TD Securities, ABN AMRO Capital, DNB Bank based in Norway, ICBC London, SMBC Nikko Securities and Société Générale. In total, Food and Water Watch estimate that $10.25 billion in loans and credit facilities from 35 banks directly supports the companies building the pipeline. Many of these banks were also responsible for the 2007 financial crises (Miles and MacMillan 2016).

Under Section 404 of the Clean Water Act and Sections 10 and 14 of the Rivers and Harbors Act of 1899, the U.S. Army Corps of Engineers (USACE) is tasked with evaluating and issuing permits for all water crossings. The USACE did not conduct an environmental assessment of the entire pipeline project, but instead was only responsible for overseeing 37 miles of the DAPL encompassing 202 water crossings within its jurisdiction (U.S. Army Corps of Engineers 2017). As required by the National Environmental Policy Act (NEPA), the Draft Environmental Assessment (EA) was prepared by Dakota Access Pipeline, LLC, and reviewed and approved by the USACE in November 2015 (U.S. Army Corps of Engineers 2015).

In response to the Draft EA, the Environmental Protection Agency (EPA), the Department of Interior (DOI) and the ACHP all issued comments objecting to the DAPL. In the first of two letters, the EPA argued that the EA does not adequately review the direct and indirect impacts of the project on the water supplies of local tribes. Moreover, the EPA questioned why the scope of the analysis was limited to small portions of the project without addressing related effects from the entire project segment (U.S. Environmental Protection Agency 2016a). In the EPA's second letter, the agency urged that the Draft EA be revised to reflect the proximity of the Standing Rock Sioux Reservation and potential impacts of a leak to the resources downstream. The Draft EA, however, lacked any reference to the reservation, which was omitted from maps and analysis in violation of environmental justice policies. The EPA recommended that alternative routes and crossing points along the Missouri River be explored that would minimize threats to water resources and drinking water supplies (U.S. Environmental Protection Agency 2016b).

The DOI's public comment argued that the USACE did not sufficiently explain why it did not analyse the impacts and consequences for spills along the length of the pipeline as might be justified as "connected actions." Moreover, the DOI contended that the USACE's conclusion that there would be no significant impact on the local environment and community was not supported by data or analysis. The 29 March 2016 letter further makes clear that formal tribal consultation had not yet occurred despite requests from multiple tribes (U.S. Department of Interior 2016). Similarly, the Advisory Council on Historic Preservation (2016) comments on the DAPL also stressed that the USACE's findings were premature and were not sufficiently informed by the knowledge and perspective of federally recognized tribes who attribute religious and cultural significance to the affected properties.

Failing to adequately address the concerns raised by the EPA, DOI, ACHP and tribal governments, based on the Final EA in July 2016 the USACE issued a "Finding of No Significant Impact" for the project, meaning that the project would not have any adverse impacts on federally endangered species or habitats, historic properties and local communities. After determining the project to not be injurious to the public interest, the USACE concluded that the preparation of a more comprehensive Environmental Impact Statement was not required (U.S. Army Corps of Engineers 2016). As a result, the DAPL project was permitted to move forward.

### Water Protectors stand with Standing Rock Sioux Tribe

Located less than a mile downstream from where the DAPL crosses under Lake Oahe is the water intake for the SRST. The SRST and other neighbouring tribal governments expressed concerns throughout the environmental review process that a leak or rupture would contaminate the river and the tribe's drinking water supply. Neighbouring tribes also argued that cultural and sacred resources in the area could be destroyed by a potential pipeline spill. Comprising all of present-day South Dakota west of the Missouri River and including the sacred Black Hills, the boundaries of Great Sioux Reservation, which includes the Standing Rock Sioux Reservation, were established in Article 2 of the Treaty of Fort Laramie of 29 April 1868. In violation of Article 12 of the treaty, the U.S. Congress unilaterally passed the Act of 28 February 1877, which removed the Black Hills from the reservation without consent three-fourths of the Sioux. As an independent sovereign nation, the SRST staunchly asserts that these treaty rights continue to remain in effect, and the tribe maintains jurisdiction on all reservation lands (Standing Rock Sioux Tribe 2017).

Although there have been conflicts at multiple points along the pipeline, the most intense resistance has been concentrated at the point pipeline's crossing at Lake Oahe (a segment of the Missouri River) just north of the Standing Rock Sioux Reservation in North Dakota. Rooted in the historical struggle between Indigenous people and the U.S. federal government, the resistance at Standing Rock is unprecedented. Allies from other movements, including environmentalists, Black Lives Matter and Code Pink, have also joined forces in support of the SRST and other tribal nations (Donnella 2016). Situated along the convergence of the Cannon Ball River and Lake Oahe, encampments began to form in response to Dakota Access, LLC's announcement of the pipeline route. Located on the reservation, the Camp of the Sacred Stones first formed in April 2016. As support continued to grow throughout the summer, a larger camp called Oceti Sakowin Camp (or Oceti Oyate) formed in August (Sacred Stone Camp 2017). Although the population of the camps fluctuated, in September 2016 Standing Rock Sioux Chairman Dave Archambault II estimated between 3,000 and 4,000 people in the camp during the week with several thousand more on the weekends (Medina 2016). At its height, the camp housed upwards of 10,000 people (Cuevas et al. 2017). Functioning as independent communities that provided food and shelter for its inhabitants, men, women and children of all ages gathered together at the camps for peaceful, prayerful resistance.

Uniting under the principle "Mni wiconi" (pronounced "mini we-choh-nee"), which is Lakota for "water is life," those committed to resisting the DAPL do not see themselves as protesters, but instead Water Protectors. Two prophecies dating back to the 1890s foretold of the current battle against the pipeline. One leader called Black Elk prophesied that in seven generations the Native American nations would come together to save the Earth. A second legend predicted that a "black snake" would threaten the world. For many at the encampments, these two stories have come to fruition with the DAPL (Woolf 2016). Standing Rock's Historic Preservation Officer and founder of the Sacred Stone Camp, LaDonna Brave Bull Allard (2016), argues that this area is sacred territory for many Native American tribes:

> Of the 380 archeological sites that face desecration along the entire pipeline route, from North Dakota to Illinois, 26 of them are right here at the confluence of these two rivers. It is a historic trading ground, a place held sacred not only by the Sioux Nations, but also the Arikara, the Mandan, and the Northern Cheyenne.

The U.S. Army Corps and the federal government have permitted the destruction of these important cultural and spiritual areas, thereby erasing the history and identity of Indigenous people. Allard (2016) poses the question: "If we allow an oil company to dig through and destroy our histories, our ancestors, our hearts and souls as a people, is that not genocide?"

## Pipelines, presidents and people power 165

While the resistance camps grew throughout the summer and fall, the SRST, represented by Earthjustice, pursued legal action against the USACE. Alleging that the agency violated federal statutes, including the Clean Water Act, National Historic Protection Act and NEPA, when it issued the permits, the tribe filed a lawsuit in federal district court in Washington, D.C., on 26 July 2016. As construction of the pipeline continued throughout the legal battle, the SRST asked the court to grant a preliminary injunction. While awaiting a decision, Dakota Access, LLC, proceeded to bulldoze an area containing tribal sacred sites and burial grounds previously identified to the Court the day prior. To prevent further destruction of sacred and culturally significant sites, the tribe filed an emergency motion for a temporary restraining order on 6 September 2016 (Earthjustice 2017). The same day, Native American Water Protectors including men, women and children attempted to block construction of the pipeline and were brutally attacked with pepper spray and dogs by private security guards hired by Dakota Access, LLC (Goodman 2016). Originating as a U.S. military and Department of Defense contractor assisting with the global war on terror, the private security company TigerSwan used counterterrorism tactics to target Water Protectors, comparing them to jihadist insurgents as a means of justifying continued widespread and invasive surveillance of protestors (Brown et al. 2017).

On 9 September 2016, the Court denied the tribe's motion for a preliminary injunction, prompting the U.S. Army, DOI and DOJ to issue a joint statement acknowledging that the important issues raised by the tribe and other tribal nations required reconsideration of its previous decisions regarding the Lake Oahe site under the NEPA (U.S. Department of Justice 2016). Acknowledging the right of citizens to peacefully protest, the agencies urged Dakota Access, LLC, to voluntarily pause all construction activity within 20 miles east or west of Lake Oahe until a determination could be made. The company rejected the request and persisted in constructing the pipeline. Although the Court issued an administrative injunction on 16 September to provide sufficient time to consider the emergency motion filed by the tribe, the injunction was later denied on 10 October. The DOJ once again requested that the company halt construction, which the company once again defied (Earthjustice 2017).

During October, construction moved increasingly closer to the Missouri River and resistance camps. Water Protectors who sought to physically block Dakota Access, LLC, were met with escalating militarized force by Morton County Sheriff's Department. After attempting to clear encampments, officers dressed in riot gear deployed pepper spray, bean bag rounds, rubber bullets and high-pitched sound devices resulting in at least 142 arrests (Skalicky and Davey 2016). The repressive police response led Tribal Chairman Dave Archambault II to call for a DOJ investigation into civil rights violations by Morton County Sheriff's Department.

Breaking his silence on the DAPL in an interview with Now This (2016) on 2 November, President Obama stated, "My view is that there is a way for us to accommodate sacred lands of Native Americans, and I think that right now the Army Corps is examining whether there are ways to reroute this pipeline." He noted that his administration was monitoring the "challenging situation" but would "let it play out for several more weeks." Caving to presidential pressure, on 14 November 2016, the USACE announced that it would delay the decision on the easement while the SRST was consulted (U.S. Department of the Army 2016a). Dakota Access, LLC, then filed a lawsuit against the USACE for delaying easement to pipeline construction.

Throughout the end of November, clashes continued between Water Protectors, Morton County Sheriff's Department and supporting law enforcement and private security agencies. Police deployed mace, tear gas, rubber bullets and water hoses in sub-zero temperatures against an estimated 400 demonstrators. The National Lawyers Guild (2016) filed a lawsuit against the Morton County Sheriff's Department for excessive force on behalf of the more than 200 people who were injured on 20–21 November. Pledging to serve as "human shields" for the Water Protectors against the militarized police, Veterans Stand for Standing Rock organized 2,000 to 5,000 military veterans who started arriving at the camp on 2 December (Medina 2016).

Averting a major showdown, on 4 December 2016, the USACE denied Dakota Access, LLC's request for a permit to drill below Lake Oahe and instead announced that it would explore alternative routes for the pipeline's crossing which would best be accomplished by an environmental impact statement. While stressing that the USACE's previous decisions conformed to all laws and regulations, Assistant Secretary of the Army, Civil Works Department, Jo-Ellen Darcy stated,

> The robust consideration of reasonable alternatives that I am directing, together with analysis of potential spill risk and impacts, and treaty rights, is best accomplished, in my judgement, by preparing an Environmental Impact Statement (EIS) that satisfies the accompanying procedures for broad public input and analysis.
>
> (U.S. Department of the Army 2016b)

Energy Transfer Partners and Sunoco Logistics Partners (2016) promptly responded to the decision the same day stating,

> The White House's directive today to the Corps for further delay is just the latest in a series of overt and transparent political actions by an administration which has abandoned the rule of law in favor of currying favor with a narrow and extreme political constituency.

Expressing their gratitude to the Obama administration, the SRST Chairman Dave Archambault II released a statement on behalf of the tribe:

> We wholeheartedly support the decision of the administration and commend with the utmost gratitude the courage it took on the part of President

Obama, the Army Corps, the Department of Justice and the Department of the Interior to take steps to correct the course of history and to do the right thing. The Standing Rock Sioux Tribe and all of Indian Country will be forever grateful to the Obama Administration for this historic decision.

(Stand With Standing Rock 2016)

Water Protectors cautiously celebrated the Army Corps decision. Although the tribe told those remaining at the encampments to vacate, some rightfully feared that the pipeline might easily push forward under the Trump administration (Dennis and Mufson 2016).

### People power vs. executive power

During the 2016 presidential campaign, Republican nominee Donald Trump promised to rescind fossil fuel regulations and expedite the permitting process for the Dakota Access and the Keystone XL pipelines. Set to personally profit from the DAPL project, financial disclosure forms showed that Trump had between $500,000 and $1 million invested in Energy Transfer Partners, with an additional $500,000 to $1 million invested in Phillips 66, which has a 25% stake in the pipeline (Milman 2016). However, he reportedly sold his shares in Energy Transfer Partners during summer 2016 (Mufson 2016). A fervent Trump supporter, Energy Transfer Partners' CEO Kelcy Warren donated $100,000 to the Trump Victory Fund, an additional $3,000 directly to the Trump campaign and two donations to the Republican National Committee totalling $66,800. Following Trump's Electoral College victory, Warren stated "I'm 100 percent sure that the pipeline will be approved by a Trump administration ... I believe we will have a government in place that believes in energy infrastructure" (Medina and Sottile 2016).

Fulfilling his campaign promise, four days into his term Trump swiftly signed a Presidential Memorandum (2017) that directed the USACE to review and approve the DAPL project in an expedited manner. Citing the President's Memorandum, the new acting Assistant Secretary of the Army, Civil Works, Douglas Lamont informed Congress of the Army's intent to terminate a plan to prepare an Environmental Impact Statement for the DAPL crossing at Lake Oahe (U.S. Department of the Army 2017a). Skipping the customary 14-day notification period, on 7 February the USACE issued the easement for the DAPL crossing without fulfilling their promise to consult with tribal governments, considering alternative routes or conducting an Environmental Impact Statement (U.S. Department of the Army 2017b).

Citing concerns over flooding, North Dakota's governor declared an emergency evacuation order requiring everyone to leave the camp prior to 22 February 2017. However, some Water Protectors choose to remain until the end and torched the remaining structures at the camp before leaving. As of 2:00 p.m. on 23 February, the Morton County Sheriff's office announced that the camp had been cleared. In total, more than 700 people were arrested at the Standing Rock resistance (Cuevas et al. 2017).

The SRST has vowed to continue fighting the DAPL through the courts. Rather than return to the resistance camps, the tribe has turned its attention towards Congress and the Trump administration and organized a Native Nations March on Washington on 10 March 2017 (Stand With Standing Rock 2017). Moving beyond the Standing Rock Reservation, the fight against DAPL has gained national and international support. Campaigns such as #DefundDAPL (2017) encourage divestment from the 17 major banks funding the project. Moreover, #NoDAPL Solidarity (2017) also serves as a coordinating hub for actions against the primary institutions supporting the pipeline such as the banks, Energy Transfer Partners and USACE, among other responsible government and corporate agencies.

As the Trump administration imposes energy infrastructure through Presidential Memorandums, the successes of Blockadia are being tested. Not only did the DAPL project receive fast-track approval via Presidential Memorandum, but Trump simultaneously invited TransCanada to resubmit their application for the Keystone XL pipeline and directed federal agencies to expedite the approval process (Presidential Memorandum-Keystone XL 2017). With the appointment of former Exxon Mobil CEO Rex Tillerson as Secretary of State, as well as the selection of climate change denier and friend of the fossil fuel industry, Scott Pruitt, to head the EPA, it is clear that the new administration intends to cater to the desires of the oil industry.

## Conclusions

Regardless of the political party or candidate occupying the government, the powerful interests of the oil industry work to ensure continued reliance on fossil fuels in the face of the dire consequences of climate change. Although each presidential administration may take a seemingly more conciliatory or confrontational approach to the interests of oil industry elites, the industrial capitalist economy – and the American way of life – is fundamentally powered by its dependence on fossil fuels. The fact that the state was compelled to take action against corporate interests demonstrates the growing power of the Indigenous and environmental activists. However, the decision to pause construction of the DAPL gave the façade of government regulation while imposing negligible tangible challenges to powerful oil industry interests. Although the actions of the Obama administration gave the appearance of conflict between the state and capitalist interests, intervention occurred reluctantly, following intense resistance by activists, and only after the incoming pro-oil Republican administration had secured electoral victory. The meagre actions of the state were a symbolic gesture that did little to halt construction of the DAPL and future oil infrastructure development in the long term. United in their commitment to capitalism, profit and continued support of fossil fuel extraction in the face of catastrophic climate change, the difference between the decisions of Democratic and Republican presidential administrations are essentially moot.

As Pearce astutely points out in *Crimes of the Powerful*, the state functions to divert attention towards less threatening issues, such as protests against fossil fuel infrastructure, rather than address the crux of the problem at hand: the inherent contradictions of capitalism. Without confronting the dominance of oil industry elites at the heart of modern industrial capitalism, state-facilitated corporate environmental crimes perpetuated by the oil industry will continue, though not without sustained resistance from the growing movement of Indigenous peoples and environmental activists waging Blockadia in retaliation.

## References

Advisory Council on Historic Preservation. (2016) Letter to General Bostick, "Ref: Dakota Access Pipeline." 19 May. Online. Available HTTP: https://assets.documentcloud.org/documents/3036069/Ex-32-ACHP-Objection-Letter-DAPL.pdf (accessed 1 February 17).

Agnew, R. (2011) "Dire Forecast: A Theoretical Model of the Impact of Climate Change on Crime." *Theoretical Criminology*, 16(1): 21–46.

——— (2012) "It's the End of the World as We Know It: The Advance of Climate Change from a Criminological Perspective," in R. White (ed.) *Climate Change from a Criminological Perspective*, 13–25. New York: Springer.

——— (2013) "The Ordinary Acts that Contribute to Ecocide: A Criminological Analysis," in N. South and A. Brisman (eds.) *Routledge International Handbook of Green Criminology*, 58–72. London: Routledge.

Allard, Ladonna Brave Bull. (2016) "Why the Founder of Standing Rock Sioux Camp Can't Forget the Whitestone Massacre." *Yes! Magazine*, 3 September. Online. Available HTTP: www.yesmagazinc.org/people-power/why-the-founder-of-standing-rock-sioux-camp-cant-forget-the-whitestone-massacre-20160903 (accessed 10 February 2017).

Barak, G. (ed.) (2015) *The Routledge International Handbook of the Crimes of the Powerful*. New York, NY: Routledge.

Bradshaw, E. (2014) "State-Corporate Environmental Cover-up: The Response to the 2010 Gulf of Mexico Oil Spill." *State Crime Journal*, 3(2): 163–181.

——— (2015a) "Obviously, We're All Oil:' The Criminogenic Structure of the Offshore Oil Industry." *Theoretical Criminology*, 19(3): 376–395.

——— (2015b) "Blockadia Rising: Rowdy Greens, Direct Action and the Keystone XL Pipeline." *Critical Criminology*, 23(4): 433–448.

Brisman, A. and South, N. (2015) "New "Folk Devils," Denials and Climate Change: Applying the Work of Stanley Cohen to Green Criminology and Environmental Harm." *Critical Criminology*, 23: 449–460.

Brown, A., Parrish, W. and Speri, A. (2017) "Leaked Documents Reveal Counterterrorism Tactics Used at Standing Rock to 'Defeat Pipeline Insurgencies.'" *The Intercept*, 27 May. Online. Available HTTP: https://theintercept.com/2017/05/27/leaked-documents-reveal-security-firms-counterterrorism-tactics-at-standing-rock-to-defeat-pipeline-insurgencies/ (accessed 2 June 2017).

Cuevas, M., Sidner, S. and Simon, D. (2017) "Dakota Access Pipeline Protest Site is Cleared." *CNN*, 23 February. Online. Available HTTP: www.cnn.com/2017/02/22/us/dakota-access-pipeline-evacuation-order/ (accessed 23 February 2017).

Dennis, B. and Mufson, S. (2016) "Army Corps Ruling Is a Big Win for Foes of Dakota Access Pipeline." *The Washington Post*, 5 December. Online. Available HTTP: www.

washingtonpost.com/news/energy-environment/wp/2016/12/04/army-will-deny-easement-halting-work-on-dakota-access-pipeline/?utm_term=.6382778c93e0 (accessed 1 February 2017).

Donnella, L. (2016) "The Standing Rock Resistance Is Unprecedented (it's Also Centuries Old)." *NPR,* 11 November. Online. Available HTTP: www.npr.org/sections/codeswitch/2016/11/22/502068751/the-standing-rock-resistance-is-unprecedented-its-also-centuries-old (accessed 10 February 2017).

Doyon, J. and Bradshaw, E. (2015) "Unfettered Fracking: A Critical Examination at Hydraulic Fracturing in the United States," in Gregg Barak (ed.) *The Routledge International Handbook of the Crimes of the Powerful,* 235–246. New York, NY. Routledge.

Earth Justice. (2017) "FAQ: Standing Rock Litigation." Online. Available HTTP: http://earthjustice.org/features/faq-standing-rock-litigation (accessed 25 January 2017).

Eilperin, J. (2017) "Former Interior Secretary Jewell says Army is Reneging on its Commitments on Dakota Access Pipeline." *The Washington Post,* 8 February. Online. Available HTTP: www.washingtonpost.com/news/energy-environment/wp/2017/02/08/former-interior-secretary-jewell-says-army-is-reneging-on-its-commitments-on-dakota-access-pipeline/?utm_term=.c7327e43b737 (accessed 10 February 2017).

"Energy Transfer Partners and Sunoco Logistics Partners Respond to the Statement from the Department of the Army." (2016) *Business Wire,* 4 December. Online. Available HTTP: www.businesswire.com/news/home/20161204005090/en/Energy-Transfer-Partners-Sunoco-Logistics-Partners-Respond (accessed 12 February 2017).

Goodman, A. (2016) "Full Exclusive Report: Dakota Access Pipeline Co. Attacks Native Americans with Dogs & Pepper Spray." *Democracy Now!* 6 September. Online. Available HTTP: www.democracynow.org/2016/9/6/full_exclusive_report_dakota_access_pipeline (accessed 1 December 2017).

Klein, N. (2014) *This Changes Everything: Capitalism vs. the Climate.* New York, NY: Simon and Schuster.

Kramer, R. (2012) "Carbon in the Atmosphere and Power in America: Climate Change as State-corporate Crime." *Journal of Crime and Justice,* 36(2): 1–18.

——— (2013) "Public Criminology and the Responsibility to Speak in the Prophetic Voice Concerning Global Warming," in E. Stanley and J. McCulloch (eds.) *State Crime and Resistance,* 41–53. London: Routledge.

——— (2014) "Climate Change: A State-corporate Crime Perspective," in T. Spapens, R. White and M. Kluin (eds.) *Environmental Crime and Its Victims: Perspectives within Green Criminology,* 22–39. Burlington, VT: Ashgate.

Kramer, R. and Michalowski, R. (2012) "Is Global Warming a State-corporate Crime?" In White, R. (ed.) *Climate Change from a Criminological Perspective,* 71–88. New York: Springer.

Lynch, M., Burns, R. and Stretesky, P. (2010) "Global Warming and State-corporate Crime: The Politicization of Global Warming under the Bush Administration." *Crime, Law, Social Change,* 54: 213–239.

Lynch, M. and Stretesky, P. (2010) "Global Warming, Global Crime: A Green Criminological Perspective," in R. White (ed.) *Global Environmental Harm: Criminological Perspectives,* 62–84. Portland, OR: Willan Publishing.

Medina, D. (2016) "Standing Rock Protest: Veterans Pledge to Protect Protesters." *NBC News,* 2 December. Online. Available HTTP: www.nbcnews.com/storyline/dakota-pipeline-protests/brutal-winter-conditions-deepen-pipeline-protesters-resolve-n690791 (accessed 10 February 2017).

Medina, D. and Sottile, C. (2016) "What Will a Trump Presidency Mean for the Dakota Access Pipeline." *NBC News,* 12 November. Online. Available HTTP: www.nbcnews.com/storyline/dakota-pipeline-protests/what-will-trump-presidency-mean-dakota-access-pipeline-n682746 (accessed 10 February 2017).

Michalowski, R. and Kramer, R. (2006) *State-corporate Crime: Wrongdoing at the Intersection of Business and Government.* New Brunswick: Rutgers University Press.

Miles, J. and MacMillan, H. (2016) "Who's Banking on the Dakota Access Pipeline?" *Food and Water Watch,* 6 September. Online. Available HTTP: www.foodandwaterwatch.org/news/who%27s-banking-dakota-access-pipeline (accessed 10 February 2017).

Milman, O. (2016) "Dakota Access Pipeline Company and Donald Trump Have Close Financial Ties." *The Guardian,* 26 October. Online. Available HTTP: www.theguardian.com/us-news/2016/oct/26/donald-trump-dakota-access-pipeline-investment-energy-transfer-partners (accessed 1 February 2017).

Mufson, S. (2016) "Trump Dumped His Stock in the Dakota Access Pipeline Owner Over the Summer." *The Washington Post,* 23 November. Online. Available HTTP: www.washingtonpost.com/news/energy-environment/wp/2016/11/23/trump-dumped-his-stock-in-dakota-access-pipeline-owner-over-the-summer/?utm_term=.baf0653cb1f2 (accessed 5 January 2017).

National Lawyers Guild. (2016) "Water Protectors Legal Collective Files Suit for Excessive Force Against Peaceful Protesters." 28 November. Online. Available HTTP: www.nlg.org/water-protector-legal-collective-files-suit-for-excessive-force-against-peaceful-protesters/ (accessed 1 January 2017).

Pearce, F. (1976) *Crimes of the Powerful: Marxism, Crime Deviance.* London: Pluto Press.

Presidential Memorandum Regarding Construction of the Dakota Access Pipeline. (2017) Memorandum for the Secretary of the Army, Subject: Construction of the Dakota Access Pipeline. The White House, Office of the Press Secretary. 25 January. Online. Available HTTP: www.whitehouse.gov/the-press-office/2017/01/24/presidential-memorandum-regarding-construction-dakota-access-pipeline (accessed 25 January 2017).

Presidential Memorandum Regarding Construction of the Keystone XL. (2017) Memorandum for the Secretary of the Army, Subject: Construction of the Dakota Access Pipeline. The White House, Office of the Press Secretary. Online. Available HTTP: www.whitehouse.gov/the-press-office/2017/01/24/presidential-memorandum-regarding-construction-keystone-xl-pipeline (accessed 25 January 2017).

Rothe, D. and Kauzlarich, D. (2016) *Crimes of the Powerful: An Introduction.* New York: Routledge.

Sacred Stone Camp. (2017) "Frequently Asked Questions." Online. Available HTTP: http://sacredstonecamp.org/faq/ (accessed 10 February 2017).

Skalicky, Sue and Davey, Monica. (2016) "Tension Between Police and Standing Rock Protesters Reaches Boiling Point." *The New York Times,* 28 October. Online. Available HTTP: www.nytimes.com/2016/10/29/us/dakota-access-pipeline-protest.html?_r=0 (accessed 1 February 2017).

Smandych, R. and Kueneman, R. (2010) "The Canadian-Alberta Tar Sands: A Case Study of State-corporate Environmental Crime," in R. White (ed.) *Global Environmental Harm: Criminological Perspectives,* 87–109. Portland, OR: Willan Publishing.

Spapens, T., White, R. and Kluin, M. (eds.) (2014) *Environmental Crime and Its Victims: Perspectives within Green Criminology.* Burlington, VT: Ashgate.

Stand With Standing Rock. (2016) "Standing Rock Sioux Tribe's Statement on U.S. Army Corps of Engineers Decision to Not Grant Easement." 4 December. Online. Available

HTTP: http://standwithstandingrock.net/standing-rock-sioux-tribes-statement-u-s-army-corps-engineers-decision-not-grant-easement/ (accessed 1 February 2017).

——— (2017) "Standing Rock Denounces Army Easement Announcement, Vows Court Challenge." 7 February. Online. Available HTTP: http://standwithstandingrock.net/standing-rock-denounces-army-easement-announcement-vows-court-challenge/ (accessed 10 February 2017).

Standing Rock Sioux Tribe. (2017) "History." Online. Available HTTP: http://standingrock.org/history/ (accessed 10 February 2017).

Stretesky, P., Long, M. and Lynch, M. (2014) *The Treadmill of Crime: Political Economy and Green Criminology*. New York: Routledge.

Stretesky, P. and Lynch, M. (2009) "A Cross-national Study of the Association between per capita Carbon Dioxide Emissions and Exports to the United States." *Social Science Research*, 38: 239–250.

U.S. Army Corps of Engineers. (2015) *Draft Environmental Assessment: Dakota Access Pipeline Project Crossings of Flowage Easements and Federal Lands*. Prepared by Dakota Access, LLC. For U.S. Army Corp of Engineers, Omaha District. November 2015. Online. Available HTTP: http://cdm16021.contentdm.oclc.org/cdm/ref/collection/p16021coll7/id/2426 (accessed 1 February 2017).

——— (2016) *Final Environmental Assessment: Dakota Access Pipeline Project Crossings of Flowage Easements and Federal Lands*. Prepared by Dakota Access, LLC. For U.S. Army Corp of Engineers, Omaha District. August 2016. Online. Available HTTP: http://cdm16021.contentdm.oclc.org/cdm/ref/collection/p16021coll7/id/2426 (accessed 1 February 2017).

——— (2017) "Dakota Access Pipeline." Online. Available HTTP: www.usace.army.mil/Dakota-Access-Pipeline/ (accessed 10 February 2017).

U.S. Department of the Army. (2016a) "Statement Regarding the Dakota Access Pipeline." Office of the Assistant Secretary. 14 November. Online. Available HTTP: http://earthjustice.org/sites/default/files/files/NRS-1125496-v1-Standing_Rock_-_11_14_16_Statement-letter.pdf (accessed 13 February 2017).

——— (2016b) Memorandum for Commander, U.S. Army Corps of Engineers. Subject: Proposed Dakota Access Pipeline Crossing at Lake Oahe, North Dakota. Office of the Assistant Secretary, Jo-Ellen Darcy. 4 December. Online. Available HTTP: www.army.mil/e2/c/downloads/459011.pdf (accessed 1 February 2017).

——— (2017a) Memorandum: Notice of Termination of the Intent to Prepare an Environmental Impact Statement in Connection with Dakota Access, LLC's Request for an Easement to Cross Lake Oahe, North Dakota. Douglas Lamont, Office of the Assistant Secretary. 7 February. Online. Available HTTP: http://earthjustice.org/sites/default/files/files/EIS-termination0.pdf (accessed 13 February 2017).

——— (2017b) Memorandum for Record. Subject: Compliance with Presidential memorandum (24 January 2017). Douglas Lamont, Office of the Assistant Secretary, Civil Works. 7 February. Online. Available HTTP: http://earthjustice.org/sites/default/files/files/Memo-Feb7-0.pdf (accessed 1 February 2017).

U.S. Department of Interior. (2016) "Comments on Army Corps of Engineers Environmental Impact Statement for DAPL." 29 March. Online. Available HTTP: https://assets.documentcloud.org/documents/3036070/DOI-MARCH-Letter-to-Corps.pdf (accessed 12 Feburary 2017).

U.S. Department of Justice. (2016) "Joint Statement from the Department of Justice, the Department of the Army and the Department of the Interior Regarding Standing Rock Sioux Tribe v. Army Corps of Engineers." Department of Justice, Office of Public Affairs.

9 September. Online. Available HTTP: www.justice.gov/opa/pr/joint-statement-depart ment-justice-department-army-and-department-interior-regarding-standing (accessed 25 January 2017).

U.S. Department of State. (2014) Ch4: Greenhouse Gases and Climate Change. Final Supplemental Environmental Impact Statement, Keystone XL Project. Bureau of Oceans and International Environmental and Scientific Affairs.

U.S. Environmental Protection Agency. (2016a) Comments on Dakota Access Pipeline Draft Environmental Assessment. 8 January. Online. Available HTTP: www.epa.gov/sites/ production/files/2016-11/documents/dakota_access_pipeline_dea_cmts_1-8-16.pdf (accessed 25 January 2017).

———— (2016b) "Re: Additional Comments on Dakota Access Pipeline Draft Environmental Assessment." Srobel, Phillip (Director, NEPA Compliance and Review Program). 11 March. Online. Available HTTP: www.epa.gov/sites/production/files/2016-11/docu ments/dakota_access_2nd_dea_cmts_3-11-16.pdf (accessed 25 January 2017).

White House, Office of the Press Secretary. (2015) "Statement by the President on the Keystone XL Pipeline." President Barak Obama. 6 November. Online. Available HTTP: https://obamawhitehouse.archives.gov/the-press-office/2015/11/06/statement-presi dent-keystone-xl-pipeline (accessed 1 February 2017).

White, R. (2009) "Climate Change and Social Conflict: Toward an Eco-global Research Agenda," in K. Kangaspunta and I. Marshall (eds.) *Eco-Crime and Justice: Essays on Environmental Crime*. Turin, Italy: United Nations Interregional Crime Research Institute (UNICRI).

———— (2011) *Transnational Environmental Crime: Toward an Eco-global Criminology*. New York: Routledge.

———— (ed.) (2012) *Climate Change From a Criminological Perspective*. New York: Springer.

———— (2013) "Environmental Activism and Resistance to State-corporate Crime," in E. Stanley and J. McCulloch (eds.) *State Crime and Resistance*, 128–140. London: Routledge.

White, R. and Kramer, R. (2015) "Critical Criminology and the Struggle Against Climate Change Ecocide." *Critical Criminology*, 23: 383–399.

Woolf, N. (2016) "North Dakota Oil Pipeline Protesters Stand their Ground: 'This is Sacred.'" *The Guardian*. 16 August. Online. Available HTTP: www.theguardian.com/us-news/2016/aug/29/north-dakota-oil-pipeline-protest-standing-rock-sioux (accessed 1 February 2017).

#DefundDAPL. (2017) Online. Available HTTP: https://actionnetwork.org/event_cam paigns/nodapl-2017-action-hub (accessed 1 February 2017).

#NoDAPL Solidarity. (2017) Online. Available HTTP: https://nodaplsolidarity.org/ (accessed 1 February 2017).

Chapter 13

# Pesticideland
## Brazil's poison market

*Stéfanie Khoury*

Brazil underwent a "Green Revolution" in the second half of the 20th century.[1] Its agricultural market was transformed from import intensive to one of the leading agro-economies in the world. By the 2000s, Brazil had become the global leader in agro-toxin consumption, and it has relied upon agro-toxins to remain highly competitive despite the effects upon human health and the environment.[2] In its aim to become a global agricultural leader, the Brazilian state has permitted and facilitated the use of agro-toxins that have in many cases been banned in its competitors' markets. Karen Friederich, a researcher from the Brazilian Association of Collective Health, has recently suggested that at least one-third of agro-toxins used in Brazil have been banned in the EU and the USA due to their impacts on human health and the environment (teleSUR 2016). The pervasiveness of the Brazilian biotechnological "experiment" gained global attention with the 2015–2016 Zika virus epidemic. Contrary to the mainstream explanation that the Zika virus was responsible for the surge in infants born with microcephaly, a small group of doctors and some activists asserted that agro-toxins were in fact the source of the epidemic (REDUAS 2016; Robinson 2016).

This chapter examines the state–agribusiness relationship in Brazil. The chapter argues that the case of Brazil's export-led agricultural market, characterized by its use of agro-toxins, exemplifies the partnership between state and capital in the reproduction of the capitalist social order. Building upon Pearce's (1976) notion of the "imaginary social order," the chapter argues that the neo-liberal practices and policies of the Brazilian state have cultivated its globally competitive agribusiness by enabling the (ab)use of the Brazilian agricultural market as a giant laboratory. The chapter explores how the state has supported and reinforced the hegemony of agribusiness for the pursuit of the long-term economic and political interests of the dominant class.

## Brazil: the leading global consumer of agro-toxins

Until the 1960s, Brazil's agricultural sector used a traditional system of production with limited applications of modern technologies. Brazil's economy centred upon the exporting of primary resources to the Global North and, in a typically colonial dynamic, was reliant upon the import of more expensive manufactured goods. But through the 1970s and early 1980s, Brazil began a process of "modernization," which Peter Evans (1979) coined as "dependent development." He argued that in its process of accumulation, Brazil included a substantial degree of industrialization, a more complex internal division of labour and increased productivity. By the mid-20th century, Brazil began to affirm its independence, like many other so-called "developing" nations, and embarked upon import-substitution industrialization (ISI) policies meant to foster the development of national industry (Hopewell 2014). But Brazil's ISI policies relied heavily on foreign investment, particularly from large transnational corporations (TNCs).

Hopewell (2014: 3), following Evans (1979), outlines the growing relationship between the state, multinational and local capital that can be characterized by both conflict and cooperation. During this period of "dependent development," the state was heavily interventionist and went to great lengths to manage the economy. But the advent of neoliberalism in Brazil, with the transition to democracy in the 1980s, could not allow such "conscious interventionism" (Evans Ibid.: 86) by the state. Immediately after the 1985 elections, the government announced that it would resort to International Monetary Fund (IMF) loans and comply with its stabilization programme (Mainwaring 1986: 170). Through international financial institution (IFI) loans and structural adjustment programmes (SAPs), controlled primarily by the USA and UK, neoliberalism and free market ideology began transforming both the global economy and national economic policies, including Brazil's. These changes, together with major policy reforms effecting the agribusiness sector throughout the 1980s and 1990s, have transformed Brazil into a leading global exporter of soybeans, corn, sugar, orange juice, beef, poultry, coffee and ethanol. Brazil's export market has undergone unprecedented growth since the implementation of foreign investment liberalizations, domestic market deregulations and SAPs, together with the creation in 1991 of the Latin American open-market MERCOSUR.

In her analysis of the transformation of state and capital relations in Brazil, Hopewell (2014) notes that "Brazilian agribusiness has emerged as a key driver of Brazilian trade policy" (2014: 4). She identifies the roots of the agribusiness' rise to dominance in Brazil during the 1980s economic crisis. Like many other developing economies, Brazil was hit by hyperinflation and a debt crisis. In response to the economic crisis, Brazilian policy makers opted to move away from ISI with the once "inward-looking economy with substantial state intervention to promote industrial development" towards "a major program of neoliberal economic restructuring" (Hopewell 2014: 5). The restructuring of the economy included opening it up to foreign direct investment (FDI) and directing its agribusiness towards an export-led strategy, thus, moving the agri-industry away from tropical product exports (coffee, tea, sugar, bananas, etc.) to producing and exporting commodities in direct competition with the USA and EU (soybeans, cotton, corn, beef, chicken, pork, etc.).

The Brazilian government has not been a passive actor in the neoliberal market restructuring of its economy. Rather, with the SAPs, Brazil's elite stood to gain much as Brazil emerged as a strong and significant player in the global political economy. Over the course of the next few decades, with the intensification of financial globalization and the restructuring of the global economy through new forms of market liberalization, there were massive influxes of international funds into so-called emergent markets. The influx of international capital ushered in a change in the financing of economic activities in Brazil from national financial contributions (i.e. state-led development or local capital) to transnational or "globalized" capital (i.e. free-market development or FDI). FDI in Brazil has been particularly focused upon export-oriented agriculture, which has had an important impact on the policies adopted to remain competitive globally and continue to attract foreign investors. In practice, this has meant state endorsement for changes in policy and regulations to facilitate the expansion of foreign investment and the growth of Brazil's export-led economy.

In the 1990s, Brazil stepped up its science and technology investments and has since dedicated substantial resources to increasing its agricultural production (Rada and Valdes 2012). Much of these resources have included massively investing in the use of agro-toxins. This is a trend that has only intensified since the 2000s. According to a report by the Brazilian Association of Public Health (ABRASCO), the use of agro-toxins in Brazil has grown by more than 162% from 2000 to 2012, making it the leading consumer of agro-toxins worldwide (Alves 2015; see also Rigotto et al. 2014). This means that since 2000, Brazil's agro-toxin imports have grown faster than anywhere in the world (Da Rocha Franco and Pelaez 2016). ABRASCO has reported that the Brazilian agricultural sector purchased over 823,000 tons of agro-toxins in 2012, surpassing the USA to become the world's largest purchaser of agro-toxins. The state heavily subsidizes and fully encourages the use of agro-toxins (Farah 1994).

In the state of Mato Grosso in mid-west Brazil, agribusiness is the main economic activity; it is also Brazil's leading consumer of agro-toxins. In 2009, the national average consumption of agro-toxins was roughly 3.7 L per inhabitant, whereas the state of Mato Grosso went through just over nine times as much, averaging roughly 34.1 L per inhabitant (Ueker et al. 2016: 2). Because of the economic importance and dependence upon export-agriculture in Brazil and particularly in the Mato Grosso region, there has been massive use of agro-toxins, including ones that are banned for the same crops in other areas of the world; at least four major producers of agro-toxins sell products in Brazil that are no longer legal in their domestic markets (Prada 2015). These include USA-based FMC Corporation, Denmark's Cheminova A/S, Germany's Helm AG and Swiss agribusiness giant Syngenta AG. According to Reuters (Prada 2015), compounds such as paraquat, considered to be "highly poisonous" by USA regulators, and banned in the EU, are still being sold in Brazil by Syngenta and Helm. A 2011 USA National Institute of Health study showed a link between paraquat use and Parkinson's disease in farm workers (Tanner et al. 2011). Paulo Peterson, director of the Brazilian Agro-Ecology Association, asserts that almost half of the main active ingredients used in agro-toxins in Brazil today – 22 of 50 ingredients – are now banned in most other countries. He places fault upon a lack of adequate monitoring by the state and lax controls of existing legislation (Alves 2015).

Controversy over Brazil's approach to agro-toxin use came under global scrutiny during the 2015–2016 Zika virus epidemic, labelled by the World Health Organization (WHO) as a global world health emergency. The epidemic, spread by the *Aedes aegypti* mosquito, originated in Brazil. The mainstream explanation was that the virus was the cause of the large numbers of reported cases of microcephaly, a congenital condition associated with a lack of fetal brain development and an abnormal smallness of the infant's head. These claims were disputed in a controversial report by a group of Argentine doctors, Physicians in the Crop-Sprayed Towns (PCST). They argued that the surge in numbers of infants born with microcephaly was not due to the Zika virus; instead, they claimed that there were indications that the larvacide pyriproxyfen (manufactured by the Japanese company Sumitomo Chemical, a subsidiary of Monsanto) used in the area to attack Zika-carrying mosquitoes may have been the real source of the problem (Aranda 2016). The PCST reported that the Brazilian Ministry of Health had added the larvacide to drinking water reservoirs in the state of Pernambuco where the numbers of affected babies were the highest. The claim that a larvacide was the cause of microcephaly was ferociously criticized and contested by the agri-industry and biotech companies, as well as by the Brazilian government – although it did suspend the use of pyriproxyfen, supposedly to allay fears. Without dwelling on the controversy here, there were several conflicting experts and divergent scientific knowledge, with opposing groups defending various stakeholders: farmers, local communities and environmentalists, on one hand, and the agri-industry and biotech companies, on the other.

Agro-ecology activists have linked the massive increases in the use of agro-toxins to the expansion of monoculture crops and genetically modified (GM) seeds (Ibid.). The commercial sale of GM crops was first introduced in 1994 by the company Calgene, a subsidiary of the agro-industry and biotechnology giant, Monsanto. GM crops have been touted as a way to lower the use of agro-toxins because, in theory, they are more resistant to disease and infestations. But there is now evidence that the opposite has transpired, and that agro-toxins are now being used in greater quantities in areas that have focused upon monoculture and GM crops (Benbrook 2012; Food & Water Watch 2013). Monoculture farming and the intensification of the use of agro-toxins in Brazil has grown hand-in-hand with the strengthening of powerful pressure groups, such as the Brazilian Agriculture and Live-Stock Confederation (a union of employers), which lobbies the government on territorial rights of Indigenous populations and slave descendants, land reform, forests, water, minerals, biodiversity and the right to work and health (Rigotto *et al.* 2014).

## Regulating agro-toxins

The current regulatory framework for agro-toxins in Brazil was adopted in the 1990s with a tripartite structure of three different ministries: the Ministry of Agriculture, Livestock and Supplies (MAPA); the Ministry of Health; and the Ministry of Environment. The regulation of agro-toxins falls under Federal Law 7802/89 adopted in 1989. Da Rocha Franco and Pelaez (2016: 213) point out that the law was drafted "in a context of intense pressure from interest groups with conflicting rationales: one pushing the intensive use of agricultural inputs to boost agribusiness yields, *versus* the preservation of human health and the environment by means of controlling that production model." Officially, the law requires a danger assessment by prohibiting the registration of agro-toxins that are carcinogenic, teratogenic, mutagenic or hormone disruptors (Da Rocha Franco and Pelaez 2016: 219). Da Rocha Franco and Pelaez (2016) note that the approval of that requirement was quite avant garde because similar criteria were only adopted by the EU in its Regulation (EC) No. 1107/2009, which only came into effect in June 2011. The regulatory bodies are meant to consider the agro-toxins' agronomic performance (i.e. its economic effectiveness) and toxicological limits (i.e. its impact on human health and environment); however, there is a non-negligible prevalence of economic over social-environmental interests (Pelaez et al. 2013). The centralization of the assessment of pesticides to a single body is under discussion in the Brazilian Senate under the project PLS 209/2013. The proposal foresees creating conditions similar to the procedures regarding transgenic seeds at the National Technical Committee on Biosafety (CTNBio), a body that has never refused a request made by industry (Rigotto et al. 2014).

There are strong tensions and palpable power struggles between the ministries visible in the example of the 2013 Law n. 12,873/13 and Decree n. 8,133/13 (regulating Law n. 12,873/13) (for a discussion see Tavares 2013, in Portuguese). The Law and Decree gave the Ministry of Agriculture the power to introduce previously banned pesticides in Brazil in order to respond to a potential epidemiological "emergency" situation, which was categorized as an imminent risk of the introduction of an exotic disease or agricultural pest. The Ministry of Agriculture claimed that the importation of agro-toxins affected by this law *should* be approved in member states of the OECD and *should* follow the UN's Food and Agriculture Organisation's International Code of Conduct on the Distribution and Use of Pesticides. Ultimately, the Ministry of Agriculture was given discretion on the importation of previously banned agro-toxins. The law was passed in under one month through the Chamber of Deputies and the Senate. Despite major concerns and opposition from various groups, including from within one of the three ministries responsible for the regulation of agro-toxins, the law received expedited presidential approbation. The Ministry of Health, the National Health Regulatory Agency (ANVISA, equivalent to the FDA in the USA)[3], and NGOs ABRASCO, Advisory and Services to Projects in Alternative Agriculture (AS-PTA), Family Agriculture and Agroecology and the Permanent Campaign Against Agrochemicals were all against giving these "emergency" powers to the Ministry of Agriculture. One objection was that the law was vague; it established few criteria and no objective parameters of what constitutes an "emergency" situation, allowing for wideranging discretion by the MAPA. According to one activist from AS-PTA, the law enables the "endanger[ment of] human and environmental health for the benefit of a group of companies that plan to export soy, corn and cotton" (Tavares 2013, transl. by author). The passing of this law highlights the asymmetric power dynamic both between the ministries and between varying social agents in Brazil; the power to import, manufacture, market and use agro-toxins lies with MAPA, at the expense of the assessments and integrity of health and the environment. At the same time, although several initiatives have been taken to facilitate the importation and use of agro-toxins and GMOs, the government approved the National Policy on Agro-ecology and Organic Production (PLANAPO). This policy allocated R$8.8 billion towards agricultural credits, financing of sustainable systems. and the extension of technical assistance for "agro-ecological," rural and organic initiatives. The Brazilian state is thus passing laws and policies that are at once wholly incongruent and contradictory: it is doing everything possible to increase agro-toxin use whilst simultaneousy endorsing agro-ecology and organic foods.

Registration of a new pesticide product is granted if the agro-toxins' toxic effect upon humans and the environment is verifiably equal to or less than that of products already registered for the same use (Tucker and Brown 1995–1996: 91). One of the problems with agro-toxin regulation in Brazil is that Law 7802/89 allows for an indefinite registration; this means that once the agro-toxin is accepted, it becomes extremely difficult – indeed virtually impossible – to remove it from exploitation. When there is doubt as to the effects on health or the environment of an agro-toxin, the burden of proof lies with the regulatory agencies. Part of the difficulty in ascertaining the real effects of endocrine disruptions caused by agro-toxins is that the regulatory agency – in this case the Ministry of Health or the Ministry of Environment – must "demonstrate that the assessment criteria used to grant the original registration either were mistaken or have become outdated with new scientific evidence on a particular active ingredient" (Da Rocha Franco and Pelaez 2016: 220). The problem is the evidence is hardly independent. All the information available to the regulatory bodies is provided by the applicants themselves. In other words, the data (including agronomic performance and human and environmental toxicity) upon which regulations are decided, are provided for by the biotech companies and the agri-industry themselves (Ibid.).

The dependence upon corporate partnership in its own regulation reflects what Pearce (1976) described with regard to corporate participation and cooperation with the state over 40 years ago. In his example, it was creating anti-trust legislation because it "provided a means by which monopoly capital could be achieved against dangerous competitors . . . without danger of popular reactions" (Pearce 1976: 87). Pearce's explanation for how the general population could permit this situation was that the state and big business effectively create and maintain an "imaginary social order" (Ibid.: 94). Thus, in his examination of anti-trust laws in the USA, he showed that although these laws appeared to be in the interest of the general public, large businesses were in fact key in their administration. A small number of token prosecutions for abuses served to uphold this "imaginary social order." One of Pearce's key contributions was that he demystified corporate crime by contrasting the "imaginary social order" with the "real social order." He argued that laws regulating corporate behaviour are written or implemented in ways that make them virtually unenforceable. The regulation of agro-toxins in Brazil is predicated upon avant garde laws that are considered to be highly restrictive and protective of society and the environment (Da Rocha Franco and Pelaez 2016). The remainder of this chapter will argue that that those laws in fact enable the state to perform its "objective function" in order to guarantee "the reproduction of the economic system" (Ibid.: 61). Thus, although there is some "regulation," this is enacted, and to a limited extent enforced, to give semblance of a legitimate system that applies to all, including the powerful, but which has the objective of preserving the dominance of the capitalist social order.

## The "imaginary social order" in Brazil

In the early 1990s, Brazil restructured its economy and opened its markets. It became dependent upon large inflows of FDI, largely from firms based in the USA and EU, as well as from its Latin American neighbours (Jank et al. 2001). Major TNCs, including Nestlé, Parmalat, ADM, Cargill, Unilever, Bunge, Dreyfus, Carrefour, Ahold, Danone and Sara Lee, undertook mergers and acquisitions of various subsectors of the Brazilian agro-industry. These TNCs, amongst others, took advantage of the Washington Consensus that underscored the economic restructuring of the Global South during the 1990s. During this period, there was a concentration and internationalization of the agri-industry in Brazil (Jank et al. 2001). However, Hopewell (2014) contends that since the 2000s, Brazilian firms have made dramatic developments in gaining market shares. She notes that of the 40 leading agribusiness companies operating in Brazil, 35 are now Brazilian in origin; and many have internationalized, becoming global leading competitors and taking large shares of the global market and its revenues (Ibid.: 7). Hopewell's argument is that with the emergence of Brazil's aggressive export-oriented agribusiness, there has been a transformation in the relationship between state and capital. She points to an independent, private-sector lobby with considerable influence on the state. Hopewell concentrates on what impact this has had for Brazil internationally and particularly in trade negotiations at the WTO. For our purposes, we consider what this has meant internally – that is the political participation of the agri-industry and its impact upon agro-toxin regulation in Brazil.

The agribusiness lobby in Brazil is organized through the *bancada ruralista* (the rural bench), a powerful congressional bloc that represents the interests of large landowners. Currently, half of Brazil's 594 lawmakers identify themselves with the agribusiness lobby (Brandào and Schoneveled 2015: 10). In 2008, Katia Abreu, an agribusiness leader, was appointed Minister of Agriculture, a clear demonstration of the influence of the agribusiness lobby in Brazilian politics. According to one study, agricultural and food companies contributed 25% of former President Dilma Rousseff's electoral funding (Prada 2015). The financial contributions of agribusiness to electoral campaigns has undoubtedly had an influence on the congressional agenda that promotes the interests of large industry groups, particularly from the agricultural sector. Brazilian agronomist and member of the country's GMO regulatory body, Prof. Leonardo Melgarejo, represents the Ministry of Agrarian Development. He has expressed concern that Brazilian lawmakers are overly influenced by powerful agricultural lobbying groups and have been undermining efforts to regulate the use of agro-toxins (teleSur 2016).

A concept that comes to mind in the Brazilian case is that of "regulatory capture": the idea that the targeted industry actively participates in creating the content of its regulation for its own benefit (Bernstein 1955). Capture theory became popular in liberal circles in the 1970s, with one of its most famous pundits being George Stigler, who wrote extensively on the subject. However, more critical scholars, many of whom have been influenced by Pearce's work in the same period, point out the flaws in capture theory. Regulatory capture theorists apply the concept to identify how states are actively engaged in enabling corporate/industry advantages and interests. Crouch (2011: 72) has argued that "capture" happens because "often the only expertise available about a field of activity is held within the firms concerned, so government is dependent on them for advice about how to exercise its regulation." This seems to apply in the case of Brazil where, as we have seen, the information available to the regulatory bodies is provided by the applicants themselves. Capture theory is ultimately a kind of "consensus" theory, whereby a wide-ranging group of stakeholders comes together in the decision-making process to find a solution that best responds to the needs of the society. But rather than working towards a collective good, the main motivation for this consensus is self-interest.

Tombs and Whyte (2007: 153–160) point out that according to the "compliance school" of regulation literature, the most successful regulatory strategies are those that encourage self-regulation. This perspective views corporations as both willing and capable of responsible and moral decision making; for compliance-style regulation to work, the broad agreement and political support of the "regulatory community" must be achieved. In their analysis of "compliance theory," Pearce and Tombs (1990) argue that it supports the view that regulatory officials and agencies must act as consultants rather than as supervisors and enforcers of regulation, thus leaving regulation in the hands of those meant to be regulated. Corporations develop, execute and enforce their own "codes of conduct." These codes rely upon an inherent voluntarism, which depends upon the goodwill of companies to fulfil their engagements. This is indeed the case of Brazil, which is cited as having restrictive regulation in the use and sale of pesticides (Sabino et al. 2011; Pelaez et al. 2013), despite a reliance on self-regulation and industry partnership. The safe and proper distribution and use of pesticides remains, for example, heavily reliant upon the industry's promotion[4]: for example, the Brazilian Code of Advertising Self-Regulation, which includes general rules that govern the advertising of specific products, including pesticides. The self-regulation of advertising different agro-toxins is significant given the impact of advertising and marketing practices on the enjoyment of human rights (see UN 2014).

Although the concept of "regulatory capture" may be convenient, Tombs and Whyte (2007) comment that as a consensus theory, it has played into neoliberal deregulation strategies. For one, it is "incapable of producing an alternative to the domination of the regulatory system by corporate interests" (Ibid.: 165). It is theory rooted in defeatism: the perspective that the corruption of state regulation by the market is both inevitable and unalterable – the classic neoliberal idea of TINA, "There Is No Alternative." Moreover, it does not explain why governments sometimes impose stricter regulations upon industry that might negatively affect corporate profits. One explanation is what Pearce (1976) described as state intervention in activities which undermine the capitalist social order. The capitalist state intervenes in the market or imposes regulations upon industry not to penalize business (and not even necessarily in the "public interest") but rather to save capitalism from itself. When the legitimacy of the capitalist state is at risk, the state steps in to safeguard the system. In this process of self-preservation by the state, the general public mostly sees a different picture; that is regulation is the state responding to its demand – which has often followed "public interest theory" (Pigou 1932). According to "public interest theory," regulations are prepared in the public interest when they are demanded by the public for correcting inefficient practices. It is often contrasted with Stigler's (1971) "public choice theory," the notion that regulations are prepared when the public demands the efficient allocation of resources. However, Pearce (1976: 94) suggested that it is neither of these, but rather a general mystification of the general public that makes them believe that regulations are good. Part of this mystification is due to the state and big businesses' creation and maintenance of an "imaginary social order," in which law has a central role to play and for which the state seeks to present the market as a just and effective regulator of business.

A mechanism related to regulatory capture is the "revolving door," which describes the ebb and flow of various forces that affect regulation, such as government officials who oscillate to and from the public to private sectors. The concern is that the exchange of personnel between the public and private sectors hinders the objectivity and independence of the regulator because she or he may have a direct interest in the regulated industry – for example, the appointment by President Lula of a former Monsanto lawyer, Beto Ferreira Martins Vasconcelos, to the post of executive secretary of the Biosecurity Council (2006–2010). Although Vasconcelos' role was formally advisory – he did not have a formal vote – he was a key contributor to the drafting of the 2005 Biosecurity Law which regulates GMOs in Brazil. Following his advice, the council approved Monsanto's GM maize, despite strong opposition, including from ANVISA and the environmental protection agency IBAMA (equivalent to the EPA in the USA), which is part of the Ministry of Environment.[5] The result of these political manoeuvres was that the *bancada ruralista* and pro-agribusiness groups worked to legitimize and legalize GMOs. With some GM crops permitted in neighbouring Argentina, many seeds entered Brazil illegally. The existence of transgenic crops in Brazil, despite their illegality at the time, was used by the *bancada ruralista* and Vasconcelos to argue that it was necessary to adapt the legislation to an already existing situation.

If a major flaw in capture theory is its defeatism, it is a defeatism that does not translate to the reality on the ground. There are numerous social movements and resistances against the business-friendly outputs of regulatory agencies, the agribusiness and the bio-tech industry. In the case of Brazil, the inadequacy of capture theory can be seen in the tensions between the economic push for agricultural productivity versus the safeguarding of health and environmental sustainability that pit varying social agents within and without the ministries against one another. Thus, as Rigotto et al. (2014) have noted, diverse social agents are struggling for distinct, often contradictory projects and interests. They point out that on one hand there are social agents focused upon the acceleration of agricultural production, including the modernization of farming and a focus upon the production of commodities in Brazil. As the authors note, this includes the oligopolies of the chemical, metal-mechanics and seed industries; big landowners; and an important participation of the financial sector, which all have strong ties with the executive, legislative and judiciary branches of the state to exert influence. On the other hand, there are social movements that have come together to resist and confront agribusiness and agro-toxin use in Brazil. These groups, such as the Permanent Campaign Against Pesticides and For Life, bring together over 100 social organizations, including ABRASCO who published the *ABRASCO Report*, in which public health professionals made public their commitment to making the scientific evidence of agro-toxin hazards available to the wider general population (Rigotto et al. 2014). However, unlike the TINA perspective, there is real potential in these distinct forces

## Conclusion

The issue of the importation, use and regulation of pesticides in Brazil is one that is deeply divisive. And this divide is marked throughout the social strata: from the grassroots through to branches of government that are in opposition with one another. On one hand, there are those segments of Brazilian society that view agro-toxins as necessary to ensuring the competitiveness and sustainability of the Brazilian economy. These groups include large landowners of the *banca ruralista* who are supported by large biotech firms and many key politicians, including the powerful Ministry of Agriculture. These groups have worked together to construct a regulatory framework that relies upon corporate participation and cooperation with the state. A notable example, as we saw, is that the information about agro-toxins that is available to the regulatory bodies and upon which policies and regulations are decided is produced and made available by the agribusiness and biotech companies themselves. On the other hand, there are activists, scientists, Indigenous populations and various public agents who oppose the abusive overconsumption of agro-toxins in Brazil. These different perspectives on agro-toxin use are thus marked by an asymmetrical power struggle between large, corporate-influenced power; regulatory agencies with economic priorities; and agro-activists, concerned citizens, Indigenous populations and public agents from weaker ministries.

In the second half of the 20th century, Brazil's economy was transformed from an import-intensive country to one of the world's largest food exporters. This chapter has argued that the Brazilian state has cultivated its globally competitive agribusiness by turning the Brazilian agricultural market into a giant laboratory. By so doing, it has privileged capital gain over human and environmental sustainability and integrity. Forty years after Frank Pearce exposed the "imaginary social order," his findings still hold true. In the case examined in this chapter, the semblance of a restrictive and protective regulatory framework for agro-toxins in Brazil is undermined by what is in fact a permissive regime more interested in expanding and accelerating Brazil's share in the global agricultural market than in safeguarding workers' health and safety, Indigenous lands and the environment. The situation in Brazil is a reminder that serious study of the state and its agents, and the activities of the ruling class remains, perhaps more than ever, relevant and necessary in order to identify and exploit the vulnerabilities of the neoliberal state and the capitalist social order. Furthermore, as Pearce (1976: 159) concluded, "the distance between rhetoric and action becomes manifest when contrasting the publicly stated purpose of legislation and the actual targets in mind when it was framed and implemented."

## Notes

1 The "Green Revolution" increased agricultural productivity with the introduction of agro-toxins, new management and technological techniques and the use of high-yield grain varieties.
2 The term agro-toxins is borrowed from the Brazilian term *agrotóxicos*, referring to the various categories of chemicals used by the agro-industry; these include herbicides, pesticides, larvacides and insecticides. The Stockholm Convention on Persistent Organic Pollutants identifies 10 of the 12 most dangerous organic chemicals as pesticides (http://chm.pops.int/TheConvention/ThePOPs/The12InitialPOPs/tabid/296/Default.aspx).
3 ANVISA is a governmental regulatory agency established in 1999 that is connected to the Ministry of Health. According to its website (http://portal.anvisa.gov.br/contact-us), ANVISA's primary goal is to protect and promote public health by exercising health surveillance over products and services, including processes, ingredients and technologies that pose any health risks.
4 In June 2016, Brazil's Ministry of Environment proposed a bill targeting the production, import and use of agro-toxins that would establish a regulatory regime consisting of registration and reporting requirements, substance risk assessments and risk management measures in order to monitor, evaluate and control the use of industrial chemicals produced in or imported into Brazil.
5 According to GMWatch (2014), ANVISA stated in its report that the data provided by Monsanto were inconclusive regarding the risk of the GMO MON810 for human and animal consumption. In 2014, a Federal Court of Appeals of the 4th Circuit unanimously ruled to annul a decision that would have allowed the TNC Bayer to commercialize "Liberty Link," a GMO corn. The decision was encouraging for environmentalists and activists who hope for a nationwide review of GMO crops and eventual proscriptions.

## References

Alves, L. (2015) "Brazil Shown to Be Largest Global Consumer of Pesticides." *The Rio Times*, 5 May. Online. Available HTTP: http://riotimesonline.com/brazil-news/rio-politics/brazil-is-largest-global-consumer-of-pesticides-shows-report/.

Aranda, D. (2016) "Pesticides Spraying in the Crosshairs." *GMWatch*, 10 March. Online. Available HTTP: www.gmwatch.org/news/latest-news/16790-microcephaly-pesticide-spraying-once-again-in-the-crosshairs.

Benbrook, C.M. (2012) "Impacts of Genetically Engineered Crops on Pesticide Use in the U.S. – The First Sixteen Years." *Environmental Sciences Europe*, 24: 24–37.

Bernstein, M. (1955) *Regulating Business by Independent Commission*. Princeton, NJ: Princeton University Press.

Brandào, F. and Schoneveled, G. (2015) "The State of Oil Palm Development in the Brazilian Amazon: Trends, Value Chain Dynamics and Business Models." Centre for International Forestry Research, Working Paper 198.

Crouch, C. (2011) *The Strange Non-Death of Neo-Liberalism*. Cambridge: Polity Press.

Da Rocha Franco, C. and Pelaez, V. (2016) "(De)Constructing the Political Agenda of Control over Pesticides in Brazil." *Ambiente & Sociedade*. São Paulo v. XIX, No. 3, pp. 215–232.

Evans, P. (1979) *Dependent Development: The Alliance of Multinational, State and Local Capital in Brazil*. Princeton, NJ: Princeton University Press.

Farah, J. (1994) "Pesticide Policies in Developing Countries: Do they Encourage Excessive Use?," World Bank Discussion Paper WDP238, The World Bank, Washington, DC.

Food & Water Watch (July 2013) "Superweeds: How Biotech Crops Bolster the Pesticide Industry." 1–16. Online. Available HTTP: www.foodandwaterwatch.org/sites/default/files/Superweeds%20Report%20July%202013.pdf

GMWatch. (2014) "Brazil's Food Safety Agency Warned in 2007 that MON810 Maize Not Proven Safe to Eat." 25 February. Online. Available HTTP: www.gmwatch.org/news/archive/2014/15329-brazil-s-food-safety-agency-warned-in-2007-that-mon810-maize-not-proven-safe-to-eat

Hopewell, K. (2014) "The Transformation of State-Business Relations in an Emerging Economy: The Case of Brazilian Agribusiness." *Critical Perspectives on International Business*, 10(4): 291–309.

Jank, M.S., Leme, M.F.P., Nassar, A.M. and Filho, P.F. (2001) "Concentration and Internationalization of Brazilian Agribusiness Exporters." *International Food and Agribusiness Management Review*, 2(3/4): 359–374.

Mainwaring, S. (1986) "The Transition to Democracy in Brazil." *Journal of Interamerican Studies and World Affairs*, 28(1) (Spring, 1986): 149–179.

Pearce, F. (1976) *Crimes of the Powerful: Marxism, Crime, and Deviance*. London: Pluto Press.

Pearce, F. and Tombs, S. (1990) "Ideology, Hegemony and Empiricism: Compliance Theories of Regulation." *British Journal of Criminology*, 30(4): 423–443.

Pelaez, V., Rodrigues da Silva, L. and Borges Araújo, E. (2013) "Regulation of Pesticides: A Comparative Analysis." *Science and Public Policy*, 40: 644–656.

Pigou, A.C. (1932) *The Economics of Welfare*. London: Macmillan and Co.

Prada, P. (2015) "Why Brazil Has a Big Appetite for Banned Pesticides" *Reuters Online*, 2 April. Online. Available HTTP: www.dailymail.co.uk/wires/reuters/article-3023304/Why-Brazil-big-appetite-banned-pesticides.html#ixzz4YkQMoW8F

Rada, N. and Valdes, C. (July 2012) "Policy, Technology, and Efficiency of Brazilian Agriculture." *US Department of Agriculture Research Service Economic Research Report No.* (ERR-137) 1–43 pp., Online. Available HTTP: www.ers.usda.gov/webdocs/publications/err137/28921_err137_reportsummary.pdf

REDUAS. (2016) "REPORT From Physicians in the Crop-Sprayed Town Regarding Dengue-Zika, Microcephaly, and Massive Spraying with Chemical Poisons." *Red Universitaria de Ambiente y Salud*, 9 February. Online. Available HTTP: http://reduas.com.ar/report-from-physicians-in-the-crop-sprayed-town-regarding-dengue-zika-microcephaly-and-massive-spraying-with-chemical-poisons/

Rigotto, M.R., Paixão e Vasconcelos, D. and Rocha, M.M. (July 2014) "Pesticide Use in Brazil and Problems for Public Health." *Cadernos de Saúde Pública*, 30(7): 1360–1362.

Robinson, C. (2016) "Argentine and Brazilian Doctors Name Larvicide as Potential Cause of Microcephaly." *GM Watch*, 10 February. Online. Available HTTP: www.gmwatch.org/news/latest-news/16706-argentine-and-brazilian-doctors-name-larvicide-as-potential-cause-of-microcephaly.

Sabino, B.; Rozenbaum, H. and Oliveira, A. (2011) "A Forensic View of Pesticide Poisonings in Brazil," in M. Stoytcheva (ed.) *Pesticides in the Modern World – Effects of Pesticides Exposure*. Intech Open Access Online. Available HTTP: www.intechopen.com/books/pesticides-in-the-modern-world-effects-of-pesticides-exposure/a-forensic-view-of-pesticide-poisonings-in-brazil.

Stigler, G.J. 1971. "The Theory of Economic Regulation." *The Bell Journal of Economics and Management Science*, 2(1) (Spring, 1971): 3–21.

Tanner, Caroline M., Kamel, G.F., Ross, W., Hoppin, J.A., Goldman, S.M., Korell, M., Marras, C., Bhudhikanok, G.C., Kasten, M., Chade, A.R., Comyns, K., Barber Richards,

M., Meng, C., Priestley, B., Fernandez, H.H., Cambi, F., Umbach, D.M., Blair, A., Sandler, D.P. and Langston, J.W. (June 2011) "Rotenone, Paraquat, and Parkinson's Disease." *Environmental Health Perspective*, 119(6): 866–872.

Tavares, V. (2013) "Portaria libera uso de agrotóxico proibido no Brasil" Escola Politecnica de Saude Joaquim Venancio – Fiocruz, 7 November. Online. Available HTTP: www.epsjv. fiocruz.br/noticias/reportagem/portaria-libera-uso-de-agrotoxico-proibido-no-brasil.

teleSUR. (2016) "Seventy Percent of Brazilian Food Contaminated by Agrochemicals." *Global Research: Centre for Research on Globalization,* 17 June. Online. Available HTTP: www.global research.ca/seventy-percent-of-brazilian-food-contaminated-by-agrochemicals/5531682

Tombs, S. and Whyte, D. (2007) *Safety Crimes.* Collumpton, UK: Willan Publishing.

Tucker, J.C. and Brown, M.A. (1995–1996) "Comparative Analysis of Pesticide Regulatory Programs in the United States and Brazil." *Loyola of Los Angeles International and Comparative Law Journal*, 18: 81–108.

Ueker, M.E., Monteiro Silva, V., Pedroso Moi, G., Pignati, W.A., Echenique Mattos, I. and Cândido Silvo, A.M. (2016) "Parenteral Exposure to Pesticides and Occurrence of Congenital Malformations: Hospital-based Case-control Study." *BMC Pediatrics*, 16 Online. Available HTTP: http://bmcpediatr.biomedcentral.com/articles/10.1186/s12887-016-0667-x

UN. (2014) "New Issue in Focus: The Impact of Advertising and Marketing Practices on the Enjoyment of Cultural Rights." UN Human Rights Office of the High Commissioner, Online. Available HTTP: www.ohchr.org/EN/NewsEvents/Pages/DisplayNews. aspx?NewsID=15864&LangID=E; www.ohchr.org/EN/Issues/CulturalRights/Pages/ impactofadvertisingandmarketing.aspx

# Chapter 14

# No criminology of wage theft
## Revisiting "workplace theft" to expose capitalist exploitation

*Paul Leighton*

Discussions of workplace theft routinely focus on employees victimizing employers, even though employers also financially victimize employees. Employers use a variety of legal and criminal wage-suppression tactics, and wage theft involves the non-payment of wages due under laws and contractual agreements. Although some of these violations are resolved through civil suits, federal law and the laws of many states have specific criminal statutes for wage theft, which involves aspects of fraud, abuse of power and violations of trust.

Indeed, wage and hour laws – especially those setting a minimum wage and higher rates for overtime – are meant to ensure "a fair day's pay for a fair day's work," so their violation strikes deep at the personal dominion of workers. Wage theft disproportionately affects low-income workers, who experience an economically precarious existence. Wage theft can force them into stressful decisions about which needs of their family – housing, food or health care, for example – they will do without. This situation can lead to, or aggravate, mental health and/or substance abuse problems, especially when workers know they have been ripped off but feel powerless to do anything about it.

Further, by redistributing from workers to business owners, wage theft directly contributes to inequality and wage stagnation. Some workers who are victims of wage theft are forced onto various social welfare programmes, thus channelling taxpayer money to support businesses that systematically skim money from their employees. And wage theft spreads perniciously because businesses that do it have a competitive advantage with lower prices and/or higher profits compared to firms that obey the wage laws and regulations. When wage and hour violators are not identified and held accountable, competitors are either forced out of business or adapt by also engaging in wage theft. If enough businesses in an industry are skimming from their employees' paycheques, then wage theft becomes a required business practice.

In spite of the criminal laws and the real harm done by wage theft, there is virtually no mention of wage theft in criminology journals and textbooks, even ones about white-collar crime. Perhaps that is an unfortunate consequence of criminal prosecutions being infrequent, pursued by a few states and typically against smaller local or regional businesses rather than national or multinational corporations.

However, further investigation reveals contradictions that should be of concern to those within criminology and beyond. The rhetoric of politicians that praises working people and the annual American parade to honour labour does not translate into criminal or even vigorous regulatory enforcement of wage theft laws. Indeed, the regulatory regime is generally weak and under-resourced, with the Wage and Hour Division of many U.S. states best described as intentionally ineffective. Universities want to prepare their graduating students for the job market, but they do so with no mention of wage and hour regulations, the policing of wage and hour violations or what students should do in the likely event they face economic exploitation. That there is little help with this type of victimization would be useful knowledge and foster critical thinking about the economic arrangements surrounding the workforce they will be joining. Thus, the absence of wage theft reproduces the ideology that Young says "insists that the interests of the bourgeoisie are the national interest, [and] that exploitation is, in fact, a fair return for a fair day's work" (in Pearce 1976: 17).

Further, Pearce's book, by analysing the crimes of the powerful, forces criminologists to look at the discipline in relation to power and capitalism because "more powerful individuals will not only attempt to impose their values on the other people in society generally, but also on those who study social life" (1976: 42). Indeed, when I started talking to other criminologists – including theoretically critical colleagues – about wage theft, the typical answer was, "Interesting . . . what is it exactly?" I discussed the non-payment of wages due under federal and state laws, such as not paying overtime, finding ways to pay less than minimum wage and forcing employees to work off the clock. I provided an example of a manager of a pizza place I worked at who simply did not pay me for all the hours I worked and how challenging him was difficult because I depended on him for enough hours of work to support myself. Everybody not only quickly understood the problem, but had examples of their own. Somehow, although many criminologists have been victimized by wage theft, it becomes forgotten as a crime and has failed to become a topic of criminological interest, even within the field of white-collar and corporate crime.

As a start on correcting the criminological neglect of wage theft, this chapter seeks to lay out a foundation based on Pearce's *Crimes of the Powerful*. The first section contextualizes wage theft as the neglected aspect of "workplace theft," and which is treated much differently in the media than employee theft. The second section demonstrates the neglect of wage theft in the criminological literature (even though it is punishable by imprisonment and thus a "real" crime that can be studied even by those who do not like to see the discipline incorporate analogous social harms). Even with the marginalization of white-collar and corporate crime, the absence of material on wage theft is striking. The third section discusses how wage theft applies to the idea of an "imaginary social order" that Pearce develops in *Crimes of the Powerful* and his analysis of Roosevelt's New Deal being tough medicine to ensure the health of capitalism.

The chapter closes with four reasons why there is no criminology of wage theft, which are also the four reasons it should be developed so that criminology no longer mindlessly mimics bourgeois values: that it is a crime of the powerful, that it will help students understand exploitation in the job market, that it will encourage critical thinking about the circumstances of workers under contemporary capitalism and that it is also about regulation.

## The two sides of "workplace theft"

Just as "insurance fraud" is usually taken to mean false claims by individuals against insurance companies, "workplace theft" becomes synonymous with employees stealing from their employer. When popular media discusses lawsuits by employees about the non-payment of wages, the discussion is very different from stories of employees getting arrested for stealing from employers. Consider the wage theft claims against retailer Wal-Mart and the treatment of "Oreo Grandma," an employee arrested for stealing snacks from Wal-Mart.

In 2008, retailer Wal-Mart settled 63 lawsuits over its wage practices that workers had filed in federal and 42 state courts. Wal-Mart would have to pay between $352 and $640 million (depending on how many workers in the class action would file claims for recovery) for "forcing employees to work unpaid off the clock, erasing hours from time cards and preventing workers from taking lunch and other breaks that were promised by the company or guaranteed by state laws" (Greenhouse and Rosenbloom 2008).

Two weeks prior, Wal-Mart had settled with 100,000 Minnesota employees for $54 million in a case where the judge estimated there were 2 million violations of state law (Bustillo 2008). Wal-Mart still had 12 suits outstanding, including appeals in wage lawsuits they lost: a 2005 California verdict for $172 million and a 2006 Pennsylvania case for $188 million. In 2009, they settled a Massachusetts case for $40 million and another California case in 2010 for $86 million (Broudway 2012). There's a 2004 settlement in Colorado for $50 million (Joyce 2006). Wal-Mart settled a 2012 federal suit for the failure to pay overtime for $4.8 million in back pay and damages to employees and $464,000 in penalties, which the Department of Labor (2012) reports "stem[s] from the repeat nature of the violations."

In addition to this intentional, systematic and pervasive pattern of wage violations, Wal-Mart has settled suits involving the hiring of illegal immigrants, sex discrimination, child labour violations (in 2000 and 2005), unfair labour practices to prevent unionization and even preventing the collective airing of grievances (National Labor Relations Board 2013; Frank 2006; Greenhouse 2005). Additional lawsuits are against Wal-Mart subcontractors because of "rampant safety and wage and workplace violations," and one federal judge has allowed Wal-Mart to be named as a defendant because of the high degree of control they exert over supply chain subcontractors (Hartman 2013).

In contrast, police charged a 63-year-old Wal-Mart employee with felony theft after surveillance video showed the maintenance worker eating a package of Oreo cookies she had not paid for. After authorities confronted her, she admitted engaging in the practice for years at another Wal-Mart. Apparently, after her son had an accident, they lived only on her $11.40 an hour (in 2013) and "simply did not have the monies to legitimately purchase the food items." But the total losses over time from cookies, gum and potato chips once or twice a week were enough so "Walmart charges Grandma with felonious Oreo eating" (Scott 2013; see also CBS 2013 and Jennings 2015: 202).

Some articles about Oreo Grandma note that at $11.40 an hour, she was making more than minimum wage and more than the usual Wal-Mart associate (Scott 2013; Jennings 2015: 202). Employee theft, the reader is reminded, is a $50 billion a year problem (CBS 2013) with Wal-Mart losing $3 billion to theft – either "a good chunk of that to employee theft" (CBS 2013) or all of it (Jennings 2015: 202).

News stories about Wal-Mart never quoted anyone saying Wal-Mart was engaged in a crime, nor did any media outlet even feel the need to explain why there were no criminal charges against Wal-Mart executives. Press coverage noted Oreo Grandma's wages were more than minimum wage and more than other Wal-Mart employees, apparently so readers should question her "need" to steal. But Wal-Mart's profitability, which grew every single year from $2.7 billion in 1995 to $17 billion in 2012 (Miglani 2015), is not mentioned in reports about wage violation suits against Wal-Mart, nor are their other abuses of labour connected to a "need" for profit. Oreo Grandma is shown to be part of a larger, multibillion-dollar problem that faces Wal-Mart and other retail stores, and Wal-Mart's wage theft is never linked to a larger "crisis of wage theft" (Bobo 2011) or $50 billion "epidemic of wage theft" (Meixell and Eisenbrey 2014; Bernhardt et al. 2013).

## No criminology of wage theft

A basic requirement of scholarly writing is a literature review in some form to contextualize the topic and outline the state of knowledge in the field to which the author is adding. This requirement represents a problem with the criminology of wage theft – and one that should be dealt with by examining the marginalization of the topic within criminology rather than overanalysing occasional passing references to wage theft.

Using the full text search feature through my university library, I conducted searches for "wage theft" and "wage and hour." The quotation marks used in the search limit results to the words used as a phrase, with the latter phrase to ensure the inclusion of results related to wage and hour violations (the more formal term for wage theft) and the Wage and Hour Division (that investigates and enforces the relevant law).

The work of McGurrin et al. (2013) provides a basis for a sample of journals because they analysed the most prestigious criminology journals plus a selection of international journals and critical ones. To their work, I have added *Contemporary Justice Review* and *Critical Criminology*. The full list and time frames includes the following:

> *Criminology* 1997–2016
> *Justice Quarterly* 1997–2016
> *Journal of Research in Crime and Delinquency* 1999–2016
> *Law and Society Review* 1996–2016
> *Journal of Criminal Law and Criminology* 1997–2016
> *Crime and Delinquency* 1999–2016
> *Criminology and Public Policy* 2001–2016
> *Journal of Quantitative Criminology* 1997–2016
> *Theoretical Criminology* 1999–2016
> *Criminal Justice and Behavior* 1999–2016
> *Social Justice* 1995–2016
> *Crime, Law, and Social Change* 1997–2016
> *The British Journal of Criminology* 1996–2016
> *Canadian Journal of Criminology and Criminal Justice* 2003–2016
> *The Journal of Criminal Justice* 1995–2016
> *Contemporary Justice Review* 2002–2016
> *Critical Criminology* 1997–2016

Out of these 17 leading criminology and justice journals, the *only* article about wage theft was a book review by Michael Lynch (2011) of Kim Bobo's *Wage Theft in America* (2011) that appeared in *Contemporary Justice Review*. Although sad, this result is perhaps not surprising given the marginalization of white-collar crime within criminology. What is still noteworthy, though, is that for 13 of the journals, a search for "wage theft" turned up *no results at all*.[1] One could read 13 of the top journals in our field for about the last 20 years and have no consciousness of wage theft. Thus, in spite of wage theft being a crime punishable by imprisonment, with costs greater than the amount of property crime reported by the FBI, and many criminologists themselves victimized by this crime, the vast majority of criminology and justice journals make *no mention* of wage theft or wage and hour violations. The 11 results for "wage theft" and "wage and hour" in the other four journals over the last 20 years tend to be passing references, usually in the context of immigrants, migrant workers and human trafficking.[2] (The consciousness of wage theft is that it happens to already marginalized others and, by implication, did not happen to me at the shopping mall pizzeria even if it felt like wage theft to me).

The criminological consciousness of wage theft is only marginally improved when books and white-collar crime texts are added into the literature review. In his review of Bobo's wage theft book, Lynch notes that "Even Friedrichs who has written what I consider the most comprehensive book on white collar and corporate crime, *Trusted Criminals*, includes only a modest discussion of wage theft" (2011: 255). Payne's 700-page book, *White-Collar Crime: A Text/Reader* (2012), has no mention of wage theft or wage and hour violations. His *White-Collar Crime: The Essentials* mentions that there is a Wage and Hour Division (2017: 319), but in a table of 29 policing/regulatory agencies; readers would need to type in the URL to find out more because there is no actual text about the agency or what it does. Rosoff, Pontell and Tillman's *Profit Without Honor* (2010) also does not mention wage theft in its 600 pages. The only book on wage theft is Bobo's (2011), who is not a criminologist but the executive director of Interfaith Worker Justice, a social justice and worker advocacy organization.

All of the white-collar criminology textbooks mentioned have discussions of employee theft, just not wage theft, and Friedrichs, who has a short discussion of wage theft, devotes more space to employee theft. Further, none of those discussions of employee theft reference the idea of controlled larceny, whereby low-level supervisors allow employees to steal office supplies, raw materials and/or goods to help offset the employees' low wage or other workplace injustice (Nadisic 2008: 129; Greenberg 1997: 89). In many ways these white-collar crime textbooks fall into the pattern critiqued by Snider (2001, 2002) in her work about the easy acceptance of claims about the "theft" of time by workers from employers. Some knowledge claims, she argues, generate more power because of their link to the structural dominance of capital.

Certainly wage theft suffers from the same "cyclical dilemma" that McGurrin et al. note for white-collar crime in general – namely, that "scholarship is only minimally conveyed to undergraduate and graduate students in their courses, texts, and journals, which in turn impacts the white collar crime knowledge base and future entry into this essential subfield of study" (2013: 12).

## Wage theft and the *Crimes of the Powerful*

One of the enduring contributions of *Crimes of the Powerful* is an articulation of the idea of an "imaginary social order" (1976: 94) to help understand hegemony. When people believe that this picture of the imaginary social order is real, then the laws and structures necessary to reproduce the capitalist economic system are legitimated. With wage theft, the imaginary social order is that the Fair Labor Standards Act (FLSA) of 1938 was passed to help workers and that enforcement of the law through federal and state Wage and Hour Divisions is aimed at upholding a fair day's pay for a fair day's work. In the imaginary social order, government enforcement catches the "bad apples" that exploit workers, while other businesses fail to comply with the law because of mistakes and confusing government regulations.

Examining this imaginary social order through the lens of the *Crimes of the Powerful* reveals a different picture that lays bare the darker truths about capitalism. Of course, the imaginary social order is not a total fantasy, or it would be dismissed as such, but there is more to the facts and interpretation than the hegemonic conventional wisdom suggests.

For example, when President Roosevelt introduced the FLSA, he stated: "A serf-supporting [sic] and self-respecting democracy can plead no justification for the existence of child labor, no economic reason for chiseling workers' wages or stretching workers' hours" (1937). Written into the law itself is a congressional finding of "the existence . . . of labor conditions detrimental to the maintenance of the minimum standard of living necessary for health, efficiency, and general well-being of workers" (29 USC § 202; see also Nordlund 1997). The combination of a minimum wage and time and a half for overtime was meant to encourage business to spread the labour over more workers and combat the "evil of 'overwork'" and "underpay" (quoted in *Overnight Motor Transportation Co., Inc. v. Missel* 316 US 572 at 578 [1942]).

However, Pearce sees minimum wage laws as being about government trying to protect capitalism from itself rather than as a pro-worker "bug" within capitalism. In discussing Roosevelt's New Deal, Pearce notes that "there was never any doubt of Roosevelt's commitment to capitalism, but in order to save it from itself he was forced to give it some rather unpalatable medicine" (1976: 43). Another scholar similarly noted that "Roosevelt's goal was not a more equitable economy, but merely less visible evidence of its inequity" (Seybold 2017). Indeed, that author quotes Mark Twain as saying that the president "persisted in attacking the symptoms and letting the disease carefully alone."

Because workers do not own the means of production from which they can draw rent or a profit, they are forced to sell their labour on the market (Pearce 1976: 53). Minimum wage laws enable capitalism by ensuring that wages and hours are sufficient for workers to be able to get enough food and rest to be able to continue work over the longer term. Wage and hours laws thus recognize a level of exploitation beyond which social policy does not reproduce "*healthy, loyal and obedient workers and soldiers*" (1976: 57; emphasis original) – and when laws do not support efficient production, "they have been ignored" (1976: 97).

This background helps make sense of why the criminal law has not been used, even against the most rampant violations – and why the powers and resources of Wage and Hour divisions seem to mock the idea of a fair day's pay for a fair day's work. For example, five states do not do any enforcement of wage laws at the state level, and they only help refer workers to the federal Wage and Hour Division (Meyer and Greenleaf 2011: 13 and 16). Another state "appears to rely exclusively on voluntary compliance" (2011: 24 and 82). Many state agencies are understaffed: Idaho had three employees to police employer compliance with wage laws, and other states relied partly on senior citizen volunteers. In response to political pressures state wage and hour divisions have been totally or partially defunded for one or more years (Lurie 2011). Further, "agencies in Michigan, Oklahoma and Texas lacked authority to initiate investigations, so all their activity was in response to worker claims," which is much less efficient than investigating businesses that are typically at the highest risk for wage theft (Lurie 2011: 422). Indeed, it means that if an employee calls to complain about wage and hour violations, those state agencies cannot ask other employees at the business if they received their full wages.

The federal government had just over 1,000 federal investigators to cover more than 7 million workplaces (Levin, Silverstein and Fowler 2014). That is after the Obama administration hired several hundred inspectors, so the number is back up to what it was in 1948, when the United States had one-sixth the number of workers (Galvin 2016b: 325). The transition from the "progressive" Obama administration to the *Insane Clown President* (Taibbi 2017) does make many people substantially more vulnerable to economic exploitation and harassment, but more fundamentally, Pearce would point out that both Republicans and Democrats support a "neo-corporate feudal order" (Pearce 1976: 98).

Neither political party nor their candidates question "whether the free enterprise system is really the best choice for America or whether our political and legal arrangements systematically promote the domination of society by the owners of big business" (Reiman and Leighton 2017: 183). But having a state apparatus to enforce wage laws reinforces beliefs about the legitimacy of a government that is working to protect the interests of workers; it also supports the neocorporate feudal order by highlighting the unacceptable conduct of the "bad apples" caught by the regulatory system, while normalizing the remaining widespread exploitation.

Further, business interests suggest that "wage theft" is a wrong and pejorative name for the problem because it implies intentionality, and in the imaginary social order mistakes and confusion about the regulations are the cause of wage non-payment. But most of the law around minimum wage and overtime is quite clear, if inconvenient for employers. Certainly a company with resources like Wal-Mart has no excuse for violations of wage – or child labour – laws. It is well known that employers can set piece rates to encourage productivity, but those rates must be above minimum wage. So there is no reason that the Department of Labor should find violations in 93% of 1,500 investigations of garment manufacturing businesses (Department of Labor 2013), with one using payroll software to generate falsified records that indicated compliance with minimum wage laws (Levin et al. 2014).

Certain areas of the wage law are complicated, but not widely applicable, like the "doffing and donning" rules about when workers are paid to put on protective gear. Classification as a worker or an independent contractor is complex, but the gains to employers from having an independent contractor instead of an employee are substantial. Thus, outsourcing and "sharing economy" apps routinely turn workers into independent contractors, with contractual relationships that give the employer as much control as they have over employees, but without responsibility for minimum wage, overtime, benefits or payroll taxes. Rather than wage theft as an innocent mistake, the Wage and Hour Division's ex-deputy administrator said, "[S]ome businesses may take that kind of calculated risk because the likelihood of being investigated is actually so low" (Levin et al. 2014).

The evidence from collecting wage theft judgments against employers also speaks to bad faith. In California, between 2008 and 2011, only 17% of workers who prevailed in wage claims were able to collect *any* amount, and often that was substantially less than the amount of the judgment (Cho et al. n.d.: 2; Meyer and Greenleaf 2011: 24). Perpetrators are completely escaping accountability in 83% of the cases where workers won a wage theft claim before the state's Division of Labor Standards Enforcement. Employers declare strategic bankruptcies and use disposable corporate shells to keep the ill-gotten gains of wage theft.

## Conclusion: why there isn't/should be a criminology of wage theft

Jock Young, in his foreword to *Crimes of the Powerful*, discusses the transformation of criminology "from parodying the most conventional prejudices of bourgeois society to becoming a significant cockpit of theoretical debate" (in Pearce 1976: 11). However, a parody requires an exaggeration for comic effect, and being akin to satire, it "blends a critical attitude with humour and wit to the end that human institutions or humanity may be improved" (quoted in Harris 2004). Like "honey and medicine," the humour helps make the critique more palatable, while the basis for humour is an exaggeration that "seeks to create a shock of recognition and to make vice repulsive so that the vice will be expunged from the person or society" (Harris 2004). But this certainly does not describe the current state of criminology with respect to wage theft; it is less a parody of bourgeois values than criminology aping (mindlessly mimicking) bourgeois values. The fact that wage theft deals with the crimes of the powerful and labour exploitation explain why there is no criminology of the topic – and at the same time neatly explains why there should be.

First, wage theft is a crime of the powerful. White-collar crime research is marginalized, and crimes of the powerful more so. For example, McGurrin et al. (2013) found that only 6.3% of the articles were about white-collar crime in their sample of 15 journals from 2001 to 2010, with the bulk of those in *Crime, Law & Social Change*. Only 3.4% of the articles in the high-prestige journals focused on white-collar crime (2013: 9). Those figures include white-collar crime with business as a victim, as well as articles about powerful organizations victimizing workers, consumers and the environment. The crimes by the powerful are likely to represent a minority of articles on white-collar crime, yet these are some of the worst forms of mass victimizations.

Criminology should embrace the study of wage theft because it cannot proceed "as if Sutherland never gave his 1939 Presidential address to the American Sociological Society that brought 'white collar crime' into the English language" (Braithwaite 2003) – and criminologists cannot proceed as if the study of white-collar crime is only about respectable people victimizing businesses.

Further, criminology itself is impoverished when it avoids the crimes of the powerful and misses an important way to be relevant because "the most important things done for good or ill... [are] done by corporate rather than individual actors" (Braithwaite 2003).

Wage theft is a particularly important crime of the powerful to study because the basic idea behind those laws is "a fair day's pay for a fair day's work." Getting defrauded when selling one's labour to make a living violates a person's integrity at a fundamental level and is a mass victimization experienced by millions. Talking about the financial fraud of wage theft keeps criminology real with respect to the economy and the lived experience of our students.

Second, wage theft is about regulation. With its emphasis on street crime, criminology rarely discusses regulation, and even with white-collar crime, much of the analysis stays with criminal law instead of civil law and regulation. But textbooks about policing generally discuss the public order functions of officers, and sub-misdemeanour policing is an emerging area of importance because it generates fees for governments (while raining injustice on the community). Unfortunately, the word *regulation* has a negative, even pejorative, connotation, that can turn off people from studying it. Regulation sounds boring. However, "today we live in a world where criminal action is increasingly embedded in organizational action" (Braithwaite 2003).

Criminology requires an understanding of how criminal law mixes with civil law and regulations to create social control for both natural and corporate persons. With wage theft, violations of the FLSA include six months in prison for a second conviction (29 USC § 216a) and civil action for the back wages plus a 100% penalty payable to the workers (29 USC § 216b). There is an assumption that civil suits will control corporate misbehaviour because they allow for financial penalties, and increasing the penalty from 100% to 300% reduced wage theft (Galvin 2016a). But private actions have limitations because the recovery from small employers or certain groups of low-wage employees may not be enough to motivate lawyers and "because businesses may be judgment-proof due to bankruptcy, the concealment of assets, or an inability to make the payments required" (Meyer and Greenleaf 2011: 10).

Third, studying wage theft would help prepare students for the workplace by raising questions about economic exploitation. Criminology, like many other disciplines in our increasingly corporatized universities, is working to prepare students for the job market: prepare a resume, practice presentations, discuss dress and practice interview questions. But criminology, like many other disciplines, is not warning students about the widespread workplace scam called wage theft that might victimize them. Nor is it talking about the subsidization of businesses through internships where the intern is replacing some work done by a paid employee rather than getting a full eductational experience. Criminology and universities generally are focused on preparing students to fit into the existing labour market rather than giving them an understanding of economic exploitation that could empower them and their communities by teaching about wage theft and the regulatory structure that polices wage and hour violations. All of the preparation "for the real world" should include the laws that give them rights over what they earn, how to challenge the theft of their earnings and the current structural limits of self-empowerment.

Fourth, wage theft would teach students to think critically. Universities in general like to claim that they teach students to think critically, and this goal is shared by criminology and criminal justice programs. "Thinking critically" about crime and justice often means exposing the injustice of harsh punishments for the poor – just without exposing the hypocrisy of a system with little accountability for the powerful. Discussing the limits of wage theft enforcement – how weak the policing and enforcement are by design – will have students thinking critically about economic exploitation in the workplace and larger questions about the conditions of labour within and outside of the criminal justice professions. Critical thinking questions like, "Why do some state Wage and Hour Divisions that police business have no investigative power?" and "Why do some states not police wage theft?" leads to "Why don't we take 'a fair day's pay for a fair day's work' seriously?" and "What are other wage suppression mechanisms?" and "Is the lack of worker protection a bug in the system or a feature?"

None of the hyped educational technologies that aim to increase engagement and personalize learning are likely to bring attention to wage theft and exploitation either. The corporate interests and venture capital behind such technology will gamify and promote more engagement with content that reinforces the imaginary social order. But what students need to know is that the federal Wage and Hour Division has the same number of investigators as 1948; that many states do not enforce wage and hours and defund the policing agencies for political reasons; that employers understand but do not always like the laws that require them to pay employees at a minimum wage, for all hours worked and time-and-a-half for hours beyond 40 in a week; that 13 main criminology journals have never published the phrase "wage theft" or "wage and hour violations" in the last two decades; that white-collar crime books give more coverage to employee theft from employers and may not even mention wage theft by employers; and that universities and criminology programs want to teach students to think critically and be prepared for the job market, but not expose them to information about wage theft or economic exploitation.

## Notes

1 The *British Journal of Criminology* had an article that turned up in the search results because several of its references had titles that included the term, but because the body text of the article itself did not mention wage theft, it is not included for purposes of this sentence. In summarizing conclusions about the criminological consciousness about wage theft, it does not seem appropriate to count an article whose authors read about wage theft but excluded the topic from their article.

2 I only counted articles that had a whole sentence about the search term or a parenthetical remark that included a citation. This rather minimal constraint did change the number reported.

## References

Bernhardt, A., Spiller, M.W. and Polson, D. (2013) "All Work and No Pay: Violations of Employment and Labor Laws in Chicago, Los Angeles and New York City." *Social Forces*, 91(3): 725–746. doi: 10.1093/sf/sos193

Bobo, K. (2011) *Wage Theft in America* (revised ed). New York: The New Press.

Braithwaite, J. (2003) "What's Wrong with the Sociology of Punishment?" *Theoretical Criminology*, 7(1): 5–28.

Broudway, I. (2012) "Labor Disputes, the Walmart Way." 23 December. Online. Available HTTP: www.businessweek.com/articles/2012-12-13/labor-disputes-the-walmart-way.

Bustillo, M. (2008) "Wal-Mart to Settle 63 Suits Over Wages." 24 December. Online. Available HTTP: https://www.wsj.com/articles/SB123007820184231721.

CBS. (2013) "Wal-Mart Worker Admits Swiping Junk Food – For Four Years." 19 February. Online. Available HTTP: http://chicago.cbslocal.com/2013/02/19/wal-mart-worker-admits-swiping-junk-food-for-four-years/.

Cho, E.H., Koonse, T. and Mischel, A. (n.d.) "Hollow Victories. National Employment Law Project and UCLA Labor Center." Online. Available HTTP: http://nelp.3cdn.net/b5cea6550994c2358d_15m6id1ha.pdf.

Department of Labor. (2012) "US Department of Labor Recovers $4.83 Million in Back Wages, Damages for More than 4,500 Wal-Mart Workers." 1 May. www.dol.gov/opa/media/press/whd/WHD20120801.htm

——— (2013) "Federal Court Orders Forever 21 to Surrender Supply Chain Information Subpoenaed by US Department of Labor." 14 March. Online. Available HTTP: www.dol.gov/whd/media/press/whdpressVB3.asp?pressdoc=Western/20130314.xml.

Frank, T.A. (2006) "Everyday Low Vices." Online. Available HTTP: http://web.archive.org/web/20160323031946/www.washingtonmonthly.com/features/2006/0604.frank.html.

Galvin, D. (2016a) "Combating Wage Theft under Donald Trump." 22 December. Online. Available HTTP: http://prospect.org/article/combatting-wage-theft-under-donald-trump.

——— (2016b) "Deterring Wage Theft." *Perspectives on Politics*, 14(2): 324–350. doi:10.1017/S1537592716000050

Greenberg, J. (1997) "The STEAL Motive," in Robert Giacalone and Jared Greenberg (eds.) *Antisocial Behavior in Organizations*. Thousand Oaks: Sage.

Greenhouse, Steven. 2005. "Wal-Mart Agrees to Pay Fine in Child Labor Cases." 12 February. Online. Available HTTP: www.nytimes.com/2005/02/12/national/12wage.html.

Greenhouse, S. and Rosenbloom, S. (2008) "Wal-Mart Settles 63 Lawsuits Over Wages." 23 December. Online. Available HTTP: www.nytimes.com/2008/12/24/business/24walmart.html

Harris, R. (2004) "The Purpose and Method of Satire." Online. Available HTTP: www.virtualsalt.com/satire.htm.

Hartman, M. (2013) "Walmart Can Be Sued Over Abuse of 'permatemps' in California Warehouse." Online. Available HTTP: www.marketplace.org/2013/05/16/wealth-poverty/numbers/walmart-can-be-sued-over-abuse-permatemps-california-warehouse.

Jennings, M. (2015) *Business Ethics* (8th ed.). Stamford, CT: Cengage.

Joyce, A. (2006) "Wal-Mart Workers Win Wage Suit." 13 October. Online. Available HTTP: www.washingtonpost.com/wp-dyn/content/article/2006/10/12/AR2006101201608.html.

Levin, M., Silverstein, S. and Fowler, L. (2014) "How Corporations Get Away with Rampant Wage Theft." 17 May. Online. Available HTTP: https://www.salon.com/2014/05/17/report_regulators_cant_stop_wage_theft_partner/.

Lurie, I. (2011) "Enforcement of State Minimum Wage and Overtime Laws." *Employee Rights and Employment Policy Journal*, 15(2): 411–442.

Lynch, M. (2011) "Wage Theft in America (Why Millions of Working Americans Are Not Getting Paid – and What We Can Do about It)." *Contemporary Justice Review*, 14(2): 255–258.

McGurrin, D., Jarrell, M., Jahn, A. and Cochrane, B. (2013) "White Collar Crime Representation in the Criminological Literature Revisited, 2001–2010." *Western Criminology Review*, 14(2): 3–19. Online. Available HTTP: www.westerncriminology.org/documents/WCR/v14n2/McGurrin.pdf.

Meixell, B and Eisenbrey, R. (2014) "An Epidemic of Wage Theft Is Costing Workers Hundreds of Millions of Dollars a Year." Online. Available HTTP: www.epi.org/publication/epidemic-wage-theft-costing-workers-hundreds/.

Meyer, J. and Greenleaf, R. (2011) "Enforcement of State Wage and Hour Laws: A Survey of State Regulators." Columbia Law School, National State Attorney General Program. Online. Available HTTP: www.law.columbia.edu/sites/default/files/microsites/attorneys-general/files/Wage%20and%20Hour%20Report%20FINAL_0.pdf.

Miglani, J. (2015) "Amazon vs Walmart Revenues and Profits 1995–2014." 25 July. Online. Available HTTP: http://revenuesandprofits.com/amazon-vs-walmart-revenues-and-profits-1995-2014/.

Nadisic, T. (2008) "The Robin Hood Effect," in Stephen Gilliland, Daniel Skarlicki and Dirk Douglas Steiner (eds.) *Justice, Morality, and Social Responsibility*. Charlotte: Information Age Publishing.

National Labor Relations Board. (2013) "NLRB Office of the General Counsel Authorizes Complaints against Walmart, Also Finds No Merit to Other Charges." Online. Available HTTP: https://www.nlrb.gov/news-outreach/news-story/nlrb-office-general-counsel-authorizes-complaints-against-walmart-also.

Nordlund, W. (1997) *The Quest for a Living Wage*. Westport: Greenwood Press.

Payne, B. (2012) *White-Collar Crime: A Text/Reader*. Los Angeles: Sage.

——— (2017) *White-Collar Crime* (2nd ed.). Los Angeles: Sage.

Pearce, F. (1976) *Crimes of the Powerful: Marxism, Crime and Deviance.*. London: Pluto Press.

Reiman, J. and Leighton, P. (2017) *The Rich Get Richer and the Poor Get Prison* (11th ed.). New York: Routledge.

Roosevelt, F. (1937) "Message to Congress on Establishing Minimum Wages and Maximum Hours." Online. Available HTTP: www.presidency.ucsb.edu/ws/?pid=15405.

Rosoff, S., Pontell, H. and Tillman, R. (2010) *Profit Without Honor* (5th ed.). Boston: Prentice Hall.

Scott, M. (2013) "Walmart Charges Grandma with Felonious Oreo Eating." Online. Available HTTP: http://madmikesamerica.com/2013/02/walmart-charges-grandma-with-felonious-oreo-eating/.

Seybold, M. (2017) "Barnum Presidents and Benevolent Monopolists: Mark Twain, Amazon, and the Futility of Antitrust." Online. Available HTTP: https://lareviewofbooks.org/article/barnum-presidents-and-benevolent-monopolists-mark-twain-amazon-futility-antitrust/#!.

Snider, L. (2001) "Crimes Against Capital: Discovering Theft of Time." *Social Justice*, 3: 105–120.

——— (2002) "Theft of Time: Disciplining through Science and Law." *Osgoode Hall Law Journal*, 40(1): 89–112.

Taibbi, M. (2017) *Insane Clown President*. New York: Spiegel & Grau.

# Chapter 15

# Prying into the pockets of public figures

*Scott Poynting*

In June 2016 former New South Wales (NSW) government minister and right-wing Australian Labor Party "numbers man" Eddie Obeid was convicted in the Supreme Court of NSW of wilful misconduct in public office, and he was sentenced in December to a maximum of five years imprisonment. The NSW Independent Commission Against Corruption (ICAC) earlier found that Obeid acted corruptly as a member of Parliament in relation to the matter at hand: to benefit his family's (undisclosed) interests in harbourside cafés leased from a government instrumentality, the Maritime Authority. ICAC also found over 2012–2014 that Obeid had misused his public position for his family's private benefit in relation to a water infrastructure company and in relation to a private health company and a $30-million-plus coal mining deal. Corruption charges have been laid over the last three alleged offences; at the time of writing in 2017 these are awaiting trial.

Yet this is small change compared to large-scale corporate corruption. The Obeid family is not General Electric or Westinghouse. The public theatre may spotlight the crooked millions of a nefarious family and their "mates" at various levels of politics and business, but the routine corruption of transnational corporations is business as usual. The chapter argues, following Frank Pearce (1976), that such anti-corruption charades act out the fantasy that the normal workings of capitalism are uncorrupted and that abnormal aberrations can be rooted out, to the public benefit: "*It is not possible to explain . . . systematic continuous* [corrupt] *behaviour in terms of the 'greed' of a few individuals*" and that anti-corruption prosecutions "by condemning an infraction as illegal and abnormal serve to *dramatise an imaginary social order*" (Pearce 1976: 93, original italics).

The earlier cartels and anti-competitive price fixing of monopoly capitalism so revealingly shown by Pearce to be endemic are now supplemented by newer corporate criminal opportunities under neoliberalism. In the focus on the lining of private pockets, our view is averted from the larger damage to public wellbeing of deregulation, privatization and contracting out of public resources – such as energy, minerals, water, transport and other infrastructure – and of services and also, of course, the damage to the natural and built environment through untrammelled land and property development where planning for human need is derailed by graft to maximize profits.

## Deterrence and denunciation of harm to the community

Edward Moses Obeid (once "The Honourable" and Member of the Order of Australia) is now in prison for corruption. The 73-year-old former NSW Labor upper house member and government minister is serving a five-year sentence (with three years non-parole) for the common-law offence of wilful misconduct in public office (R v Obeid 2016). More court proceedings are to come, likewise ensuing from lengthy and painstaking investigations by the NSW Independent Commission Against Corruption (ICAC).

The sentencing judge, Beech-Jones J, remarked that "[c]orruption by elected representatives consumes democracies. It destroys public confidence in democratic institutions" (R v Obeid 2016: #137). The prison sentence accordingly reflected "the need for general deterrence, denunciation and recognition of the harm done to the community" (R v Obeid 2016: #138).

Justice Beech-Jones had earlier observed that "[c]ourts do not determine sentences by consulting opinion polls or surveying the views of the political commentariat" (R v Obeid 2016: #133). Fortunately so, for Obeid: NSW Premier, Liberal Party leader Mike Baird, commented to the press on the day of the sentence, "The crimes of Eddie Obeid and his cronies are the most serious instance of official corruption we have seen in our lifetime" (Loussikian and Fox Koob 2016). Such hyperbole begs some history.

## Context and proportion

The premier may not have "seen" this, though his young lifetime did include most of the period (1965–1975) of the NSW government of his fellow Liberal Party premier, Sir Robert Askin, a by-word for official corruption and infamous for brown paper bags of money making their way to his desk from gambling, prostitution and other crime rackets.[1] Baird was himself dubbed "Casino Mike" (ABC News 2016) after his exceptional liquor licensing provisions favouring Sydney's casino, and also "Teflon Mike" (nothing sticks to him) (Seccombe 2016). Yet he had gained the premiership in 2014 with a reputation as a "cleanskin," in a conservative coalition government which had itself won office on an anti-corruption ticket following the opprobrium attached to Labor in the wake of the public revelations about Obeid and his connections. (More, later, on the irony of this anti-corruption presentation.) Baird resigned suddenly less than three years later, in February 2017, "for family reasons," and within six weeks had taken a million-dollar-plus job with a major bank (Clennell and Godfrey 2017).

I do not suggest here that Baird is personally corrupt. There are, rather, three points to make. First, the short term of Baird's historical memory of NSW politics is not credible: his father was a Liberal cabinet minister not a decade after Askin's departure and at one time himself candidate for premier. Although it is convenient for his party that the voting public have short memories, Baird must himself know better. Second, the turbo-charging of neoliberalism makes lubrication via the contents of brown paper bags rather an old-school technology. Australia's richest men can these days reap their casino superprofits legally (if at times marginally so at best) and be championed openly in their business expansion by political leaders; the same goes for developers and the other beneficiaries of deregulation and privatization. Having privatized the generation and transmission of electricity, the state's ports and $500 million of public housing and home care for the aged and disabled, Baird's government went on to privatize the state's Land Titles Office, which generates some $60 million per annum of revenue. As the Australian Greens [political party] spokesman David Shoebridge notes, "It puts a corruption risk at the heart of land titles in NSW" (Seccombe 2016). Where arguably it has ever been since colonization, because land expropriated from Indigenous people was "granted" by the Crown to those favoured by the colonial regime, leading rapidly to speculation and enriching a manipulative cohort. In the current era, neoliberalism legalizes harmful acquisition of, and speculation in, real property and supercharges the process while helping to hide it. The third point is that all of this constitutes corruption in the broader, more sociological, sense of "distortion and subversion of the public realm in the service of private interests" (Beetham 2015: 41) and the more powerful explanatory understanding of how this is endemic to capitalist social relations and, indeed, how this accelerates and extends into new spheres under neoliberal regimes. Eddie Obeid's peddling of influence (what else does a "power broker" do?) and envelopes stuffed with cash do not tell us much about how our contemporary society works or how it could be transformed for the better. As Antonio Gramsci noted in another context (of polemicizing against economism), those who lack a historical materialist understanding of the deeper workings of social relations are reduced to "prying into the pockets of public figures" (1971: 378). Baird is not alone in his lack of historical perspective and proportionality.

## Corruption "unexceeded since the Rum Corps"

Geoffrey Watson SC, the counsel assisting the ICAC inquiry dealing with corruption surrounding the granting of coal exploration licences in NSW, in which the Obeid family made a secret $30-million profit and was set to gain $30 million more, announced in his opening address in November 2012 that the ICAC investigation had uncovered "corruption on a scale probably unexceeded since the days of the Rum Corps" (McClymont and Besser 2012). The colonial military, the NSW Corps, responsible for law and order in the early years of NSW, had become known by that name because of its control over corrupt monopoly trade in alcohol (which became almost a *de facto* currency) virtually from its arrival in 1790 until its recall to England in 1810: a period that included a mutiny in 1808 that later became known as the "Rum Rebellion," which overthrew the governor to secure the power and profits of the military and the civilian colonist cabal most closely associated with them in business and politics. Benefiting from early speculation in land expropriated from Aborigines, as well as the exploitation of convict slave labour, the Rum Corps and their cronies established an early pattern of corrupt super-profits at the height of this period of primitive accumulation during which modern capitalism was coming into being. The Rum Corps is another by-word for corruption in Australian history; there is no shortage of such by-words.[2] Watson's pronouncement, as well as being studied hyperbole, was thus a witty and headline-ready piece of theatre. And theatre it was: crowds queued on city pavements outside the inquiry to sit in on the public spectacle; there was regular laughter and even applause from the public gallery. Dramatic news footage and column inches were provided day by day. ICAC's State Counsel was dubbed "Hollywood Watson" (McClymont and Besser 2014: 346, 387).

The popular impact of the inquiry, and others by ICAC before and after, was artfully orchestrated and timed by ICAC. Of course it drew attention to the commission's function in exposing unlawful corruption to the spotlight, subjecting it to censure and calling some of its notable protagonists to account.

## Raising ravens

ICAC was set up in 1989 by the Greiner Liberal (conservative coalition) government, amid pervasive perceptions of endemic and systemic corruption in NSW under the previous (Wran, Labor) government, which from 1976 had followed the Askin Liberal government and 15 months of its two immediate Liberal successors.[3]

Premier Nick Greiner was hoist with his own petard in 1992 when found to be corrupt by the very ICAC that he had brought into being. He had rigged the appointment of an independent MP as a senior state official in order to gain his seat for the Liberal Party and break the hung Parliament; he had lied about this to the ICAC inquiry, during which he suffered many "memory lapses." Though this corruption finding was later overturned on appeal over a jurisdictional technicality (Greiner v ICAC 1992) – an anomaly that was later rectified in subsequent legislation – the finding forced his resignation and ended his premiership.

Greiner was not the last Liberal Party premier to have ICAC blow up in his face. In 2014, NSW Premier Barry O'Farrell was also called before ICAC and suffered a "massive memory fail" over his receiving the gift of a $3,000 bottle of 1959 vintage luxury wine, which had not been declared as required by law. He resigned in shame, when his thank-you note for the gift which he had denied, was produced to ICAC (ABC 2014). The gift and the note were proffered by millionaire Nick Di Girolamo, executive of Australian Water Holdings (AWH), a company with which the state government, through the Sydney Water Corporation, had been doing business regarding the privatization of water infrastructure. Clearly, Di Girolamo must have been deeply disappointed with the premier when he was moved to jog his memory in this way. Ironically, Di Girolamo had been a partner with Eddie Obeid in some potentially highly lucrative ventures of AWH involving public–private partnerships (McClymont and Besser 2014: 360–377).

There is no doubt that Nick Greiner, in establishing ICAC, had sought to catch out the network of Labor "mates" and their enablers in public office. By the 1980s, however, the sort of corruption that was known to distort government across Australia was not so much based on illegal gambling and prostitution, as in Askin's time – though large-scale production, smuggling and sale of illicit drugs such as cannabis and heroin were indeed facilitated through connections in the police, the judiciary and politics. More importantly, corrupt practices within licit business sectors such as property development, construction, transport, finance, media and mining had become normalized, with bribes and clandestine political "donations" widespread. This involved key players in both major political parties, whose business cronies thrived in the 1980s "economic rationalist" climate of deregulation and privatization.[4] If ICAC had teeth, it was inevitable that both sides of politics would be bitten. Since it came into being in 1989, ICAC has been fiercely independent of the government of the day, as shown by Liberal premiers Greiner's and O'Farrell's experiences, as well as those of the seriously corrupt Obeid and his fellow Labor minister (convicted and imprisoned in 2017), Ian Macdonald. Although ICAC shows no fear or favour to public officials, when it comes to private-sector corruption, however, it cannot really come to grips. It is set up not to.

## Official function and operation of ICAC

When the ICAC Act was passed into law in NSW in 1988, there were two notable forerunners existing in Commonwealth countries: Singapore (since 1952) and Hong Kong (since 1974) (Johnston 1999). The more recent and relevant example was Hong Kong's ICAC, whose name was even adopted by NSW. In addition to its investigative role, it has an important pedagogical function, offering preventative advice to firms and organizations and mounting "innovative public education programs" (Johnston 1999: 217). Like the Singapore bureau, it was independent of police (corruption of which had been a concern in both places, as in NSW), and it could investigate corruption in public and private sectors.

NSW's ICAC has investigative, prevention and community/public-sector education functions, and is independent of the police. It covers public-sector corruption only. It does not conduct prosecutions, though it can refer cases, with recommendations for prosecution, to the Director of Public Prosecution

(DPP). It does not deal with police corruption, which is dealt with (since 1997) by a separate body, the Police Integrity Commission, but ICAC can investigate police involvement in corruption of public officials.

ICAC can execute search warrants and can sequester documents and data. It can compel parties to attend for interviews or hearings and can recommend prosecution if evidence of a suspected crime has been uncovered, even if the suspect is not a public servant – as in the case of Eddie Obeid's son, Moses. For instance, in 2015, Moses Obeid was charged along with his father and former mining minister Ian Macdonald over an alleged conspiracy to commit misconduct in public office in relation to the granting of a coal mining licence directly over the Obeid family property at Mt Penny in the Bylong Valley, west of the Upper Hunter region, resulting in a $30 million "windfall" to the Obeids. These charges were proffered by the DPP after the referral from ICAC following its extended investigation into the matter (Whitbourn and McClymont 2016).

## ICAC's ideological function: theatre and fantasy

The investigation and prosecution over the alleged Mt Penny conspiracy, in addition to the theatricality over the worst corruption "since the Rum Corps," were reported in the media in terms of the grossest venality (Minister Macdonald) and the basest of greed (the Obeids) – as if greed of these individuals were the key to understanding systematic and continuous corruption. Reportage of long luxurious lunches (accompanied by footage of the bellies that received them), huge restaurant bills, expensive wines, paid sexual services with gratuitously published commentary from the servicing prostitute: the abundance of such details may well have distracted and disgusted readers, listeners and viewers (see, e.g., McClymont 2017).

There is doubtless truth and some newsworthiness in these stories, but it is small beer compared to the environmental damage wrought by coal mining and energy corporations (see Poynting and Whyte 2017; White 2017, especially in respect of the Adani corporation), or the distortions imposed through the enormous influence they wield, which was never an issue in these corruption cases and media stories about them, and nor can it be. To observe this is not to minimize the magnitude and reach of the corruption of Eddie Obeid, his family and his political and business cohorts in NSW of the late 1990s and early 2000s, nor the enormous work and important public service performed by ICAC in uncovering it. Investigative journalists such as – and especially – Kate McClymont, have also done sterling work in exposing this corruption and helping to make it a priority of ICAC and then reporting ICAC's investigations and hearings and subsequent court proceedings. But McClymont and her co-author Linton Besser (2014: 386) tend to individualize – possibly for dramatic effect – the causes of the corruption:

> Following the ICAC's investigations and the corruption they exposed, the electorate's level of trust in politicians and parties and the entire democratic

process hit a new low. Much of this scepticism must be sheeted back to one man: Edward Moses Obeid OAM.

Yet over the same period, Liberal Party senator, Arthur Sinodinos, who was also federal assistant treasurer, had a series of embarrassing and implausible memory lapses during an ICAC appearance. ICAC cannot do much about the memories of those compelled to appear, though witnesses give evidence under oath and can be prosecuted for perjury. Sinodinos denied any recall of a $74,000 donation to the political party of which he was finance director for NSW (Jabour 2014), by Australian Water Holdings (the company mentioned earlier, in which Obeid was secretly and corruptly involved), of which he, Sinodinos, was actually deputy chairman – with a salary of $200,000 a year that would seem to indicate a serious fiduciary duty. ICAC was told in 2014 that AWH had been seeking an enormously profitable public–private partnership with the NSW government which, had it gone ahead, would have netted Sinodinos himself between $10 million and $20 million, and the Obeids some $100 million (Jabour 2014). AWH's chief executive, Nick Di Girolamo, was the very same who had gifted the "forgotten" $3,000 bottle of wine to NSW Liberal premier, Barry O'Farrell. Sinodinos resigned as assistant treasurer after his excruciating memory failures over financial matters, but was later restored to the federal ministry under the Turnbull government. In fact, including Sinodinos, no fewer than 10 Liberal Party MPs, were forced to resign as a result of ICAC operations over the same period, with most of these instances similarly involving political donations (Harris 2014; Chen 2014). Eddie Obeid and his network of Labor Party cronies clearly did not invent this level of corruption in NSW, nor were their team the only players.

In his second reading speech to the NSW parliament in legislating for ICAC, Premier Nick Greiner (1988) announced that "the measure of its success will be the enhancement of integrity and, most importantly, of community confidence in public administration in this State." By McClymont and Besser's assessment of "a new low" in this respect, over a quarter of a century of ICAC has not delivered its crucial and explicit objective. Could its real function, rather, be "to *dramatise an imaginary social order*," as Pearce (1976: 93, original italics) puts it, in which capitalist social relations can be purged of corruption? As I finish this chapter, the "Paradise Papers" have had the mass media revealing details of the use of offshore tax havens – just as the Panama Papers leaks did the previous year. "Cows go moo," commented one Australian cartoonist, suggesting that the discovery was no surprise. Although it is indeed public knowledge that this happens systematically, commentators and politicians persist in the fantasy that the tax system can be fixed to patch the loopholes. For exigencies of space, this single example must serve to instance how corruption is widely reduced to spectacle, cleansing the imagined social order that could be rid of it.

## "Where there's smoke, there's Eddie"

The picture of Eddie Obeid offered upon his conviction in 2016 by former premier Kristina Keneally, whom Obeid, as the dominant right-wing faction leader in NSW Labor, had shoehorned into office in 2009, as a "one-in-100-year flood of corruption" (Hoerr 2016), presents corruption as an unusual deviance from the normally orderly, lawful and beneficent functioning of Australian society. The characterization the same day by earlier premier Morris Iemma, similarly supported for the premiership within the Labor caucus in 2005 by Obeid as the leading "numbers man," of Obeid's behaviour as "one of the worst and most grotesque breaches of public trust" (Hoerr 2016), likewise paints such corruption as abnormal and exceptional.

Iemma would know better. He had served his "political apprenticeship" (McClymont and Besser 2014: 230) as a staffer to Senator Graham Richardson, widely known as a "numbers man" and "power broker" (terms that would come to apply to Obeid) within the right-wing NSW branch of the Labor Party. Obeid likewise learned the political ropes as an "acolyte" of Richardson (McClymont and Besser 2014: 231). *He Who Must Be Obeid* in fact demonstrates clearly that Eddie Obeid was no aberration within the NSW Labor Party; he learnt the dark arts of branch stacking, organizing the numbers, political donations, influence peddling, power broking and indeed self-enrichment under the tutelage of "Richo," who quickly realized the "recruitment" utility of Obeid's connections within the Lebanese immigrant population, which was numerous and mobilizing in Sydney when Obeid was a Labor neophyte and the influence of the Arabic press that Obeid came to dominate (McClymont and Besser 2014). The book is thus an empirically rich and fine-grained case study of the making of a corrupt "numbers man" and "bagman" out of circumstances that were given and directly inherited from the past. Eddie Obeid did not bring large-scale corruption to public life in NSW, though he did take to it with all of the persistence and application that McClymont and Besser show. Also, yes, avarice: but that does not mean that the avarice explains the corruption.

When Obeid came to the Labor Party, via approaches to local government over council permits for his printing business, he was an impecunious, if ruthless, small businessman running an ethnic press and printery in need of expanding its space and hours of operation, against the wishes of local residents in an inner-city council area that had become notorious for branch stacking, corruption and indeed associated violence. Obeid quickly learned about the exercise of influence in local government and the role of party factions, managed by the head office, in allocating party candidacy for local elections. The head office was overwhelmingly interested, as Richardson had learnt all too well, in donations to the party and favoured those local party activists who could garner these. Property developers were always keen to secure influence through such brokers, on both "sides" of politics. Obeid would come to play the dual role of property developer and bagman.

Obeid benefited on several occasions (1982, 1992 and 1993) from insurance payouts for fires at his printing establishments. One business, Offset Alpine, was staggeringly overinsured, with the policy secured shortly before the unfortunate fire (McClymont and Besser 2014: 89). The insurance company, FAI, was also a shareholder in Offset Alpine, with 1.45 million shares acquired the day before the fire (McClymont and Besser 2014: 90). Another shareholder – clandestinely so – was Graham Richardson. Richardson denied this under oath when questioned by the Australian Securities Commission, and had the enormous profits from the fire deposited in a Swiss bank, thus avoiding tax (McClymont and Besser 2014: 94). In 2010, Richardson settled a case with the Australian Taxation Office for $2.3 million, indicating that the taxable amount must have been considerably larger (McClymont and Besser 2014: 96). The intermediary for these monies was apparently the colourful stockbroker Rene Rivkin, who suicided in 2005 after he was convicted for insider trading in Qantas shares (McClymont and Besser 2014: 94). Richardson had also sent $1 million, apparently of the Offset Alpine proceeds, to a bank in Lebanon – on the instructions of Rivkin, he claimed – to close associates of the Obeid family (McClymont and Besser 2014: 97). Liberal Party Police Minister Mike Gallacher quipped in parliament in 2012, "Where there's smoke, there's Eddie" (McClymont and Besser 2014: 98).

Two points can here be made about the Offset Alpine episode. First, none of these events come under the purview of ICAC. They do not involve public officials acting in their capacity as such. Indeed, although insurance fraud is a serious crime in NSW – and this case has never been tested in court as such – insurance and financial fraud is not generally referred to as "corruption" in Australia, even when it involves ongoing and systematic harm in these sectors of the economy.

Second, Eddie Obeid's manifest sense of impunity was not an irrational vanity; it had some basis in reality. Throughout his entire business career, he had cultivated connections, including clandestine business collaborations, with some of the country's most powerful and influential personages in both politics and business. The fact that if he were to go down, there was too much risk that they would go down with him, might be seen to lend him a measure of protection practically bordering on impunity. Beneficiaries in the Offet Alpine payout, apart from Obeid, Rivkin and Richardson, included Trevor Kennedy, Rodney Adler, Sean Howard, Bill Hayden and Ray Martin (West 2013). I am not suggesting that any of these persons were involved in fraud in this case, merely that their involvement in the investment must have given Obeid considerable confidence, as well as capital.

Trevor Kennedy owned 12% of Offset Alpine (Lampe 2004). He is a businessman and company executive, who as a "pillar of Sydney society," has served on the boards of many big Australian firms, including AWA, Qantas and chairmanship of Oil Search, which "effectively controlled most of the oil and gas resources of Papua New Guinea" (Chenoweth 2006: 3), and Consolidated Press, where he was managing director, and "right hand man" (Barry 2009: 142) to Kerry Packer, sometime Australia's richest man. He was also a business associate of high-flying lawyer and corporate banker Malcolm Turnbull, who is currently the prime minister of Australia. Turnbull served as Packer's lawyer and represented him, among other things, at the Costigan Royal Commission in 1980–1984, where he was investigated over tax avoidance, including in a scandalous scheme called "bottom of the harbour" (which is where the tax monies went). Packer was never convicted over this, or anything else. Kennedy was investigated by the Australian Investment and Securities Commission (ASIC) over the Offset Alpine and Swiss banks matter and denied under oath that he had held any ownership of the company. In 2003, his Swiss bank account holdings were all over the front pages, and he resigned his directorships in seven public companies. In 2010, however, ASIC gave up the chase over the missing monies: "Kennedy's offshore structures were disguised by an impenetrable labyrinth of entities which stretched from the British Virgin Islands to the Bahamas, and through a chain of corporate trusts in Liechtenstein and Scottish partnership" (West 2013).

Graham Richardson was, as noted, a senator and leading "enforcer" in the right wing of the Australian Labor Party, and renowned as the party's "kingmaker": titles that would accrue to Obeid in the NSW branch. As such, Richardson had delivered the caucus numbers for leadership of the parliamentary party, and hence prime ministership, for PMs Hawke, and later, Keating. The sudden instalment of Hawke in the lead-up to the 1983 election had seen the toppling as Labor Party leader of Bill Hayden, later to be the Queen's representative as Governor-General of Australia. Bill Hayden was also an investor in Offset Alpine. After his political career, Richardson held a regular political commentary show on Packer's Channel Nine, and later on Channel Seven and SKY News.

Famous and flamboyant stockbroker and entrepreneur Rene Rivkin – celebrated as "Stockbroker of the Year" in 1985 (ABC 2005) – was the major shareholder and indeed chairman of Offset Alpine, which he had bought from Kerry Packer for $15.3 million and floated on the stock exchange in 1992 (West 2013). The insurance bonanza was $53 million, leading Kerry Packer to joke that it was a "very good fire" (McClymont and Besser 2014: 89). Rivkin was a close associate of Richardson, who had appointed him to the board of the National Gallery of Australia (McClymont and Besser 2014: 85). He was convicted of insider trading in Qantas in 2003, and banned from stockbroking, though he continued to trade unlawfully while under weekend detention, and was under investigation when he suicided in 2005. He died owing the Australian Tax Office $18 million in taxes and fines.

Rodney Adler was chief executive of FAI Insurance since 1988, at one time Australia's third largest general insurer, and as such was in the "rich list" of

Australia's 200 wealthiest throughout the 1990s. He was on Sydney's and Melbourne's "society" A-list: "A 1997 fund-raiser in his honour was attended by Australia's rich and powerful. Tributes to him flowed thick and fast, including one by video from US millionaire Donald Trump"; Rene Rivkin paid tribute there in person (*The Age* 2005). Adler was to go on to become a director of HIH insurance, for the defrauding of $2 million from which, along with his failure there of his duties as a director, he was convicted in 2005, and served two and a half years in prison.

Sean Howard, another of *Business Review Weekly*'s "Rich List 200," is an Internet entrepreneur and founder of OzEmail, at one stage Australia's biggest Internet business. In 1994, Malcolm Turnbull and Trevor Kennedy became investors in OzEmail. White (2015) records that this delivered Turnbull "his first serious fortune," with Howard boasting: "He gave me $500,000 in 1994 and five years later I gave him $55m."

Ray Martin is a household name in Australia as a television "personality" on Packer's Nine Network. Like fellow Offset Alpine investors Kennedy, Adler, Howard, Hayden and Obeid himself, he has been awarded the Order of Australia.

So Obeid was well connected enough to believe he was beyond reach – and he may well have been had it not been for the loose talking of his second son, Moses, whose bankruptcy in a crooked deal involving council light-poles/flagpoles led to the family's business networks coming under the microscope (McClymont and Besser 2014). This leads us to our concluding point: that, beyond insurance scams, most of Obeid's sharp business dealings – be they in council light poles, favoured leases of government property, purchase of real estate from the Housing Commission and sale of constructions to it, local and state rezoning of land for development, construction of a marina on a public waterway, privatized supply and public private partnerships in water infrastructure, rezoning of land in relation to mining, proposed provision of human resources management software to health authorities and all the rest of the money-spinning schemes meticulously detailed by McClymont and Besser (2014) – have arisen in the context of neoliberalism, with its deregulation, privatization of public assets and contracting out by the state to private suppliers.

## Conclusion: "somebody's got to get paid"

Although neoliberalism provides new opportunities for, and new forms of, corruption, the old ideological smoke-and-mirrors ploys continue to distract the populace from the real mechanisms of corruption in the broad social-scientific sense: not the narrow sense defined by ICAC. These mechanisms arise in the normal workings of capitalism, and theatrics purporting that its social relations can be cleaned up to some pure, ideal, non-corrupt form are sheer fantasy.

Prying into pockets of public figures 213

In a cabinet meeting in 2002, Obeid was exasperated by his fellow ministers' overreaction, as he saw it, to widespread and troublesome "allegations that local councillors were on the take and that developers offered bribes," exclaiming matter of factly, "someone has got to get paid!" One observer told McClymont and Besser (2014: 154) that they interpreted Obeid's response as a retort that his interlocutors were "living in a fantasy land." It is not difficult to see so many of Obeid's actions as wrongful, his self-justifications as wrong-headed and his lack of scruples as simply wrong. But about the workings of really existing capitalism in the historical and actual state of NSW, he was perversely right in this observation. The fantasy which he scorned is one that is useful for the maintenance of that very capitalism.

ICAC provides an important public service, and one that I do not wish to belittle. Yet, as argued, it also functions very effectively, while drawing attention to certain forms of rightly criminalised corruption, to distract from broader and deeply entrenched forms of more insidious corruption, and to convey the impression that something is indeed being done that will help to prevent it. This is indicative of an enduring contradiction in regulation. This contradiction itself arises from the contradictions in social relations that the regulatory system must deal with.

Pearce (1976) directs our attention to the systematic, rather than individual, nature of corruption under monopoly capitalism, and I have argued this remains so in its neoliberal phase. He adverts us to the over-dramatization that we need to beware of in publicized cases that function as a show. In this way, prying into the pockets of public figures can distract us from the corruption structured into capitalism itself.

## Notes

1 See, for example, Mick Young, MP, in Parliament of Australia, House of Representatives Hansard, 23 April 1985, p. 1642. Immediately following Askin's death – and therefore immune from defamation prosecution – journalist David Hickie wrote in his *National Times* story, "Askin: Friend of Organised Crime":

> While Sir Robert Askin was in power, organised crime became institutionalised on a large scale in New South Wales. Sydney became, and has remained, the crime capital of Australia. Askin was central to this. His links with three major crime figures, Perce Galea, close friend Joe Taylor, and another, allowed the transformation of Sydney's baccarat clubs into fully-fledged casinos. Askin's links with corrupt police allowed those casinos and SP betting to flourish. The corrupt police included commissioners Allan and Hanson.

See also Hickie (1985). The unnamed crime figure was clearly Abe Saffron; see McClymont (2008).

2 Among these by-words, in more recent history: "The Moonlight State" of Queensland police corruption under National Party premier Joh Bjelke-Petersen (Four Corners 1987) and the "white shoe brigade" (property developers in coastal Queensland under Bjelke-Petersen), and WA, Inc. (the cosy relationships between the Labor government of

## 214 Scott Poynting

Brian Burke in Western Australia and a number of spectacularly failed companies, including investment banks, in the 1980s).

3 Ironically, the government of the notoriously corrupt Bob Askin had been elected to replace a Labor government, which political scientist Murray Goot (2007) records as being "seen as 'worm-eaten' by 'graft, corruption, nepotism and general chicanery'" [original quotation marks]. *Plus ça change!*

4 John Pilger's (1990: 235–311) chapter, "Mates," gives a very good sense of this, especially on the Labor side.

## References

ABC News. (2005) "Rene Rivkin Dead." Online. Available HTTP: www.abc.net.au/news/2005-05-01/rene-rivkin-dead/1562144 (accessed 22 May 2017).

ABC News. (2014) "NSW Premier Barry O'Farrell to Resign Over 'massive memory fail' at ICAC." *ABC News*, 17 April. Online. Available HTTP: www.abc.net.au/news/2014-04-16/nsw-premier-barry-ofarrell-to-resign-over-icac-grange-wine/5393478 (accessed 10 May 2017).

ABC News. (2016) "NSW Premier Mike Baird Faces Backlash Over "arrogant" Graffiti Removal Facebook Post." *ABC News*, 31 October. Online. Available HTTP: www.abc.net.au/news/2016-10-30/mike-baird-criticised-forgraffiti-removal-facebook-post/7978604 (accessed 14 April 2017).

The Age. (2005) "Rocket Rod Crashes to Earth." *The Age*, 17 February. Online. Available HTTP: www.theage.com.au/news/National/Rocket-Rod-crashes-to-earth/2005/02/16/1108500151281.html (accessed 22 May 2017).

Barry, P. (2009) *Who Wants to be a Billionaire?: The James Packer Story*. Sydney: Allen and Unwin.

Beetham, D. (2015) "Moving Beyond a Narrow Definition of Corruption," in Whyte, D. (ed.) *How Corrupt is Britain?* London: Pluto Press, 41–46.

Chen, P.J. (2014) "A Growing Body Count By ICAC Hasn't Hurt the NSW Liberals – Yet." *The Conversation*, 18 August. Online. Available HTTP: https://theconversation.com/a-growing-body-count-by-icac-hasnt-hurt-the-nsw-liberals-yet-30560 (accessed 19 May 2017).

Chenoweth, N. (2006) *Packer's Lunch: A Rollicking Tale of Swiss Bank Accounts and Money-Making Adventurers in the Roaring 90s*. Sydney: Allen and Unwin.

Clennell, A. and Godfrey, M. (2017) "Mike Baird Reveals Why He Took $1 Million Plus National Australia Bank Job." *Daily Telegraph*, 1 March. Online. Available HTTP: www.dailytelegraph.com.au/news/nsw/mike-baird-reveals-why-he-took-1-millionplus-national-australia-bank-job/news-story/448fddd4f2e81dee6118e1a6468e41b1 (accessed 14 April 2017).

*Four Corners* (1987) "The Moonlight State." *ABC Television*, 11 May. Online. Available HTTP: www.abc.net.au/4corners/stories/2011/08/08/3288495.htm (accessed 19 May 2017).

Goot, M. (2007) "Askin, Sir Robert William (Bob) (1907–1981)." *Australian Dictionary of Biography*, Vol. 17. Online. Available HTTP: http://adb.anu.edu.au/biography/askin-sir-robert-william-bob-12152 (accessed 19 May 2017).

Gramsci, A. (1971) *Selections from the Prison Notebooks*. London: Lawrence and Wishart.

Greiner, N. (1988) "Second Reading Speech of the ICAC Act: Except from Hansard, Legislative Assembly." 28 May. Online. Available HTTP: www.icac.nsw.gov.au/about-the-icac/legislation/second-reading-speech (accessed 10 May 2017).

Greiner v Independent Commission Against Corruption, Moore v Independent Commission Against Corruption. (1992) Judgment of Gleeson CJ, Mahoney JA, Priestley JA/ Court of Appeal. New South Wales Court of Appeal.

Harris, M. (2014) "ICAC: Strike – 10th Liberal MP Skittled at Inquiry." *Newcastle Herald*, 14 August. Online. Available HTTP: www.theherald.com.au/story/2489538/icac-strike-10th-liberal-mp-skittled-at-inquiry/ (accessed 19 May 2017).

Hickie, D. (1985) *The Prince and the Premier: The Story of Perce Galea, Bob Askin and the Others who Gave Organised Crime its Start in Australia*. Sydney: Angus and Robertson.

Hoerr, K. (2016) "Eddie Obeid Found Guilty of Misconduct in Public Office While Member of NSW Upper House." *ABC News*, 28 June. Online. Available HTTP: www.abc.net.au/news/2016-06-28/eddie-obeid-found-guilty-of-misconduct-in-public-office/7545632 (accessed 19 May 2017).

Independent Commission Against Corruption, New South Wales (2013) *Fact Sheet: Investigation into the Conduct of Moses Obeid, Eric Roozendaal and Others*, 31 July.

Jabour, B. (2014) "Arthur Sinodinos Denies Knowledge of $74,000 AWH Donation to NSW Libs." *The Guardian*, 3 April. Online. Available HTTP: www.theguardian.com/world/2014/apr/03/arthur-sinodinos-denies-knowledge-of-74000-awh-donation-to-nsw-libs (accessed 19 May 2017).

Lampe, A. (2004) "Kennedy Takes Another Hit in ASIC Battle." *The Age*, 3 May. Online. Available HTTP: www.theage.com.au/articles/2004/05/06/1083635280860.html?from=story rhs (accessed 22 May 2017).

Loussikian, K. and Fox Koob, S. (2016) "Eddie Obeid Jailed For Minimum Three Years for Misconduct Conviction." *The Australian*, 15 December. Online. Available HTTP: www.theaustralian.com.au/national-affairs/state-politics/eddie-obeid-jailed-for-minimum-three-years-for-misconduct-conviction/news-story/64cebe1a0b9c213609cc47fdd9da33b3 (accessed 14 April 2017).

McClymont, K. (2008) "Saffron's Son: Dad Paid Off Askin and Lent Packer Money." *Sydney Morning Herald*, 28 July. Online. Available HTTP: www.smh.com.au/news/national/dad-paid-off-askin-and-lent-packer-money/2008/07/27/1217097059696.html (accessed 11 May 2017).

McClymont, K. (2017) "Ian Macdonald Set to Share Porridge and Water, Not Pig and Wine, with Eddie Obeid." *Sydney Morning Herald*, 30 March. Online. Available HTTP: www.smh.com.au/nsw/ian-macdonald-set-to-share-porridge-and-water-not-pig-and-wine-with-eddie-obeid-20170330-gv9wdo.html (accessed 19 May 2017).

McClymont, K. and Besser, L. (2014) *He Who Must Be Obeid: The Untold Story*. Sydney: Vintage Books.

McClymont, K. and Besser, L. with Nicholls, S. (2012) "Coal Corruption Worst Scam 'since Rum Corps'." *Sydney Morning Herald*, 13 November. Online. Available HTTP: www.smh.com.au/national/coal-corruption-worst-scam-since-rum-corps-20121112-298vv.html (accessed 15 April 2017).

Pearce, F. (1976) *Crimes of the Powerful: Marxism, Crime and Deviance*. London: Pluto Press.

Pilger, J. (1990) *A Secret Country*. London: Vintage Books.

Poynting, S. and Whyte, D. (2017) "Introduction: Corruption Downunder." *International Journal for Crime, Justice and Social Democracy*, 6(4): December.

R v Obeid (No. 12) (2016) NSW Supreme Court [NSWSC] 1815, 15 December. Online. Available HTTP: www.austlii.edu.au/au/cases/nsw/NSWSC/2016/1815.html (accessed 14 April 2017).

Seccombe, M. (2016) "NSW Premier Mike Baird's Flaws Beginning to Show." *The Saturday Paper*, Issue 112, 11 June. Online. Available HTTP: www.thesaturdaypaper.com.

au/news/politics/2016/06/11/nsw-premier-mike-bairds-flaws-beginning-show/14655672003359 (accessed 14 April 2017).

West, M. (2013) "Trevor Kennedy Fought Hard to Maintain Secrecy of His Business Dealings." *Sydney Morning Herald*, 3 December. Online. Available HTTP: www.smh.com.au/business/trevor-kennedy-fought-hard-to-maintain-secrecy-of-his-business-dealings-20131203–2yp2h.html (accessed 22 May 2017).

Whitbourn, M. and McClymont, K. (2016) "Eddie Obeid and son Moses Charged Over $30 Million Coal Deal." *Sydney Morning Herald*, 19 July. Online. Available HTTP: www.smh.com.au/nsw/eddie-obeid-and-son-moses-charged-over-30-million-coal-deal-20160706-gpzycv.html (accessed 19 May 2017).

White, A. (2015) "Sean Howard, Malcolm Turnbull's OzEmail Partner, Is in Start-up Mode Again." *The Australian*, 16 October. Online. Available HTTP: www.theaustralian.com.au/business/the-deal-magazine/sean-howard-malcolm-turnbulls-ozemail-partner-is-in-startup-mode-again/news-story/b83e619f01d198c0829931f3bc281e9a (accessed 22 May 2017).

White, R. (2017) "Corruption and the Securitisation of Nature." *International Journal for Crime, Justice and Social Democracy*, 6(4): December.

# Chapter 16

# The crimes of the powerful and the Spanish crisis

*Ignasi Bernat*

The financial and economic crisis has hit Spain unexpectedly hard since 2007. This fact brought several economic and social issues to the surface: massive unemployment; youth emigration; draconian cuts to education, health and welfare; labour counter-reforms; hundreds of thousands of evictions; and so on. At the same time, new scandals have been continuously exposed since the beginning of the crisis. They are often understood as a continuum of bad practices and wrongdoing by politicians and business leaders who are either inefficient or directly corrupt. This particular idea has been known as the "Transition Culture" (Fernández – Savater 2013) and – despite its negative meaning – is also being widely promulgated as an explanation of the crisis. More and more people are stating that the entire political regime born in the aftermath of Franco's dictatorship needs to be transformed.

This explanation of the current crisis in Spain has the value of enabling us to understand that crimes of the powerful are not an isolated element, but sit on a continuum in the Spanish system. Nevertheless, it has the limitation of conceiving them as the result of a political culture lacking in ethical values. In fact, a new penal populism seems to be rising – but this time directed against corrupt politicians and businesspeople (*eldiario.es* 25 February 2015).[1] But are we just facing a problem of "rotten apples"? To solve this problem, do we need more or better accountability? Is it a problem based simply on a lack of regulation and enforcement?

I will address the most widespread form of corporate crime before and during the Spanish crisis as a case study – the mortgage lending concession to benefit banks and other corporations involved in this form of accumulation by financial dispossession (Bernat 2015). But to do so, I will focus on some lessons from Frank Pearce's book to suggest one possible interpretation of the unpunished crimes (Jiménez 2014: 96) of the powerful.

Since 2013 the Court of Justice of the European Union (CJEU) has ruled several times against the Spanish state on several dimensions of the mortgage issue according to the strand of jurisprudence that protects consumers from judicial procedures regarding the interpretation of the general contracting conditions' directive (Directive 93/13). Mostly, the Court ruled on the lack of protection of the consumer in the foreclosure procedure, claiming that Spanish law had to be amended in order to strengthen the position of the consumer in regard to the banks (Sentence 14 March 2013). Thus, the Spanish legislator urgently introduced a new law in May 2013 (Law 1/2013). This legal reform of the Spanish government has opened new prejudicial questions due to the lack of sensitivity to the CJEU jurisprudence. Again, the Court has questioned the limitations of the Spanish law and opened the possibility of appeal for consumers (Sentence 29 October 2015). At the same time, the Court has ruled against Spain because of the high interest rates in cases of non-payment, claiming that they are too rigid and not fair considering the costs that banks should assume (Sentence 26 October 2016). It has been very critical of the Spanish Supreme Court (Sentence 21 December 2017) in limiting the time of a judge to expel land clauses, and it has warned that judges have the power to nullify land clauses[2] and also to prevent other banks from introducing abusive clauses (Sentence 26 January 2017).

However, without denying the political and ethical corruption of the Spanish elites, we want to focus our attention on the specific regime of power that arises from the financialization of the economy as a political process (Harvey 2010), which has reshaped previous power relations and the access to rights and services. This power reconfiguration enables crimes involving several predatory practices (Taylor 1997). This new regime of power is the result of the assemblage of an increasingly financialized *political economy* (Lapavitsas 2013a), the peculiarities of the Spanish *spatial fix* (López and Rodríguez 2011) and an institutional architecture characterized as an "incomplete democracy" (Navarro 2002) from its origins – but in a current process of de-democratization (Tilly 2010: 43) due to the corporate power attack. Thereby, corruption or corporate crime is not a pathology of the system, but just another mechanism to accumulate capital (Pearce 1976). This chapter approaches the social agreement that conceals corporate power and the structure of impunity that fosters the crimes of the powerful as an outcome and a means to further concentrate class power (Whyte 2015: 26).

Nonetheless, before scrutinizing these mortgage concessions as predatory practices of accumulation by dispossession (Harvey 2004: 186), the chapter now turns to the financialization of the economy, the Spanish subsidiary position within the EU and the institutional role of the Spanish state in fostering corporate power in order to locate the relationship between the state and the corporation within the overall social structure (Pearce 1976: 105) that gave momentum to the crimes of the powerful.

## Financialization and the European arrangement

Financial capital has been gaining strength over productive capital throughout the history of capitalism (Arrighi 1999; Foster 2010), although this tendency seems to have gathered momentum since 1970 with the drop in productivity and real accumulation (Lapavitsas 2009a). This recent period of capitalist history is characterized by financialization (Lapavitsas 2013a: 169). Nevertheless, the process that made financial capital paramount is clearly linked to political power and the hegemonic change that started in the 1970s and consolidated in the 1980s with the Regan and Thatcher victories that strengthened the neo-liberal project of the Western elites (Harvey 2010). The consensus established after WWII in the midst of the Roosevelt era (Hagan 2010) was replaced by the new Washington consensus inspiring a set of financial changes to foster financial institutions (Aglietta and Moatti 2002). The myth of market efficiency (Harcourt 2010) has been the leading force in the Reagan era (Hagan 2010) seeking to redirect all human action to the exchange sphere (Ruggiero 2013). This shift towards financialization was marked symbolically and significantly with the derogation of the Glass–Steagall Act in 2000 by Clinton, when commercial banks turned definitively to the financial market (Lapavitsas 2009b; Hagan 2010).

The financial sector has penetrated all domains of Western societies (Lapavitsas 2009a), gaining institutional salience through state efforts at economic re-regulation (Harcourt 2010: 85). There have been institutional and technological changes fostering financial innovation, but also growth in the size of the markets and the institutions participating in them, in the number of employees and in the volume of profits (Lapavitsas 2009b). Financial profit is the broad term used to refer to the multiplicity of forms to obtain revenues with return on capital (Lapavitsas 2013a), although the most important change has been in the financial expropriation from working people (Lapavitsas 2009a, 2013a). The nature of capital accumulation has been altered due to the patently subsidiary position of goods and services production and distribution with regard to finance (Foster 2010; Lapavitsas 2013a). Financial accumulation originates in the sphere of distribution and not in the production, the former requiring financial institutions trading with loanable capital. Financial accumulation needs increasing financial flows of loanable capital and not industrial stocks, neither value nor surplus value production (Lapavitsas 2013a: 202).

The American real estate bubble is the outcome of this accumulation process. The bubble resulted from the drop of interest rates by the Federal Reserve since 2001 to avoid recession after 9/11 and the failure of the dot.com economy (Lapavitsas 2009a). This rate drop allowed wider sectors of the population to gain access to credit, but this supposed democratization of money meant expanding financial expropriation towards more vulnerable populations, converting them into a source of profit for banks and other financial institutions through fees, tariffs and commissions (Lapavitsas 2011, 2009b). A shift in banking towards family assets and revenues occurred via the provision of household services and credit, such as mortgages, education, health, insurance or pensions, etc. (Lapavitsas 2011). This false credit democratization maintained private demand in a context of wages stagnation since the 1970s. The financial sector mediated as a provider of goods and services to homes which financialized everyday life (Lapavitsas 2013a). Housing access became the key element in this process due to the dependency on banks to provide housing financing. Mortgages exponentially increased household indebtedness, albeit with international and intranational variations (Lapavitsas 2013a). Further, because financial expropriation is more likely in a context of scarce social rights or when these need to be complemented through the market (Taylor 1997), financialization and the withdrawal of the social state have to be understood as intertwined trends. Moreover, it cannot be denied that financial expropriation from the working classes had racialized aspects in many countries as those groups who were previously excluded from certain goods were now included as consumers – if, in fact, targeted as more vulnerable groups (Dymski 2009; Bernat 2014).

The immediate causes of the financial crisis of 2007 in the United States, which spread globally, have to be located in the sinking of subprime mortgages (Mazzucato 2013; Toussaint 2014). These mortgages ultimately polluted the entire financial sector of the Western world (Lapavitsas 2013b), with nothing more than the conversion of loans to poor families into financial assets, reducing passive investment and encouraging speculation (Toussaint 2014). Even with the elaborate financial engineering of banks, the burst of the construction bubble exposed European banks, the Germans particularly, as the number of assets accumulated (Lapavitsas 2013b). American banks were having problems due to the fall in valuation of real estate assets and also because many households had trouble meeting mortgage payments. Most European banks continued to loan money and to invest in the European periphery until the bankruptcy of American banks in September 2008 and in Europe thereafter (Lapavitsas 2013b). Banks from the core of the Eurozone loaned massive sums to those on the periphery, believing that they were stable markets after their incorporation into the euro, but the real estate bubbles burst one after another because of the private debt held mainly by banks (Aglietta and Brand 2015; Mazzucato 2013).

A complementary element in the theoretical explanation of the crisis is provided by economic geography (Krugman 1992). This would see the genesis of the crisis in Europe rooted in the industrial polarization between the core and the periphery of the European region (Aglietta and Brand 2015). According to this geographical interpretation, the key element to understand the depth of the crisis in the Southern European periphery would be the regional inequality and industrial polarization (Krugman 2012). In this regard, the problems faced by Spain are also the result of the European spatial agreement reinforcing the uneven spatial division prior to the euro, which increased the existing trend towards deindustrialization and financial speculation in the periphery of the EU (Aglietta and Brand 2015). This agreement facilitates industrial disinvestment in the South because it is less competitive with rising labour costs and, thus, trade deficits because of the negative trade balance between exports and imports (Krugman 2012). At the same time, it consolidates the North of the EU, particularly Germany, but also Austria and Finland, and those under their influence such as the Czech Republic, Poland and Slovakia (Aglietta and Brand 2015).

The uneven development between regions is based on the cumulative effect of rising outcomes, that is, the interaction between demand, transport costs and rising outcomes that reinforces regional inequalities (Krugman 1992). Therefore, if there is not a coordinated policy at a European level of industrial investment in the South, existing inequalities in the industrial sectors are reinforced by scale economies and the agglomeration effects (Aglietta and Brand 2015; Mazzucato 2013). Monetary union is ensuring that the countries with a productive advantage can improve their position, reinforcing their competitiveness and productivity, whereas the opposite occurs in the less competitive territories. The euro made for a false monetary stability that reduced interest rates and flooded the banks of South Europe with largely French and German capital in search of profits, inflating the real estate bubble (Krugman 2012). In other words, it could not have reached such a size without the millions allocated to the most profitable activity, the construction sector in all its domains, that is, construction companies, real estate agencies, promoters and mortgage concessions (García-Montalvo 2008). We cannot forget that this sector represented 60% of all bank credits in 2007 (García-Montalvo and Raya 2012: 22). The bubble-related sky-rocketing of prices produced inflation, the increase in household debt, the fall in the value of savings, the rise of labour costs and the drop in investment in the industrial sector (Aglietta and Brand 2015; Aguilera and Naredo 2009). Therefore, the uneven spatial division has stimulated industrial concentration, with processes of specialization in Germany and its satellites driven by industrial restructuring. Unequal political power held by certain European states, influencing the policy making of the EU, lies behind this understanding of the crisis in the Eurozone (Aglietta and Brand 2015).

## The Spanish spatial fix

The Spanish spatial fix has relied on financialization and territory-based tourism, construction and ownership promotion as competitive advantages to foster asset price Keynesianism[3] (López and Rodríguez 2010). In this spatial fix have been two constant elements: infrastructure development and the promotion of city making. In the first place, the construction of infrastructure aimed to foster a *sui generis* Keynesianism to catalyze the economy, creating employment and increasing internal demand. Another objective was to make tourist arrivals easier through several means of transport to attract capital for investment and consumption because of the weakness of internal demand (López and Rodríguez 2010). At the same time, tourism allowed the Spanish housing market to enter into the global financial flow. This tight net also aimed to produce the interconnection of every territory of the state which allowed the valorization of every area entering in several economic bubbles (1975–1985, 1986–1991, 1996–2007) that fostered economic growth and the recessions afterwards. This model is not only the result of the late development of Francoism, but there has been a strong continuity during different governments after the transition to democracy (López and Rodríguez 2011). It is for this reason that Spain holds a wide network of high-speed trains and airports in every region built with the European cohesion funds from 1986 to 2004 (López and Rodríguez 2010; Fernández Durán 2006). The *quid pro quo* was accepting deindustrialization to avoid competition with existing EU members. This model required huge building companies and strong banks to carry out such projects which created tremendous financial power (Rodríguez 2015). The former electric and telecommunication national monopolies were privatized, benefiting national and financial powers. That is, the state action and corporations allowed the "democratization" of oligarchical power. Infrastructures, megaprojects and privatization have fostered powerful groups backed by the state (Naredo 2009).

Second, the promotion of cities as "growth machines" (Molotch 1976: 360) has been another key element in the Spanish territorial specialization (López and Rodríguez 2010). This model is based on territorial administrative decentralization where regional and local bodies have greater autonomy in urban issues. Actually, an important part of their budget comes from the added value of rezoning land and the taxes it generates (López and Rodríguez 2010). Municipalities are fiscally subordinated to the revenues of real estate markets through taxation upon assets, the selling of urban land, licenses to build or reform and so on. In this model, land is a market commodity which provides power and economic resources (López and Rodríguez 2010; Molotch 1976), but the right to housing is dismissed (Fernández Durán 2006). Municipalities are then trapped in a race to create monopolistic rents over land and urban brands to attract capital investment and visitors (Harvey 2005). That is the reason why urban events are so important: music festivals, business fairs, summits, sporting events, marketing, etc. In this way powerful groups shape priorities and decisions affecting urban life and public budgets, enabling them to obtain huge profits from housing speculation and rent extraction with banks, builders, construction firms and promoters (Naredo 2010; Harvey 2005). Indeed, this growth model and its two main features have been devastating for the environment, criss-crossing territory with highways and train lines, airports not always well planned and promoting urban sprawl with the car and fossil fuel dependency at its centre (López and Rodríguez 2010; Fernández Durán 2006).

Although regions and municipalities are very important in the making of the bubble, we cannot forget the central administration's role in the final outcome. The last bubble (1996–2007) has to be understood as the result of the economic and political conditions that allowed every piece of land to become a growth machine, from big cities to tourist regions and even remote areas (López and Rodríguez 2010). The extension of urbanization allows the capture of surplus capital in order to delay the crisis of under-consumption (Harvey 2010). This is key to analysing all of the measures taken by the Spanish state: promotion of ownership instead of renting, land liberalization, deregulation of the mortgage market, fiscal subvention to the real estate sector and building infrastructure to inflate the bubble and to foster strong territorial cohesion (López and Rodríguez 2011). Actually, urban and real estate sectors are strongly regulated in each domain (García-Montalvo 2008). In this sense the co-production of the state in promoting a Keynesianism of price assets can be discussed as a crime of the powerful exemplified in the following case study.

## Case study: mortgages

The case we want to explore is the most paradigmatic state–corporate crime (Michalowski and Kramer 2006) in the financialization context. Provision of mortgages can be considered crimes during the 1996–2007 bubble for two main reasons: first, because of the way the state paved the conditions for this massive approval of mortgages; and second, because of the wrongdoing of all the corporations involved in this context. These crimes have produced not only the eradication of the right to housing, but also the variety of social harms associated with eviction (Bernat 2014; Forero 2014).

As mentioned earlier, the crisis has its immediate origin in subprime mortgages (Mazzucato 2013; Lapavitsas 2013b; Toussaint 2014). In the Spanish case we have three years in a row of more than 1.5 million mortgages, and during the triennium 2005–2007 (Figure 16.1), Spain built more houses than Germany, France and Italy put together, even though each country alone has a greater population than Spain (Akin et al. 2014). Such volume of construction was the catalyst of the Spanish economy, representing 20% of gross domestic product (GDP) and receiving 60% of banking credits (García-Montalvo and

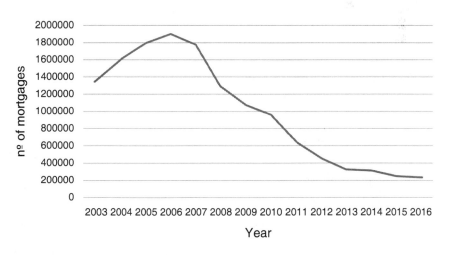

*Figure 16.1* Spanish mortgages 2003–2016
Source Instituto Nacional de Estadística (National Institute of Statistics)

Raya 2012). Mortgages and financial mechanisms such as securitization made the ongoing transfer from the working wages towards financial institutions possible (López and Rodríguez 2010); through mortgages, working wages went to financial institutions and in this way the main way accumulation occurred is by financial dispossession (Bernat 2015).

In order to understand how the right to housing has been turned into an inaccessible commodity, we need to understand the state co-production of the crime. In fact, we reached this point precisely through several measures implemented by the state administration. The situation was so worrying that in the middle of the bubble the United Nations rapporteur for housing urged the Spanish government to tackle the situation (Kothari 2008). But now we will focus on those policies deployed by the central administration in this context.

### The role of the state

First, there was the housing policy implemented by the late Franco's regime to foster ownership as a primary way of accessing housing, which is in contrast to other countries. A key point in understanding the scale of the problem is that even public housing was aimed at turning renters into owners (Observatori Desc 2013). Two reasons lay behind this: politically this allows the subjection of and governing of working people (Stavrakakis 2013), but economically it fosters asset price Keynesianism (López and Rodríguez 2010). Housing policies, like housing plans and urban renting laws, were addressed at discouraging renting, while creating an unstable situation due to the liberalization of the urban rental market (López and Rodríguez 2010; Observatori Desc 2013).

Second, the market for land was another key element in creating the bubble. A law passed in 1998 and known as "all developable" was aimed at the supply side. This supply policy made the assumption that liberalizing land, that is, supplying more and more land, would result in price decreases. Yet the opposite happened, because when there is an expectation of housing revalorization, prices increase (López and Rodríguez 2010). This situation cannot be explained as the result of fundamental factors such as the income per capita, construction costs or demographic growth and the real need for first or second residences. The explanation is that housing became an investment instead of a good to be used (García-Montalvo 2008). In the decision to buy, the potential value was more important than the actual use value that the buyer would attribute to it. This is a clear indicator that we were in a bubble (García-Montalvo 2008).

The direct influence of the state in the creation of the bubble can also be seen in two further factors associated with the gradual introduction of the Spanish mortgage market into the global financial markets. This incorporation occurred at two key stages. First in 1981 when it was allowed by law to increase the amount borrowed and the variable credit rate increased to 80%, which facilitated longer loans to return the capital and transferring the risk to households. Second, in 1992, when the hedge funds and the securitization funds were regularized in order that mortgages could be sold into to the financial global market, which established the basement to the economic cycle 1995–2007 boosted by construction and mortgages. Securitization allowing more mortgages was granted under the wrong assumption that risk was neutralized (López and Rodríguez 2010).

The last big expansion of the bubble came through fiscal relief for house-buying, that is, public subsidies for real estate purchases instead of promoting other forms of access to housing, even including second and third residences (Observatori Desc 2013). Lastly, state influence was extended to the construction of infrastructure that we have analysed earlier, which generated the territorial homogenization allowing every area to become part of the bubble and the promotion of growth machines to maintain high demand for housing and land (López and Rodríguez 2010).

A further element showing state complicity in the production of social harm lies in evictions that followed the mortgages. Data on housing evictions are shocking; according to the INE (National Institute of Statistics)[4] from 2014 to the third quarter of 2016 some 161,648 evictions were initiated in Spain. These routine practices of corporations were facilitated by the state: a mortgage law dating from 1909 had established that in the case of non-payment eviction is almost immediate and that even after returning the mortgaged property the debt is not cancelled. If the auction of the asset has no buyer, the bank keeps it for 70% of the valuation amount, but when the debt is not fully covered, it produces new interest to be repaid by the mortgage holder (Colau and Alemany 2013).

### The role of corporations

Having discussed the different dimensions of state involvement, now we turn to the role of corporate actors, including banks, real estate agencies, taxation companies and notaries involved in the production of harm through their modus operandi. These routine practices of corporations were possible because of the state setting a framework of permission. At the same time, as we mentioned earlier, the eurozone ensured that banks enjoyed massive liquidity coming from other European banks and hedge funds (Krugman 2012). The Spanish bubble was a great opportunity to put up great amounts of money which gave the banks huge sums to borrow at a low interest rate (Ballbé and Caicedo 2012, *El País*), but increased competition for new customers. This process made the goal of getting new clients paramount, and banks and real estate agencies proliferated throughout Spain. To increase their volume of business, banks used several dubious (at best) practices. First, customers were not sufficiently aware of the conditions of their mortgage (García-Montalvo 2008), not least the fact that banks would cover their costs and then begin to make profits after just three years of repayments by the lender. Second, banks gave mortgages in certain periods based on the sole aim of increasing the volume of business in their balance sheets (Bernat 2014). Third, they accepted dirty money for the repayment of mortgages (García-Montalvo 2008). Fourth, much of the wrongdoing by banks was directed at their own customers, namely the inclusion of products of scarce utility that the mortgage applicant signed unknowingly, such as swaps; mortgages that a few years after signing, people were paying sometimes double the amount; guarantees by relatives, friends or sometimes unknown people; and promoting bridging loans in order to access better houses that ended up with many people being doubly mortgaged (Colau and Alemany 2012; Observatori Desc 2013).

Valuation agencies also had a key role in creating the bubble due to appraisal value being used as a proxy of the value of a property in the market and which either stimulated or disincentivized a transaction (García-Montalvo and Raya 2012). But these companies are dependent on banks as customers when they are not directly outsourced from them. The most common predatory practice was inflating valuations in order that mortgage credit was inferior to the 80% under the Bank of Spain's guidelines; in this way, subprime mortgages were camouflaged. Appraisal value was manipulated according to the necessities of those involved in the transaction. A good proxy of this is comparing the average of the loan with the transaction price, which was over 100% (García-Montalvo and Raya 2012). This exemplifies the overvaluation of the balance sheets of the Spanish banks at the time.

Real estate agencies have also been implicated because of a list of bad practices in the network of offices throughout Spain (Akin et al. 2014), influencing every last town and operating sometimes without license. Among their practices they falsified pay slips and promoted cross-guarantees to secure mortgage approvals by banks, as well as contracting migrants with influence in their communities to cheat their compatriots (Bernat 2014), and engaging in racist discrimination involving offering property in certain neighbourhoods only for migrants (Observatori Desc 2013).

## Conclusion

For a better understanding of the permanent crisis in Spain (Agamben 2014), this chapter has discussed two paramount elements. The first of these elements is the relationship between the state and the corporation within the overall social structure (Pearce 1976: 105). In this context, Pearce emphasizes the impossibility of successfully studying the crimes of the powerful as isolated acts. Today, this forces us to locate the crimes of the powerful within the financialization of the economy as a resource to squeeze yet more corporate profitability within the frame of the neoliberal turn (Laval and Dardot 2013). In this regard, a critical analysis of the role of the state in financialization is essential. Thus, this analysis has considered the relationship between the public and the private sectors as an instance where corporate crime is shaped and gathers momentum. Financialization has ended up blurring the dichotomy between the public and the private (Tombs 2012; Tombs and Whyte 2015) that works in the imaginary social order (Pearce 1976). Certainly, the crimes of the powerful are produced in an era where there is a tendency to underestimate the state prevalence in many analyses of economic globalization. As we have seen, the state is a key player in such offences, establishing ideal conditions for corporate power to conquer new domains in which to do business and to foster higher levels of corporate profitability (Whyte 2014).

The second element of analysis echoes another point of emphasis of Pearce. He stressed the need to take into account "the international nature of the capitalist system to wholly understand the crimes of the powerful" (Pearce 1976: 105). In the peripheral and semi-peripheral countries of global capitalism, this statement is essential to capture the dynamics of corporate regulation and its crimes at the local level; thus international financial institutions are key players to study as to how regulation that addresses economic growth – ignoring social development – is produced (Friedrichs and Friedrichs 2002; Wonders and Danner 2006). What is more, in the Spanish case the political economy is shaped by international relations that restrain – *de iure* and *de facto* – its sovereignty in many senses. Indeed, institutions and treaties of the European Union pave the road to a neoliberal agenda that fosters the power of capital, allowing and securing its investments at a regional and global level (Etxezarreta 2002). EU institutions and actions – such as the European Commission; the Single European Act in 1986; the liberalization of capital; and the treaties of Maastricht, Amsterdam, Nice, Lisbon or Dublin, as well as some directives as the Bolkestein Directive for the liberalization of services, the Directive on Working Hours or the enacted measures of the European Central Bank – promote norms which benefit corporate power, an ongoing regional regulation which is a way to increase corporate power. Despite this we cannot ignore that this process is an outcome of power relations inside the EU, as it is shown by an economic geography (Krugman 1992) that establishes a strong core, but with the southern and eastern peripheries that keep their markets open to economic and financial power in neocolonial dynamics (Fernández Durán 2006: 67).

Therefore, corporate crime and victimization – not least in the form of mortgages and evictions – should be understood as a process instead of the summation of several events. In this way, we can locate corporate crime within a wider political economy and a set of social relationships that relegates rights (Bernat and Whyte 2017). Corporate crimes then play a key role within the ongoing process of accumulation of power and wealth (Whyte 2015). In this sense, corporations are not only institutional actors, but institutionalized power relations where profit accumulation takes place. Although this is a domain for struggle, resistance and challenge, different rules apply to each set of actors in the field. The limits and rules in this terrain are framed and established by the crimes of the powerful, allowing corporate players to accumulate through financial dispossession. In this sense, corporations have proved the capacity to have laws passed on their behalf, to threaten governments, to deploy unlawful practices, to neglect rights and to dispossess people as possessing a sort of criminal capital that guarantees impunity for their behaviour and a steady rhythm for wealth accumulation.

## Notes

1 Although there are only 82 people imprisoned for corruption, which perhaps means that it is only a discourse.
2 Land clauses were introduced by banks to ensure that interest rates could not go down in any case, but could only go up linked to the main proxies of the market such as Euribor or Libor.
3 By asset price Keynesianism, López and Rodríguez (2010: 110) refer to policies aiming to convert real estate assets into liquidity to promote investment and consumption, that is, to turn savings into effective demand.
4 Before 2014 data are not available. Only after huge pressure by social movements did the Spanish authorities start to gather the data.

## References

Agamben, G. (2014) *Archeologia della Politica*. Seminar at University of Girona, May 2014.
Aglietta, M. and Brand, T. (2015[2013]) *Un* New Deal *para Europa. Crecimiento, euro, competitividad*. Madrid: Traficantes de sueños.
Aglietta, M. and Moatti, S. (2002[2000]) *El FMI: Del orden monetario a los desórdenes financieros* (2ª ed.). Madrid: Ediciones Akal.
Aguilera, F. and Naredo, J.M. (2009) "Introducción," in Federico Aguilera (Coordinador), *Economía, poder y megaproyectos*, 3–18. Lanzarote: Fundación César Manrique.
Akin, O., Montalvo, J.G. Villar, J.G., Peydró, J.-L. and Raya, J.M. (2014) "The Real Estate and Credit Bubble: Evidence from Spain." *SERIEs*, 5(2-3): 223–243.
Arrighi, G. (1999[1994]) *El largo siglo xx: Dinero y poder en los orígenes de nuestra época*. Madrid: Akal.
Ballbe, M. and Caicedo, Y. (2012) "*El ataque alemán desahucia a España*." noviembre 29, El País.
Bernat, I. (2014) "Desahuciando a inmigrantes: una etnografía en una comunidad dañada." *Crítica Penal y poder*, 7: 35–63.
——— (2015) "Entendiendo los desahucios: financiarización, poder corporativo y derechos mercantilizados." *Sortuz*, 7(2): 88–104.
Bernat, I. and Whyte, D. (2017) "State-corporate Crime and the Process of Global Accumulation." *Critical Criminology*, 25: 71–86.
Colau, A. and Alemany, A. (2012) *Vides Hipotecades. De la bombolla hipotecària al dret a l'habitatge*. Barcelona: Angle.
——— (2013) *¡Sí se puede! Crónica de una pequeña gran victoria*. Barcelona: Destino.
Dymski, G. (2009) "Racial Exclusion and the Political Economy of the Subprime Crisis." *Historical Materialism*, 17: 149–179.
*eldiario.es* (2015) "Un populismo punitive contra las elites." febrero 25.
Etxezarreta, M. (2002) "Europa S.A.," in Gemma Galdón (ed.) *Mundo S. A.*, 151–159 Barcelona: La tempestad.
Fernández Durán, R. (2006) *El tsunami urbaizador: Sobre sus causas y repercusiones devastadoras, y la necesidad de prepararse para el previsible estallido de la burbuja inmobiliaria*. Barcelona: Virus.
Fernández-Savater, A. (2013) "La cultura de la transición y el nuevo sentido común." *Cuadernos de eldiario.es*, 1: 16–18.

Forero, A. (2014) "Soberanía limitada, delitos estatal-corporativo y daño social: los desahucios y suicidios en España," in Iñaki Rivera Beiras (ed.) *Delitos de los Estados, de los mercados y daño social*, 167–181. Barcelona: Anthropos.

Foster, J.B. (2010) "The Financialization of Accumulation." *Monthly Review*, 62(5): 1–17.

Friedrichs, D. and Friedrichs, J. (2002) "The World Bank and the Crimes of the Globalization: A Case Study." *Social Justice*, 29 (1–2): 13–36.

García Montalvo, J. (2008) *De la Quimera Inmobiliaria al Colapso Financiero*. Barcelona: Bosch.

García Montalvo, J. and María Raya, J. (2012) "What is the Right Price of the Spanish Real State." *Spanish Economic and Financial Outlook*, 1(3): 22–28.

Hagan, J. (2010) *Who Are the Criminals? The Politics of Crime Policy From the Age of Roosevelt to the Age of Reagan*. New Jersey: Princeton University.

Harcourt, B. (2010) "Neoliberal Penality: A Brief Genealogy." *Theoretical Criminology*, 14(1): 74–92.

Harvey, D. (2004[2003]) *El Nuevo Imperialismo*. Madrid: Akal.

———— (2005) "El arte de la renta: la globalización y la mercantilización de la cultura," in David Harvey et al. (eds.) *Capital financiero, propiedad inmobiliaria y cultura*. Barcelona: Macba.

———— (2010) *The Enigma of Capital and the Crisis of Capitalism*. New York: Oxford University.

Jiménez, D. (2014) "Crímenes que producen castigo. Sobre el sentido del jubileo en una administración general del daño." *Crítica Penal y Poder*, 7: 85–121.

Kothari, Miloon. (2008) *Informe del relator especial sobre una vivienda adecuada como elemento integrante del derecho a un nivel de vida adecuado* A/HRC/7/16/Add 2, de 7 de Febrero, Naciones Unidas.

Krugman, P. (1992[1991]) *Georgrafía y comercio*. Barcelona: Bosch.

———— (2012[2012]) *¡Acabad ya con esta crisis!* (3ª ed.). Barcelona: Crítica.

Lapavitsas, C. (2009a) *El capitalismo financiarizado: expansión y crisis*. Madrid: Maia Ediciones.

———— (2009b) "Financialised Capitalism: Crisis and Financial Expropriation." *Historical Materialism*, 17: 114–148.

———— (2011) "Theorizing Financialization." *Work, Employment and Society*, 25(4): 611–626.

———— (2013a) *Profiting Without Producing: How Finance Exploits us All*. London: Verso.

———— (2013b[2012]) *Crisis en la Euro zona*. Madrid: Capitán Swing.

Laval, C. and Dardot, P. (2013[2010]) *La Nueva Razón del Mundo*. Madrid: Gedisa.

López, Isidoro, Emmanuel Rodríguez y Hernández. (2010) *Fin de ciclo. Financiarización, territorio y sociedad de propietarios en la onda larga del capitalismo hispano (1959–2010)*, Madrid: Traficantes de sueños.

———— (2011) "The Spanish Model." *New Left Review*, 69: 5–28.

Mazzucato, M. (2013) *The Entrepreneurial State: Debunking Public vs. Private Sector Myths*. London: Anathem.

Michalowski, R. and Kramer, R. (2006) "The Critique of Power," in R. Michalowski and R. Kramer (eds.) *State-Corporate Crime: Wrongdoing at the Intersection of Business and Government*, 1–18. Brunswick: Rutgers.

Molotch, H. (1976) "The City as a Growth Machine: Toward a Political Economy of Place." *American Journal of Sociology*, 82(2): 309–332.

Naredo, J.M. (2009) "Economía y poder. Megaproyectos, recalificaciones y contratas," in *Economía, poder y megaproyectos*, 19–52. Lanzarote: Fundación César Manrique.

———— (2010) "El modelo inmobiliario español y sus consecuencias," in *Coloquio sobre urbanismo, democracia y mercado: una experiencia española (1970–2010)*, 13–27.

Navarro, V. (2002) *Bienestar insuficiente, democracia incompleta*. Barcelona: Anagrama.

Obsevatori Desc. (2013) *Emergencia habitacional en el Estado espanol: La crisis de las ejecuciones hipotecarias y de los desalojos desde una perspectiva de los derechos humanos*. Online. Available HTTP: http://observatoridesc.org/sites/default/files/2013-Emergencia-Habitacional.pdf

Pearce, F. (1976) *The Crimes of the Powerful. Marxism, Crime and Deviance*. London: Pluto.

Rodríguez, E. (2015) *Por qué Fracasó La Democracia en España. La transición y el régimen del '78*. Madrid: Traficantes de Sueños.

Ruggiero, V. (2013) *I crimini dell'economia: Una lettura criminologica del pensiero economico*. Milano: Feltrinelli.

Stavrakakis, Y. (2013) "La sociedad de la deuda. Grecia y el futuro de la postdemocracia," in Alain Badiou et al. (eds.) *El sintoma griego*, 7–28.

Taylor, I. (1997) "The Political Economy of Crime," in Mike Maguire et al. (eds.) *The Oxford Handbook of Criminology* (2nd ed.), 265–303. Oxford: Oxford University.

Tilly, C. (2010[2007]) *Democracia*. Madrid: Akal.

Tombs, S. (2012) "State-Corporate Symbiosis in the Production of Crime and Harm." *State Crime*, 1(2): 170–195.

Tombs, S. and Whyte, D. (2015) *The Corporate Criminal: Why Corporations Must be Abolished*. London: Routledge.

Toussaint, É. (2014[2014]) *Bancocracia*. Barcelona: Icaria.

Wonders, N. and Danner, M. (2006) "Globalization, State-corporate Crime, and Woman," in Raymond Michalowski and Ronald Kramer (eds.) *State-Corporate Crime*, 98–115. Rutgers, Brunswick.

Whyte, D. (2014) "Regimes of Permission and State-corporate Crime." *State Crime Journal*, 3(2): 237–246.

———— (2015) "Introduction: A Very British Corruption," in David Whyte (ed.) *How Corrupted is Britain?* 1–37, London: Pluto.

# Chapter 17

# Crimes of globalization and Asian dam projects
## Powerful institutions and slow violence

*David O. Friedrichs*

Well into the second decade of the 21st century, it is a somewhat dishearten-ing fact that the field of criminology continues to be principally focused on crimes of the power*less* and the control of such crime. But on the other side of this, there is now increasing attention to crimes of the power*ful* and the control of such crime. More specifically, a form of "crimes of the powerful" that was quite invisible to criminologists in that earlier time but is important to address in the world we live in today is identified and discussed. These crimes are the "crimes of globalization" perpetrated by immensely powerful international financial institutions such as the World Bank, with specific attention to Asian dam projects that are one significant manifestation of such crime. If mainstream criminology has greatly attended to "fast violence" – for example, conventional forms of homicide, mass shootings and the like – the claim here is that the field needs to attend much more fully to "slow violence" that takes place incremen-tally, for the most part, but has hugely harmful consequences.

## Crimes of the powerful, crimes of globalization and an imaginary social order

Some forms of "crimes of the powerful" have been long recognized within criminology, especially the crimes of capitalist corporations. As early as 1845 Friedrich Engels alleged that such corporations engaged in the "murder" of their workers. In the first half of the 20th century Willem Bonger and Edwin Sutherland were two prominent criminologists who called attention to the crimes of capitalist corporations. The concept of "crimes of the powerful" – as set forth in Frank Pearce's 1976 book – provided a potent conceptual framework for understanding connections between different manifestations of such crimes. The core argument of this chapter is that in an increasingly globalized world of the late 20th century and early 21st century more recent manifestations of crimes of the powerful require the attention of contempo-rary criminologists. And a sophisticated understanding of the crimes of glo-balization addressed in this chapter needs to incorporate at least some core elements of Marxist theory. Most Western criminologists have either wholly disregarded or have specifically rejected Marxist theory. In part, this stance can be attributed to the horrific histories of the so-called Marxist states of the 20th century – notably the Stalinist Soviet Union and the Maoist People's Republic of China – and so this is the "baggage" that broadly constrains receptivity to anything characterized as a "Marxist" analysis. This proposition may be considerably more pronounced in the American than in the European context. Americans, in particular, during the long course of the "Cold War" were relentlessly exposed to the horrors of "communism" as practiced in the Soviet Union, the People's Republic of China and elsewhere. So it tends to be a relatively small proportion of self-identified criminologists who – for various reasons, sometimes quite serendipitously – are receptive in differing degrees to Marxist analysis. The present author has long regarded Marxist analysis as a potent intellectual project for making sense of our political economy, and specifically a capitalist society. At the same time he has never identified himself as a "Marxist," and is leery of *any* form of totalistic theory for making sense of the endlessly complex and often contradictory nature of contemporary social reality. Some theoretical frameworks are more potent and fundamental than others – and Marxist analysis belongs in this former category – but variable insights from many other theoretical paradigms (including but hardly limited to symbolic interactionism and structural functionalism) can advance our understanding of at least some dimensions of this social reality. The present author is also leery of "utopianism," if that term is understood as positing the possibility of establishing an "ideal" or even "perfect" society. There is a long and tragic history of the failure of such projects, with the Marxist versions of utopias among these spectacular failures. Human beings have demonstrated over and over again their vulnerability to being "corrupted" in relation to honourable, constructive behaviour toward other human beings. Dostoyevsky's (1864, 1960) protagonist in *Notes from Underground* surely had it right here, about the endless perversity of human beings, their frequent resistance to adopting policies and practices that can be shown to be in their interest and their ultimate resistance as well to living in a "crystal palace." That said, it is surely possible to realize a more just, equitable and human social order than that characterizing many Western nations, including the United States. The Scandinavian countries, for many – including the present author – exemplify this possibility (e.g. Partenu 2016). These countries have incorporated the most humane dimensions of the socialistic model along with productive dimensions of free markets, although they have hardly been immune to some of the more pernicious forces of neoliberalism. In relation to the adoption of the Scandinavian model by other countries historical, cultural and demographic dimensions come into play and compromise the practical realization of the adoption of this model by non-Scandinavian countries.

But the ongoing broadly diffused resistance to Marxist analysis is especially unfortunate early in the 21st century because some core current developments within Western capitalist countries are anticipated and well understood (at least partially) by Marxist analysis. As Terry Eagleton (2011) has suggested, "Marx was right." He was right about the polarization between the haves and have-nots – the dramatic expansion of socioeconomic inequality – and about the ongoing, relentless drive on the part of capitalist corporations to maximize profits, trumping all other societal objectives and values. And Frank Pearce's (1976: 66) notion of an "imaginary social order" could hardly be more timely at the outset of the Trump era in the United States and the post-Brexit era in the UK:

> According to the "imaginary social order" Britain and America are societies where the people have freely chosen via the democratic processes to have a free enterprise system humanized by elements of a mixed economy. The "real social order" is a monopoly capitalist system with a certain degree of state control of the industrial infrastructure, but where the state itself is ultimately dominated by the ruling class.

In the United States and the UK a nostalgia for an imagined mid-20th-century version of industrial capitalism persuaded large numbers of voters to support "faux populism," advancing nationalistic (and economic elitist) agendas. In a global context an "imaginary social order" regards the activities of international financial institutions as beneficial to (and appreciated by) the peoples of the Global South, when in fact they disproportionally favour the interests of "the ruling class." Frank Pearce's Marxist framework on "crimes of the powerful" provides one core point of departure, then, for understanding crimes of globalization.

## The criminology of crimes of the powerful today

In the second half of the second decade of the new century there is a long-overdue upsurge of attention to crimes of the powerful. Gregg Barak's (2015) edited anthology, *The Routledge International Handbook of the Crimes of the Powerful* is one indicator of this interest. Dawn Rothe and David Kauzlarich's (2016) text, *Crimes of the Powerful* – the first comprehensive criminological survey of the topic – is another. Vincenzo Ruggiero's (2015) *Power and Crime* – an erudite examination of the historical roots of attempts throughout Western history to understand in some sense the role of power in relation to "crime" – is still one more indicator of this resurgent interest. The enduring definitional issues relating to the concept of "crime" provide a core starting point for any treatment of crimes of the powerful (Friedrichs 2015). The conventional criminological adoption of a standard "legalistic" definition of crime has inevitably skewed criminological attention toward the crimes of the powerless, not the powerful. Frank Pearce's (1976) analysis in *Crimes of the Powerful* provided a core foundation for the re-conceptualization of crime in Marxist terms, and is relevant to an understanding of "crimes of globalization" specifically as crime.

## Crimes of globalization as a contemporary form of organized crime

The concept of "crimes of globalization" is literally a 21st-century product, since it was first coined by the author in the first year of this new century, in 2000. Crimes of globalization have been defined as the demonstrably harmful policies and practices of institutions and entities that are specifically a product of the forces of globalization. Accordingly, crimes of globalization intersect with, but should not be confused with, the globalization of crime (Aas 2013). Some specific forms of crimes of globalization include the imposition of odious debt, mineral resource extraction projects, pipeline projects, water availability projects, relocation projects and dam projects, principally in the Global South. As to the origins of this concept, the author's daughter Jessica spent her junior year (1999–2000) of college in Thailand, and while there lived among river fishing people in northeast Thailand whose way of life was being destroyed by a World Bank–financed dam, the Pak Mun dam. She returned to the United States somewhat earlier than originally planned to make a presentation on the Pak Mun dam protest movement at a so-called anti-globalization protest rally in Washington, D.C., in April 2000. The author was moved to co-author a paper with his daughter, presented at the 2000 American Society of Criminology Meeting in San Francisco – and subsequently published in 2002 in *Social Justice* – where he provided a criminological framework for her "case study" of the Pak Mun dam protest (Friedrichs and Friedrichs 2002). The "harms" associated with the Pak Mun dam project, as well as other such projects in the developing world, include but are not limited to destruction of a way of life for Indigenous peoples; forced relocations; violent repression of protests; and huge, enduring environmental damage (Khagram 2004; Leslie 2014; Molle et al. 2014; Zeller 2015). Public pressure and protests from the mid-1990s on led the World Bank to scale back on its funding of mega-dam projects and to focus on the repairs of existing hydropower projects. But by the middle of the second decade of the current century the World Bank – following the lead of new financiers from China and Brazil – returned to backing the construction of mega-dams. This revival of attention has been attributed to institutional self-interest, but reflects a general disregard for the environment and the Indigenous communities that continue to be adversely affected by the mega-dam projects.

Whereas criminologists have a long history of attention to such phenomena as inner-city street gangs and to organized crime entities, they have directed virtually no attention to the immensely harmful activities of international financial institutions such as the World Bank and the International Monetary Fund. Although the original conception of crimes of globalization was limited to demonstrable harms perpetrated by international financial institutions that operate on a global scale, a broader application of the term – to demonstrable harms specifically attributable to the conditions of globalization – is possible. Somewhat alternative conceptions of crimes of globalization have been set forth. For example, Moises Naim (2006) has applied this term to illegal trade in drugs, arms, intellectual property, people and money occurring globally. He has noted that like the war on terrorism, the fight to control these illegal markets pits governments against agile, stateless and resourceful networks empowered by globalization. But the present author favours the term "transnational crime" for enduring types of illegal activity – including trade in drugs and arms – that in the context of a globalized world increasingly occurs across borders.

Frank Pearce (1976), in *Crimes of the Powerful*, did not systematically address the activities of international financial institutions. He did devote some attention to the increasingly significant international dimension of crime and noted that

> In any *examination* of the international context, care must be taken to deal with what is actually being done, by governments and by international corporations and agencies such as the International Monetary Fund, as well as what is presented by various governments as the rationale for their action.
>
> (Pearce 1976: 147)

Pearce did address at length organized crime – specifically, in its syndicated form – which has been one long-standing preoccupation of criminologists, but he challenged the mainstream interpretation of such crime by framing it in relation to capitalist interests, with some attention to its increasing international context. Just as Sutherland suggested that corporate crime could be viewed as a form of organized crime, so, too, one can suggest that the crimes of international financial institutions can be viewed this way as well. Since the beginning of the new century various criminologists have examined different dimensions and cases of crimes of globalization, with much of this research reviewed and summarized in Dawn Rothe and David Friedrichs' (2015) *Crimes of Globalization*. It reviews a range of manifestations of crimes of globalization in relation to a ferry sinking in Senegal, the Rwandan genocide and the Congo wars, genocidal actions in Timor-Leste and mineral extraction projects in Africa, Asia and elsewhere, among other illustrative cases.

The study of crimes of globalization, then, is best understood as an extension of "crimes of the powerful" into a realm largely neglected until recently by criminological students of such crime. Whether or not those who address crimes of globalization explicitly invoke Pearce's Marxist analysis of crimes of the powerful, they at a minimum do so implicitly. Arguably the more explicit application of this Marxist framework would be beneficial.

## Crimes of the powerful and slow violence

On the forms of violence perpetrated by the powerful, some of it is "fast" by any standard, exemplified by forms of state crime such as genocide and crimes against humanity and on the lower levels of state action abuses of power by the police and other such state actors. But much of it is "slow violence," a concept introduced by Rob Nixon (2011). Some conspicuous forms of fast violence (e.g. gun-related violence) are disproportionally committed by the powerless. But hugely harmful forms of slow violence (e.g. environmentally harmful activity) are disproportionally committed by the powerful. As Nixon notes, fast violence is much more easily and readily represented in the media – pervasively so – whereas the effective representation of slow violence is much more of a challenge. In November 2015, a dramatic form of fast violence – a terrorist attack, leaving 130 people dead and many more seriously injured – occurred in Paris. This incidence of violence, committed by marginalized, relatively powerless (in conventional terms) terrorists, was massively represented by the media. But a month later in Paris a meeting of leaders of large countries to address the challenges of global climate change – a hugely threatening form of slow violence – was only covered by the media in a far more limited way, and, of course, climate change as slow violence presents huge challenges in terms of effective representation. In a somewhat parallel vein, in the highly unusual and often surreal U.S. presidential campaign of 2016 Donald Trump was highly successful in focusing attention of the alleged threats of violence from potential Muslim terrorists and illegal immigrants. Senator Bernie Sanders had a heartening level of success in focusing on the structural harms emanating out of Wall Street and a capitalist system rigged to the advantage of the rich, but this type of threat and harm is less easily represented in a dramatic and effective form. Frank Pearce's book was one seminal contribution to the need to address structural sources of harm relative to the dramatic, certainly traumatic and heinous, but ultimately more limited, forms of harm associated with conventional or street crime. His notion of an "imaginary social order" and the illusions aligned with such an order also provides a point of departure for addressing the "false consciousness" that privileges some forms of violence as public concerns over other forms that are in fact demonstrably more harmful in the long run.

## Crimes of globalization, international financial institutions and Asian dam projects

In a celebrated essay in *Life* magazine publisher Henry Luce (1941) famously declared the 20th century to be "the American century." It seems unlikely that in 2014 the 21st century will be declared to be the American century, although it may be called "the Asian century" (or the Chinese century). The Asian region has for some time been increasingly dynamic and consequential in the global political economy and in international affairs (Pieterse and Kim 2012). On the other side of this it has been estimated that approximately one half of the world's poorest people live in South Asia alone.

Although the field of criminology has been a predominantly Western enterprise, we now have the emergence of Asian criminology. The Asian

Criminological Society held its eighth annual meeting in Beijing, in 2016. The Third International Conference of the South Asian Society of Criminology and Victimology also took place in 2016, in Goa, India. The author here draws upon presentations made at the Seventh Annual Meeting of the Asian Criminological Society in Hong Kong, as well as a keynote opening presentation made at the Goa Conference. At both conferences he made the case for the adoption of a cosmopolitan framework for an emerging Asian criminology and the need to transcend conventional criminological concerns in Asia and elsewhere. A 21st-century criminology would need to engage fully with the evolving forces of globalization. And such a criminology would need as well to engage increasingly with the "voices" of the Global South. And as Frank Pearce presciently argued, such a criminology would increasingly need to attend to the crimes of the powerful, both within a domestic and within a global framework.

The World Bank was a central focus of the original paper on crimes of globalization. The World Bank was established in 1945, at the end of World War II, with the key purpose of contributing to the stabilization of economies severely disrupted by the war (Babb 2009; Fujita 2013; Weaver 2008). Over time, its focus increasingly shifted to the promotion of "development" in so-called "developing" countries – or the Global South. The World Bank as well as the International Monetary Fund – also established at the 1945 Bretton Woods Conference to foster global economic growth – have been the target of a range of criticisms (Sarfaty 2012; Shaman 2009; Weaver 2008). These international financial institutions have primarily dealt with dictators and economic elites in the Global South, rather than legitimate representatives of the peoples of these countries. Despite the professed objective of providing economic aid to Global South countries, the projects funded by the international financial institutions all too often greatly facilitate the flow of money out of these countries into the coffers of Western-based transnational corporations that receive contracts to carry out the projects. The ordinary citizens of these countries benefit little, if at all, from many of these projects – as opposed to corrupt political and business entities as well as multinational corporations – and in too many cases are significantly harmed by the projects (Khagram 2004; McCully 2001; Rich 1994). The agenda of the international financial institutions is skewed to Western interests and reflective of Western values, with little, if any, meaningful input from Indigenous peoples (i.e. the powerless) in Global South countries. Accordingly, the international financial institutions are profoundly non-democratic. The voting power for the projects of the international financial institutions is very disproportionately exercised by representatives of the most powerful (e.g. G7) countries, rather than by representatives of the relatively powerless Global South countries. Altogether, the World Bank has been justly criticized as paternalistic in relation to Global South countries, hypocritical in relation to the gap between professed goals and actual policy priorities and actions and complicit in genocidal activities carried out in these countries. The global divide between the rich and the poor is exacerbated rather than reduced by the activities of the

World Bank. And too many of its projects contribute to long-term and profoundly consequential economic damage.

The professed goal of the World Bank to reduce global poverty has, by many measures, failed in various respects. The structural adjustment agreements imposed on Global South countries (especially, in this case, by the International Monetary Fund) have been hugely damaging (Shandra, Shircliff and London 2011). The building of dams has been complicit in ongoing forms of harm, including but hardly limited to, the destruction of a way of life for Indigenous peoples, forced relocations, violent repression of protests and huge, enduring environmental damage (Leslie 2014; Nijhuis 2015). In sum, if one accepts the foregoing analysis of the activities of international financial institutions such as the World Bank, is it then accurate and warranted to characterize it as a "criminal enterprise," a global form of organized crime? Obviously any such claim is going to be hotly contested. By any measure, however, the policies and practices of the international financial institutions are subjected to remarkably little effective oversight. Altogether, the claim made here is that these policies and practices are usefully addressed within the broad framework of an analysis of "crimes of the powerful" as pioneered by Frank Pearce, among others.

There are now other international financial institution entities that have a far lower profile than the World Bank and the International Monetary Fund, but that require the attention of students of crimes of globalization. The International Finance Corporation (IFC) is a branch of the World Bank that finances private-sector activities in developing countries. It is at least formally committed to the professed World Bank goal of reducing poverty globally. This entity has grown dramatically since 2005 and has been reporting huge profits (e.g. $1.5 billion in 2014). Critics of the International Finance Corporation contend that it backs multinational corporations and elite business projects in developing countries, displacing small, family-run businesses. Accordingly, the principal benefactors of its financing are these multinational corporations and wealthy businesses based in Global South countries. Furthermore, it privileges a good return on investments over social and environmental standards being met by the projects it funds. In Africa it has funded for-profit health care, but no benefit is realized by poor Africans as a consequence. In April 2015, in Gujarat, India, a group of farmers and fishermen filed a historic (first-ever) lawsuit against the International Finance Corporation. The claim was that the IFC financing of a mega-power plant in Gujarat was wrecking the livelihoods of the plaintiff farmers and fishermen. This claim, then, is a classic allegation of a crime of globalization.

The Asian Development Bank (ADB) is the second-largest development institution in Asia. It was established in 1966, so approximately a half-century ago. It has 48 member countries in the Asia/Pacific Rim area, a professional staff of some 3,000 people over 100 active projects and assets of some $12 billion. It is dominated by its Japanese member partner. This bank is colloquially referred to as the "Dam & Bridge" bank because hard infrastructure projects are a priority among its project. The ADB follows the lead of the World Bank in avoiding involvement in civil and political issues in the countries where it funds projects. It has been harshly criticized for being complicit in gross violations of human rights (e.g. in Myanmar/Burma). Although its original guidelines called for Indigenous populations to provide "consent" on projects, this was more recently altered to a call that these populations be "consulted" on projects. Altogether, its safeguard policies place principal emphasis on the needs of the borrower countries. For example, China successfully pressured the ADB to lower safety standards for projects it was funding in that country. The internal culture of the ADB resists the creation of inspection mechanisms, which in the view of some commentators may reflect Japanese cultural biases. The bank's priorities are the quick disbursement of big loans, and its staff is rewarded for getting these loans out efficiently. This is a core criminogenic dimension of the international financial institutions. The negative impact of projects on Indigenous peoples are both demonstrable and of little direct or clear concern to the bank's officials. And as with the World Bank and the International Monetary Fund, there is no effective mechanism of accountability for the Asian Development Bank's policies and practices.

The Asian Infrastructure Investment Bank is a new development bank established by China in 2015, with an anticipated $100 billion starting capital (Perlez 2015a, 2015b). The establishment of this bank was opposed by the United States, due to a concern that it had the potential to undermine the World Bank and the Asian Development Bank. Its proponents claim that it will be organized to avoid the large bureaucratic structure, filled with political appointees, characterizing these established international financial institutions. It aspires to be "lean, clean and green" and to make appointments based on ability, not political connections. The founders of this new bank claim that it will adhere to zero tolerance for corruption, will integrate local communities into its decision making and will ensure that people displaced by its projects will be taken care of properly. U.S. critics of the bank are concerned that China will use the bank to advance its own global agenda, and will in fact forego environmental and human rights protections, with anti-corruption measures evaded. China's "track record" of giving loans to unstable governments, all too often for demonstrably bad projects, with villagers not infrequently uprooted with little meaningful compensation, is invoked in this context.

Finally, we have the establishment of the New Development Bank (NDB), formerly the BRICS Development Bank (Desai and Vreeland 2014). Its stated goal is to mobilize resources for infrastructure and sustainable development projects in the BRICS countries (Brazil, Russia, India, China and South Africa). The BRICS countries presently compose some 43% of the world's population, but only about 22% of the gross domestic product (GDP). The premise for the establishment of this bank is that the World Bank and the International Monetary Fund have failed to give a fair voice to the BRICs nations. The claim of its proponents is that it will complement the existing international financial institutions, but will be more agile and less bureaucratic. It also has a stated goal of supporting sustainable development. This bank was officially launched in July 2015, with initial capital of $50 billion. All of the member countries are supposed to have an equal voice in its policies and practices, with the presidency rotating among these countries (the first president is from India). The first loan, issued in April 2016, was granted in Chinese currency, and the headquarters of the bank are located in Shanghai. Some commentators express a concern over potential Chinese domination of this bank.

Is a development bank that is authentically committed to productive development, with authentically democratic input and the promotion of human values, possible? Can institutions which perpetrate crimes of globalization be replaced in Asia by institutions that foster the common good? This remains to be seen. The ongoing historical tension between profitability (and jobs) and long-term sustainability is a core dimension of the challenges involved in all of this. Powerful institutions and individuals have always had – and continue to have – a disproportionate voice in policies and practices adopted in response to these challenges, but their claims of acting responsibly in relation to broader interests are largely belied by history. The inevitable depletion of finite natural resources in conjunction with the relentless pursuit of profit by transnational corporations – and international financial institutions – is quite certain to be a formative theme of the grand narrative of the 21st century. Criminologists can play a role in monitoring the demonstrable harm (crime) emanating from the activities of the newly established international financial institutions. Criminologists can address the question of which forms of crimes of globalization are most and least prevalent in Asia. They can also address how crimes of globalization in Asia compare with such crimes in other parts of the world. How do public and political responses to crimes of globalization in Asia compare to the responses in other parts of the world?

## Conclusion: building on the legacy of Frank Pearce's *Crimes of the Powerful*

Criminology early in the 20th century was very different from what it had become early in the 21st century, and we can safely say that criminology early in the 22nd century will be very different from what it is today. A remark attributed (correctly or not) to the physicist Niels Bohr holds that "prediction is difficult, especially about the future." So we cannot pretend to know exactly how criminology will be transformed in the decades ahead, or even whether it will survive as a recognizable academic endeavour. But it seems highly likely that the crimes of the power*less*, and the control of such crime, will – and certainly should – become proportionally less of a focus going forward. Clearly, many conventional forms of crime are migrating from "the street" (or real space) to cyberspace (Goodman 2015). And it seems reasonable to surmise that those forms of conventional crime that continue to occur in real space will become progressively less viable, with the ever-expanding network of "surveillance," broadly defined, and the massive collection of personal data. Obviously one hopes that the conditions – socio-economic, socio-psychological and so forth – will be transformed in positive ways to diminish the motivating forces that give rise to criminal behaviour. Also, one can hope that social control policies are transformed in constructive ways, based upon reliable evidence, rather than in the form of an ever-expanding carceral state. It is necessary to acknowledge, however, that various social and political conditions could give rise to upward spikes of at least some forms of conventional crime. But the most fundamental criminological challenges, going forward, are likely to be in the realm of crimes of the powerful. An increasingly well-informed populace is likely to become ever more aware of the structural forces giving rise to such crime and the vast range of harms emanating from such crime. Specifically, there is reason to anticipate growing awareness of crimes of globalization. The perception of corrupt dealings by the Egyptian government of Mubarak with the International Monetary Fund was a contributing factor to the Arab Spring uprising in that country in 2011 (Marfleet 2013). We have strong indicators that crime and its control will increasingly be conceived of as transnational and global phenomena. If the foregoing projections are correct, Frank Pearce's *Crimes of the Powerful* is likely to be viewed as one of the seminal works providing a foundation for an evolving 21st-century criminology.

## Author's note

This chapter draws upon David O. Friedrichs, Dawn L. Rothe, and Olivia Salama, "Crimes of Globalization in Asia: An Overview and an Agenda," Asian Criminological Society 7th Annual Conference, Hong Kong, 24–27 June 2015, and David O. Friedrichs, Dawn L. Rothe and Jessica Friedrichs, "Asian Dam Projects and Crimes of Globalization: Slow Violence as Crime and as Victimization," Third International Conference of the South Asian Society of Criminology and Victimology, Goa, India, 28–29 January 2016. Steve Bittle's comments on an earlier version of this chapter were very helpful. The author's Distinguished Professor stipend facilitated his participation in the Hong Kong and Goa conferences where the themes addressed in this chapter were first presented.

## References

Aas, K. (2013) *Globalization and Crime* (2nd ed.). Los Angeles: Sage.

Babb, S. (2009) *Behind the Development Banks: Washington Politics, World Poverty, and the Wealth of Nations*. Chicago: University of Chicago Press.

Barak, G. (ed.) (2015) *The Routledge International Handbook of the Crimes of the Powerful*. London: Routledge.

Desai, R.M. and Vreeland, J.R. (2014) "What the New Bank of BRICS Is All About." *The Washington Post*, 17 July.

Dostoyevsky, F. (1864, 1960) *Notes From Underground & The Grand Inquisitor*. New York: E.P. Dutton & Co.

Eagleton, T. (2011) *Why Marx Was Right*. New Haven: Yale University Press.

Friedrichs, D.O. (2015) "Crimes of the Powerful and the Definition of Crime," in G. Barak (ed.) *The Routledge International Handbook of the Crimes of the Powerful*. London: Routledge.

Friedrichs, D.O. and Friedrichs, J. (2002) "The World Bank and Crimes of Globalization: A Case Study." *Social Justice*, 29: 1–12.

Fujita, S. (2013) *The World Bank, Asian Development Bank and Human Rights*. Cheltenham, UK: Edward Elgar.

Goodman, M. (2015) *Future Crimes*. New York: Doubleday.

Khagram, S. (2004) *Dams and Development: Transnational Struggles for Water and Power*. Ithaca, NY: Cornell University Press.

Leslie, J. (2014) "Large Dams Just Aren't Worth the Cost." *New York Times*, 24 August: 5.

Luce, H.R. (1941) "The American Century." *Life*, 17 February.

Marfleet, P. (2013) "Mubarak's Egypt – Nexus of Criminality." *State Crime*, 2: 112–134.

McCully, P. (2001) *Silenced Rivers: The Ecology and Politics of Large Dams*. London: Zed Books.

Molle, F., Foran, T. and Kakonen, M. (2014) *Contested Waterscapes in the Mekong Region: Hydropower, Livelihoods and Governance.* London: Routledge.

Naim, M. (2006) *Illicit: How Smugglers, Traffickers, and Copycats are Hijacking the Global Economy*. New York: Anchor Books.

Nijhuis, M. (May 2015) "Harnessing the Mekong or Killing It?" *National Geographic*, 110–129.

Nixon, R. (2011) *Slow Violence and the Environmentalism of the Poor*. Cambridge, MA: Harvard University Press.

Partenu, R. (2016) *The Nordic Theory of Everything: In Search of a Better Life*. New York: Harper & Collins.

Pearce, F. (1976) *Crimes of the Powerful: Marxism, Crime and Deviance*. London: Pluto Press.

Perlez, J. (2015a) "New China-led Bank Pledges to Fend Off Corruption." *New York Times*, 12 April: 13.

Perlez, J. (2015b) "Beijing's Rival to World Bank: Moves Forward Without U.S." *New York Times*, 5 December: A1.

Pieterse, J.N. and Kim, J. (eds.) (2012) *Globalization and Development in East Asia*. New York: Routledge.

Rich, B. (1994) *Mortgaging the Earth: The World Bank, Environmental Impoverishment, and the Crisis of Development*. Boston: Beacon Press.

Rothe, D.L. and Friedrichs, D.O. (2015) *Crimes of Globalization*. London: Routledge.

Rothe, D.L. and Kauzlarich, D.L. (2016) *Crimes of the Powerful: An Introduction*. London: Routledge.

Ruggiero, V. (2015) *Power and Crime*. London: Routledge.

Sarfaty, G.A. (2012) *Values in Transition: Human Rights and the Culture of the World Bank*. Stanford: Stanford University Press.

Shaman, D.I. (2009) *The World Bank Unveiled: Inside the Revolutionary Struggle for Transparency*. Little Rock, AR: Parkhurst Brothers, Inc.

Shandra, J.M., Shircliff, E. and London, B. (2011) "The International Monetary Fund, World Bank, and Structural Adjustment: A Cross-National Analysis of Forest Loss." *Social Science Research*, 40: 210–225.

Weaver, C. (2008) *Hypocrisy Trap: The World Bank and the Poverty of Reform*. Princeton: Princeton University Press.

Zeller, N.R. (2015) "Doing a Dam Better? Understanding the World Bank's eco-Governmentality in Lao Hydropower Development." *Journal of Lao Studies* Special Issue: 161–180.

# Section III

# New developments in crimes of the powerful research

This third and final section showcases some of the new directions which studies of the powerful have taken in the 40 years since the publication of *CotP*. Thus, Dawn L. Rothe and Victoria E. Collins focus on "our" complicity in reproducing and perpetuating the inherently violent hyper-neoliberal system that allows us to enjoy "mediated comfortable lives" of consumerism and consumption. Then, in an exploration of an oft-ignored and pernicious aspect of consumerism, Susanne Soederberg exposes the expansion and legitimation of the payday loan industry which exploits low-income workers by lending money at usurious rates, showing how *debtfarism*, an integral component of financialized capitalism, is a mode of governance facilitated and legitimated by the neoliberal state. Laura Finley argues that the failure of capitalist states to protect victims of domestic violence is an offence against human rights, a state crime and a crime of the powerful. Jon Burnett's chapter examines the resurgence and (re)application of neoliberal capitalism's assumption that the interests of labour and capital are the same through a case study of Britain's Conservative government's embracing of workfare, prison labour and unpaid work as reformative devices for the unruly and unwaged or under-waged. This strategy reflects the "intensified valorization" of work that is essential to neoliberal capitalism. By contrast, Biko Agozino, following a review of some of the literature on corporate crimes, argues that the lenience extended by the state to crimes of the powerful should be applied to crimes of the poor; he recommends the adoption of restorative justice, penal abolition and peace making as dominant modes of social control for all law-breakers. Meanwhile, Jose Atiles applies elements of Pearce's theoretical framework to de-naturalize colonial state crimes, then develops an ambitious research agenda for future scholars. The final chapter by Dean Curran links Pearce's depiction of the "organized irresponsibility" that characterizes capitalist corporations to Beck and Luhmann's theorization of complexity as an enabler of irresponsibility to understand how the collective agency without culpability enjoyed by corporations encourages reckless risk taking; moreover, the hugely unequal distribution of this ability of collective actors to extract private gains at social risk exacerbates inequality.

# Chapter 18

# An extension of Frank Pearce's work on crimes of the powerful

## "Demystification" and the role of our consent

*Dawn L. Rothe and Victoria E. Collins*

> *Crimes of the Powerful*, its actual underpinning assumption is that the social world is a creation of social beings in relationships.
>
> Frank Pearce (2015)

This quote includes what Pearce referred to as the imaginary social order where the harms and crimes of the powerful are part and parcel of the banality of everyday life. As such, our primary focus in this chapter is to "demystify" the "imaginary social world" by recognizing our own role in the reification and facilitation of these harms in the era of neoliberal consumerism. After all, the neoliberal consumerism of today is qualitatively different from the past in that it is has embedded itself wholly into the cultural and social fabric of society and is seen as a "natural" normality of everyday life. We argue that we, as citizens, perpetuate the crimes of the powerful through consumerism and the willing consumption of hegemonic ideology in a system of totality that is part and parcel of the banality of everyday life. Having said this, we limit our discussion to the hegemonic ideology of neoliberalism and consumption with examples of commodified surveillance, technologies, military violence and corporations' exploitation and use of slave labour.

## Hegemony and consent

> We never see beyond the choices we don't make.
>
> The Oracle in *The Matrix* film (Silver et al. 1999)

As this quote suggests, not recognizing our role in the perpetuation of crimes of the powerful prevents us from seeing beyond the box of hyper-capitalism that is ensured its "legitimacy" through mystification wherein hegemony and hegemonic discourse serve to ensure domination by consent. The concept of ideological and cultural hegemony, as conceptualized by Antonio Gramsci (1971), is especially relevant. For Gramsci, ideological hegemony is where a particular ideology is reflected throughout society, permeating all institutions and social relations, making it appear as innate and the only way it should be or common sense. Yet common sense can be profoundly misleading, obfuscating or disguising a more heinous "truth": the violence and harm of the system itself. This violence then becomes banal, disavowed, depoliticized and normalized through cultural hegemony and hegemonic discourse (Neocleous 2008: 73–74). Cultural hegemony refers to "the 'spontaneous' consent given by the great masses of the population to the general direction imposed on social life" (Gramsci 1971: 12). Given that hegemony is tied directly to capital accumulation – "the profit-seeking process at the heart of the world economy" and our "advanced consumer capitalism as a way of life" – consent is thus organized around consumption and consumerism (Carroll and Greeno 2013: 122–124). Furthermore, hegemonic discourse represents the dominant ideology (neoliberalism, consumerism), justifying the social, political and economic status quo while masking the violence of the system and the powerful. The discourse is "intended to sustain the pre-existing modes of hegemonic dominance" (Pearce and Tombs 2006: 1). The following section delves into this hegemonic discourse that supports the inept status quo and the violence and harms of the powerful.

## Hegemony, culture, ideology and hegemonic discourse

We agree with Young (1976) in his foreword to Frank's Pearce's book when he argues that it is "the system itself that must be investigated" (p. 11). While recognizing the inherent complexities of our global neoliberal capitalist system, the entrenchment of profit making as the "imaginary social order" as it is reinforced through consumerism should be unpacked. As noted by Renner (2002: 53) "most consumers don't know that a number of common purchases bear the invisible imprint of violence." But consumption takes many forms spanning from the use of everyday products to purchasing entertainment that blatantly objectifies and reifies inequalities. As Baudrillard (1998: 31) argues consumption "is governed by magical thinking" as it is both an objective process and lived as a myth creating a "fantasy of goods and services" (Ritzer 1998). This is disconnected from how and by whom the product is made, as well as any broader social meaning. From a structural perspective, that consumption is language, a mode of discourse that conveys messages and symbols as a means of communication. The commodity itself then becomes greater than its intended use, as its value is associated with what it signifies. Whereas Baudrillard argues this allows the consumer to read the system of consumption (i.e. knowing what to consume and when) ultimately resulting in an inability to satisfy their want for commodities, we argue that the language of consumption has greater applicability. Through consumption, broader ideologies and structures are propagated and reified. In this sense, we use the term reification as conceptualized by Lukács: "the structural process whereby the commodity form permeates life in capitalist society" (Zuidervaart 1991: 76).

It has been well established that metrics for success in modern society are commonly defined within capitalist parameters (Merton 1938; Messner and Rosenfeld 1994; Wacquant 2009). Consider that in the United States and many other countries across the globe, "success" is often achieved through the acquisition of material wealth, such as houses, cars and job security (often a career), as well as other goods that are symbolic of having "made it." You need only glance at commercials for high-end vehicles to observe that it is not just the car that as being sold, but also the imagery and status associated with driving a Cadillac, Lexus, BMW, Lotus or Ferrari. For example, the recent commercial for the new Lexus RX, begins with a Caucasian man and woman dressed in white, sitting in an all-White luxurious apartment. The man glances at the woman as he strides out of the room, an image of the front of a Lexus vehicle flashes on the screen followed by the words "Elegance can have edge." The man walks through the wall into another room, this one all blue. This room is occupied by two women, one Caucasian one Black, the screen again flashes between the room and the front of a blue Lexus car, before blinking the words "Sophistication can have attitude." The pattern repeats with a room that is all red and the words "Refinement can be daring," and then silver before flashing the words "It's time for luxury to be more expressive" (Toyota 2015). The consumer is being sold a luxury vehicle to fulfil the practicalities of travel, as well as the cultural messaging that particular choice conveys to others – what Veblen (1994) termed "conspicuous consumption."

As argued by Veblen (1994),

> The motive that lies at the root of ownership is emulation. . . . The possession of wealth confers honor; it is an invidious distinction. Nothing equally cogent can be said for the consumptions of goods, nor for any other conceivable incentive to acquisition, and especially not for any incentive to the accumulation of wealth.
>
> (17)

Although human agency plays its part in the pursuit of the accumulation of wealth – or goods that signify belonging to a particular class of wealth – these ideals of status acquisition do not develop in a vacuum. To assure clarity, we are not arguing that commercial culture manufactures ideology, rather, it "*relays* and *reproduces* and *processes* and *packages* and *focuses* ideology that is constantly arising both from social elites and from active social groups and movements throughout society" (Gitlin 1979: 253). Hegemonic discourse, or in the case of our advertising example used earlier, propagates ideals of success centring on goods that have been interwoven into the constructions of status identity. Therefore, there exists a hegemonic discourse that aptly crafts and defines "success" and by proxy individual worth within structured parameters that emphasizes capital acquisition above all else. In this instance, success evokes a certain iconography, a pre-scripted visual imagery that enforces and then re-enforces the cultural hegemony.

Media provides one platform for the dissemination of a hegemonic discourse that promotes capitalism as *the* way of life. From product placement in television shows and films that utilize non-advertising media to sell goods to the audience (Hackley, Tiwsakul and Preuss 2008; Herman and McChesney 2004), to choices made about what is deemed newsworthy (Bicket and Wall 2007; Cushion and Lewis 2009; Douglas 2006; Esser 2008; Hickey 1998), to the way characters are presented in television shows (Gitlin 1979), the content of media extends beyond simple entertainment to reify the hegemonic status quo. For instance, characters and plotlines in popular television are formulaic. The characters are interchangeable following a standardized plot over the course of 50 to 60 minutes providing a social rigidity that is both familiar and new. Favoured characters are often steadily employed, have positive relationships and have sustainable material wealth (i.e. a place to live, a vehicle or transportation, nice clothes and other artefacts that assist them in their lives). As argued by Gitlin (1979) primetime television content "match[es] the intertwined processes of commodity production, predictability and obsolescence, in a high-consumption society" (254). There is a replication and reinforcement of what is right or natural in the world.

Contained within the familiar narrative of television programming is the conveyance of an understanding of acceptable (and expected) behaviour within the parameters of our current capitalist system. The economic elite have the power to colonize our consciousness as we are bombarded with messaging (advertisements, product placement, etc.) that we consent to both as it relates to its domination of time and public space. Time, therefore, does not belong to the individual. The audience gives tacit consent adopting the common sense ideology that they are choosing to be entertained. However, the capitalist purpose has become the media's purpose (Exoo, 2010), and there is simultaneous confirmation of both elite authority and consumer choice as leisure itself becomes routinized, industrialized and homogenized (Gitlin 1979).

Similarly, the emulation of wealth through the process of consumption, which leads to the broader public consenting to the cultural hegemony that promotes capitalist markets, can be observed in the public's fixation with celebrities. An individual gains celebrity status for having an exceptional skill or talent; however, their "success" in a capitalist system also garners them public praise and recognition. Success then is predominantly associated with wealth – whether real or perceived – as opposed to having other forms of capital: emotional, political, social, cultural, spiritual and familial. Yet celebrities represent exceptionalism, a status that cannot be readily achieved by the average citizen. However, aspects of "celebrity" can be emulated through consumerism – that is, by possessing the same commodities and goods that are symbolic of celebrity success. The average citizen can also purchase fashion apparel, vehicles, homes and vacations that are representative of the lifestyle and status of those who have bested the capitalist system. However, this often comes at a great financial cost, a detail that is often excluded from the discourse and quietly addressed through the acquisition and accumulation of debt.

In the United States in 2015, the average household has $132,069 of debt with $15,310 of that being in credit card debt alone. This translates to a total of $712 billion owed by U.S. consumers (Issa 2016). The debt itself further supports the crimes of the powerful where predatory lending practices such as subprime mortgages, payday loans and debt conciliation firms (Friedrichs 2009) allow for the exploitation of vulnerable people who, due to the relatively easy access to credit, accumulate debt that they cannot pay off (see also Soederberg on debtfarism in this volume). This understanding of material consumption, however, is missing from the hegemonic discourse surrounding wealth and success, and when it does emerge it is presented as being the result of individual flaws as opposed to the consequences of a unfair system. Individuals facing financial ruin are ostracized for being irresponsible and greedy, as any possibility at counter-hegemony is absorbed into the dominant discourse surrounding the issue. Those in power not only benefit from the massive amounts of debt that is accumulated, but also from the pervasive false consciousness. This process supports a criminogenic system that benefits the wealthy where the access and use of credit to purchase particular products and the status meaning associated with them – image, branding and success – has become banal. Here, the harm caused by capitalism has been packaged and re-packaged to reinforce that "success" can only be achieved through consenting to neoliberalist consumerism.

Another such example is the "shopping mall," a location advertised to be a central location of convenience that offers the "world's abundance and variety" (Crawford 2000: 126) in product choices. Here products associated with cultural ideals of fashion, beauty and an ascetically pleasing home are sold to the consumer as a unique display in choice that they then exercise. Yet underneath the constructed veneer of global variety, the shopping mall is a generic type containing the same few shops, many of which are based in the United States. For example, the Simon Property Group is the largest U.S. shopping mall owner with more than 325 properties in the United States and internationally (Simon Property Group 2016). Boosting "superior shopping" (Achara in Wahba 2015) this corporation brands itself as being innovative, emphasizing consumer choice through their marketing caption "Find it. Love it" (Simon Property Group 2016). However, the choice offered is illusory as there is little variation between shopping malls as one mall contains the same shops as the next, owned by the same few multinational corporations, in many of the same countries (predominantly the United States and other Global North countries). Therefore, it is not the consumer who has any real choice; rather it is the productive forces of global capital that have considerable influence not only over which products are constructed and sold, but also over who has the right to access and enjoy them (i.e. pricing). This again hides the massive amounts of harm and systemic violence that occur in providing the material goods that are then consumed.

Missing from the hegemonic discourse are the larger globalized contexts that allow for the mass consumption of goods, including the harms committed against large groups of people. The dominant discourse that promotes capitalist engagement creates a *Zerrspiegel* of sorts, a distorting mirror where certain images are enhanced while others are suppressed. The global systems of capital that lead to the massive social harms, human rights abuses and economic exploitation (Bauman 1998; Nagle 2008) are hidden beneath the shiny veneer of material possessions, status identity and entertainment. This is not something that the audience questions due to the pervasive nature of the neoliberal system that promotes the prioritization of capital.

Buried beneath the façade of normality, capitalist economies thrive on blatant inequalities. From the indentured servitude of those trapped in factories, sweatshops or fishing industries to the conflict over resources such as oil, gold, diamonds and coltan, the violence of consumerism is pervasive and structural (Renner 2002). Therefore, there exists a false consciousness about the origins of the goods that are selected for purchase and the violence used to produce them in their mass quantities. There exists a gross irony when the consumer, through their false consciousness, purchases material goods for the status identity that they convey, while remaining ignorant to the pain, abuses and hardships suffered by others in their production. They are giving their consent to violence that has become banal, disavowed, depoliticized and normalized through cultural hegemony and hegemonic discourse. They have accepted the common sense ideology that has been "negotiated by unequal forces in a complex process through which the subordination and resistance of the worker is created and recreated" (Simon 1982: 64).

It is here we suggest that attention should be given to the role of consumption in an effort to "demystify" the dominant hegemonic discourse and our own role in reproducing the imaginary social order that supports and facilitates crimes of the powerful. After all, consumption of the crimes of the powerful is present every day and has come to be seen as a "fact of life" that "nicely captures the dominant social meaning of banal goods" (Goold, Loader and Thumala 2013: 978). Nonetheless, there is little recognition by most scholars and students of the relationship between the harms and violence of the powerful and our own consumption, pacification, tacit support and facilitation of these crimes. This is not to say that we have done so wittingly; rather, it occurs and is reaffirmed in our everyday lives and our consumption of education, propaganda, the "need" for the latest consumer goods and a multitude of actions we take and choices we make every day without thinking of how we are complicit in the perpetual cycle of crimes of the powerful (Rothe and Kauzlarich 2016).

## Consumption, consent and reification of crimes of the powerful

We partake in our own oppression, supporting the system that perpetuates crimes of the powerful, the neoliberal capitalistic agenda, the state, the corporations, the elite in general. Consider the common reaction when many of us first heard about the National Security Agency (NSA) "sweeping" data collections from emails, text messages, phone records, search engines and social media outlets, all in the name of surveillance for security. This was followed by revelations that the United States was not alone in this project; countries, including New Zealand, Australia and the United Kingdom, to mention, a few had been activly collecting such data in the name of national security. Shortly after these revelations, we were told about the massive numbers of fusion centres bridging corporate interests with state surveillance, primarily located in the United States. We were outraged when we learned governments, in the United States and abroad, had databases of citizen personal information while simultaneously logging into to our Facebook, Twitter or Instagram accounts to express our outrage or just posting our latest daily deed. We Google the latest products available for consumption, purchase our spot in the "cloud," join OnStar, use our Google locater app or friends' "hangout" apps and use our car and phone GPS. This is all to say that we are linked in to the very things that control us under the promise of liberation and freedom.

We willingly join supermarket and grocery store loyalty card programmes that trade our personal information and surveillance of shopping habits for a minimal discount on groceries. We carry our charge cards, using them to play in the land of consumerism. We jump on the bandwagon to use fingerprint identification or iris identification to shorten lines at airports or on our cell phones for "security." We think nothing of the cameras in the store that monitor our every move – rather, we are outraged if a "crime" occurs and the store cameras were not turned on. We run out to purchase our own "toy" drones, legitimating their use, thus in return validating the government's use of them for our own surveillance. We purchase home security systems that are wired into our cell phones to monitor any activities, regulate our heat or turn off the lights. And the list goes on for how we, as citizens, willingly accept surveillance and being monitered in our lives, actively participating and facilitating technological advances that are believed to make our lives "better." These products and "security" features we endure everyday have come to be seen as a "fact of life" that "nicely captures the dominant social meaning of banal goods" (Goold et.al. 2013, p. 978). It is, as argued by Boghosian (2013, "normalizing cultural obedience through surveillance" (26) to which we are active participants.

In addition, there is little to no recognition of the structural arrangement of capitalism that benefits those in positions of power, nor is there any acknowledgement of the criminogenic structures that allow for the maintenance of a system that benefits a few and exploits many. Let us consider another aspect of our role briefly mentioned in the previous section. Nearly all of our techno-gadgets require coltan and other natural minerals. We not only purchase all of the new cell phones, latest gadgets, smart tablets, iPads, etc., we do not think of our relationship to the corporate and elite harms and crimes that are associated with their extraction. Instead, it is consumption and having the latest, best and/or making our lives simpler and easier. There is an entire e-waste industry that dumps illegal surplus in Global South countries, lending to harmful toxins destroying waterways, land and people as children and those looking for scraps to sell filter through harmful leftover products. Additionally, consider that at the time of this writing Apple has just released its latest iPhones – the iPhone 7 and 8 – amidst much media coverage and speculation (Criddle 2016; Curtis 2016; McCann 2016). This has amounted to sales of over 32.3 billion phones just from the latest iphone 8 and 8 plus. Furthermore, the company's total revenue has increased by 30% year-over-year to a total of $74.6 billion (49 billion pounds) (Rougeau 2015). While Apple's success is celebrated, or even taken for granted, by the larger public, there has been lesser attention to the massive amounts of tax fraud the company has committed in Europe where Ireland has been permitted by European anti-trust regulators to collect 13 billion euros for tax avoidance over the last 10 years (Couturier 2016). There is also relatively little consumer concern about the worker conditions at the Pegatron factories in Shanghai, where Apple was found to be violating regulations on worker hours, dormitory standards, ID cards, juvenile workers and work meetings. The awful conditions were highlighted in the suicides of 14 workers at Foxconn, Apple's biggest supplier, in 2010 (Bilton 2014). It seems such human rights violations and systemic violence have had little to no impact on Apple's profits. Rather, Apple, and their economic success, fits within the cultural hegemony as through the continued purchasing of Apple products the great masses have given "spontaneous" consent "to the general direction imposed on social life" (Gramsci 1971: 12). This consumption of the latest and best gadgets, vying for the latest Apple product or smaller and smarter phone, makes us complicit in the process of living in these neoliberal capitalistic consumption states.

On the other hand, we are outraged, even if momentarily, when we hear of tainted products by corporations or the use of slave labour or unpaid wages to workers, again, at least for a moment. Yet we continue to shop at stores or buy corporate products from known habitual offenders. For example, Hormel supports inhumane factory farming or Nestle aggressively takes over family farms and has been linked to child slavery. Consider the food products we consume as well from meat to seafood products. "Labor abuses in the fishing industry, stretching from Southeast Asia to America's own waters" (Associated Press 2016: 1) continues as we write this chapter. Foreign fishermen are confined to boats for years at a time where they are often abused and living in squalor conditions, catching valued swordfish and ahi tuna. "Their catch ends up at restaurants and premium seafood counters across the country, from Whole Foods to Costco, and is touted by celebrity chefs such as Roy Yamaguchi and Masaharu Morimoto" (Associated Press 2016: 2). Few humans in the Global North are not a part of the crimes of the powerful, if only because they consume products that are likely somehow linked to human suffering or exploitation. To be connected in a modern society is often to be connected with corporations who exist only to make a profit and reify the capitalistic exploitive system, not to satisfy real human needs.

State violence is also consumed by us daily in more subtle ways, even celebrated without our considering or perhaps knowing that we are doing just that, often in the name of patriotism, nationalism or as a spectacle/carnival of entertainment. Consider the number of military airshows across the globe where millions flock to see the "awe" of fighter jets, without ever considering the real meaning of violence and death behind them that countries and regions such as Iraq, Syria and Palestine witness daily. In cities across the Global North, as the military prepares for the exercise of state power and violence, citizens consume and enjoy, much like a carnival, the awe of the jets as they fly overhead, taking pictures and buying military products and souvenirs.

Living in and being a part of the imaginary social order where the profits, harms and violence that are inherent in this hegemonic neoliberal capitalistic order dissuade us from demystifying our own roles in the perpetuation of the harms of the powerful and the system they thrive in. Living in the imaginary social world dissuades us from disavowing our mediated comfortable lives. Nonetheless, we hope this chapter contributes to some discussion of our roles in the consent and consumption of the harms of the powerful

## Conclusion

We are reminded of the two main characters in the novel, *The Iron Heel*, by Jack London (1908), Ernest Everhard and Avis Cunningham. Ernest, in an effort to expose the blood and violence behind Cunningham's capitalistic successes, tells Avis that everything in her home is dripping with blood, from the beams to her expensive gown.

> Except that the gown you wear is stained with blood. The food you eat is bloody stew. The blood of little children and of strong men is dripping from your very roof-beams. I can close my eyes, now, and hear it drip, drop, drip, drop, all about me.
>
> (39)

Initially rejecting this statement, Avis decides to take to the streets and look at society's ills and the harms perpetrated on the lower class. Soon she saw through the mystification of the imaginary social order created and sustained by the elite and tells Ernest she sees they [the working class and impoverished] have been badly treated, "I-I think some of their blood is dripping from our roof beams . . . I shall never be able to take pleasure in pretty gowns again." Earnest responds, "Nor will you be able to take pleasure in sackcloth" (41).

We hope that more active, informed and deliberate consumption will recognize how the connections to the violence of the state and lining the pockets of the powerful at the expense of the many are related. For certain, to live an active, engaged life outside the imaginary social order is a difficult task. Yet we should not lose sight of the relationship between the state and its subjects – to not obfuscate the materiality of violence and domination of the imaginary social order. For us, this begins by demystifying our role in the harms and violence of the powerful, to "see the blood dripping from our beams," to begin to imagine a state and social order where inequality is unacceptable and where humanism replaces the dogma of neoliberalism, consumption and unwitting consent. Thus, replacing one dogmatic ideology of neoliberal consumerism that includes the thought of something new – to develop a new political and economic form that looks beyond "the capitalist horizon" that regretfully, we believe, will only occur when the existing system collapses (Žižek 2009).

## References

Associated Press. (2016) "Hawaiian Seafood Caught by Foreign Crews Confined Boats." 8 September. Online. Available HTTP: http://nbc4i.com/2016/09/08/hawaiian-seafood-caught-by-foreign-crews-confined-on-boats/

Baudrillard, J. (1998) *The Consumer Society: Myths and Structures*. London, UK: Sage. Online. Available HTTP: http://cnqzu.com/library/Economics/marxian%20economics/Baudrillard,%20Jean-The%20Consumer%20Society.Myths%20and%20Structures.pdf

Bauman, Z. (1998) *Globalization: The Human Consequence*. New York, NY: Columbia University Press.

Bicket, D. and Wall, M. (2007) "Circling the Wagons." *Journal of Communication Inquiry*, 31, 206–221.

Bilton, R. (2014) "Apple 'Failing to Protect Chinese Factory Workers'." 18 December. Online. Available HTTP: www.bbc.com/news/business-30532463

Boghosian, H. (2013) *Spying on Democracy: Government Surveillance, Corporate Power and Public Resistance*. San Francisco, CA: City Light Books.

Carroll, W.K. and Greeno, M. (2013) "Neoliberal Hegemony and the Organisation of Consent," in *Managing Democracy, Managing Dissent,* 121–135. London: Freedom Press.

Couturier, K. (2016) "How Europe Is Going after Apple, Google and Other U.S. Tech Giants." 30 August. Online. Available HTTP: www.nytimes.com/interactive/2015/04/13/technology/How-Europe-Is-Going-After-U.S.-Tech-Giants.html?_r=0

Crawford, M. (2000) "'The World in a Shopping Mall': From Variations in a Theme Park," in M. Miles and T. Hall (eds.) *The City Cultures Reader,* 125–114. New York, NY: Routledge (Taylor and Francis Group).

Criddle, C. (2016) "iPhone 7: Best New Features, UK Price and Apple's Release Date." 12 September. Online. Available HTTP: www.telegraph.co.uk/technology/0/iphone-7-full-specs-apples-key-features-uk-price-and-release-dat/

Curtis, S. (2016) "iPhone 7: Release Date, UK Price, Pictures, Specs and Key Features of Apple's New iPhone." 12 September. Online. Available HTTP: www.mirror.co.uk/tech/iphone-7-release-date-specs-8131852

Cushion, S. and Lewis, J. (2009) "Towards a 'Foxification' of 24-hour News Channels in Britain?: An Analysis of Market-driven and Publicly Funded News Coverage." *Journalism*, 10: 131–153.

Douglas, S.J. (2006) "The Turn Within: The Irony of Technology in a Globalized World." *American Quarterly*, 1: 619–638.

Esser, F. (2008) "Dimensions of Political News Cultures: Sound Bite and Image Bite News in France, Germany, Great Britain, and the United States." *International Journal of Press/Politics*, 13: 401–442.

Exoo, C. (2010) *The Pen and the Sword: Press, War and Terror in the 21st Century*. Oakland, CA: Sage.

Friedrichs, D.O. (2009) *Trusted Criminals: White Collar Crime in Contemporary Society* (4th ed.). Belmont, CA: Wadsworth.

Gitlin, T. (1979) "Prime Time Ideology: The Hegemonic Process in Television Entertainment." *Social Problems*, 26(3): 251–266.

Goold, B., Loader, I. and Thumala, A. (2013) "The Banality of Security: The Curious Case of Surveillance Cameras." *British Journal of Criminology*, 53(6): 977–996.

Gramsci, A. (1971) *Selections Form the Prison Notebooks*. New York, NY: International Publishers.

Hackley, C., Tiwsakul, R. and Preuss, L. (2008) "An Ethical Evaluation of Product Placement: A Deceptive Practice?" *Business Ethincs*, 17(2): 109–120.

Herman, E.S. and McChesney, R.W. (2004) *The Global Media: The New Missionaries of Corporate Captialism*. New York, NY: Continuum.

Hickey, N. (1998) "Money Lust: How Pressure For Profit is Perverting Journalism." *Columbia Journalism Review*, Jul–Aug, 28–36.

Issa, E.E. (2016) "2015 American Household Credit Card Debt Study." Online. Available HTTP: www.nerdwallet.com/blog/credit-card-data/average-credit-card-debt-household/

London, J. (1908) *The Iron Heel*. London, UK: London Press.

McCann, J. (2016, September 10) "iPhone 7 News and Features: All you Nto Know About the New iPhone Online." Available HTTP: www.techradar.com/news/phone-and-communications/mobile-phones/iphone-7-1328149

Merton, R. (1938) "Social Structure and Anomie." *American Sociological Review*, 3: 672–682.

Messner, S.F. and Rosenfeld, R. (1994) *Crime and the American Dream* (4th ed.). Thomas Wadsworth.

Nagle, L.E. (2008) "Selling Souls: The Effect of Globalization on Human Trafficking and Forced Servitude." *Wisconsin International Law Journal*, 26(1): 131–162.

Neocleous, M. (2008) *Critique of Security*. Edinburgh, Scotland: Edinburgh University Press.

Pearce, F. (1976) *Crimes of the Powerful: Marxism, Crime and Deviance*. London, UK: Pluto Press.

——— (2015, February 3) "Marxism and Corporate Crime in the 21st Century: An Interview with Frank Pearce." Online. Available HTTP: http://redquillbooks.com/interview-frank-pearce/

Pearce, F. and Tombs, S. (2006) "Hegemony, Risk and Governance: 'social regulation' and the American Chemical Industry." *Economy and Society*, 25(3): 428–454.

Renner, M. (2002) *The Anatomy of Resource Wars*. Washington, DC: Worldwatch Institute.

Ritzer, G. (1998) *The McDonaldization Thesis: Explorations and Extensions*. London: Sage Publications.

Rothe, D.L. and Kauzlarich, D. (2016) *Crimes of the Powerful: An Introduction*. New York, NY: Routledge.

Rougeau, M. (2015, January 27) "Apple Just Made a Mind-blowing Amount of Money." Online. Available HTTP: www.techradar.com/news/phone-and-communications/mobile-phones/apple-just-made-a-mind-blowing-amount-of-money-1282408

Silver, J. (Producer), and Wachowski, L. and Wachowski, L. (Directors) (1999) *The Matrix* (Motion picture). United States: Warner Brothers.

Simon, R. (1982) *Gramsci's Political Thought*. London, UK: Lawrence and Wishart.

Simon Property Group. (2016) "Simon Property Group: The World's Largest Publicly Traded Real Estate Company." Online. Available HTTP: http://investors.simon.com/phoenix.zhtml?c=113968&p=irol-IRHome

Toyota. (2015, April 1) *New lexus rx commercial* [Video file]. Online. Available HTTP: www. youtube.com/watch?v=dFbHb9uwQiI

Veblen, T. (1994) *The Theory of the Leisure Class (Dover Thrift Editions)*. New York, NY: Dover Publications.

Wacquant, L. (2009) *Punishing the Poor: The Neoliberal Government of Social Insecurity*. Durham: Duke University Press.

Wahba, P. (2015, April 22) "Top U.S. Mall Owner Simon Taps Tech, Loyalty to Boost Own Brand." Online. Available HTTP: http://fortune.com/2015/04/22/mall-owner-simon-brand/

Žižek, S. (2009) *The Sublime Object of Ideology*. London, United Kingdom: Verso.

Zuidervaart, L. (1991) *Adorno's Aesthetic Theory: The Redemption of Illusion*. Cambridge, MA: MIT Press.

# Chapter 19

# Debtfarism, predatory lending and imaginary social orders

## The case of the U.S. payday lending industry

*Susanne Soederberg*

Over the past two decades, an increasing number of low-income households in the United States – as elsewhere – have come to depend on expensive credit to meet basic survival needs (e.g. rent, food, medicine, transportation, day care and so forth). Of the vast array of financial products targeting the poor, payday loans have come under the greatest public scrutiny for their predatory lending practices, including their exorbitant interest rates and penalty fees (Soederberg 2014). Payday loans refer to small, short-term, unsecured (non-collateralized) cash advances, which are due on the borrower's next payday (usually two weeks). There are now almost as many payday storefronts and online payday venders as McDonald's and Starbucks combined (CFSA 2016). Although there are different types of cash advance providers, 17 large companies dominate the industry, with the largest market share belonging to Advance America (National People's Action 2012). According to Advance America, the corporation's rapid growth and high levels of profitability are the result of decreasing availability of short-term consumer credit alternatives from traditional banking institutions, the relatively low costs of entry and the regulatory safe harbour that many state statutes provide for cash advance services (Advance America 2010: 5). There is, however, a darker side to the industry's economic success.

Although the size of the payday loan permitted varies by state jurisdiction and ranges from $50 to $1,000, with $325 being typical, several studies indicate that general average payday loan rates range anywhere from 364% to 550% annual percentage rate (APR), not including common charges such as late fees and bounced cheques fees, which can cost nearly as much, or even more, as the loan itself (Graves and Peterson 2005: 661; Peterson 2007). The highly lucrative nature of payday companies is due to their ability to trap low-income customers into spiralling debt cycles, or what is referred to in the industry as rollover loans (Damar 2009). Findings have revealed that 75% of payday debtors are unable to repay their loan within two weeks and are forced to get a rollover loan at additional costs (Chin 2004; Graves and Peterson 2005; Consumer Financial Protection Bureau 2013). If the borrower agrees to pay the rollover fee, by contrast, the loan is usually extended for another two weeks. "Nearly 90 percent of payday lending revenues are based on fees stripped from borrowers who have flipped loans and are trapped in a cycle of debt. The typical payday borrower will have an outstanding payment for 30 weeks" (Jory 2009: 319).

Rollover loans are particularly perilous for the customer base of payday lenders, who live from paycheque to paycheque (or from government benefit to government benefit). Most borrowers, for instance, are disproportionately female, with single mothers – many of whom are reliant on welfare provisioning – making up a key segment of the industry's customers. African American and Latino customers also comprise an overwhelming number of payday borrowers (National People's Action 2012: 6). Pensioners form another large segment of borrowers, with over one-quarter of all bank payday borrowers being Social Security beneficiaries (CFPB 2013; CLR 2013).

Drawing on Marxian insights, I explore how state interventions have facilitated the expansion and legitimation of the payday lending in the United States, despite its well-publicized predatory lending practices. I argue that the regulative and rhetorical nature of *debtfarism* – that is, a mode of neoliberal governance in the age of financialized capitalism – has served to normalize and naturalize payday lending as a convenience of modern life for low-income people (Soederberg 2014). By exploring various regulatory provisions, I reveal how the debtfare state plays an integral role in establishing what Pearce (1976) refers to as an *imaginary social order*. In so doing, I demonstrate how the debtfare state serves to depoliticize the violence entailed in payday lending, whilst facilitating the industry's expansion through the democratization of credit – a trope that dominates the imaginary social order of payday lending.

I develop this argument in three main sections. In the first section, I explore the analytical contours of this argument by contextualizing it in the dominant debates. In the second section, I focus on a concrete discussion of the regulatory and rhetorical features of debtfarism the establishment of the imaginary of the democratization of credit by at least three ways: (1) the use of voluntary codes of conduct; (2) the distortion of usury laws; and (3) the rhetorical use of consumer protection law. In the third section, I conclude by summarizing my argument.

## Debtfarism and the democratization of credit: the imaginary social order of payday lending

### Debating predation

Legal and economic scholars have argued that payday lending is either welfare enhancing (Morgan and Strain 2008) or that it is welfare destroying (Carrell and Zinman 2008). On the first view, it is believed that payday loans can help distressed individuals to smooth liquidity shocks without incurring the more expensive costs of overdraft fees and interests, bounced cheques, late fees and/or getting evicted or foreclosed upon (Zinman 2010). Here, payday loans fill an important void in the existing credit system, which is evidenced by strong consumer demand for convenient, small amounts of short-term credit at high rates of interest (Morse 2009; Drysdale and Keest 2000). On the welfare reducing provision of credit such as payday loans, critics point to the adverse economic effects of the predatory nature, including over-lending, over-charging, deception and targeting certain consumer segments such welfare recipients, military personnel and so forth (Morgan 2007).

Those who question the welfare-enhancing features of payday loans highlight the exorbitant interest rates attached to these loans and the ensuing debt trap that occurs when many borrowers cannot make their payment and thus select to roll over their loan for longer periods, incurring more interest and fees. For these authors, the predatory nature of payday loans is inappropriate based on grounds of the moral predicate (Chin 2004; Morgan 2007). As a corrective, these scholars champion the reform of usury laws, which they regard as a feature of consumer protection law that serves to "protect the needy from the greedy" (Drysdale and Keest 2000: 657). The lending system would thus become more moral through the enactment of laws that encourage more effective and fair ways of determining whether a loan is appropriate for a borrower on the basis of their capacity to make the required repayments (Austin 2004; Woolston 2010).

These readings and resolutions to predatory lending fail to grapple with the inherent social structures and processes that lead to, and, in turn, perpetuate payday lending. Or, as Pearce warns, greed in itself is not a necessary explanatory factor in understanding corporate malfeasance (1976). Drawing on Pearce, I fill this gap in the literature and thereby provide a more complete understanding of the role of power and state intervention. I identify a core assumption which the earlier debates about payday lending uncritically rehearse: the uncritical liberal embrace of the market as a naturally evolving arena marked by individualized expressions of liberty, equality and freedoms (based on legal contract and private property). This assumption forms the backbone of what Pearce refers to as "imaginary social order in America – portrayed as a pluralist, democratic, free-enterprise society" (1976: 80). The trope of the democratization of credit is often employed by the payday lending industry and its trade associations (e.g., Community Finance Services of America and Financial Service Centres of America, or FiSCA).

### Democratization of credit as an imaginary social order

> Just as many consumers prefer the convenience of specialty stores to large department stores, many consumers prefer the efficiency and convenience of financial service centers over banks. They prefer transacting at FiSCA member stores because of their neighborhood locations and longer hours of operation, and the friendly service they receive.
>
> *Financial Service Centres of America* (FiSCA)[1]

> I turned to Advance America not because I was frivolous or careless with money. I turned to them because at the time I didn't have the funds available. We are

> Americans who work hard and live right. Things happen. And when you have places like Advance America that can help everyday people, that's a good thing.
>
> *Advance America Customer*, Advance America (2010: ii)

The convenience and accessibility of credit are important elements of the trope of the democratization of credit (Advance America 2010). According to FiSCA and other reports, for instance, the ease of payday loans helps to "bridge the unexpected need for short-term credit when other options are not available" (FiSCA 2012). Some scholars have suggested that the only factors a payday borrower takes into consideration are convenience of location, simplicity of process and speed of approvals, and not the interest rate (FDIC 2009). On this view, payday lenders are providing a valuable and necessary service to its customers. The root causes of poverty (e.g. lack of living and/or social wages) and its gendered, racialized and class expressions have also been conveniently erased in this imaginary social order marked by the democratization of credit (Soederberg 2014).

The imaginary social order is constructed and reconstructed through a complex and multifaceted set of practices and processes (Pearce 1976), one important feature of which is the capitalist state. As Pearce suggests, "[s]tate institutions are not separate from society, over and above it, but are an integral part of the mode of production, although their role and relative importance may vary under different conditions" (1976: 58). Since the early 1990s, neoliberal forms of state intervention have been marked by pro-market regulations and privatization schemes (Peck and Tickell 2002). As I have discussed elsewhere, a key mode of neoliberal governance has been debtfarism (Soederberg 2014). Debtfarism is articulated through rhetorical and regulatory forms of intervention that not only reproduce the power inherent in payday lending, but also the large Wall Street banks that back them. In the next section, I explore several concrete ways the debtfare state assists in this process through the continual reproduction of the imaginary social order marked by the democratization of credit.

## Debtfare state and the facilitation of payday lending

### Unmasking "predators who care" and best practices

Following the general neoliberal trend of corporate caring and good citizenship – or what I have elsewhere referred to as the marketization of social justice (Soederberg 2010) – the payday industry has engaged in aggressive campaigning to rebrand itself as a respectable lending institution that is engaged in "helping hardworking Americans meet their financial obligations" through the creation of programmes such as the 2010 *America Needs a Raise* campaign in which the corporation does not recognize and award Americans for their "extraordinary service" in their spaces of employment, but rather outside of the workplace (Advance America 2010). By establishing the façade of the corporation as a friendly neighbour assisting the middle class to make ends meet, our gaze is moved away from the wider dynamics of capital accumulation in which these workers earn their low wages or the exploitative relations in which payday lenders extract their revenue.

The payday industry is also vested in signalling its good citizenship by adhering to consumer protection laws and meeting other requirements set by regulators. In the attempts to curtail meaningful regulation regarding its interest rates and fees, for instance, the payday lobby organization CFSA has announced its strong support of the Consumer Financial Protection Bureau's (CFPB) recommendations for a principles-based reform approach to ensure fair treatment for all customers through the focus on disclosure (CFPB 2013). Advance America has stressed it will meet these requirements "by promoting transparency on all aspects of lending practices, improving and streamlining disclosures to enable customers to easily compare borrowing options, and ensuring that similar products are regulated in an equitable manner to support market competition" (Advance America 2010: iii). To this end, FiSCA lists a "Code of Conduct,"[2] and the CFSA has devised a "Customer Bill of Rights," including a list of coercive collection practices that they dissuade their members from considering or using as a threat toward a customer (US Department of Defense 2006; cf., Picciotto 2011).[3]

These absences of legally binding rules in consumer finance – authored by the debtfare state and its preferences for market-friendly regulation – have resulted in not only higher-priced credit for the poor, but also inferior legal protections (Drysdale and Keest 2000). Legal obligation continues to act as a coercive and ideological frame governing the relations between debtors and creditors, whilst the latter are able to evade any meaningful legal obligation, and, as we will see, are even permitted to distort the meaning of legal obligation in the same manner as the salary lenders. For instance, although the CFSA's list of "best practices" prohibits the threat of prosecution as a collection tactic, many payday lenders use this approach to collect past due accounts. What is more, some lenders do not limit themselves to merely threatening debtors with criminal prosecution, but also moving forward with this threat in court. In one Dallas, Texas precinct in one year, payday lenders filed over 13,000 criminal charges with law enforcement officials against their consumers (Drysdale and Keest 2000: 610).

What is not well known among payday loan borrowers – despite the financial education services that the payday lending industry allegedly offers – is that a post-dated cheque given to someone who knows that it will not clear rarely supports criminal prosecution. As a federal district court in Tennessee noted, one should assume that the borrower does not have enough money in the bank to cover the cheque – otherwise they would not be in court: "Certainly a lender's exaction of a fee to 'defer' deposit signifies the requisite acceptance on

# 262 Susanne Soederberg

his part necessary to remove the transaction from the realm of the criminal bad cheque statute" (Drysdale and Keest 2000: 611). Notwithstanding the absence of criminal prosecution threats, however, payday debtors who default on loans are subject to punitive charges in the form of delinquency and collection fees. Payday loans are the only type of consumer debt that can trigger treble damage penalties upon default (Drysdale and Keest 2000).

### Rhetorical payday bans and salience distortion

A narrow definition of usury is the taking of more for the use of money than the law allows. Usury laws – a key domain of the debtfare state – are believed to protect against the oppression of debtors through excessive rates of interest charged by lenders. Because there is no federal usury law, each state has its own percentage rate that is considered a *de facto* usury rate (Jory 2009: 321). But for the most part, usury laws have failed to regulate the payday lending industry (Peterson 2007). Thirty-six percent (APR) is the limit set by the Federal Deposit Insurance Corporation's (FDIC) Responsible Small Dollar Lending Guidelines and is double the cap for federally chartered credit unions. A majority of states have statutes regulating what loan terms are permitted and prohibited.[4] The statutes also entail penalties for non-compliance. Many of these states even cap the interest or fees lenders can charge to consumers (Plunkett and Hurtado 2011). Most of these states limit the number of loans that can be made or renewed with the aim of reducing predatory cycles of debt (Johnston 2010).

Yet debtfarism – in both its federal and state articulations – has facilitated the evasion of usury laws by payday lenders. After conducting a rigorous empirical study of 50 state usury laws, legal scholar Christopher L. Peterson concludes that since 1965 usury law has become more lax, more polarized and more misleading. He refers to this trend as "salience distortion" (Peterson 2007: 5). Seen from our theoretical frame, Peterson's views reflect wider attempts by the debtfare state to assist payday lenders by depoliticizing increasing public criticism and controversy regarding the industry's disregard for consumer protection laws and the creation of so-called debt traps (i.e. rollover loans). In what follows, I outline some examples of salience distortion exercised by debtfare practices with regard to usury laws.

When faced with usury caps or an outright ban of payday lending from state legislatures in the early 2000s (e.g. Georgia and North Carolina banned payday lending in 2004), payday lenders created "rent-a-bank" partnerships with nationally chartered banks (Soederberg, 2014). This move was largely facilitated by previous debtfare interventions, such as the Marquette decision of 1978 (*Marquette Nat. Bank of Minneapolis v. First of Omaha Service Corp.*), which allowed banks to circumvent state usury laws (Johnston 2010). Briefly, the Marquette Decision represented an attempt by the U.S. federal government to displace state regulation (Mann and Hawkins 2007). The U.S. Supreme Court ruled that lenders in a state with liberal usury laws (e.g. Delaware and

South Dakota) could apply rates to workers residing in states with more restrictive usury ceilings (Peterson 2007).

Significantly, the Marquette decision served to undermine usury protection, which was a vital step in the growth of secondary forms of exploitation. The American state thus effectively legalized usury in 1978. From this time onward, any national bank was permitted "to charge an interest rate as high as the maximum rate permitted by the laws of the state where the bank is located" (Mann and Hawkins 2007: 871). And although this pertained to national banks, it played a major role in normalizing usury across the United States, allowing national banks to charge, among other things, over 4,000% (median) interest rates on overdraft cheques (i.e. in excess of 20 times that of payday loans), creating a ludicrous situation in which payday loans become a cost-effective alternative (Fusaro 2008).

Seen from this perspective, the beneficiaries of interest rate caps on payday loans across several states[5] are national banks. Around the time of the start of various payday bans in 2004, the bounced cheque rates in both Georgia and North Carolina increased. Eager to take advantage of this new opening, the federal government passed the Cheque Clearing for the 21st Century Act in 2003 (or "Check 21"), which came into effect in 2004 (Morgan and Strain 2008). One of the features of this new law effectively enhances bank profitability with regard to bounced cheques. For instance, the act allows depository institutions to debit payers' accounts more quickly (using electronic presentment) without crediting payees' accounts more promptly. Less "float" for cheque writers means more bounced cheques revealing the social power of money through its temporal dimension (Morgan and Strain 2008: 14).

To avoid heavy-handed regulation, some payday lenders shut down their physical offices in states with severe restrictions and began conducting payday lending via the Internet, where they charge higher rates and issue loans in greater amounts than their brick-and-mortar stores (Johnston 2010). Since 2006, for example, the state of California's Department of Corporations has been trying to force these unlicensed, Internet-only businesses to adhere to the same rules that govern the state-licensed (brick-and-mortar) payday loan stores that offer short-term, unsecured loans of up to $300 and cap the annualized percentage rate at 459% for a maximum 31-day period. Internet payday lenders have been allowed to circumvent state law by claiming that they are associated with sovereign Aboriginal nations that operate outside of California and are thus immune from state regulation. Authorities estimate that these Aboriginal-based, Internet-only lending companies involve thousands of websites that generate billions of dollars in revenue nationwide ("Internet payday lenders with ties to Indians dodge California regulators," *LA Times*, 13 April 2009, cited in Soederberg 2014).

Other online competitors are also attempting to reconfigure the spatio-temporal dimensions of short-term loans and, in doing so, may affect the dominant position of virtual payday lending. ZestCash, an online small-loans lending company established in 2009 by former Google executive Douglas Merrill, raised $73 million of funding in early 2012 to expand the company's operations ("Former Google CIO Raises $73 Million to Reform Payday Loans with Data-Driven Startup ZestCash," *TechCrunch*, 19 January 2012; zestcash.com). ZestCash offers loans of up to $800 but, unlike payday lenders, allows the loans to be repaid over a period of months, as opposed to weeks. According to its website, by using "analytical techniques," ZestCash suggests that it is able to offer a fair, lower-cost alternative to people "who do not have access to traditional credit." Yet like payday borrowers, these lenders require a bank account and a source of income. Moreover, ZestCash still charges triple-digit interest rates when computed in terms of APR. Although it markets its product as 50% cheaper (for those with relatively better credit ratings) than traditional payday lenders, ZestCash loans, according to the company's website, average 365% APR as opposed to 480% APR of payday loans (Soederberg 2014).

Two further examples of how payday lenders have circumvented state usury laws due to the existence (and maintenance) of loopholes are worth mentioning here (Woolston 2010). The first is the case of Ohio. In 2008, and in response to increasing pressure from constituents and consumer advocates, the Ohio State Legislature passed and signed into law the Short-Term Loan Act to curb predatory payday lending. The act essentially capped the maximum loan amount at $500, limited the APR on loans at 28% and made the maturity date a minimum of 30 days. Additionally, the act banned lenders from issuing more than four loans per year to the same borrower. The statute also addresses a common circumvention technique of out-of-state lenders – issuing loans via the Internet or telephone – by banning out-of-state lenders from issuing loans to Ohio residents (Johnston 2010). After mounting a $20 million campaign to overthrow the new law through a voter initiative on the November 2008 ballot, Ohio voters overwhelming defeated the industry's initiative.

The payday lenders, however, quickly found legal loopholes through salience distortion (Peterson 2007; Johnston 2010). Whereas only 19 lenders, for instance, obtained a licence under the new law, the majority of lenders were licensed under either Ohio's Mortgage Loan Act, which does not require issuance of an actual mortgage and does not place limits on the interest rates that can be charged, or under Ohio's Small Loan Act, which permits payday lenders to charge 423% APR, even higher than the 391% allowed under the repealed payday lending statute (Johnston 2010). In a 2009 study, *every* payday lender surveyed in Ohio charged triple-digit interest rates and required loans to be paid back within two weeks or less. Furthermore, the majority issued loans in amounts exceeding $500 (Johnston 2010: 12–26). Yet to date, neither the state of Ohio nor the federal government has enacted any meaningful laws or regulations that curtail this practice (Woolston 2010).

Texas also provides a good example in which to gain insight into the loopholes involved when banning or mitigating payday lending in the name of consumer protection. To overcome the rent-a-bank prohibition, payday lenders

Debtfarism 265

in Texas have been exploiting a loophole in a broadly worded statute that allows them to operate as "credit service organizations" (or CSOs) (Mann and Hawkins 2007). CSOs were originally established in the state to improve a customer's credit rating. In Texas, CSOs are legally required to pay a $100 registration fee to the secretary of state, post a $10,000 bond for each store, disclose contract terms and costs to borrowers and permit borrowers three days to cancel a contract ("The Perils of Payday," *The Texas Observer*, 30 April 2009 cited in Soederberg 2014). Payday lenders use the CSO status to process loans from third parties and then collect fees – not interest – thereby evading usury laws (Johnston 2010: 17). Targeting low-income neighbourhoods in the state, payday lenders grew from 1,513 storefronts in 2005 to more than 2,800 in 2009. Like the rest of the United States, the payday lending business was extremely lucrative in the wake of the 2008 recession ("The Perils of Payday," *The Texas Observer*, 30 April 2009).

### Consumer protection in democratized credit

> The CFPB [Consumer Financial Protection Bureau] has a statutory obligation to promote markets that are fair transparent, and competitive.
> CFPB, *Payday Loans and Deposit Advance Products: A White Paper of Initial Data Findings* (2013: 4)

In the aftermath of the 2007 subprime crisis, and in the renewed spirit of reforming the predatory practices of consumer finance, two legislative bills were introduced in 2009 to reform the payday lending industry: the Payday Loan Reform Act and the Protecting Consumers from Unreasonable Credit Rates Act. Notably, neither bill has been enacted at the time of writing. As we will see, each bill has a built-in loophole that not only allows the payday lending industry to engage in business-as-usual behaviour, but also does little to radically alter the existing conditions and violent nature of payday lending practices in the United States. The proposed bills – informed by the central trope of consumer protection – do not challenge the disciplinary and exploitative nature of dispossessive capitalism, but rather aid in the remaking of the illusions of the community of money.

Introduced by U.S. Representative Luis Gutiérrez (D-Illinois), head of the House Financial Services Subcommittee on Financial Institutions and Consumer Credit, the Payday Loan Reform Act of 2009 requires lenders to provide specific disclosures to payday loan customers and claims to extend protections of the Military Lending Act to all Americans (Johnston 2010). There are very useful features of the proposed bill, particularly with regard to collection practices (Soederberg 2014). Under the bill, for instance, payday lenders are not permitted to threaten or seek to have consumers prosecuted in criminal court to collect outstanding loans. In addition, the bill forbids lenders from taking a security interest in property to secure the loan (Johnston 2010). For legal scholar Creola Johnson, however, the bill provides the following loophole: "It shall be unlawful for a payday lender to require a consumer to pay interests and fees that, combined, total more than 15 cents for every dollar loaned in connection" (Johnston, 2010: 24). This provision will, in effect, grant congressional approval to lenders that charge triple-digit interest rates for payday loans. Thus, the bill is "an ersatz reform that would allow payday lenders to charge at what amounts to an APR of 390 percent" (Johnston 2010: 24; "391 Percent Payday Loan," *New York Times*, 12 April 2009).

The Protecting Consumers from Unreasonable Credit Rates Act of 2009 was introduced by Senator Richard J. Durbin (D-Illinois) to establish "a national usury rate for consumer credit transactions."[6] In contrast to the Gutiérrez bill, consumer protection proponents support Durbin's bill. Like the Military Lending Act, Durbin's bill would cap interest rates at 36% percent. Although there are some strengths of the bill, it falls short in terms of providing needed consumer protection. A critical component of the bill, for instance, is section 141(b)(2) under the heading "Tolerances." This section provides that the definitions of "fee" and "interest rate" do not include "credit obligations that are payable in at least three fully amortizing installments over at least 90 days" (Johnston 2010: 27). In addition, for loans of $300 or more, payday lenders are permitted to charge additional fees, which include origination fees of no more than $30, as well as late fees of either $20, or a fee authorized by state law. As history has shown, lenders will draft loan contracts to circumvent the purpose of the legislation (Johnston 2010).

The fact that neither bill has been enacted – despite their industry-friendly formulations – is telling. The payday lending industry is central not only to highly lucrative forms of secondary exploitation, but also to the commodification of social reproduction in the United States as a disciplinary device. Moreover, it is telling that the debates remain within the moral bounds of usury law, which, as many authors have noted, has been a historical source of conflict that predates capitalism (Peterson 2007; Graeber 2011).

What is omitted in these reforms are the relations of power that have a vested interest in constructing and reproducing a social reality in which the working poor are made dependent on private credit as a primary means of obtaining economic security. This position is mirrored in a 2013 study on the payday loan industry by the CFPB. The report begins by uncritically accepting the existence of payday loans. "The CFPB recognizes that demand exists for small dollar credit products. These types of credit products can be helpful for consumers if they are structured to facilitate successful repayment without the need to repeatedly borrow at a high cost" (CFPB 2013). The report goes on to investigate and suggest various ways payday loans can be transformed into what they refer to as "sustained use" (CFPB 2013).

Issues that remain out of bounds in terms of discussing (let alone achieving) a *reasonable* interest rate, include living wages with mandatory social benefits by employers, as well as adequate state provisioning of education, housing, health, old age and child care and so forth. This is symptomatic of a major trend in advanced forms of neoliberalization, namely the neglect of poverty and how to address it. According to Randy Albelda (2012: 11), this has been not figured prominently on the national agenda since the "welfare reform" debates in the 1980s and 1990s.

## Conclusion

In this chapter, I have employed my concept of debtfarism, as a key component of neoliberal interventions, and Pearce's notion of imaginary social order to reveal how the reliance of the working poor on private provisioning in the form of payday loans for basic subsistence needs is a construction imbued with power rooted in capitalist society. In so doing, I have attempted to reveal that the dominant debates about the payday lending industry are devoid of considerations of class relations and state power in the wider processes of capital accumulation. These criticisms are thus are unable to provide an adequate explanation as to why – despite public outcry and continual attempts at legal reform – payday lending not only continues to thrive, but also has proven to be wildly lucrative (Peterson 2007; National People's Action 2012).

The legal and political framings of debtfarism have been successfully employed to bolster the payday loan industry and the underlying dynamics of capital accumulation dominated by financial logics, such as the poverty industry. Since the 2007 subprime meltdown and subsequent recession, annual earnings for the country's (publicly traded) payday corporations (e.g. Advance America, Cash America, Dollar Financial, EZ Corp, First Cash Financial, QC Holdings) have risen to their highest levels on record.

> Annual filings show that the nation's major payday lenders collectively earn more from their high-cost cash advances than before the financial crisis. From 2007 to 2010 their combined revenues from payday lending have increased 2.6 percent, or some $30 million in annual revenues.
>
> (National People's Action 2012: 10)

The payday lending industry is also a thriving business in Canada, the United Kingdom, New Zealand, South Africa and South Korea (Aitken 2010; Bond 2013). Although geographically distinct, the regulatory and rhetorical features of new modes of governance such as debtfarism are also more than likely mediating and facilitating the rise of the poverty industry and the imaginary social orders in which it thrives.

## Notes

1 "FiSCA History." Available at: <www.fisca.org/Content/NavigationMenu/About-FISCA/FiSCAHistory/default.htm> (accessed 20 April 2012).

2 FiSCA "Code of Conduct." Available at: <www.fisca.org/Content/NavigationMenu/AboutFISCA/CodesofConduct/default.htm> (accessed 30 April 2012).
3 CFSA Customer Bill of Rights. Available at: <http://cfsaa.com/cfsa-member-best-practices/cfsa-customer-bill-of-rights.aspx> (accessed 20 April 2012).
4 Seven states (Arkansas, Connecticut, Maryland, New Jersey, New York, Pennsylvania and Vermont) plus the federal district of Washington, D.C., protect consumers against abusive practices in small loan products (Plunkett and Hurtado 2011: 37–38). Yet five states set no usury caps for small loans, including Delaware, Idaho, South Dakota, Utah and Wisconsin (Plunkett and Hurtado 2011).
5 Since the subprime housing debacle of 2007 and the subsequent recessionary environment, several states have increased regulatory pressure on payday lending, including Arizona, Arkansas, Colorado, Montana, New Hampshire, Ohio and Oregon – home to over 3,400 payday loan stores issuing over $3 billion in payday loans annually. These seven states have limited small-dollar loan interest rates between 17% and 45% APR, effectively ending or severely limiting payday lending (National People's Action, 2012).
6 <www.govtrack.us/congress/bills/111/s500/text> (accessed 12 May 2012).

# References

Advance America. (2010) *2010 Annual Report*. Spartanburg, SC: Advance America Cash Advance Centre.

Aitken, R. (2010) "Regul(ariz)ation of Fringe Credit: Payday Lending and the Borders of Global Financial Practice." *Competition and Change*, 14(2): 80–99.

Albeda, R. (2012) "Same Single-Mother Poverty: Fifteen Years of Welfare Reform." *Dollars & Sense*, January/February: 11–17.

Austin, R. (2004) "Of Predatory Lending and the Democratization of Credit: Preserving the Social Safety Net of Informality in Small-loan Transactions." *American University Law Review*, 53(6): 1217–1257.

Bond, P. (2013) "Debt, Uneven Development and Capitalist Crisis in South Africa: from Moody's Macroeconomic Monitoring to Marikana Microfinance Mashonistas." *Third World Quarterly*, 34(4): 569–592.

Carrell, S. and Zinman, J. (2008) "In Harm's Way? Payday Loan Access and Military Personnel Performance." *Working Paper, No. 8–18*, Philadelphia, PA: Federal Reserve Bank of Philadelphia.

CFSA [Community Finance Services Association] (2016) "About the Payday Advance Industry." Online. Available HTTP: http://cfsaa.com/about-the-payday-advance-industry.aspx (accessed 3 January 2016).

Chin, P. (2004) "Payday Loans: The Case for Federal Legislation." *University of Illinois Law Review*, 3: 723–754.

CLR [Centre for Responsible Lending] (2013) *Triple-Digit Danger: Bank Payday Lending Persists*. Durham, NC: Centre for Responsible Lending

Consumer Financial Protection Bureau (CFPB) (2013) *Payday Loans and Deposit Advance Products – A White Paper of Initial Data Findings*. Washington, DC: Consumer Financial Protection Bureau.

Damar, E.H. (2009) "Why Do Payday Lenders Enter Local Markets? Evidence from Oregon." *Review of Industrial Organization*, 34(2): 173–191.

Drysdale, L. and Keest, K.E. (2000) "The Two-Tiered Consumer Financial Services Marketplace: The Fringe Banking System and its Challenge to Current Thinking about the Role of Usury Laws in Today's Society." *South Carolina Law Review*, 51: 589–669.

FDIC [Federal Deposit Insurance Corporation] (2009) *National Survey of Unbanked and Underbanked Households,* Washington, DC: FDIC.

FiSCA. (2012) "Consumer Fact Sheet." Online. Available HTTP: www.fisca.org/Content/NavigationMenu/ConsumerCenter/ConsumerFactSheet/default.htm (accessed 24 April 2012).

Fusaro, M.A. (2008) "Hidden Consumer Loans: An Analysis of Implicit Interest Rates on Bounced Checks." *Journal of Family and Economic Issues,* 29(1): 251–263.

Graeber, D. (2011) *Debt: The First 5,000 Years,* Brooklyn, NY: Melville House Publishing.

Graves, S.M. and Peterson, C.L. (2005) "Predatory Lending and the Military: The Law and Geography of 'payday' Loans in Military Towns." *Ohio State Law Journal,* 66(5): 653–832.

Johnston, C. (2010) *Dear President Obama: You Protected the Troops; Now Fulfill Your Promise to Protect All Americans from Payday Loans.* Online. Available HTTP: http://works.bepress.com/creola_johnson/1 (accessed 4 April 2012).

Jory, K. (2009) "Mandatory Arbitration Clauses in Payday Lending Loans: How the Federal Courts Protect Unfair Lending Practices in the Name of Anti-protectionism." *Ohio State Journal on Dispute Resolution,* 24(2): 315–380.

Mann, R.J. and Hawkins, J. (2007) "Just Until Payday." *UCLA Law Review,* 54(4): 855–912.

Morgan, D.P. (2007) "Defining and Detecting Predatory Lending." *Federal Reserve Bank of New York Staff Reports No. 273,* New York: Federal Reserve Bank of New York.

Morgan, D.P. and Strain, M.R. (2008) "Payday Holiday: How Households Fare after Payday Credit Bans." *Federal Reserve Bank of New York Staff Reports, No. 39,* New York: Federal Reserve Bank of New York.

Morse, A. (2009) *Payday Lenders: Heroes or Villains?,* Chicago: Booth School of Business, University of Chicago.

National People's Action. (2012) *Profiting from Poverty: How Payday Lenders Strip Wealth from the Working-poor For Record Profits.* Chicago: National People's Action.

Pearce, F. (1976) *Crimes of the Powerful: Marxism, Crime and Deviance.* London: Pluto Press.

Peck, J. and Tickell, A. (2002) "Neoliberalizing Space." *Antipode: A Radical Journal of Geography,* 34(3): 380–404.

Peterson, C.L. (2007) "Usury Law, Payday Loans, and Statutory Sleight of Hand: An Empirical Analysis of American Credit Pricing Limits," in *Selected Words of Christopher L. Peterson.* Gainsville, FL: University of Florida.

Picciotto, S. (2011) *Regulating Global Corporate Capitalism.* Cambridge: Cambridge University Press.

Plunkett, L.A. and Hurtado, A.L. (2011) "Small Dollar Loans, Big Problems: How States Protect Consumers From Abuses and How the Federal Government Can Help." *Suffolk University Law Review,* XLIV(31): 31–88.

Soederberg, S. (2010) *Corporate Power and Ownership in Contemporary Capitalism: The Politics of Resistance and Domination.* London: Routledge.

Soederberg, S. (2014) *Debtfare States and the Poverty Industry: Money, Discipline and the Surplus Population.* London: Routledge.

US Department of Defense. (2006) *Report on Predatory Lending Practices Directed at Members of the Armed Forces and their Dependents,* Washington, DC: Department of Defense.

Woolston, A.S. (2010) "Neither Borrower Nor Lender Be: The Future of Payday Lending in Arizona." *Arizona Law Review,* 52(3): 853–887.

Zinman, J. (2010) "Restricting Consumer Credit Access: Household Survey Evidence on Effects around Oregon Rate Cap." *Journal of Banking & Finance,* 34(1): 546–556.

Chapter 20

# Failure to protect

## State obligations to victims and state crime

*Laura Finley*

The World Health Organization (WHO) found in 2013 that nearly one-third of the world's women had endured physical or sexual intimate partner violence, and as much as 38% of all murders of women around the globe are domestic violence related (WHO 2013). According to a study by the WHO, women are at greater risk in the home than in any other location (Garcia-Moreno et al. 2005). Domestic violence kills more women worldwide than civil wars (Parker 2014). Dr Margaret Chan, the director-general of the WHO, described domestic violence as a "global health problem of epidemic proportions" (Park 2013).

This chapter focuses on domestic violence as a human rights problem that states are obligated to address. Although these are pernicious global problems, the chapter will focus on the United States and the UK. After a review of the scope and extent of domestic violence in both places, the chapter addresses states' obligations as determined by international human rights treaties and court decisions. It then includes an assessment of the failure to enact and enforce adequate appropriate legislation, the failure of police to adequately respond in domestic violence cases, the problems with how these cases are addressed in courts and limitations in the provision of services by domestic violence shelters. The chapter concludes that these failures can be viewed as crimes of the state, or crimes of the powerful. Although domestic violence was not part of Pearce's work initially, I contend that it should be, given the responsibilities of the state and the concomitant failures to address the issue appropriately. Such a view is consistent with Pearce's critique of lawmakers and their ability to label others' activity as deviant while disregarding their responsibilities.

## Scope and extent of domestic violence

In the United States, one in four women and one in seven men will be victims of domestic violence, and every nine seconds a woman is physically assaulted by an intimate partner. Domestic violence is the most common cause of injury for women in the United States aged 15 to 44, some 1,300 people are killed each year by abusers in the United States alone (Chemaly 2012) Far more people in America, largely women, have been killed by their partners than were U.S. forces in the wars in Iraq and Afghanistan combined. American women are twice as likely to suffer domestic violence as breast cancer (Chemaly 2012). In the United States, more women are injured from domestic violence than from car accidents, rapes and muggings combined (Murray 2008). Rates are similarly high in the UK, where every 30 seconds the police receive a call for assistance relating to domestic abuse (Laville 2014).

## The costs of domestic violence

Domestic violence is tremendously costly in a variety of ways, but in particular how it affects communities. The Centers for Disease Control (CDC) has estimated domestic violence costs $8.3 billion per year. Approximately $5.8 billion of that is in medical costs, with another $2.5 billion in lost productivity. Victims of domestic violence use emergency health care services eight times more frequently than do non-victims, which incurs both personal and societal costs (Chelala 2016). Women who have been abused are 70% more likely to have heart disease, 80% more likely to have a stroke, 60% more likely to develop asthma during their lifetime, three times more likely to suffer from depression, four times more likely to commit suicide and suffer from post-traumatic stress disorder (PTSD) at six times the rate of non-victims. Studies have found that the increased health care costs for victims can persist for as long as 15 years after the abuse (Pearl 2013). Additionally, some 64% of domestic violence victims say the abuse has affected their work, and it is estimated that victims lose 8 million paid days of work annually, and homicide by an intimate partner is the second-leading cause of death for women in the workplace (Day, McKenna and Bowlus 2005; Workplace Statistics 2016).

Data are clear that domestic violence is costly in other countries and regions as well. A 2004 study of domestic violence in England and Wales included three types of costs: 1) services, including criminal justice, health care, social services, housing, and civil legal assistance; 2) economic output losses, both for the victims and their families as well as for employers; and 3) human and emotional costs to the victim. It found that, for one year, the cost to the criminal justice system is around £1 billion, which is approximately one-quarter of the criminal justice system's annual budget for violent crime. Health care costs for physical injuries were estimated at £1.2 billion, with an addition £176 million for mental health care. Nearly £.25 billion is spent annually on social services, and an estimated £.16 billion is spent on housing for victims. Civil legal services cost an estimated £.3 billion. Lost economic output was estimated to be at least £2.7 billion. The biggest cost, however, was the emotional toll that domestic violence takes on victims, which is measured at £17 billion. Altogether, the cost of domestic violence in England and Wales totals a staggering £23 billion annually (Walby 2004).

## States' obligations to address domestic violence

In the late 1960s and into the 1970s, domestic violence emerged as a social issue, first in the UK and then in the United States. Initially, efforts were focused on getting victims to safety, followed by holding abusers accountable through the criminal justice system. As legislation was enacted to criminalize domestic violence, police and courts were required to treat the issue far more seriously. Yet decades later, there remain many weaknesses in the ways that states have responded to domestic violence.

Bettinger et al. (2011) note that states are obligated to respond to domestic violence, and that poorly trained police, under-prosecution of offenders and inadequate victim services are in violation of the fundamental human rights of women. According to international human rights agreements, states also have a duty to prevent domestic violence. In the Americas, this duty can be found in the American Declaration on the Rights and Duties of Man and other human rights documents. The United Nations Committee on the Elimination of Racial Discrimination has also recognized that violence against women is a violation of human rights and that states are obligated to protect and provide access to justice for victims, particularly women of colour, who face additional barriers in obtaining safety (Domestic Violence and Access to Justice 2008; Libal and Parekh 2009). Additionally, the International Covenant on Civil and Political Rights (ICCPR), adopted in 1966 and entered into force in 1976, requires member states to take steps to maintain gender equality and to protect people from victimization.

The UN Convention on the Elimination of All Forms of Discrimination Against Women (CEDAW) does not specifically address domestic violence, but the Committee on the Elimination of Discrimination Against Women, charged with overseeing CEDAW, was the first intergovernmental human rights organization to consider domestic violence to be a denial of human rights and to recommend states take preventive measures. Article 4 does articulate that states must exercise due diligence to prevent and investigate all acts of violence, whether those acts are perpetrated by private individuals or the state. It also requires that states develop "penal, civil, labour and administrative sanctions" in their domestic legislation to assist women who are victims to violence. The Committee on the Elimination of Discrimination Against Women also explained that member nations may be responsible for private acts of abuse if they fail to enact preventative programs, to respond effectively and to provide compensation to victims (Domestic Violence and Access to Justice 2008).

Paragraph 124(d) of the Beijing Platform for Action (BPfA), adopted by the Fourth World Conference on Women, calls for states to have programmes and policies for women who have been victims of violence to obtain and maintain safety, including compensation (Access to Justice for Women Victims of Violence in the Americas 2007: 32). The American Convention on Human Rights, the American Declaration on the Rights and Duties of Man and the

Convention of Belem do Para also require that member states establish effective judicial remedies to violence against women. All major countries in the Organization of American States (OAS) have ratified the Inter-American Convention on the Prevention, Punishment, and Eradication of Violence Against Women, which is the only international treaty specifically addressing violence against women. The treaty allows groups or individuals to petition the Inter-American Commission on Human Rights (IACHR) for redress of human rights violations (Bettinger et al. 2011).

## Inadequate laws

The primary piece of federal legislation related to domestic violence in the United States is the Violence Against Women Act (VAWA), which was originally enacted in 1994 and has been reauthorized several times since. According to Bettinger et al. (2011), VAWA fails to accomplish three critical objectives: (1) it does not authorize a direct remedy when abusers or police officers violate victims' rights; (2) there is no requirement that all states participate or that they monitor their progress; and (3) it does not adequately fund all the services that are needed to ensure victim safety.

The 1994 version of VAWA authorized federal lawsuits against those who "commit a crime of violence motivated by gender," and the attorneys general of 38 states supported this measure because the state courts were incapable of addressing gender-based violence adequately. In its original intent, then, VAWA provided battered women with an important federal remedy against their perpetrators. In 2000, however, in *United States v. Morrison*, the Supreme Court invalidated this portion of VAWA, holding that Congress did not have the authority to create such a remedy. No other federal remedies have been authorized, which clearly violates the human rights treaties cited previously (Bettinger et al. 2011).

VAWA provides funding for domestic violence advocacy and for victims of domestic violence. Yet this funding merely encourage states, localities and agencies to act on a voluntary basis. It does not mandate that individual states provide comprehensive services. As such, VAWA does not fulfil the United States' duty to protect the human rights of women, as the human rights treaties described earlier did not obligate states to help only if they feel like it. The voluntary nature of VAWA grants also means that money often fails to reach those who are most in need (Bettinger et al. 2011).

Although guns are more heavily controlled in the UK, the United States has a tremendous problem with gun violence in general. Guns increase the likelihood that someone will be killed in a domestic violence situation by at least five times (Jeltsen 2016). One problem with the federal law is the definition of domestic abuse that is used, which requires that the couple be currently or formerly married, cohabiting or the parents of shared children. This "boyfriend loophole" means that many abusers who do not live with their victims are exempt (unless they are prohibited due to a different conviction). The federal gun ban also does not address guns already owned by the abuser.

Some local and state governments have passed laws that force convicted domestic abusers or subjects of domestic violence restraining orders to turn in their guns. Research has shown these to be effective, with studies showing a 25% lower murder rates in those states compared to those that don't require abusers to relinquish their weapons (Domestic violence and firearms, n.d.). Still, only nine states have relinquishment laws, and enforcement of relinquishment laws or of the federal gun ban for domestic abusers is woefully inadequate (Domestic violence and firearms, n.d.).

The result is that, despite the bans, many perpetrators continue to keep or are allowed to purchase new weapons. A March 2013 investigation by the *New York Times* found that more than 50 people in Washington State were arrested on gun charges in 2011, even though those individuals were subject to protective orders. In a three-year period, more than 30 people in Minnesota were convicted of an assault with a dangerous weapon against a partner while subject to protective orders (Luo 2013). Many judges fail to order perpetrators to relinquish their weapons, and police are not generally trained or authorized to seize them. One study by Everytown for Gun Safety found that judges ordered defendants to surrender their guns in only 5% of qualifying domestic violence cases between 2012 and 2014, and even when the judge knew the offender had access to weapons the study found that only 13% of the time did a judge order a defendant to surrender his weapons in domestic violence cases (Cauterucci 2015; Mascia 2015).

## Police failure to protect

Police, judges and other criminal justice personnel are often not adequately trained. Consequently, they are not prepared to provide appropriate remedies to victims. Police officers in the United States and UK still treat domestic violence informally, sometimes failing to even produce a report of the incident. In 10% of cases across the United States, police failed to respond at all to reports of domestic violence and in 30% of cases in which victims request police assistance no official report is made. They often do not arrest perpetrators even in cases where the evidence is clear that an arrest could be made. Results from the National Violence Against Women Survey show that arrests are made in less than half of all cases, and even less frequently in cases of sexual assault and stalking. Police are still less likely to make an arrest when a husband feloniously assaults his wife than in other felony assault cases (Bettinger et al. 2011).

Police also often fail to respond to restraining order violations. An IACHR commission noted that women are often killed despite having contacted police, as they fail to enforce protective orders or other legislation. The case of Jessica Lenahan-Gonzales highlights this problem. In 1999, Jessica Lenahan-Gonzales's estranged husband, Simon Gonzales, took her three girls from their yard where they were playing. This was a violation of a permanent restraining order due to Simon's abuse. The order required him to remain at least 100 yards from Jessica and her children unless it was a scheduled visitation, which it was not. Jessica contacted the police multiple times, even visiting the Castle Rock police station, and was told despite her growing despair about what might happen that no action would be taken. In the early hours of the morning, Simon Gonzales pulled up to the police station and opened fire. Police officers returned fire, killing Gonzales. They also found that the three girls were dead in his vehicle as well. Jessica's legal case against the police for their failure to protect her and her girls reached the Supreme Court, which ruled 7–2 that Castle Rock and its police could not be sued for their failure to protect her by refusing to enforce the restraining order. Upset but not willing to quit, Jessica's attorneys brought the case before the IACHR in 2011. That court held that the United States failed to protect both Lenahan and her daughters from domestic violence and to provide equal protection before the law, both human rights violations (Finley 2010a).

Additionally, many officers still encourage victims to work out their issues with abusers, rather than providing them the required legal assistance. In one study, 40% of police departments explicitly encouraged mediation, and one half had no formal policy on domestic violence. Police frequently tell the parties simply to "cool off," as if there is no obligation to take the matter seriously (Bettinger et al. 2011).

Sometimes police do respond but fail to conduct adequate investigations or keep appropriate records. This lack of an extensive paper trail can seriously impede the victims' short-term and long-term access to various remedies. A 2002 study found that in almost half of the cases, officers did not take photographs, even though victims had visible injuries, and in 27% of the cases, officers did not ask victims about the perpetrator's history of abuse (Bettinger et al. 2011). This is in spite of sufficient data showing that domestic violence is patterned behaviour that escalates over time.

Another concern is mandatory arrest policies In the 1980s, the Minneapolis Domestic Violence Experiment conducted by Sherman and Berk resulted in mandatory arrest policies being enacted across the United States. Critics note, however, that mandatory arrest policies place victims in danger of retaliatory violence, and that they disempower victims who may not actually want their abuser arrested. In some cases in which it is difficult to determine who the aggressor is, police may make dual arrests, which then re-victimizes the party who was not at fault (Celik 2013). Victims have been arbitrarily arrested in conjunction with, or in some cases instead of, their abusers. These women are subjected to additional violence at the hands of the state, in the form of force during arrest, threats to remove and actual removal of children into the hands of the state, strip searches and other degrading conditions of confinement. This is even worse for women of colour, who are more likely to be arrested as a result of mandatory arrest policies than are Caucasian women (Police Violence &

Domestic Violence n.d.). It's also unclear that mandatory arrest works, as some studies have found that victims are more likely to be killed if their abuser was arrested and incarcerated rather than being warned and returned to the home (Sherman and Harris 2014).

Yet another issue is the over-representation of police officers as abusers. Two studies found that law enforcement families endured abuse at rates four times those of the general public. Another study focusing only on older, more experienced officers found 28% more domestic violence (Pyke 2015). Yet accusations against officers are often handled informally, and few who are found guilty suffer any serious sanction (Friedersdorf 2014). Rarely do these allegations result in prosecution. In 1998–1999, there were 23 domestic violence complaints levied against Boston police yet not one resulted in criminal prosecution. A study of the Los Angeles Police Department found 91 cases of domestic violence between 1990 and 1997, but in more than three-quarters of those cases, the allegations were not even mentioned in the officer's performance review. Twenty-nine percent of the officers facing allegations were promoted, with some being promoted within two years of the alleged incident (Police Family Violence Fact Sheet n.d.). Shockingly, a 1995 study found only 19% of surveyed departments reported that an officer would be terminated as a result of a second allegation of domestic violence. Despite the gun prohibition for domestic abusers, police officers who are convicted of abuse are rarely asked to relinquish their weapons (Finley 2010a).

Despite being particularly vulnerable to abuse, Native American women living on reservations suffer disproportionally from the states' failure to protect them from domestic violence. Laws prevent tribal police from acting on complaints in felony cases or when the situation involves a non-Native, thus leaving it to federal authorities, who do not adequately respond (Bhungalia 2001). Further, the time it takes for such a response means that many Native women suffer more serious injuries or even killed before law enforcement arrives. Many Native women describe being re-victimized by law enforcement (Bhungalia 2001). Because issues of jurisdiction are so complicated between reservations and state and federal law, many times law enforcement officers simply choose not to get involved (Bhungalia 2001).

Immigrant women, especially those who are undocumented, are at greater risk for enduring abuse and yet are less protected. When they report domestic violence to police, they risk being arrested and deported. The lack of interpreters also results in difficulties for immigrant victims, documented or not. Law enforcement often ride along with Border Patrol in border states like California, Texas and Arizona, so victims are simply afraid to call the police for help (Police Violence and Domestic Violence n.d.). Arab, Arab American and Muslim women have been refused help by police, who make derogatory comments about them. They have also been turned away from shelters because staff are concerned they will draw attention from the police (Police Violence & Domestic Violence n.d.).

In 2012, *The Guardian* reported that, in the four years prior, there were 56 cases in the UK involving police officers and a handful of community support officers who either were found to have abused their position to rape, sexually assault or harass women and young people or were investigated over such allegations (Laville 2012).

In 2014, then-home secretary Minister Theresa May vowed to take over how police handle domestic violence after a report by Her Majesty's Inspectorate of Constabulary (HMIC) found that only 8 out of 43 forces responded well to domestic violence. The report identified "poor attitudes, ineffective training and inadequate evidence gathering" and called for a dramatic change in police response. The report also documented a "considerable lack of empathy" in the handling of domestic violence cases, citing a case in which officers were overheard calling a victim a "fucking slag." Police did not take victims seriously and failed to use basic investigative techniques in numerous cases. For example, they found that photographs of injuries were taken in only half of 600 domestic abuse cases in which bodily harm was a factor (Laville 2014).

As should be clear, and has been noted by prominent domestic violence scholars, these problems go beyond any individual officer or department. Rather, they are systemic and, as such, indicative of the state's failure to protect victims per international human rights law (Stark 2007). As Pearce pointed out, these system failures are quite often by design, as in one way or another they benefit the status quo. In this case, it is easy to see that aggressive police hungry for power and control are, if not literally, figuratively comparable to abusers.

## Court failures

The inadequate treatment of domestic violence cases in court begins with the process of obtaining restraining or protective orders. Traumatized victims find it difficult to recount the terror of their situations to a degree that the courts will grant the order, especially when so many go it alone. There is a scarcity of advocates who can accompany victims in this process. When a victim does obtain a hearing, it is often cursory, which means the full scope of the threat rarely emerges (Waldron 2015). Further, although courtroom procedures are often intimidating, in these cases abusers are sometimes able to confront their victims beforehand, given the layout of courtrooms (Finley 2010b). Sometimes judges place limitations on the evidence they will allow, failing to consider the unique circumstances of a specific case (Bettinger et al. 2011). These hearings are especially difficult for victims who need interpreters, most frequently immigrant women, because finding an interpreter uses up more of the few minutes that a victim may have to tell her story.

In addition, judges often encourage survivors to negotiate with their batterers. This is in spite of research that documents the power and control exercised by abusers and shows the difficulties victims face due to their subordinate position (Bettinger et al. 2011). Importantly, abusers are rarely prosecuted at all, let alone convicted. In a 2002 Department of Justice study of 16 large urban counties, about half of domestic violence offenders facing prosecution were convicted, and only 18% of those defendants were convicted of felonies. Regardless of the prosecution and conviction rates, victims often decide not to report because they believe it to be ineffective (Bettinger et al. 2011).

Supreme Court rulings have also affected the likelihood that a domestic violence victim will receive appropriate remedy in court. In the 2004 case of *Crawford v. Washington*, the Court decided that in cases in which testimonial statements are to be admitted at trial without the in-court testimony of the declarant, the accused must have the opportunity to confront the declarant before the trial. The result of this decision is that if a woman refuses to testify because she is afraid of seeing her abuser in the courtroom, the case could be dismissed because the accused did not have the opportunity to confront beforehand. This case and its companion decisions have increased the opportunities for domestic violence offenders to intimidate witnesses and tamper with evidence. Research shows that 80% to 90% of abuse victims are unwilling to testify at trial, so their cases are likely to be dismissed on the grounds of this Confrontation Clause (Bettinger et al. 2011).

In England and Wales, only one in eight reported domestic violence cases went to trial in 2004, and 5.4% resulted in conviction (Making the Grade? 2007). Despite signing the Beijing Platform for Action, the 2007 Making the Grade Report, sponsored by End Violence Against Women (EVAW), found that government activity to reduce violence against women in the UK was still inadequate.

## Failure to fully provide for victim services

In some cases, it seems as though states have shifted their responsibility for addressing violence against women to non-profit organizations or nongovernmental organizations (NGOs). Although non-profits and NGOs have developed some very useful responses, this is a huge abdication of the states' responsibility (Finley 2010b; Finley and Esposito 2011). Further, there simply are not enough non-profits or NGOs offering the needed services. Each year the National Network to End Domestic Violence (NNEDV) conducts a 24-hour census of requests for help, and each year it finds some 11,000 or even more victims are turned away due to restrictions on what can be provided, capacity issues or funding concerns (Jeltsen 2016). President Trump has pledged to cut funding for federal programmes that support domestic violence victims, including the grants that are administered by the Department of Justice (Caldwell 2017).

In the UK, budget cuts are reducing services for victims and perhaps even closing shelters. In November, activist group Sisters Uncut blocked bridges in November 2016 to protest the cuts. Reports have shown that two-thirds of survivors are turned away by shelters, due to reasons like lack of space, language barriers and an inability to meet victims' needs. The numbers are much higher among Black and ethnic minority women, with support services turning away 80% of survivors (WITW Staff 2016). If these cuts are made, Sunderland will be to the only major city in the UK without a domestic violence shelter (McIntyre 2017).

## Conclusion

In sum, the failure to protect victims from domestic violence and to adequately assist those who have been victimized is a form of state crime. State crime occurs when the state acts against its own citizens or the citizens of another country during the course of a conflict, or when the state fails to act when it is obligated to do so (Green and Ward 2004; Kramer 1994; White 2008). As this chapter shows, states clearly have an obligation to protect women from domestic violence. When they fail to do so, it can be considered an example of state crime (Finley 2010a). The powerful have the means and responsibility to do far more to protect women from domestic violence and to assist those who have been victimized. Yet as Pearce so clearly articulated, their deviance may be that of commission, but it can also be that of omission, or failing to do what is required.

As Stark (2007) explained, states should honour those human rights treaties they have adopted and consider adopting legislation that fully supports victims of domestic violence. According to the IACHR, the failure to investigate and prosecute cases of violence against women rises to the level of systemic impunity which perpetuates violence against women. The United States definitely needs to ratify CEDAW, given that Richards and Haglund (2015) found that adoption of international human rights law, in particular, the Convention on the Elimination of All Forms of Discrimination Against Women (CEDAW) results in stronger domestic laws and better protections for women.

Just as Pearce called for a "serious study of the state and its agents and of the activities of the ruling class" (1976: 158), I call on radical criminologists to include in their examination of crimes of the powerful the harmful policies and practices that leave women in desperate fear.

## References

Access to Justice for Women Victims of Violence in the Americas. (2007, January 20). *Rapporteurship on the Rights of Women.* Available HTTP: https://www.cidh.oas.org/women/access07/tocaccess.htm (accessed 28 March 2018).

Bettinger-Lopez et al. (2011) "Domestic violence in the United States: A Preliminary Report Prepared for Rashida Manjoo." U.N. Special Rapporteur on Violence Against Women. Online. Available HTTP: www.reproductiverights.org/sites/crr.civicactions.net/files/newsletter/DV%20in%20the%20US_Br%20Paper%20to%20SR%20on%20VAW.pdf (accessed 28 January 2017).

Bhungalia, L. (2001) "Native American Women and Violence." *National NOW Times,* Spring. Online. Available HTTP: www.now.org/nnt/spring-2001/nativeamerican.html (accessed 14 February 2011).

Caldwell, P. (2017) "Donald Trump Might Cut Violence Against Women Programs." *Mother Jones*, 19 January. Online. Available HTTP: www.motherjones.com/politics/2017/01/donald-trump-end-violence-against-women-grants (accessed 31 January 2017).

Cauterucci, C. (2015) "How Domestic Violence Abusers Get to Keep their Guns." *Slate*, 28 October. Online. Available HTTP: www.slate.com/blogs/xx_factor/2015/10/28/how_convicted_domestic_abusers_get_to_keep_their_guns.html (accessed 31 January 2017).

Çelik, A. (2013) "An Analysis of Mandatory Arrest Policy on Domestic Violence." *International Journal of Human Sciences*, 10(1): 1503–1523.

Chelala, C. (2016) "The Public Health Impact of Domestic Violence." *Counterpunch*, 5 February. Online. HTTPS: www.counterpunch.org/2016/02/05/the-public-health-impact-of-domestic-violence/ (accessed 31 January 2016).

Chemaly, S. (2012) "50 Actual Facts about Domestic Violence." *Huffington Post*. Online. Available HTTP: www.huffingtonpost.com/soraya-chemaly/50-actual-facts-about-dom_b_2193904.html (accessed 31 December 2016).

Day, T., McKenna, K. and Bowlus, A. (2005) "The Economic Costs of Violence against Women: An Evaluation of the Literature." *UN Women Watch*. Online. Available HTTP: www.un.org/womenwatch/daw/vaw/expert%20brief%20costs.pdf (accessed 31 December 2016).

Domestic Violence & Access to Justice: Response to the Periodic Report of the United States to the United Nations Committee on the Elimination of Racial Discrimination (2008, February) U.S. Human Rights Network. Online. Available HTTP: www.ushrnetwork.org/files/ushrn/images/linkfiles/CERD/15Domestic%20Violence.pdf (accessed 7 January 2012).

Finley, L. (2010a) *Examining Domestic Violence as a State Crime: Nonkilling Implications.* Global Nonkilling Working Paper #2.

——— (2010b) "Where's the Peace in this Movement? A Domestic Violence Advocate's Reflections on the Movement." *Contemporary Justice Review*, 13(1): 57–69.

Finley, L. and Esposito, L. (2011). "Neoliberalism and the Non-Profit Industrial Complex: The Limits of a Market Approach to Service Delivery." *Peace Studies Journal*, 5(3): 4–26.

Friedersdorf, C. (2014, September 19). "Police Have a Much Bigger Domestic-Abuse Problem Than the NFL Does." *The Atlantic*. Available HTTP: https://www.theatlantic.com/national/archive/2014/09/police-officers-who-hit-their-wives-or-girlfriends/380329/ (accessed 29 March 2018).

Garcia-Moreno, C., Jansen, H., Ellsberg, M., Heise, L. and Watts, C. (2005). *WHO Multi-Country Study on Women's Health and Domestic Violence Against Women.* Geneva: World Health Organization.

Green, P. and T. Ward (eds.) (2004). *State Crime: Governments, Violence and Corruption.* London: Pluto Press.

Jeltsen, M. (2016) "Supreme Court Affirms that Even "reckless" Domestic Abusers Should Lose Gun Rights." *Huffington Post*, 27 June. Online. Available HTTP: www.huffingtonpost.com/entry/supreme-court-domestic-violence-gun-rights_us_5771293fe4b0dbb1bbbb0e63 (accessed 31 January 2017).

Kramer, R. C. (1994). "State Violence and Violent Crime." *Peace Review* 6 (2): 171–175.

Laville, S. (2012) "Revealed: The Scale of Sexual Abuse by Police Officers." *The Guardian*, 29 June. Online. Available HTTP: www.theguardian.com/uk/2012/jun/29/guardian-investigation-abuse-power-police (accessed 28 January 2017).

Laville, S. (2014) "Police Failures Over Domestic Violence Exposed in Damning Report." *The Guardian*, 27 March. Online. Available HTTP: www.theguardian.com/society/2014/mar/27/police-failures-domestic-violence-damning-report (accessed 28 January 2017).

Libal, K. and Pareck, S. (2009). "Reframing Violence Against Women as a Human Rights Violation: Evan Stark's Coercive Control." *Violence Against Women*, 15(12): 1477–1489.

Luo, M. (2013, 2017) "In Some States, Gun Rights Trump Orders of Protection." *The New York Times*, March. Online. Available HTTP: from www.nytimes.com/2013/03/18/us/facing-protective-orders-and-allowed-to-keep-guns.html?pagewanted=all&_r=0 (accessed 31 January 2017).

Making the Grade? (2007). *End Violence Against Women*. Available HTTP: http://www.evaw intl.org/makingthegrade (accessed 29 March 2018).

Mascia, J. (2015) "Domestic Abusers Frequently Get to Keep their Guns: Here Are the Big Reasons Why." *The Trace*, 26 October. Online. Available HTTP: www.thetrace.org/2015/10/domestic-abuse-guns-boyfriend-loophole/ (accessed 31 January 2017).

McIntyre, S. (2017) "Sunderland Set to Become UK's Only Major City Without Any Domestic Violence Refuges For Women." *The Independent*, 2 January. Online. Available HTTP: www.independent.co.uk/news/uk/home-news/sunderland-domestic-violence-womens-refuges-wearside-women-in-need-a7506186.html (accessed 28 January 2017).

Murray, A. (2008) *From Outrage to Courage: Women Taking Action For Health and Justice*. Monroe, ME: Common Courage.

Park, M. (2013) "WHO: 1 in 3 Women Experience Physical or Sexual Violence." *CNN*, 20 June. Online. Available HTTP: www.cnn.com/2013/06/20/health/global-violence-women/ (accessed 28 January 2017).

Parker, C. (2014) "Women and Children Bear Brunt of Domestic Violence, Stanford Scholar Says." *Stanford Report*, 24 September. Online. Available HTTP: http://news.stanford.edu/news/2014/september/domestic-violence-toll-092314.html (accessed 31 December 2016).

Pearl, R. (2013) "Domestic Violence: The Secret Killer that Costs $8.3 Billion Annually." *Forbes*, 5 December. Online. Available HTTP: www.forbes.com/sites/robertpearl/2013/12/05/domestic-violence-the-secret-killer-that-costs-8-3-billion-annually/#2f126413c136 (accessed 31 December 2016).

Pearce, F. (1976). *Crimes of the Powerful: Marxism, Crime and Deviance*. London: Pluto Press.

Pyke, A. (2015) "New Report on Police Deaths Comes With Grim Revelations." *Think Progress*. Online. Available HTTP: from https://thinkprogress.org/new-report-on-police-deaths-comes-with-grim-revelations-516b20b0dff7#.o9v1lcn45 (accessed 31 December 2016).

Richards, D. and Haglund, J. (2015, February 11). "How Laws Around the World Do and Do Not Protect Women From Violence." *Washington Post*. Available HTTP: https://www.washingtonpost.com/news/monkey-cage/wp/2015/02/11/how-laws-around-the-world-do-and-do-not-protect-women-from-violence/?utm_term=.f721084fb9d4 (accessed 29 March 2018).

Sherman, L. and Harris, H. (2014) "Increased Death Rates of Domestic Violence Victims From Arresting vs. Warning Suspects in the Milwaukee Domestic Violence Experiment (MilDVE)." *Journal of Experimental Criminology*, 1–20.

Stark, E. (2007) *Coercive Control: How Men Entrap Women in Personal Life*. New York: Oxford University Press.

Walby, S. (2004) "The Cost of Domestic Violence." *England's Women and Equality Unit*. Online. Available HTTP: http://citeseerx.ist.psu.edu/viewdoc/download?doi=10.1.1.393.886&rep=rep1&type=pdf (accessed 25 November 2016).

Waldron, T. (2015) "Why Victims of Domestic Violence Don't Testify, Particularly Against NFL Players." *Think Progress*, 11 February. Online. Available HTTP: https://thinkprogress.

org/why-victims-of-domestic-violence-dont-testify-particularly-against-nfl-players-qe76fe2e39165#.v41nm3ffr (accessed 31 December 2016).

WHO. (2013) "Global and Regional Estimates of Violence Against Women: Prevalence and Health Effects of Intimate Partner Violence and Non-partner Sexual Violence." Online. Available HTTP: http://apps.who.int/iris/bitstrcam/10665/85239/1/9789241564625_eng.pdf (accessed 31 December 2016).

White, R. (2008). "Depleted Uranium, State Crime, and the Politics of Knowing." *Theoretical Criminology*, 12, 31–54.

WITW Staff. (2016) "U.K. Activist Group Blocks Bridges While Protesting Cuts to Domestic Violence Services." *New York Times*, 21 November. Online. Available HTTP: http://nytlive.nytimes.com/womenintheworld/2016/11/21/u-k-activist-group-blocks-bridges-while-protesting-cuts-to-domestic-violence-services/ (accessed 28 January 2017).

Workplace Statistics. (2016). *Corporate Alliance to End Domestic Violence*. Available HTTP: from http://www.caepv.org/getinfo/facts_stats.php?factsec=3 (accessed 29 March 2018).

# Chapter 21

# "Punitive reformation"

## State-sanctioned labour through criminal justice and welfare

*Jon Burnett*

This chapter examines an aspect of the "imaginary social order" that was integral to the analysis within *Crimes of the Powerful*, but has rarely been adequately explored: the "belief that the interests of labour are essentially the same as the interests of capital" (Pearce 1976: 98). As Frank Pearce powerfully demonstrated, considerable ideological work went into constructing and reproducing the idea that the relationship between labour and capital was basically consensual, and certainly democratic, in the forms of social order that were the subject of his analysis. Yet despite the importance of this insight – not least for its contribution to the theorization of the state within *Crimes of the Powerful* – it is an observation that some four decades later needs expansion. Against the backdrop of the sustained neoliberal revolution that has swept through the political and cultural landscape, unwaged or-sub-waged labour has been (re)embedded and reformulated in the delivery of mainstream welfare and criminal policy: through an explosion of workfare, through a resurgent enthusiasm for prison labour and through a commitment to unpaid work as an element of community sentencing. And in this context, it is not just the interests of labour that are portrayed as being the same as the interests of capital. So, too, are the interests of labour forms mandated or administered through the delivery of criminal justice and social policy.

Building on this analysis, this chapter examines the delivery and development of these labour forms by taking a specific historical juncture as a starting point: the formation in the UK of a Conservative-led coalition government in 2010. This, of course, does not mark the beginning of any of these initiatives. They all have long and varying histories. But it does mark a stage where there were concerted attempts to intensify their use, whilst linking them in political discourse through several intertwining themes including the valorization of "work" in terms of tackling poverty, affecting health and wellbeing (see Jones 2010; Patrick 2014) and as a form of character reformation (Ministry of Justice 2010). At the same time, this period also marks a key juncture in which already existing moves to open up these forms of labour to private enterprise have been further entrenched, coming together to transform them into significant sources of profit.

As such, what follows begins by providing a brief descriptive overview of the scale of these schemes and how they have been developed under the most recent Conservative and Conservative-led governments. It discusses how workfare and criminal justice policies produce a sub-section of the UK's labour force that although marginal, is nonetheless significant. Tens of thousands of people per year work in such contexts, providing millions of hours of unwaged or sub-waged labour for charities, local authorities, community projects and businesses across the UK, as well as those companies that have swooped in to take advantage of the ongoing shift towards contracting out its delivery. And this chapter attempts to show how the analysis embedded in *Crimes of the Powerful* provides a basis for developing a way of thinking about these forms of labour *as a labour force*. Indeed, it is the contention of this chapter that examining these things as a form of labour reveals something about the contemporary "real," as opposed to "imagined," social order.

## The (re)construction of a state-sanctioned workforce

In 2010, the Conservative Party returned to electoral power in Britain, forming a coalition government with the Liberal Democrats and ending nearly two decades of Labour rule. The coalition lasted five years. And in this time it embarked upon a programme of criminal justice and welfare reform which sought to place work at its centre and has continued (albeit not uncontested) since. Within this context, the commitment to workfare, to penal labour and to unpaid labour as a part of community sentencing was clear.

A key driver of this programme was the promise of a "rehabilitation revolution": among the first major pledges of the coalition government. A Green Paper published in 2010 – *Breaking the Cycle: Effective Punishment, Rehabilitation and Sentencing of Offenders* – set out the scope of this ambition clearly, arguing that the "administration of punishment" was going to be transformed in order to become "more robust and credible." "Prisons will become places of hard work and industry, instead of enforced idleness," the Green Paper suggested. "There will be greater use of strenuous, unpaid work as part of a community sentence alongside tagging and curfews, delivered swiftly after sentencing." These measures should not be viewed "in isolation," it went on to explain. For they stood alongside reforms relating to policing, welfare changes "to encourage employment and dramatically reduce the number of workless households" and "early intervention with children most at risk," so as to reduce the chance they would follow "criminal paths" (Ministry of Justice 2010: 1–2). Criminal justice reform, in other words, was seen in conjunction with broader aspects of social policy, and the government made clear that it wanted to revolutionize their delivery by opening them up (more than already was the case) to private enterprise.

### Prison labour

A desire to put "hard work and industry" at the core of the prison system is, of course, nothing new. Indeed, when setting out its penal policy a few years earlier, the Conservative Party had implied that it would be the heir to a much longer sense of mission, claiming that "In the 19th century prisons became the pioneers of social reform" (The Conservative Party 2008: 2). But although prison labour has a long history, what was in the offing was a thorough examination of its role. *Breaking the Cycle* indicated that more prisoners would be expected to work a full working week in a "structured and disciplined environment," that provisions of the Prisoners' Earnings Act 1996 would be implemented so as to allow deduction of wages that could be transferred to a Victims' Fund as "reparations" and that the private, voluntary and community sectors would be harnessed to provide expertise in developing "working prisons" (Ministry of Justice 2010: 14). In order to achieve these aims, it was deemed necessary to "develop the market," overcoming "the barriers that prevent independent providers from getting involved in prison industry," and ultimately open up much more prison labour to the private sector. In this context:

> Prison should be a place where work itself is central to the regime, where offenders learn vocational skills in environments organised to replicate, as far as practical and appropriate, real working conditions.
>
> (Ministry of Justice 2010: 15)

Within a few years, these plans were being given a more concrete feel. In 2012 Justice Secretary Ken Clarke claimed that he would double the prison workforce, from 10,000 to 20,000 prisoners working full time, arguing that: "Right now, prisoners are simply a wasted resource – thousands of hours of manpower sitting idle" (cited in Whitehead 2012). The Prison Industries Unit was rebranded as One3One Solutions, part of the National Offender Management Service (NOMS), encouraging more businesses to use prison labour in their supply chains and it, in turn, pledged to massively expand revenue by 2021 (Wright 2012). According to its promotional material: "Our flexibility and our commitment to offer more work opportunities to prisoners means that we are ready right now to offer more to business" (One3One Solutions 2013: 3). But this is a form of flexibility for which prisoners themselves bear the cost. As the Industrial Workers of the World (IWW) Incarcerated Workers Organising Committee has emphasized, some prisoners only command wages of £4 per week (if working full time), with others earning up to £25 per week in workshops run by private companies. But even with such small financial rewards, working is frequently necessary to try and secure the basic means to procure essential items, and if prisoners refuse to work they can be "punished via the IEP (Incentives and Earned Privileges Scheme), and can have visits, association (time outside in a courtyard or out of cell) and other 'privileges' [taken] away from them" (Incarcerated Workers Organising Committee 2017).

By the time that the (then) Home Secretary Liz Truss promised to give prisons "the biggest overhaul in a generation" then, in November 2016, promising £1.3 billion investment against the backdrop of a prison "crisis," the market for prison labour was becoming much more well established (BBC 2016). The target for 20,000 prisoners may not have been met, with around 11,000 prisoners working equating to around 13% of the prison population. But the infrastructure was certainly showing signs of expansion. In the financial year 2015–2016, One3One Solutions' financial data showed more than 350 contracts worth well over £5 million, with customers including sports clubs, book distributors, hospitals, laundry services, recycling companies, textile companies, government departments, call centres and diecasters. The labour that prisoners provided ranged from recycling work, to general assembly and packing, to laundry work, agricultural work, call centre operation, textiles, printing and woodwork (One3One Solutions 2017). Prisoners worked around 16 million hours in 2015–2016 (Prison Reform Trust 2016: 46). And although elements of the Conservative prison reform agenda are certainly contested, as the Empty Cages Collective (2017: 19) has discussed, prison labour remains integral. Of six new "mega-prisons" that have been announced, for example, the "centre-piece" of them are their "workshops," with one having the capacity to employ some 800 prisoners at any given time.

### Unpaid work

But if this indicates a commitment to contracting out prison labour, it is only one part of a much bigger shift within criminal justice in which the role of "work" is central. At around the same time that the Coalition government was pledging to place "hard work" at the crux of prison policy, it was crystallizing already-existing moves to further embed competition in probation, privatize around 70% of probation services and "reform" the role of unpaid labour in the community. The publication of a series of consultations and strategy documents, including a Competition Strategy for Offender Services and Transforming Rehabilitation: Strategy for Reform, made clear what these plans would look like, as well as the delivery of unpaid work within them (Bardens and Garton Grimwood 2013). And in 2012, the Ministry of Justice announced that global outsourcing giant Serco, working with the London Probation Trust, had won a four-year £37 million contract to oversee unpaid labour schemes in London, with the company promising to deliver savings of some £25 million. "This partnership will bring innovation and deliver a tougher, swifter Community Payback service that offers real value for the taxpayer," said the Minister for Probation Jeremy Wright (cited in Ministry of Justice 2012b). Yet just two years later, the contract was ended early, with whistle-blowers claiming that there were inaccuracies in the recording of placements (Sofos 2013), the probation and family court union NAPO stating that it had been a "scandalous waste of public money" and the government saying that the exercise would be incorporated into the broader "transforming rehabilitation programme" (Brown 2014). Under this programme, by 2014, 35 individual Probation Trusts had been amalgamated into a National Probation Service and 21 Community Rehabilitation Companies (CRCs), the latter of which were mandated to manage offenders defined as low-to-medium risk across 21 "contract package areas" in England and Wales. CRCs were formed as partnerships led frequently by the private sector merged with public-sector agencies, social enterprises and charities (for details see Clinks 2014). From this point onwards, they would deliver unpaid work in a context where its role was, and continues to be, under development (see Her Majesty's Inspectorate of Probation 2016).

Part of this development was a commitment to ensuring that unpaid work would be more punitive. And in doing so, this continued a trajectory embedded by the previous government, which some years earlier had rebranded unpaid work as *community payback* along similar lines. But if these provided some of the starting points of the coalition's reforms, they were taken further. In 2011, Minister for Prisons and Probation Crispin Blunt announced that more offenders given community sentences would be forced to do "hard labour" and that they would begin much sooner after sentencing. Unemployed offenders would be forced to work a minimum of 28 hours per week, with an added greater emphasis on job hunting when not working. "If you are unemployed and on Community Payback," Blunt suggested, "you shouldn't be sitting idle at home watching daytime television or hanging about with your mates on a street corner, you should be out paying back to your community through hard, honest work" (cited in Ministry of Justice 2011). These suggestions are now integrated into policy. And part of this "paying back" involves attempts to ensure that unpaid work is much more visible (through greater emphasis on pre-existing requirements for offenders to wear clothing with "community payback" branded on the back), that (as already stated) work is "harder," that work is more intensive and that communities have a much greater role in directing where and how offenders should be put to work (again, this built on already existing measures). Thus, interested groups are encouraged to put forward ideas for labour projects, with local newspapers circulating call-outs for their readers (see, as one example, Bath Chronicle 2013), and a government website enabling interested groups to submit suggestions online. One promotional document tells potential beneficiaries that the scheme provides "each community with a free workforce each year" (Hampshire Probation Trust 2015: 5). And although the use of unpaid work is decreasing in some contexts, it is, per a thematic inspection of unpaid work published in 2016, the most frequently imposed component of community sentences. In 2014, for example, unpaid work was imposed as part of over 70,000 community sentences, and it was the sole component in around 36,500 of them (Her Majesty's Inspectorate of Probation 2016: 10).[1]

Some estimates equate that to around 7 million hours of unpaid labour per year, worth more than £50 million per year if the minimum wage were paid, on things like environmental projects, litter picking, building and landscaping projects, painting and decorating jobs and for retail businesses. The maximum time that people can work is 300 hours, and the stipulations for these projects are that they benefit the local community, do not take paid work away from others and do not make a profit for anyone. But there appears to be one caveat. The National Audit Office (2016: 4) estimates the value of these contracts for the bodies that have won them (of which unpaid work components are only one part) at around £259 million. "Essentially," says one CRC run by the training and skills provider Seetec, "we provide free labour" (Surrey and Sussex Community Rehabilitation Company 2017: 4).

### Intensifying workfare

According to David Skinns (2016: loc 3638), in an overview of the coalition government's penal policies, the "rehabilitation revolution" was driven in practice by an ideological commitment to opening up more business opportunities, a punitive philosophical bent and a desire to transform the way the services were delivered. And in this context, the government saw the administration of services on a "payment-by-results'" basis as fundamental. But in rolling out these mechanisms, it was able to draw on experience developed through the simultaneous delivery of other policy frameworks, not least of which was through its commitment to "workfare."

The coalition government was almost evangelical in its devotion to workfare when it came to power, introducing a plethora of different schemes over the next few years. For all this zeal though, the ground had undoubtedly already been paved. For if the beginnings of a modern-day workfare regime had been established in the 1980s, they were made real by Tony Blair's New Labour from 1997 onwards, with the then prime minister pledging in his first major speech that "[t]his will be the Welfare to Work government" (for discussion, see Peck 2001: 262). What the coalition government did, and the current government has attempted to continue, was to extend conditionality in the welfare system to a greater range of people and in a greater range of situations. "Workfare," the essence of which is described by the geographer Jamie Peck as "the imposition of a range of compulsory programs and mandatory requirements for welfare recipients with a view to *enforcing work while residualizing welfare*" (Ibid: 10, emphasis in original), has been one of the core mechanisms through which Conservative welfare reform has been driven. And it has ensured the availability of a substantial, permanently available, and super-exploitable labour force.

This has been fostered in several ways. The seemingly continual churn of new schemes and new ways to embed workfare ensures that its scope has followed a generally expansionist trajectory. The introduction of the flagship Universal

Credit, for example, has been key in an attempt to establish in-work conditionality. And effectively this raises the spectre of extending workfare from the unemployed to those in precarious, low-paid work (see Stone 2016). The introduction of a Work and Health Programme in 2017, meanwhile, has refocused the way workfare affects those with health conditions or disabilities and the long-term unemployed (see Mirza-Davies and McGuinness 2016). Although there is not the space here to discuss in detail the shifting parameters of workfare and its ideological drivers, it is salient to point out that this general direction of policy has been massively contested and in terms of *certain* programmes has been rolled back (see Boycott Workfare 2015, for example). But nonetheless, those who have benefitted from the mandatory free labour that workfare provides over the last few years has included, and in some cases still includes, a range of bodies such as charities, aid organizations, local authorities, businesses, social enterprises and so on.

At the same time, this has coincided with a broadening of the scope of those facilitating this coercive power – continuing a desire already in place to involve the private and third sector in delivering workfare. And in turn, this has been backed up by the intensification of the length and the quantity of sanctions and workfare requirements, meaning that people can be forced to work unpaid for longer and under threat of longer punishment. With some workfare schemes having enabled unpaid "placements" of up to six months and an overall thrust towards more intensive conditionality, this has had the impact of strengthening their coercive power. According to David Webster (2015) of the University of Glasgow, by 2013 benefit sanctions were being applied at such rate that there were more that year (over 1 million) than there were fines imposed by magistrates' and sheriff courts.

All of this has operated within the context of a bonanza for those companies circling for the lucrative contracts to be "providers." From the £400 million contract awarded to Atos (later awarded to Maximus) for carrying out fit-to-work assessments, to the £130 a year allocated for the Work and Health Programme (Mirza-Davies and McGuinness 2016), the market for workfare profiteering, certainly already established, has exploded over the last few years. And it is in this milieu, ultimately, that workfare polices ensure a sustained supply of unpaid labour. According to the Department of Work and Pensions, there were 1.81 million people referred to one of its major schemes, the Work Programme (later replaced by the Work and Health Programme) between June 2011 and December 2015 (cited in Learning and Work Institute 2016). Not all of these referrals, of course, will have necessarily led to workfare "placements." But nonetheless, the Work Programme was only one among several workfare schemes. According to the Office for National Statistics' UK labour market statistics in March 2017 (the most recent statistics at the time of writing), there were some 91,000 people, at that point, on "government-supported training and employment programmes" (Office for National Statistics 2017).

## Underpinning social order

What the following discussion has attempted to do is sketch out a very rough picture of the size of – and *some* of the immediate policies underpinning – three forms of labour as they have developed since the coalition government came to power in 2010. At the same time, it has attempted to show how the reforms that have been put in place since this point have built on an institutional framework already in place to ensure that this labour force provides an opportunity for capital – either through the substantial contracts for the delivery of these programmes, or through the availability of an unwaged or-sub waged workforce. This account, necessarily descriptive, is nonetheless partial. It is not an overarching historical overview of their development, which goes back much further than the coalition government. Nor is it an analytical account of policy formation. Rather, it gives some indication of the size of a sub-section of the "labour force" that, although undoubtedly marginal, is still important. Indeed, it points to tens of thousands of people per year working, no matter how temporarily, under the auspices of state-sanctioned labour schemes either administered or mandated through the criminal justice and the welfare systems.

In government literature, policy documentation and communications materials, work, in these contexts, has a practical, utilitarian function. All of these labour forms are described as providing skills necessary for the contemporary workplace, and thus offering a pathway for "reintegration." They are discussed as a way to build skills and confidence, for example, or to instil discipline, whilst at the same time having some form of reparative function. But what follows in the remainder of this chapter attempts to go beyond the *stated* aims of these labour forms and assess, in conjunction, their role and purpose as a labour *practice*. It examines their development, as stated in the introduction, against the backdrop of the sustained neoliberal revolution embedded within UK policy making. Drawing on *Crimes of the Powerful*, it looks at the ways these labour practices can be analysed as one component of a "real," as opposed to "imagined" social order.

## The interests of labour and capital

*Crimes of the Powerful* spanned an impressive historical sweep, drawing on the development of anti-trust laws in the late 19th century to moral crusades against certain forms of crime in the late 1960s. But although its scope was panoramic, it was written in, and spoke to, a particular historical moment in capitalist development, marked – in the UK at least – by what was depicted as a "crisis" of the post-war settlement and its Keynesian welfare state. In other words, it spoke to a particular time of struggle in which the ideological currents that would later usher in a period of neoliberalism were apparent, if not yet realized. And it was in this context that for Pearce, the construction of the notion that labour had the same interests as capital was central to the "imagined" social order he was analysing. For it was "[a]ccording to the capitalist worldview," he stated, that "labour is merely a factor of production, and like all such factors, it is desirable that it should be calculable and controllable." Furthermore: "If labour does not accept such an interpretation of itself certain problems may be created which the ruling class will then solve pragmatically, according to their perception of the realities of the situation" (Pearce 1976: 98–99).

These suggestions are instructive for the discussion here. All of the forms of labour described earlier contain within them traces of a series of historical, at times contradictory, ideas, including moves towards decarceration, the imposition of discipline, shifting ideological aims of imprisonment and pre-welfare state work philosophies. They speak simultaneously to punitive demands and rehabilitative visions. In this context their roles should not be seen as uniform or static, for they shift in conjunction with political, cultural and economic changes. But despite these swirling philosophical concerns, they are all depicted as forming one part of a "pragmatic" response to offending and unemployment or under-employment. And in the process, they feed into a neoliberal worldview that presumes an alliance of interests of its own: between recipients, "providers," beneficiaries and society as a whole. In this worldview then, it is not just labour, but sub-waged or un-waged labour sanctioned or facilitated by the state that is articulated as sharing an interest with capital. And in this context, they embody the intensified valorization of work and capital that is central to neoliberalism.

So, for example, workfare schemes draw explicitly on the idea that "work" is the most effective mechanism to combat poverty: depicted as being beneficial, without question, for one's health, one's relationships, one's future and for wider society. According to a 2007 Green Paper, for instance: "Work is the main route out of poverty for all groups within society. *Work is good for you*" (cited in Jones 2010: 15. Emphasis in original). For former Welfare Minister Iain Duncan Smith, unemployed people need "to learn that it's the right thing to go to work" (cited in Goulden 2012). While more latterly, according to Jones (2016), the government has announced its intention to "signpost the importance of employment as a health outcome in mandates, outcomes frameworks, and interactions with Clinical Commissioning Groups" (primarily for its Work and Health workfare programme). In a similar context, former Prisons Minister Crispin Blunt has argued: "Working in prisons is good for business, good for prisoners and good for society" (Ministry of Justice 2012a), sometime after pledging to make Britain a "global leader" in providing businesses with "effectively free labour" (see Wheeler 2010). And regarding unpaid labour as part of sentencing, he stated: "The introduction of regular, meaningful hard work is proven to help break the cycle of crime and encourage a law-abiding life." In conjunction with embedding greater competition to "drive efficiencies in public protection," this means "fewer victims of crime and much reduced costs for the taxpayer – a wholly positive result for society" (Ministry of Justice 2012a), according to Blunt. Indeed, there are significant attempts to assert that such forms of work would not able to realize their stated, disciplinary roles, *without* being opened up to capital to unprecedented degrees.

At the same time, though, these labour strategies are linked to an understanding that their recipients require a series of interventions, aimed at correcting what are perceived to be *personal* failings. And in this way they co-exist along with and alongside what has been termed in other contexts as a "new behaviourism" marked, among other things, by an emphasis on influencing behaviour though imposed duties and responsibilities, rather than enhancing social rights; conjoined attempts to incentivize, redirect and discipline people underpinned by their "failures" at individual levels and a downgrading of structural concerns "in favour of a focus on individual 'agency' and social pathologies" (see Harrison and Hemingway 2014: loc. 709; for earlier discussion of this concept, see Cohen 1985). That is, the dislocations underpinned by the destructive impacts of neoliberalism – the sustained assault on employment protections, for example, or the mass increase in inequality engendered by the revamping of the welfare state – are reasserted as individual moral deficits. And thus, just as Pearce critiqued deviancy theorists for developing an analysis of power without comprehending the materialist basis in which power was rooted, attempts to cohere work as a form of punitive reintegration can reinforce the notion that lack of work is indicative of a series of what are depicted as personal deficits. Or in other words, although the imposition of unwaged or sub-waged labour as a central aim of welfare and policy has a long history, the more recent commitment to it in its current form, and the attempts to blend punishment, profit and control into a heady mix, corresponds exactly to the core facets of neoliberal ideology: the reification of personal responsibility, the worship of capital as a *de facto* social good, the elevation of competition to virtue, the disciplining of recalcitrant populations, the desire to revamp the contours of the state and so on.

And it is in this context that these labour forms should be analysed in the way they constitute a particular labour *force*. Of course, to reiterate, this is not to suggest a simple uniformity in all of these forms of work. But it is notable that this is a labour force that has little ability to unionize, little ability to organize, little ability to exert control over its working environment and little public support in doing so. It is a labour force that commands no wages, or only tokenistic wages, and has next to no choice about where it is put to work. With regard to prison labour and workfare, specifically, when part of a supply chain, workers can quite simply keep costs down, and their wages (or lack of) can be utilized as a key part of a business model. For access to a workforce with little to no bargaining power enables businesses to offset the financial risks they face by passing them on to such employees. But even when workers are not of economic "use" in this way, their very existence transforms them into profit for those companies that have secured contracts to facilitate their work. And regardless of the economic value that can be extracted from them, such labour forms can be understood not just in terms of their immediate economic benefit, but in terms of their regulatory roles and broader functions as forms of social control. As Dario Melossi and Pavarini Massimo (1977/1981) observed in their landmark study of the origins of the prison and the factory some 40 years ago, for example, the core function of punitive labour is not always to produce, but to teach the *will* to produce. At the same time, it serves as a warning of the fate that could befall others. Indeed, it is this that goes some way to explaining the reasons why states tolerate the staggering sums – far more, in some cases, than will be made back through the value of labour – for the outsourcing of labour programmes.

Understanding all of these things requires going beyond an analysis which simply evaluates these labour forms on their own stated terms. It requires – in fact – looking at the way they underpin and are underpinned by a "real," as opposed to "imagined," social order. Of course, the trajectory of this is not set in stone. Despite the popularity of unpaid work within community sentencing, for example, community sentences as a whole are on a general downward spiral. Many of the probation privatization reforms, meanwhile, are falling apart even on their market terms (Garside 2016). At the same time, workfare programmes are undergoing a process of constant change, with some schemes collapsing and others expanding in their reach. And the role of prison labour, meanwhile, has to be set against a programme of prison "reform" which is by no means certain. But despite these shifting directions, the use of labour remains a key feature of criminal justice and welfare policies as they interact with each other. The lessons of *Crimes of the Powerful* are surely that understanding this demands a "mode of analysis" which considers the state's interactions with the economy, as well as their broader cultural functions as forms of social control. It requires a mode of analysis which examines the extent to which these interactions inform a production of knowledge around the role of "labour," "work" and the response to social insecurities and inequities. It demands an understanding of the ideological functions of law, and, certainly at the moment, it requires a mode of analysis linking the role of these programmes both historically and in the context of contemporary neoliberal order, with the way they are depicted officially as a kind of punitive reformation.

## Note

1 Unpaid work can be ordered as part of a community order or suspended sentence order, which can include one or more of the following: unpaid work (community payback); curfew; rehabilitation activity; programme (a course addressing specific offending behaviour); mental health treatment; drug rehabilitation; alcohol treatment; prohibited activity (for example, being banned from entering a licensed premises); exclusion (being banned from entering a specific place); or residence (a requirement to live at a specified address). All offenders serving a community order or suspended sentence order must also seek permission from their responsible officer to change residence); attendance centre (under 25s only); and restrictions on travel abroad (Ministry of Justice 2013: 13).

## References

Bardens, J. and Garton Grimwood, G. (2013) *Introducing "Payment by Results" in Offender Rehabilitation and other Reforms*, House of Commons Standard Note: SN/HA/6665. London: House of Commons.

Bath Chronicle. (2013) "Ideas Wanted for Offenders on Bath Community Payback Scheme." *Bath Chronicle*, 28 September, Online. Available HTTP: www.bathchronicle.co.uk/ideas-wanted-offenders-bath-community-payback/story-19846494-detail/story.html.

BBC. (2016) "Prisons to Get 'biggest overhaul in a generation'." *BBC News*, 3 November, Online. Available HTTP: www.bbc.co.uk/news/uk-37854358.

Boycott Workfare. (2015) "Mandatory Work Activity and Community Work Placements to Go! But What's Coming Next?" *Boycott Workfare*, 1 December, Online. Available HTTP: www.boycottworkfare.org/mandatory-work-activity-and-community-work-placements-to-go-but-whats-coming-next/.

Brown, J. (2014) "London Unpaid Work." *On Probation*, 2 March, Online. Available HTTP: http://probationmatters.blogspot.co.uk/2014/03/london-unpaid-work.html.

Clinks. (2014) *The Transforming Rehabilitation Programme: The New Owners of the Community Rehabilitation Companies*. London: Clinks. Online. Available HTTP: www.clinks.org/sites/default/files/table-of-new-owners-of-crcs.pdf.

Cohen, S. (1985) *Visions of Social Control: Crime, Punishment and Classification*. London: Polity.

Conservative Party. (2008) *Prisons With a Purpose: Our Sentencing and Rehabilitation Revolution to Break the Cycle of Crime*, Security Agenda Policy Green Paper No. 4, London: The Conservative Party.

Empty Cages Collective. (2017) "The Empty Cages Collective." *Organise!*, No. 88, 19–20.

Garside, Richard. (2016) "Let them Fail." *Centre for Crime and Justice Studies*, 27 October, Online. Available HTTP: www.crimeandjustice.org.uk/resources/let-them-fail

Goulden, C. (2012) "Work Is the Best Route Out of Poverty – Half the Time." *Joseph Rowntree Foundation*, 26 October, Online. Available HTTP: www.jrf.org.uk/blog/work-best-route-out-poverty-%E2%80%93-half-time

Hampshire Probation Trust. (2015) *Getting the Most Out of Community Payback*. Hampshire: Hampshire Probation Trust.

Harrison, M. and Hemingway, L. (2014) "Social Policy and the New Behaviourism: Towards a More Excluding Society," in Malcolm Harrison and Teela Sanders (eds.) *Social Policies and Social Control: New Perspectives on the "not-so-big society"*. Bristol: Policy Press.

Her Majesty's Inspectorate of Probation. (2016) *A Thematic Inspection of the Delivery of Unpaid Work*. Manchester: Her Majesty's Inspectorate of Probation.

Incarcerated Workers Organising Committee. (2017) "Making Prisons Work: The Rising Tide of Prison Labour in the UK." *Incarcerated Workers Organising Committee*, 8 July. Online. Available HTTP: http://incarceratedworkers.noflag.org.uk/2017/07/08/making-prisons-work-the-rising-tide-of-prison-labour-in-the-uk/

Jones, N. (2010) "Work: The Best Route Out of Poverty?" *Child Poverty Action Group Poverty Magazine*, No. 137, 15–17.

Jones, S. (2016) "Work Is Not a 'health' outcome." *Welfare Weekly*, 15 December, Online. Available HTTP: https://www.welfareweekly.com/work-is-not-a-health-outcome.

Learning and Work Institute. (2016) "Work Programme Statistics – March 2016." *Learning and Work Institute*, March, Online. Available HTTP: www.learningandwork.org.uk/resource/work-programme-statistics-march-2016/

Melossi, D. and Pavarini, M. (1977/1981) *The Prison and the Factory: Origins of the Penitentiary System*. London: Macmillan.

Ministry of Justice. (2010) *Breaking the Cycle: Effective Punishment, Rehabilitation and Sentencing of Offenders*, Cm 7972. London, Ministry of Justice.

Ministry of Justice. (2011) "Offenders to Go Full Time on Community Payback." *Ministry of Justice Press Release*, 24 August. Online. Available HTTP: www.gov.uk/government/news/offenders-to-go-full-time-on-community-payback

Ministry of Justice. (2012a) "New Work in Prisons Enterprise Launched." *Ministry of Justice Press Release*, 24 May. Online. Available HTTP: www.gov.uk/government/news/new-work-in-prisons-enterprise-launched

Ministry of Justice. (2012b) "New Approach to Community Payback Begins in London." *Ministry of Justice Press Release*, 31 October. Online: HTTP: www.gov.uk/government/news/new-approach-to-community-payback-begins-in-london

Ministry of Justice. (2013) *Target Operating Model: Rehabilitation Programme*. London: Ministry of Justice.

Mirza-Davies, James and McGuinness, Feargal. (2016) "Work and Health Programme." *House of Commons Briefing Paper Number 7845*. London: House of Commons.

National Audit Office. (2016) *Transforming Rehabilitation*, HC 951 Session 2015–16. London: Ministry of Justice.

Office for National Statistics. (2017) "UK Labour Market: Mar 2017 Statistical Bulletin." *Office for National Statistics*, March, Online. Available HTTP: www.ons.gov.uk/employmentandlabourmarket/peopleinwork/employmentandemployeetypes/bulletins/uklabourmarket/mar2017#employment

One3One Solutions. (2013) *Prospectus*. London: One3One Solutions, Online. Available HTTP: http://one3one.justice.gov.uk/downloads/prospectus.pdf

One3One Solutions. (2017) *One3One Solutions Customers and Sales 2015–2016*. London: One3One Solutions.

Patrick, R. (2014) "Welfare Reform and the Valorisation of Work: is Work Really the best form of Welfare?," in Malcolm Harrison and Teela Sanders (eds.) *Social Policies and Social Control: New Perspectives On the "not so big society"*. Bristol: The Policy Press, pp. 55–70.

Peck, J. (2001) *Workfare States*. New York: The Guilford Press.

Pearce, F. (1976) *Crimes of the Powerful: Marxism, Crime and Deviance* (2nd ed.). London: Pluto Press.

Prison Reform Trust. (2016) *Bromley Prison Briefings Factfile Autumn 2016*. London: Prison Reform Trust.

Skinns, D. (2016) *Coalition Government Penal Policy 2010–2015: Austerity, Outsourcing and Punishment*. London: Palgrave Macmillan.

Surrey and Sussex Community Rehabilitation Company. (2017) *Information for Providers*. Kent: Surrey and Sussex Community Rehabilitation Company, Online. Available HTTP: http://ksscrc.co.uk/content/documents/2017-01-20-community-payback-brochure-.pdf

Sofos, D. (2013) "Whistle-blowers Criticise Privatised Probation Service." *BBC News*, 21 November. Online. Available HTTP: www.bbc.co.uk/news/uk-25035850

Stone, J. (2016) "DWP Punishing the Working Poor" with New Sanctions in Universal Credit System." *The Independent*, 15 April. Online. HTTP: www.independent.co.uk/news/uk/politics/dwp-punishing-the-working-poor/-with-sanctions-in-new-universal-credit-system-a6985461.html

Webster, D. (2015) "Benefit Sanctions: Britain's Secret Penal System." *Centre for Crime and Justice Studies*, 26 January, Online. Available HTTP: www.crimeandjustice.org.uk/resources/benefit-sanctions-britains-secret-penal-system

Wheeler, B. (2010) "Prison Factory Plan 'to cut reoffending', Says Minister." *BBC News*, 4 October, Online. Available HTTP: www.bbc.co.uk/news/uk-politics-11463182

Whitehead, T. (2012) "Ken Clarke to Double Number of Prisoners Working Fulltime." *Daily Telegraph*, 12 January, Online. Available HTTP: www.telegraph.co.uk/news/uknews/law-and-order/8984942/Ken-Clarke-to-double-number-of-prisoners-working-full-time.html

Wright, O. (2012) "Plan For Cheap Prison Work 'May Cost Thousands of Jobs'." *The Independent*, 4 June, Online. Available HTTP: www.independent.co.uk/news/uk/politics/plan-for-cheap-prison-work-may-cost-thousands-of-jobs-7815140.html

# Chapter 22

# Imperialism
## The general theory of crimes of the powerful

*Biko Agozino*

With *Crimes of the Powerful: Marxism, Crime and Deviance*, Frank Pearce (1976) contributed what critics called an innovative "landmark in the creation of a Marxist criminology" (McMullen 1978: 376). Pearce rejected the obsession of the discipline with street criminality and the control of relatively powerless groups of people. He also pushed critical criminology away from conceptual clarifications towards a more empirical examination of the links between organized criminals and corporate criminals. W.E.B. Du Bois pioneered this line of critique in his 1899 social study of *The Philadelphia Negro* in which he found that the newly emancipated former slaves were banned from going to the public parks, were intimidated by political clubs to disenfranchise them and were arrested and incarcerated for the purpose of selling their labour to slave-like chain gangs while the law-enforcement agencies overlooked the crimes of the business class. Pearce stated at the "Revisiting *Crimes of the Powerful* Conference" (York University, Canada, 25–26 May 2017) that if he were to rewrite the book today, he would give more centrality to anti-racism and anti-sexism rather than continue to insist that racism and sexism could be represented by class struggles, using the orthodox mode of production analysis. The book was theoretically framed from the very first page – Jock Young's preface, though Young went on to opine that the radicalism of Black Power did not excuse the "petty theft . . . in (Black) lumpenproletarian areas" – to the penultimate page of the book's conclusion with reference to Black Power activists and drugs-dependent "white radicals" as "Dangerous Special Offenders." These references misrepresented Black Power simply as part of the lumpenproletarian class struggles without emphasis on race–class–gender articulation or intersectionality. The application of classical Marxism to criminology by Pearce was a breath of fresh air to demonstrate that concepts like "mode of production, surplus value and class struggle" are relevant to the theory of corporate criminality (Ruggiero 2015: 105). I suggest that struggles against racism and sexism are articulated with class struggles and should not be neglected in the analysis.

A lot of what Pearce went on to argue in parts two and three of the book are more consistent with the critique of a racist (and not just class-based) criminal justice system that was articulated with business interests and with the interests of politicians as empirically detailed by Du Bois. Had Pearce articulated the foundational work of Du Bois, Frantz Fanon and Stuart Hall, he would not have concluded that "within sociology, particularly within criminology, the serious study of the state and its agents and the activities of the ruling class is virtually non-existent" (Pearce 1976: 158). The critique of crimes of the powerful needs to be attentive to race-class-gender articulation of power and criminality the way that Du Bois (1904) demonstrated and Stuart Hall (2016), Paul Gilroy (1982), Kimberley Crenshaw (1989), Biko Agozino (2003) and many others advanced.

The perceptive critique of oppressive criminal justice administration was generally ignored by criminologists until Edwin Sutherland echoed the critique but without any reference to Du Bois in his 1939 Presidential Address to the American Sociological Society in the city of Philadelphia. Sutherland (1949) called on criminologists to look beyond street criminality and start addressing "white-collar crimes" that cost society more than small-time criminals. The difference between white-collar crime and crimes of the powerful is that Frank Pearce saw the reality that powerful criminals could be multinational corporations and that governments cannot be characterized as white- or blue-collar criminals. Both Sutherland and Pearce, however, failed to recognize that what they were calling for was already inaugurated by Du Bois (1904) in his 1896 doctoral dissertation at Harvard University where he focused attention on *The Suppression of the African Slave Trade* as an example of the crimes of the powerful, a foundational text in human rights criminology (Agozino 2017). The important critique of corporate crime will be stronger if articulated with the criticism of racism and sexism in society.

The blind spot in studies of white-collar criminality that ignored human rights crimes by the state may be as a result of the influence of the individualist jurisprudence of Western criminology with its exclusive focus on the punishment of individual offenders (Garland 1990). Frank Pearce critiqued the inadequacy of this criminological individualism by departing from the liberal perspective of labelling with its penchant for mitigating the criminalization of underdogs rather than theorizing the defiance of the underdogs fighting back against repressive state and powerful corporate criminals (Becker 1967; Gouldner 1968). The mode of production approach to crimes of the powerful was illustrated by Pearce with a detailed study of the case of Al Capone and his alliance with corporate racketeers during Prohibition. This approach needs to be rescued from a possible charge of crude economism by extending the critique to the imperialist-racist-sexism that was rampant not only among Detroit executives and federal officials who bribed union leaders but also among poor White workers and their White-supremacist trade unions (Foner 1974).

My conceptualization of power as a relationship that is apparent in all crimes – the idea that all crimes are crimes of the powerful – comes from my awareness that no people are completely powerless. Even among the relatively powerless, those who are more likely to commit offences are those who have the unaccountable power to invade the private and public spaces of others and try to colonize them. What the rapist, the pickpocket, the murderer, the fraudster, the genocidist, the enslaver, the exploiter, the oppressor and the colonizer have in common is the will to transgress the spaces of others and try to control them. Thus, I contend that imperialism is the general form of all criminality (Agozino 2003).

The implication of this observation for the crimes of the powerful paradigm is huge. If "[t]here is no doubt that Capone was a powerful man," according to Pearce (1976), if all crimes are crimes of the powerful, then the expected responses to the crimes of the powerful will need to be reconsidered. Pearce insisted that the state could handle corporate crime punitively. This raises the suspicion that the revolutionary theory of the crimes of the powerful runs the risk of being co-opted by the punitive state to entrench penal retentionism as the ideal form of legalism, whereas penal abolitionism might be a more promising strategy for holding power more accountable in democratic societies. Giannacopoulos (2011) has warned that nomophilia, or the insane love of law, could lead to what I call nomophilitis if constitutional recognition is regarded as the only way to protect indigenous rights under imperialist White supremacy.

## Contemporary debates on crimes of the powerful

In their "Introduction" to *Corporate Crime: Ethics, Law, and the State* Pearce and Snider promised a book that looked at all aspects of corporate crime with a focus on the "causes, extent, and control." They observed that there is a consensus on the pervasiveness and dangerousness of corporate crime. There is also "much less agreement on remedies and praxis" concerning the variable lack of adequacy in efforts to control it; there is a "paucity of deterrent mechanisms, and the mildness of the sanctions imposed relative to the harms done" (Pearce and Snider 1995: 3).

In Chapter 2, the editors reflected on the difficulties of regulating capitalism in an era when imperialism enabled corporations to operate across national boundaries, thereby rendering the regulatory powers of the nation state relatively redundant while neoliberal policies effectively undermine the existing powers of the state in the quest for smaller government and unregulated enterprises. Advocacy of more effective regulations of the malfeasance of limited liability companies is hampered by the fact that residents of the rich industrialized countries realize they have better standards of living than residents of poorer countries and they see entrepreneurship as a major contributor to their better living standards compared to 100 years previously.

Also significant portions of the population have bought shares to have a stake in capitalism even if corporate shareholders continue to control the vast majority of shares. The Chicago University School of Economics rationalized this pattern of *laissez faire*-ism by arguing that market forces are the best regulators of economic behaviour and recommended that the state should leave corporations and individuals to pursue their self-interests within the law in accordance with the mystical hand of order theorized by Adam Smith. The consequence is that as the state declined in significance, the power of the multi-national corporation increased exponentially, making some corporations more powerful than many state governments and thereby placing them relatively above the laws of the nation-state. The models differed from the free-market economies of the United States and the UK to the Asian Tiger economies under authoritarian political regimes, to the social democracy model in Sweden where state regulation allowed for the highest-paid workers and highest level of social welfare coverage while still leaving international capital free reign. Pearce and Snider conclude that the state should be encouraged to "include state planning, state ownership of enterprises, particularly 'natural' monopolies, a welfare state based on universalistic principles" (Pearce and Snider 1995: 43). No word directly against racism and imperialism here despite the call for "universalistic principles" (Kitosa 2012; Feagin et al. 2014).

These observations about the declining significance of state regulatory powers over increasingly internationalized power of global capitalism and the suggestion that the state should actively participate in the economy for the purpose of retaining the goal of public good through public policy suggest that the criminological obsession with the punishment of offenders needs to be revised in support of penal abolitionism. The problem this formulation raises is that it represents the state as the arbiter or regulator of corporate criminality, albeit an ineffective regulator in the face of transnational corporate delinquency that is not easily subjected to the punitive rules of any one country. The problem with the formulation also includes the fact that the state is not just a neutral arbiter but also an active committee for the settlement of the affairs of the bourgeoisie and in that process remains an active machinery for the oppression of the other classes. In other words, the focus on the regulation of capitalism by the state relatively neglected the crimes of the state that also tend to be difficult to subject to penology. This calls for creative responses by societies subjected to jungle justice under the hegemony of the capitalist state. Roosevelt gave poor Whites the New Deal but gave African Americans the "raw deal" by, for example, opposing legislation to make lynching a federal offence (Trotter 1995).

In this same book John Braithwaite attributed the relative success of the Australian regulation of nursing homes to the fact that the regulators spent more time listening to the perspectives of the residents (Braithwaite 1995: 65). He also suggested that the self-regulation of Australian pharmaceutical companies in response to professional opinions from doctors could be seen as an example of "communitarian control of corporate crime" that could be applicable to "trans-national corporate crimes that are beyond the reach of the state" (68). Braithwaite's formulation is not satisfactory precisely because he never raised in his chapter the issue of diversity along with liberty, equality and fraternity in a country like Australia that is a notorious settler-colonial location where the Indigenous people continue to be treated as viruses to be eradicated with the help of the criminal justice system that incarcerated them disproportionately (Cunneen and Tauri 2016). Writing only a few years after the landmark decision of *Mabo* in which the High Court finally accepted the principle that Mr. Mabo and Torres Straights islanders had a right to their ancestral land (even if non-continuity of land title by the Indigenous peoples supposedly eroded such rights), Braithwaite's republicanism was mum on this issue (although he addressed it elsewhere). Furthermore, invoking self-regulation as a dialogic principle applicable to trans-national corporations without extending the same principle of self-regulation to the Indigenous and poor working-class youth who appear to be hounded by the control-freak state over the possession of small quantities of drugs suggests that the criminological republicanism of Braithwaite was not sensitive to the need to decolonize the criminal justice system for the benefit of all. He called for diversion and restorative justice elsewhere while presumably leaving the settler-colonial prohibition system intact (Braithwaite 2002). Finally, by focusing exclusively on the regulation of businesses by state agencies, the chapter falls into the same trap of seeing the state as a neutral arbiter when the settler-colonial state is an active participant in organized crimes against Indigenous people and working people.

Following the definition of corporate crime by Steve Box (1983) as "acts of commission or omission" against the law, Steve Tombs (1995) detailed his study of British Chemical Industries to show that they may be seen as examples of new forms of organization with emphases on decentralization, commodification of services, greater autonomy and the contracting out of tasks that include health and safety. Consequently, according to Tombs, accountability in health and safety violations is not easy to determine with regards to the individual responsibility of employees and the collective responsibility of the far-from-rational bureaucratic corporations. He concluded that the diversity in the forms of organizations and the increased autonomy with which they operate may offer an opportunity for an increased democratization of corporate accountability by empowering "outside" stakeholders to play a role in the policing of criminal corporations that violate health and safety rules. This is an interesting approach because it does not obsess with how to "punish" corporate crimes but seeks how to regulate them with the view of preventing crimes in the first place. I believe that this approach is consistent with penal abolitionism at the level of individual offenders too.

The difficulties in the penological approach to crimes of the powerful are illustrated by Pearce and Tombs (1993) in their study of the 1984 "accidental" violations of health and safety regulations by Union Carbide in Bhopal, India. They assert that such a disaster occurred despite growing propaganda about corporate responsibility and the promise of "safety at any cost" by capitalist corporations that proclaimed to offer environmentally friendly products or to provide wood boxes for wildlife to nest on their premises. When a multinational company such as Union Carbide invested in a Third World country such as India, it was seen as doing the country a favour, and so regulations were usually relaxed in order to attract more such investments. When the "accident" occurred, the parent company in the United States offered a character defence by asserting that it had an excellent safety record and it blamed the accident on the "cultural backwardness" of India that supposedly failed in maintenance of the plant. Yet a similar accident had happened in the parent company in West Virginia but with fewer damages. In the case of Bhopal, the accident was waiting to happen because of the structural design of the company that brought the water hose in close proximity to the carbide which eventually caused the leak that killed an estimated 2,500 to 8000 poor people living close to the dangerous plant, contrary to safety requirements. The authors considered the conspiracy theory of sabotage as the cause and rejected it before considering the miserly settlement that the company reached with the victims of the disaster. They concluded by suggesting that preventive regulation of corporate crime may help to reduce or eliminate the frequent deaths of workers and poor people in the community, deaths caused by the negligence of corporations that are driven by the profit motive while paying lip service to health and environmental safety. Again the emphasis is not on imposing punishment for corporate crimes against companies that are not necessarily rogue corporations, but on prevention and reparations as is assumed in penal abolitionism.

Lauren Snider (1993) exposed the difficulties of relying on punishment as the main instrument for the control of corporate crime, given that the reality of political economy means that state watchdogs are not all that autonomous from the big corporations that they are supposed to regulate. As can be expected, smaller corporations are investigated more frequently and penalized more severely, whereas the more powerful corporations tend to get away with murder. In contrast to street crimes that were expected to cost $4 billion annually in the United States alone (at that time), corporate crimes were estimated to cost five times that annually. Compared to the 20,000 annual homicides in the United States, corporate violations of health and safety rules claimed an estimated 14,000 lives, plus 30,000 deaths from unsafe or defective products, and over 600,000 deaths from tobacco-related causes and environmental pollution by corporations. Using the example of Drexel Burnham, which defrauded investors with a fraudulent junk bond scheme, Snider showed that the director of the company faced charges while the company pleaded guilty and was fined $650 million. Yet the crime led to over 300 savings and loan companies defaulting and it would cost $300 billion to $1.5 trillion dollars to rescue those companies. This indicates that even when civil, administrative and criminal procedures are used in the control of corporate crimes those controls are "woefully ineffective," focus on the corporate actors that do the least wrong and impose meagre fines relative to the assets, according to Snider. The conclusion is that we need to understand the processes that defeated past reform efforts as we fight for the success of control mechanism targeting corporate crimes. My suggestion is that whatever works in the control of corporate crime should be

# Imperialism 303

abstracted and applied to street crimes rather than rely exclusively on criminal law when dealing with the poor.

Furthermore, Steve Tombs and David Whyte (2015) highlighted the fact that 40 years after the rise of what Stuart Hall (2016) articulated as Authoritarian Populism under the neoliberal ideology of Thatcherism, corporate crime was widespread in Britain as evident in illegal phone tapping investigations of newspapers and £297 million fine of Glaxo-Smith Kline with several executives given suspended sentences by Chinese courts. While Barclays Bank was fined £290 million and the Royal Bank of Scotland was fined £300 million by British courts, HSBC was fined US$2 billion for money laundering in the United States, among other "lowlights from the cesspit of corporate crime" (Tombs and Whyte 2015: 1–2). However, Tombs and Whyte blame the turn to Lyotard's post-modernism for the neglect of *Crimes of the Powerful*, yet Pearce told the conference on "Revisiting *Crimes of the Powerful*" that he saw himself as a post-structuralist though he was not a fan of French theory. Derriderian deconstruction, especially on *Specters of Marx* (Derrida 1993; Agozino 2011), suggest that a post-modern discourse that is antagonistic to race–class–gender oppression could enrich the critique of crimes of the powerful beyond political economy and class struggles (Saleh-Hanna 2015).

## The withering away of the law thesis

The danger that threatens the crimes of the powerful thesis is that it runs the risk of normalizing the commodity fetishism of the legal form under bourgeois dictatorships. According to Marx (1954), just because the philistine bourgeoisie is used to signing contracts in commercial relations, they came to the conclusion that the basis for civil society was a social contract and not the slavery, theft, force and violence that historical materialism documents as the roots of primitive accumulation of capital. Pashukanis (1924) inferred from this that commodity fetishism is evident in the legal form and not just in the commercial relations. As a result of this commodity fetishism, courts supposedly seek to impose punishment that is deemed to be equitable to the gravity of the offences. This is one way that the economic substructure relatively determines the forms of the legal superstructure, but Pashukanis added that the legal superstructure also relatively determined the outcome of commercial contracts, and so the mutual determination of outcomes is evident in the dialectical relationships between the infrastructure and the superstructure. Moreover, according to Pashukanis, the commodity fetishism that insists on equal exchanges in the market is extended to penal law by insisting that the offenders must "pay" for their crimes through a fine of equal value or through the loss of liberty for a period of time calibrated to be a just recompense for the harm caused.

The conclusion by Pashukanis (1924) was that when the dictatorship of the proletariat succeeded in smashing the dictatorship of the bourgeoisie as predicted by Marx, Engels and Lenin, then the commodity fetishism form of bourgeois law would be smashed along with the bourgeois state. But although the dictatorship of the proletariat pursues the task of building a classless society or communism, it would still be necessary to retain repressive laws to defend the revolution against counter-revolutionaries. However, when the communist society arrives and repressive law withers away to make way for administrative law on the basis of "from each according to their abilities and to each according to their needs," the state and the legal form of commodity fetishism would wither away because there would be no more classes to be repressed with the power of the state and with punitive law.

The problem for Pashukanis, according to David Garland (1990), was that this style of the critique of state capitalism under Joe Stalin was not funny given that the commodity fetishism form that was supposedly characteristic of bourgeois legalism retained the dominant form of legalism long after the overthrow of the dictatorship of the bourgeoisie and its replacement with the dictatorship of the proletariat. Rather than witness the withering away of the law, more repressive laws were imposed on the workers and the calibration of punishment in keeping with commodity fetishism retained the form of criminal legalism by making some corrupt officials pay with their lives when even bourgeois countries punished such crimes more leniently. Stalin may have understood the unflattering critique by Pashukanis because the young jurist was purged from the party and executed in 1937 (Head 2004).

The question is whether the crimes of the powerful paradigm dictates more severe calibrations of punishment for relatively powerful offenders based on the fact that the crimes of the relatively powerless received more severe sentences. If so, critical perspectives on the crimes of the powerful are in danger of perpetuating the commodity fetishism form of legalism that was imposed under the capitalist mode of production that should be allowed to wither away. The alternative question is whether societal responses to the crimes of the powerful should be adapted as the model for the responses to all crimes as a step towards penal abolitionism. The following conclusion answers this question in the affirmative.

## Conclusion

Neo-Classical theories have not proven effective for all crimes, leading to calls for reparative justice and penal abolitionism and for the adoption of peace making, diplomacy or love as better philosophies of justice (Pepinsky 1991). These are broadly applicable to corporate crimes and crimes of the state because corporations and states cannot be executed or incarcerated the same way that individual officials or offenders may be jailed for crimes of powerful organizations. The argument in this chapter is that the reparative, diplomatic or administrative mechanisms reserved for powerful corporations and for the state should be extended to individuals who break the law.

The chapter also argues that research on crimes of the powerful should extend the focus beyond corporations and look at powerful individuals like police officers and military officers whose crimes tend to be attract administrative sanctions at most. The Black Lives Matter movement is enough to convince us that law enforcement officers and private security agents or vigilantes are powerful arms of the corporatist state who engage in crimes of the powerful and who are treated like officials of powerful corporations, but they are not often included in the focus of researchers on crimes of the powerful. Dave Whyte (2007) attempted this when he addressed the commercial war crimes committed by troops and corporations during the invasion of Iraq, though he, too, focused on economic crimes and relatively neglected the slaughter of human beings that accompanied the invasion. I am encouraging theorists of crimes of the powerful to extend to the poor the same penal abolitionism that was used when responding to the crimes of the powerful invaders of Iraq and to the genocidist states in Africa. Because there is evidence that arms of the state engage in drugs running while other arms wage war on drugs as Pearce pointed out, then the theory of crimes of the powerful should embrace activism against the war on drugs and call for legalization and education towards harm reduction (Reiman and Leighton 2010; Agozino 2003).

Similarly, the crimes committed by terrorist organizations are not usually included in the focus of research on crimes of the powerful. The crimes committed by powerful gangs in inner cities, by neo-fascists and by warlords in developing countries should also be covered by research on crimes of the powerful (Oriola 2012). Child abusers, murderers, arsonists, drug dealers, rapists, armed robbers, burglars and car snatchers are all relatively powerful groups and individuals who could benefit from the policy implications of research on crimes of the powerful. If corporate criminals tend to be treated with mainly administrative rules and fines, then maybe these other forms of crimes of the powerful should also be treated with non-penal sanctions towards the withering away of punitive law. It is true that some crimes are so vile that some punishment would be justified and yet, in the final analysis, almost all offenders re-enter society following the abolition of the death penalty in almost all industrialized countries. Thus we should be thinking of ways to move beyond punishment towards reparations and community healing through love and forgiveness.

These conclusions could be challenged for seeming to retain the commodity fetishism of capitalist legal forms by suggesting that the way that corporate crime is treated under capitalism should become the standard for responding to all crimes. It would have been better to do away with the capitalist legal standards in entirety as ineffective regulatory mechanisms, but it is also true that the response to crimes of the powerful departs from the commodity fetishism by calibrating punishment below the equivalence of the harm done. Thus, abstracting the lenient administrative rules reserved for crimes of the powerful and applying them to all crimes would pave the way for penal abolitionism and possibly for administrative law to replace criminal law in general. The alternative would be to generalize the punitive and severe responses to the crimes of the poor for all crimes whereas those responses were based on the false standards of bourgeois commodity fetishism and class antagonism as Pashukanis suggested.

Related to the suggestion of penal abolitionism is the philosophy of non-violence that is common in the Africana tradition. This is evident in the fact that people of African descent endured crimes of the powerful for centuries during slavery, colonialism and apartheid but without obsessing about the need for punishment or vengeance against the perpetrators of those crimes against humanity. Instead, people of African descent are demanding reparations as suitable responses to those crimes of the powerful because no punishment would ever fit the crimes against humanity. Desmond Tutu (Tutu and Tutu 2014) said that he is often asked how South Africans could forgive the unforgivable crimes of apartheid and he always responded that there is nothing that is unforgivable; everyone deserves to be forgiven something.

Derrida (2001) examined the hypothesis that forgiveness comes from the theologies of the religions of the book or the Abrahamic religions of Judaism, Christianity and Islam. But he found that each of these religions, although preaching forgiveness, also insisted that there was something that was unforgiveable, whereas people of African descent do not appear to hold grudges on the basis that something is unforgivable. Mandela believed that loving all human beings was part of what made him human and that he would never allow any human being to deprive him of the ability to love the whole of humanity lest they deprive him of some of his humanity. According to Mandela (1994), resentment is like a poison you take and hope that it kills your enemy.

## References

Agozino, B. (2003) *Counter-Colonial Criminology: A Critique of Imperialist Reason*. London: Pluto Press.
———— (2011) "The Africa-Centered, Activist, and Critical Philosophy of Derrida," in *International Journal of Baudrillard Studies*, Volume 8–1 (Jan.).
———— (2017) "The Africana Paradigm, W.E.B. Du Bois as a Founding Father of Human Rights Criminology," in L. Webber, E. Fishwick and M. Marmo (eds.) *The Routledge International Handbook of Criminology and Human Rights*, New York: Routledge.
Becker, H.S. 1967. "Whose Side Are We On?" *Social Problems*, 14 (Winter): 239–248.
Box, S. (1983) *Power, Crime and Mystification*. Tavistock: London.
Braithwaite, J. (1995) "Corporate Crime and Republican Criminological Praxis," in F. Pearce and L. Snider (eds.) *Corporate Crime: Contemporary Debates*. Toronto: University of Toronto Press.
———— (2002) *Restorative Justice and Responsive Regulation*. New York: Oxford University Press.
Crenshaw, K. (1989) "Demarginalizing the Intersection of Race and Sex: A Black Feminist Critique of Antidiscrimination Doctrine, Feminist Theory and Antiracist Politics." *University of Chicago Legal Forum*, 139.
Cunneen, C. and Tauri, J. (2016) *Indigenous Criminology*. Bristol: Policy Press.

Derrida, J. (2001) *On Cosmopolitanism and Forgiveness*. New York: Routledge.

———— (1993) *Specters of Marx: The State of the Debt, the Work of Mourning and the New International*. New York: Routledge.

Du Bois, W.E.B. (1904) *The Suppression of the African Slave-Trade to the United States of America: 1638–1870*, Harvard Historical Studies, Vol. 1, Cambridge: Harvard University.

———— (1899) *The Philadelphia Negro: A Social Study*. Philadelphia: University of Pennsylvania Press.

Feagin, J., Hernan, V. and Kimberley, D. (2014) *Liberation Sociology* (3rd ed.). Boulder: Paradigm Publishers.

Foner, P.S. (1974) *Organized Labor and the Black Workers. 1619–1973*. New York: International Publishers.

Garland, D. (1990) *Punishment and Modern Society: A Study in Social Theory*. Oxford: Clarendon.

Giannacopoulos, M. (2011) "Nomophilia and Bia: The Love of Law and Violence." *Borderlands*, 10(1).

Gilroy, P. (1982) "The Myth of Black Criminality." *The Socialist Registrar*, 19

Gouldner, A. (1968) "The Sociologist as Partisan: Sociology and the Welfare State." *American Sociologist* (May), 103–116

Hall, S. (2016) *Cultural Studies 1983: A Theoretical History*. Durham: Duke University Press.

Head, M. (2004) "The Rise and Fall of a Soviet Jurist: Evgeny Pashukanis and Stalinism." *Canadian Journal of Law and Jurisprudence*, 17(2): 269–294.

Kitosa, T. (2012) "Criminology and Colonialism: Counter Colonial Criminology and the Canadian Context." *Journal of Pan African Studies*, 4(10): January.

Mandela, N. (1994) *Long Walk to Freedom: The Autobiography of Nelson Mandela*. Boston: Little Brown & Co.

Marx, K. (1954) *Capital: A Critique of Political Economy*. Moscow: Progress Press.

McMullan, J.L. (1978) "Review of Frank Pearce, *Crimes of the Powerful: Marxism, Crime and Deviance*," in *The Canadian Journal of Sociology/Cahiers canadienns de sociologie*, 3(3): Summer.

Oriola, T. (2012) *Criminal Resistance? The Kidnapping of Oil Workers*, Aldershot: Ashgate.

Pashukanis, E.B. (1924) *Law and Marxism: A General Theory*. Moscow: Progress Press.

Pearce, F. (1976) *Crimes of the Powerful: Marxism, Crime and Deviance*. London: Pluto Press.

Pearce, F. and Snider, L. (1995) "Regulating Capitalism," in F. Pearce and L. Snider (eds.) *Corporate Crime: Contemporary Debates*. Toronto: University of Toronto Press.

Pearce, F. and Tombs, S. (1993) "US Capital versus the Third World: Union Carbide and Bhopal," in Frank Pearce and Michael Woodwiss (eds.) *Global Crime Connections: Dynamics and Control*. Toronto: University of Toronto Press.

Pepinsky, H. (1991) *The Geometry of Violence and Democracy*. Bloomington: Indiana University Press.

Reiman, J. and Leighton, P. (2010) *The Rich Get Richer and the Poor Get Prison: Ideology, Class, and Criminal Justice*. New York: Allyn & Bacon.

Ruggiero, V. (2015) "Ethics and Crimes of the Powerful." *The Howard Journal*, 54(1): February.

Saleh-Hanna, V. (2015) "Black Feminist Hauntology: Rememory the Ghosts of Abolition," in *Penal Field, Vol. XII, Abolitionism*. Online. Available HTTP: http://champpenal.revues.org

Snider, L. (1993) "The Politics of Corporate Crime Control," in Frank Pearce and Michael Woodwiss (eds.) *Global Crime Connections: Dynamics and Control*. Toronto: University of Toronto Press.

Sutherland, E.H. (1949) *White Collar Crime*. New York: Holt, Rinehart & Winston.

Tombs, S. (1995) "Corporate Crime and New Organizational Forms," in F. Pearce and L. Snider (eds.) *Corporate Crime: Contemporary Debates*. Toronto: University of Toronto Press.

Tombs, S. and Whyte, D. (2015) "Introduction to the Special Issue on 'Crimes of the Powerful'." *The Howard Journal*, 54(1): February.

Trotter, J. W. (1995) "From a Raw Deal to a New Deal?" *Vol' 8: African Americans in Depression and War, 1929–1945*, New York: Oxford University Press.

Tutu, Desmond and Tutu, Mpho. (2014) *The Book of Forgiving: The Fourfold Path for Healing Ourselves and Our World*. New York, HarperOne.

Whyte, D. (2007) "The Crimes of Neo-Liberal Rule in Occupied Iraq." *British Journal of Criminology*, 47: 175–195.

# Chapter 23

# Frank Pearce and colonial state crimes

## Contributions to a research agenda

*Jose Atiles*

> Again many British fortunes have been built on the terrorisation of colonial peoples as earlier the aristocracy had become rich through forced enclosures. But we do not have enough detailed work on either the present activities or the growth of the major corporations.
>
> (Pearce 1976:159)

Crimes of the powerful are an integral part of the history and of the political, socio-legal and economic daily experiences of the Global South[1] and of colonial contexts. Years of colonial regimes, dirty wars, systematic violations of human rights, paramilitarism, corruption and plundering by local elites and transnational corporations have become the day-to-day of the Global South. That is, on the one hand, what is considered exceptional in the Global North, in the South and in the colonies is normal or a part of everyday life; and, on the other hand, the history of the crimes of the powerful in the Global South and in the colonies has been defined by an intense relation between the global and the local, as well as being the result of a capitalist world-system and of a series of colonial epistemologies.

Despite the quotidian nature of the crimes of the powerful in the Global South, the local experiences with state violence and criminality have been systematically interpreted from conceptual categories coming from the Global North. An example of this is how dictatorship regimes of Latin America have become the example *par excellence* of many scholars (particularly for those in human rights, transitional justice and orthodox criminological[2] traditions) committed to interpreting and defining state crimes as an endemic phenomenon of the Global South. Conveniently, these traditions exploited examples of state crimes in the Global South, while simultaneously silencing the long history of the Global North's involvement in and support of state crimes in the Global South. As a result of this short-sighted framework, Global North scholars have made a tradition of employing reductionist and colonial interpretations of the diverse Global South histories and complex realities.

This hegemonic epistemological and methodological approach to state crimes is what I will call the criminology and the sociology of the exceptions. That is, a hyper-emphasis on what seems abnormal, different or the exceptional case that proves the norm. My contention is that this approach cannot be applied to the Global South, because it silences the reasons behind state criminality. In the colonies and in the Global South, sociology and criminology have to focus on what has been constituted as part of everyday life, instead of looking at what is exceptional from the experiences of the Global North. Additionally, a critical approach to these experiences would not only attempt to articulate reality, but would try to think of ways in which such reality could be transformed.

This chapter aims to apply Pearce's (1976) critical methodology and a Marxist theoretical framework to the development of the concept of colonial state crimes. By doing this, the chapter will show how, even though Pearce (1976) does not develop a colonial perspective in his analysis of the crimes of the powerful, his theory and his methodological emphasis in the study of what has been normalized constitute a foundational contribution to the development of the colonial perspective in the analysis of state crimes. In this way, I intend to contribute to the development of a better understanding of the experiences of the Global South with regards to the crimes of the powerful.[3]

My contention is that Pearce's (1976) contribution to the critical analysis of state criminality, and especially the study of how domination and criminality have become an integral part of capitalism, can be expanded when it is explored from a colonial perspective. As Agozino (2003) has shown, colonialism was fundamental in the development of contemporary criminology. That is, criminology was implemented to regulate the lives, bodies and resistances of colonial subjects. Furthermore, the common sense (knowledge) produced by criminologists served to legitimize metropolitan interests in colonial territories and to depoliticize anticolonial mobilizations. As Fanon (1999, 2009) shows, anticolonial mobilizations were quickly transformed into behavioural, legal and psychological problems. Hence, criminology played a key role in colonialism, but also, colonialism transformed criminology.[4]

This colonial approach will be developed into three general sections. The first section is devoted to the exposition of the concept of state crimes. The second section discusses the relation between the anticolonial tradition and state crimes. The third section presents the concept of colonial state crimes as a notion that can portray the Global South experience with regard to state violence and criminality. That is, in this third part, I expose what could be considered an approach to colonial state crimes from the perspective of the sociology and criminology of everyday life. Therefore, the intention is to show how Pearce's (1976) analysis and methodology have contributed to the development of the colonial state crimes concept, allowing for a better understanding of colonial violence.

## Crimes of the powerful: state and critical criminology

Crimes of the powerful and critical state crime approaches are relatively new in the socio-legal and criminological traditions.[5] In this sense, Pearce's (1976) contribution helped to give form to this tradition within sociology and criminology. Looking back at the impact of his book, Pearce comments that it "was a tentative beginning of analysis, which could be built upon to develop more comprehensive accounts of State(s), economy(ies), society(ies) and ideology(ies)" (Pearce 2015: 4). As is well known, Pearce (1976) managed to lay down the foundations for the development of a critical approach to these institutions and to the detailed explorations of the mechanisms that explain these correlations. Furthermore, Pearce's (1976) analysis and methodology can be understood as some of the most important critiques to the sociology and the criminology of exceptions. That is, Pearce's (1976) emphasis on historical, political, socio-legal and economic aspects of state–corporate criminality aimed to show that the crimes of the powerful are only possible if there is a permanent structure of power – they are not a result of specific actors or specific time periods, contrary to what sociology of exceptions claims.

My focus here is on one of the challenges proposed by Pearce (1976) which has been relatively neglected; that is, the relationship between the state, colonialism and corporations – with some important exceptions – has not been properly developed by the crimes of the powerful tradition. Hence, I will return to Pearce's (1976) text through a perspective of colonialism and in search for the development of a colonial state crimes research agenda.

In what follows, I will briefly describe some key concepts set out by Pearce (1976), starting by analysing the concept of the powerful. It is my contention that the questions of the constitution of the powerful and of the relation between the powerful and the powerless remain important for colonial contexts; in the latter, the ontological definition of the powerful is not as clear-cut as it seems. An easy answer is that in a colonial society, the powerful are the colonizers, but this is a reductionist answer. Thus, when one is to study the crimes of the powerful in a colonial society, one has to start by looking at the process of ontological definition by the powerful and the powerless. That is, one has to look at the colonial history, at the configuration of the colonial society and at the distribution of power, but also, one has to look at the negotiations and dialogue among local colonized elites and the colonizers. The key question is how colonialism has been established and what has been the role that corporations, local elites, colonizing countries and the colonized state itself has played.

A second aspect to consider is the relation between state and criminality. My contention is that the Marxist reading of the state proposed by Pearce (1976) continues to be pertinent for the analysis of state crimes in colonial contexts. For Pearce, one of the major problems in criminology and sociology at the time was the poor theorization about the state. Hence, the author pointed out that "the concept of the state itself must be in part reconsidered, and finally the relationship between crime, law and the state clarified" (Pearce 1976: 52). For Pearce,

> the state institutions are not separate from society, over and above it, but are an integral part of the mode of production [. . .]. The state apparatuses have been developed as instruments of the ruling-class interests and cannot simply be treated as tools – to be taken over by this or that group.
>
> (Pearce 1976:58)

Hence, it can be argued that the state is a formal and informal structure in which a series of public and private institutions converge; in which the monopoly of violence is executed; and in which a series of hegemonic discourses, ideologies and technologies of power determine life in a specific political context.

This definition allows us, in turn, to understand how states operate even in colonial contexts. In colonial contexts, the state operates as power structures that, given their anti-democratic configuration, systematize, institutionalize and normalize the oppression of colonized subjects. The colonial state is the dispositive/apparatus that makes possible the domination of a country or nation by an empire. In this sense, colonial states are the other, yet equally modern, side of the bourgeois state[6] widely analysed by Pearce (1976), because they were born from the same matrix of power. Therefore, any effort to understand state crimes, both in the Global North and in the South, should not overlook the definition of the state, as it is the dispositive that defines and naturalizes the exercise of power since modernity.

Moving forward in the analysis of ideology, economy and law, Pearce (1976) suggested that the state, as any power structure and as a system of hegemonic reproduction of the interests of the ruling classes, operates through ideological, economic and violent apparatuses. In this sense, the law and the rule of law play an ideological and violent role in the reproduction of ruling class interests. The law and the ideology of rule of law serve as tools that depoliticize conflicts, simultaneously creating the false image of neutrality and objectivity, even leading the oppressed classes to guarantee the interests of the elites and the state through recognition of the law.

As Pearce points out, the state is responsible, through its structures, for guaranteeing the economy and the functioning of capitalism. At the same time that the state approves laws that guarantee the production and reproduction of life, the state is an essential part of the modes of production. Thus, "its objective function is to help guarantee the reproduction of the economic system. It will not be the only nexus of institutions responsible for this task nor will its functionaries necessarily be the major beneficiaries of the system it protects" (Pearce 1976: 61). A clear example of these processes of transformation and normalization of violent practices initiated by the state is found in various forms of slavery legislation and their subsequent abolition (Beckles 2013). In these cases, one can see how the state produces the reality through the law while simultaneously adapting it to the economic and political interests of a given period.

In this sense, economics and the law go hand in hand with capitalist societies. This is the case with colonial territories as well. Unsurprisingly, this link between capital, the law and the state structures creates conditions for criminal practices. "Corruption and partiality within the police, the class bias of the judiciary, and the use of harassment, terror and violence of both a legal and illegal kind against socialists better describes the working of the law within these societies" (Pearce 1976: 51). It can be noted that state corruption and the repression of social movements go hand in hand, constituting an example or a manifestation of state crimes.

The analysis of what seems normal or natural, and the ways in which the state reproduces the interests of the powerful, is precisely what Pearce (1976) aims to show as problematic. Likewise, Green and Ward (2012) argue that modern states claim for themselves the monopoly over the use of legitimate violence, but at the same time, they are the main perpetrators or instigators of the most serious uses of illegitimate violence, causing suffering, injury and death in contravention of their own laws. Additionally, Green and Ward (2004) evidence how states that claim to be democratic (as does the United States) are serious offenders of their own laws and have become criminal states.[7] In their study, the authors broadly describe the exercise of state violence, defined within the framework of state terrorism and support to pro-state terrorism, torture, genocide, war crimes and police violence, both in the local and international sphere.

Critical studies of state crimes show that there is a critical consensus on the violent and repressive nature of democratic states. However, cases of studies and empirical research have focused on the Global South and in what seems exceptional and not on everyday violence. As will be shown, this disproportionate approach in the experiences of the Global South obeys the *coloniality of knowledge*[8] constitutive of the criminology and sociology of the exceptions.

Finally, Pearce (1976) had shown that capitalist societies, by their own structure of power and corrupt nature, allow and even encourage state–corporate criminality. Some fifteen years later, the concept of "state–corporate crime" was identified, in 1990, when Michalowski and Kramer defined this phenomenon as signifying "illegal or socially injurious actions that occur when one or more institutions of political governance pursue a goal in direct co-operation with one or more institutions of economic production and distribution" (2006: 15). More recently, Tombs and Whyte (2015a) have argued that there is a complicit relation between state and corporate crimes and harm and also have shown that in the state–corporate crimes tradition there exists a consensus regarding the colonial origins of this complicity. Corporations have played a key role in colonialism, and in some colonial contexts some corporations operated as states. My contention here is that the colonial role of corporations remains a key aspect of their contemporary existence. That is, the legal, ontopolitical and economic nature of corporations are embedded in their colonial origins.

## State crimes and the anticolonial tradition

Studies on colonialism have shown that this phenomenon exemplifies the utmost expression of violence and power impositions on subjects and spaces. In colonial territories and in the Global South, we find the normalization of everything that is considered exceptional in the Global North. As Maldonado-Torres (2007) proposes, colonial territories are spaces where the normalization of the non-ethics of war takes place. Césair (2000) and Fanon (1999, 2009) have clearly exemplified the strategies of power and subordination imposed through colonialism. The authors have shown how colonies are constituted in contact zones between geopolitical and biopolitical forms of power. That is, colonial practices are not limited to the control of a specific territory outside of the metropolitan state, but that the imposition of epistemologies, the introduction of forms of social organization and of legal transplant and the reduction of the colonized to a being less than human are key strategies of domination implemented in the colonies. My understanding is that colonialism operates as an *ontopolitical* system of domination. Thus, colonialism manifests itself in a four-dimensional way.

First, as I mentioned before, colonialism implies the geopolitical control of territory. This is the definition of the classical colonial practices implemented by European empires in the Americas, the Caribbean, Africa and Asia from the 16th century to the present. This involves taking control over the territory; transforming the landscape; plundering natural, mineral and fossil resources; and carrying out the genocide of the Indigenous inhabitants and their replacement either by slaves or indentured labour. In the geopolitical practices, one can find the first manifestation of colonial state crimes, because the processes of land acquisition and power imposition require systematic use of violence.

Second, colonialism implies a biopolitical form of domination, that is, the construction of a truth and the promotion of the idea of the racial, epistemological, economic and socio-legal superiority of the metropolis (Mbembe 2003). Thus, biopolitical domination is not only external or imposed from without, but it is also internal or from within, as it produces colonized subjectivities. Through biopolitics, colonialism breaks into the totality of the space of life, constituting itself in the truth of the colonized being. As a result, as Fanon (2009) shows, the colonizer and the colonized cannot perceive reality beyond the conceptual framework constituted by colonialism. This aspect has been widely studied by the currents of thought denominated *coloniality of power, of knowledge and of being* (Maldonado-Torres 2007). These traditions show that colonialism operates as an ontological form of subjection and interpretation of reality, and despite political and legal emancipation, the Global South and North continue to be intertwined through the colonial logic inaugurated by modernity.

Third, colonialism uses the law and the state of exception as dispositives of regulation and administration of the colonized territory and subjects (Atiles-Osoria 2016). The law normalized the violence of colonialism through the design of a legal truth about the colonial subject and the political alternatives. Elsewhere, I have shown that the colonial state of exception has served as a dispositive of legitimation and normalization of the exceptionality that takes place in colonial territories (Atiles-Osoria 2016). That is, the colonial state of exception has become the norm in colonies, which entails that the law in colonial territories always operates in exceptional ways. Furthermore, the colonial state of exception has been used to criminalize and to repress anticolonial movements. Thus, the law and colonial state of exception play key roles in colonial societies, since they make possible the domination of colonial subjects.

Fourth, colonialism also implies a series of indirect mechanisms and administration techniques. Traditionally, these techniques of indirect ruling have been categorized within the framework of neocolonialism, and they refer mainly to economic domination. However, it is important to note that these forms of economic colonial power are not limited to neocolonialism, but include practices of economic domination that existed during the colonial era and that continue to exist today. Moreover, colonial domination was not limited to the government of colonies, but colonial states made systematic use of national and transnational corporations and local elites to ensure the survival of colonial rule.

Not surprisingly, Marx and Engels (1968) made multiple references to colonialism, mostly associated to the role of corporations in the colonies. In addition, as shown by Tombs and Whyte (2015a), British public and private corporations (e.g. British East India Company) played a central role in the colonization of India and various African countries. These corporations behaved like states in the colonies – developing, in many cases, armies, collecting taxes, organizing commercial relations and local and international political relations – even though colonial sovereignty belonged to the British crown.

As Pearce (1976) has shown, this is one of the areas to be developed by the crimes of the powerful tradition, because corporations functioned in multiple colonial contexts as proto-states. As noted earlier, corporations and corporate criminality developed jointly or at the same time with colonialism and colonial state crimes. For this reason, one cannot define colonial state crimes without referring to the centrality of corporations.

Postcolonial criminology has, to a certain extent, sought to address central aspects of the crimes committed by colonial states. For example, McLaughlin (2001) suggests that a broader definition of postcolonial criminology would involve the analysis of the relations that persist between the colonial and postcolonial, pointing to new forms of thinking that emerge in a heterodox way. For McLaughlin (2011) when reading the texts of contemporary postcolonial criminology, one notices the plurality of cultural meanings, mostly problematic, applied to concepts and words usually used in criminology, such as crime, criminal, law, state, rule of law, culture and justice. For this reason, McLaughlin

(2001) considers it pertinent to transform criminology and the dominant criminological practices in the orthodox academy. Despite its important contribution, postcolonial criminology approach is problematic because it assumes that colonialism has ended and thus omits an analysis of colonial state crimes as current phenomena.

Finally, it is interesting to note that theories on state crimes have not considered colonialism as a form of criminality, even though it is widely acknowledged that colonialism is a crime against humanity (Beckles 2013). As Ward (2005) shows, violence in colonial territories was not generated by excesses of certain state representatives or by corporations, but it was a part of systematic and organized practices for the attainment of colonial domination. In this sense, the concept of colonial state crimes recognizes that violence in the colonial context has been legitimized through various discourses of power. Blakeley (2009) has pointed out that the record of European and U.S. colonial powers is extremely violent. Many of the strategies they used, both to acquire territory and to exploit their resources, involved the use of state violence on a mass scale. In the early stages, this was justified as part of the *civilizing mission*. Colonial state crimes were then justified in order to stop the decolonization of territories dominated by colonial powers. At present, state criminality is legitimized through economic discourses and relies on the need to maintain the colonial regime in order to guarantee economic development.

Therefore, the study of colonial state crimes should emphasize colonialism as a *dominating rationality* (that is, not just how power has been imposed and how the powerful perceive themselves, but also how the colonized or powerless perceive those in power) and as a part of an epistemic regime that determines the relations between the Global North and South. Furthermore, it is important to note that colonialism has a dynamic character; therefore, its study should not be limited to the interpretations or theorizations of the criminology of the exceptions, but rather it should denounce state crimes, even if they happened in the past. In this sense, I consider that it is necessary to assume a colonial perspective in the analysis of the Global South realities.

## Colonial state crimes: a research agenda

The concept of colonial state crimes, as has been shown, is based on Marxist and anticolonial studies traditions. Thus, it is based on the emphasis of critical analyses of what has been normalized or naturalized in colonial contexts. This critical analysis is done not only with the intention to explain the histories of state criminality, but to transform such realities. Thus, with the concept of colonial state crimes, I am proposing an epistemological and methodological framework that allows us to explain what has become normal in a way that one can denaturalize it and change power relations. In what follows, I am going to set out some general ideas of the concept of colonial state crimes, which will serve for the future development of a research agenda.

First, colonial state crimes operate within the *dominating rationality* and/or through an epistemological form that assumes, at the outset, the inferiority of colonized people. Thus, the Global South and its inhabitants are a space and subjects of domination. This aspect is what has been named as *coloniality*, which entails the ontopolitical definition of one being inferior for mere reasons such as race, gender or precedence. If a being is dehumanized, then the uses of violence against it do not constitute a crime in terms of the *dominating rationality*. In other words, colonial subjects and territories cannot be victims of the crimes of the powerful, because they are not seen as human beings. This rationality has made possible colonial crimes such as slavery, genocide and colonialism itself.

This first point emphasizes the ontopolitical analysis of the imposition and the definition of power in colonial societies. As can be noted, in colonial societies, power is constituted in a different manner than in the Global North. That is, ontopolitical definitions of reality must be highlighted from the very beginning of any research on colonial state crimes. Thus, when orthodox scholars look at the Global South and argue that a specific state is a criminal state, they are probably overlooking many aspects of day-to-day experiences with violence. Therefore, in a society where the non-ethics of war and the colonial state of exception are the norm, it is important to look at what has been naturalized, rather than looking at what appears as exceptional. Furthermore, colonial state crimes, as manifestations of the crimes of the powerful, operate through the confluence between local and global interests. As Pearce (1976) reminds us, this aspect must be considered from an international or global perspective.

Second, the concept of colonial state crimes begins with the recognition that the terms "crime" and "state terrorism," as orthodox studies have understood them, are reductionist, and do not recognize the socio-historical roots of the conflicts they seek to define. Hence, when studying colonial state crimes, one must look at how certain practices have been defined in colonial societies and how that reflects a better understanding of state violence. As has been stated, the normalization of exceptionality and state violence in colonial societies makes it very difficult to define certain practices of state violence as crimes.[9]

Additionally, the colonial state crimes concept acknowledges that a frequent error in the studies on colonialism is to equate state terrorism with state crimes. My contention is that state terrorism refers to very specific strategies implemented by the colonizer and colonized states to ensure their domination. Elsewhere, I have shown that colonial state terrorism refers to the systematic use of repression, criminalization, and support of pro-state organizations to delegitimize anticolonial mobilizations (Atiles-Osoria 2016). Colonial state terrorism is located within the matrix of colonial state crimes, but it is not comparable to the totality of forms of violence that colonial state crimes entail.

Third, the concept of colonial state crimes is based on the political understanding of the use of state violence, which means that the latter is instrumental and used as a repressive and criminalizing dispositive. Therefore, the concept proposes to avoid the depoliticization of violence and state criminality. Colonial state crimes are always political; therefore, legitimations of state actions under the alleged technical, bureaucratic, and security discourses operate as depoliticizing strategies. In this sense, when looking at colonial state crimes, one must emphasize what has been constructed as technical or as not problematic. In that way, one can re-politicize state criminality and human suffering in colonial contexts.

Fourth, the concept of colonial state crimes does not make a distinction between manifestations of political violence exercised by governments, the paramilitary and pro-state organizations and corporations. Paramilitary and corporate actions, in most cases, take place under the auspices of colonial states. In colonial societies, crimes and political violence always take place within the umbrella of *dominating rationality*, so there is an intense relation between pro-state, corporate and state interests and uses of violence. For this reason, one must emphasize the intertwined relations between multiples actors.

Fifth, colonial state crimes involve the use of the state's economic and administrative resources either for the enrichment of elites or to facilitate and sponsor the repression of anticolonial movements. An example of the previous is the implementation of the diversion of funds for the purchase of equipment and subsidies from pro-state organizations or from state special military forces to deal with the alleged terrorist threats of anticolonial movements (Atiles-Osoria 2012). Therefore, when analysing colonial state crimes, one has to look not just at the specific cases of corruption, but also at what is considered as corruption in local contexts. For many colonial states, the uses of public funds in the repression of anticolonial and social movements are not seen as corruption, but rather as part of the normal function of the state. Highlighting such practices must be a key aspect of the research on colonial state crimes.

Sixth, colonial state crimes emphasize the depoliticizing capacity of counterterrorist policies. One must bear in mind that colonial states interpret any group that opposes colonial rule as an enemy or as a terrorist. By showing how counterterrorism and counterinsurgent practices are forms of state terrorisms, colonial state crimes re-politicize descriptions of state violence. A key aspect here is to show how the so-called terrorists are ontopolitically constituted and how those practices tend to depoliticize and criminalize sociopolitical sectors that are not necessarily armed movements (Atiles-Osoria 2013, 2014).

Finally, it is important to note that colonial state crimes are dynamic; they cannot be understood as static practices, but rather as being transformed at the same time that historical reality changes. The proposed concept of colonial state crimes simultaneously contemplates the exercise of violence by state power structures and by its legal and economic systems, and admits the historical fluidity of its manifestations. Therefore, I understand that the concept of colonial state crimes is the one that best represents and defines the complex history of violence in colonial contexts.

## Conclusion

This chapter has proposed a general definition of the concept of colonial state crimes, starting with the foundational analysis of Frank Pearce (1976). The long history of state criminality and impunity in colonial contexts and in the Global South shows that it is necessary to develop a concept that allows us to understand the experiences of the Global South from their own categories and from a perspective that prioritizes what has become normal, rather than prioritizing the exceptions.

Additionally, I consider that for the development of the concept of colonial state crimes, it is pertinent to conduct, as Pearce (1976) suggested in his book, empirical investigations into colonial contexts. In my own work on the Puerto Rican colonial context, I have shown how this concept operates (Atiles-Osoria 2012, 2013, 2014); however, it is necessary to expand the case studies. For example, I have focused on state crimes resulting from political repression, but I have not developed a deep analysis of colonial state–corporate crimes; economic crimes; or systematic violations of the human, civil and political rights of Afro-descendant and migrant communities. My contention is that these possible case studies will show that colonialism is central to all manifestations of state political violence, because, although the cases do not seem to be related or exceptional, they are the product of a colonial system. Hence, the concept of colonial state crimes may involve these areas of analysis.

As has and should continue to be done in Puerto Rico, I believe that the concept of colonial state crimes can be applied to other areas of the Global South. It is only in this way that we will be able to establish an area of criminological and socio-legal research that reflects Global South and colonial experiences with regards to oppression, such as the one Pearce (1976) foresaw forty years ago.

## Notes

1  I am using Santos' (2009) descriptions of the Global North and South.
2  I am using Chambliss, Michalowki, and Kramer's (2010) definition of orthodox criminology.
3  Iadicola (2010) and Lasslett (2012) have made important contributions into the colonial approach to crimes of the powerful.
4  For a similar analysis, see Kitossa (2012).
5  There is a long tradition of analysis of state violence in both the Global North and South. These analyses came from different academic traditions; however, what makes the crimes of the powerful approach relevant is the efforts to show the intertwined relationship between the local and the global, the state and the corporations, the class interests and the reproduction ideologies (Tombs and Whyte 2003, 2015b; Whyte 2009).
6  For a similar analysis, see Mignolo (2005).
7  Elsewhere, I have made an analysis of U.S. colonial state crimes (Atiles 2012, 2016).
8  For a detailed analysis, see Maldonado (2007).
9  A current example of such difficulties can be found in the CARICOM mobilization for reparation for years of British slavery, genocide and colonialism. Great Britain has refused

even to apologize for these crimes against humanity because they claim their action were not crimes, because slavery was legal in that time (Beckles, 2013). Here we have a clear example of colonial state crime in which concepts, as defined by orthodox scholars, do not allow us to deal with colonial violence and to resolve such injustices.

## References

Agozino, B. (2003) *Counter Colonial Criminology: A Critique of Imperialist Reason*. London: Pluto Press.

Atiles-Osoria, J. (2012) "Pro-State Violence in Puerto Rico: Cuban and Puerto Ricans Right-Wing Terrorism." *Socialism and Democracy*, 26(1): 127–142.

——— (2013) "Neoliberalism, Law and Strike: Law as Instrument of Repression in the Student Strikes at the University of Puerto Rico between 2010 and 2011." *Latin American Perspectives*, 40(5): 105–117.

——— (2014) "The Criminalization of Socio-environmental Struggles in Puerto Rico." *Oñati Socio-Legal Series*, 4(1): 85–103.

——— (2016) "Colonial State Terror in Puerto Rico: A Research Agenda." *State Crime Journal*, 5(2): 221–242.

Beckles, H. (2013) *Britain's Black Debt: Reparations for Caribbean Slavery and Native Genocide*. Kingston: University of the West Indies Press.

Blakeley, R. (2009) *State Terrorism and Neoliberalism: the North in the South*. London and New York: Routledge.

Césaire, A. (2000) *Discourse on Colonialism*. New York: Monthly Review Press.

Chambliss, W., Michalowki, R. and Kramer, R. (eds.) (2010) *State Crime in the Global Age*. Devon and Portland: Willian.

Fanon, F. (1999) *Los condenados de la tierra*. Nafarroa: Txalaparta.

——— (2009) *Pieles negras, máscaras blancas*. Madrid: Akal.

Green, P. and Ward, T. (2004) *State Crime: Government, Violence and Corruption*. London: Pluto Press.

——— (2012) "State Crime: A Dialectical View," in M. Maguire, R. Morgan and R. Reiner (eds.) *The Oxford Handbook of Criminology*, 717–740. Oxford: Oxford University Press.

Iadicola, P. (2010) "Controlling Crime of Empire." *Social Justice*, 37(2): 98–110.

Kitossa, T. (2012) "Criminology and Colonialism: Counter Colonial Criminology and the Canadian Context." *The Journal of Pan African Studies*, 4(10): 204–226.

Lasslett, K. (2012) "State Crimes by Proxy: Australia and Bougainville Conflict." *British Journal of Criminology*, 52: 705–723.

Maldonado-Torres, N. (2007) "On the Coloniality of Being." *Cultural Studies*, 21(2): 240–270.

Marx, K. and Engels, F. (1968) *On Colonialism*. Moscow: Foreign Languages Publishing House.

Mbembe, A. (2003) *Necropolítica*. Tenerife: Melusina.

McLaughlin, E. (2001) "Postcolonial Criminology," in E. McLaughlin and J. Muncie (eds.) *The Sage Dictionary of Criminology*, 214. London: Sage.

Michalowski, R.J. and Kramer, R.C. (2006) "The Critique of Power," in R.J. Michalowski and R.C. Kramer (eds.) *State-Corporate Crime*, 1–17. New Jersey: Rutgers University Press.

Mignolo, W. (2005) *The Idea of Latin America*. Malden, Oxford and Victoria: Blackwell Publishing.

Pearce, F. (1976) *Crime of the Powerful: Marxism, Crime and Deviance*. London: Pluto Press.

———— (2015) "Marxism and Corporate Crime in the 21st Century." *Red Quill Books Interview Series #3*. Interviewed by Steve Bittle. Posted on 2 February.

Santos, B. (2009) *Sociología jurídica crítica: Para un nuevo sentido común en el derecho*. Madrid and Bogota: Trotta/ILSA.

Tombs, S. and Whyte, D. (eds.) (2003) *Unmasking the Crime of the Powerful: Scrutinizing States and Corporations*. New York and Oxford: Peter Lang.

———— (2015a) *The Corporate Criminal. Why Corporations Must be Abolished?*. London and New York: Routledge.

———— (2015b) Introduction to the Special Issue on "Crimes of the Powerful." *The Howard Journal*, 54(1): 1–7.

Ward, T. (2005) "State Crime in the Heart of Darkness." *British Journal of Criminology*, 45: 434–45.

Whyte, D. (2009) *Crimes of the Powerful: A Reader*. London: Open University Press.

Chapter 24

# Organized irresponsibility, corporations and the contradictions of collective agency and individual culpability

*Dean Curran*

In thinking about ways to build on *CotP*, it may be said that from Pearce's *CotP* (1976) to Tombs and Whyte's (2015) *The Corporate Criminal* that an impressive amount of research has been developed on the contemporary corporation as a criminogenic social unit. As Pearce (1976: 90) highlights, it is only the yawning chasm between *actionable* criminal acts and *actual* criminal prosecutions that hides the fact that "corporations provide the most efficient and largest examples of organised crime in America" (Pearce 1976: 78).[2] From skirting anti-trust rules, taxation rules or cutting corners on safety and health regulations (Pearce and Tombs 1998), as Pearce (1976: 105) emphasizes, criminal activity is often simply one amongst many other potential strategies by corporate actors. Pearce and his co-authors have sought to explore the systemic manner in which corporations are able to create structures of relationships that enable them to avoid responsibility for the damages caused by their actions (Pearce and Tombs 1998; Pearce 2001a), culminating in a discussion where Pearce's work is described as an analysis of corporate "organized irresponsibility" (Tombs and Whyte 2015: 107–120). The analysis of the criminogenic nature of the corporation has recently led to the argument that in fact the corporation needs to be "abolished" (Tombs and Whyte 2015).

Creatively building upon Pearce's work on corporate crime and *The Radical Durkheim* (2001b) as well as on the social theory of risk, this chapter develops an analysis of the relationship between corporations in contemporary capitalism and organized irresponsibility.[3] The chapter proceeds as follows. First, this analysis of corporate "organized irresponsibility" (Pearce 2001a; Tombs and Whyte 2015) is outlined and is linked to Pearce's *CotP* (1976). Second, this analysis of the corporate form is linked to Beck's theorization of "organized irresponsibility" (Beck 1995 [1988]), to identify how corporations instantiate a particularly pernicious form of *complexity as the opportunity for irresponsibility*, which Beck elucidates in his creative re-thinking of Luhmann's (1995 [1984]) systems theory to understand contemporary environmental risk (Beck 1995 [1988]). Finally, the source of this organized irresponsibility is traced to a particular dysfunctional amalgam of individualism and collectiveness in the law that enables collectivities to act, but only places culpability with specific individuals who can be shown to be responsible for the socially damaging outcomes.

## Capitalist corporations and criminal irresponsibility

In *CotP*, Pearce (1976) identifies how the "real social order" violates many core elements of the "imaginary social order." One of the most significant of these violations is in the relationship between organized crime and capitalist institutions. For Pearce (1976), criminal activity, whether it be corporate crime or of illegal organizational units commonly described as "organized crime," must be situated in the larger capitalist social order. For both of these types of organizations, Pearce (1976) focuses on what might be called the *differential license* between the potentially criminally prosecutable behaviour and the prosecution of these offences to the full extent permitted within the law. For Pearce (1976) this differential license is not random, but rather is highly correlated with the extent to which the criminal activities do or do not threaten the reproduction of core capitalist institutions. Whereas the state is often very permissive on anti-trust issues – where greater monopolization does not threaten the capitalist order – embezzlement crimes, which if widespread could fundamentally undermine trust and functioning of capitalist markets and corporations, tend to be prosecuted in a much more vigorous fashion (Pearce 1976).[4] Likewise when organized crime was engaged in practices that busted unions or co-opted them, or crimes such as bootlegging, which did not threaten the existing social and economic order, a much more permissible attitude to criminal prosecution was taken. Yet when Capone's activities in Chicago began to threaten the existing function of the social order, he was pursued in much more vigorous terms by the state (Pearce 1976). In this way, Pearce argues that this differential license to commit *actionable* crimes without being prosecuted is highly dependent on whether the actions threaten interests that are bound up with the reproduction of the state and capitalism.

In this vein, it might be said that the global financial crisis of 2007–2008 further extended the scope of differential license, with the emergence of *necessary license*, in which *not* prosecuting the actionable financial crimes in the United States following the crisis was a necessity for the reproduction of the existing social and economic order. Criminalizing large parts of the American financial system, after almost 30 years of glorification of Wall Street as the bastion of American capitalism, would have been a massive blow to the existing "cultural imaginary" of capitalism and wealth (see also Johnson and Kwak 2010; Will et al. 2013).

Of course, when discretion is possible in terms of boundary decisions, congruence with the interests of decision makers and those who influence those decision makers is a key means of ending up on the right side of the boundary. There are significant *prima facie* cases where criminal behaviour is simply not prosecuted, especially when the crimes are congruent with the interests of elite decision makers – as was the case with the lack of prosecution of financial crimes in the lead-up to the financial crisis (Morgenson and Story 2011). Nevertheless, the systemic nature of avoidance of criminal responsibility for harms created by corporations suggests that there is a social process in play beyond the systemic bias of decision makers regarding the status of the potential subject of investigation. As Pearce has highlighted in his work, corporate crimes manifest key features that make them different than many other criminal activities.

In terms of how corporate crimes should be understood differently, Pearce argues that "Corporate crimes are, above all, organizational crimes" (Pearce 1993: 138; see also Pearce 2001a). In particular, contrary to the dominant focus in criminal law on *mens rea* and *actus rea*, the "organizational production" of crimes creates a situation in which crimes are often not caused by personal motives, but rather result from organizational goals (Pearce 2001a: 36–37). Moreover, the whole idea of defined goals or motives of specific individuals generating specific *intentions*, which then lead to particular *acts* that then have definable *consequences* is particularly inappropriate to corporate-caused harms, even if this triplet of individual *intention-act-consequence* is core to criminal reasoning (see Pearce 2001a: 36–37). As Pearce argues, the fit between corporate organizational structures and the way the law adjudicates criminality is particularly poor: "The criminal law, rather than recognising the fact that decisions are the product of systemic processes, focuses on individual intentionality" (Weait 1992 in Pearce 2001a: 38). Often intention for acts carried out in the corporation's name is impossible to ascribe to the corporation as a totality (representing the five core elements of the corporation)[5] or with any one of these elements as a collectivity, such as the senior executives as a group, who are closest to a "controlling mind" of the corporation. Yet the corporation as a unit still produces massive harmful outcomes.

Driving home the point regarding the poor fit between the presuppositions of criminal law and the legally constituted organizational structure of the corporation, Pearce (2001a) argues that the criminal focus on *intention-act-consequence* embodies an extremely simple theory of causation. In particular, the issue of aggregation is faced in the application of corporate criminal law in particularly exigent terms. The individualism of criminal law cannot capture the dynamics of corporate criminality "because the way that responsibilities are distributed through a corporate body makes it extremely unlikely that the necessary fault will ever reside entirely in a single identifiable person" (Slapper 1993 in Pearce 2001a: 39). The advantages of aggregation in facing an individualistic, empiricist legal theory of causation is manifested in concrete terms in that by the end of the 20th century the only two convictions for corporate manslaughter in England and Wales were against small companies where it was relatively simple to link the controlling mind to the harms caused (Pearce 2001a: 39).[6]

Large corporations are able to benefit from a situation in which the various causes and conditions that result in significant harms are able to be distributed in such a manner that legal responsibility is extremely difficult to ascribe. Citing the catastrophic consequences of Bhopal,[7] the capsizing of the Herald of Free Enterprise ferry[8] and the Piper Alpha explosion in the North Sea,[9] Pearce (1993: 136) points out that in all of these cases the accidents occurred in a subdivision of a large company,[10] that the legal penalties on the parent company were relatively trivial and in all of these cases "neither the companies nor their chief executives have been convicted of felonies" (Pearce 1993: 136). In each of these cases, existing safety procedures were not properly used and "safety was compromised for the sake of profits," yet although corporate strategy and financial control ultimately flow from executives (Pearce 2001a: 44), low level-employees were held responsible for these disasters (Pearce 1993: 136). Being unable in these cases to move from the harmful consequences back to the specific act and ultimately to the intention that produced these outcomes, corporate executives are able to avoid responsibility for massive corporate-caused social harms.

## Rethinking organized irresponsibility

Pearce's discussion of how corporate legal forms create a form of "structural irresponsibility" (Pearce 2001a: 46) has been particularly influential. Tombs and Whyte (2015) in their ground-breaking *The Corporate Criminal*, build on Pearce's (2001a) discussion under the guise of discussing the "organized irresponsibility" of contemporary corporations. Undoubtedly, these insights are important, but in thinking further about "organized irresponsibility" and how corporations manifest a type of causality that is not captured by the legal reasoning underpinning contemporary criminal law, it may be helpful to step back and reflect on more general analyses of "organized irresponsibility" in social life. C. W. Mills used the concept of "organized irresponsibility" several times in his *The Power Elite* (1956: 338, 342, 357, 361), linking the concept to the impunity in which American elites acted. In discussing "organized irresponsibility," Mills (1956: 342) declared that it is the "mindlessness of the powerful that is the true higher immorality of our time." Linking organized irresponsibility specifically to corporate power, he then proceeded to associate this "higher immorality" with "the organized irresponsibility that is today the most important characteristic of the American system of corporate power" (Mills 1956: 342).

Although Mills' discussion of organized irresponsibility is highly innovative, his theoretical articulation of the concept has several limitations for our purposes. While using the concept to describe systemic impunity, it is not an organizing concept for his analysis of elites, but rather functions as a systemic outcome of his analysis of American corporate (and state) elites. Thus, although as a metaphor it is evocative, its theoretical articulation is limited. Second, Mills tended to employ the term in a moralistic and individualistic manner, referring to the poor behaviour of individuals, without linking the concept to the systems that in fact tend to nullify individual agency (as discussed earlier).

Thirty years later another social theorist, Ulrich Beck, developed a conceptualization of "organized irresponsibility" that was to become a key pillar of his social theory (Beck 1995 [1988]). Despite some limitations of Beck's utilization of the concept, which are discussed later, this formulation provides two important advantages over Mills' formulation. First, Beck moved away from a primarily individualistic and moral account of organized irresponsibility by tying it more closely to an analysis of how structures and systems tend to generate organized irresponsibility. Second, although Mills did an impressive job in linking organized irresponsibility to power and to socially irresponsible behaviour, Beck specifically linked it to the production of risk, and thus ultimately *social harm*, which better explains why this irresponsibility is so socially dysfunctional.

Beck's account of organized irresponsibility is primarily developed in *Ecological Politics in an Age of Risk* (1995 [1988])[11] and *World Risk Society* (1999), though the foundations of the analysis are ultimately in Beck's *Risk Society*'s (1992a [1986]) discussion of structures of irresponsibility. For Beck, organized irresponsibility occurs when agents are able to collectively create risks for which each of them are able to avoid culpability due to the difficulties in attributing specific consequences to specific actors (Beck 1995). Beck specifically links organized irresponsibility to the way in which contemporary law is creating "organized non-liability" because of its inability to adequately capture address the level of complexity of the contemporary configurations of the productive potential of modern economies (Beck 1995). In this vein, it is Beck's creative re-interpretation of Luhmann's (1995 [1984]) systems theory that develops this conception of organized irresponsibility and identifies the conditions for its development. As Strydom puts it: "In the buildup toward the threshold, however, *no individual decisions can be isolated, but only the accumulation of effects of decision-making*, the long-term consequences of decisions no longer identifiable, over-complex and indistinct causal relations" (Strydom 2002: 68, emphasis added). As societies continue to see greater levels of functional differentiation of production and ensuing complexity from this functional differentiation, the opportunities grow for a type of systemic causality, which eludes the identification of specific agents as responsible for the damages wreaked by collective actions. What we see here in Beck's work, like in Pearce's discussion though in a different form, is the idea that the types of causation that are manifested in contemporary society are not adequately addressed by contemporary law (Beck 1995: 134–135). The complexity of causal chains and how they generate organized irresponsibility ties into Beck's discussion of the "problem of attribution" and how the "relations of definition" of risk in terms of how responsibility for risks are ascribed is becoming a key fulcrum of social power (Beck 1995: 77, 110).[12]

For Beck, this widespread condition of organized irresponsibility is central to the massive growth in environmental risk and the potential catastrophes embodied in the contemporary production of goods. Although Beck's theory of the unintended production of social risk as a critique of existing legal frameworks remains primarily unexplored in the existing literature, he views the lack of appropriate fit between contemporary complex causality and contemporary configurations of the law as central to the production of heightened environmental risk. As Beck (1995: 69) asks: "[W]hat good is a legal system that prosecutes technically manageable small risks, but legalizes large-scale hazards on the strength of its authority, foisting them on everyone, including even those multitudes who resist them?"

Beck's thinking on organized irresponsibility has significant potential to illuminate a variety of different topics, including contemporary finance (Curran 2015), environment (Curran 2016) and, as this chapter argues, corporate crime; nevertheless, some modifications of Beck's specific understanding of "organized irresponsibility" are necessary before this task can be achieved.[13] First, the conceptual tools that Beck provides to analyse contemporary risk, including the social production and distribution of risk, private escape routes from risk, relations of definition of risk and organized irresponsibility, can be utilized to analyse contemporary risk irrespective of the larger "epochal" question of the "risk society thesis" (see Beck 1992a, 1999; Strydom 2002; Mythen 2007). That is, one can be agnostic regarding the epochal question of whether risks work in a fundamentally different way in contemporary society that has resulted in a new form of modernity (see Beck 1992a) while still considering Beck's conceptual tools as a useful paradigm or approach for risk research (see Curran 2016, 2017).[14]

Second, Beck's interpretation of organized irresponsibility tends to negate how power relations are imbricated with organized irresponsibility and hence needs to be revised. In particular, Beck increasingly focused on the non-knowingness associated with risk society processes, such that even those who initially benefitted from organized irresponsibility would ultimately be overwhelmed by these processes (Beck 1999, 2004). In this vein, Beck came to view risk emerging from organized irresponsibility as completely uncontrollable and hence, rather than being a power dimension, it became a kind of collective failure to manage a collective action problem (see Beck 1999: 6–7). This totalizing uncontrollability, however, is clearly overstated. Even with the global financial crisis of 2007–2008, which was admittedly unexpected by the vast majority of actors,[15] and in which, once the crisis began, many of its elements were difficult to control, this does not entail total uncontrollability. The shift from partnerships to shareholder companies, the way in which pay was structured, as profit share but not loss share, suggests that even within complex networks of causation and out-of-control effects, there is significant scope for modifying one's *risk position*; therefore, power relations continue to be a key part of organized irresponsibility (Curran 2015). It may be said that organized irresponsibility actually stands between complete uncontrollability, where all would equally face social harm blindly, and total controllability, where the consequences for these processes would be fully controllable, and hence responsible agents could be identified. It is this *in-between space* that is key to how organized irresponsibility functions as a power relation in contemporary society.

Third, Beck tended to analyse organized irresponsibility in terms of the logics of institutions or organizations, usually placing the relation of organized irresponsibility at the level in which several organizations, such as corporations, cumulatively create environmental damages, in which any specific damage cannot be attributed to any specific corporation (see Beck 1992b). Undoubtedly, Beck's insight that organized irresponsibility can function at the intercorporate level is an in important insight, yet, his focus on institutional logics of science or of industry focuses on risk and irresponsibility as the product of a generic type of instrumental rationality (Beck 1992a: ch 7). By focusing on merely disembodied logics of organization, Beck importantly neglects how *interests* are intertwined with the complex logics of causation and avoidance of liability associated with organized irresponsibility. But the opposite model, rational choice theory and the associated individualistic mentality of culpability of *mens rea*, is inadequate as well, as discussed earlier. Rather what is needed is to situate interests, power and the distribution of agency within the organizational and larger capitalist institutional setting, as Pearce (1976) has emphasized. Having delineated an account of organized irresponsibility suited to the purposes of this chapter, the next section utilizes this concept to dig deeper to analyse how contemporary corporations embody a particularly dysfunctional form of organized irresponsibility.

## Organized irresponsibility and the dysfunctional dialectic of individual and collective

As this chapter proposes, there may be advantages to analysing the socially dysfunctional impacts of the contemporary capitalist corporation through the prism of "organized irresponsibility." The specific terms of the failure to hold responsible corporations and those within corporations who implement socially damaging actions is important and has been discussed extensively in the literature. An individualistic law, which tends to require *actus reus* and *mens rea* be identified for specific members to be held responsible creates massive problems in identifying responsible agents in extremely complex corporate structures. In corporations, the cause of an outcome may involve a whole variety of individuals and groups contributing in different ways to latent conditions that make a disaster likely and then different groups of individuals generating the actual actions or omission of actions that directly lead to the damages. The complexity of contemporary corporations makes a "corporate veil" (Wormser 1912; see also Tombs and Whyte 2015: 91–115) that is extremely difficult to move behind.

On the other hand, when alternative bases of judgement are used and corporations as a whole are criminally prosecuted even if specific individuals or

Organized irresponsibility 329

groups within the corporation cannot be identified as responsible, the burden tends to fall on those who are least aware of the conditions and least *directly* responsible for the outcomes: the shareholders.[16] Even if ultimately pressure from shareholders for higher returns plays a key role in intensifying fragility and the risk of catastrophe, as was the case with unreasonably high expectations of the return on equity of banks in the lead-up to the crisis (see Engelen et al. 2011: 108–111), this is really the responsibility of a shareholder *qua* shareholder, which *ceteris paribus* seeks maximal returns on his or her investments. Simply put, in a situation of knowing very little about the corporation that they (part) own, shareholders cannot distinguish between high returns based on excellent management and high returns based on negligence of care or, alternatively, between lower returns based on greater stability and care and lower returns based on poor management. Of course, playing a fundamental role in this dysfunctional structure in which corporate decision makers can dump responsibility for poor behaviour onto shareholders is the fact that the limited liability legal status of corporations generates a certain position of complacency of shareholders because there are strict limits to what a shareholder can lose, which is nothing more than what they have put into the company.[17]

The value of the concept of "organized irresponsibility" is, in large part, its ability to bring together a whole series of apparently independent processes and identify an important dimension of similarity that these processes exhibit. In this case, what the concept of "organized irresponsibility" zeroes in on is the dysfunctional dialectic of individual and collective that these cases manifest. The specific problem is not simply the individualistic nature of the law – the law does allow for the creation of innumerable collective agencies. Neither is the problem simply the collective nature of the law – collective organizations, such as private corporations, play a key role in managing the intense complexity of contemporary supply and consumption chains, which would not become significantly less complex even with a transition to a different economic system (Pearce 2001b). Although power relations played a role in the generation of these large corporate actors, as Sennett (2006) has emphasized in his discussion of the emergence of Bismarckian corporate capitalism, less complex, individual and family firms have found it extremely difficult to manage the complexity of 20th-century industrialism. Much of this complexity is a product of the pursuit of exchange value; however, Pearce (2001b) in the *Radical Durkheim* has also powerfully argued that a successful socialism would need to directly face the problem of complexity generated from high levels of functional differentiation emerging from high productivity and the diversity of different products currently produced. Facing this problem via either a multitude of atomistic families and individuals or through the centralized state without intermediate associations is, as de Tocqueville and Durkheim have emphasized, likely to lead to social dysfunction and the undermining rather than enhancement of autonomy (see Pearce 2001b: 160).

Consequently, what the concept of "organized irresponsibility" can help to identify is that the problem is neither solely in the individualism of the law nor in the collectivism of the law, but rather in the dysfunctional combination of the two. In particular, the problem is that whereas collective organizations are created, such as corporations, private think tanks, producer and trade bodies, and are able to act as collective agents, they are not fully collective bodies in which individuals are integrated together to create a new entity. That is, when culpability is to be distributed, the individuals who occupy the collective agencies are able to revert to their individual identity and disavow the actions of the collective agencies. It is this incoherent amalgam of collectivism of agency, but not of culpability, that creates the particular dysfunction of contemporary corporations. "Organized irresponsibility" can help elucidate the dual-sided nature of this process, the creation of collective actors that are directed by the individuals who occupy them, alongside individuals' potential disavowal of this collective agency if it is disadvantageous. This dysfunctional couplet of collective agency without culpability *ex ante* tends to encourage reckless processes that often ultimately lead to catastrophic social consequences.

This process creates not only systemic risk, but also the intensification of inequalities, a set of processes recently discussed as differential *risk classes* (Curran 2013, 2016, 2018; see also Beck 2013). The power to create and occupy collective actors that can be used as a means of extracting private gains, while also being able to dis-identify with the collective organization when the expected disbenefits of being associated with it exceeds its benefits, is clearly highly unequally distributed. For most of the disadvantaged in society, there are very few opportunities to occupy legal collective vehicles that create social risk while appropriating private benefit. These less advantaged individuals would need to commit an individual and often violent (and highly punished) crime to engage in the similar process of private benefit at social risk.

## Conclusion

Frank Pearce's *Crimes of the Powerful* (1976) was a ground-breaking book that helped to advance the critical study of corporations (and organizations more broadly) as units that are particularly adept at committing crimes without being held responsible for them. Pearce has continued to make important contributions to the study of corporate crime (Pearce 1993, 2001a; Pearce and Tombs 1996, 1998, 2012) and to the study of social theory, in particular, how the threads of Marxist and Durkheimian social theory can speak to each other (Pearce 2001b), upon which this chapter has sought to build. The relationship between the sociology of risk, specifically, the approach to risk that is most explicitly oriented to risks as real, future, possible and uncertain damages (Beck's risk society) (Curran 2016), and the critical study of corporate crime has been minimally investigated in the literature. Yet as this chapter argues, a rethinking of Beck's core concept of organized irresponsibility creates an important space for a dialogue between the critical study of corporate crime *á la* Pearce and the study of Beck's analysis of risk through the paradigm of the social production and distribution of risk in contexts of widespread organized irresponsibility.

As argued here it is not merely the individualistic nature of legal responsibility, nor simply the power to create collective agents that is the problem. It is the dysfunctional combination of the highly flexible ability of individual agents to combine to create collective agency in terms of corporations, but then to disassociate from this collective agency when damages arise, that creates a systematic gap between the power to produce risk and the power to assign culpability for risk that constitutes contemporary organized irresponsibility. In this space, a certain *risk arbitrage*[18] for the already powerful is intensifying two of the fundamental problems of our age, inequality and global systemic environmental and financial risk. Ultimately, re-evaluating how the law institutionalizes forms of collective and individual action and responsibility is absolutely central to addressing these problems. In pursuing this goal, as argued here, a meeting of the minds of the sociology of risk, specifically a critical rethinking of risk society, and the critical study of corporate crime, specifically Frank Pearce's work, have the potential to significantly contribute to this aim of rethinking the collective and individual dimensions of the law.

## Notes

1 I am grateful for this opportunity to write for this collection. I am particularly pleased to contribute to this collection due to my gratitude to Frank Pearce as a teacher and someone who has helped me improve my own work and understanding of the intersections of social theory and social life. This is not to suggest, though, that Frank Pearce would agree with the specific argument developed in this chapter.

2 On this chasm, see also Sutherland (1945).

3 The analysis of corporate crime and law in this chapter focuses specifically on Anglo-American (common law–based) legal systems, though many of the points regarding organized irresponsibility also apply to other types of legal systems (as Beck emphasized in his discussion of pollution in Germany (Beck 1992b)).

4 Sutherland (1940) has an alternative, interesting theory of this differential in terms of the level of organization of the criminal versus the level of organization of those who are harmed by the criminal activity. In embezzlement, a single actor faces a large corporation from which he or she has misappropriated funds, whereas in many other cases where the criminal activity goes weakly or un-punished, the corporation as a whole causes harms that are widely distributed amongst a large group of unorganized and weak individuals. Sutherland's (1940) insight here speaks in particular to the illegal foreclosures that continued to be imposed on weak and disparate individuals post-crisis, though it is likely that both of these views (Pearce 1976 and Sutherland 1940) explain different dimensions of this *differential license*.

5 Pearce (2001a: 38) highlights that these five elements of the corporation are (1) the legal personality of the corporation, (2) its shareholders, (3) its directors, (4) its managers and (5) its low-level employees.

6 The potential for prosecution for corporate manslaughter under common law in England and Wales was affirmed in a 1990 judgement in the Free Enterprise Ferry case. A new statutory law, The Corporate Manslaughter and Corporate Homicide Act (2007), was brought into law in 2008. Changes made to the originally proposed statutory law

after consultations with industry made the law's scope much narrower than originally proposed (McShee 2008) and the new law's lack of deviation from the "identification principle" has led many to consider the law too narrow to adequately capture the diverse ways in which senior executives contribute to harm and accidents (see Horder 2016: 172–3; see also Holmes 2017).

7　In 1984, an accident in a Union Carbine plant in Bhopal, India, caused the release of about 30 tons of highly toxic gases, causing approximately 15,000 deaths, though the number severely affected was much higher (Taylor 2014)

8　In 1987, a ferry travelling from Zeebrugge, Belgium, to Dover capsized, leading to 193 deaths (Holmes 2017).

9　In 1988, 167 workers were killed by an oil rig accident in the North Sea (Macalister 2013)

10　In describing these occurrences as "accidents" the intention is to indicate that the specific disaster was not intended by the relevant parties within the corporation who caused the disaster, which in no way precludes the fact that agents for the corporation intended the actions that constituted the conditions for the accidents to occur and for their damaging consequences to be as extensive as they were.

11　The original German title of *Ecological Politics in an Age of Risk* (1995 [1988]) better highlights the focus on organized irresponsibility in the text, which was "Counterpoisons: the organized irresponsibility" (Lash 2000: 61).

12　For an excessive claim in this vein, see Beck (2009: 31–32).

13　In a recent book I worked to elucidate how many elements of Beck's work, suitably reconstructed, can provide a powerful critique of contemporary risk and inequality and capitalism (Curran 2016). When, as a graduate student, I explained to one of my fellow students this project, he exclaimed, "It is like Frank [Pearce's] *Radical Durkheim*, but for Beck," which, again, suggests just one of the many ways that Pearce's teaching and research has both explicitly and implicitly affected my research.

14　In Beck (1989) he describes risk society as a "paradigm," though this historical disjuncture thesis is clearly there in his risk writings (see Beck 1992, 1995, 1999, 2009).

15　See Lewis (2011) for some of the key exceptions. Moreover, and more notably, the effort that Goldman made to extricate themselves from exposure to many of the worst mortgage-based special-purpose vehicles a year prior to the crisis suggests that there were significant warning signs, hence suggesting that "non-knowingness"(Beck 2004) is not an adequate way to characterize greater risk and complexity in finance (or environment).

16　In terms of the lack of responsibility for the damages from financial risk, it has been recently noted how with respect to the 2008 global financial crisis there has developed "an exceptional criminogenic environment. There were no criminal referrals from the regulators. No fraud working groups. No national task force. There has been no effective punishment of the elites here" (William K. Black in Morgenson and Story, 2011). When penalties have been levied for illegal behaviour, it has been fines that fall on the shareholders that have been the primary means of punishment.

17　Djelic and Bothello (2013: 589) argue that the limited liability legal status of corporations leads to a "systemic inscription of instability in contemporary capitalism."

18　"Risk arbitrage" is where the private benefits of ratcheting up risk are greater than the costs of these risks for their originator, even when these risks manifest themselves in significant losses (Curran 2015, 2016).

## References

Beck, U. (1989) "On the Way to the Industrial Risk-Society? Outline of an Argument." *Thesis Eleven*, 23(1): 86–103.

Organized irresponsibility **333**

———— (1992a [1986]) *Risk Society: Towards a New Modernity*. London: Sage.

———— (1992b) "From Industrial Society to the Risk Society: Questions of Survival, Social Structure and Ecological Enlightenment." *Theory, Culture & Society*, 9(1): 97–123.

———— (1995 [1988]) *Ecological Politics in an Age of Risk*. Cambridge: Polity Press.

———— (1999) *World Risk Society*. Malden, MA: Polity.

———— (2004) "The Cosmopolitan Turn," in N. Gane (ed.) *Future of Social Theory*. London: Continuum.

———— (2009) *World at Risk*. Cambridge: Polity.

———— (2013) "Why 'Class' is too Soft a Category to Capture the Explosiveness of Social Inequality at the Beginning of the 21st Century." *British Journal of Sociology*, 64(1): 63–74.

Curran, D. (2013) "Risk Society and the Distribution of Bads: Theorizing Class in the Risk Society." *British Journal of Sociology*, 64(1): 44–62.

———— (2015) "Risk Illusion and Organized Irresponsibility in Contemporary Finance: Rethinking Class and Risk Society." *Economy and Society*, 44(3): 392–417.

———— (2016) *Risk, Power, and Inequality in the 21st Century*, Basingstoke: Palgrave Macmillan.

———— (2017) "Risk, Innovation, and Democracy in the Digital Economy." *European Journal of Social Theory*, 0(0): 1–20, early publish. http://journals.sagepub.com/doi/full/10.1177/1368431017710907

———— (2018) "Beck's Creative Challenge to Class Analysis: From the Rejection of Class to the Discovery of Risk-Class." *Journal of Risk Research*, 21(1): 29–40.

Djelic, M.L. and Bothello, J. (2013) "Limited Liability and Its Moral Hazard Implications: The Systemic Inscription of Instability in Contemporary Capitalism." *Theory and Society*, 42(6): 589–615.

Engelen, E., Ertürk, I., Froud, J., Johal, S., Leaver, S., Moran, M., Nilsson, A. and Williams, K. (2011) *After the Great Complacence: Financial Crisis and the Politics of Reform*. Oxford: Oxford University Press.

Holmes, G. (2017) "Zeebrugge Ferry Disaster, 30 Years On: Deadly Failings Behind One of UK's Worst Peacetime Maritime Tragedies." *The Independent*, 3 March. Online. Available HTTP: www.independent.co.uk/news/uk/home-news/zeebrugge-ferry-disaster-ms-herald-of-free-enterprise-uk-30-years-on-maritime-tragedy-killed-a7583131.html

Horder, J. (2016) *Ashworth's Principles of Criminal Law* (8th ed.). Oxford: Oxford University Press.

Johnson, S. and Kwak, J. (2010) *13 Bankers: The Wall Street Takeover and the Next Financial Meltdown*. New York: Pantheon Books.

Lash, S. (2000) "Risk Culture," in B. Adam, U. Beck and J. van Loon (eds.) *The Risk Society and Beyond: Critical Issues for Social Theory*. London: Sage.

Lewis, M. (2011) *The Big Short*. London: Penguin.

Luhmann, N. (1995 [1984]) *Social Systems*. Stanford, CA: Stanford University Press.

Macalister, T. (2013) "Piper Alpha Disaster: How 167 Oil Rig Workers Died." *Guardian*, 4 July. Online. Available HTTP: www.theguardian.com/business/2013/jul/04/piper-alpha-disaster-167-oil-rig

McShee, D. (2008) "The History of the Corporate Manslaughter and Corporate Homicide Act 2007," in A. Davies (ed.) *Corporate Manslaughter and Corporate Homicide Act*, 9–16. Cambridge: Workplace Law Group.

Mills, C.W. (1956) *The Power Elite*. Oxford: Oxford University Press.

Morgenson, G. and Story, L. (2011) "In Financial Crisis, No Prosecutions of Top Figures." *New York Times*, 14 April. Online. Available HTTP: www.nytimes.com/2011/04/14/business/14prosecute.html (accessed 4 April 2016).

Mythen, G. (2007) "Reappraising the Risk Society Thesis: Telescopic Sight or Myopic Vision?" *Current Sociology*, 55(6): 793–813.

Pearce, F. (1976) *Crimes of the Powerful: Marxism, Crime and Deviance*. London: Pluto.

——— (1993) "Corporate Rationality as Corporate Crime." *Studies in Political Economy*, 40 (Spring): 135–162.

——— (2001a) "Crime and Capitalist Business Organisations," in N. Shover and J.P. Wright (eds.) *Crimes of Privilege: Readings in White Collar Crime*, 35–48, Oxford: Oxford University Press.

——— (2001b) *The Radical Durkheim* (2nd ed.). Toronto: Canadian Scholars Press.

Pearce, F. and Tombs, S. (1996) "Hegemony, Risk and Governance: 'social regulation' and the American Chemical Industry." *Economy and Society*, 25(3): 428–454.

——— (1998) *Toxic Capitalism: Corporate Crime in the Chemical Industry*. Aldershot: Ashgate.

——— (2012) *Bhopal: Flowers at the Altar of Profit and Power*. Crime Talk Books (e-book).

Sennett, Richard. (2006) *The Culture of the New Capitalism*. New Haven, CT: Yale University Press.

Strydom, P. (2002) *Risk, Environment and Society*. Buckingham: Open University Press.

Sutherland, E.H. (1940) "White-Collar Criminality." *American Sociological Review*, 5(1): 1–12.

Sutherland, E.H. (1945) "Is 'White-Collar Crime' Crime?." *American Sociological Review*, 10(2): 132–139.

Taylor, A. (2014) "Bhopal: The World's Worst Industrial Disaster, 30 Years Later." *Atlantic*. Online. Available HTTP: www.theatlantic.com/photo/2014/12/bhopal-the-worlds-worst-industrial-disaster-30-years-later/100864/

Tombs, S. and Whyte, D. (2015) *The Corporate Criminal: Why Corporations Must Be Abolished*. Abingdon: Routledge.

Will, S., Handelman, S. and Brotherton, D.C. (eds.) (2013) *How They Got Away with It: White Collar Criminals and the Financial Meltdown*. New York: Columbia University Press.

Wormser, I.M. (1912) "Piercing the Veil of Corporate Entity." *Columbia Law Review*, 12: 496–518.

# Index

Abreu, K. 181
academic knowledge claims xli–xliii
*Accumulation of Capital, The* (Luxemburg) 146
Ackerman, S. 42
acting in concert 69–70
*Age of Stagnation, The* (Das) 147
Agozino, B. 298, 306
agro-toxins: consumption in Brazil 174–178; regulatory framework in Brazil 178–184
aleatory materialism 81
Althusser, L. 81
anti-trust legislation 5–6, 180
Apple, Inc. 252
Archer, M. 80
Arendt, H. 69, 147
Aristotle 69
Asian dam projects 234, 236–240
Asian Development Bank (ADB) 238–239
Asian Infrastructure Investment Bank 239

bailouts 90–91
Bankowski, Z. 15
Barak, G. 233
*Barbarians in Our Midst* (Peterson) 39
Baudrillard, J. 246
Beck, U.: analysis of risk 330–331; conceptualization of organized irresponsibility 322, 326–328; *Ecological Politics in an Age of Risk* 326; *Risk Society* 326; *World Risk Society* 326
Beijing Platform for Action (BPfA) 272
Bell, D. 47
Berk, R. 275
Bhopal disaster 301–302
Black Lives Matter movement 305
Blair, T. 288

Blakeley, R. 316
blame 96–97, 138–140
blaming the victim 137–140
Blockadia 160–162, 168
Blunt, C. 291
Boggs, H. 39
Boghosian, H. 251
Bonger, W. 231
Bougainville 126–129
Bougainville Copper Limited (BCL) 126–129
Box, S. 301
Brazil: agro-toxin consumption 174–178; genetically modified crops 177; imaginary social order in 180–184; import-substitution industrialization policies 175; regulatory framework for agro-toxins in 178–184; state and capital relations in 175–176; Zika virus epidemic 177
*Breaking the Cycle* (Green Paper) 284, 285

Calder, J.D. 33
Canada: Charbonneau Commission 46–47, 49, 54; construction industry/political corruption schemes 47–48, 54; criminal association legislation 48–50; exclusion of lawyers from mandatory suspicious reporting 51–53; failure to make beneficial ownership structure of corporations transparent 50–51; Gomery Commission 54; nuclear waste storage 82; "participation/facilitation" offense 48–49; political "use" of corruption inquiries 53–55; "sham" offshore tax scheme involving CRA and KPMG International 52–53, 54
Canada Revenue Agency (CRA) 52–53, 54

capital: accumulation of 146–147; capitalist state's relationship to criminalization and the economies of 145–149; conception of 123–124; global 144–145; rigging of interbank interests rates 149–153; "secret" and "hidden rationality" of 13; state-corporate crime and organic composition of 126–129; violence and accumulation of 61

*Capital* (Marx) 119–125, 129

capitalism: development of 63; influence on types of crimes and crime control 145–149; privilege of 63; regulatory law and 27–29; social embeddedness of 46–47; zombie 89–90

Capone, A. 32–43, 299, 323–325

capture theory 182–183

celebrity 248–249

Césair, A. 314

Charbonneau Commission 46–47, 49, 54

Chicago Crime Commission (CCC) 33–36

child labour 124–125

Christensen, J. 51

Clarke, K. 285

coercion: hegemony and 60–63; by legal intervention 25–27; power and 69–70; voluntarism and 21–25, 27–29

colonial state crimes 316–319

commodity fetishism 303–304

Comte, A. 60

concealment 64–65

consciousness 11

consensus 63–64

consent: hegemony and 245–246; reification of crimes of the powerful and 250–253

consumer protection 265–267

consumption: debt and 147; reification of crimes of the powerful and 250–253; role of 246–250

*Contribution to the Critique of Political Economy, A* (Marx) 120

Coolidge, C. 33

cooperation 60–61

corporate crime: contemporary debates on 299–303; definition of 301; enablers of 45–46; as form of organized crime 323–325; general theory of crimes of the powerful 297–306

*Corporate Crime* (Pearce and Snider) 299

*Corporate Criminal, The* (Tombs and Whyte) 322, 325

corporate criminal liability (CCL): blaming the victim 138–141; convictions 141; court decisions in Finland 134–140; enforcement 140–141; formulation of legislation in Finland 132–134; imaginary social order of 131–141; punishing shop floor in Finland 136–138; silencing corporate recidivism in Finland 135–136

corporate fines 134

corporate recidivism 135–136

corporations 25–27, 29, 143–144, 313–314, 322

corruption 49–50

credit: consumer protection in democratized 265–267; imaginary social order and democratization of 259–260

credit service organizations (CSOs) 264

Crenshaw, K. 298

crime control 148

*Crime in America* (Kefauver) 37

crimes of globalization: challenges 240–241; as contemporary form of organized crime 234–235; international financial institutions and Asian dam projects 236–240

*Crimes of Globalization* (Rothe and Friedrichs) 235

*Crimes of the Powerful* (Pearce) xxviii–xxx, xxxiii–xlvii, 3–4, 15–16, 20–21, 32, 42, 45, 87–89, 98, 102, 119, 141, 157, 160, 189, 233, 235, 283, 290, 297, 322, 323, 330

*Crimes of the Powerful* (Rothe and Kauzlarich) 233

criminal irresponsibility 323–325

criminology 15–17

critical realism (CR): environmental 76–78; principles of 73–74; TMSA and 73–74

Currie, E. 16

Dakota Access Pipeline (DAPL) Project: background 162–163; objections to 162–163; resistance by SRST 158–159, 163–168; standoff between Water Protectors and 158, 163–167

Das, S. 147

debt 147, 249

debtfarism: democratization of credit and 258–260; payday lending and 258, 260–267

democracy 4–5

Derrida, J. 303, 306
de Tocqueville, A. 329
Dewey, J. 63–65
dialectical materialism 12
differential license 323
discourses 74–76
discursive 74–76
domestic violence: costs of 271; court failures 277–278; failure to fully provide for victim services 278–279; failure to protect victims from 270–279; inadequate laws 273–274; police failures 274–277; scope and extent of 270–271; states' obligations to address 272–273
domination 61–62, 63–64
Dostoyevsky, F. 232
Du Bois, W.E.B.: *The Philadelphia Negro* 297–298; *The Suppression of the African Slave Trade* 298
Duncan Smith, I. 291
Durbin, R.J. 266
Durkheim, É. 92–94, 329

Eagleton, T. 233
*Ecological Politics in an Age of Risk* (Beck) 326
*Economic and Philosophical Manuscripts of 1844, The* (Marx) 121
empiricist sociology 10
enclosure 103–104, 109–110
Engels, F. 315
enmeshment: hazardous nuclear waste and 81–83; looping effects and 78–80; recombinant nature and 77
environmental activism 160–162
epistemology 14
Export Trade Act of 1918 6
expulsion 103–104, 109–110
extra-discursive 74–76

Factory Act of 1844 125
Fair Labor Standards Act (FLSA) of 1938 193–194, 197
false consciousness 62
Fanon, F. 298, 306, 314
fast violence 236
fear 67
finance 88–89
financial crisis of 2007 220
Finland: blaming the victim 137–140; CCL enforcement 140–141; CCL legislation 131–141; corporate recidivism 135–136;

court cases 134–140; criminal offence punishment 134; middle management punishment 136–137
Fischetti, C. 38
Foucault, M. 75–76
Friedrichs, D. 235

Garland, D. 304
genetically modified crops 177
*German Ideology, The* (Marx and Engels) 120
Giannacopoulos, M. 299
Gilroy, P. 298
Gitlin, T. 248
globalization: crimes of 234–241; neoliberal 104
Global South countries 237–240
Gomery Commission 54
"Gomery Effect" 54–55
Gramsci, A. 63–64, 70
Green, P. 313
Gutiérrez, L. 265

Hacking, I. 78–80, 83
Hall, S. 298, 303
Harvey, D. 148
hegemonic discourse 246–250
hegemony: coercion and 60–63, 65; consensus and 63–64; consent and 245–246; secrecy and 63–65
Hitz, F.P. 41
*Holy Family or Critique of Critical Critique, The* (Marx and Engels) 121
Homan Square detentions and interrogations warehouse 42–43
*Homo juridicus* 67–69
Hopewell, K. 180–181
humanism 80

imaginary social order: in Brazil 180–184; coercion and 60–63; concept of 7–9, 14; consumption and 246–253; crimes of globalization and 231–233; democratization of credit as 259–260; law and 7; naïve and misleading 8–9; notion of xxxiv, 7–9, 131, 202, 283, 290, 323; of payday lending 259–260; real social order and 7–9, 13, 323; violence and 235–236; workplace theft and 193–196
import-substitution industrialization policies 175

Independent Commission Against Corruption (ICAC): findings of corruption for Eddie Obeid 202–203, 209–212; formation of 205–206; ideological function 207–208; official function and operation of 206–207, 212–213
interactionism 9, 11
Inter-American Commission on Human Rights (IACHR) 273, 274–275
Inter-American Convention on the Prevention, Punishment, and Eradication of Violence Against Women 273
interbank interest rates 149–153
International Covenant on Civil and Political Rights (ICCPR) 272
international financial institutions 236–240
International Monetary Fund 238
Iran-Contra scandals 40–41
*Iron Heel, The* (London) 253

Kauzlarich, D. 233
Kefauver, E. 37–38
Kennedy, E.M. 40
Keystone XL pipeline 161–162
KPMG International Cooperative 52–53, 54
Kramer, R. 313

labelling theory xxxv–xxxvi
labour markets 64
law: corporate power and 6–7; *Homo juridicus* 67–69; imaginary social order and 7–9; as mechanism for creating "unanimity of interest" and collective consciousness 10–11; minimum wage 194–196; provisional status of 4–5; regulatory 27–29; voluntarism and 21–25
Lemert, E. 9–10
Lenahan-Gonzales, J. 274–275
Libor scandal 149–153
Loesch, F. 33–34, 36
London, J. 253
looping effects 78–80
Luce, H. 236
Luciano, C. "Lucky" 37
Luhmann, N. 322, 326
Lukács, G. 12–13
Luxemburg, R. 146
Lyotard, J.F. 303

Mafia 37–40
Mafia-type organized crime 46–47
Maldonado-Torres, N. 314
Mandela, N. 306
Marx, K.: *Capital* 119–125, 129; conception of capital 123–124; *A Contribution to the Critique of Political Economy* 120; on distribution of surplus value 124–125, 147; *The Economic and Philosophical Manuscripts of 1844* 121; *The German Ideology* 120; *The Holy Family or Critique of Critical Critique* 121; labour theory of value 122–123; notion of false consciousness 62; philosophical foundations of political economy 120–122, 129–130; *The Poverty of Philosophy* 120–121; references to colonialism 315; on roots of primitive accumulation of capital 303
Massimo, P. 293
May, T. 277
McBarnet, D. 51
McLaughlin, E. 315–316
Mead, G.H. 9
Mellon, A. 33–34
Melossi, D. 293
Merton, R.K. 45
Michalowski, R. 313
middle management punishment 136–137
Military Lending Act 265–266
Mills, C.W. 325, 326
minimum wage laws 194–196
Minneapolis Domestic Violence Experiment 275
Moran, G. "Bugs" 33
mortgages 152, 220, 223–226
Murphy, R. 76–77, 81, 83

National Network to End Domestic Violence (NNEDV) 278
Native American women 276
neoliberal globalization 104
neoliberalism xxxvi–xli
*New Criminology, The* (Taylor, Walton and Young) 3, 15–16
New Development Bank (NDB) 239–240
New South Wales (NSW): corruption in granting of coal exploration licences 204–205; formation of ICAC 205–206; ICAC findings of corruption for Eddie Obeid 202–203, 209–212; ideological function of ICAC 207–208; Rum Corps 204–205

nomophilia 299
non-Mafia-type organized crime 46–47
*Notes from Underground* (Dostoyevsky) 232
nuclear waste 81–83

Obeid, E. 202–203, 209–212
"Obligatory Sacrifice and Imperial
Projects" (Pearce) 87
Occupy Wall Street (OWS) movement
41–42
Organization of American States
(OAS) 273
organized crime: crimes of globalization as
form of 234–235; evolution of organized
crime control 32–43; as social construct
45–46; structure in America 37–39;
syndicates 38, 235; types of 46–47; U.S.
federal government perspective on
39–40; war against 40–41; World Bank as
"criminal enterprise" 238
Organized Crime Control Act of 1970
33, 40
organized irresponsibility: dysfunctional
dialectic of individual and collective and
328–330; rethinking 325–328
*Origins of Totalitarianism, The* (Arendt) 147
ostentation 65–69

Papua New Guinea 126–129
Pashukanis, E.B. 303
payday lending: consumer protection in
democratized credit 265–267; debating
predation 258–259; debtfare state and the
facilitation of 260–267; democratization
of credit as an imaginary social order
259–260; imaginary social order of
258–260; rhetorical payday bans and
salience distortion 262–265; unmasking
"predators who care" and best practices
260–262
Payday Loan Reform Act of 2009 265
Pearce, F.: concern with limitations of
labelling theory and SI xxxv–xxxvi;
*Corporate Crime* 299; corporate crimes
323–325; crimes committed by the
dispossessed and crimes committed by
the powerful 62; *Crimes of the Powerful*
xxviii–xxx, xxxiii–xlvii, 3–4, 15–16,
20–21, 32, 42, 45, 87–89, 98, 102, 119,
141, 157, 160, 189, 233, 235, 283, 290,
297, 322, 323, 330; critical realism
73–74; critique of democracy and the

rule of law 4–6, 9–14; critique of racist
criminal justice system 297–298; notion
of imaginary social order xxxiv, 7–9,
131, 202, 259–260, 267, 283; notion
of real social order xxxiv, 290, 323;
notion of structural irresponsibility 325;
"Obligatory Sacrifice and Imperial
Projects" 87; *The Radical Durkheim* 322,
329; "Revisiting *Crimes of the Powerful*"
conference 303; study of Bhopal
disaster 301–302; *Toxic Capitalism* 73;
use of methodology and framework for
development of concept of colonial state
crimes 310–314, 317, 319
Peck, J. 288
Peterson, V. 36–37
*Philadelphia Negro, The* (Du Bois) 297
Poggi, G. 67
*Policing the Crisis* (Hall) 3
*Poverty of Philosophy, The* (Marx) 120–121
power: coercion and 61–62, 69–70; fear
and 67; imbalance in criminal justice
system 42; neoliberal SSA and 107–109;
networks and 110–111; new enclosures
and 110–111
*Power and Crime* (Ruggiero) 233
*Power Elite, The* (Mills) 325
predation 258–259
prison labour 285–286
Protecting Consumers from Unreasonable
Credit Rates Act of 2009 266
"public choice theory" 182
"public interest theory" 182

Racketeer Influenced and Corrupt
Organization Statute (RICO) 47
racketeers 47–48
*Radical Durkheim, The* (Pearce) 322, 329
radicalism 10–11
Rakoff, J.S. 42
Reagan, R. xxxvii, 40
real social order xxxiv, 7–9, 13, 323
recombinant nature 76–78
regulatory capture 182–183
regulatory law 27–29
reification 13–14
Renner, M. 246
revolving door mechanism 183
*Risk Society* (Beck) 326
Rockefeller, J.D. 36
Rock Sioux Tribe (SRST) 158–159,
163–168

## 340 Index

Roosevelt, F.D. 194
Rothe, D. 233, 235
*Routledge International Handbook of the Crimes of the Powerful, The* (Barak) 233
Ruggiero, V. 233
Rum Corps 204–205
Russell, B. 60

sacrifice 92–94
sacrificers 92–94, 97–98
sacrificial discourse 94–98
sacrificial interpellators 95, 97
"sanctuary" movement 41
secrecy 63–65
"Secret Six" 34–35
shareholders 26–27
Sherman Act of 1890 6
Sherman, L. 275
shopping malls 249
Skinns, D. 288
Sloterdijk, P. 70
slow violence 235–236
Snider, L. 299, 302
social agents 74
social change 69–70, 80–81
social control 60
social institutions 12
social relations: post-capitalist 69–70; racketeering and 47–48; recombinant nature and 76–78; social structures and 74–76
social structure of accumulation (SSA) theory: background 104–106; enclosure and neoliberal 109–110; expulsion and neoliberal 109–110; neoliberal 106–107; peak and end of neoliberal 111–112; power and neoliberal 107–109
social structures 74–76, 80
society 9
Soper, K. 80
Spain: corporate crime within 226–228; crimes of powerful and financial/economic crisis 217–228; financialization and the European arrangement 218–221; mortgages 223–226; role of corporations 225–226; role of state 224–225; spatial fix 221–223
*Specters of Marx* (Derrida) 303
Spencer, H. 60
Stalin, J. 304

state–corporate crime 126–129, 159–160, 223–228
state–corporate environmental crime 157–169; climate change and 159–162; fossil fuels and 159–162
state crimes: anticolonial tradition and 314–316; colonial 316–319
"state-finance" nexus 148–149
state-initiated corporate crime 159–160
state-sanctioned labour: (re)construction of 284–289; interests of labour and capital 290–293; prison labour 285–286; underpinning social order 290; unpaid work 286–288; voluntarism and 21–25; workfare 288–289
Stigler, G. 181
*Suppression of the African Slave Trade, The* (Du Bois) 298
surveillance 251
Sutherland, E. 45, 231, 298
symbolic interactionism (SI) xxxv–xxxvi

Taylor, I. 15–16
television programming 248
Thailand 234
Thatcher, M. xxxvii
"There Is No Alternative" (TINA) 182–183
Tombs, S. 73, 181–182, 301, 303, 313, 315, 322, 325, 328
*Toxic Capitalism* (Pearce and Tombs) 73
transformational model of social action (TMSA) 73–74
Truss, L. 286

UN Convention on the Elimination of All Forms of Discrimination Against Women (CEDAW) 272
Union Carbide Corporation 301–302

Veblen, T. 247
victimization 96–97, 138–140
victim services 278–279
violence 60–63, 69–70, 235–236
Violence Against Women Act (VAWA) 273
voluntarism 21–25, 27–29

Wal-Mart 190–191
Walton, P. 15–16
Ward, T. 313, 316

Water Protectors 158, 163–167
wealth 146–147, 247–248
Weber, M. 60, 61, 62
white-collar crime 45–46, 196–197
Whyte, D. 181–182, 303, 305, 313, 315, 322, 325, 328
workfare 288–289
work-for-wages contracts 21–25
workplace theft: criminology of 191–193; criminology of wage theft 196–198; freedom in labour markets and 64;
imaginary social order and 193–196; literature review of wage theft 191–193; sides of 190–191; wage theft 193–198
World Bank 237
*World Risk Society* (Beck) 326
Wright, J. 286

Young, J. 15–16, 189, 196, 246, 297

Zika virus epidemic 177
zombie capitalism 89–90